SUICIDE SQUAD

TRIAL BY FIRE

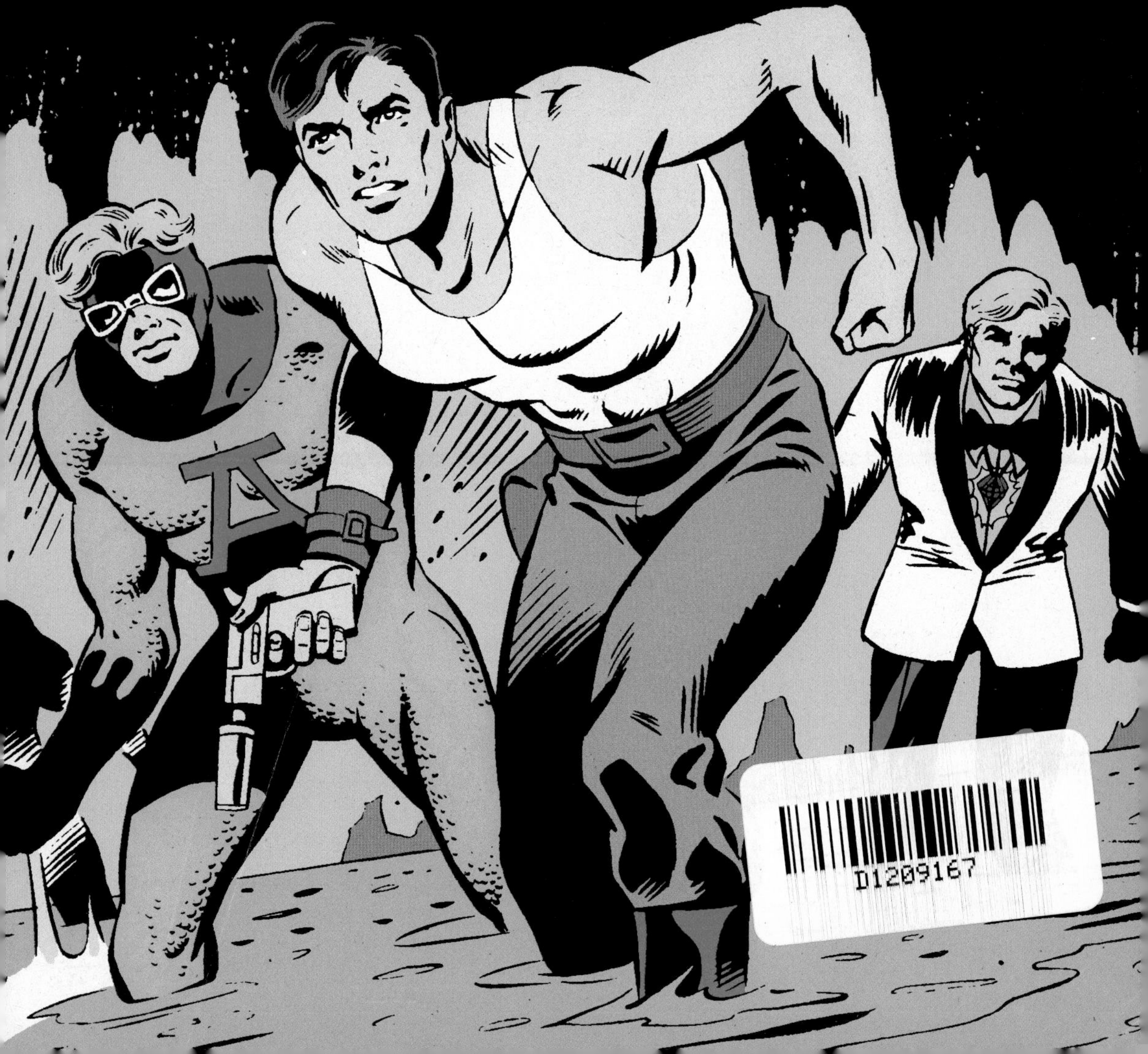

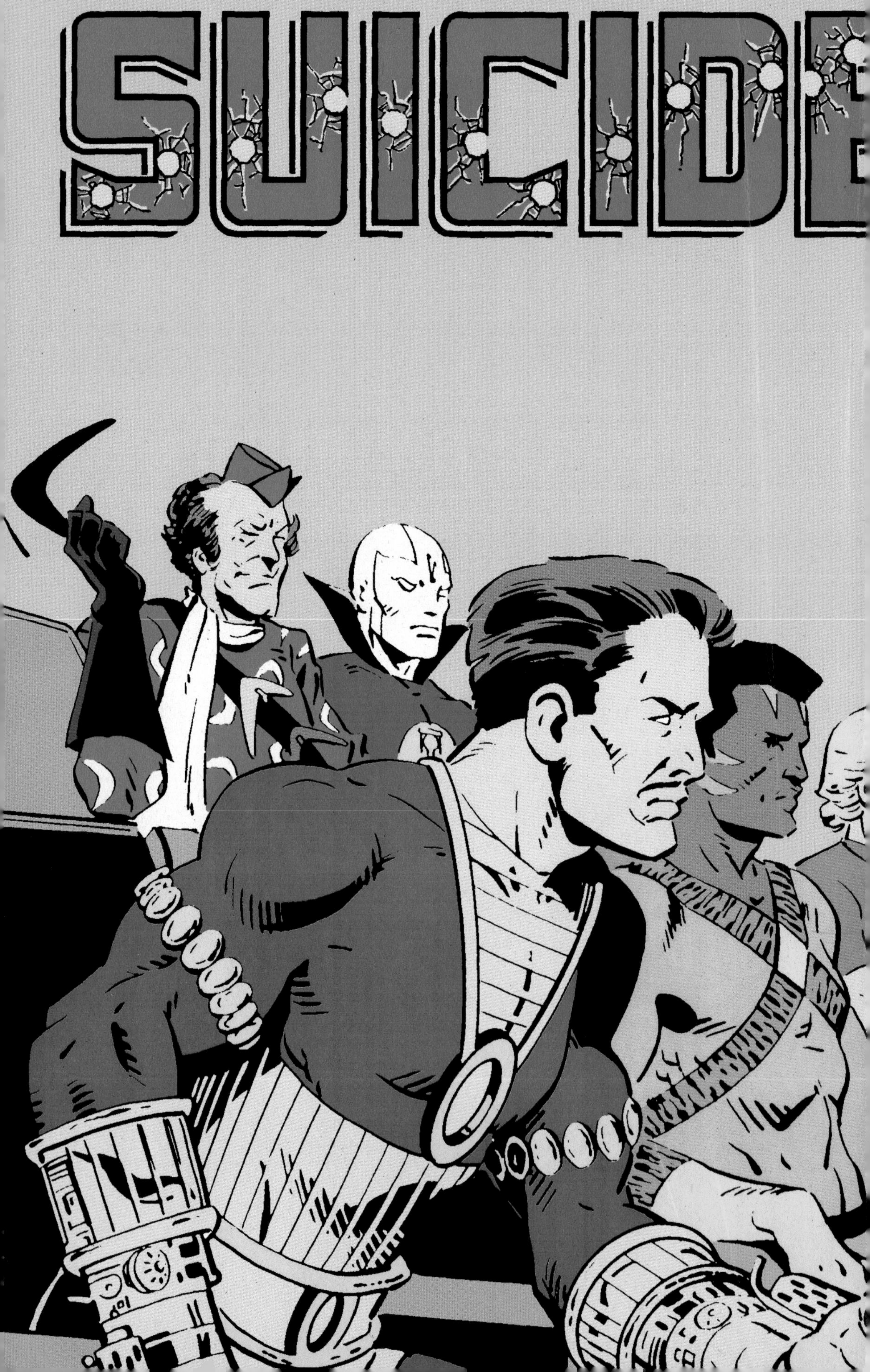
SUICIDE

SQUAD

TRIAL BY FIRE

John **OSTRANDER**
writer

Luke **MCDONNELL**   Bob **LEWIS**   Karl **KESEL**   Dave **HUNT**
artists

Carl **GAFFORD**
colorist

Todd **KLEIN**   Albert **DEGUZMAN**
letterers

Cover art by
Luke **MCDONNELL**
Karl **KESEL**

ROBERT GREENBERGER Editor – Original Series
JEB WOODARD Group Editor – Collected Editions
SCOTT NYBAKKEN Editor – Collected Edition
Steve Cook Design Director – Books

BOB HARRAS Senior VP – Editor-in-Chief, DC Comics

DIANE NELSON President
DAN DIDIO and JIM LEE Co-Publishers
GEOFF JOHNS Chief Creative Officer
AMIT DESAI Senior VP – Marketing & Global Franchise Management
NAIRI GARDINER Senior VP – Finance
SAM ADES VP – Digital Marketing
BOBBIE CHASE VP – Talent Development
MARK CHIARELLO Senior VP – Art, Design & Collected Editions
JOHN CUNNINGHAM VP – Content Strategy
ANNE DEPIES VP – Strategy Planning & Reporting
DON FALLETTI VP – Manufacturing Operations
LAWRENCE GANEM VP – Editorial Administration & Talent Relations
ALISON GILL Senior VP – Manufacturing & Operations
HANK KANALZ Senior VP – Editorial Strategy & Administration
JAY KOGAN VP – Legal Affairs
DEREK MADDALENA Senior VP – Sales & Business Development
JACK MAHAN VP – Business Affairs
DAN MIRON VP – Sales Planning & Trade Development
NICK NAPOLITANO VP – Manufacturing Administration
CAROL ROEDER VP – Marketing
EDDIE SCANNELL VP – Mass Account & Digital Sales
COURTNEY SIMMONS Senior VP – Publicity & Communications
JIM (SKI) SOKOLOWSKI VP – Comic Book Specialty & Newsstand Sales
SANDY YI Senior VP – Global Franchise Management

Cover color by Drew Moore.
Interior color restoration by David Tanguay.
Publication design by Robbie Biederman.

SUICIDE SQUAD VOL. 1 : TRIAL BY FIRE

DC Comics, 2900 W. Alameda Avenue, Burbank, CA 91505
Printed By Transcontinental Interglobe, Beauceville, QC, Canada. 1/22/16.
Second Printing.
ISBN: 978-1-4012-5831-3

Library of Congress Cataloging-in-Publication Data

Ostrander, John.
Suicide squad. Volume 1, Trial by fire / John Ostrander, Luke McDonnell.
pages cm
"Originally published in single magazine form in SECRET ORIGINS 14, SUICIDE SQUAD 1-8."
ISBN 978-1-4012-5831-3
1. Graphic novels. I. McDonnell, Luke, illustrator. II. Title. III. Title: Trial by fire.
PN6728.S825O88 2015
741.5'973--dc23

2015012143

PEFC Certified
Printed on paper from sustainably managed forests and controlled sources
PEFC
PEFC/01-31-106
www.pefc.org

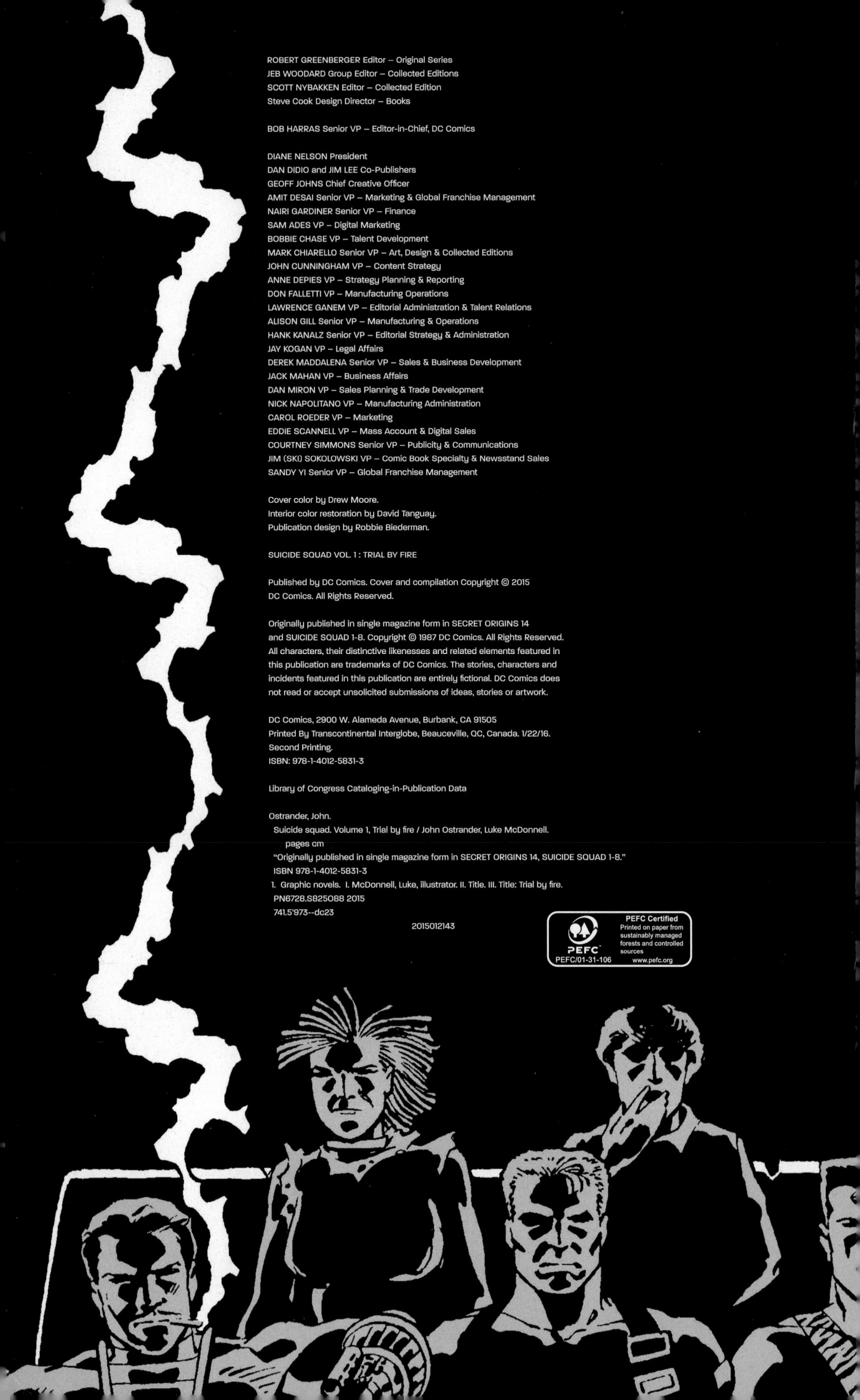

THE SECRET ORIGIN OF THE SUICIDE SQUAD p7

From SECRET ORIGINS #14, May 1987
Cover pencils by **Luke McDonnell** Cover inks by **Dave Hunt**

TRIAL BY BLOOD p46

From SUICIDE SQUAD #1, May 1987
Cover art by **Howard Chaykin**

TRIAL BY FIRE p69

From SUICIDE SQUAD #2, June 1987
Cover pencils by **Luke McDonnell** Cover inks by **Karl Kesel**

JAILBREAK p92

From SUICIDE SQUAD #3, July 1987
Cover pencils by **Luke McDonnell** Cover inks by **Karl Kesel**

WILLIAM HELL'S OVERTURE p115

From SUICIDE SQUAD #4, August 1987
Cover pencils by **Luke McDonnell** Cover inks by **Bob Lewis**

THE FLIGHT OF THE FIREBIRD p138

From SUICIDE SQUAD #5, September 1987
Cover pencils by **Luke McDonnell** Cover inks by **Bob Lewis**

HITTING THE FAN p161

From SUICIDE SQUAD #6, October 1987
Cover pencils by **Luke McDonnell** Cover inks by **Bob Lewis**

THROWN TO THE WOLVES p184

From SUICIDE SQUAD #7, November 1987
Cover art by **Jerry Bingham**

PERSONAL FILES p207

From SUICIDE SQUAD #8, December 1987
Cover art by **Jerry Bingham**

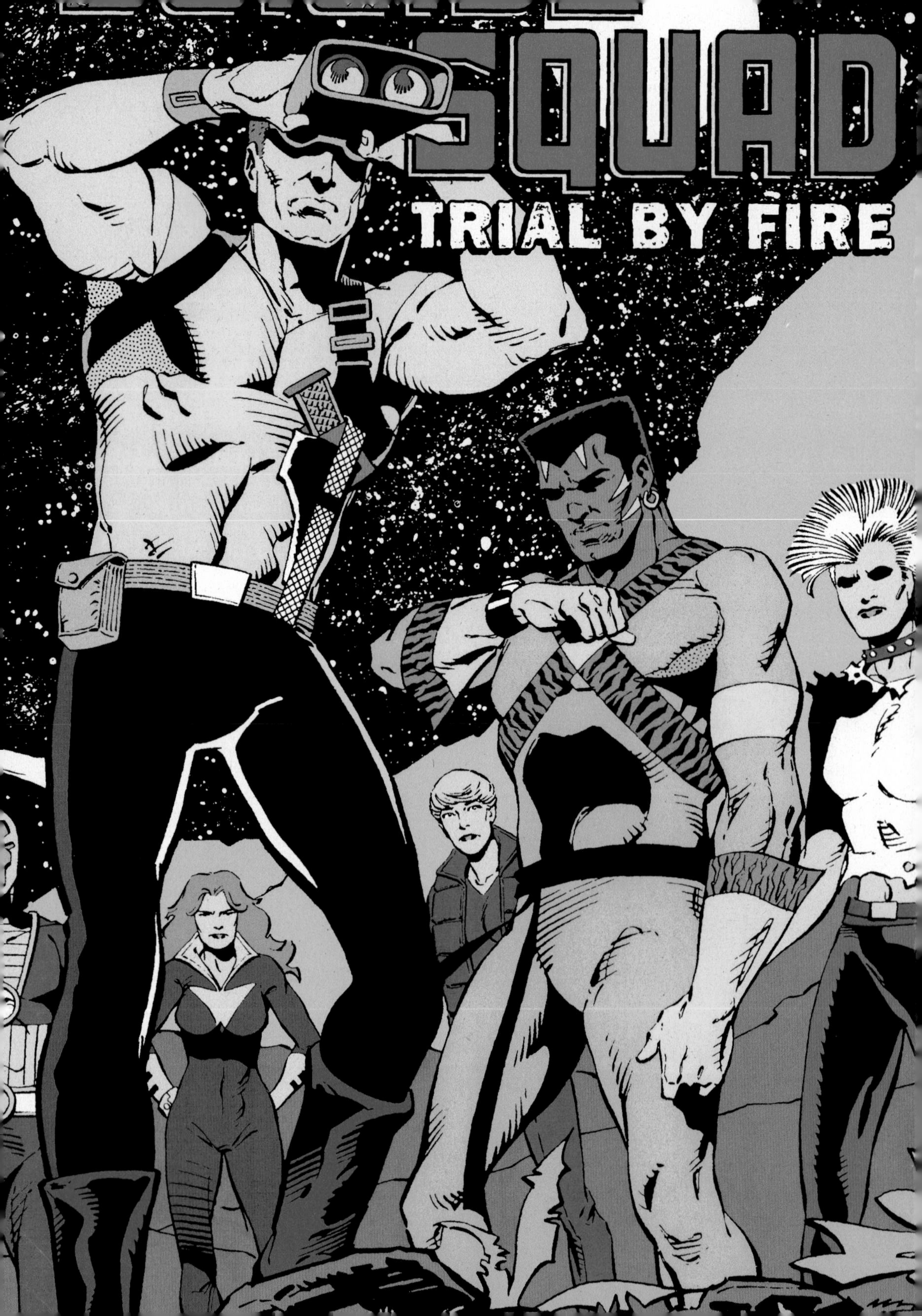
SQUAD
TRIAL BY FIRE

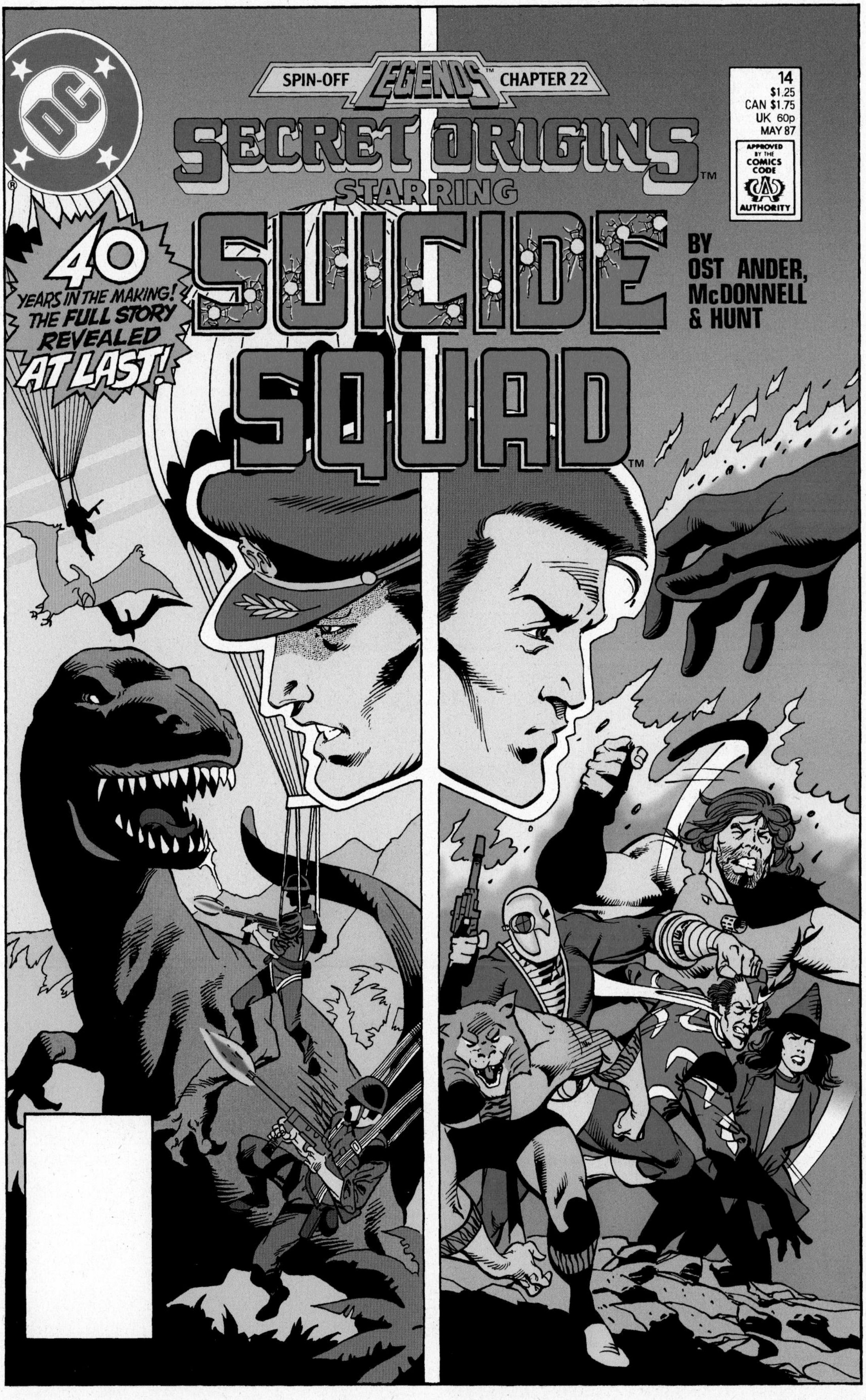

SPIN-OFF LEGENDS™ CHAPTER 22
SECRET ORIGINS™
STARRING
SUICIDE SQUAD™
14
$1.25
CAN $1.75
UK 60p
MAY 87
APPROVED BY THE COMICS CODE AUTHORITY
BY
OST ANDER,
McDONNELL
& HUNT
40 YEARS IN THE MAKING! THE FULL STORY REVEALED AT LAST!

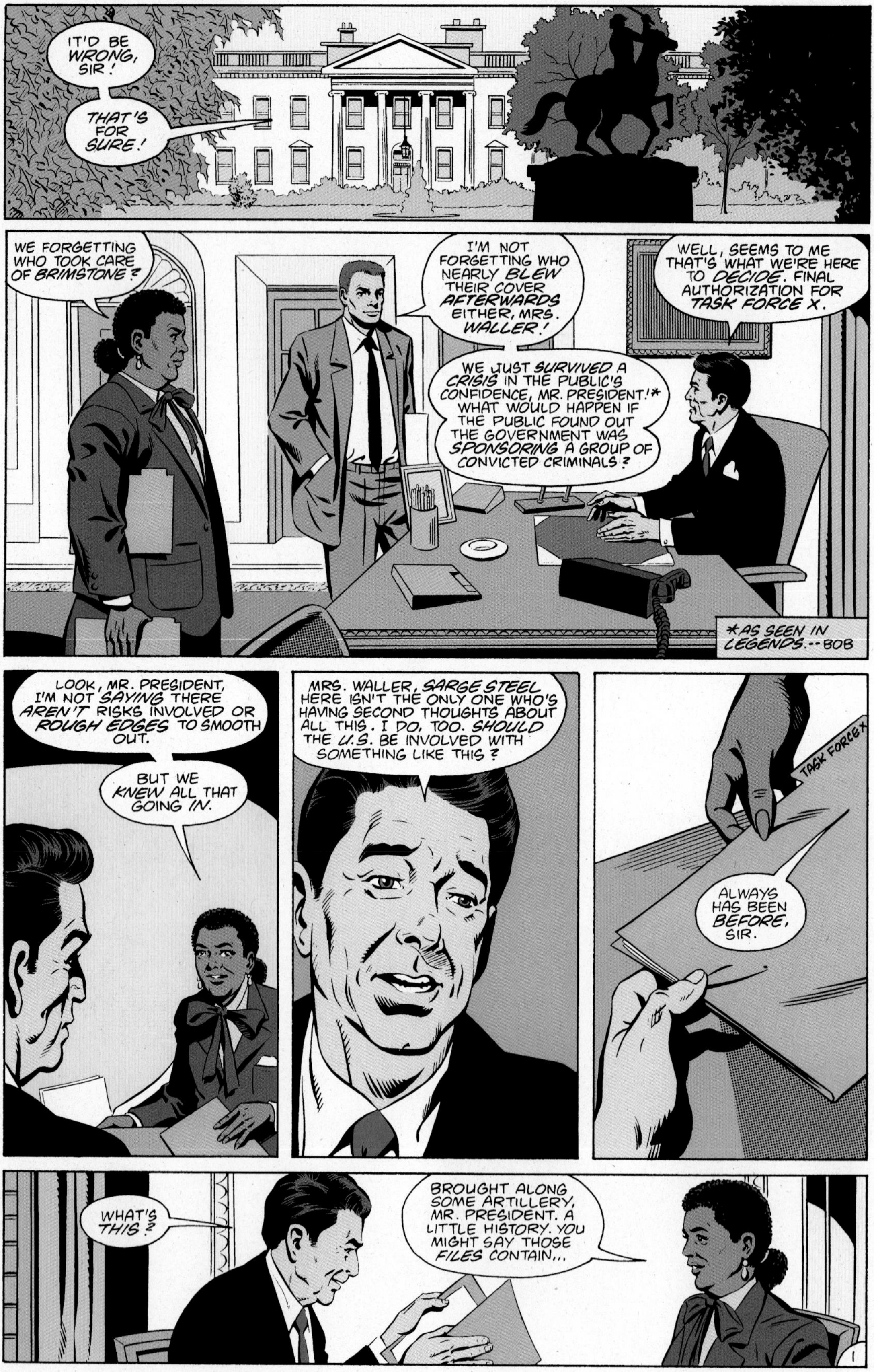
IT'D BE WRONG, SIR!
THAT'S FOR SURE!
WE FORGETTING WHO TOOK CARE OF BRIMSTONE?
I'M NOT FORGETTING WHO NEARLY BLEW THEIR COVER AFTERWARDS EITHER, MRS. WALLER!
WE JUST SURVIVED A CRISIS IN THE PUBLIC'S CONFIDENCE, MR. PRESIDENT!* WHAT WOULD HAPPEN IF THE PUBLIC FOUND OUT THE GOVERNMENT WAS SPONSORING A GROUP OF CONVICTED CRIMINALS?
WELL, SEEMS TO ME THAT'S WHAT WE'RE HERE TO DECIDE. FINAL AUTHORIZATION FOR TASK FORCE X.
*AS SEEN IN LEGENDS.--BOB
LOOK, MR. PRESIDENT, I'M NOT SAYING THERE AREN'T RISKS INVOLVED OR ROUGH EDGES TO SMOOTH OUT.
BUT WE KNEW ALL THAT GOING IN.
MRS. WALLER, SARGE STEEL HERE ISN'T THE ONLY ONE WHO'S HAVING SECOND THOUGHTS ABOUT ALL THIS. I DO, TOO. SHOULD THE U.S. BE INVOLVED WITH SOMETHING LIKE THIS?
TASK FORCE X
ALWAYS HAS BEEN BEFORE, SIR.
WHAT'S THIS?
BROUGHT ALONG SOME ARTILLERY, MR. PRESIDENT. A LITTLE HISTORY. YOU MIGHT SAY THOSE FILES CONTAIN...
1

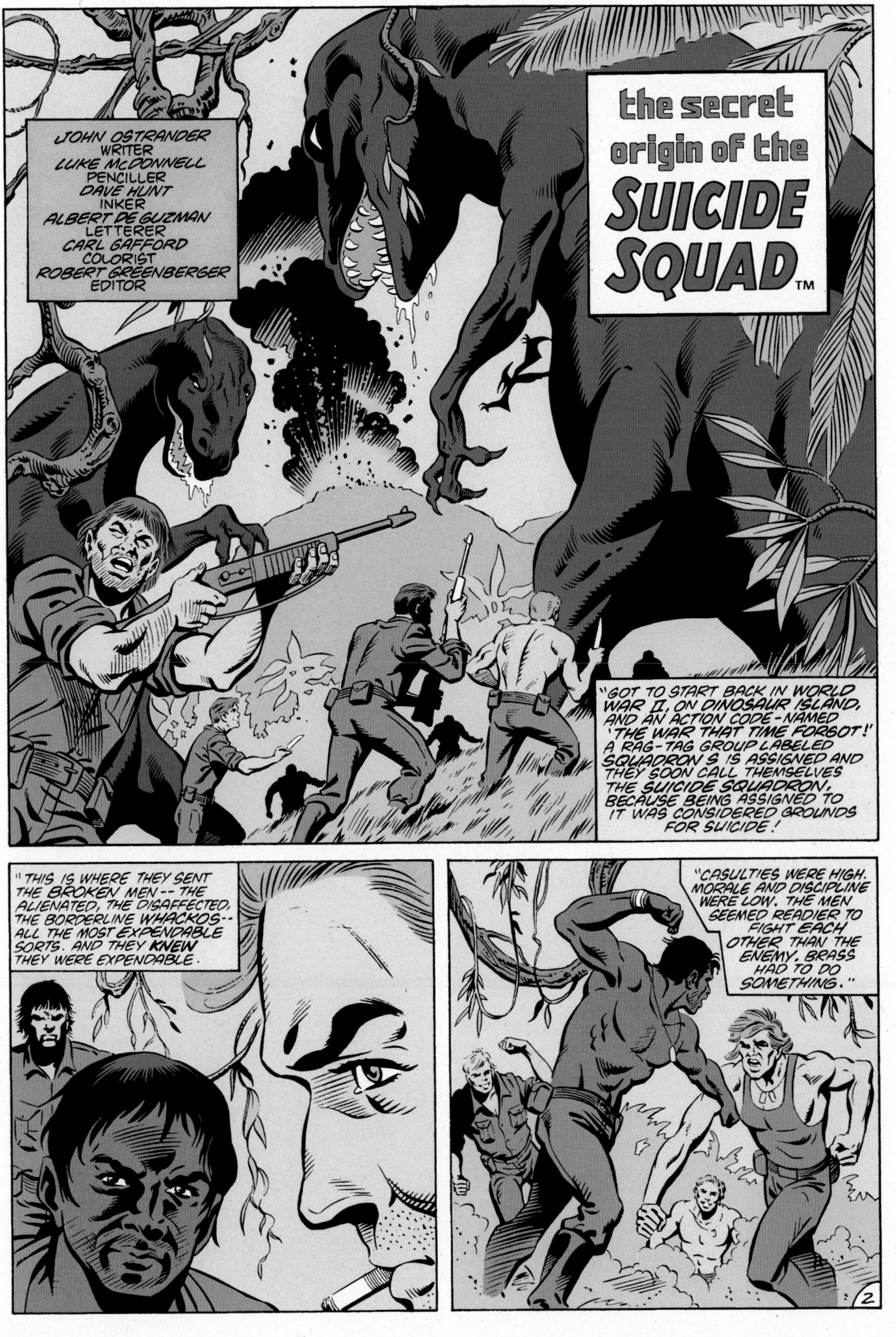
JOHN OSTRANDER
WRITER
LUKE McDONNELL
PENCILLER
DAVE HUNT
INKER
ALBERT DE GUZMAN
LETTERER
CARL GAFFORD
COLORIST
ROBERT GREENBERGER
EDITOR
the secret origin of the SUICIDE SQUAD™
"GOT TO START BACK IN WORLD WAR II, ON DINOSAUR ISLAND, AND AN ACTION CODE-NAMED 'THE WAR THAT TIME FORGOT!' A RAG-TAG GROUP LABELED SQUADRON S IS ASSIGNED AND THEY SOON CALL THEMSELVES THE SUICIDE SQUADRON, BECAUSE BEING ASSIGNED TO IT WAS CONSIDERED GROUNDS FOR SUICIDE!
"THIS IS WHERE THEY SENT THE BROKEN MEN -- THE ALIENATED, THE DISAFFECTED, THE BORDERLINE WHACKOS -- ALL THE MOST EXPENDABLE SORTS. AND THEY KNEW THEY WERE EXPENDABLE.
"CASULTIES WERE HIGH. MORALE AND DISCIPLINE WERE LOW. THE MEN SEEMED READIER TO FIGHT EACH OTHER THAN THE ENEMY. BRASS HAD TO DO SOMETHING."
2

GOOD, BAD, INDIFFERENT-- THEY'RE STILL *OUR* MEN. WE'VE *GOT* TO GIVE THEM A FIGHTING CHANCE TO SURVIVE.

THEY NEED A C.O., TOUGH, MEAN, AND COMMITTED, WHO'LL MAKE THEM WORK *TOGETHER!*

I THINK CAPT. RICHARD MONTGOMERY FLAG IS THE MAN AND HERE'S WHY.

"AS A ROOKIE FLYER, HE WAS OUT WITH HIS SQUADRON OF TBFS WHEN THEY CAME UPON A JAP FLAT-TOP."

LET'S GET THAT FLAT-TOP, GANG! USE ATTACK PLAN THREE! RICK, YOU COME IN LAST! WE'LL PAVE THE WAY!

THEY'RE TAKING ALL THE RISKS, SO THERE'LL BE LESS TO CLOBBER ME WHEN I MAKE MY RUN!

LOOK AT THAT *FLAK!*

BOOM!

BUH-BOOM

THEY'VE ALL BEEN *HIT!*

NO ONE LEFT NOW... BUT ME...!

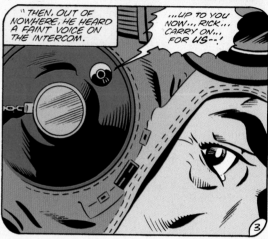

"THEN, OUT OF NOWHERE, HE HEARD A FAINT VOICE ON THE INTERCOM.

...UP TO YOU NOW... RICK... CARRY ON... FOR *US*--!

3

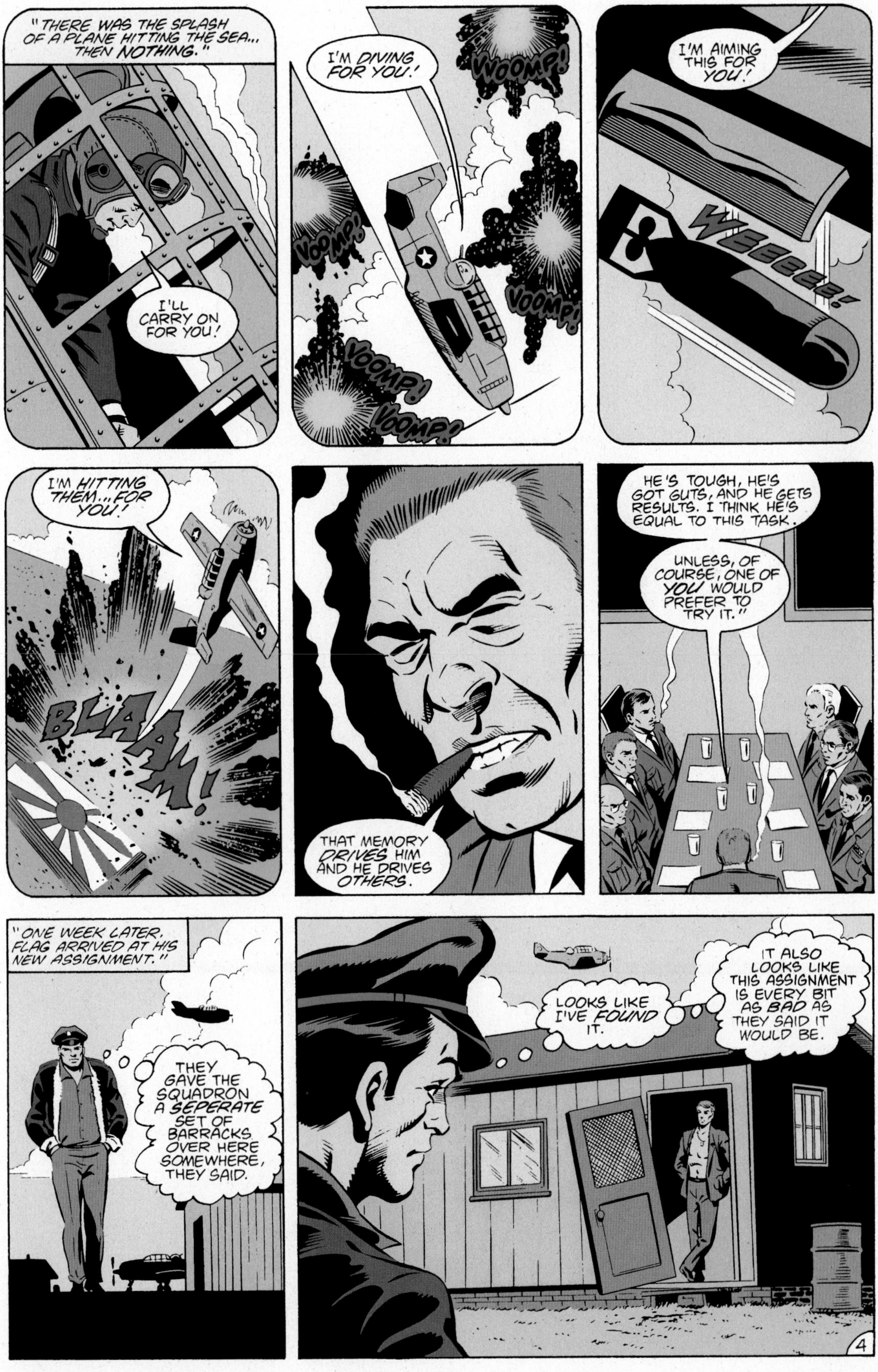
"THERE WAS THE SPLASH OF A PLANE HITTING THE SEA... THEN NOTHING."
I'LL CARRY ON FOR YOU!
I'M DIVING FOR YOU!
WOOMP!
VOOMP!
VOOMP!
VOOMP!
VOOMP!
I'M AIMING THIS FOR YOU!
WEEEEE!
I'M HITTING THEM... FOR YOU!
BLAAAM!
THAT MEMORY DRIVES HIM AND HE DRIVES OTHERS.
HE'S TOUGH, HE'S GOT GUTS, AND HE GETS RESULTS. I THINK HE'S EQUAL TO THIS TASK.
UNLESS, OF COURSE, ONE OF YOU WOULD PREFER TO TRY IT."
"ONE WEEK LATER, FLAG ARRIVED AT HIS NEW ASSIGNMENT."
THEY GAVE THE SQUADRON A SEPERATE SET OF BARRACKS OVER HERE SOMEWHERE, THEY SAID.
LOOKS LIKE I'VE FOUND IT.
IT ALSO LOOKS LIKE THIS ASSIGNMENT IS EVERY BIT AS BAD AS THEY SAID IT WOULD BE.
4

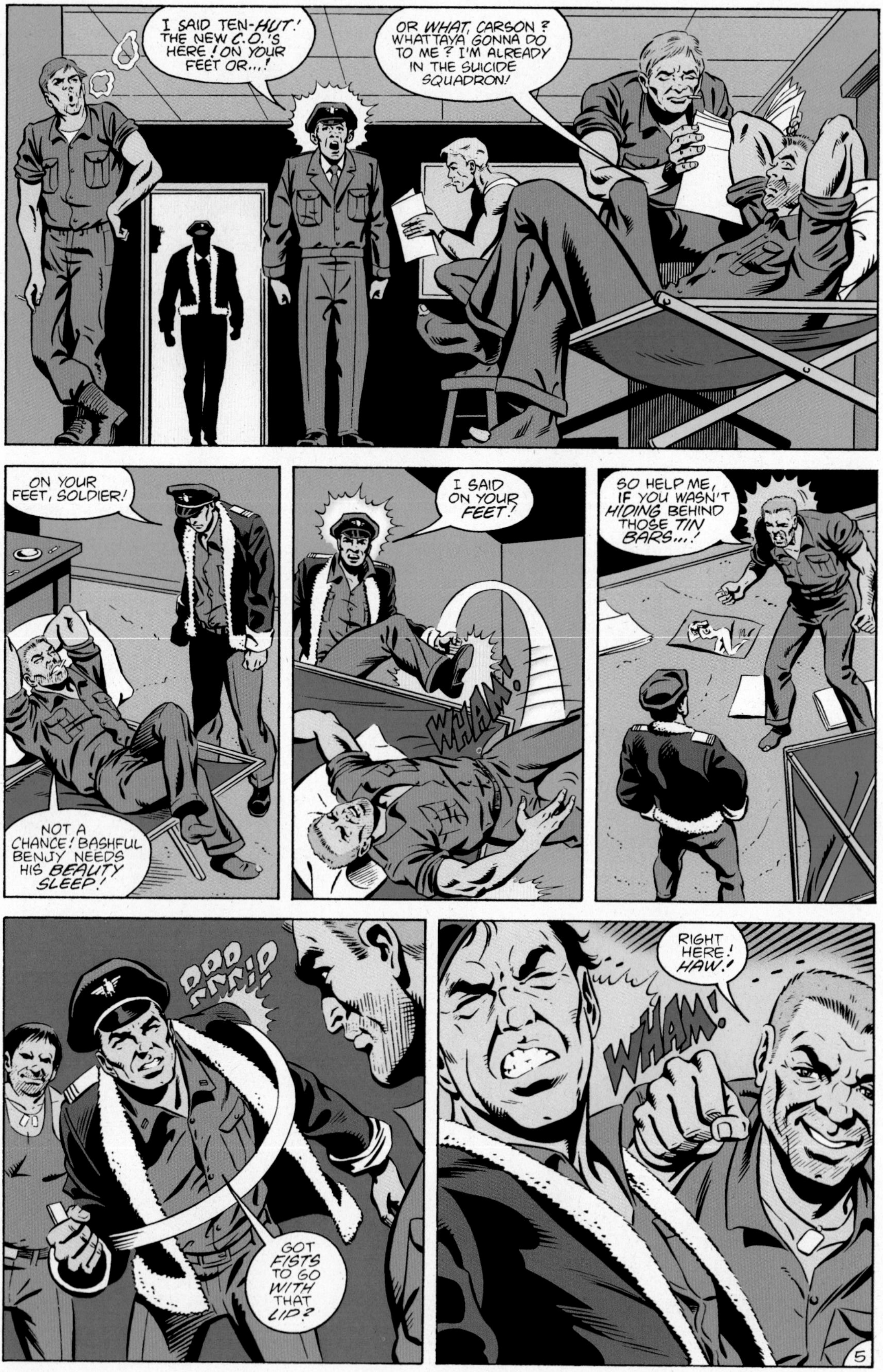
I SAID TEN-HUT! THE NEW C.O.'S HERE! ON YOUR FEET OR...!
OR WHAT, CARSON? WHATTAYA GONNA DO TO ME? I'M ALREADY IN THE SUICIDE SQUADRON!
ON YOUR FEET, SOLDIER!
NOT A CHANCE! BASHFUL BENJY NEEDS HIS BEAUTY SLEEP!
I SAID ON YOUR FEET!
WHAM!
SO HELP ME, IF YOU WASN'T HIDING BEHIND THOSE TIN BARS...!
GOT FISTS TO GO WITH THAT LIP?
RIGHT HERE! HAW!
WHAM!
5

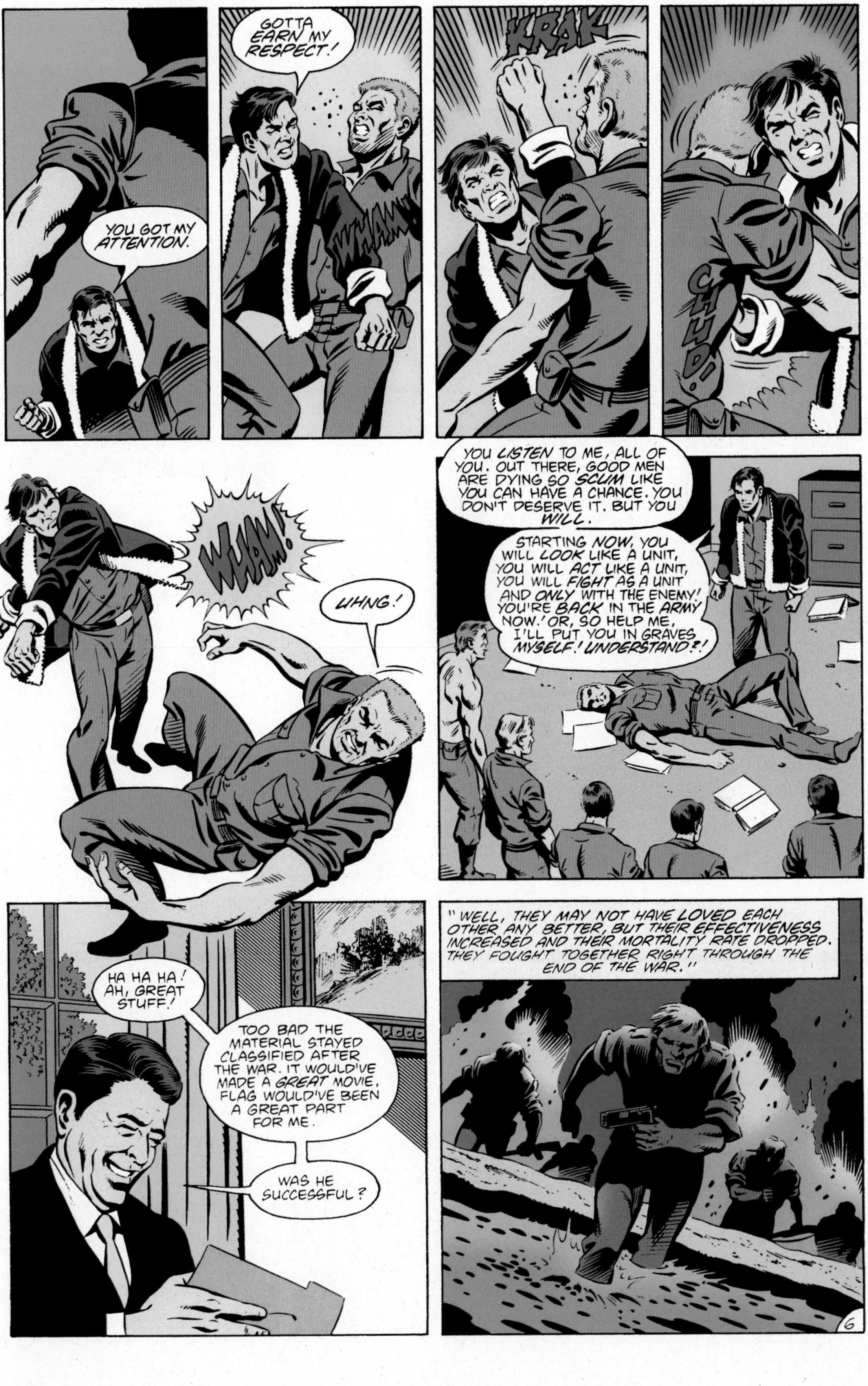
YOU GOT MY ATTENTION.
GOTTA EARN MY RESPECT!
WHAM
KRAK
CHUD!
WHAM!
UHNG!
YOU LISTEN TO ME, ALL OF YOU. OUT THERE, GOOD MEN ARE DYING SO SCUM LIKE YOU CAN HAVE A CHANCE. YOU DON'T DESERVE IT. BUT YOU WILL.
STARTING NOW, YOU WILL LOOK LIKE A UNIT, YOU WILL ACT LIKE A UNIT, YOU WILL FIGHT AS A UNIT AND ONLY WITH THE ENEMY! YOU'RE BACK IN THE ARMY NOW! OR, SO HELP ME, I'LL PUT YOU IN GRAVES MYSELF! UNDERSTAND?!
HA HA HA! AH, GREAT STUFF!
TOO BAD THE MATERIAL STAYED CLASSIFIED AFTER THE WAR. IT WOULD'VE MADE A GREAT MOVIE. FLAG WOULD'VE BEEN A GREAT PART FOR ME.
WAS HE SUCCESSFUL?
"WELL, THEY MAY NOT HAVE LOVED EACH OTHER ANY BETTER, BUT THEIR EFFECTIVENESS INCREASED AND THEIR MORTALITY RATE DROPPED. THEY FOUGHT TOGETHER RIGHT THROUGH THE END OF THE WAR."
6

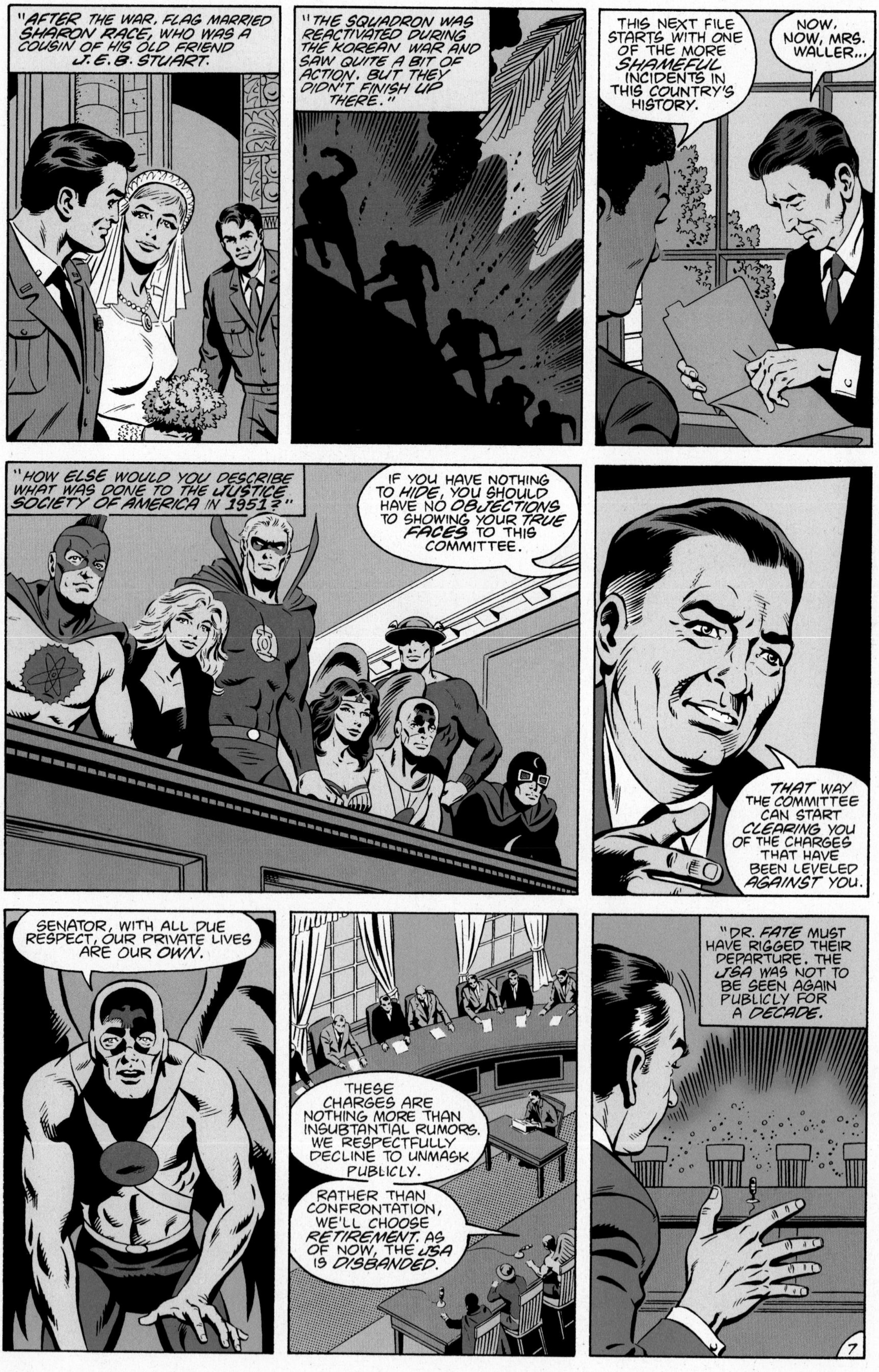
"AFTER THE WAR, FLAG MARRIED SHARON RACE, WHO WAS A COUSIN OF HIS OLD FRIEND J.E.B. STUART.
"THE SQUADRON WAS REACTIVATED DURING THE KOREAN WAR AND SAW QUITE A BIT OF ACTION. BUT THEY DIDN'T FINISH UP THERE."
THIS NEXT FILE STARTS WITH ONE OF THE MORE SHAMEFUL INCIDENTS IN THIS COUNTRY'S HISTORY.
NOW, NOW, MRS. WALLER...
"HOW ELSE WOULD YOU DESCRIBE WHAT WAS DONE TO THE JUSTICE SOCIETY OF AMERICA IN 1951?"
IF YOU HAVE NOTHING TO HIDE, YOU SHOULD HAVE NO OBJECTIONS TO SHOWING YOUR TRUE FACES TO THIS COMMITTEE.
THAT WAY THE COMMITTEE CAN START CLEARING YOU OF THE CHARGES THAT HAVE BEEN LEVELED AGAINST YOU.
SENATOR, WITH ALL DUE RESPECT, OUR PRIVATE LIVES ARE OUR OWN.
THESE CHARGES ARE NOTHING MORE THAN INSUBTANTIAL RUMORS. WE RESPECTFULLY DECLINE TO UNMASK PUBLICLY.
RATHER THAN CONFRONTATION, WE'LL CHOOSE RETIREMENT. AS OF NOW, THE JSA IS DISBANDED.
"DR. FATE MUST HAVE RIGGED THEIR DEPARTURE. THE JSA WAS NOT TO BE SEEN AGAIN PUBLICLY FOR A DECADE.
7

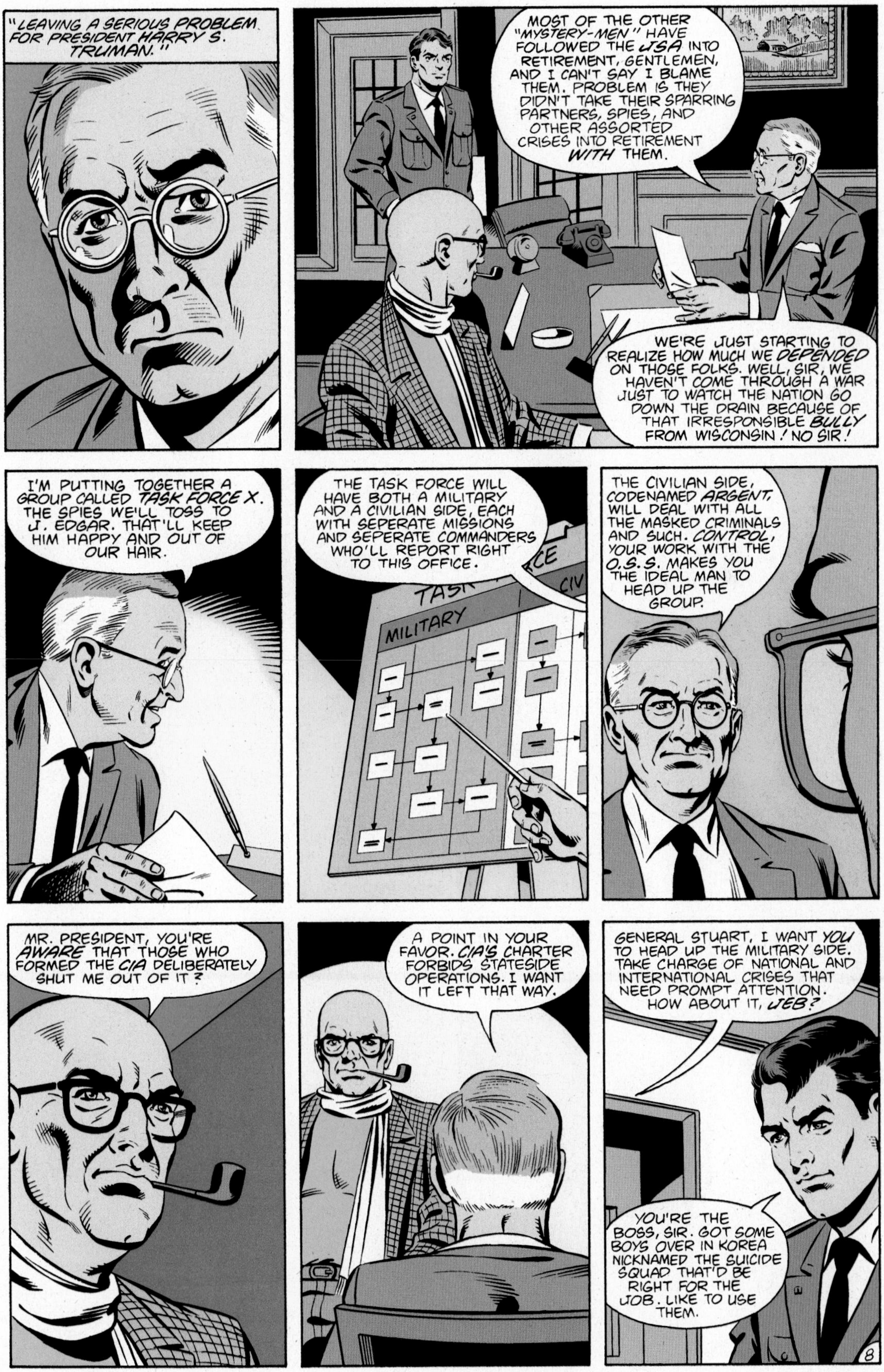
"LEAVING A SERIOUS PROBLEM FOR PRESIDENT HARRY S. TRUMAN."
MOST OF THE OTHER "MYSTERY-MEN" HAVE FOLLOWED THE JSA INTO RETIREMENT, GENTLEMEN, AND I CAN'T SAY I BLAME THEM. PROBLEM IS THEY DIDN'T TAKE THEIR SPARRING PARTNERS, SPIES, AND OTHER ASSORTED CRISES INTO RETIREMENT WITH THEM.
WE'RE JUST STARTING TO REALIZE HOW MUCH WE DEPENDED ON THOSE FOLKS. WELL, SIR, WE HAVEN'T COME THROUGH A WAR JUST TO WATCH THE NATION GO DOWN THE DRAIN BECAUSE OF THAT IRRESPONSIBLE BULLY FROM WISCONSIN! NO SIR!
I'M PUTTING TOGETHER A GROUP CALLED TASK FORCE X. THE SPIES WE'LL TOSS TO J. EDGAR. THAT'LL KEEP HIM HAPPY AND OUT OF OUR HAIR.
THE TASK FORCE WILL HAVE BOTH A MILITARY AND A CIVILIAN SIDE, EACH WITH SEPERATE MISSIONS AND SEPERATE COMMANDERS WHO'LL REPORT RIGHT TO THIS OFFICE.
MILITARY
THE CIVILIAN SIDE, CODENAMED ARGENT, WILL DEAL WITH ALL THE MASKED CRIMINALS AND SUCH. CONTROL, YOUR WORK WITH THE O.S.S. MAKES YOU THE IDEAL MAN TO HEAD UP THE GROUP.
MR. PRESIDENT, YOU'RE AWARE THAT THOSE WHO FORMED THE CIA DELIBERATELY SHUT ME OUT OF IT?
A POINT IN YOUR FAVOR. CIA'S CHARTER FORBIDS STATESIDE OPERATIONS. I WANT IT LEFT THAT WAY.
GENERAL STUART, I WANT YOU TO HEAD UP THE MILITARY SIDE. TAKE CHARGE OF NATIONAL AND INTERNATIONAL CRISES THAT NEED PROMPT ATTENTION. HOW ABOUT IT, JEB?
YOU'RE THE BOSS, SIR. GOT SOME BOYS OVER IN KOREA NICKNAMED THE SUICIDE SQUAD THAT'D BE RIGHT FOR THE JOB. LIKE TO USE THEM.
8

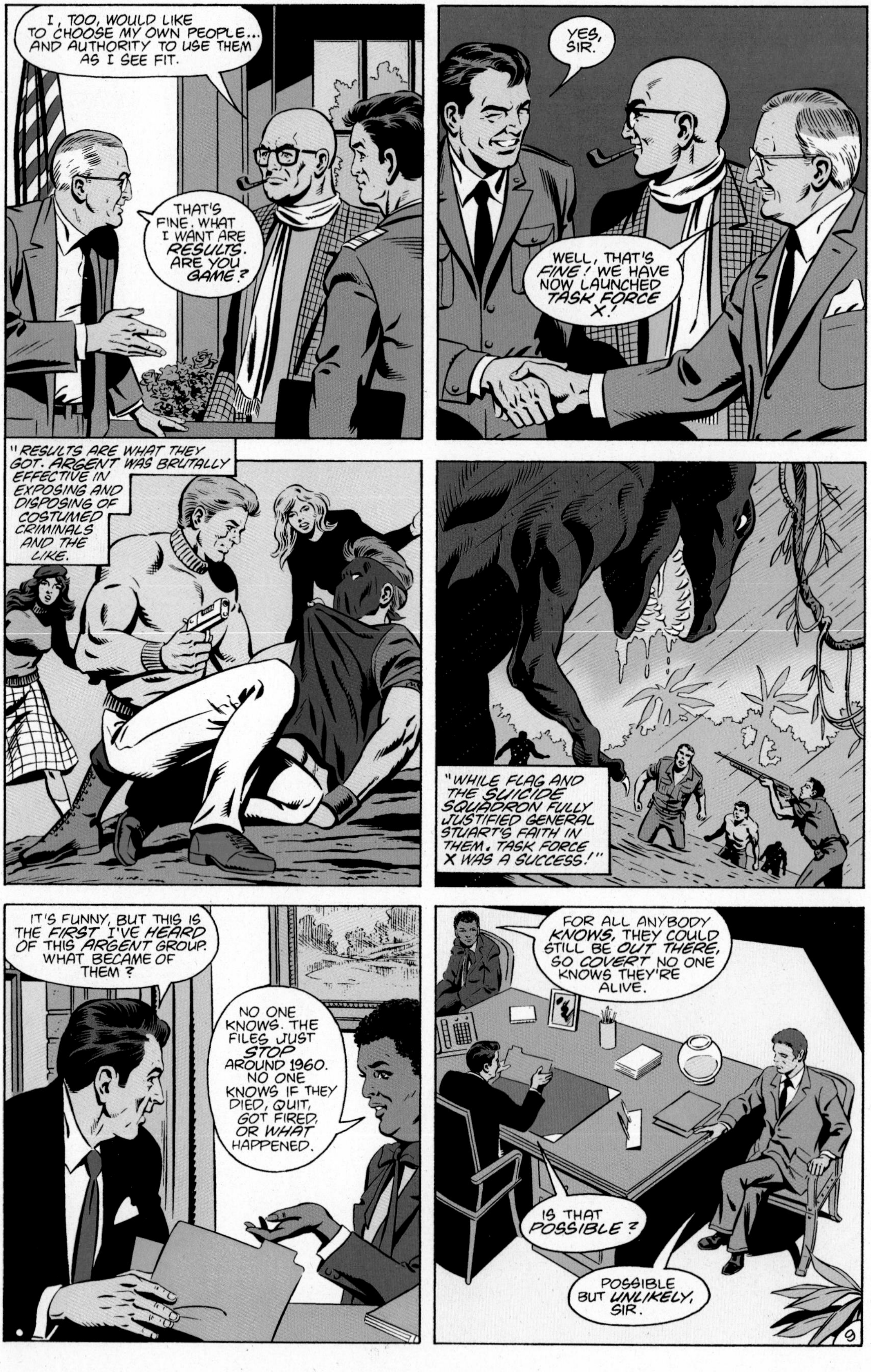
I, TOO, WOULD LIKE TO CHOOSE MY OWN PEOPLE... AND AUTHORITY TO USE THEM AS I SEE FIT.
THAT'S FINE. WHAT I WANT ARE RESULTS. ARE YOU GAME?
YES, SIR.
WELL, THAT'S FINE! WE HAVE NOW LAUNCHED TASK FORCE X!
"RESULTS ARE WHAT THEY GOT. ARGENT WAS BRUTALLY EFFECTIVE IN EXPOSING AND DISPOSING OF COSTUMED CRIMINALS AND THE LIKE.
"WHILE FLAG AND THE SUICIDE SQUADRON FULLY JUSTIFIED GENERAL STUART'S FAITH IN THEM. TASK FORCE X WAS A SUCCESS!"
IT'S FUNNY, BUT THIS IS THE FIRST I'VE HEARD OF THIS ARGENT GROUP. WHAT BECAME OF THEM?
NO ONE KNOWS. THE FILES JUST STOP AROUND 1960. NO ONE KNOWS IF THEY DIED, QUIT, GOT FIRED, OR WHAT HAPPENED.
FOR ALL ANYBODY KNOWS, THEY COULD STILL BE OUT THERE, SO COVERT NO ONE KNOWS THEY'RE ALIVE.
IS THAT POSSIBLE?
POSSIBLE BUT UNLIKELY, SIR.
9

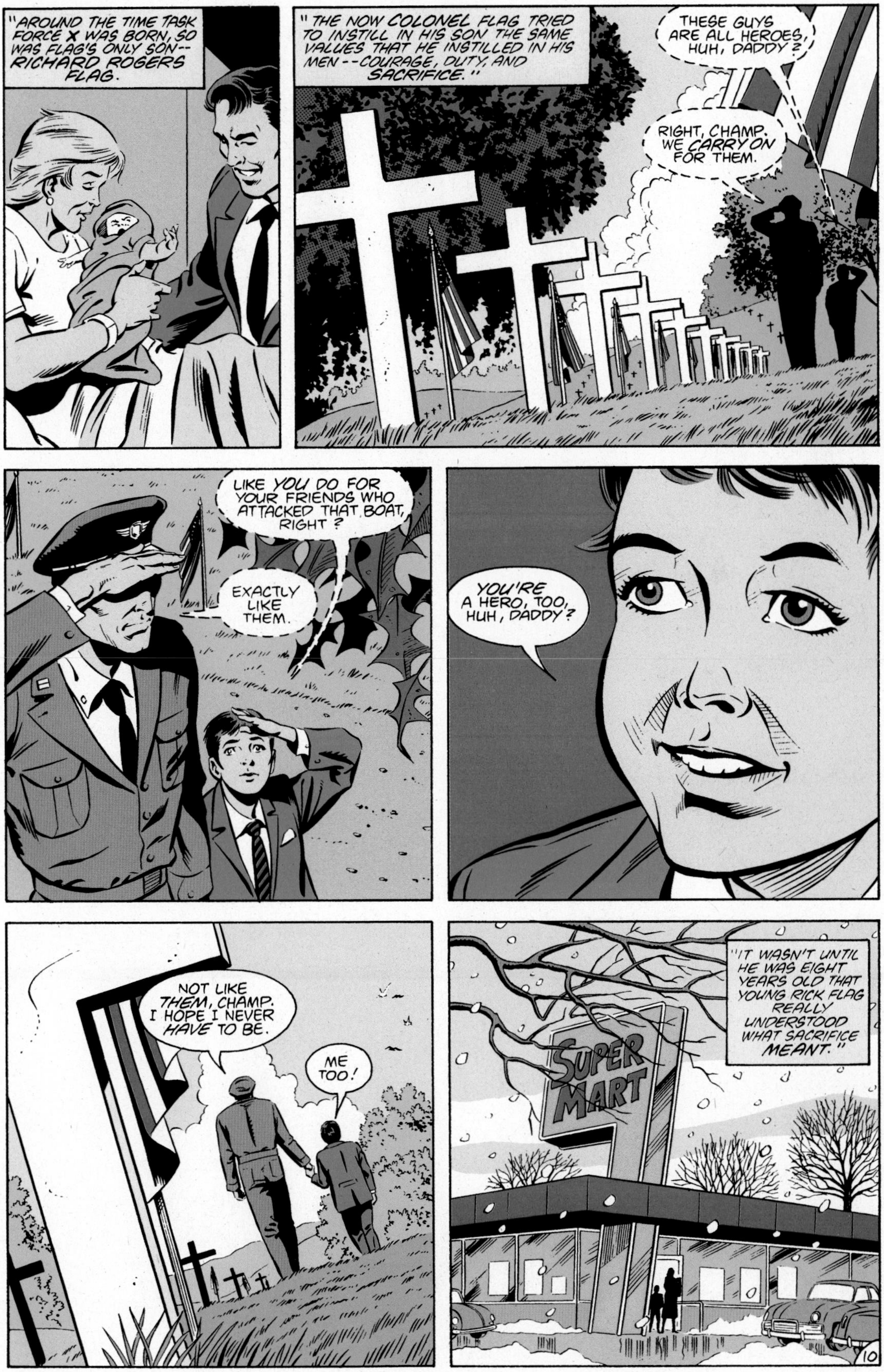
"AROUND THE TIME TASK FORCE X WAS BORN, SO WAS FLAG'S ONLY SON-- RICHARD ROGERS FLAG.
"THE NOW COLONEL FLAG TRIED TO INSTILL IN HIS SON THE SAME VALUES THAT HE INSTILLED IN HIS MEN--COURAGE, DUTY, AND SACRIFICE."
THESE GUYS ARE ALL HEROES, HUH, DADDY?
RIGHT, CHAMP. WE CARRY ON FOR THEM.
LIKE YOU DO FOR YOUR FRIENDS WHO ATTACKED THAT BOAT, RIGHT?
EXACTLY LIKE THEM.
YOU'RE A HERO, TOO, HUH, DADDY?
NOT LIKE THEM, CHAMP. I HOPE I NEVER HAVE TO BE.
ME TOO!
"IT WASN'T UNTIL HE WAS EIGHT YEARS OLD THAT YOUNG RICK FLAG REALLY UNDERSTOOD WHAT SACRIFICE MEANT."
SUPER MART
10

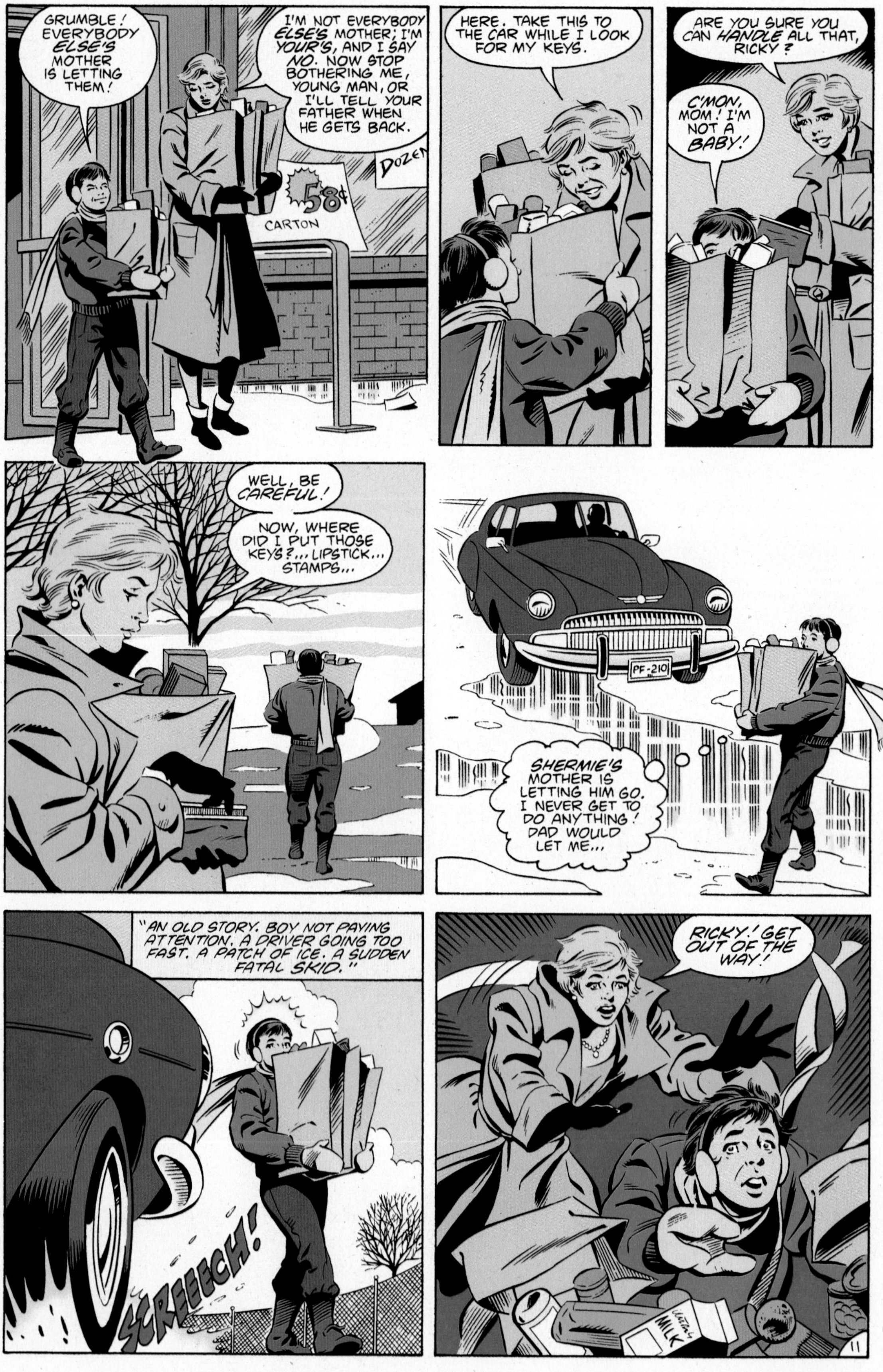
GRUMBLE! EVERYBODY ELSE'S MOTHER IS LETTING THEM!
I'M NOT EVERYBODY ELSE'S MOTHER; I'M YOUR'S, AND I SAY NO. NOW STOP BOTHERING ME, YOUNG MAN, OR I'LL TELL YOUR FATHER WHEN HE GETS BACK.
58¢
CARTON
HERE. TAKE THIS TO THE CAR WHILE I LOOK FOR MY KEYS.
ARE YOU SURE YOU CAN HANDLE ALL THAT, RICKY?
C'MON, MOM! I'M NOT A BABY!
WELL, BE CAREFUL!
NOW, WHERE DID I PUT THOSE KEYS?... LIPSTICK... STAMPS...
PF-210
SHERMIE'S MOTHER IS LETTING HIM GO. I NEVER GET TO DO ANYTHING! DAD WOULD LET ME...
"AN OLD STORY. BOY NOT PAYING ATTENTION. A DRIVER GOING TOO FAST. A PATCH OF ICE. A SUDDEN FATAL SKID."
SCREEECH!
RICKY! GET OUT OF THE WAY!
MILK
11

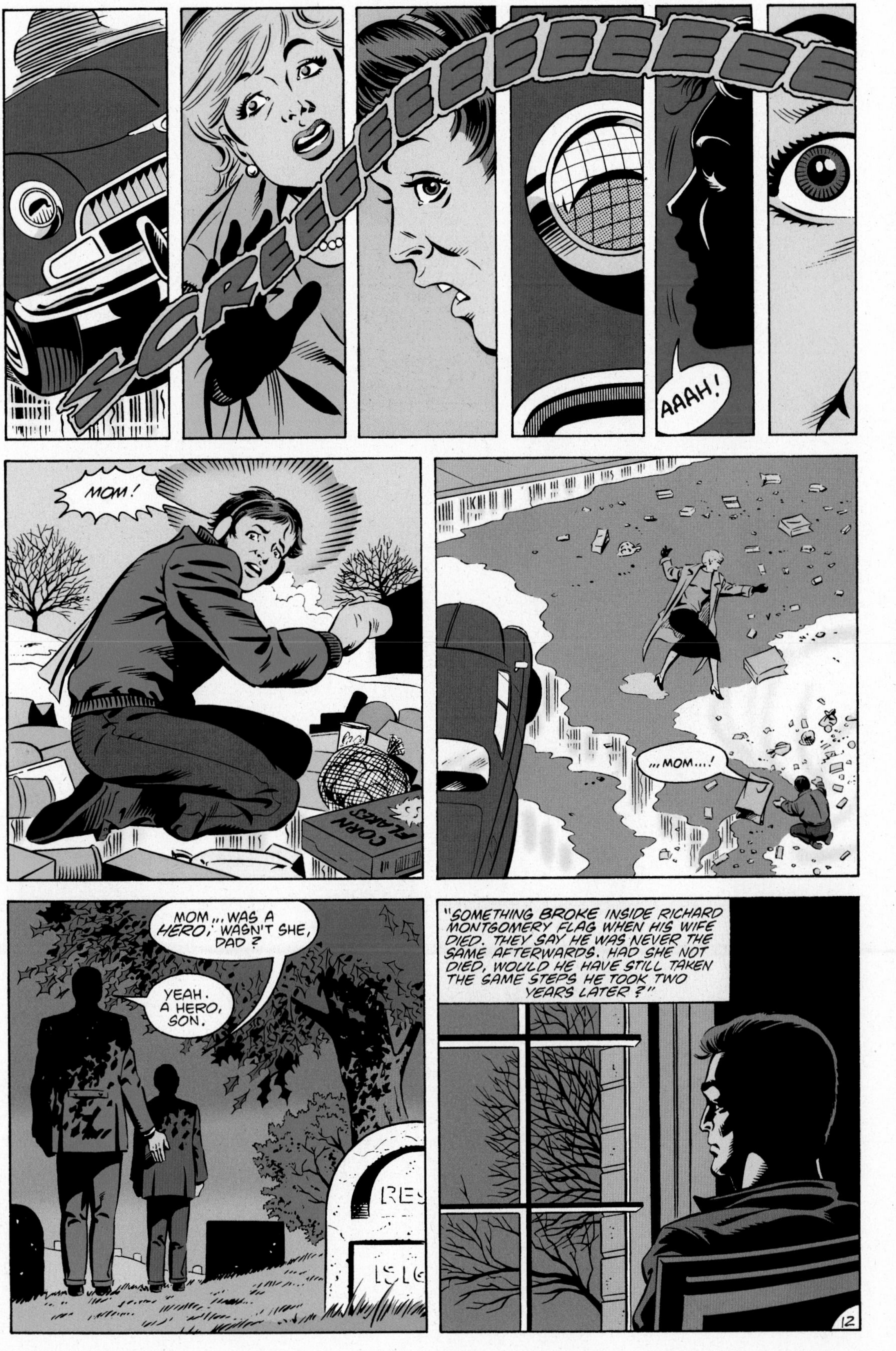
SCREEEEEEEEEEEEEE
AAAH!
MOM!
...MOM...!
MOM... WAS A HERO, WASN'T SHE, DAD?
YEAH. A HERO, SON.
"SOMETHING BROKE INSIDE RICHARD MONTGOMERY FLAG WHEN HIS WIFE DIED. THEY SAY HE WAS NEVER THE SAME AFTERWARDS. HAD SHE NOT DIED, WOULD HE HAVE STILL TAKEN THE SAME STEPS HE TOOK TWO YEARS LATER?"
12

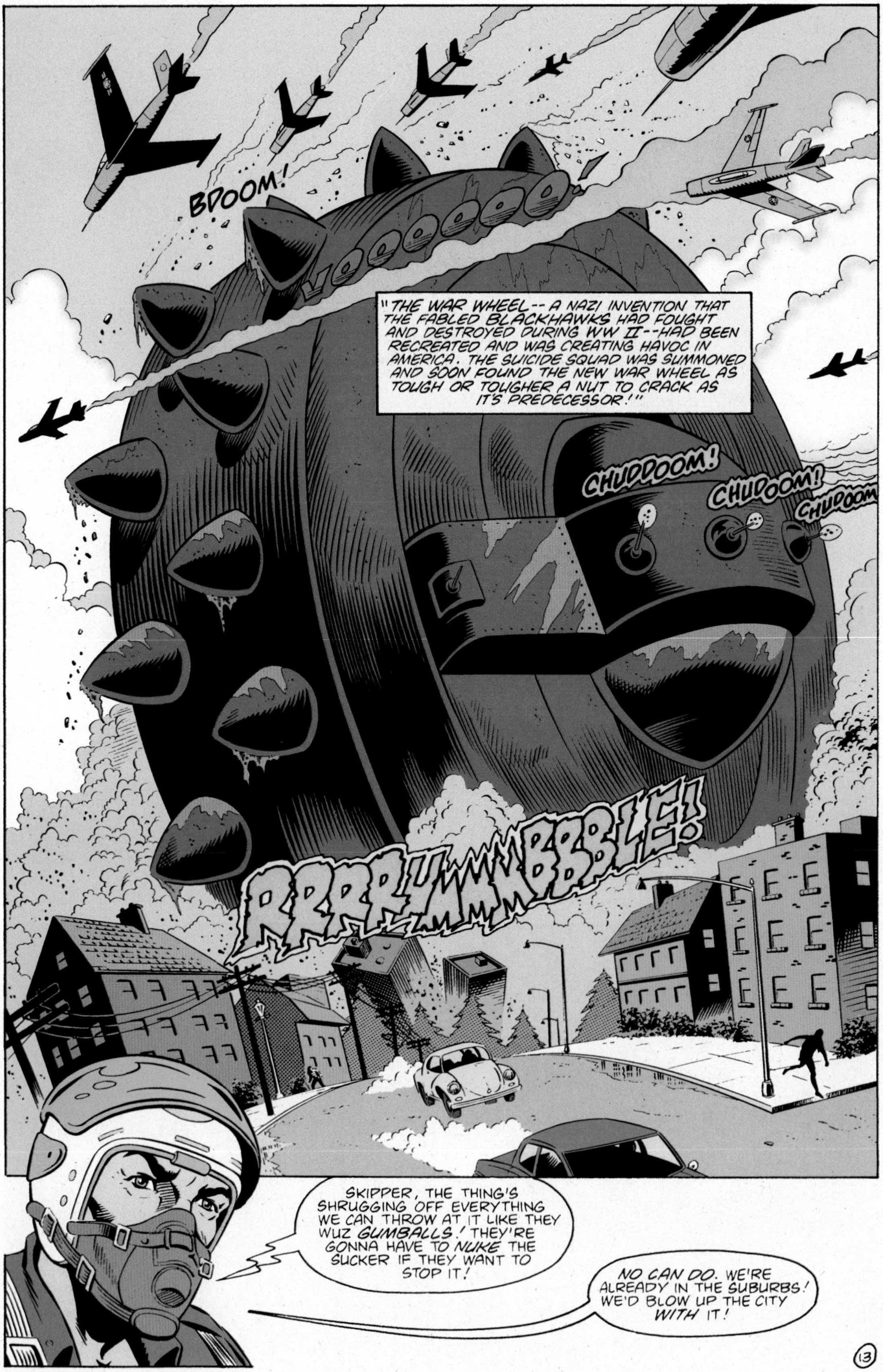
BDOOM!
VOOOOOOO!
"THE WAR WHEEL-- A NAZI INVENTION THAT THE FABLED BLACKHAWKS HAD FOUGHT AND DESTROYED DURING WW II--HAD BEEN RECREATED AND WAS CREATING HAVOC IN AMERICA. THE SUICIDE SQUAD WAS SUMMONED AND SOON FOUND THE NEW WAR WHEEL AS TOUGH OR TOUGHER A NUT TO CRACK AS IT'S PREDECESSOR!"
CHUDDOOM!
CHUDOOM!
CHUDOOM
RRRRUMMMBBBLE!
SKIPPER, THE THING'S SHRUGGING OFF EVERYTHING WE CAN THROW AT IT LIKE THEY WUZ GUMBALLS! THEY'RE GONNA HAVE TO NUKE THE SUCKER IF THEY WANT TO STOP IT!
NO CAN DO. WE'RE ALREADY IN THE SUBURBS! WE'D BLOW UP THE CITY WITH IT!
13

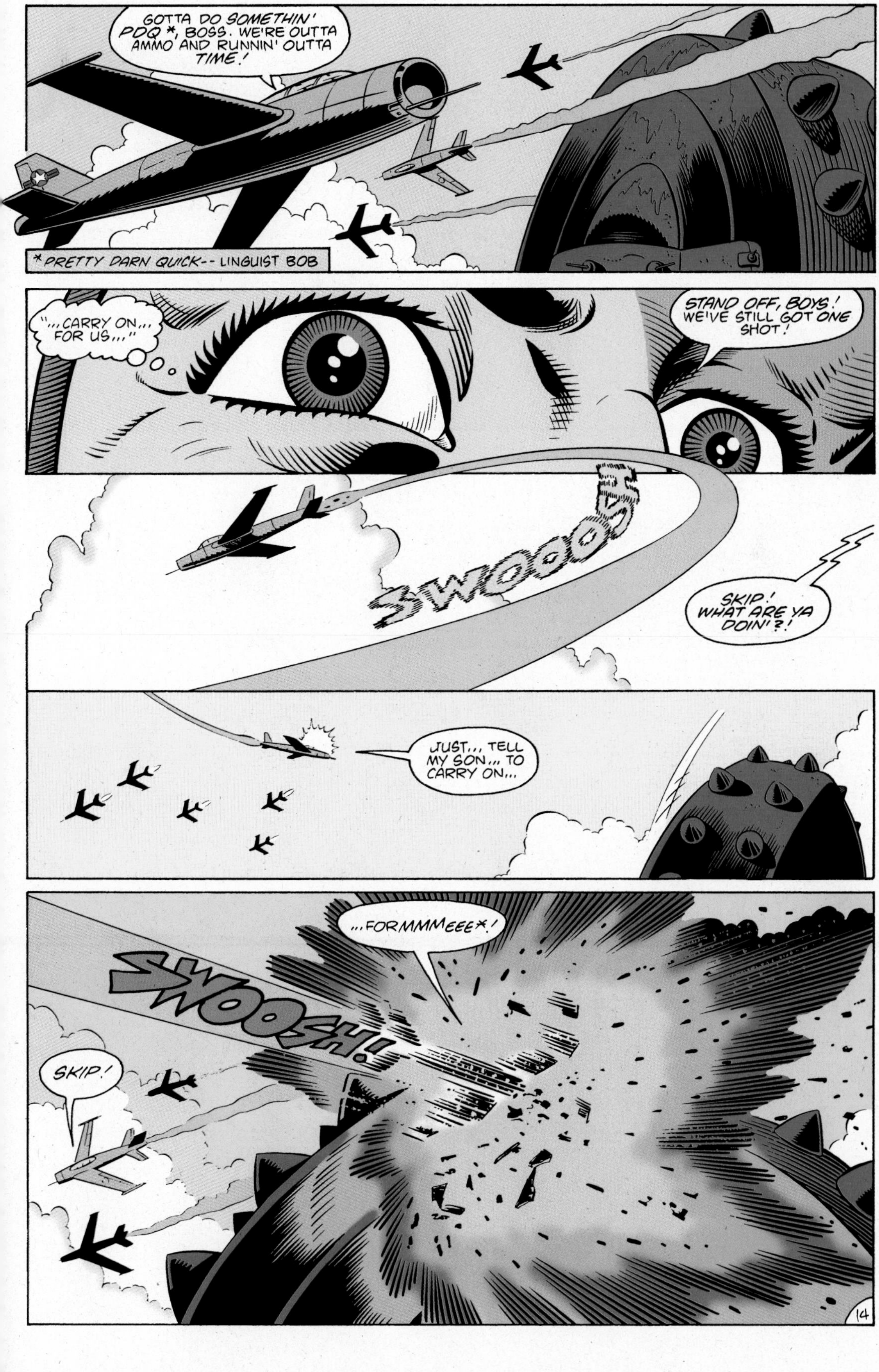
GOTTA DO SOMETHIN' PDQ*, BOSS. WE'RE OUTTA AMMO AND RUNNIN' OUTTA TIME!
*PRETTY DARN QUICK-- LINGUIST BOB
"...CARRY ON... FOR US..."
STAND OFF, BOYS! WE'VE STILL GOT ONE SHOT!
SWOOOOSH
SKIP! WHAT ARE YA DOIN'?!
JUST... TELL MY SON... TO CARRY ON...
...FORMMMEEE*!
SWOOSH!
SKIP!
14

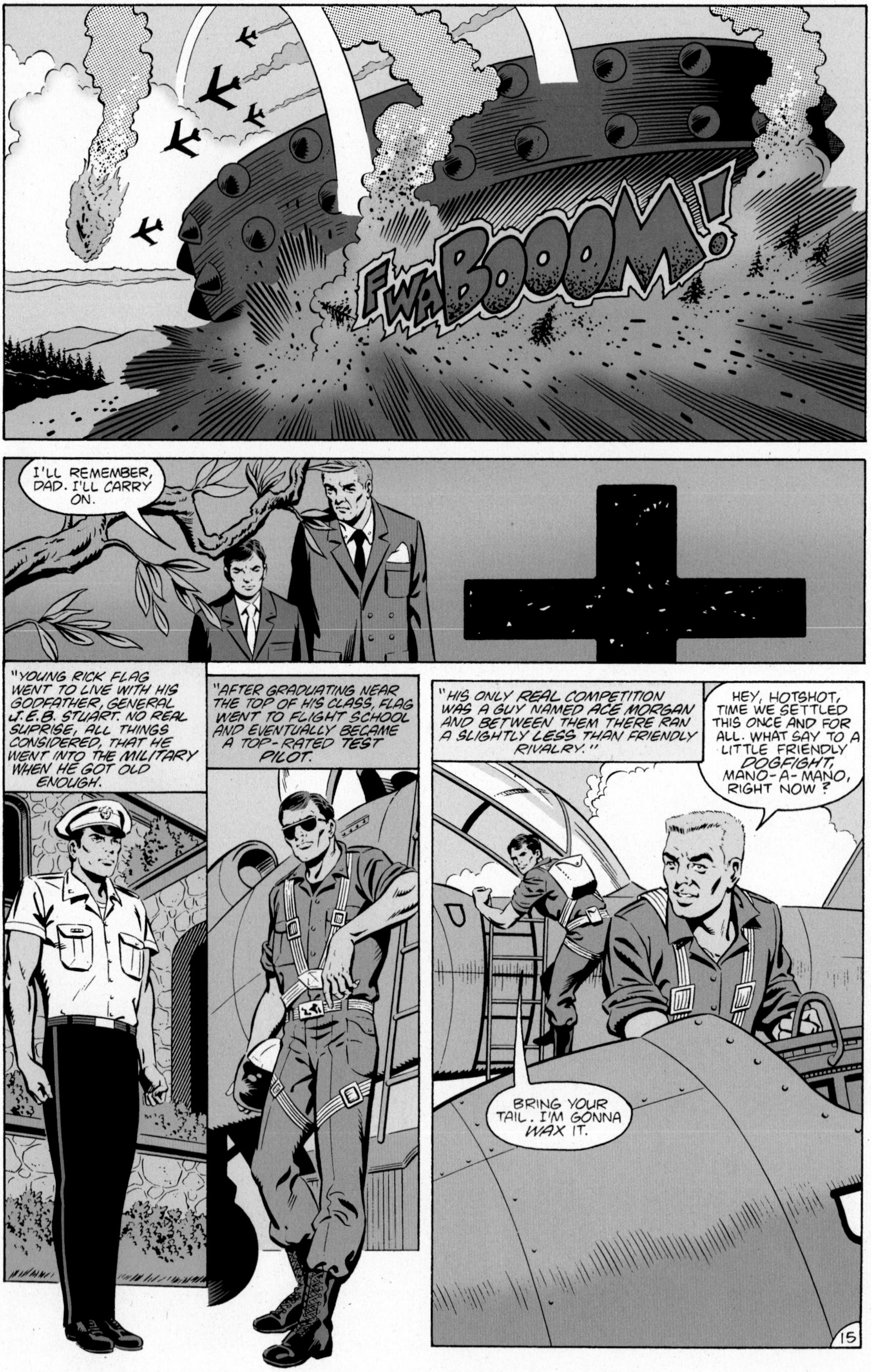
FWABOOOM!
I'LL REMEMBER, DAD. I'LL CARRY ON.
"YOUNG RICK FLAG WENT TO LIVE WITH HIS GODFATHER, GENERAL J.E.B. STUART. NO REAL SUPRISE, ALL THINGS CONSIDERED, THAT HE WENT INTO THE MILITARY WHEN HE GOT OLD ENOUGH.
"AFTER GRADUATING NEAR THE TOP OF HIS CLASS, FLAG WENT TO FLIGHT SCHOOL AND EVENTUALLY BECAME A TOP-RATED TEST PILOT.
"HIS ONLY REAL COMPETITION WAS A GUY NAMED ACE MORGAN AND BETWEEN THEM THERE RAN A SLIGHTLY LESS THAN FRIENDLY RIVALRY."
HEY, HOTSHOT, TIME WE SETTLED THIS ONCE AND FOR ALL. WHAT SAY TO A LITTLE FRIENDLY DOGFIGHT, MANO-A-MANO, RIGHT NOW?
BRING YOUR TAIL. I'M GONNA WAX IT.
15

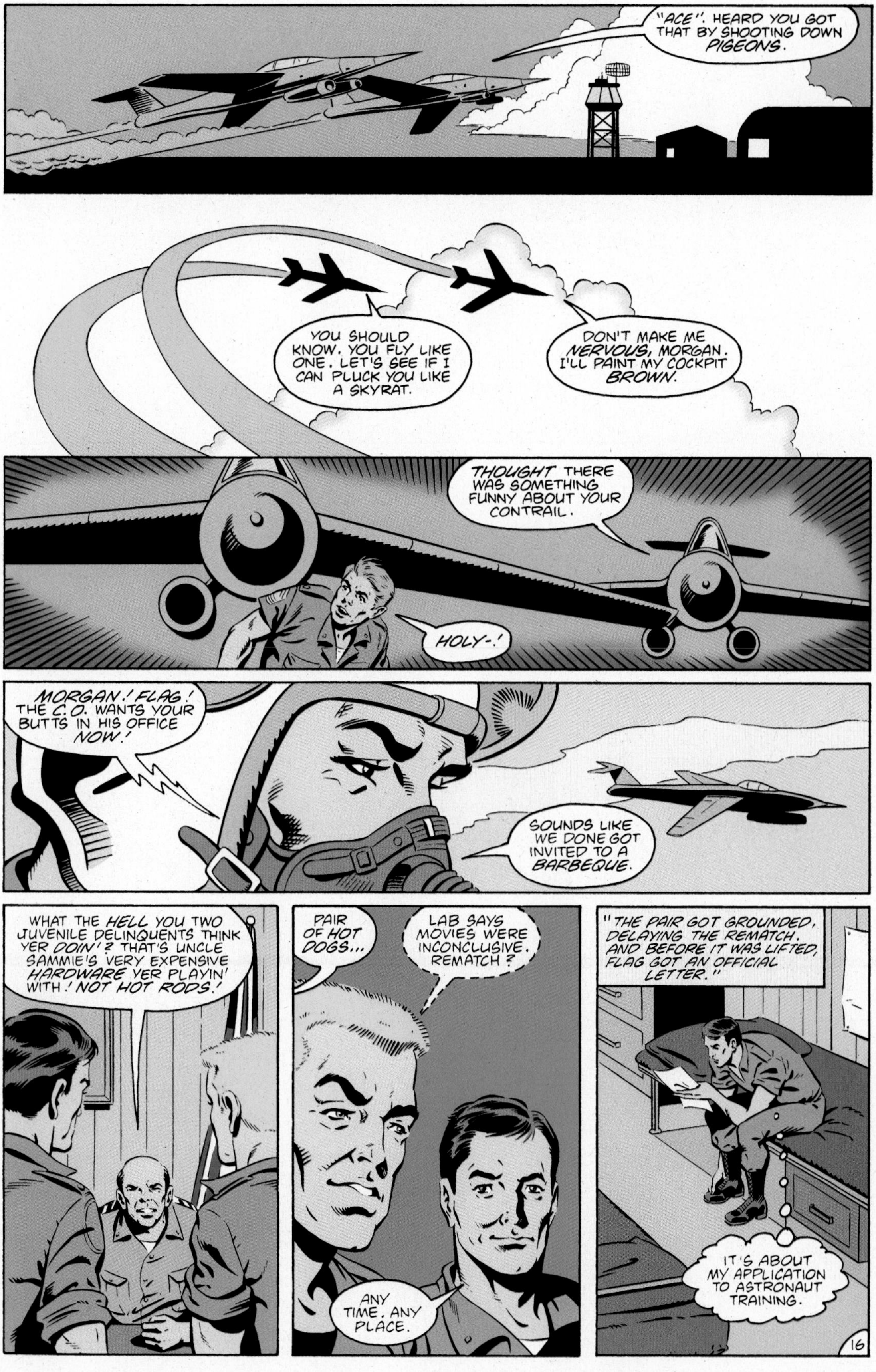
"ACE". HEARD YOU GOT THAT BY SHOOTING DOWN PIGEONS.
YOU SHOULD KNOW. YOU FLY LIKE ONE. LET'S SEE IF I CAN PLUCK YOU LIKE A SKYRAT.
DON'T MAKE ME NERVOUS, MORGAN. I'LL PAINT MY COCKPIT BROWN.
THOUGHT THERE WAS SOMETHING FUNNY ABOUT YOUR CONTRAIL.
HOLY-!
MORGAN! FLAG! THE C.O. WANTS YOUR BUTTS IN HIS OFFICE NOW!
SOUNDS LIKE WE DONE GOT INVITED TO A BARBEQUE.
WHAT THE HELL YOU TWO JUVENILE DELINQUENTS THINK YER DOIN'? THAT'S UNCLE SAMMIE'S VERY EXPENSIVE HARDWARE YER PLAYIN' WITH! NOT HOT RODS!
PAIR OF HOT DOGS...
LAB SAYS MOVIES WERE INCONCLUSIVE. REMATCH?
ANY TIME. ANY PLACE.
"THE PAIR GOT GROUNDED, DELAYING THE REMATCH. AND BEFORE IT WAS LIFTED, FLAG GOT AN OFFICIAL LETTER."
IT'S ABOUT MY APPLICATION TO ASTRONAUT TRAINING.
16

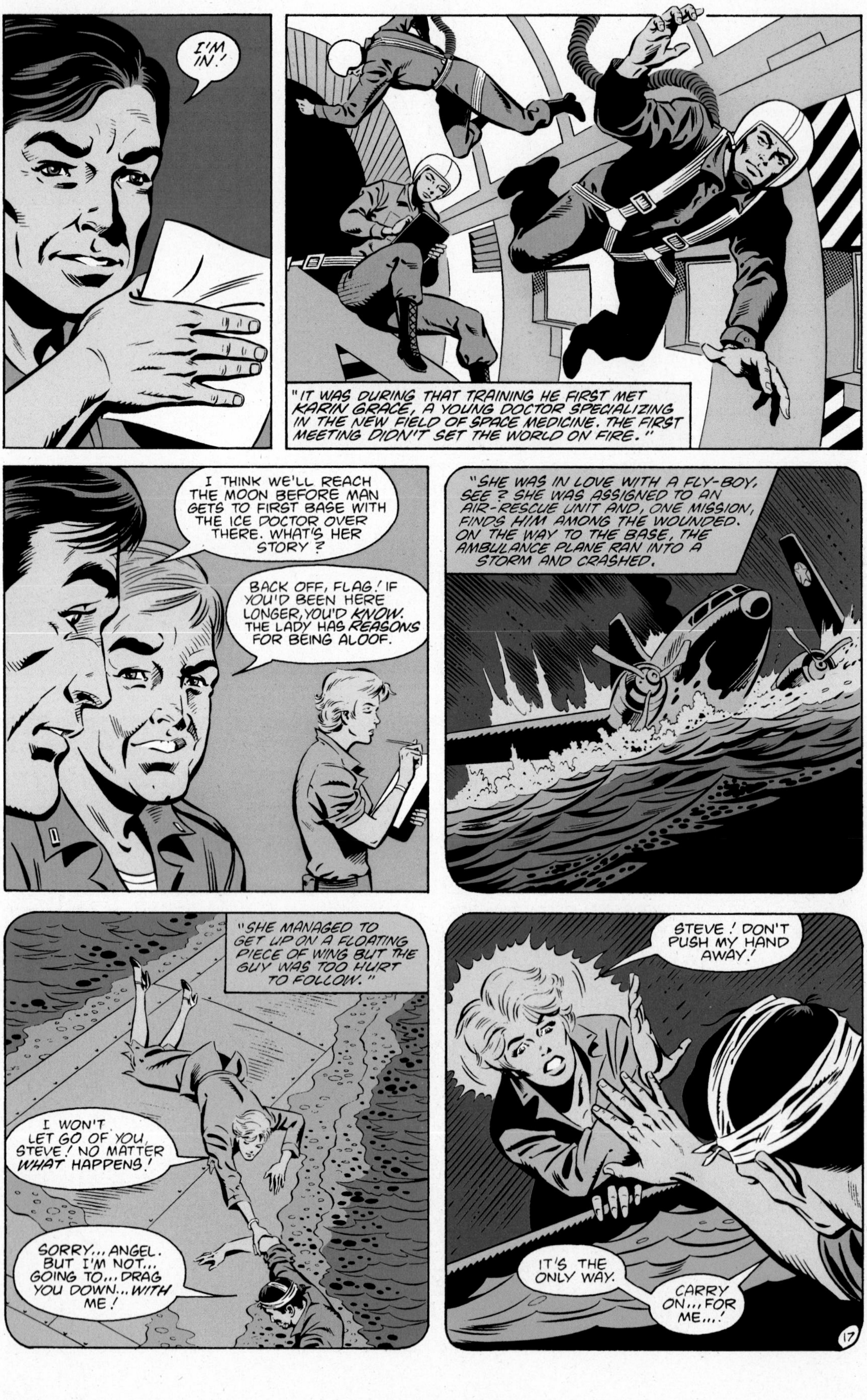
I'M IN!
"IT WAS DURING THAT TRAINING HE FIRST MET KARIN GRACE, A YOUNG DOCTOR SPECIALIZING IN THE NEW FIELD OF SPACE MEDICINE. THE FIRST MEETING DIDN'T SET THE WORLD ON FIRE."
I THINK WE'LL REACH THE MOON BEFORE MAN GETS TO FIRST BASE WITH THE ICE DOCTOR OVER THERE. WHAT'S HER STORY?
BACK OFF, FLAG! IF YOU'D BEEN HERE LONGER, YOU'D KNOW. THE LADY HAS REASONS FOR BEING ALOOF.
"SHE WAS IN LOVE WITH A FLY-BOY, SEE? SHE WAS ASSIGNED TO AN AIR-RESCUE UNIT AND, ONE MISSION, FINDS HIM AMONG THE WOUNDED. ON THE WAY TO THE BASE, THE AMBULANCE PLANE RAN INTO A STORM AND CRASHED.
"SHE MANAGED TO GET UP ON A FLOATING PIECE OF WING BUT THE GUY WAS TOO HURT TO FOLLOW."
I WON'T LET GO OF YOU, STEVE! NO MATTER WHAT HAPPENS!
SORRY... ANGEL. BUT I'M NOT... GOING TO... DRAG YOU DOWN... WITH ME!
STEVE! DON'T PUSH MY HAND AWAY!
IT'S THE ONLY WAY.
CARRY ON... FOR ME...!
17

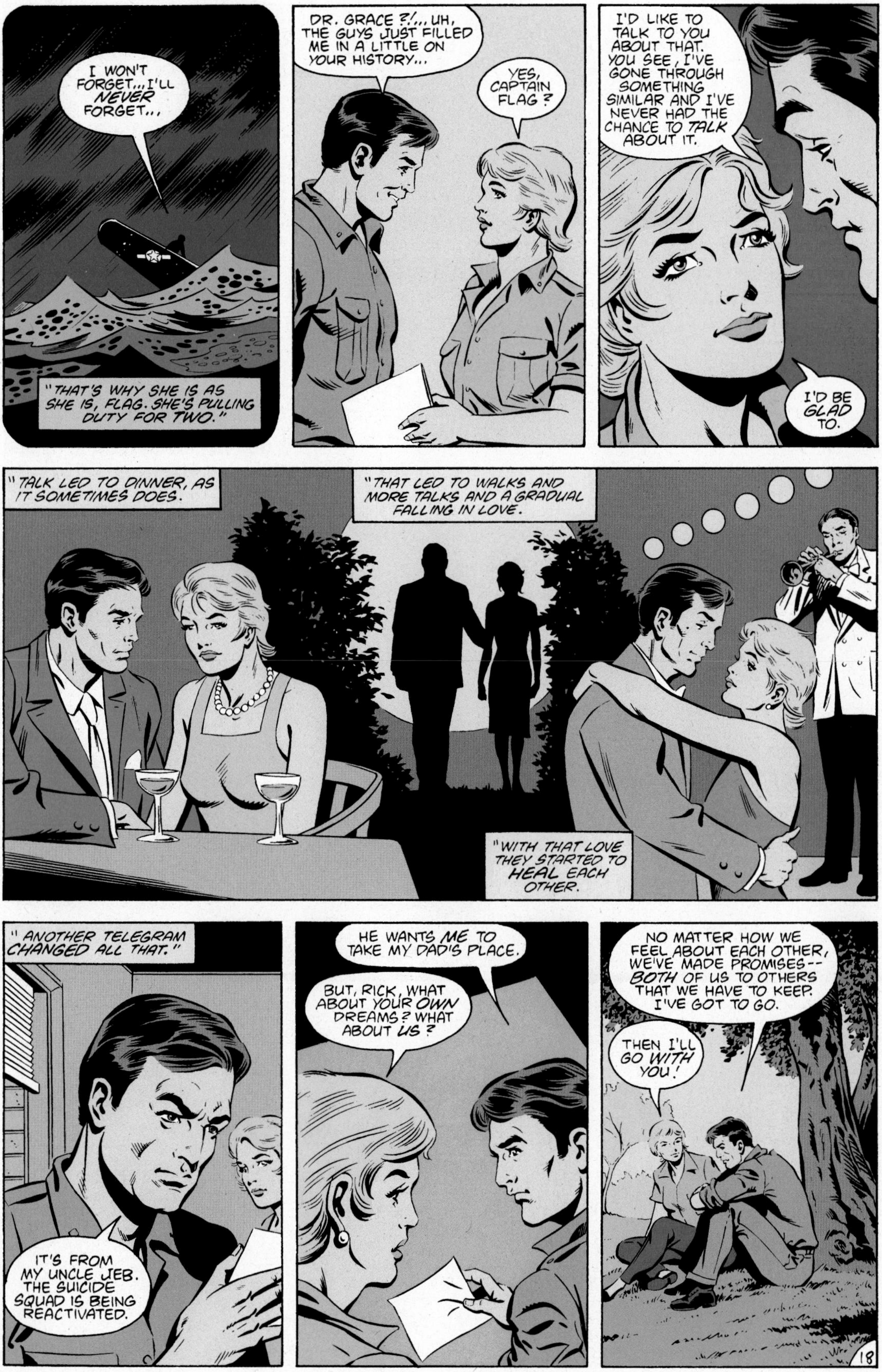
I WON'T FORGET... I'LL NEVER FORGET...
"THAT'S WHY SHE IS AS SHE IS, FLAG. SHE'S PULLING DUTY FOR TWO."
DR. GRACE ?!... UH, THE GUYS JUST FILLED ME IN A LITTLE ON YOUR HISTORY...
YES, CAPTAIN FLAG ?
I'D LIKE TO TALK TO YOU ABOUT THAT. YOU SEE, I'VE GONE THROUGH SOMETHING SIMILAR AND I'VE NEVER HAD THE CHANCE TO TALK ABOUT IT.
I'D BE GLAD TO.
"TALK LED TO DINNER, AS IT SOMETIMES DOES.
"THAT LED TO WALKS AND MORE TALKS AND A GRADUAL FALLING IN LOVE.
"WITH THAT LOVE THEY STARTED TO HEAL EACH OTHER.
"ANOTHER TELEGRAM CHANGED ALL THAT."
IT'S FROM MY UNCLE JEB. THE SUICIDE SQUAD IS BEING REACTIVATED.
HE WANTS ME TO TAKE MY DAD'S PLACE.
BUT, RICK, WHAT ABOUT YOUR OWN DREAMS? WHAT ABOUT US?
NO MATTER HOW WE FEEL ABOUT EACH OTHER, WE'VE MADE PROMISES-- BOTH OF US TO OTHERS THAT WE HAVE TO KEEP. I'VE GOT TO GO.
THEN I'LL GO WITH YOU!
18

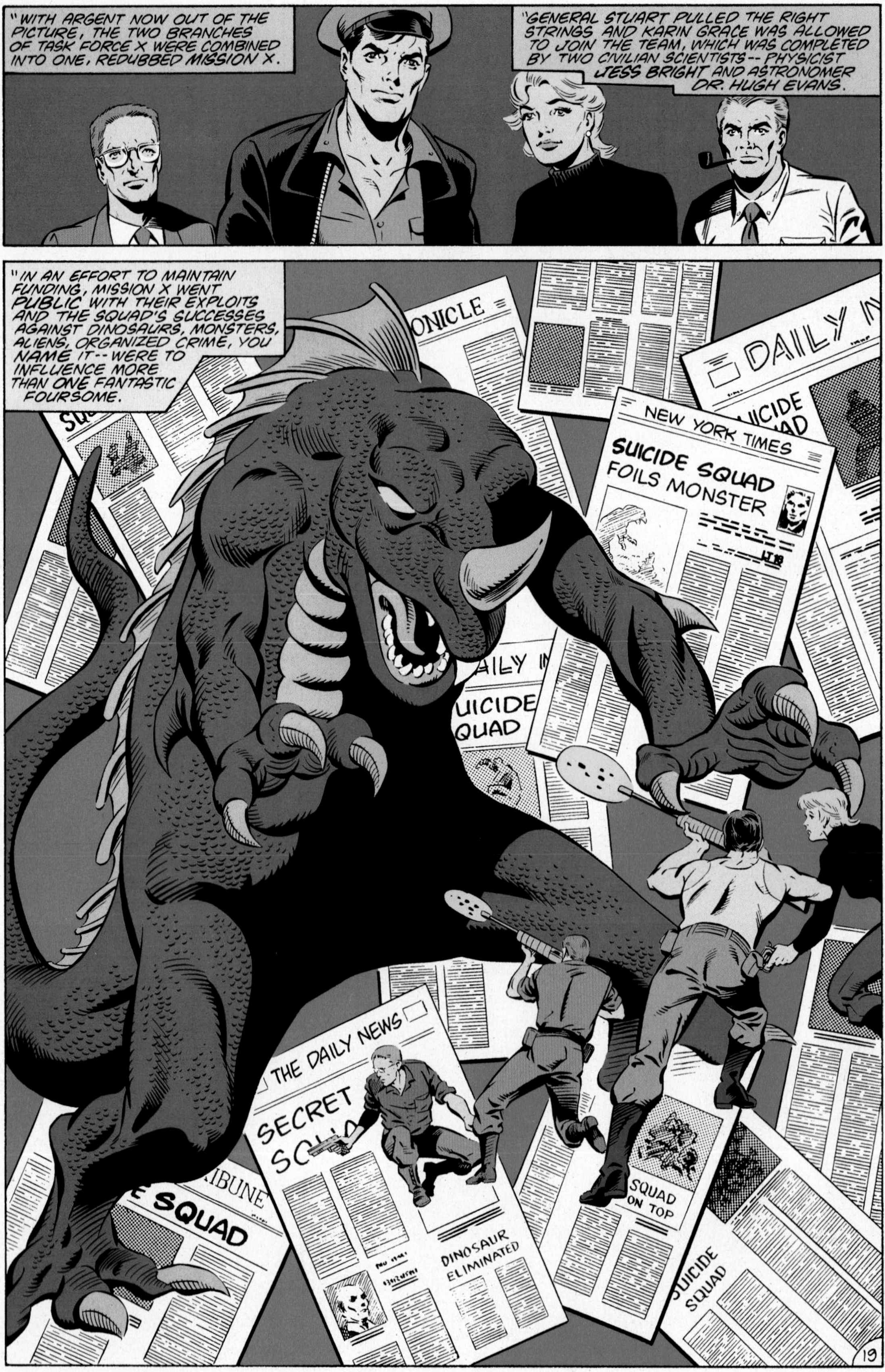
"WITH ARGENT NOW OUT OF THE PICTURE, THE TWO BRANCHES OF TASK FORCE X WERE COMBINED INTO ONE, REDUBBED MISSION X.
"GENERAL STUART PULLED THE RIGHT STRINGS AND KARIN GRACE WAS ALLOWED TO JOIN THE TEAM, WHICH WAS COMPLETED BY TWO CIVILIAN SCIENTISTS -- PHYSICIST JESS BRIGHT AND ASTRONOMER DR. HUGH EVANS.
"IN AN EFFORT TO MAINTAIN FUNDING, MISSION X WENT PUBLIC WITH THEIR EXPLOITS AND THE SQUAD'S SUCCESSES AGAINST DINOSAURS, MONSTERS, ALIENS, ORGANIZED CRIME, YOU NAME IT -- WERE TO INFLUENCE MORE THAN ONE FANTASTIC FOURSOME.
NEW YORK TIMES
SUICIDE SQUAD FOILS MONSTER
THE DAILY NEWS
SECRET
DINOSAUR ELIMINATED
SQUAD ON TOP
19

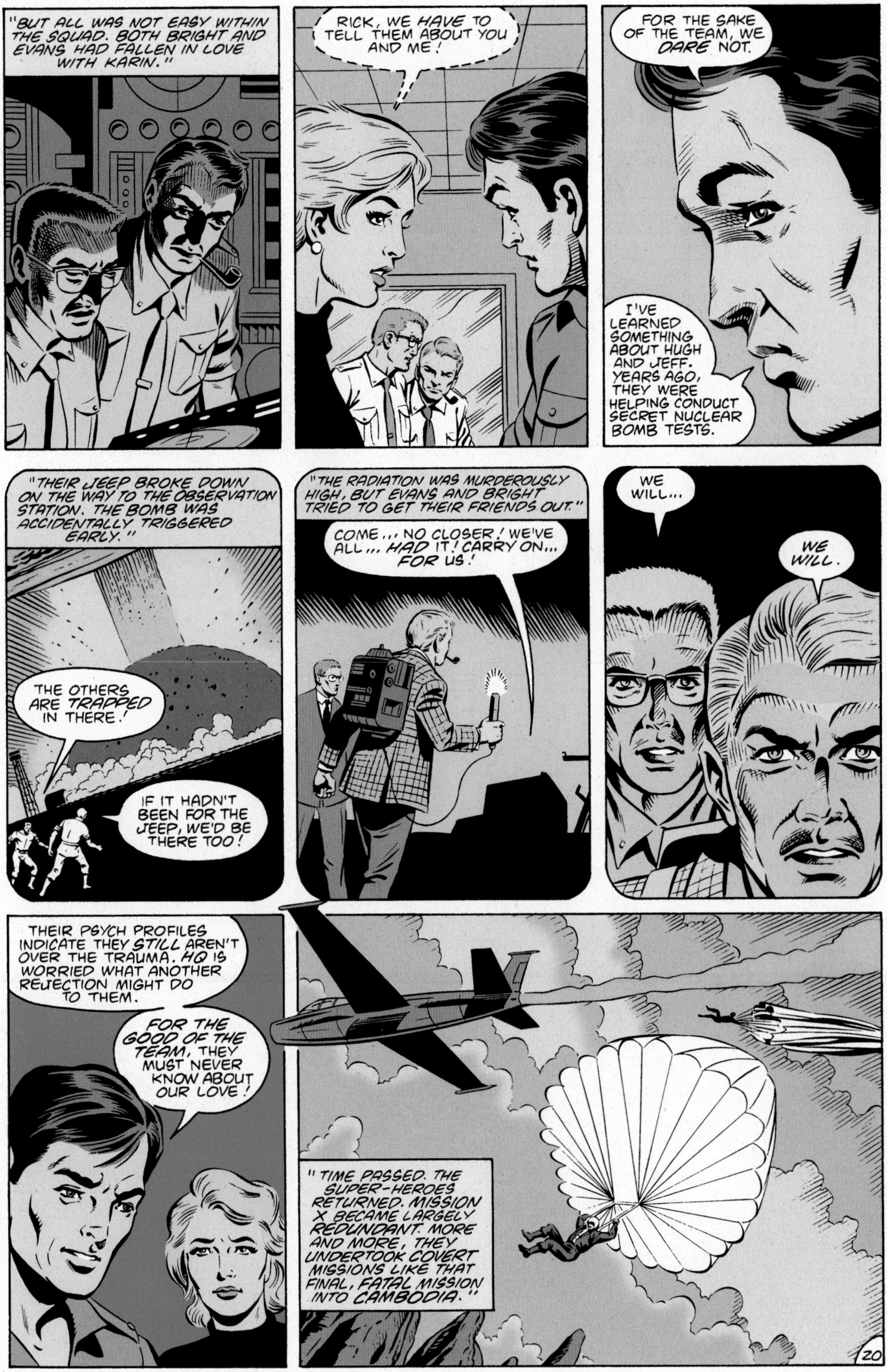
"BUT ALL WAS NOT EASY WITHIN THE SQUAD. BOTH BRIGHT AND EVANS HAD FALLEN IN LOVE WITH KARIN."
RICK, WE HAVE TO TELL THEM ABOUT YOU AND ME!
FOR THE SAKE OF THE TEAM, WE DARE NOT.
I'VE LEARNED SOMETHING ABOUT HUGH AND JEFF. YEARS AGO, THEY WERE HELPING CONDUCT SECRET NUCLEAR BOMB TESTS.
"THEIR JEEP BROKE DOWN ON THE WAY TO THE OBSERVATION STATION. THE BOMB WAS ACCIDENTALLY TRIGGERED EARLY."
THE OTHERS ARE TRAPPED IN THERE!
IF IT HADN'T BEEN FOR THE JEEP, WE'D BE THERE TOO!
"THE RADIATION WAS MURDEROUSLY HIGH, BUT EVANS AND BRIGHT TRIED TO GET THEIR FRIENDS OUT."
COME... NO CLOSER! WE'VE ALL... HAD IT! CARRY ON... FOR US!
WE WILL...
WE WILL.
THEIR PSYCH PROFILES INDICATE THEY STILL AREN'T OVER THE TRAUMA. HQ IS WORRIED WHAT ANOTHER REJECTION MIGHT DO TO THEM.
FOR THE GOOD OF THE TEAM, THEY MUST NEVER KNOW ABOUT OUR LOVE!
"TIME PASSED. THE SUPER-HEROES RETURNED. MISSION X BECAME LARGELY REDUNDANT. MORE AND MORE, THEY UNDERTOOK COVERT MISSIONS LIKE THAT FINAL, FATAL MISSION INTO CAMBODIA."
20

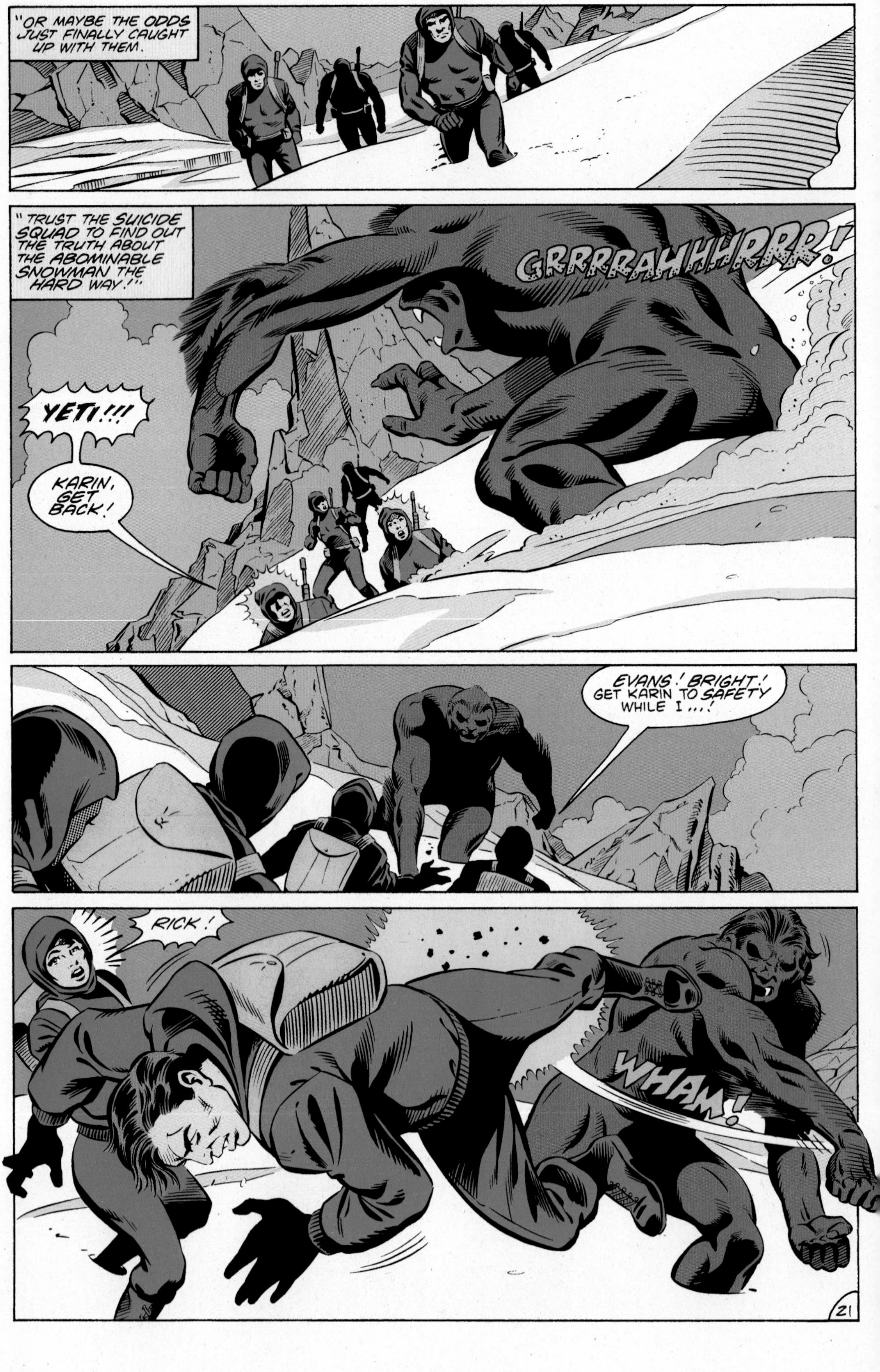

"OR MAYBE THE ODDS JUST FINALLY CAUGHT UP WITH THEM.
"TRUST THE SUICIDE SQUAD TO FIND OUT THE TRUTH ABOUT THE ABOMINABLE SNOWMAN THE HARD WAY!"
GRRRRAHHHRRR!
YETI!!!
KARIN, GET BACK!
EVANS! BRIGHT! GET KARIN TO SAFETY WHILE I...!
RICK!
WHAM!
21

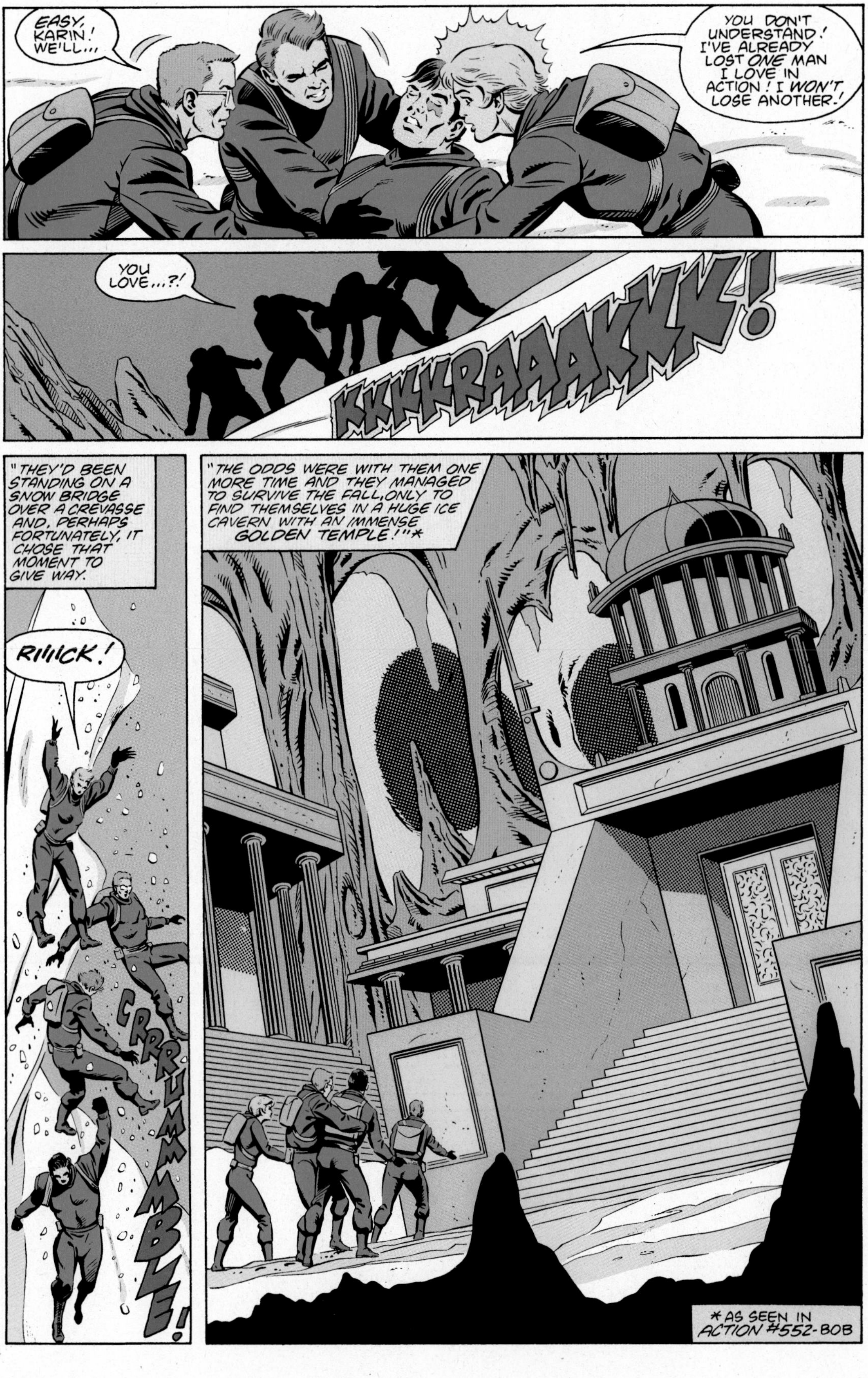
EASY, KARIN! WE'LL...
YOU DON'T UNDERSTAND! I'VE ALREADY LOST ONE MAN I LOVE IN ACTION! I WON'T LOSE ANOTHER!
YOU LOVE...?!
KKKKRAAAKKK!
"THEY'D BEEN STANDING ON A SNOW BRIDGE OVER A CREVASSE AND, PERHAPS FORTUNATELY, IT CHOSE THAT MOMENT TO GIVE WAY.
RIIICK!
CRRRUMMMBLE!
"THE ODDS WERE WITH THEM ONE MORE TIME AND THEY MANAGED TO SURVIVE THE FALL, ONLY TO FIND THEMSELVES IN A HUGE ICE CAVERN WITH AN IMMENSE GOLDEN TEMPLE!"*
*AS SEEN IN ACTION #552-BOB

"KARIN'S CONCERN FOR RICK HAD NOT GONE UNREMARKED OR MISUNDERSTOOD."

YOU AND FLAG-- THIS HAS BEEN GOING ON SINCE WE BEGAN, HASN'T IT, KARIN?

OH, PLEASE, JEFF! NOT NOW!

KARIN... DON'T... THE TEAM...!

HUSH, DARLING! IT'S OUT NOW!

WHY COULDN'T YOU JUST TELL US?

RICK...WE FELT IT WAS BETTER THIS WAY! FOR THE SAKE OF THE TEAM! HUGH, I'M SORRY!

HONESTY WOULD'VE BEEN BEST FOR THE TEAM, NOT PLAYING US FOR FOOLS!

YOU CAN TAKE THE TEAM AND SHOVE IT! WHEN WE GET BACK, I'M THROUGH!

IT'S HAPPENING JUST LIKE I FEARED. OR IS IT, DEEP DOWN, THE WAY THAT I ALWAYS WANTED?!

THE SQUAD WAS MY DUTY, NOT MY DREAM.

DEEP DOWN, HAVE I SET US UP FOR THIS FALL?

"ANGER, DOUBT, GUILT-- THE SUICIDE SQUAD WAS STARTING TO CRACK.

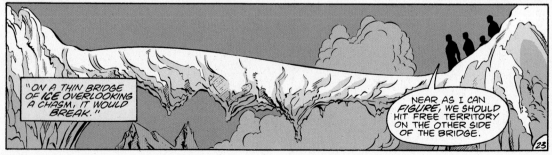

"ON A THIN BRIDGE OF ICE OVERLOOKING A CHASM. IT WOULD BREAK."

NEAR AS I CAN FIGURE, WE SHOULD HIT FREE TERRITORY ON THE OTHER SIDE OF THE BRIDGE.

23

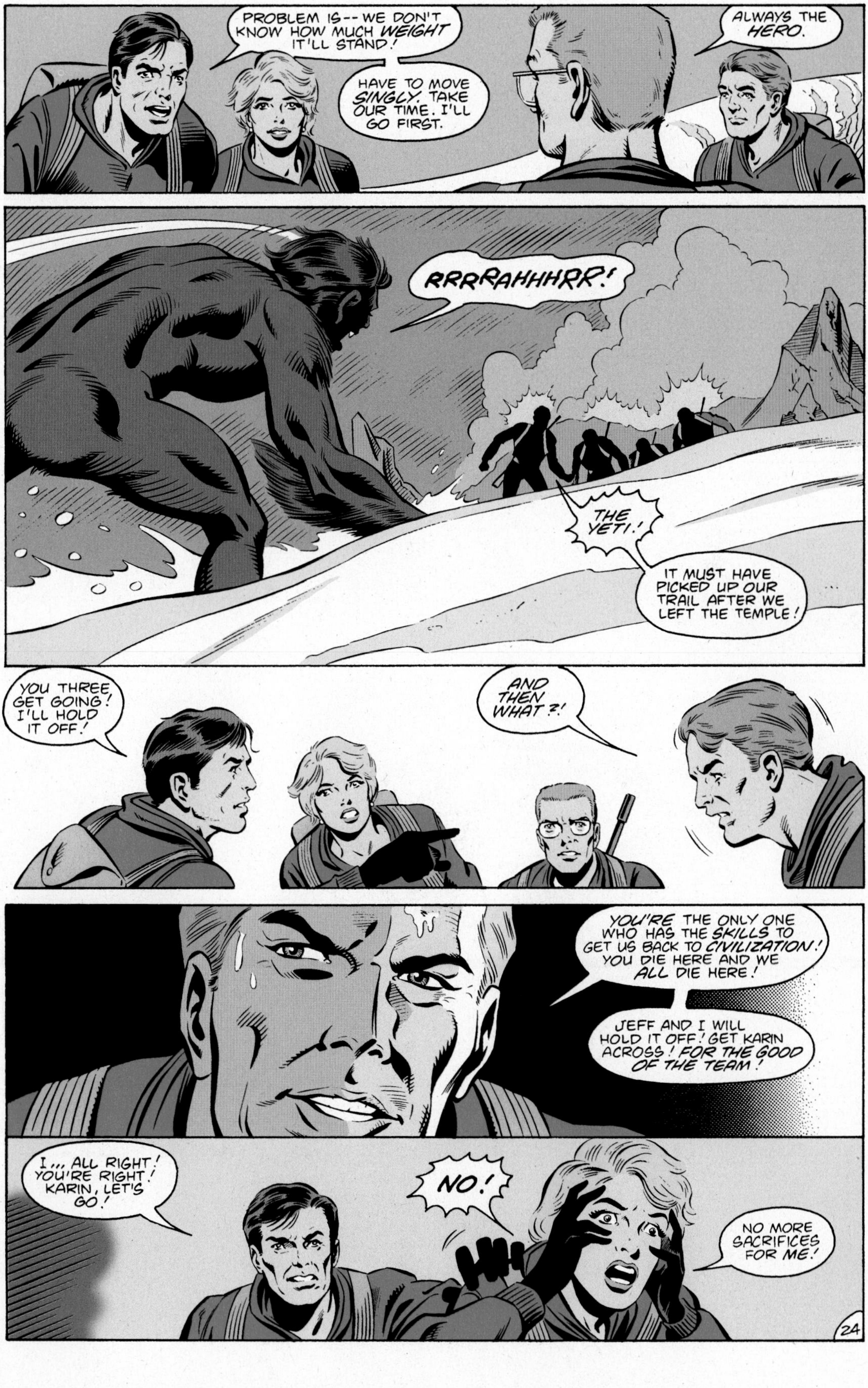
PROBLEM IS-- WE DON'T KNOW HOW MUCH WEIGHT IT'LL STAND!
HAVE TO MOVE SINGLY. TAKE OUR TIME. I'LL GO FIRST.
ALWAYS THE HERO.
RRRRAHHHRR!
THE YETI!
IT MUST HAVE PICKED UP OUR TRAIL AFTER WE LEFT THE TEMPLE!
YOU THREE GET GOING! I'LL HOLD IT OFF!
AND THEN WHAT?!
YOU'RE THE ONLY ONE WHO HAS THE SKILLS TO GET US BACK TO CIVILIZATION! YOU DIE HERE AND WE ALL DIE HERE!
JEFF AND I WILL HOLD IT OFF! GET KARIN ACROSS! FOR THE GOOD OF THE TEAM!
I... ALL RIGHT! YOU'RE RIGHT! KARIN, LET'S GO!
NO!
NO MORE SACRIFICES FOR ME!
24

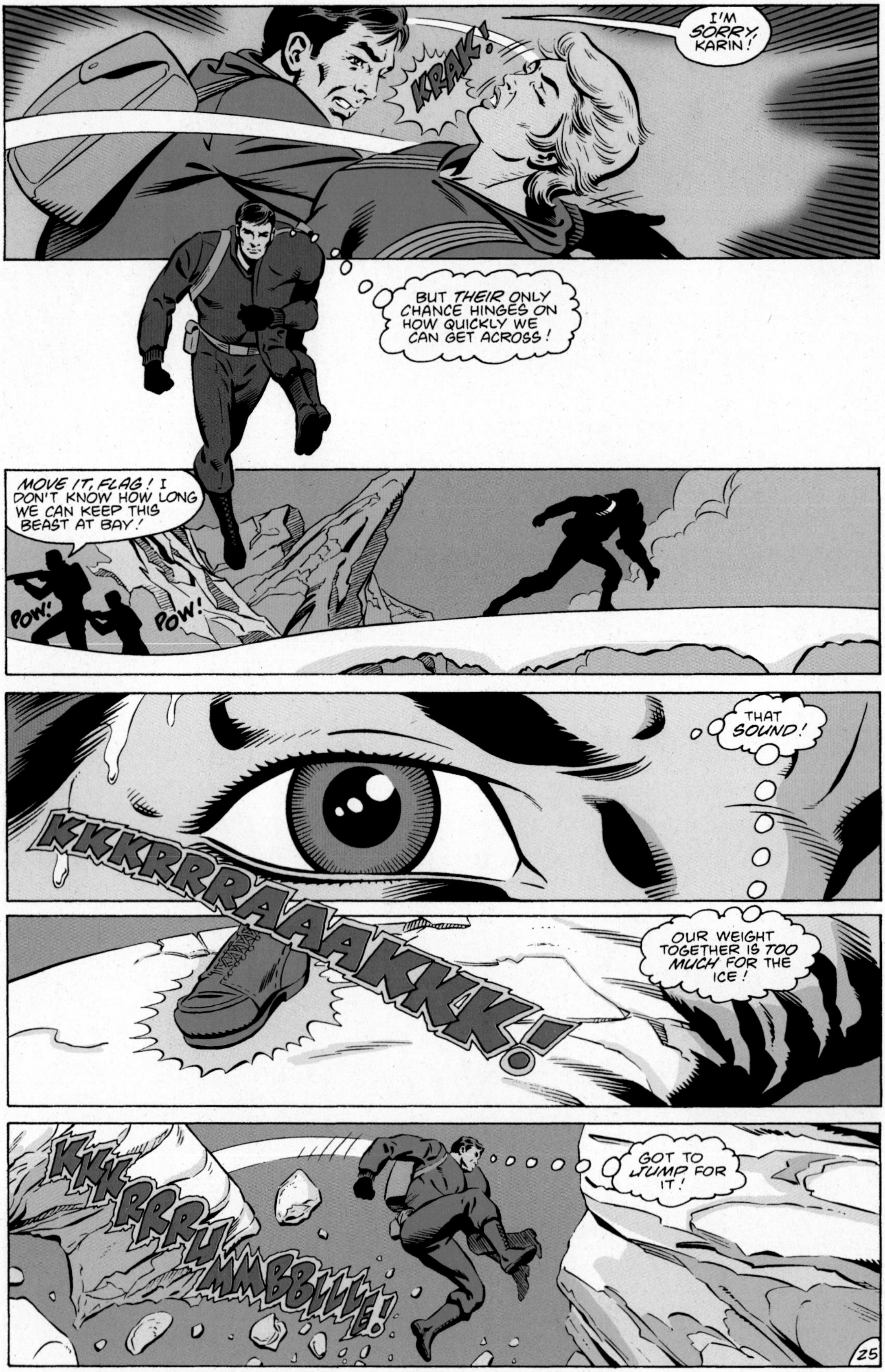
I'M SORRY, KARIN!
KRAK!
BUT THEIR ONLY CHANCE HINGES ON HOW QUICKLY WE CAN GET ACROSS!
MOVE IT, FLAG! I DON'T KNOW HOW LONG WE CAN KEEP THIS BEAST AT BAY!
POW!
POW!
THAT SOUND!
KKKRRRRAAAAKKKK!
OUR WEIGHT TOGETHER IS TOO MUCH FOR THE ICE!
KKKRRRRUMMBBLLLE!
GOT TO JUMP FOR IT!
25

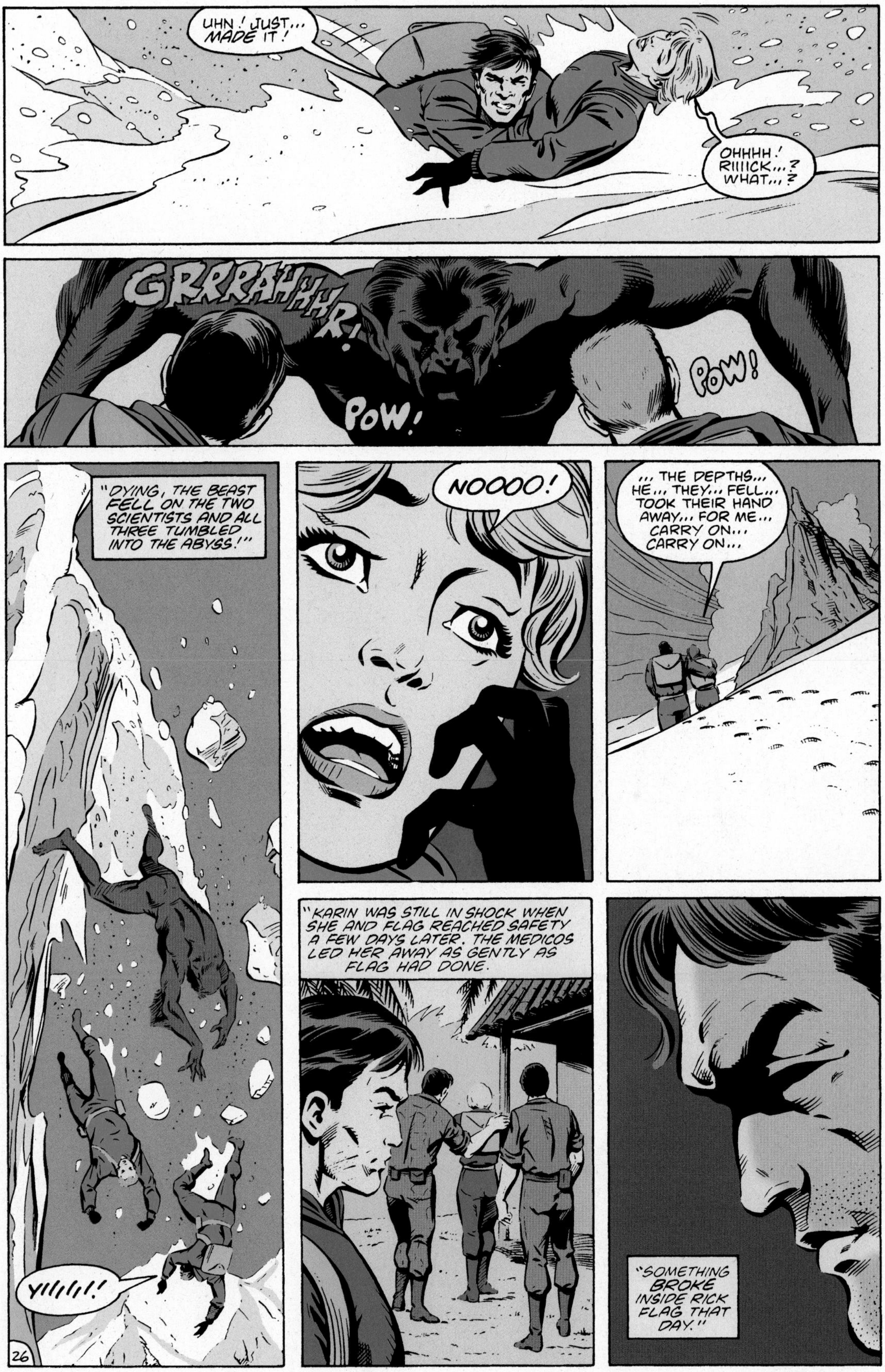
UHN! JUST... MADE IT!
OHHHH! RIIIICK...? WHAT...?
GRRRAHHHR!
POW!
POW!
"DYING, THE BEAST FELL ON THE TWO SCIENTISTS AND ALL THREE TUMBLED INTO THE ABYSS!"
YIIIII!
26
NOOOO!
... THE DEPTHS... HE... THEY... FELL... TOOK THEIR HAND AWAY... FOR ME... CARRY ON... CARRY ON...
"KARIN WAS STILL IN SHOCK WHEN SHE AND FLAG REACHED SAFETY A FEW DAYS LATER. THE MEDICOS LED HER AWAY AS GENTLY AS FLAG HAD DONE.
"SOMETHING BROKE INSIDE RICK FLAG THAT DAY."

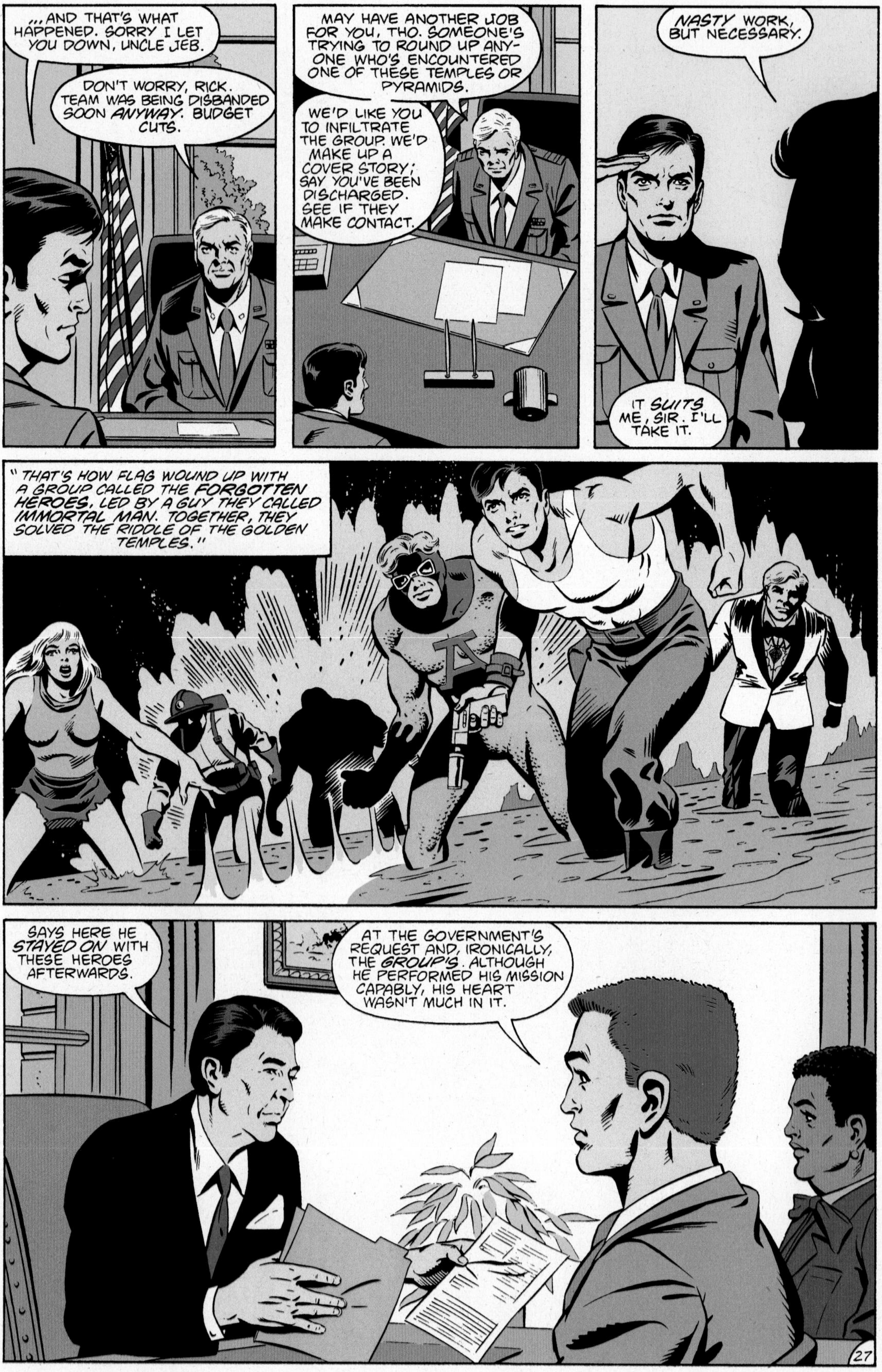
...AND THAT'S WHAT HAPPENED. SORRY I LET YOU DOWN, UNCLE JEB.
DON'T WORRY, RICK. TEAM WAS BEING DISBANDED SOON ANYWAY. BUDGET CUTS.
MAY HAVE ANOTHER JOB FOR YOU, THO. SOMEONE'S TRYING TO ROUND UP ANYONE WHO'S ENCOUNTERED ONE OF THESE TEMPLES OR PYRAMIDS.
WE'D LIKE YOU TO INFILTRATE THE GROUP. WE'D MAKE UP A COVER STORY; SAY YOU'VE BEEN DISCHARGED. SEE IF THEY MAKE CONTACT.
NASTY WORK, BUT NECESSARY.
IT SUITS ME, SIR. I'LL TAKE IT.
"THAT'S HOW FLAG WOUND UP WITH A GROUP CALLED THE FORGOTTEN HEROES, LED BY A GUY THEY CALLED IMMORTAL MAN. TOGETHER, THEY SOLVED THE RIDDLE OF THE GOLDEN TEMPLES."
SAYS HERE HE STAYED ON WITH THESE HEROES AFTERWARDS.
AT THE GOVERNMENT'S REQUEST AND, IRONICALLY, THE GROUP'S. ALTHOUGH HE PERFORMED HIS MISSION CAPABLY, HIS HEART WASN'T MUCH IN IT.
27

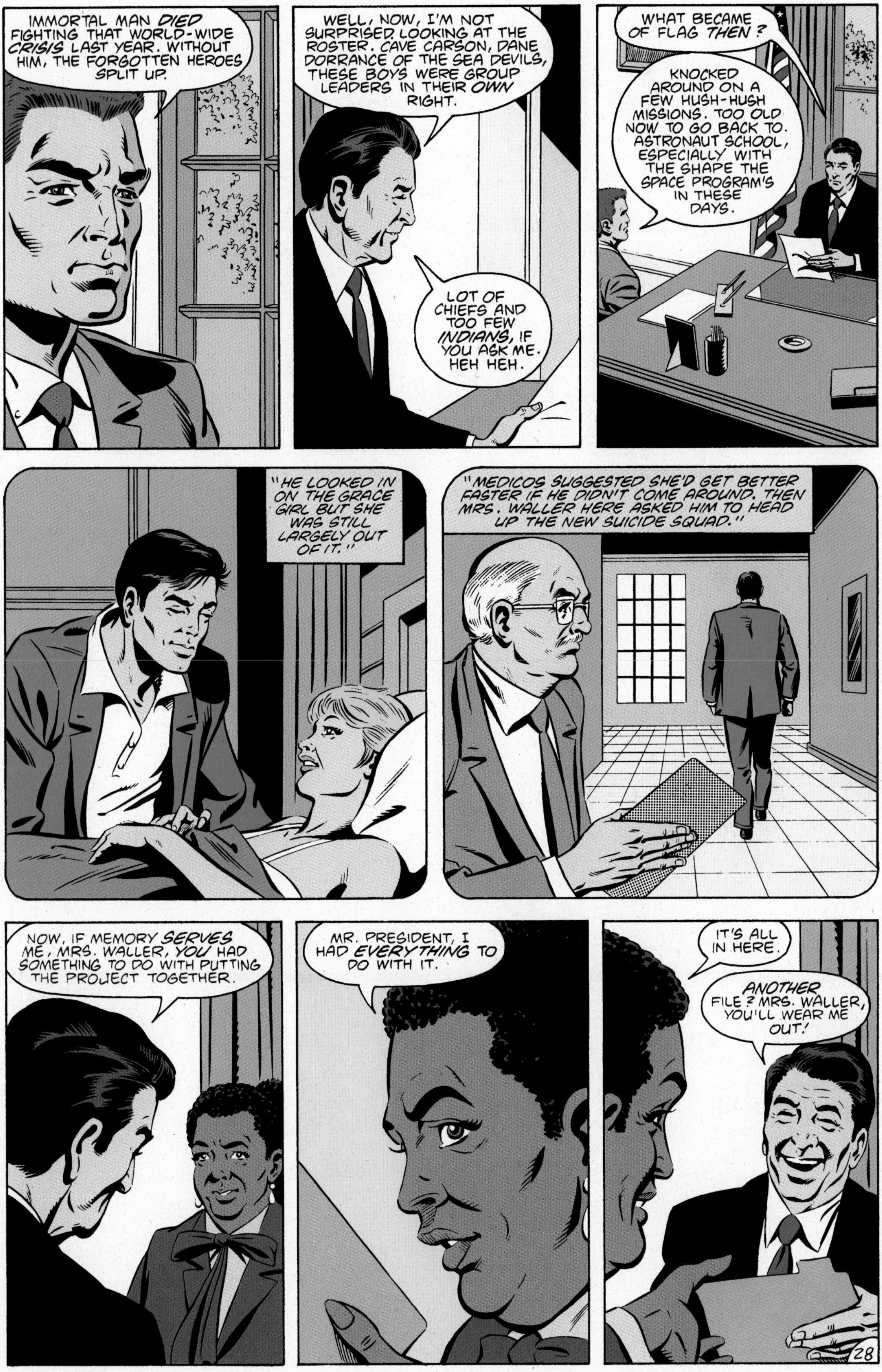
IMMORTAL MAN DIED FIGHTING THAT WORLD-WIDE CRISIS LAST YEAR. WITHOUT HIM, THE FORGOTTEN HEROES SPLIT UP.
WELL, NOW, I'M NOT SURPRISED LOOKING AT THE ROSTER. CAVE CARSON, DANE DORRANCE OF THE SEA DEVILS, THESE BOYS WERE GROUP LEADERS IN THEIR OWN RIGHT.
LOT OF CHIEFS AND TOO FEW INDIANS, IF YOU ASK ME. HEH HEH.
WHAT BECAME OF FLAG THEN?
KNOCKED AROUND ON A FEW HUSH-HUSH MISSIONS. TOO OLD NOW TO GO BACK TO. ASTRONAUT SCHOOL, ESPECIALLY WITH THE SHAPE THE SPACE PROGRAM'S IN THESE DAYS.
"HE LOOKED IN ON THE GRACE GIRL BUT SHE WAS STILL LARGELY OUT OF IT."
"MEDICOS SUGGESTED SHE'D GET BETTER FASTER IF HE DIDN'T COME AROUND. THEN MRS. WALLER HERE ASKED HIM TO HEAD UP THE NEW SUICIDE SQUAD."
NOW, IF MEMORY SERVES ME, MRS. WALLER, YOU HAD SOMETHING TO DO WITH PUTTING THE PROJECT TOGETHER.
MR. PRESIDENT, I HAD EVERYTHING TO DO WITH IT.
IT'S ALL IN HERE.
ANOTHER FILE? MRS. WALLER, YOU'LL WEAR ME OUT!
28

WON'T KEEP YOU LONG FROM YOUR *NAP*, SIR. JUST A *SHORT* AND *BITTER* STORY. MINE.

THE REPORTS OF THE CRIME AND VIOLENCE THAT OCCUR IN CHICAGO'S *CABRINI-GREEN* ARE ALL TRUE. PLACE IS ALSO HOME TO LOTS OF *GOOD, DECENT* FOLKS TRYING TO FIND A WAY *OUT* OF THE CYCLE OF POVERTY.

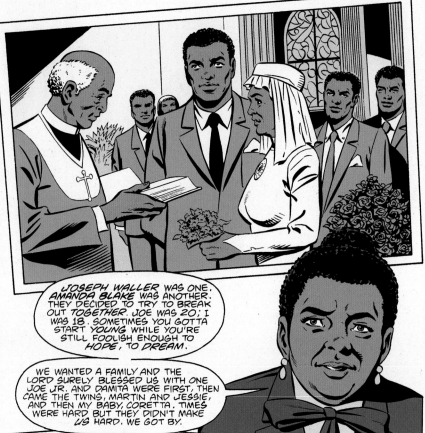

JOSEPH WALLER WAS ONE. *AMANDA BLAKE* WAS ANOTHER. THEY DECIDED TO TRY TO BREAK OUT *TOGETHER*. JOE WAS 20; I WAS 18. SOMETIMES YOU GOTTA START *YOUNG* WHILE YOU'RE STILL FOOLISH ENOUGH TO *HOPE*, TO *DREAM*.

WE WANTED A FAMILY AND THE LORD SURELY BLESSED US WITH ONE JOE JR. AND DAMITA WERE FIRST, THEN CAME THE TWINS, MARTIN AND JESSIE, AND THEN MY BABY, CORETTA. TIMES WERE HARD BUT THEY DIDN'T MAKE *US* HARD. WE GOT BY.

OF COURSE, IN THOSE DAYS WE HAD SOME SOCIAL PROGRAMS TO FALL BACK ON. YOU *DO* REMEMBER SOCIAL PROGRAMS, DON'T YOU, MR. PRESIDENT?

NOW, NOW, MRS. WALLER...

29

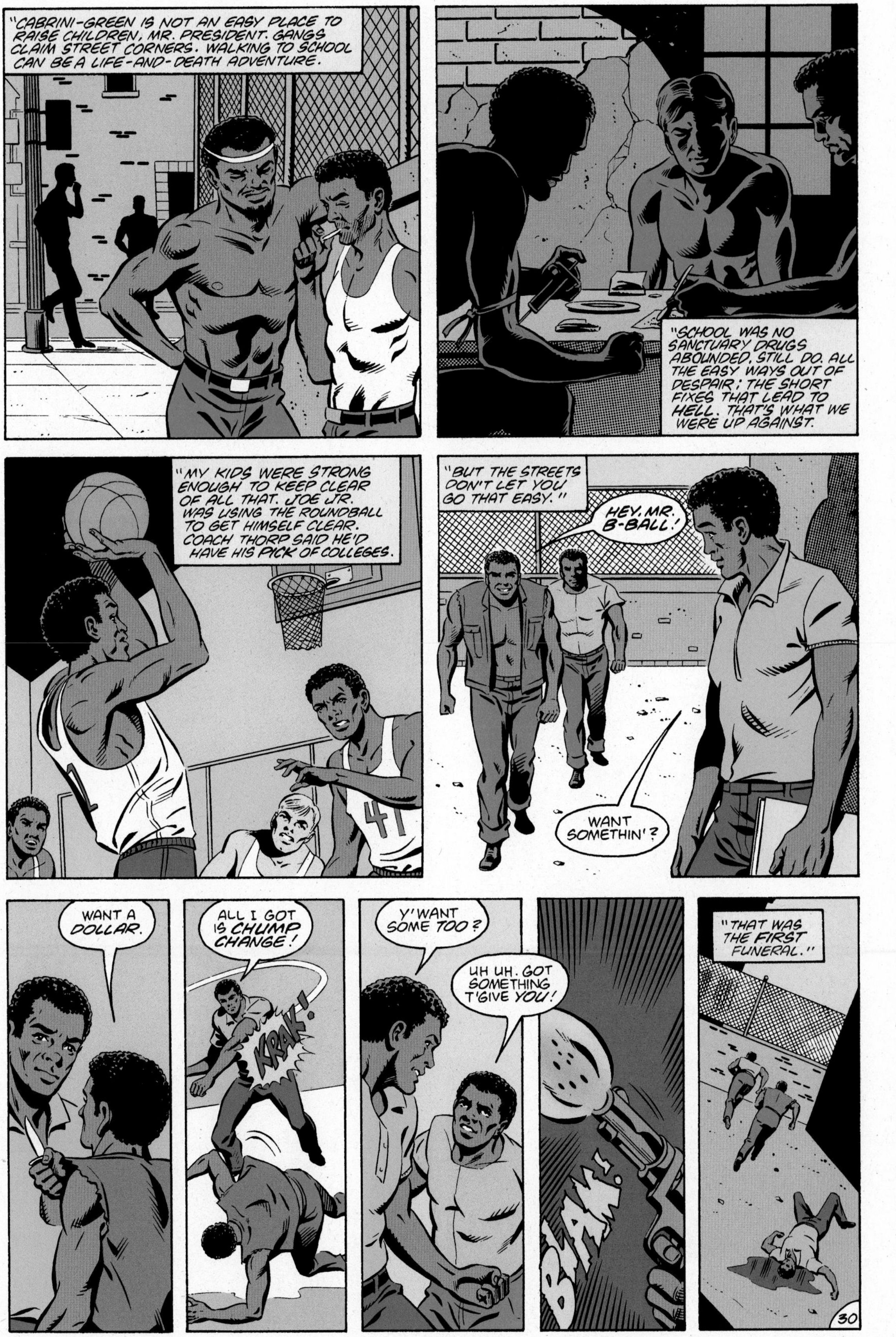
"CABRINI-GREEN IS NOT AN EASY PLACE TO RAISE CHILDREN, MR. PRESIDENT. GANGS CLAIM STREET CORNERS. WALKING TO SCHOOL CAN BE A LIFE-AND-DEATH ADVENTURE.
"SCHOOL WAS NO SANCTUARY. DRUGS ABOUNDED. STILL DO. ALL THE EASY WAYS OUT OF DESPAIR; THE SHORT FIXES THAT LEAD TO HELL. THAT'S WHAT WE WERE UP AGAINST.
"MY KIDS WERE STRONG ENOUGH TO KEEP CLEAR OF ALL THAT. JOE JR. WAS USING THE ROUNDBALL TO GET HIMSELF CLEAR. COACH THORP SAID HE'D HAVE HIS PICK OF COLLEGES.
"BUT THE STREETS DON'T LET YOU GO THAT EASY."
HEY, MR. B-BALL!
WANT SOMETHIN'?
WANT A DOLLAR.
ALL I GOT IS CHUMP CHANGE!
KRAK!
Y'WANT SOME TOO?
UH UH. GOT SOMETHING T'GIVE YOU!
BLAM!
"THAT WAS THE FIRST FUNERAL."
30

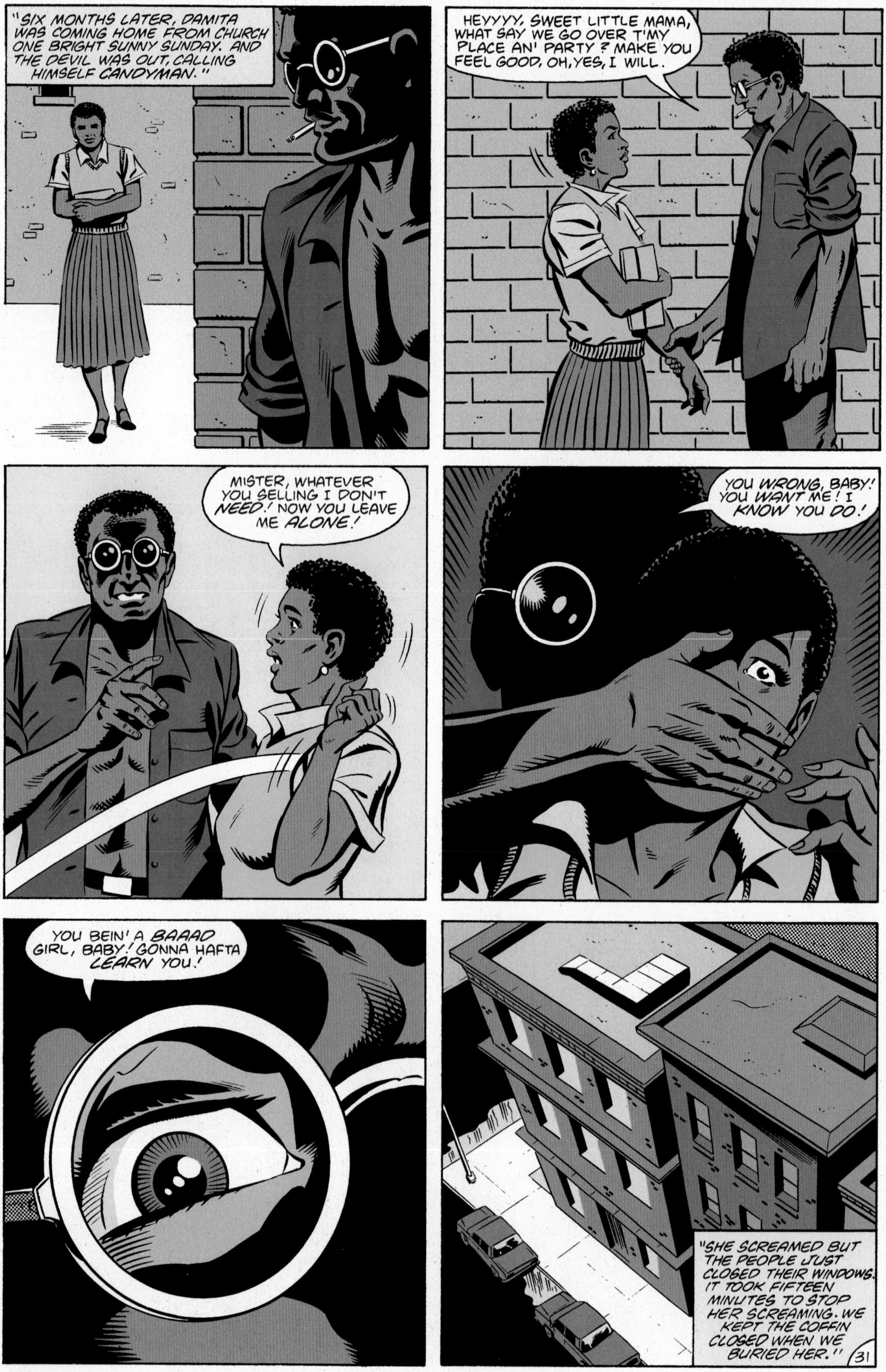
"SIX MONTHS LATER, DAMITA WAS COMING HOME FROM CHURCH ONE BRIGHT SUNNY SUNDAY. AND THE DEVIL WAS OUT, CALLING HIMSELF CANDYMAN."
HEYYYY, SWEET LITTLE MAMA, WHAT SAY WE GO OVER T'MY PLACE AN' PARTY ? MAKE YOU FEEL GOOD, OH, YES, I WILL.
MISTER, WHATEVER YOU SELLING I DON'T NEED! NOW YOU LEAVE ME ALONE!
YOU WRONG, BABY! YOU WANT ME! I KNOW YOU DO!
YOU BEIN' A BAAAD GIRL, BABY! GONNA HAFTA LEARN YOU!
"SHE SCREAMED BUT THE PEOPLE JUST CLOSED THEIR WINDOWS. IT TOOK FIFTEEN MINUTES TO STOP HER SCREAMING. WE KEPT THE COFFIN CLOSED WHEN WE BURIED HER."
31

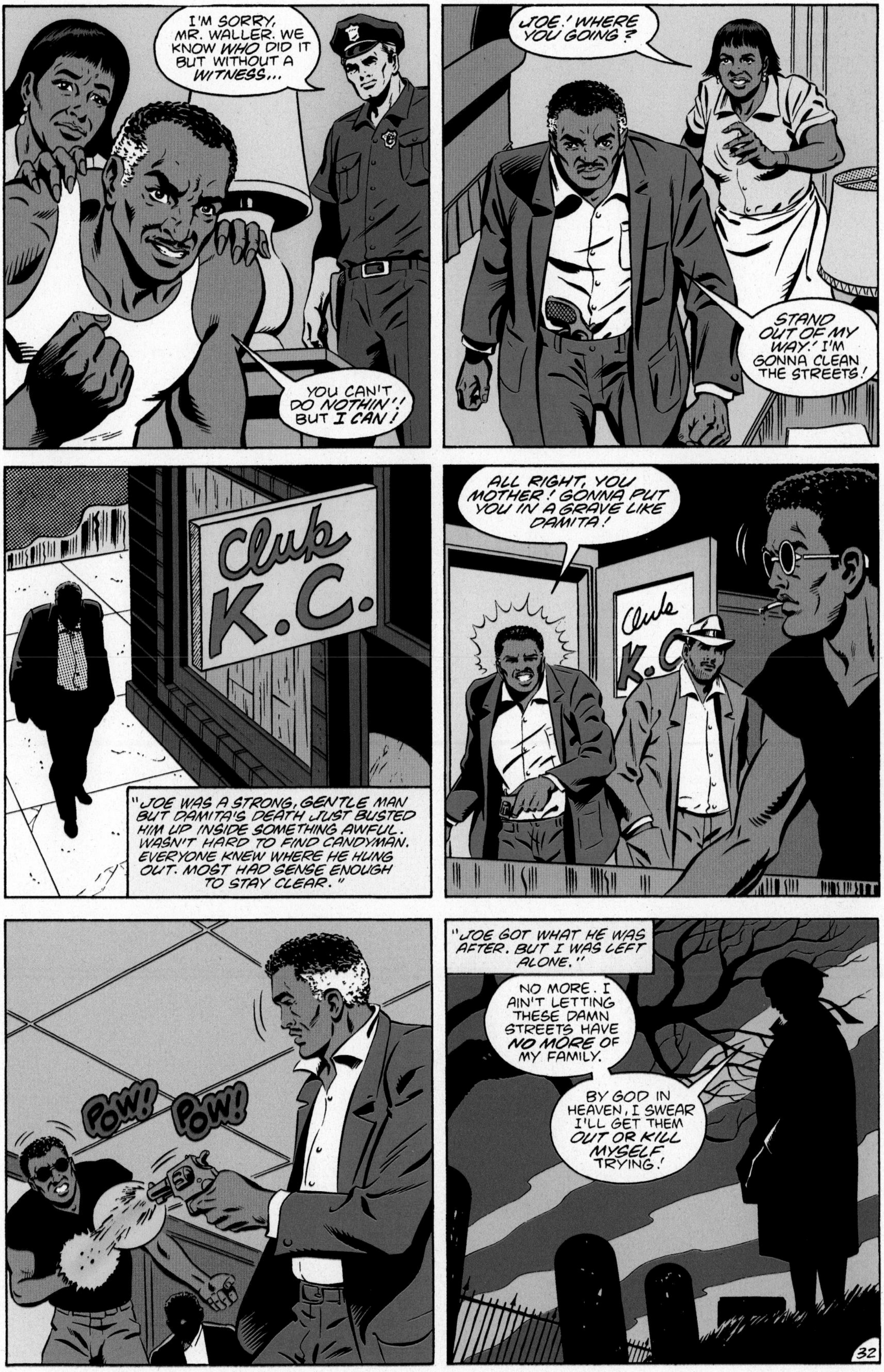

I'M SORRY, MR. WALLER. WE KNOW WHO DID IT BUT WITHOUT A WITNESS...
YOU CAN'T DO NOTHIN'! BUT I CAN!
JOE! WHERE YOU GOING?
STAND OUT OF MY WAY! I'M GONNA CLEAN THE STREETS!
Club K.C.
"JOE WAS A STRONG, GENTLE MAN BUT DAMITA'S DEATH JUST BUSTED HIM UP INSIDE SOMETHING AWFUL. WASN'T HARD TO FIND CANDYMAN. EVERYONE KNEW WHERE HE HUNG OUT. MOST HAD SENSE ENOUGH TO STAY CLEAR."
ALL RIGHT, YOU MOTHER! GONNA PUT YOU IN A GRAVE LIKE DAMITA!
Club K.C
POW! POW!
"JOE GOT WHAT HE WAS AFTER. BUT I WAS LEFT ALONE."
NO MORE. I AIN'T LETTING THESE DAMN STREETS HAVE NO MORE OF MY FAMILY.
BY GOD IN HEAVEN, I SWEAR I'LL GET THEM OUT OR KILL MYSELF TRYING!
32

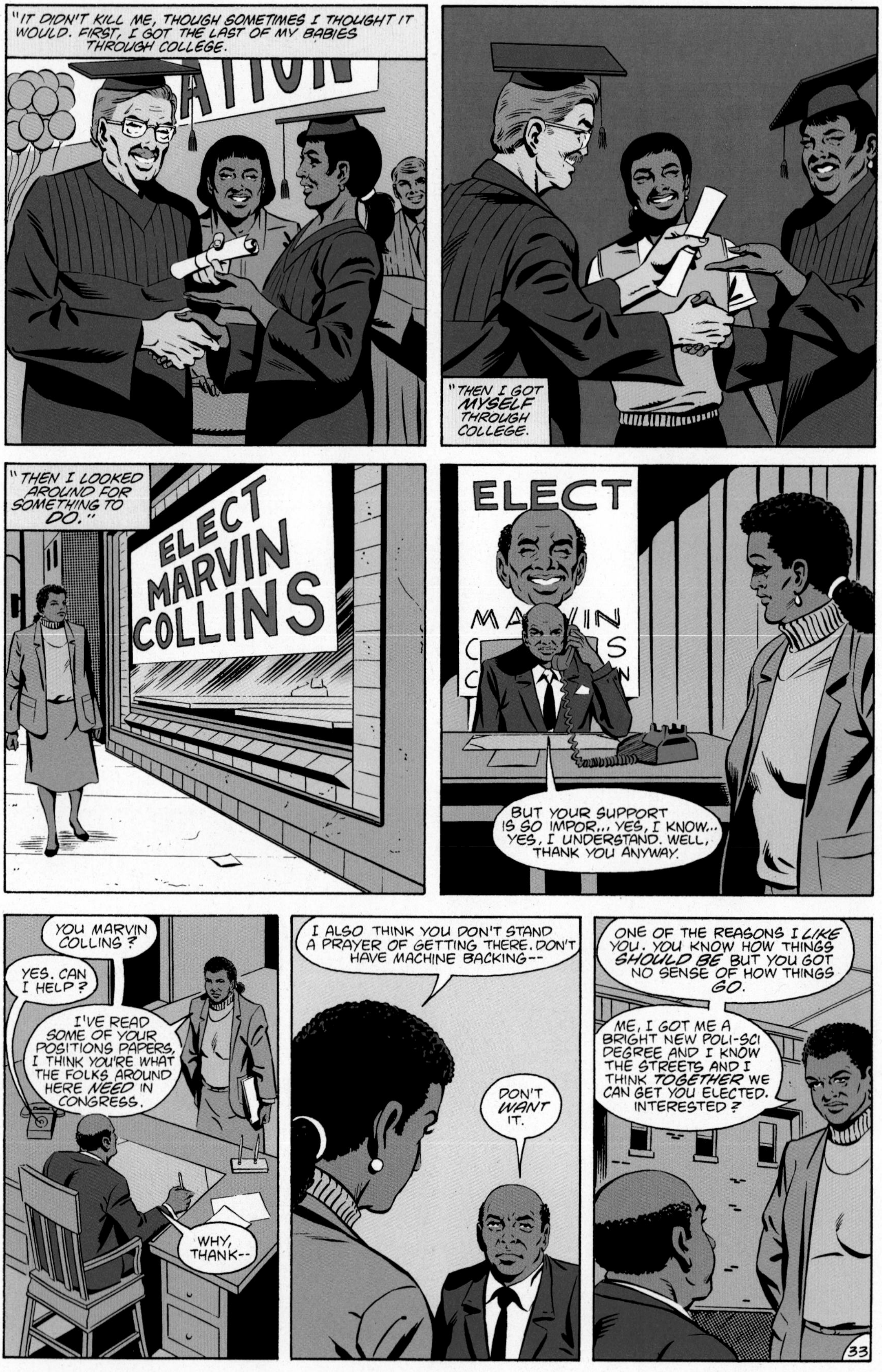
"IT DIDN'T KILL ME, THOUGH SOMETIMES I THOUGHT IT WOULD. FIRST, I GOT THE LAST OF MY BABIES THROUGH COLLEGE.
"THEN I GOT MYSELF THROUGH COLLEGE.
"THEN I LOOKED AROUND FOR SOMETHING TO DO."
ELECT MARVIN COLLINS
ELECT
BUT YOUR SUPPORT IS SO IMPOR... YES, I KNOW... YES, I UNDERSTAND. WELL, THANK YOU ANYWAY.
YOU MARVIN COLLINS?
YES. CAN I HELP?
I'VE READ SOME OF YOUR POSITIONS PAPERS. I THINK YOU'RE WHAT THE FOLKS AROUND HERE NEED IN CONGRESS.
WHY, THANK--
I ALSO THINK YOU DON'T STAND A PRAYER OF GETTING THERE. DON'T HAVE MACHINE BACKING--
DON'T WANT IT.
ONE OF THE REASONS I LIKE YOU. YOU KNOW HOW THINGS SHOULD BE BUT YOU GOT NO SENSE OF HOW THINGS GO.
ME, I GOT ME A BRIGHT NEW POLI-SCI DEGREE AND I KNOW THE STREETS AND I THINK TOGETHER WE CAN GET YOU ELECTED. INTERESTED?
33

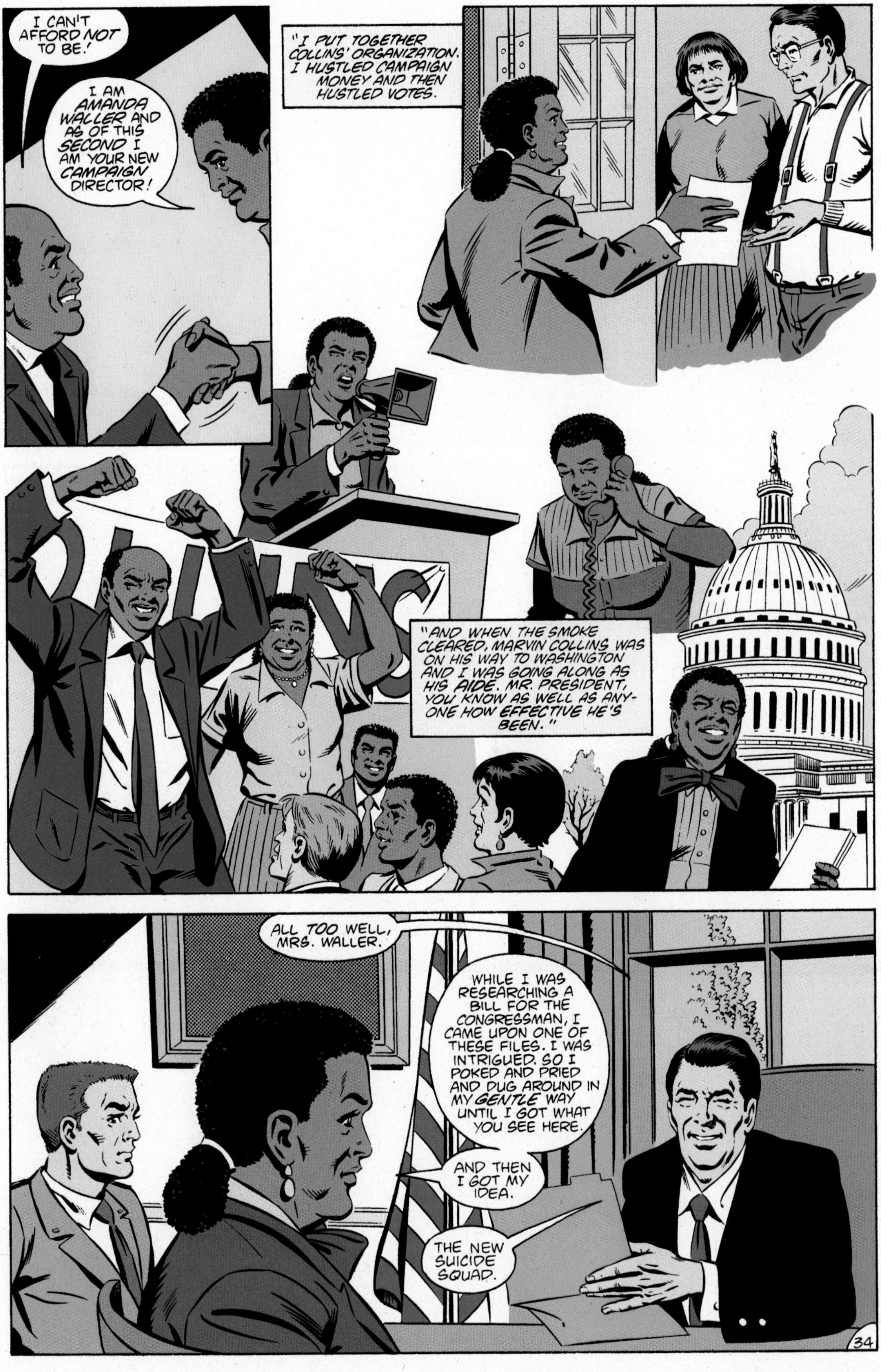
I CAN'T AFFORD NOT TO BE.'
I AM AMANDA WALLER AND AS OF THIS SECOND I AM YOUR NEW CAMPAIGN DIRECTOR!
"I PUT TOGETHER COLLINS' ORGANIZATION. I HUSTLED CAMPAIGN MONEY AND THEN HUSTLED VOTES.
"AND WHEN THE SMOKE CLEARED, MARVIN COLLINS WAS ON HIS WAY TO WASHINGTON AND I WAS GOING ALONG AS HIS AIDE. MR. PRESIDENT, YOU KNOW AS WELL AS ANYONE HOW EFFECTIVE HE'S BEEN."
ALL TOO WELL, MRS. WALLER.
WHILE I WAS RESEARCHING A BILL FOR THE CONGRESSMAN, I CAME UPON ONE OF THESE FILES. I WAS INTRIGUED, SO I POKED AND PRIED AND DUG AROUND IN MY GENTLE WAY UNTIL I GOT WHAT YOU SEE HERE.
AND THEN I GOT MY IDEA.
THE NEW SUICIDE SQUAD.
34

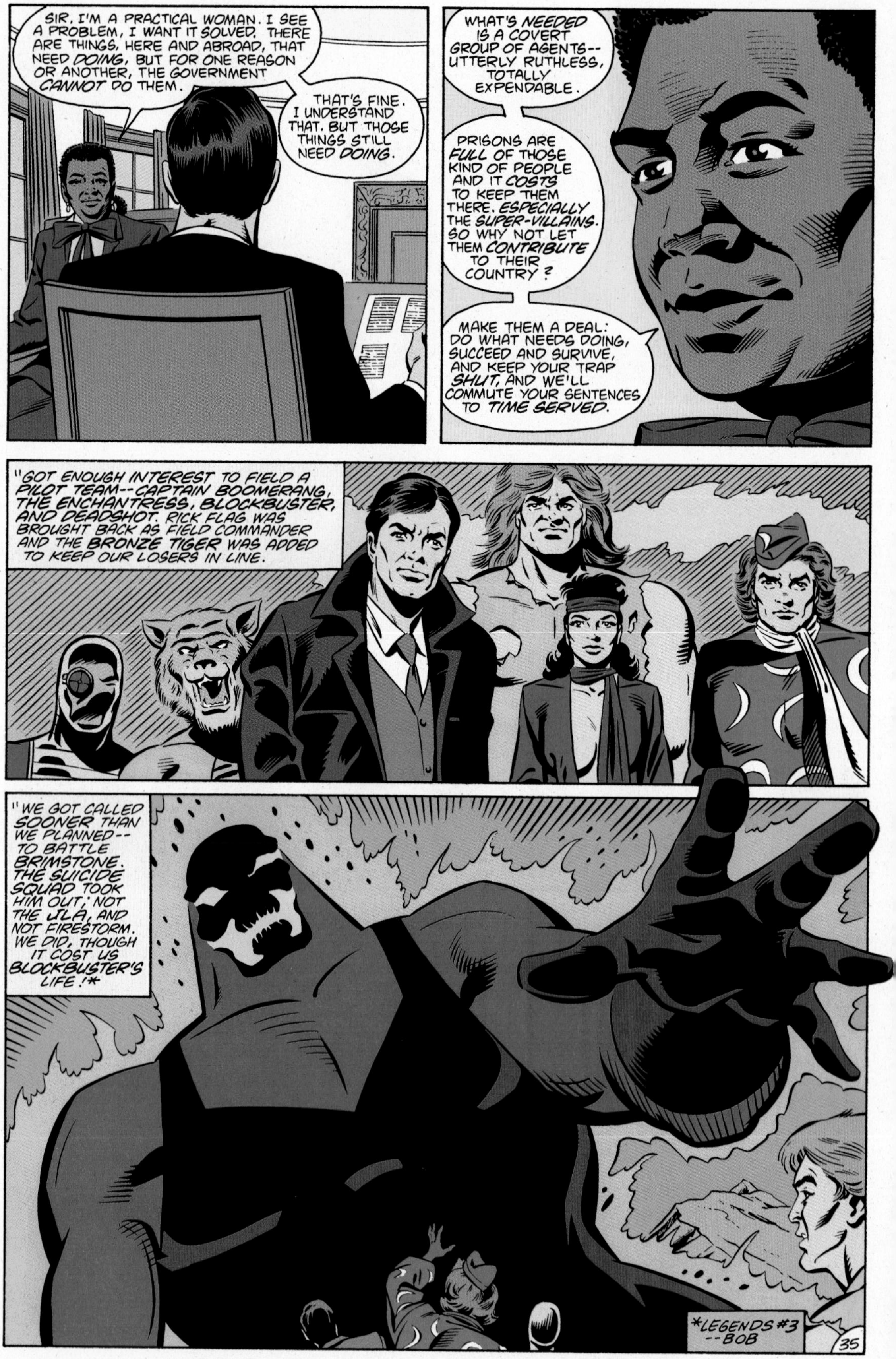
SIR, I'M A PRACTICAL WOMAN. I SEE A PROBLEM, I WANT IT SOLVED. THERE ARE THINGS, HERE AND ABROAD, THAT NEED DOING, BUT FOR ONE REASON OR ANOTHER, THE GOVERNMENT CANNOT DO THEM.
THAT'S FINE. I UNDERSTAND THAT. BUT THOSE THINGS STILL NEED DOING.
WHAT'S NEEDED IS A COVERT GROUP OF AGENTS-- UTTERLY RUTHLESS, TOTALLY EXPENDABLE.
PRISONS ARE FULL OF THOSE KIND OF PEOPLE AND IT COSTS TO KEEP THEM THERE. ESPECIALLY THE SUPER-VILLAINS. SO WHY NOT LET THEM CONTRIBUTE TO THEIR COUNTRY?
MAKE THEM A DEAL: DO WHAT NEEDS DOING, SUCCEED AND SURVIVE, AND KEEP YOUR TRAP SHUT, AND WE'LL COMMUTE YOUR SENTENCES TO TIME SERVED.
"GOT ENOUGH INTEREST TO FIELD A PILOT TEAM--CAPTAIN BOOMERANG, THE ENCHANTRESS, BLOCKBUSTER, AND DEADSHOT. RICK FLAG WAS BROUGHT BACK AS FIELD COMMANDER AND THE BRONZE TIGER WAS ADDED TO KEEP OUR LOSERS IN LINE.
"WE GOT CALLED SOONER THAN WE PLANNED-- TO BATTLE BRIMSTONE. THE SUICIDE SQUAD TOOK HIM OUT; NOT THE JLA, AND NOT FIRESTORM. WE DID, THOUGH IT COST US BLOCKBUSTER'S LIFE!*
*LEGENDS #3 --BOB
35

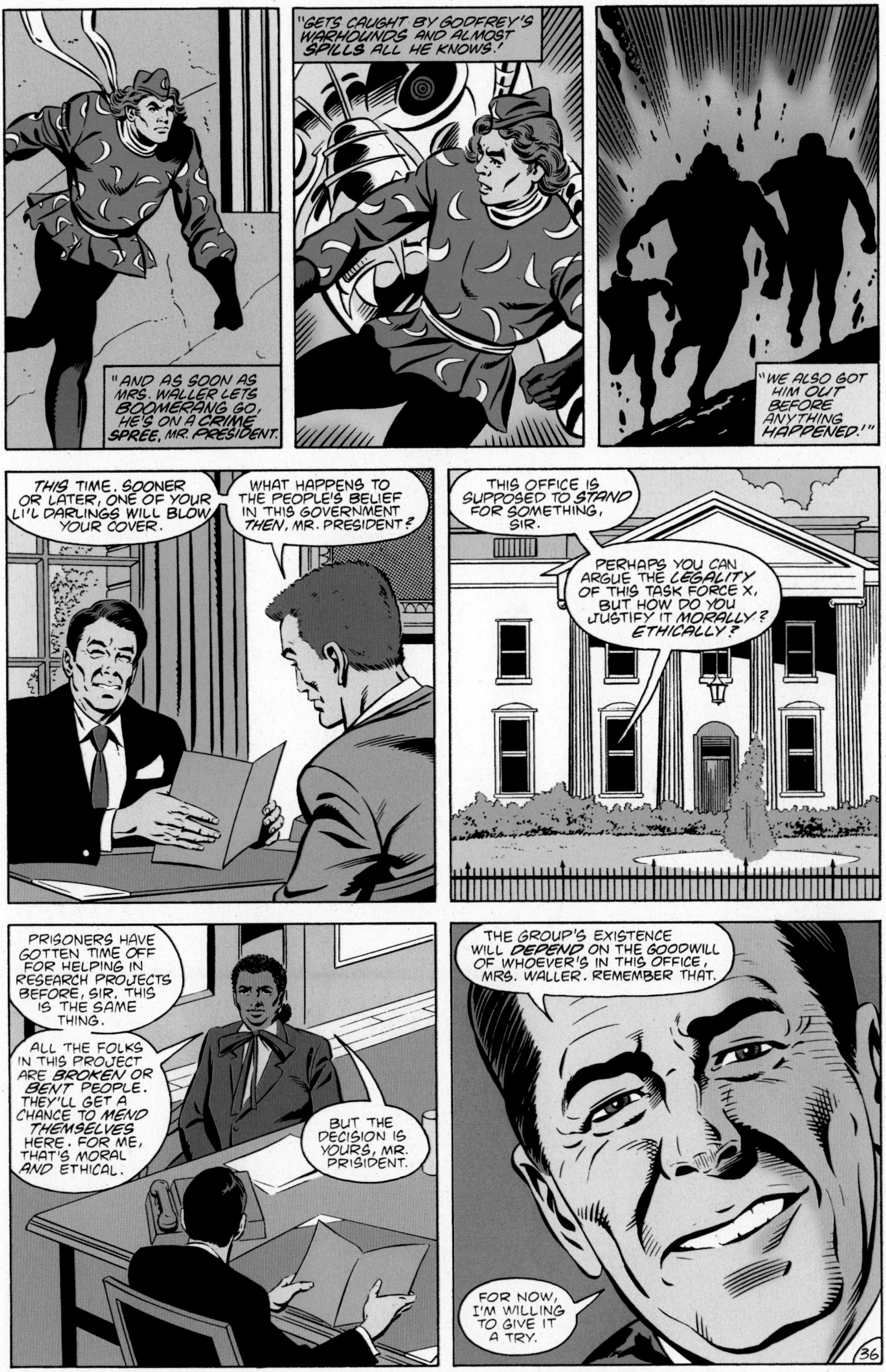
"AND AS SOON AS MRS. WALLER LETS BOOMERANG GO, HE'S ON A CRIME SPREE, MR. PRESIDENT.
"GETS CAUGHT BY GODFREY'S WARHOUNDS AND ALMOST SPILLS ALL HE KNOWS.'
"WE ALSO GOT HIM OUT BEFORE ANYTHING HAPPENED!"
THIS TIME. SOONER OR LATER, ONE OF YOUR LI'L DARLINGS WILL BLOW YOUR COVER.
WHAT HAPPENS TO THE PEOPLE'S BELIEF IN THIS GOVERNMENT THEN, MR. PRESIDENT?
THIS OFFICE IS SUPPOSED TO STAND FOR SOMETHING, SIR.
PERHAPS YOU CAN ARGUE THE LEGALITY OF THIS TASK FORCE X, BUT HOW DO YOU JUSTIFY IT MORALLY? ETHICALLY?
PRISONERS HAVE GOTTEN TIME OFF FOR HELPING IN RESEARCH PROJECTS BEFORE, SIR. THIS IS THE SAME THING.
ALL THE FOLKS IN THIS PROJECT ARE BROKEN OR BENT PEOPLE. THEY'LL GET A CHANCE TO MEND THEMSELVES HERE. FOR ME, THAT'S MORAL AND ETHICAL.
BUT THE DECISION IS YOURS, MR. PRISIDENT.
THE GROUP'S EXISTENCE WILL DEPEND ON THE GOODWILL OF WHOEVER'S IN THIS OFFICE, MRS. WALLER. REMEMBER THAT.
FOR NOW, I'M WILLING TO GIVE IT A TRY.
36

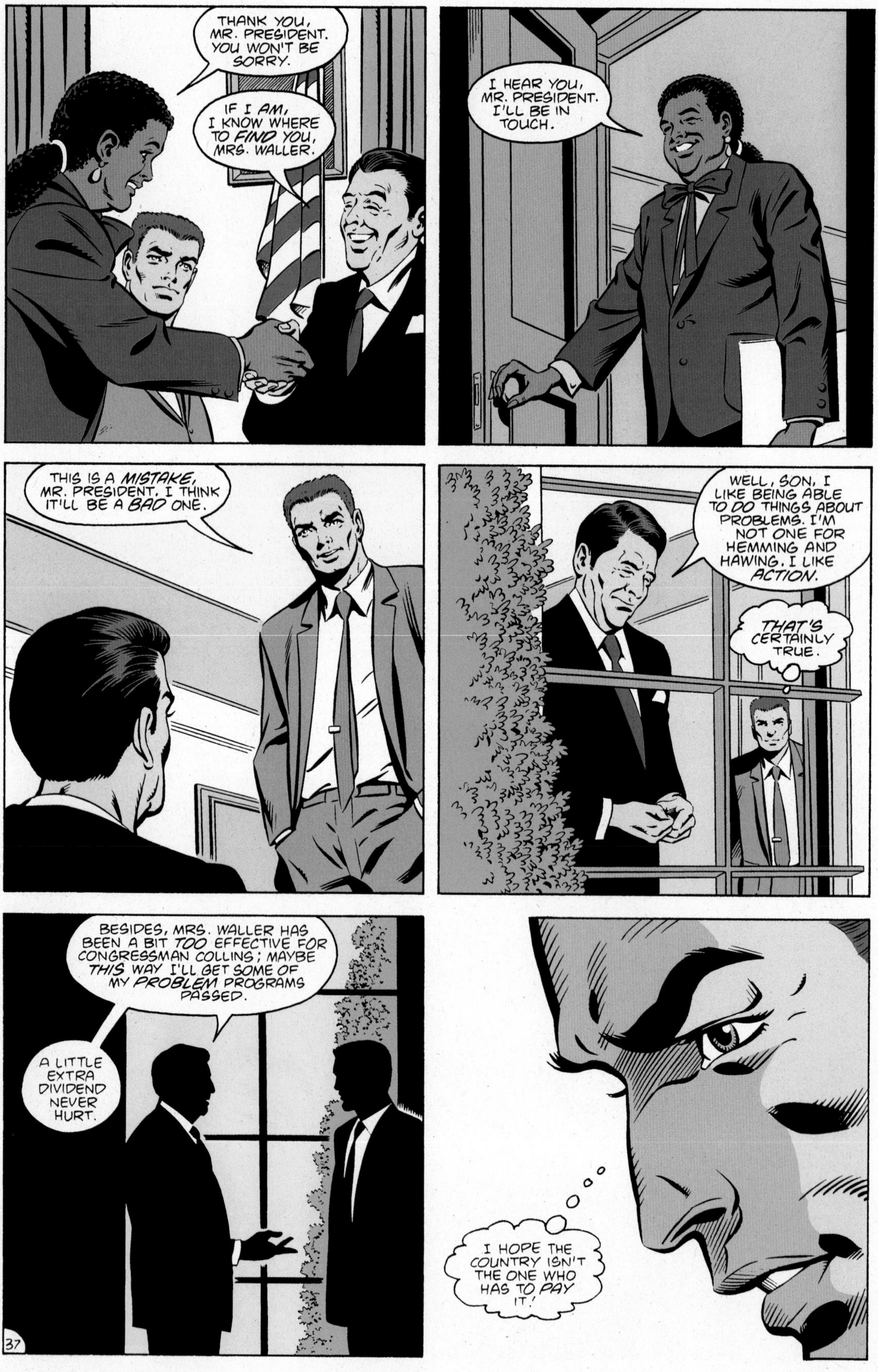
THANK YOU, MR. PRESIDENT. YOU WON'T BE SORRY.
IF I AM, I KNOW WHERE TO FIND YOU, MRS. WALLER.
I HEAR YOU, MR. PRESIDENT. I'LL BE IN TOUCH.
THIS IS A MISTAKE, MR. PRESIDENT. I THINK IT'LL BE A BAD ONE.
WELL, SON, I LIKE BEING ABLE TO DO THINGS ABOUT PROBLEMS. I'M NOT ONE FOR HEMMING AND HAWING. I LIKE ACTION.
THAT'S CERTAINLY TRUE.
BESIDES, MRS. WALLER HAS BEEN A BIT TOO EFFECTIVE FOR CONGRESSMAN COLLING; MAYBE THIS WAY I'LL GET SOME OF MY PROBLEM PROGRAMS PASSED.
A LITTLE EXTRA DIVIDEND NEVER HURT.
37
I HOPE THE COUNTRY ISN'T THE ONE WHO HAS TO PAY IT!

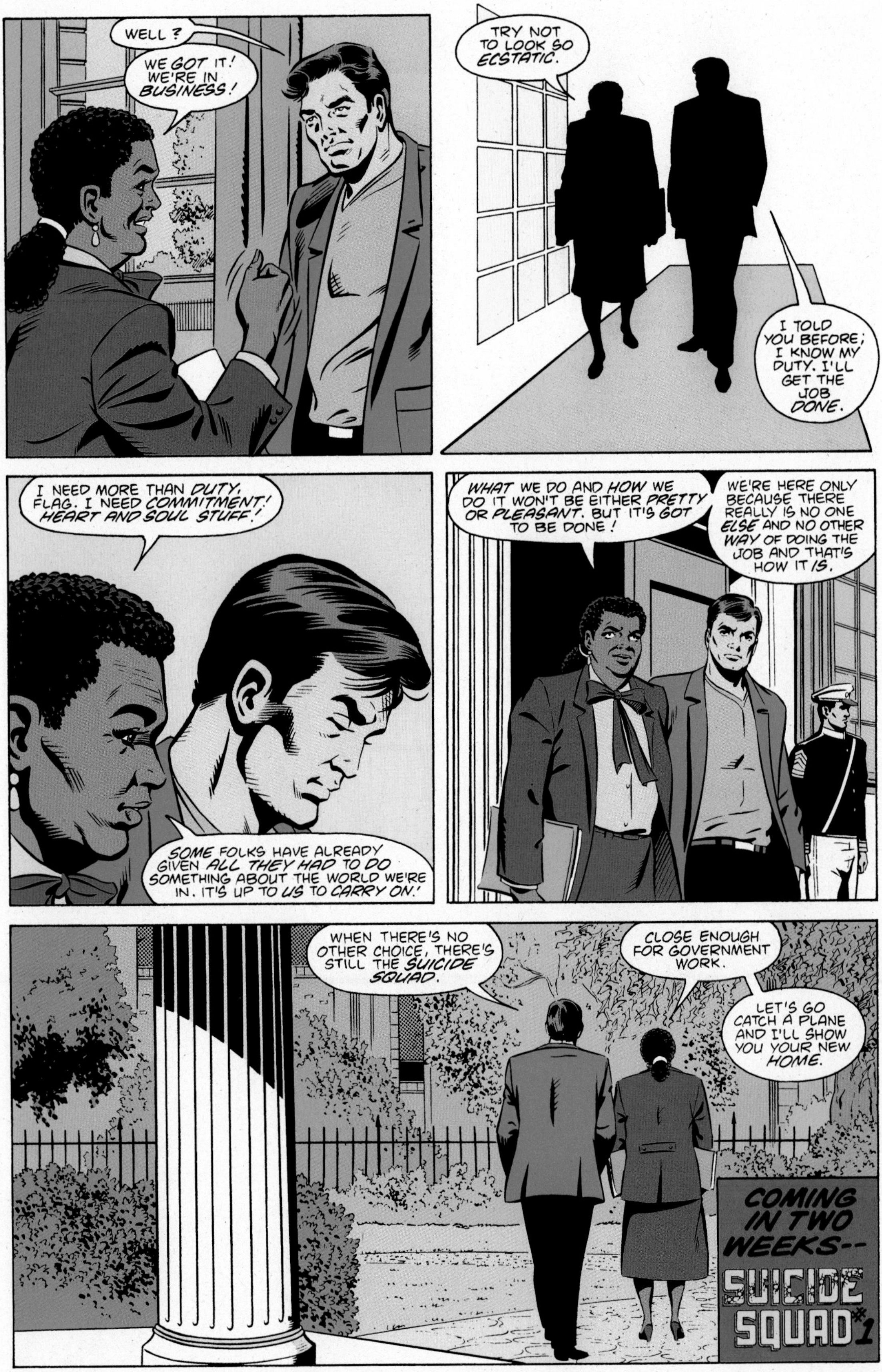
WELL ?
WE GOT IT! WE'RE IN BUSINESS!
TRY NOT TO LOOK SO ECSTATIC.
I TOLD YOU BEFORE; I KNOW MY DUTY. I'LL GET THE JOB DONE.
I NEED MORE THAN DUTY, FLAG. I NEED COMMITMENT! HEART AND SOUL STUFF!
SOME FOLKS HAVE ALREADY GIVEN ALL THEY HAD TO DO SOMETHING ABOUT THE WORLD WE'RE IN. IT'S UP TO US TO CARRY ON!
WHAT WE DO AND HOW WE DO IT WON'T BE EITHER PRETTY OR PLEASANT. BUT IT'S GOT TO BE DONE!
WE'RE HERE ONLY BECAUSE THERE REALLY IS NO ONE ELSE AND NO OTHER WAY OF DOING THE JOB AND THAT'S HOW IT IS.
WHEN THERE'S NO OTHER CHOICE, THERE'S STILL THE SUICIDE SQUAD.
CLOSE ENOUGH FOR GOVERNMENT WORK.
LET'S GO CATCH A PLANE AND I'LL SHOW YOU YOUR NEW HOME.
COMING IN TWO WEEKS--
SUICIDE SQUAD #1

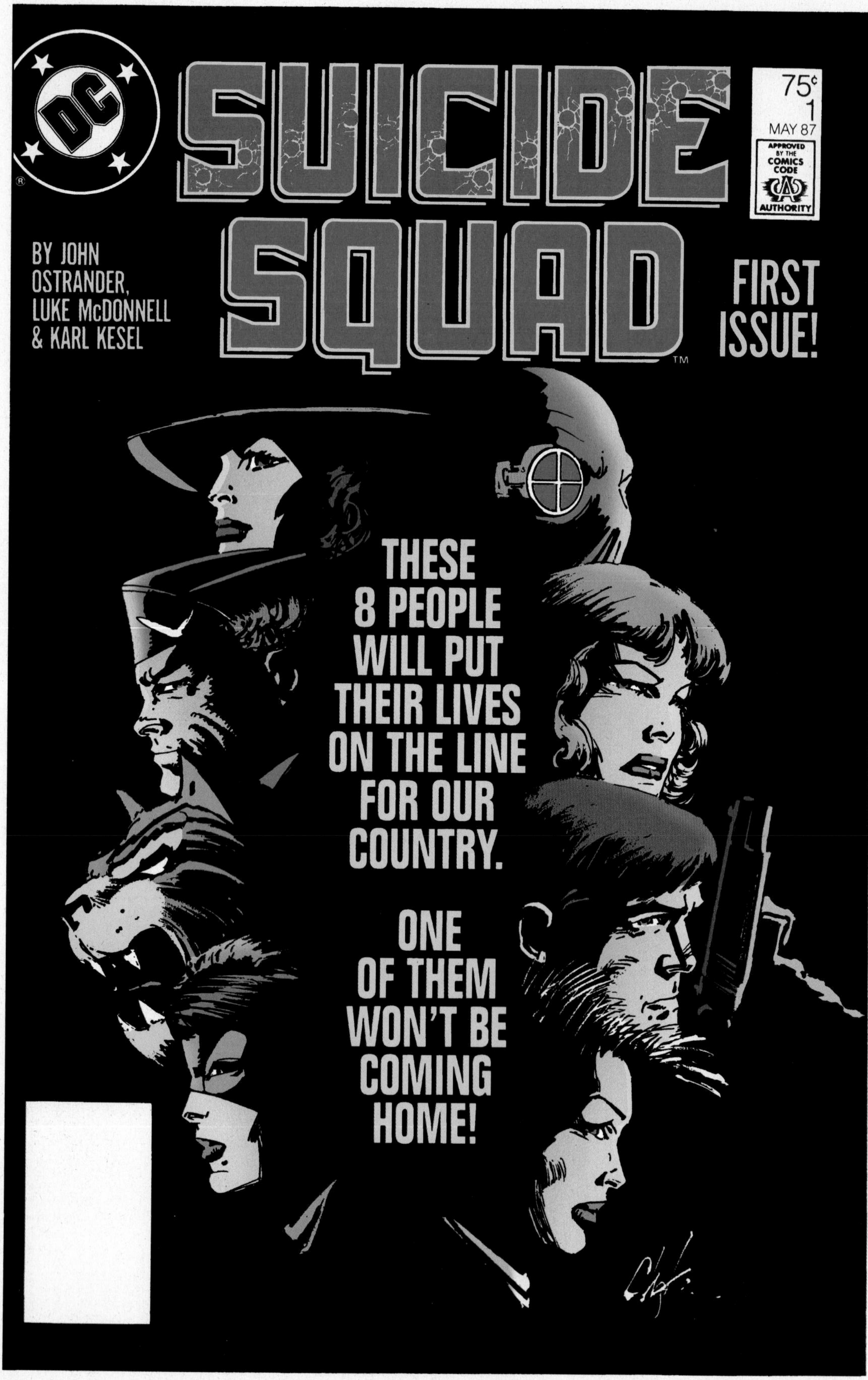
DC
SUICIDE SQUAD
75¢
1
MAY 87
APPROVED BY THE COMICS CODE AUTHORITY
BY JOHN OSTRANDER, LUKE McDONNELL & KARL KESEL
FIRST ISSUE!
THESE 8 PEOPLE WILL PUT THEIR LIVES ON THE LINE FOR OUR COUNTRY.
ONE OF THEM WON'T BE COMING HOME!

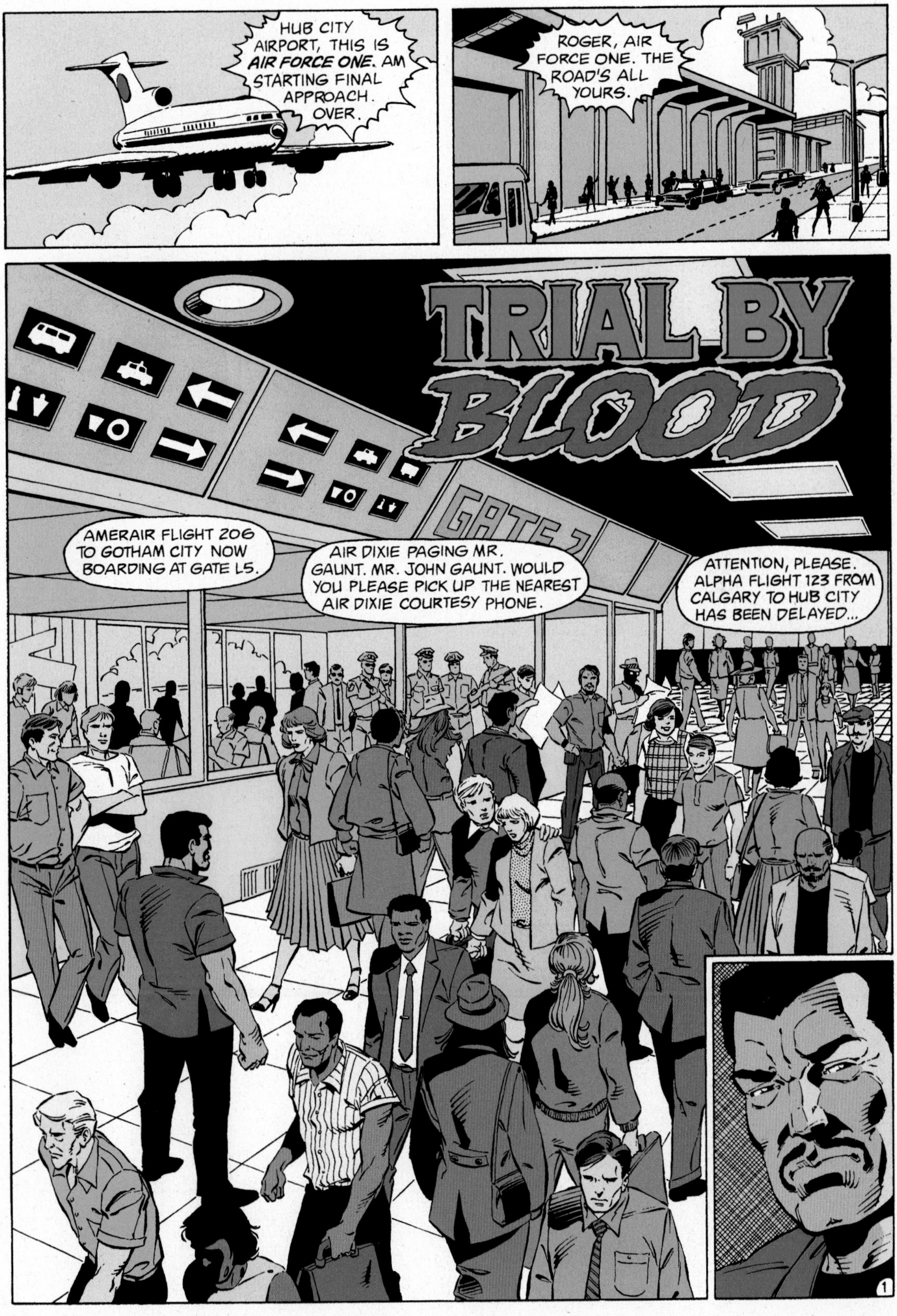
HUB CITY AIRPORT, THIS IS AIR FORCE ONE. AM STARTING FINAL APPROACH. OVER.
ROGER, AIR FORCE ONE. THE ROAD'S ALL YOURS.
TRIAL BY BLOOD
GATE 7
AMERAIR FLIGHT 206 TO GOTHAM CITY NOW BOARDING AT GATE L5.
AIR DIXIE PAGING MR. GAUNT. MR. JOHN GAUNT. WOULD YOU PLEASE PICK UP THE NEAREST AIR DIXIE COURTESY PHONE.
ATTENTION, PLEASE. ALPHA FLIGHT 123 FROM CALGARY TO HUB CITY HAS BEEN DELAYED...
1

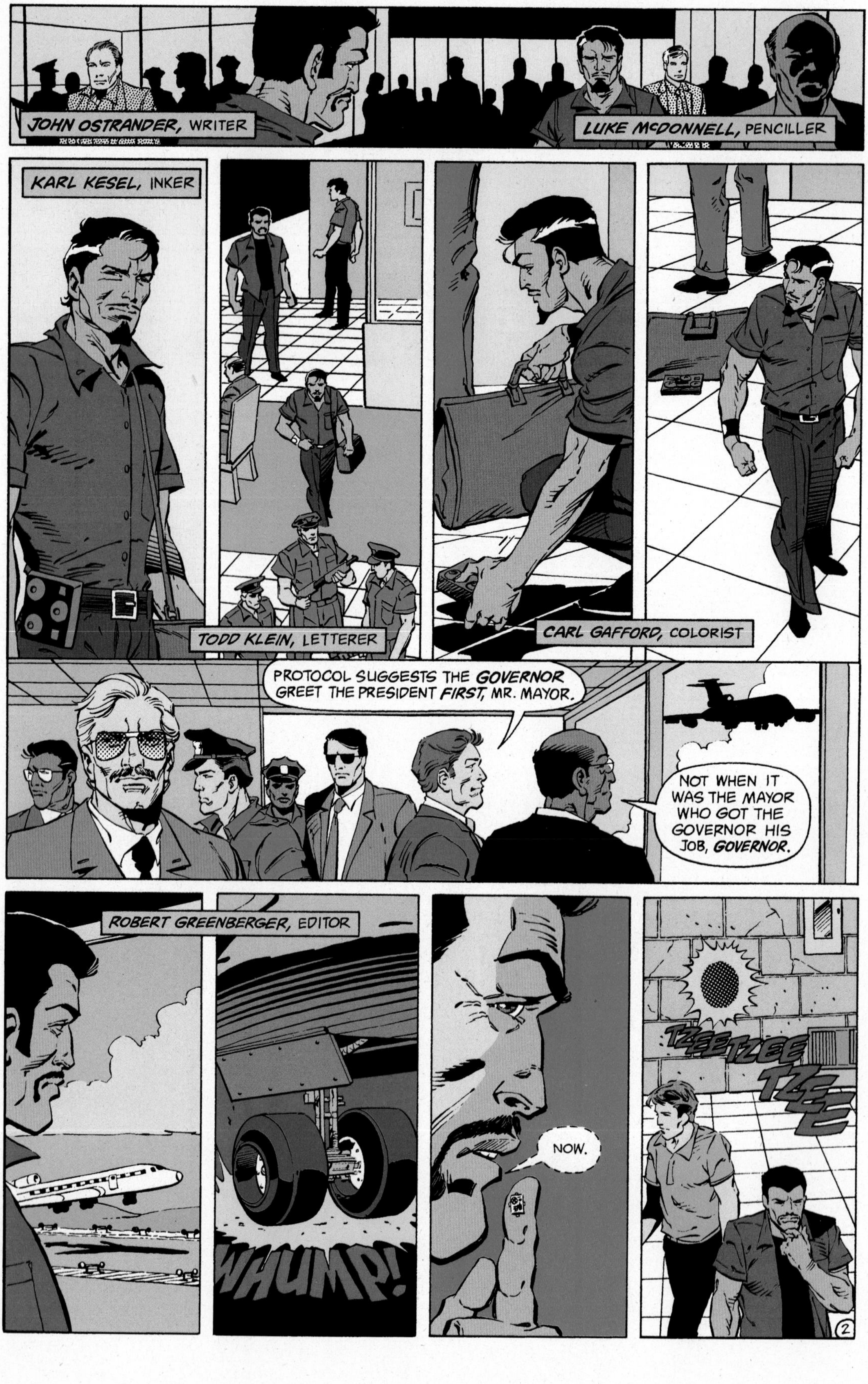
JOHN OSTRANDER, WRITER
LUKE McDONNELL, PENCILLER
KARL KESEL, INKER
TODD KLEIN, LETTERER
CARL GAFFORD, COLORIST
PROTOCOL SUGGESTS THE GOVERNOR GREET THE PRESIDENT FIRST, MR. MAYOR.
NOT WHEN IT WAS THE MAYOR WHO GOT THE GOVERNOR HIS JOB, GOVERNOR.
ROBERT GREENBERGER, EDITOR
WHUMP!
NOW.
TZEE TZEE TZEE TZEE
2

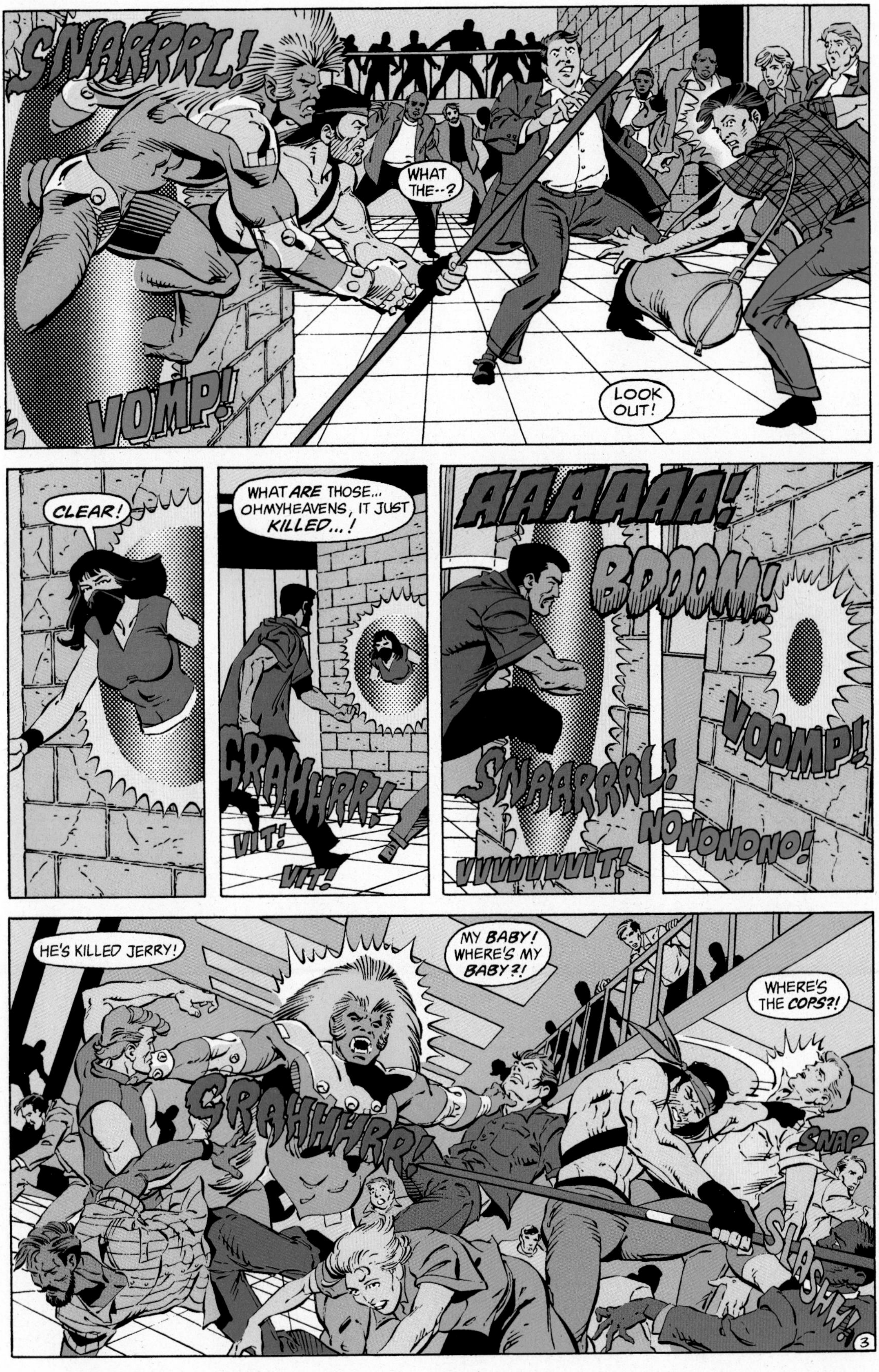
SNARRRL!
WHAT THE--?
VOMP!
LOOK OUT!
CLEAR!
WHAT ARE THOSE... OHMYHEAVENS, IT JUST KILLED...!
GRAHHHRR!
VIT!
VIT!
AAAAAA!
BDOOM!
SNAARRRL!
VVVVVVVIT!
VOOMP!
NONONONO!
HE'S KILLED JERRY!
MY BABY! WHERE'S MY BABY?!
WHERE'S THE COPS?!
GRAHHHRR!
SNAP
SLASH!
3

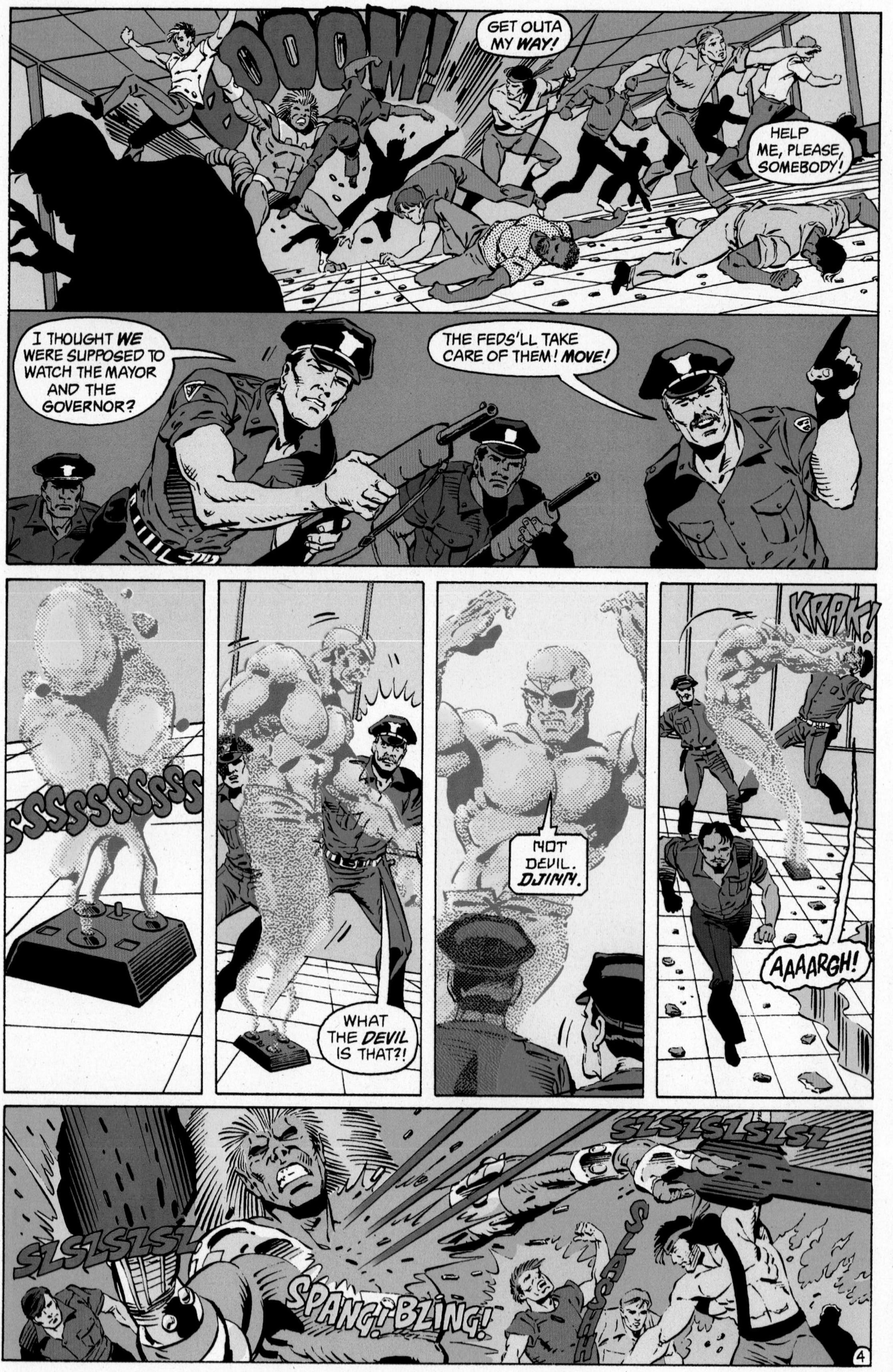
OOOOM!
GET OUTA MY WAY!
HELP ME, PLEASE, SOMEBODY!
I THOUGHT WE WERE SUPPOSED TO WATCH THE MAYOR AND THE GOVERNOR?
THE FEDS'LL TAKE CARE OF THEM! MOVE!
SSSSSSSSSS
WHAT THE DEVIL IS THAT?!
NOT DEVIL. DJINN.
KRAK!
AAAARGH!
SZSZSZSZSZ
SZSZSZSZSZ
SPANG! BZING!
SLASH
4

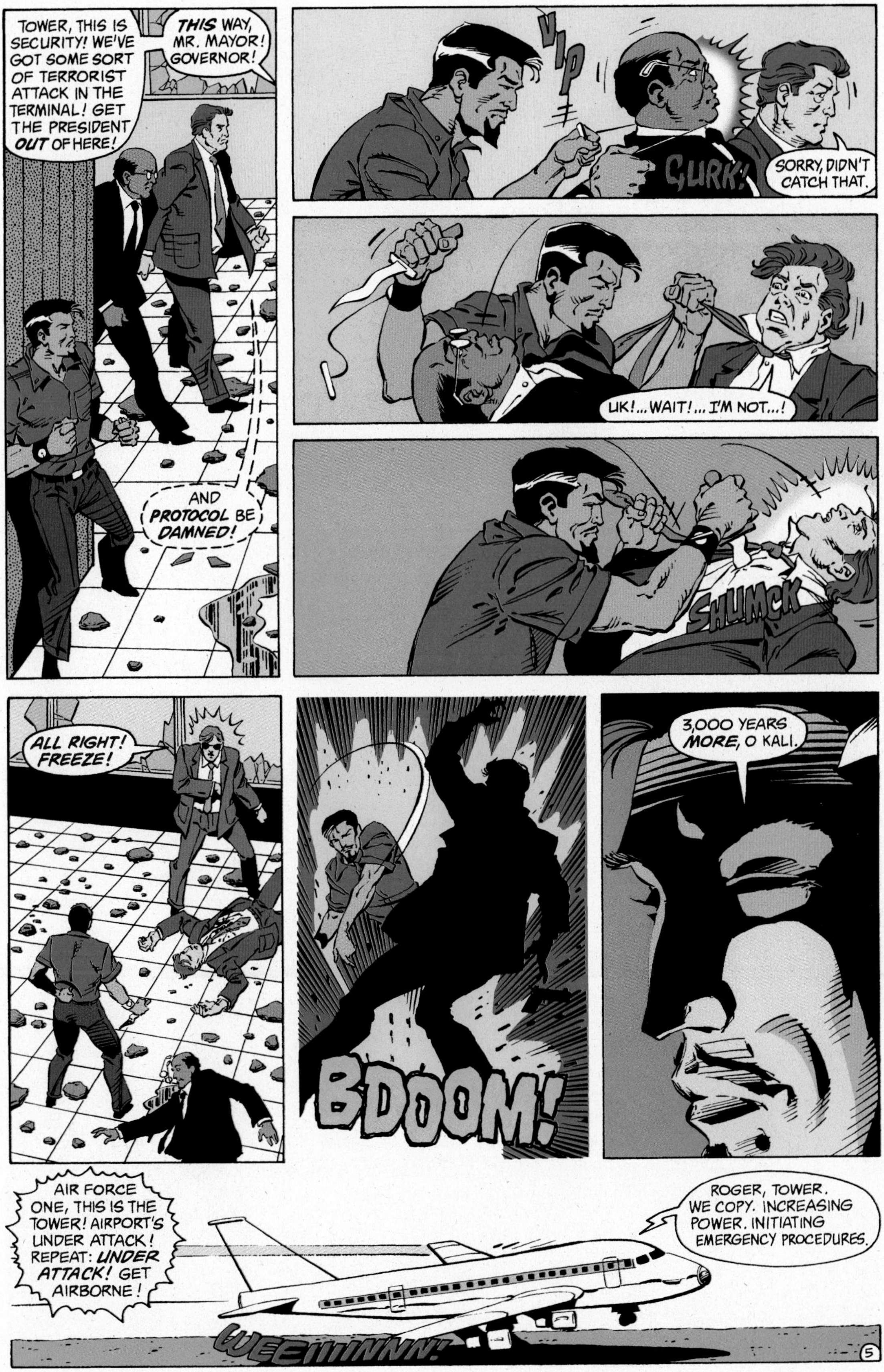
TOWER, THIS IS SECURITY! WE'VE GOT SOME SORT OF TERRORIST ATTACK IN THE TERMINAL! GET THE PRESIDENT OUT OF HERE!
THIS WAY, MR. MAYOR! GOVERNOR!
AND PROTOCOL BE DAMNED!
VIP
GURK!
SORRY, DIDN'T CATCH THAT.
UK!... WAIT!... I'M NOT...!
SHUMCK
ALL RIGHT! FREEZE!
BDOOM!
3,000 YEARS MORE, O KALI.
AIR FORCE ONE, THIS IS THE TOWER! AIRPORT'S UNDER ATTACK! REPEAT: UNDER ATTACK! GET AIRBORNE!
ROGER, TOWER. WE COPY. INCREASING POWER. INITIATING EMERGENCY PROCEDURES.
WEEIIIINNNN!
5

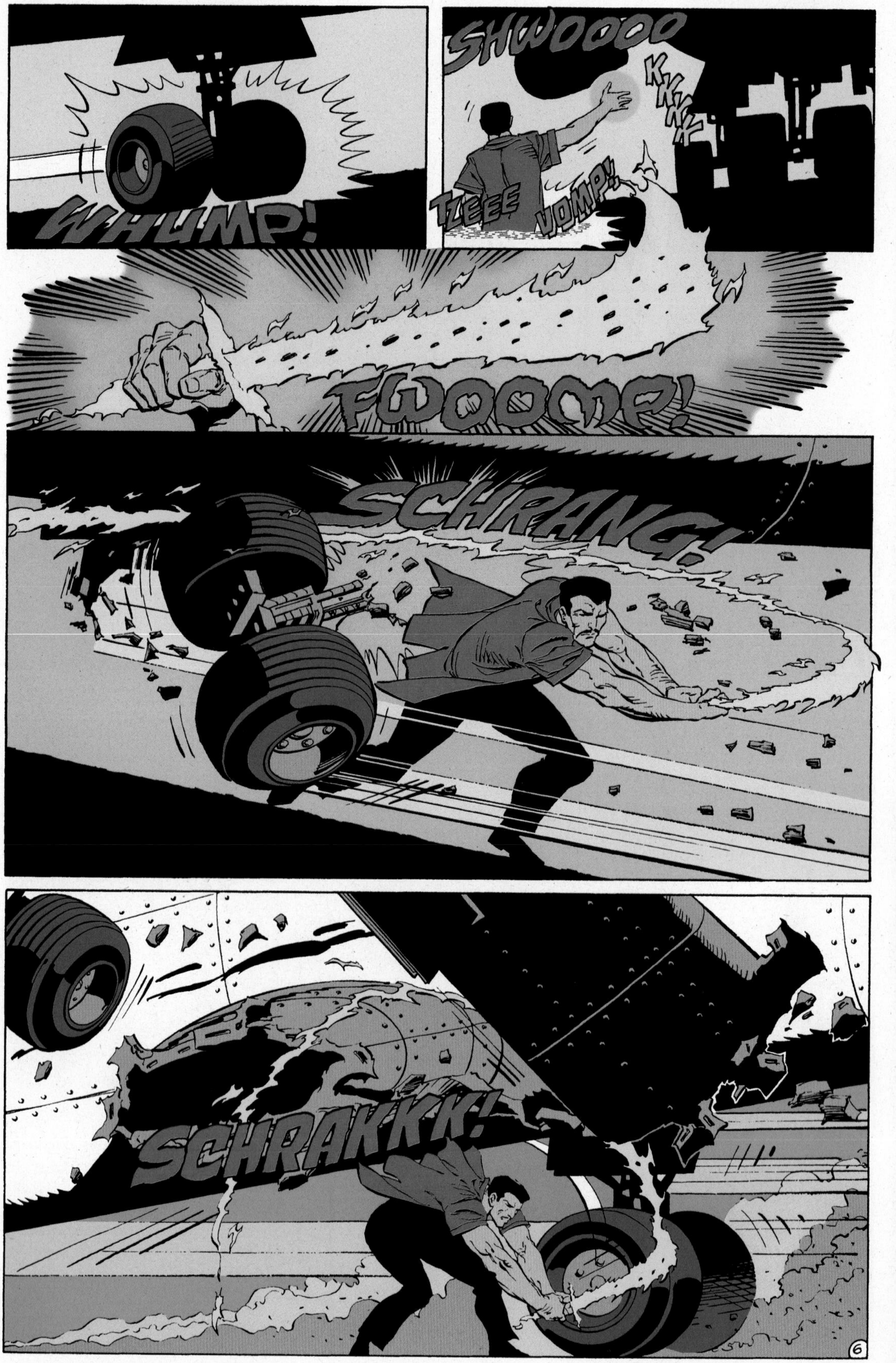
WHUMP!
SHWOOOO
KKKKK
TZEEE
VOMP!!
FWOOOMP!
SCHRANG!
SCHRAKKK!
6

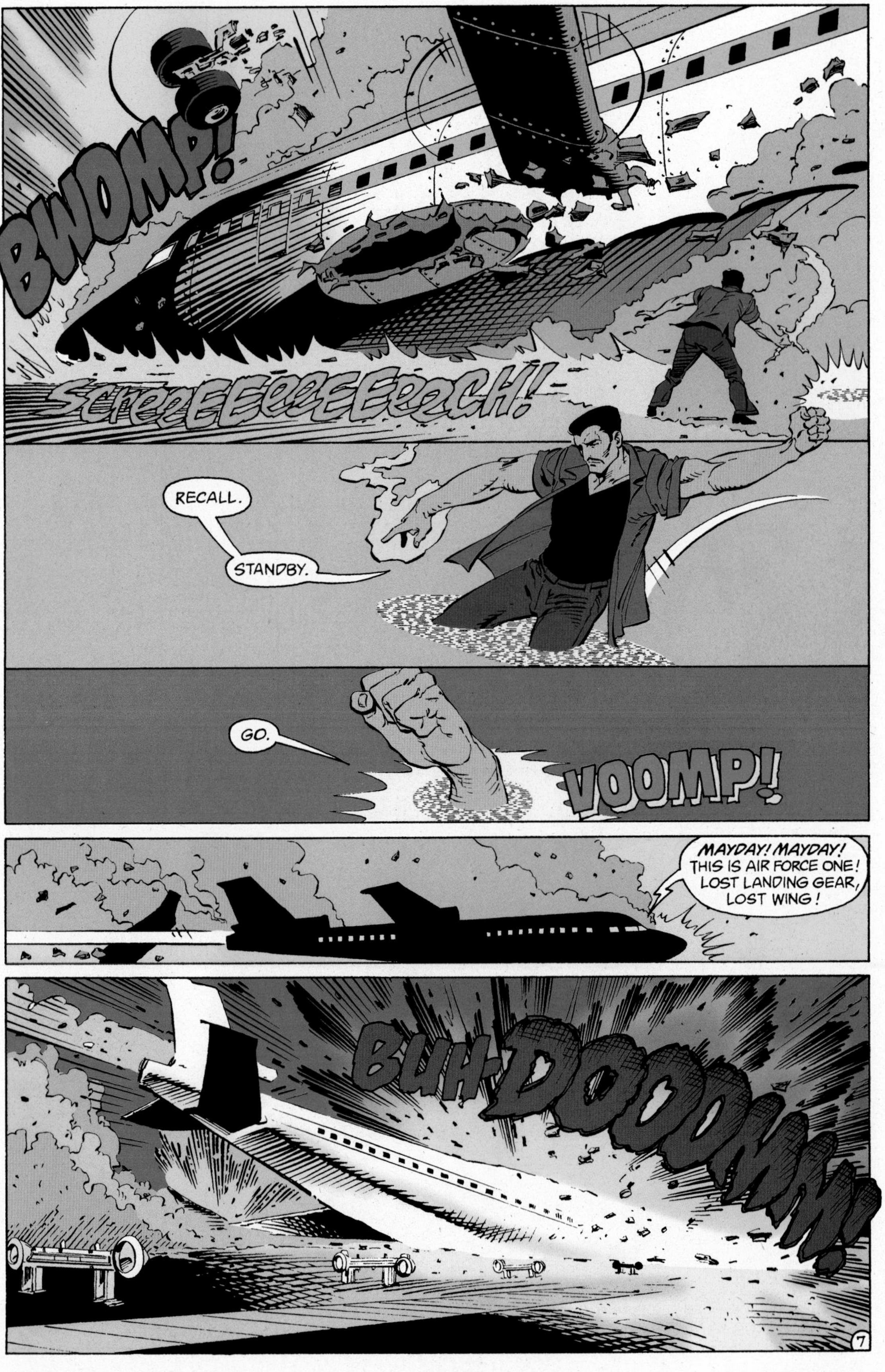
BWOMP!
ScreeEEEeeEEEeeCH!
RECALL.
STANDBY.
GO.
VOOMP!
MAYDAY! MAYDAY! THIS IS AIR FORCE ONE! LOST LANDING GEAR, LOST WING!
BUH-DOOOMM!
7

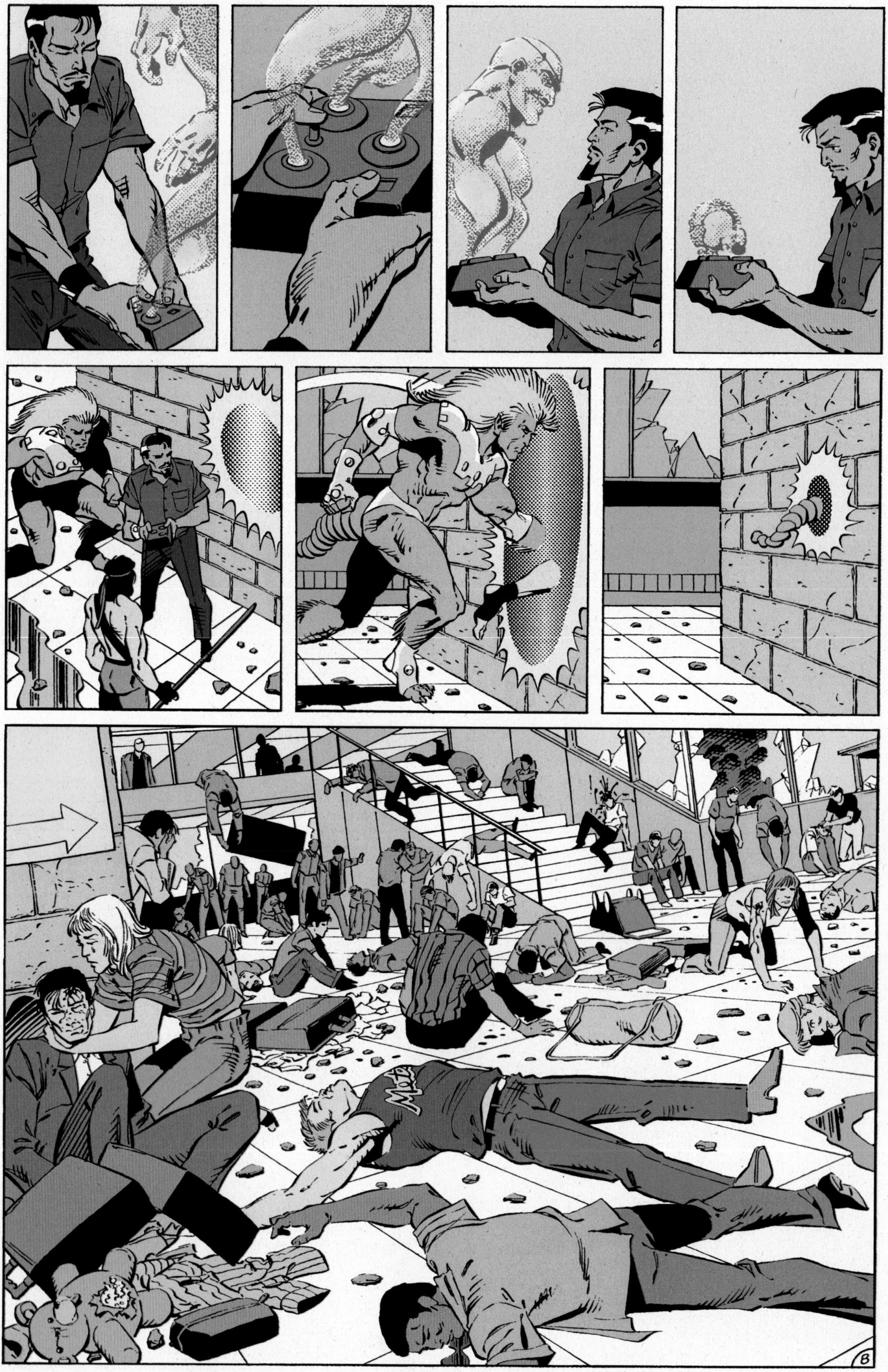

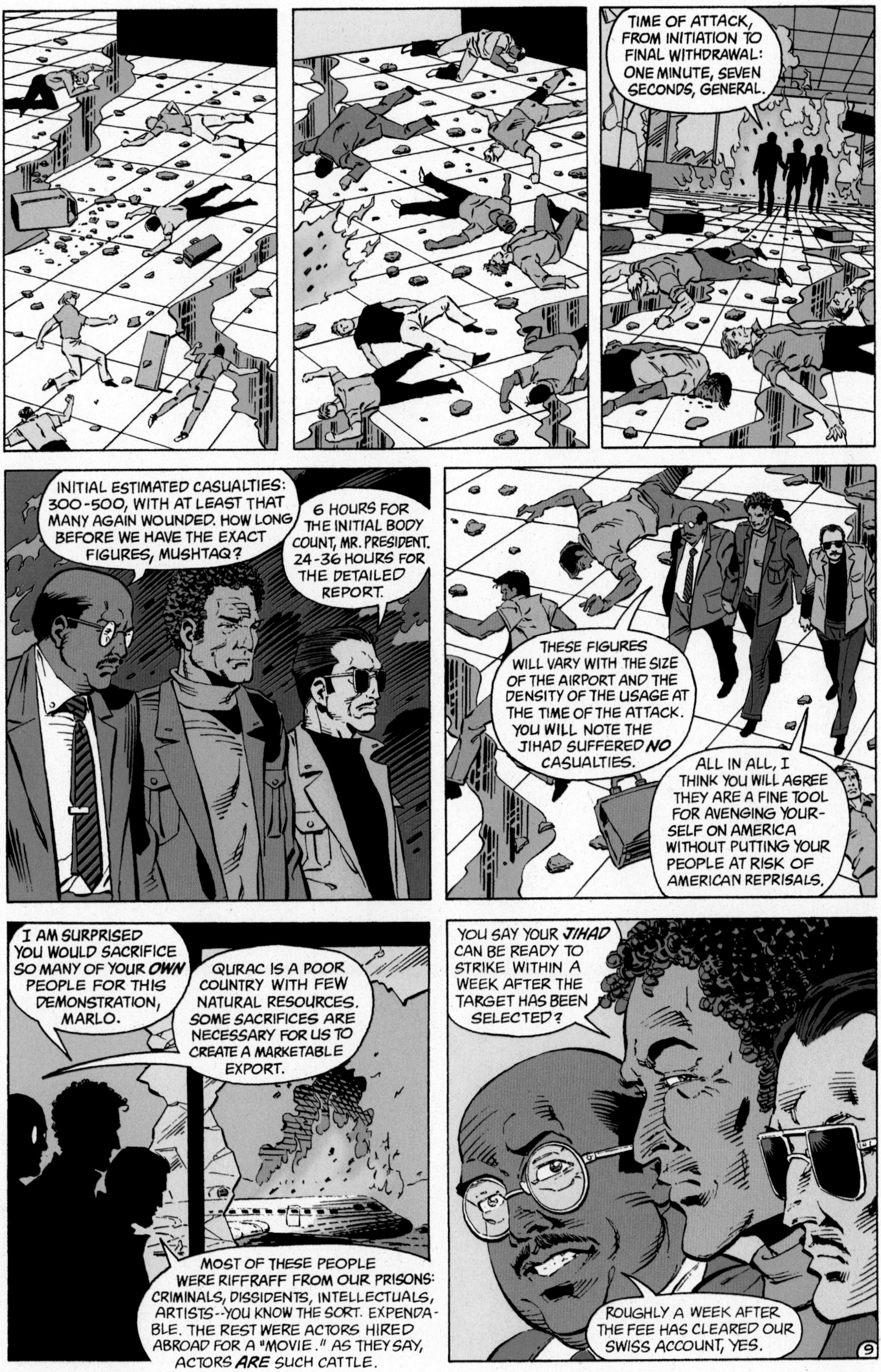
TIME OF ATTACK, FROM INITIATION TO FINAL WITHDRAWAL: ONE MINUTE, SEVEN SECONDS, GENERAL.
INITIAL ESTIMATED CASUALTIES: 300-500, WITH AT LEAST THAT MANY AGAIN WOUNDED. HOW LONG BEFORE WE HAVE THE EXACT FIGURES, MUSHTAQ?
6 HOURS FOR THE INITIAL BODY COUNT, MR. PRESIDENT. 24-36 HOURS FOR THE DETAILED REPORT.
THESE FIGURES WILL VARY WITH THE SIZE OF THE AIRPORT AND THE DENSITY OF THE USAGE AT THE TIME OF THE ATTACK. YOU WILL NOTE THE JIHAD SUFFERED NO CASUALTIES.
ALL IN ALL, I THINK YOU WILL AGREE THEY ARE A FINE TOOL FOR AVENGING YOURSELF ON AMERICA WITHOUT PUTTING YOUR PEOPLE AT RISK OF AMERICAN REPRISALS.
I AM SURPRISED YOU WOULD SACRIFICE SO MANY OF YOUR OWN PEOPLE FOR THIS DEMONSTRATION, MARLO.
QURAC IS A POOR COUNTRY WITH FEW NATURAL RESOURCES. SOME SACRIFICES ARE NECESSARY FOR US TO CREATE A MARKETABLE EXPORT.
MOST OF THESE PEOPLE WERE RIFFRAFF FROM OUR PRISONS: CRIMINALS, DISSIDENTS, INTELLECTUALS, ARTISTS--YOU KNOW THE SORT. EXPENDABLE. THE REST WERE ACTORS HIRED ABROAD FOR A "MOVIE." AS THEY SAY, ACTORS ARE SUCH CATTLE.
YOU SAY YOUR JIHAD CAN BE READY TO STRIKE WITHIN A WEEK AFTER THE TARGET HAS BEEN SELECTED?
ROUGHLY A WEEK AFTER THE FEE HAS CLEARED OUR SWISS ACCOUNT, YES.
9

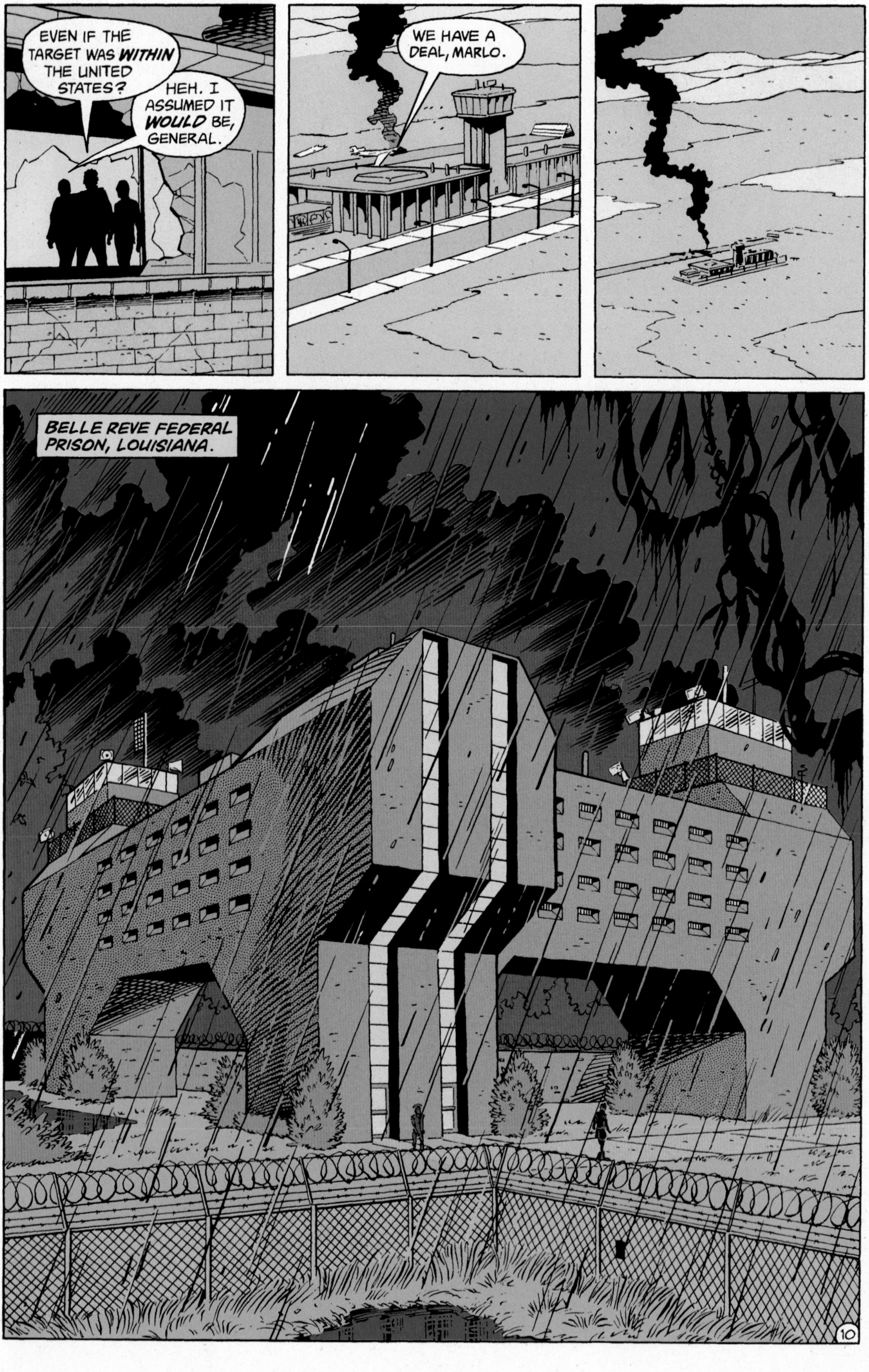
EVEN IF THE TARGET WAS WITHIN THE UNITED STATES?
HEH. I ASSUMED IT WOULD BE, GENERAL.
WE HAVE A DEAL, MARLO.
BELLE REVE FEDERAL PRISON, LOUISIANA.
10

MOST CITY AND STATE FACILITIES HAVEN'T THE MEANS OF DEALING WITH A SUPER-POWERED BEING, ACCUSED OR CONVICTED. BELLE REVE IS ONLY ONE OF A FEW FEDERAL FACILITIES WITH THOSE CAPABILITIES.

AND, AS YOU KNOW, THE KEENE ACT OF 1961 AND THE INGERSOLL AMENDMENT OF 1972 GIVES THE FEDERAL GOVERNMENT MORE LEEWAY...

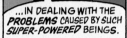

...IN DEALING WITH THE PROBLEMS CAUSED BY SUCH SUPER-POWERED BEINGS.

OVER HERE, WE HAVE A NEW PRISONER WHO JUST CAME TO US LAST NIGHT FROM PITTSBURGH. A GOOD CASE IN POINT. CALLED THE PARASITE.

GOOD HEAVENS! IS HE ALIVE?

YOU WERE SAYING THE PRISON WAS BUILT ON THE SITE OF AN OLD SOUTHERN PLANTATION, MR. ECONOMOS. THIS PLANTATION WAS BUILT IN THE SWAMP, WARDEN?

NEAR ONE THAT SEEMS TO HAVE GROWN OVER THE LAST CENTURY, MISS VALE. AND I REALLY THINK THAT AFTER ALL THE TIME WE'VE SPENT TOGETHER OVER THE PAST FEW DAYS, PUTTING THIS STORY TOGETHER FOR YOUR MAGAZINE, THAT YOU COULD CALL ME "JOHN", VICKI.

I PREFER TO KEEP THE PROFESSIONAL DISTANCE, WARDEN. NOTHING PERSONAL. YOU SAID BELLE REVE WAS DESIGNED NOT ONLY TO INCARCERATE CONVICTED SUPER-POWERED FELONS BUT TO ALSO ACT AS A HOLDING FACILITY?

YES, BUT NOT AWAKE. HE STEALS ENERGY FROM LIVING BEINGS, WHICH IS HOW HE EATS. HE KILLED ABOUT TWENTY PEOPLE THAT WAY. *

NO ONE KNOWS WHAT HE IS, TO START WITH: HUMAN, ALIEN, MUTANT. IS HE/WAS HE A CITIZEN? IF SO, WHAT JURISDICTION GETS HIM? WHAT DO YOU DO WITH HIM WHILE YOU TRY TO FIGURE IT OUT?

*SEE FIRESTORM #58-59. -- BOB

11

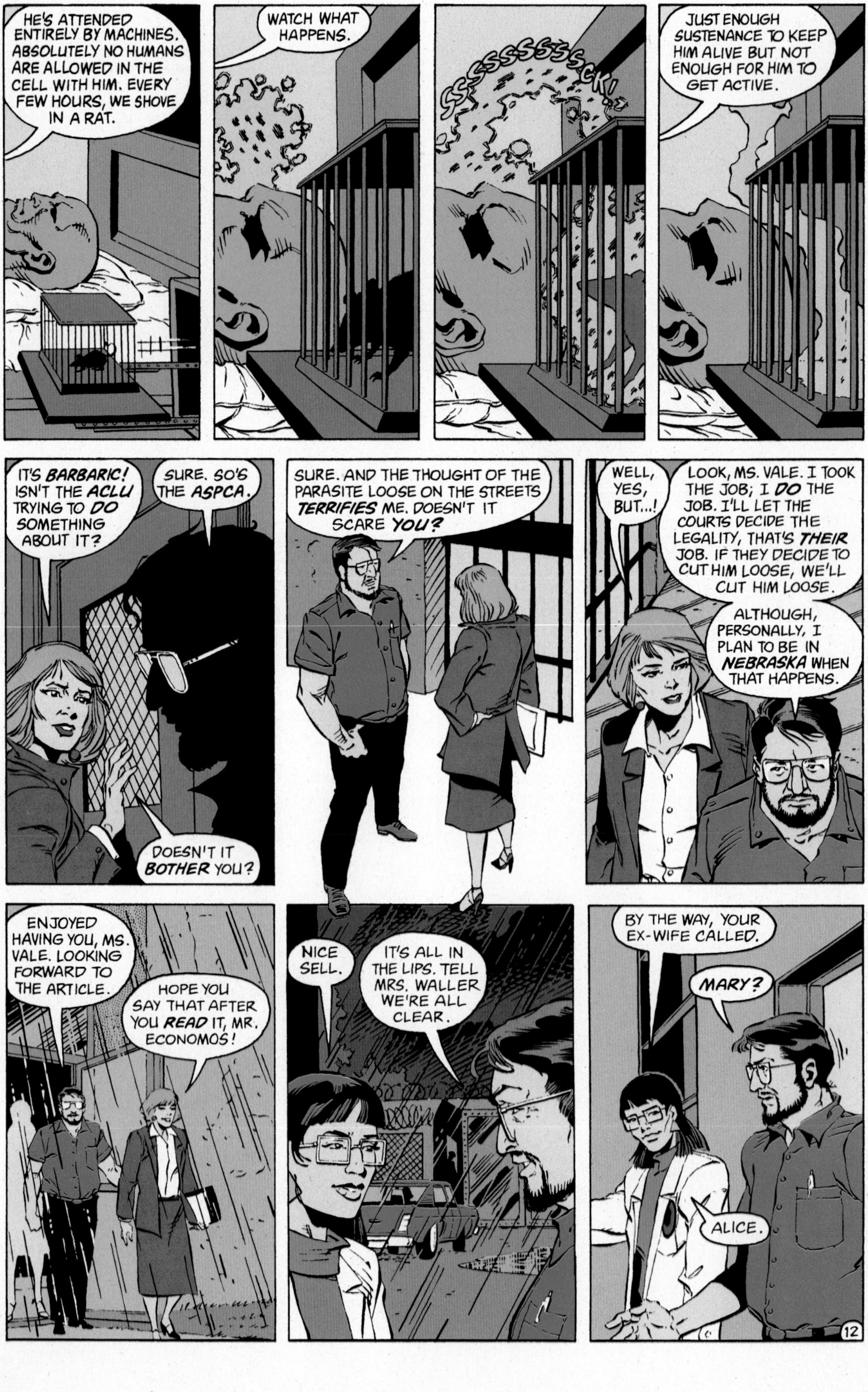
HE'S ATTENDED ENTIRELY BY MACHINES. ABSOLUTELY NO HUMANS ARE ALLOWED IN THE CELL WITH HIM. EVERY FEW HOURS, WE SHOVE IN A RAT.
WATCH WHAT HAPPENS.
SSSSSSSSSCK!
JUST ENOUGH SUSTENANCE TO KEEP HIM ALIVE BUT NOT ENOUGH FOR HIM TO GET ACTIVE.
IT'S BARBARIC! ISN'T THE ACLU TRYING TO DO SOMETHING ABOUT IT?
SURE. SO'S THE ASPCA.
DOESN'T IT BOTHER YOU?
SURE. AND THE THOUGHT OF THE PARASITE LOOSE ON THE STREETS TERRIFIES ME. DOESN'T IT SCARE YOU?
WELL, YES, BUT...!
LOOK, MS. VALE. I TOOK THE JOB; I DO THE JOB. I'LL LET THE COURTS DECIDE THE LEGALITY, THAT'S THEIR JOB. IF THEY DECIDE TO CUT HIM LOOSE, WE'LL CUT HIM LOOSE.
ALTHOUGH, PERSONALLY, I PLAN TO BE IN NEBRASKA WHEN THAT HAPPENS.
ENJOYED HAVING YOU, MS. VALE. LOOKING FORWARD TO THE ARTICLE.
HOPE YOU SAY THAT AFTER YOU READ IT, MR. ECONOMOS!
NICE SELL.
IT'S ALL IN THE LIPS. TELL MRS. WALLER WE'RE ALL CLEAR.
BY THE WAY, YOUR EX-WIFE CALLED.
MARY?
ALICE.
12

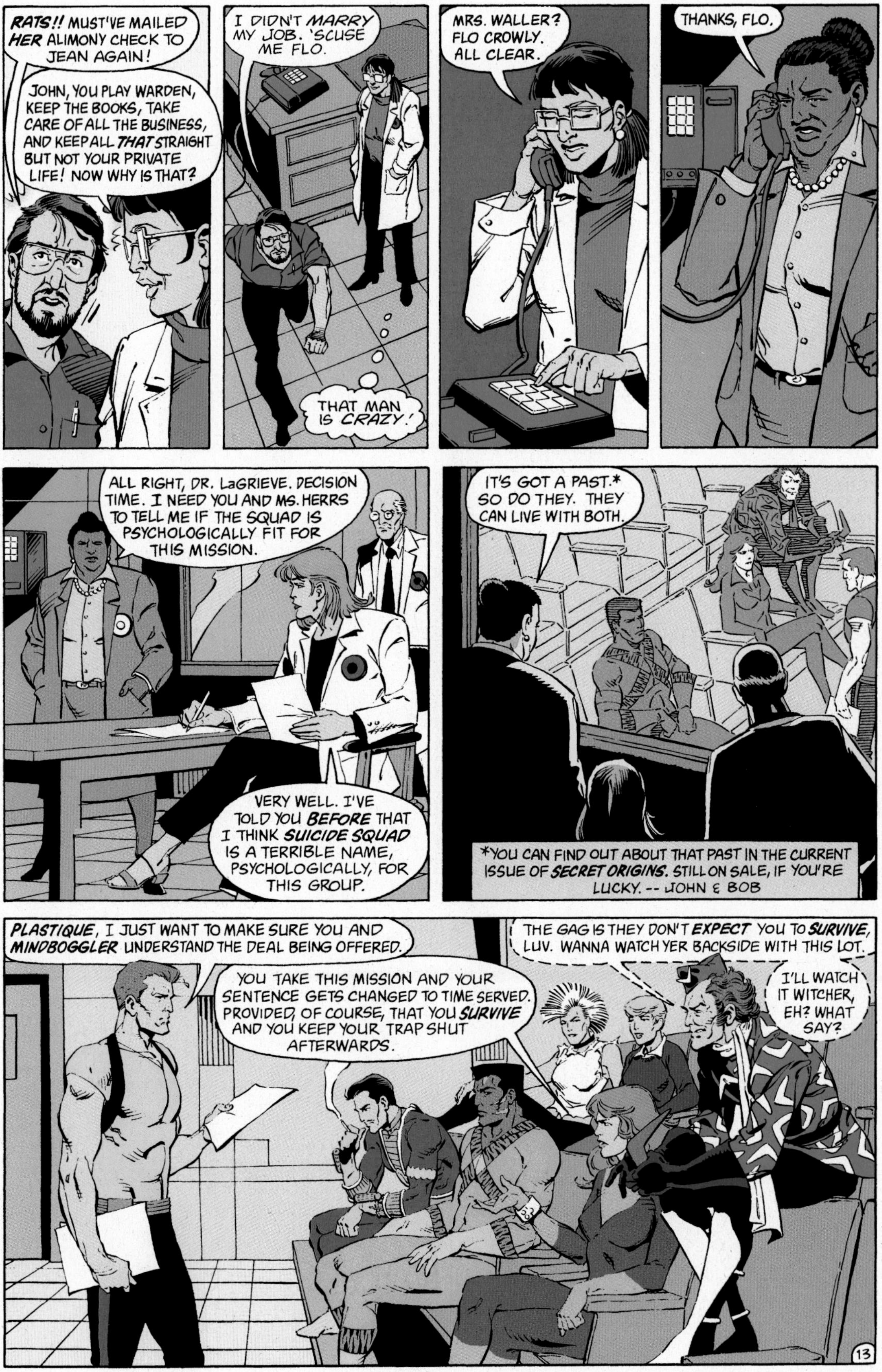
RATS!! MUST'VE MAILED HER ALIMONY CHECK TO JEAN AGAIN!
JOHN, YOU PLAY WARDEN, KEEP THE BOOKS, TAKE CARE OF ALL THE BUSINESS, AND KEEP ALL THAT STRAIGHT BUT NOT YOUR PRIVATE LIFE! NOW WHY IS THAT?
I DIDN'T MARRY MY JOB. 'SCUSE ME FLO.
THAT MAN IS CRAZY!
MRS. WALLER? FLO CROWLY. ALL CLEAR.
THANKS, FLO.
ALL RIGHT, DR. LaGRIEVE. DECISION TIME. I NEED YOU AND MS. HERRS TO TELL ME IF THE SQUAD IS PSYCHOLOGICALLY FIT FOR THIS MISSION.
VERY WELL. I'VE TOLD YOU BEFORE THAT I THINK SUICIDE SQUAD IS A TERRIBLE NAME, PSYCHOLOGICALLY, FOR THIS GROUP.
IT'S GOT A PAST.* SO DO THEY. THEY CAN LIVE WITH BOTH.
*YOU CAN FIND OUT ABOUT THAT PAST IN THE CURRENT ISSUE OF SECRET ORIGINS. STILL ON SALE, IF YOU'RE LUCKY. -- JOHN & BOB
PLASTIQUE, I JUST WANT TO MAKE SURE YOU AND MINDBOGGLER UNDERSTAND THE DEAL BEING OFFERED.
YOU TAKE THIS MISSION AND YOUR SENTENCE GETS CHANGED TO TIME SERVED. PROVIDED, OF COURSE, THAT YOU SURVIVE AND YOU KEEP YOUR TRAP SHUT AFTERWARDS.
THE GAG IS THEY DON'T EXPECT YOU TO SURVIVE, LUV. WANNA WATCH YER BACKSIDE WITH THIS LOT.
I'LL WATCH IT WITCHER, EH? WHAT SAY?
13

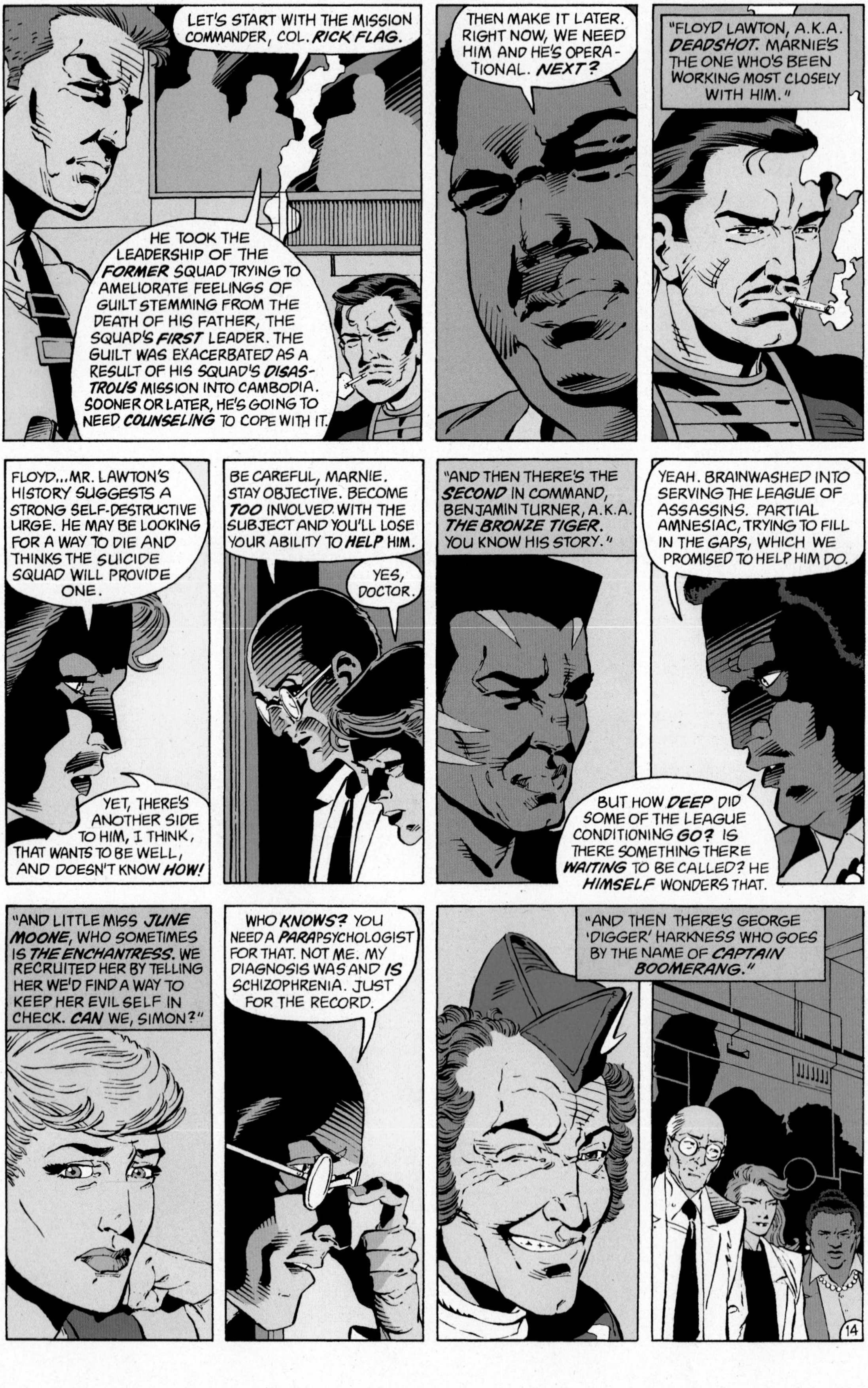
LET'S START WITH THE MISSION COMMANDER, COL. RICK FLAG.
HE TOOK THE LEADERSHIP OF THE FORMER SQUAD TRYING TO AMELIORATE FEELINGS OF GUILT STEMMING FROM THE DEATH OF HIS FATHER, THE SQUAD'S FIRST LEADER. THE GUILT WAS EXACERBATED AS A RESULT OF HIS SQUAD'S DISASTROUS MISSION INTO CAMBODIA. SOONER OR LATER, HE'S GOING TO NEED COUNSELING TO COPE WITH IT.
THEN MAKE IT LATER. RIGHT NOW, WE NEED HIM AND HE'S OPERATIONAL. NEXT?
"FLOYD LAWTON, A.K.A. DEADSHOT. MARNIE'S THE ONE WHO'S BEEN WORKING MOST CLOSELY WITH HIM."
FLOYD...MR. LAWTON'S HISTORY SUGGESTS A STRONG SELF-DESTRUCTIVE URGE. HE MAY BE LOOKING FOR A WAY TO DIE AND THINKS THE SUICIDE SQUAD WILL PROVIDE ONE.
YET, THERE'S ANOTHER SIDE TO HIM, I THINK, THAT WANTS TO BE WELL, AND DOESN'T KNOW HOW!
BE CAREFUL, MARNIE. STAY OBJECTIVE. BECOME TOO INVOLVED WITH THE SUBJECT AND YOU'LL LOSE YOUR ABILITY TO HELP HIM.
YES, DOCTOR.
"AND THEN THERE'S THE SECOND IN COMMAND, BENJAMIN TURNER, A.K.A. THE BRONZE TIGER. YOU KNOW HIS STORY."
YEAH. BRAINWASHED INTO SERVING THE LEAGUE OF ASSASSINS. PARTIAL AMNESIAC, TRYING TO FILL IN THE GAPS, WHICH WE PROMISED TO HELP HIM DO.
BUT HOW DEEP DID SOME OF THE LEAGUE CONDITIONING GO? IS THERE SOMETHING THERE WAITING TO BE CALLED? HE HIMSELF WONDERS THAT.
"AND LITTLE MISS JUNE MOONE, WHO SOMETIMES IS THE ENCHANTRESS. WE RECRUITED HER BY TELLING HER WE'D FIND A WAY TO KEEP HER EVIL SELF IN CHECK. CAN WE, SIMON?"
WHO KNOWS? YOU NEED A PARAPSYCHOLOGIST FOR THAT. NOT ME. MY DIAGNOSIS WAS AND IS SCHIZOPHRENIA. JUST FOR THE RECORD.
"AND THEN THERE'S GEORGE 'DIGGER' HARKNESS WHO GOES BY THE NAME OF CAPTAIN BOOMERANG."
14

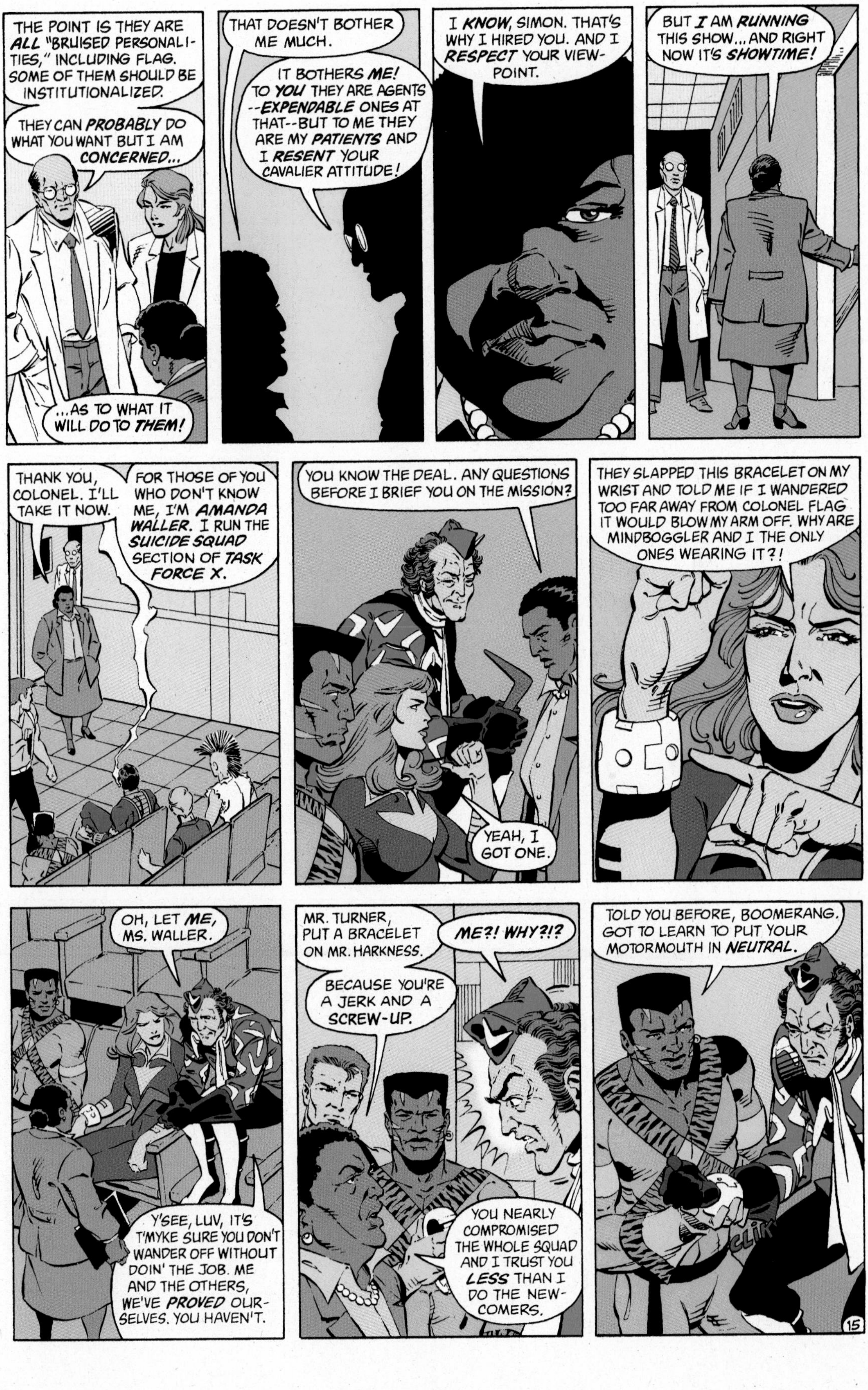
THE POINT IS THEY ARE ALL "BRUISED PERSONALITIES," INCLUDING FLAG. SOME OF THEM SHOULD BE INSTITUTIONALIZED.
THEY CAN PROBABLY DO WHAT YOU WANT BUT I AM CONCERNED...
...AS TO WHAT IT WILL DO TO THEM!
THAT DOESN'T BOTHER ME MUCH.
IT BOTHERS ME! TO YOU THEY ARE AGENTS --EXPENDABLE ONES AT THAT--BUT TO ME THEY ARE MY PATIENTS AND I RESENT YOUR CAVALIER ATTITUDE!
I KNOW, SIMON. THAT'S WHY I HIRED YOU. AND I RESPECT YOUR VIEWPOINT.
BUT I AM RUNNING THIS SHOW..., AND RIGHT NOW IT'S SHOWTIME!
THANK YOU, COLONEL. I'LL TAKE IT NOW.
FOR THOSE OF YOU WHO DON'T KNOW ME, I'M AMANDA WALLER. I RUN THE SUICIDE SQUAD SECTION OF TASK FORCE X.
YOU KNOW THE DEAL. ANY QUESTIONS BEFORE I BRIEF YOU ON THE MISSION?
YEAH, I GOT ONE.
THEY SLAPPED THIS BRACELET ON MY WRIST AND TOLD ME IF I WANDERED TOO FAR AWAY FROM COLONEL FLAG IT WOULD BLOW MY ARM OFF. WHY ARE MINDBOGGLER AND I THE ONLY ONES WEARING IT?!
OH, LET ME, MS. WALLER.
Y'SEE, LUV, IT'S T'MYKE SURE YOU DON'T WANDER OFF WITHOUT DOIN' THE JOB. ME AND THE OTHERS, WE'VE PROVED OURSELVES. YOU HAVEN'T.
MR. TURNER, PUT A BRACELET ON MR. HARKNESS.
ME?! WHY?!?
BECAUSE YOU'RE A JERK AND A SCREW-UP.
YOU NEARLY COMPROMISED THE WHOLE SQUAD AND I TRUST YOU LESS THAN I DO THE NEWCOMERS.
TOLD YOU BEFORE, BOOMERANG. GOT TO LEARN TO PUT YOUR MOTORMOUTH IN NEUTRAL.
CLIK
15

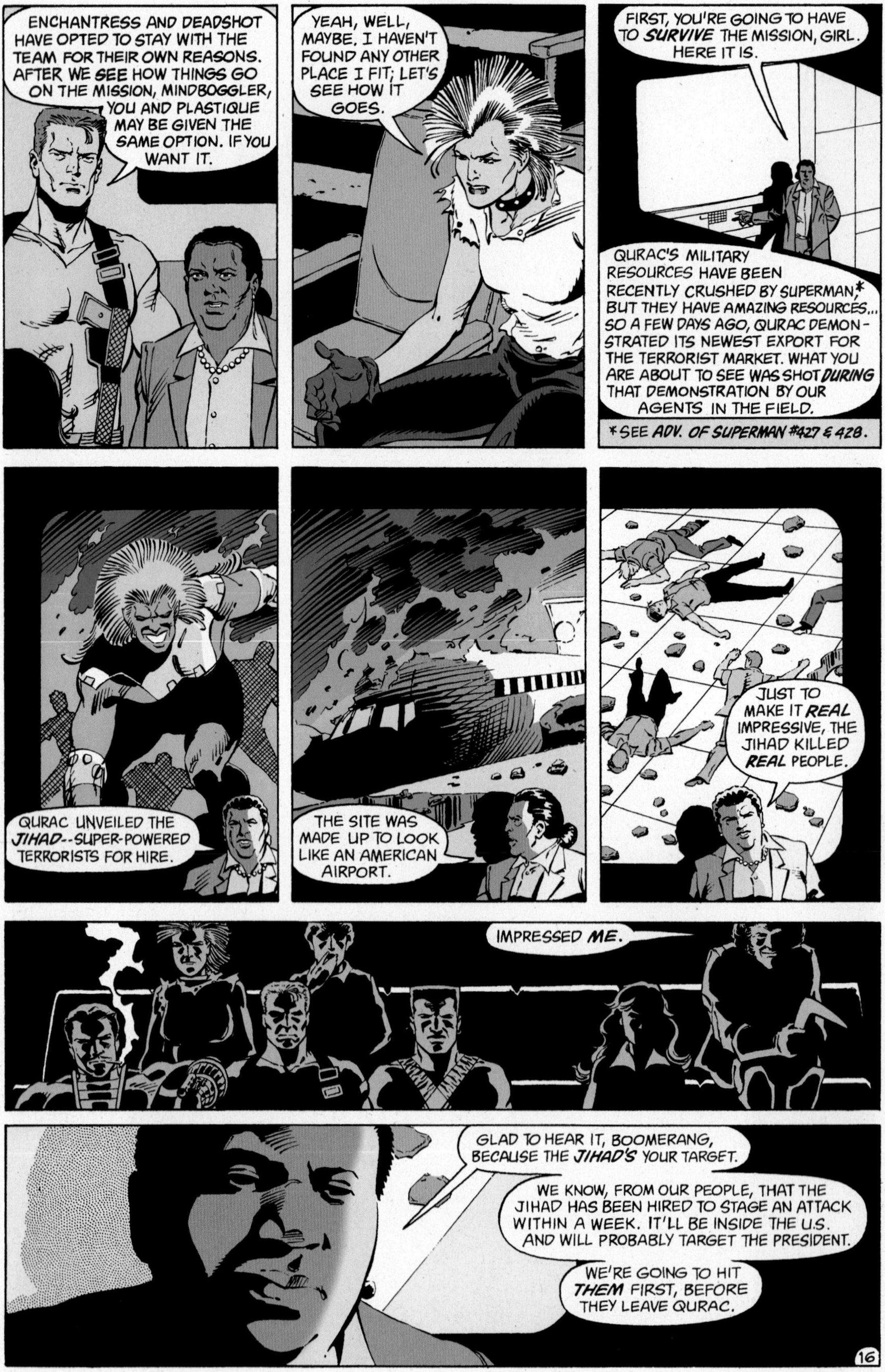
ENCHANTRESS AND DEADSHOT HAVE OPTED TO STAY WITH THE TEAM FOR THEIR OWN REASONS. AFTER WE SEE HOW THINGS GO ON THE MISSION, MINDBOGGLER, YOU AND PLASTIQUE MAY BE GIVEN THE SAME OPTION. IF YOU WANT IT.
YEAH, WELL, MAYBE. I HAVEN'T FOUND ANY OTHER PLACE I FIT; LET'S SEE HOW IT GOES.
FIRST, YOU'RE GOING TO HAVE TO SURVIVE THE MISSION, GIRL. HERE IT IS.
QURAC'S MILITARY RESOURCES HAVE BEEN RECENTLY CRUSHED BY SUPERMAN,* BUT THEY HAVE AMAZING RESOURCES... SO A FEW DAYS AGO, QURAC DEMONSTRATED ITS NEWEST EXPORT FOR THE TERRORIST MARKET. WHAT YOU ARE ABOUT TO SEE WAS SHOT DURING THAT DEMONSTRATION BY OUR AGENTS IN THE FIELD.
*SEE ADV. OF SUPERMAN #427 & 428.
QURAC UNVEILED THE JIHAD--SUPER-POWERED TERRORISTS FOR HIRE.
THE SITE WAS MADE UP TO LOOK LIKE AN AMERICAN AIRPORT.
JUST TO MAKE IT REAL IMPRESSIVE, THE JIHAD KILLED REAL PEOPLE.
IMPRESSED ME.
GLAD TO HEAR IT, BOOMERANG, BECAUSE THE JIHAD'S YOUR TARGET.
WE KNOW, FROM OUR PEOPLE, THAT THE JIHAD HAS BEEN HIRED TO STAGE AN ATTACK WITHIN A WEEK. IT'LL BE INSIDE THE U.S. AND WILL PROBABLY TARGET THE PRESIDENT.
WE'RE GOING TO HIT THEM FIRST, BEFORE THEY LEAVE QURAC.
16

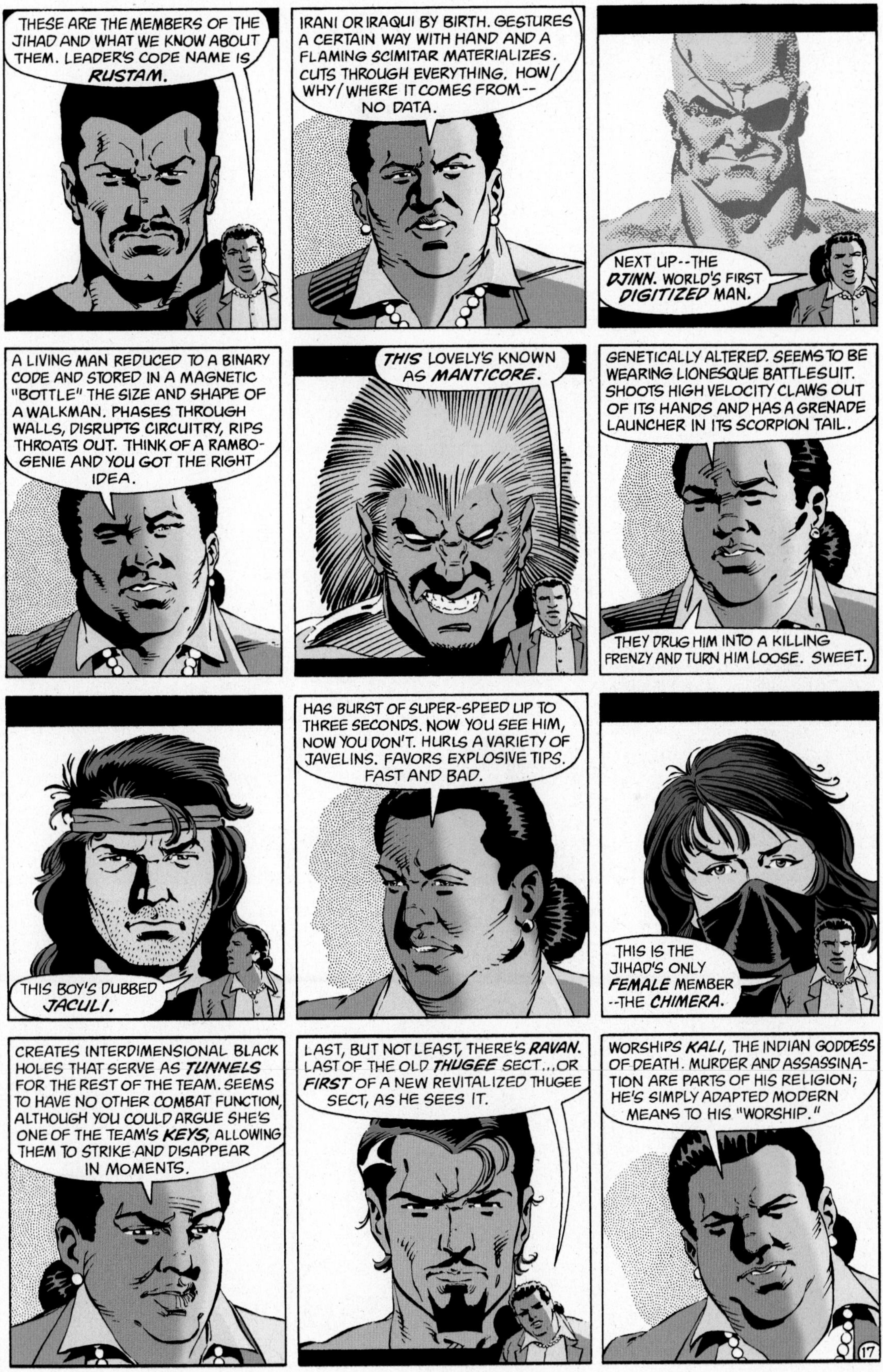
THESE ARE THE MEMBERS OF THE JIHAD AND WHAT WE KNOW ABOUT THEM. LEADER'S CODE NAME IS *RUSTAM*.
IRANI OR IRAQUI BY BIRTH. GESTURES A CERTAIN WAY WITH HAND AND A FLAMING SCIMITAR MATERIALIZES. CUTS THROUGH EVERYTHING. HOW/ WHY/ WHERE IT COMES FROM -- NO DATA.
NEXT UP--THE *DJINN*. WORLD'S FIRST *DIGITIZED* MAN.
A LIVING MAN REDUCED TO A BINARY CODE AND STORED IN A MAGNETIC "BOTTLE" THE SIZE AND SHAPE OF A WALKMAN. PHASES THROUGH WALLS, DISRUPTS CIRCUITRY, RIPS THROATS OUT. THINK OF A RAMBO-GENIE AND YOU GOT THE RIGHT IDEA.
THIS LOVELY'S KNOWN AS *MANTICORE*.
GENETICALLY ALTERED. SEEMS TO BE WEARING LIONESQUE BATTLESUIT. SHOOTS HIGH VELOCITY CLAWS OUT OF ITS HANDS AND HAS A GRENADE LAUNCHER IN ITS SCORPION TAIL.
THEY DRUG HIM INTO A KILLING FRENZY AND TURN HIM LOOSE. SWEET.
THIS BOY'S DUBBED *JACULI*.
HAS BURST OF SUPER-SPEED UP TO THREE SECONDS. NOW YOU SEE HIM, NOW YOU DON'T. HURLS A VARIETY OF JAVELINS. FAVORS EXPLOSIVE TIPS. FAST AND BAD.
THIS IS THE JIHAD'S ONLY *FEMALE* MEMBER --THE *CHIMERA*.
CREATES INTERDIMENSIONAL BLACK HOLES THAT SERVE AS *TUNNELS* FOR THE REST OF THE TEAM. SEEMS TO HAVE NO OTHER COMBAT FUNCTION, ALTHOUGH YOU COULD ARGUE SHE'S ONE OF THE TEAM'S *KEYS*, ALLOWING THEM TO STRIKE AND DISAPPEAR IN MOMENTS.
LAST, BUT NOT LEAST, THERE'S *RAVAN*. LAST OF THE OLD *THUGEE* SECT...OR *FIRST* OF A NEW REVITALIZED THUGEE SECT, AS HE SEES IT.
WORSHIPS *KALI*, THE INDIAN GODDESS OF DEATH. MURDER AND ASSASSINATION ARE PARTS OF HIS RELIGION; HE'S SIMPLY ADAPTED MODERN MEANS TO HIS "WORSHIP."
17

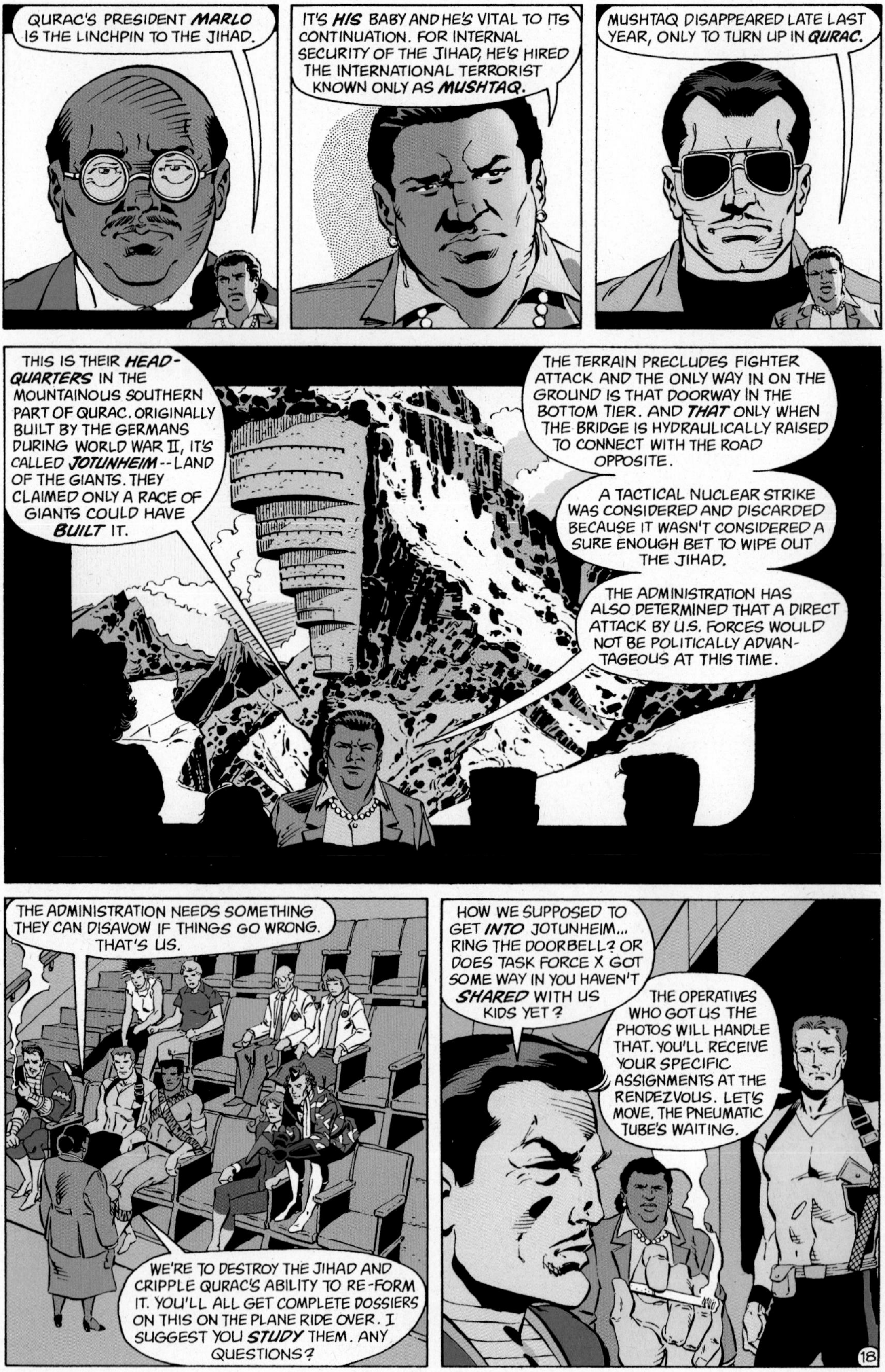
QURAC'S PRESIDENT MARLO IS THE LINCHPIN TO THE JIHAD.
IT'S HIS BABY AND HE'S VITAL TO ITS CONTINUATION. FOR INTERNAL SECURITY OF THE JIHAD, HE'S HIRED THE INTERNATIONAL TERRORIST KNOWN ONLY AS MUSHTAQ.
MUSHTAQ DISAPPEARED LATE LAST YEAR, ONLY TO TURN UP IN QURAC.
THIS IS THEIR HEAD-QUARTERS IN THE MOUNTAINOUS SOUTHERN PART OF QURAC. ORIGINALLY BUILT BY THE GERMANS DURING WORLD WAR II, IT'S CALLED JOTUNHEIM--LAND OF THE GIANTS. THEY CLAIMED ONLY A RACE OF GIANTS COULD HAVE BUILT IT.
THE TERRAIN PRECLUDES FIGHTER ATTACK AND THE ONLY WAY IN ON THE GROUND IS THAT DOORWAY IN THE BOTTOM TIER. AND THAT ONLY WHEN THE BRIDGE IS HYDRAULICALLY RAISED TO CONNECT WITH THE ROAD OPPOSITE.
A TACTICAL NUCLEAR STRIKE WAS CONSIDERED AND DISCARDED BECAUSE IT WASN'T CONSIDERED A SURE ENOUGH BET TO WIPE OUT THE JIHAD.
THE ADMINISTRATION HAS ALSO DETERMINED THAT A DIRECT ATTACK BY U.S. FORCES WOULD NOT BE POLITICALLY ADVAN-TAGEOUS AT THIS TIME.
THE ADMINISTRATION NEEDS SOMETHING THEY CAN DISAVOW IF THINGS GO WRONG. THAT'S US.
WE'RE TO DESTROY THE JIHAD AND CRIPPLE QURAC'S ABILITY TO RE-FORM IT. YOU'LL ALL GET COMPLETE DOSSIERS ON THIS ON THE PLANE RIDE OVER. I SUGGEST YOU STUDY THEM. ANY QUESTIONS?
HOW WE SUPPOSED TO GET INTO JOTUNHEIM... RING THE DOORBELL? OR DOES TASK FORCE X GOT SOME WAY IN YOU HAVEN'T SHARED WITH US KIDS YET?
THE OPERATIVES WHO GOT US THE PHOTOS WILL HANDLE THAT. YOU'LL RECEIVE YOUR SPECIFIC ASSIGNMENTS AT THE RENDEZVOUS. LET'S MOVE. THE PNEUMATIC TUBE'S WAITING.
18

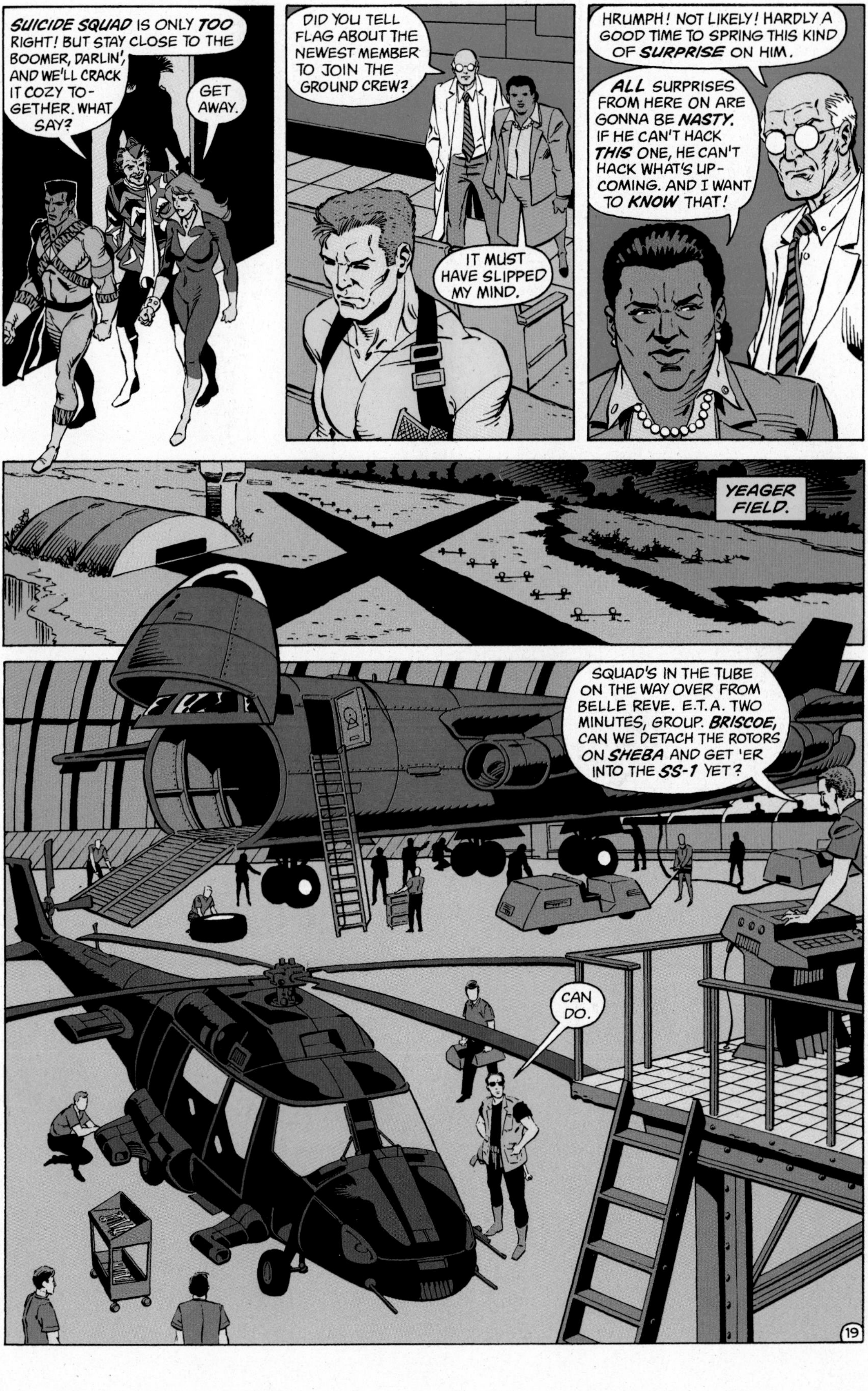
SUICIDE SQUAD IS ONLY TOO RIGHT! BUT STAY CLOSE TO THE BOOMER, DARLIN', AND WE'LL CRACK IT COZY TOGETHER. WHAT SAY?
GET AWAY.
DID YOU TELL FLAG ABOUT THE NEWEST MEMBER TO JOIN THE GROUND CREW?
IT MUST HAVE SLIPPED MY MIND.
HRUMPH! NOT LIKELY! HARDLY A GOOD TIME TO SPRING THIS KIND OF SURPRISE ON HIM.
ALL SURPRISES FROM HERE ON ARE GONNA BE NASTY. IF HE CAN'T HACK THIS ONE, HE CAN'T HACK WHAT'S UPCOMING. AND I WANT TO KNOW THAT!
YEAGER FIELD.
SQUAD'S IN THE TUBE ON THE WAY OVER FROM BELLE REVE. E.T.A. TWO MINUTES, GROUP. BRISCOE, CAN WE DETACH THE ROTORS ON SHEBA AND GET 'ER INTO THE SS-1 YET?
CAN DO.
19

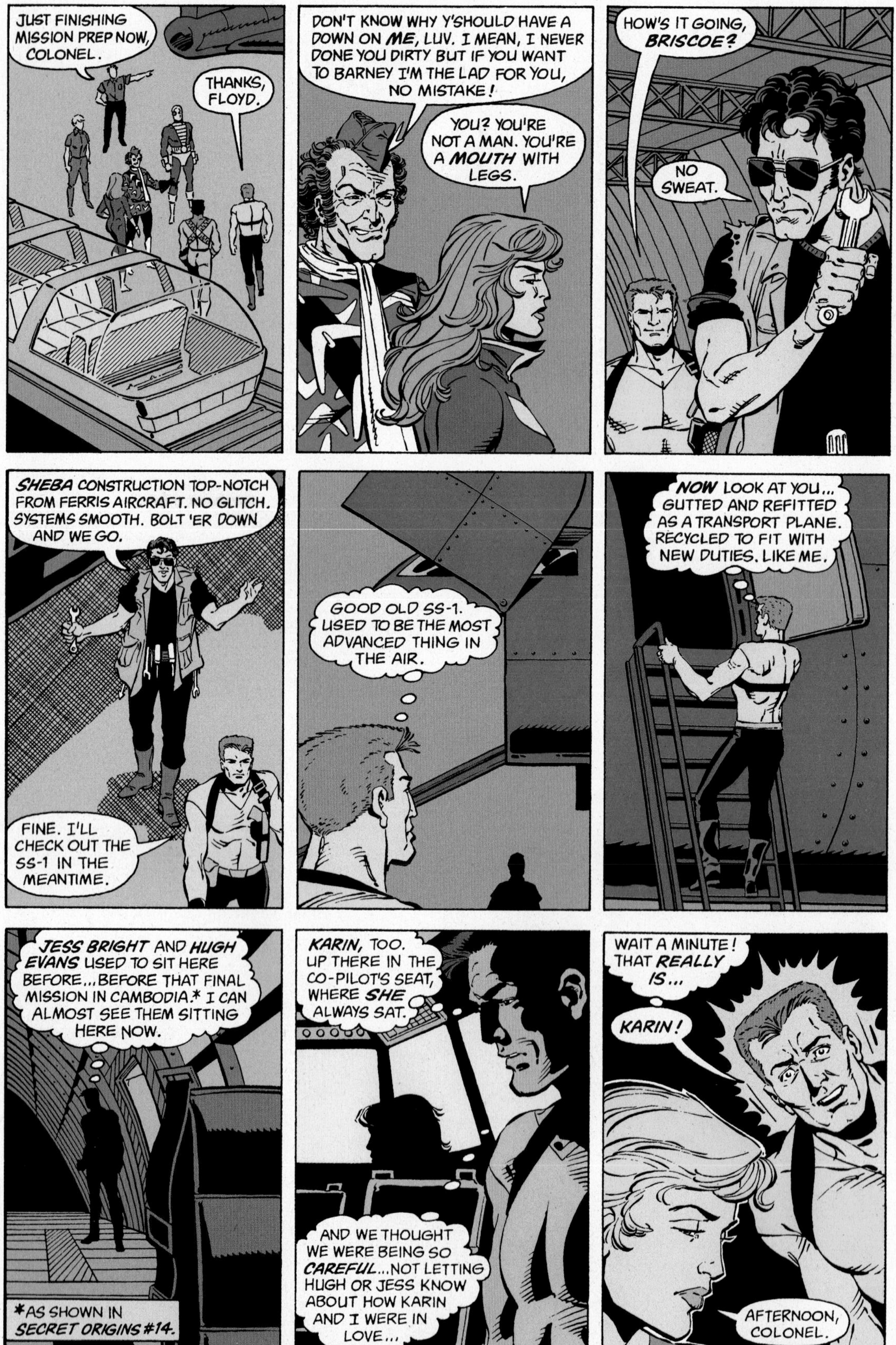
JUST FINISHING MISSION PREP NOW, COLONEL.
THANKS, FLOYD.
DON'T KNOW WHY Y'SHOULD HAVE A DOWN ON ME, LUV. I MEAN, I NEVER DONE YOU DIRTY BUT IF YOU WANT TO BARNEY I'M THE LAD FOR YOU, NO MISTAKE!
YOU? YOU'RE NOT A MAN. YOU'RE A MOUTH WITH LEGS.
HOW'S IT GOING, BRISCOE?
NO SWEAT.
SHEBA CONSTRUCTION TOP-NOTCH FROM FERRIS AIRCRAFT. NO GLITCH. SYSTEMS SMOOTH. BOLT 'ER DOWN AND WE GO.
FINE. I'LL CHECK OUT THE SS-1 IN THE MEANTIME.
GOOD OLD SS-1. USED TO BE THE MOST ADVANCED THING IN THE AIR.
NOW LOOK AT YOU... GUTTED AND REFITTED AS A TRANSPORT PLANE. RECYCLED TO FIT WITH NEW DUTIES. LIKE ME.
JESS BRIGHT AND HUGH EVANS USED TO SIT HERE BEFORE... BEFORE THAT FINAL MISSION IN CAMBODIA.* I CAN ALMOST SEE THEM SITTING HERE NOW.
*AS SHOWN IN SECRET ORIGINS #14.
KARIN, TOO. UP THERE IN THE CO-PILOT'S SEAT, WHERE SHE ALWAYS SAT.
AND WE THOUGHT WE WERE BEING SO CAREFUL...NOT LETTING HUGH OR JESS KNOW ABOUT HOW KARIN AND I WERE IN LOVE...
WAIT A MINUTE! THAT REALLY IS...
KARIN!
AFTERNOON, COLONEL.
20

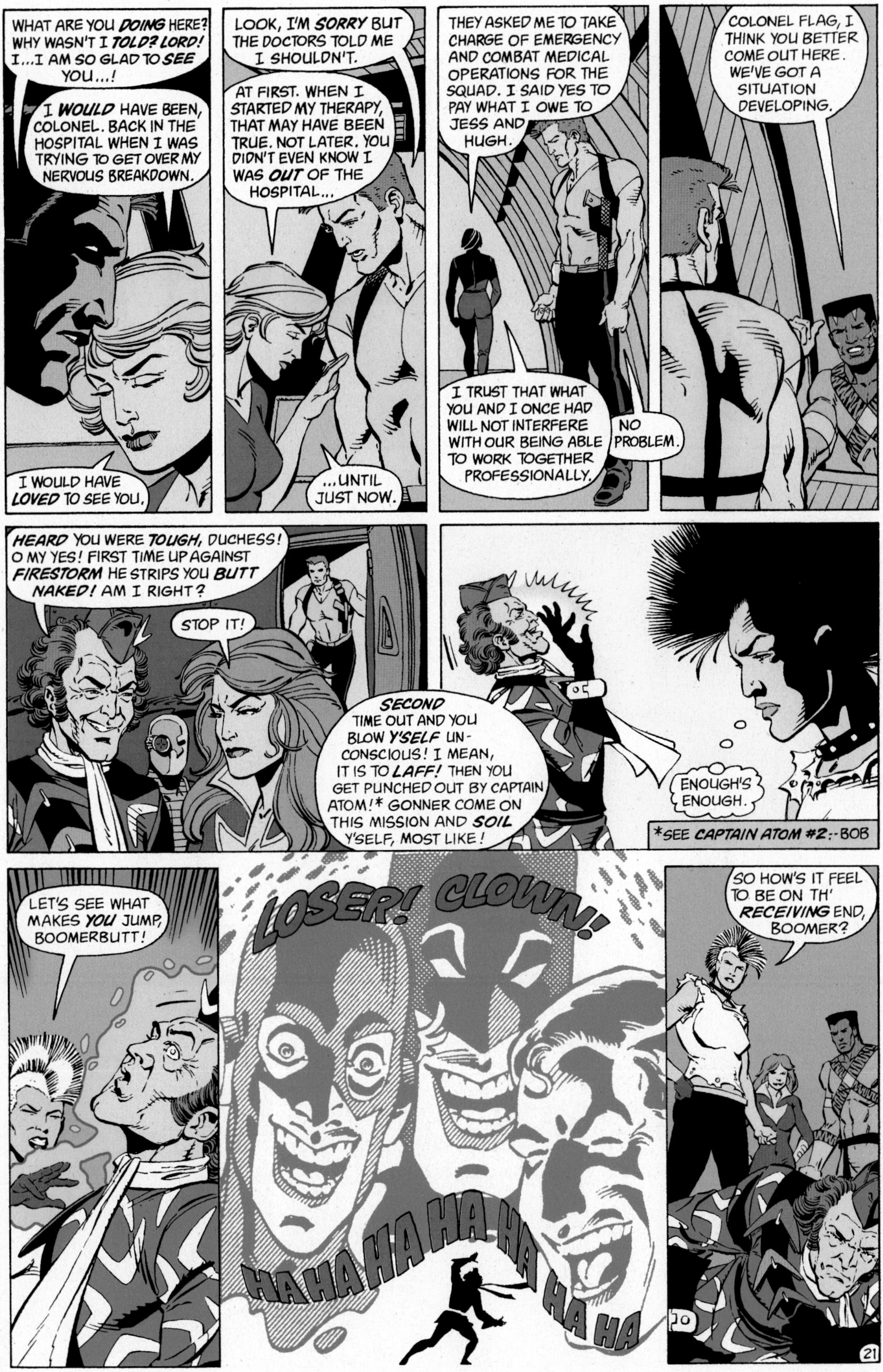
WHAT ARE YOU DOING HERE? WHY WASN'T I TOLD? LORD! I...I AM SO GLAD TO SEE YOU...!
I WOULD HAVE BEEN, COLONEL. BACK IN THE HOSPITAL WHEN I WAS TRYING TO GET OVER MY NERVOUS BREAKDOWN.
I WOULD HAVE LOVED TO SEE YOU.
LOOK, I'M SORRY BUT THE DOCTORS TOLD ME I SHOULDN'T.
AT FIRST. WHEN I STARTED MY THERAPY, THAT MAY HAVE BEEN TRUE. NOT LATER. YOU DIDN'T EVEN KNOW I WAS OUT OF THE HOSPITAL...
...UNTIL JUST NOW.
THEY ASKED ME TO TAKE CHARGE OF EMERGENCY AND COMBAT MEDICAL OPERATIONS FOR THE SQUAD. I SAID YES TO PAY WHAT I OWE TO JESS AND HUGH.
I TRUST THAT WHAT YOU AND I ONCE HAD WILL NOT INTERFERE WITH OUR BEING ABLE TO WORK TOGETHER PROFESSIONALLY.
NO PROBLEM.
COLONEL FLAG, I THINK YOU BETTER COME OUT HERE. WE'VE GOT A SITUATION DEVELOPING.
HEARD YOU WERE TOUGH, DUCHESS! O MY YES! FIRST TIME UP AGAINST FIRESTORM HE STRIPS YOU BUTT NAKED! AM I RIGHT?
STOP IT!
SECOND TIME OUT AND YOU BLOW Y'SELF UN-CONSCIOUS! I MEAN, IT IS TO LAFF! THEN YOU GET PUNCHED OUT BY CAPTAIN ATOM!* GONNER COME ON THIS MISSION AND SOIL Y'SELF, MOST LIKE!
ENOUGH'S ENOUGH.
*SEE CAPTAIN ATOM #2:-BOB
LET'S SEE WHAT MAKES YOU JUMP, BOOMERBUTT!
LOSER! CLOWN!
HA HA HA HA HA HA HA HA HA
SO HOW'S IT FEEL TO BE ON TH' RECEIVING END, BOOMER?
21

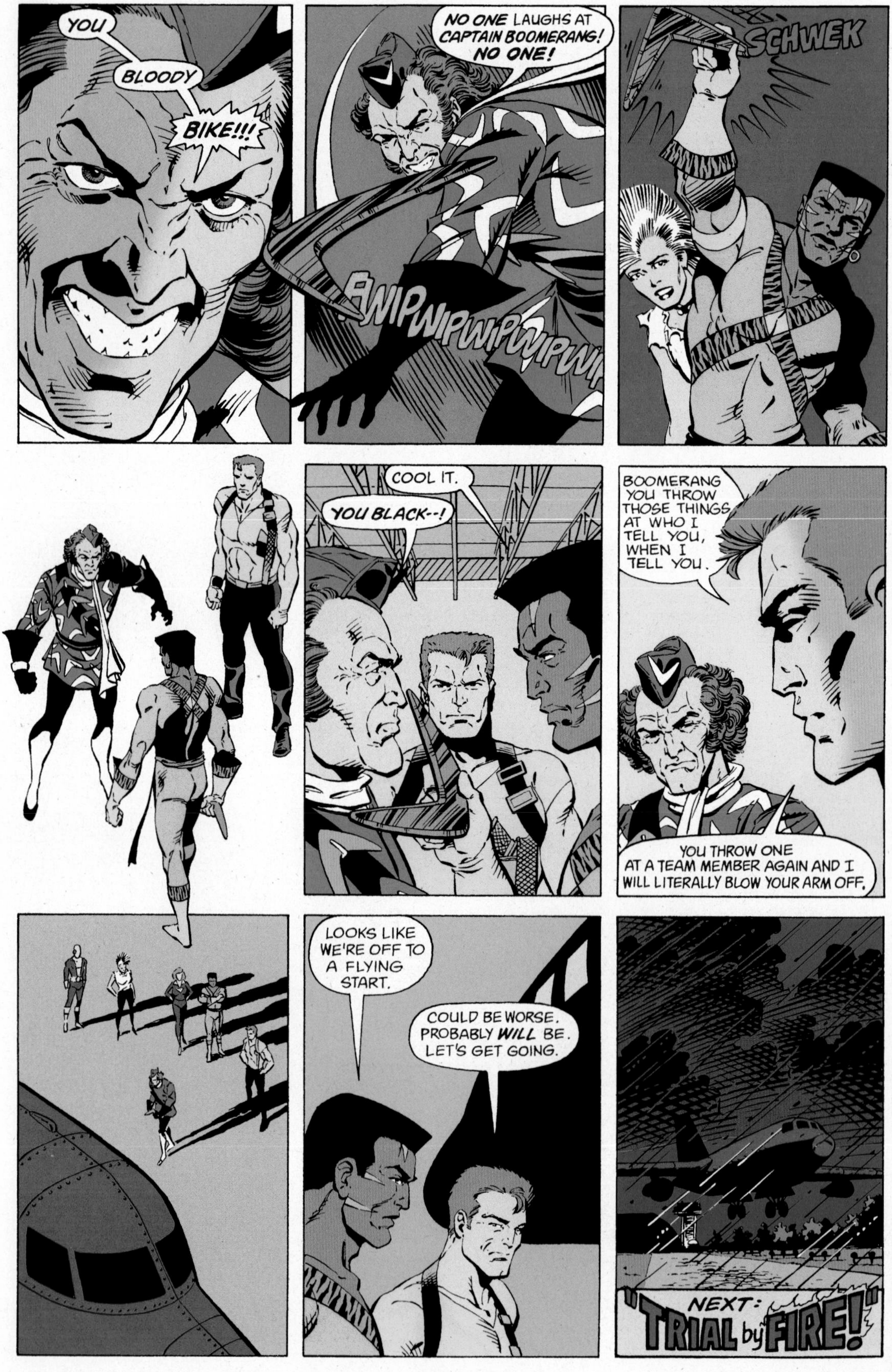
YOU
BLOODY
BIKE!!!
NO ONE LAUGHS AT CAPTAIN BOOMERANG! NO ONE!
WIPWIPWIPWIPWIPWI
SCHWEK
COOL IT.
YOU BLACK--!
BOOMERANG YOU THROW THOSE THINGS AT WHO I TELL YOU, WHEN I TELL YOU.
YOU THROW ONE AT A TEAM MEMBER AGAIN AND I WILL LITERALLY BLOW YOUR ARM OFF.
LOOKS LIKE WE'RE OFF TO A FLYING START.
COULD BE WORSE. PROBABLY WILL BE. LET'S GET GOING.
NEXT: "TRIAL by FIRE!"

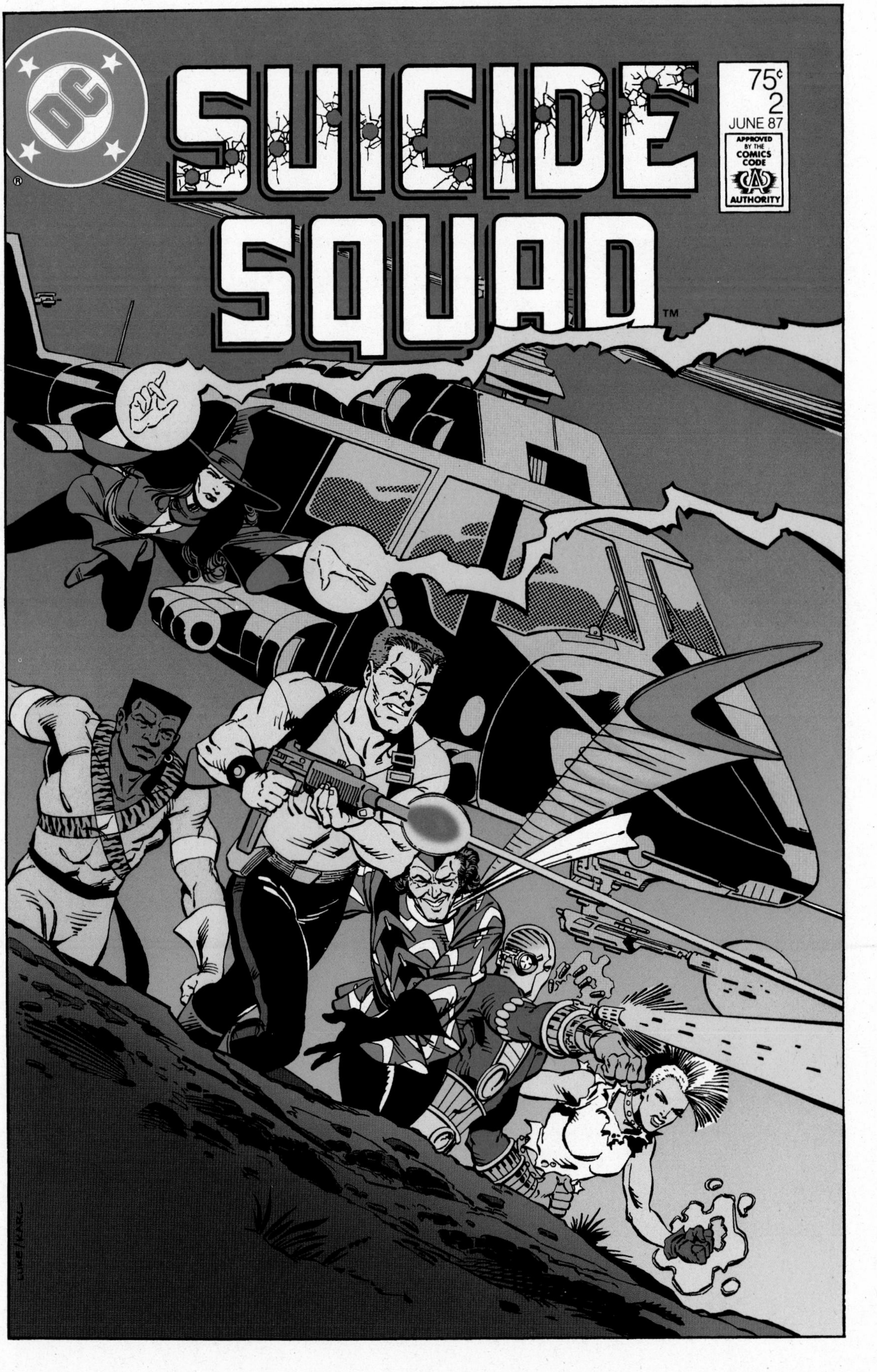

SUICIDE SQUAD
75¢
2
JUNE 87
APPROVED BY THE COMICS CODE AUTHORITY

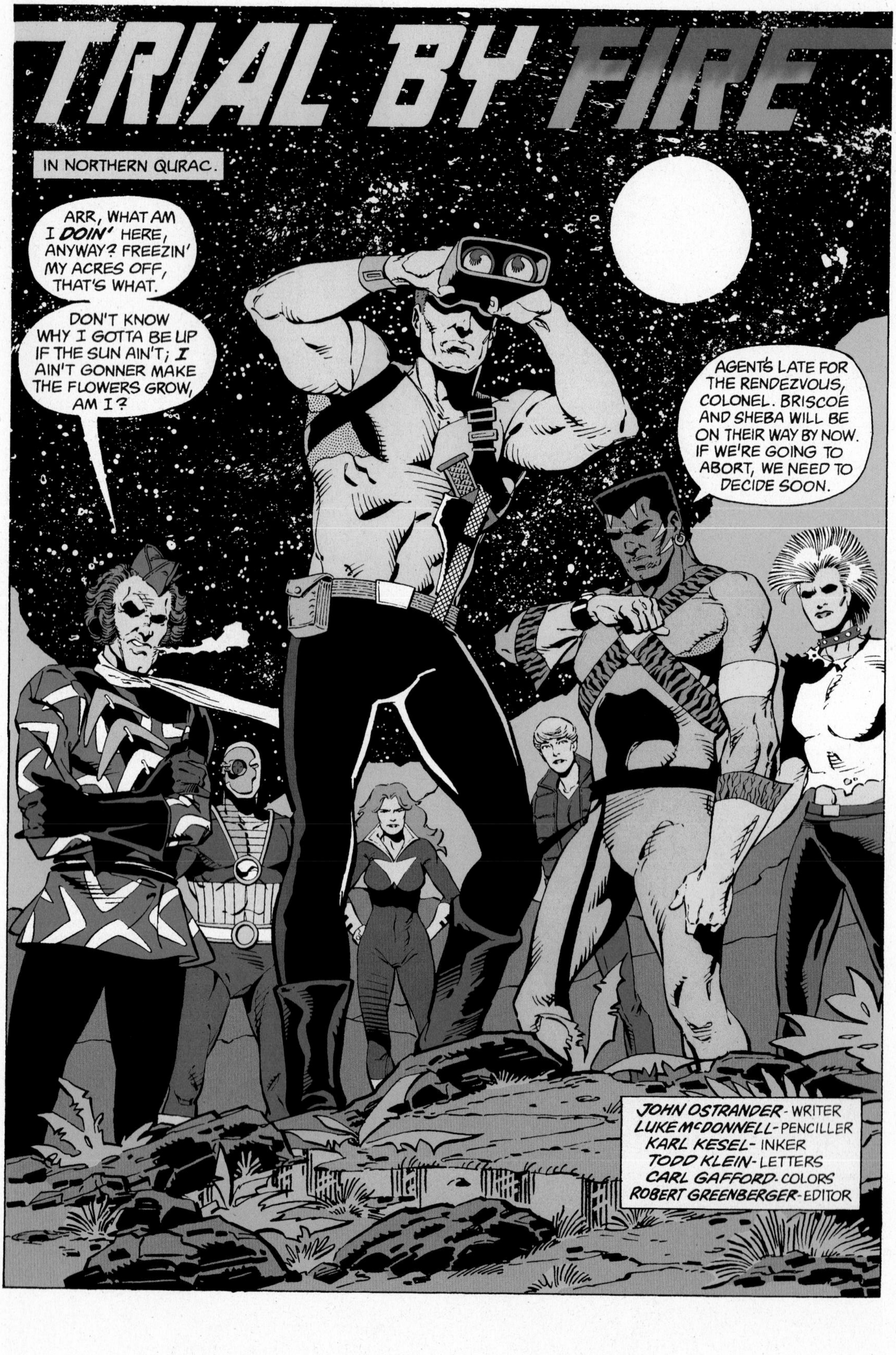
TRIAL BY FIRE
IN NORTHERN QURAC.
ARR, WHAT AM I DOIN' HERE, ANYWAY? FREEZIN' MY ACRES OFF, THAT'S WHAT.
DON'T KNOW WHY I GOTTA BE UP IF THE SUN AIN'T; I AIN'T GONNER MAKE THE FLOWERS GROW, AM I?
AGENT'S LATE FOR THE RENDEZVOUS, COLONEL. BRISCOE AND SHEBA WILL BE ON THEIR WAY BY NOW. IF WE'RE GOING TO ABORT, WE NEED TO DECIDE SOON.
JOHN OSTRANDER-WRITER
LUKE McDONNELL-PENCILLER
KARL KESEL-INKER
TODD KLEIN-LETTERS
CARL GAFFORD-COLORS
ROBERT GREENBERGER-EDITOR

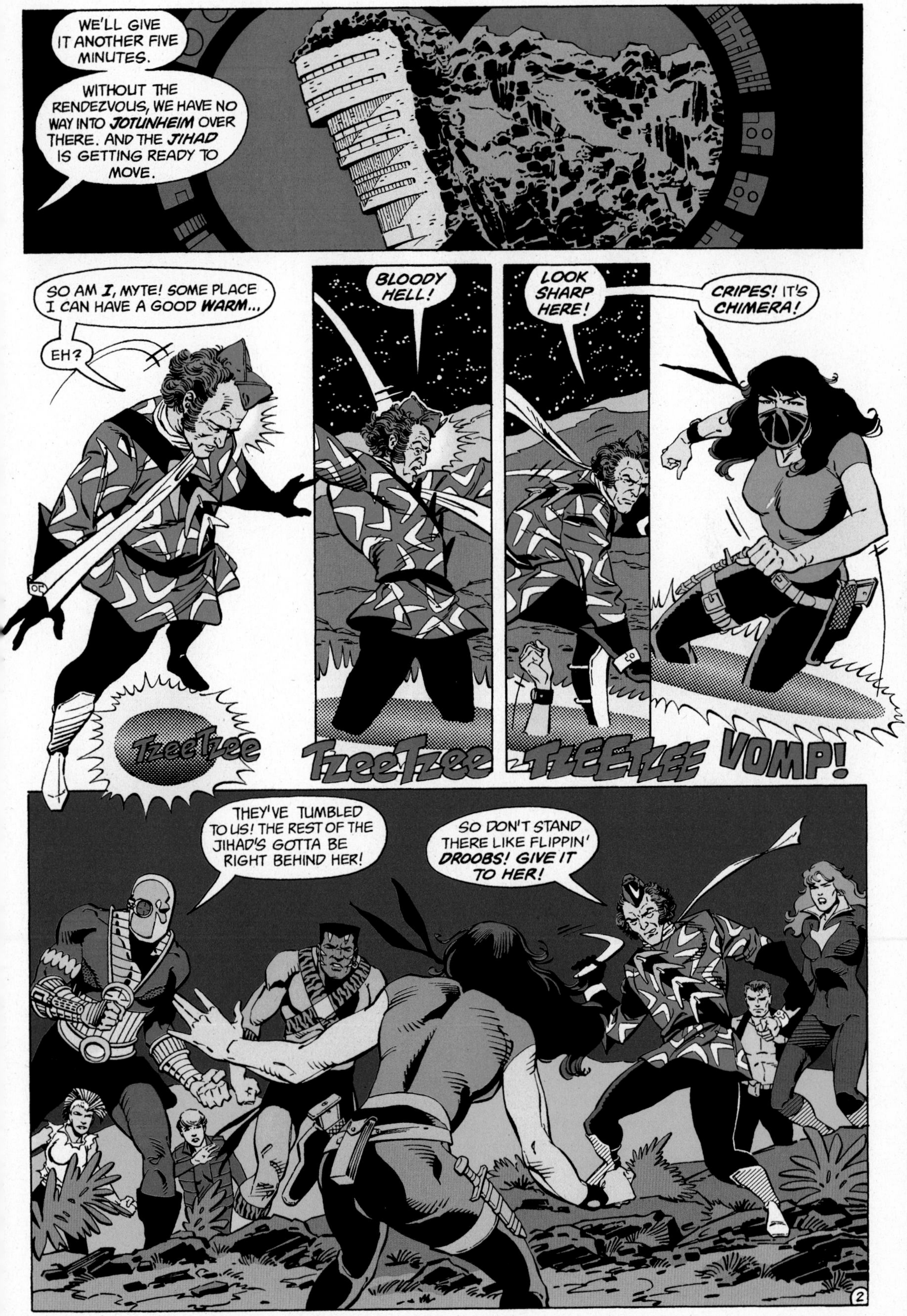
WE'LL GIVE IT ANOTHER FIVE MINUTES.
WITHOUT THE RENDEZVOUS, WE HAVE NO WAY INTO JOTUNHEIM OVER THERE. AND THE JIHAD IS GETTING READY TO MOVE.
SO AM I, MYTE! SOME PLACE I CAN HAVE A GOOD WARM...
EH?
TZEETZEE
BLOODY HELL!
TZEETZEE
LOOK SHARP HERE!
CRIPES! IT'S CHIMERA!
TZEETZEE
VOMP!
THEY'VE TUMBLED TO US! THE REST OF THE JIHAD'S GOTTA BE RIGHT BEHIND HER!
SO DON'T STAND THERE LIKE FLIPPIN' DROOBS! GIVE IT TO HER!
2

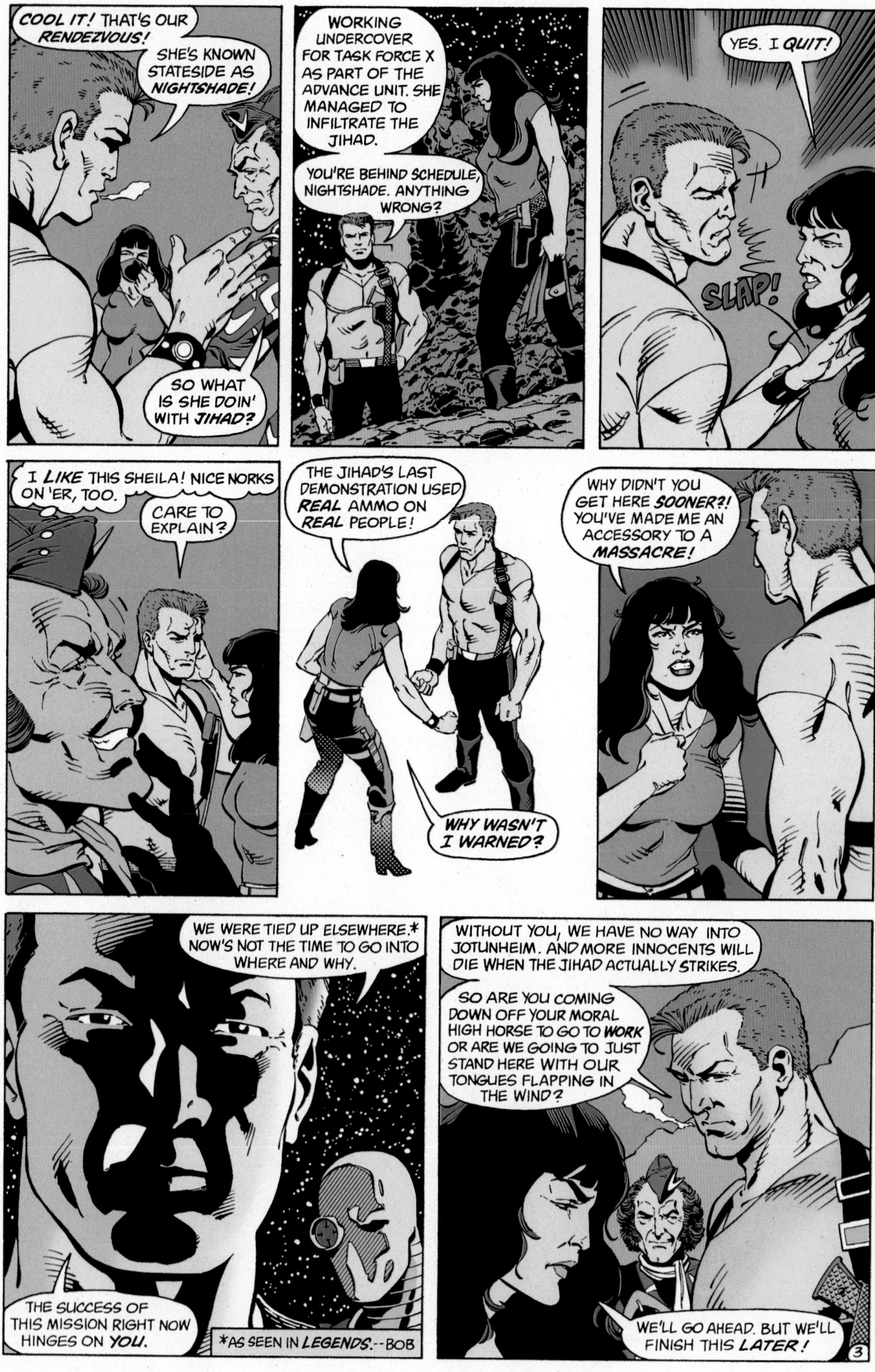
COOL IT! THAT'S OUR RENDEZVOUS!
SHE'S KNOWN STATESIDE AS NIGHTSHADE!
SO WHAT IS SHE DOIN' WITH JIHAD?
WORKING UNDERCOVER FOR TASK FORCE X AS PART OF THE ADVANCE UNIT. SHE MANAGED TO INFILTRATE THE JIHAD.
YOU'RE BEHIND SCHEDULE, NIGHTSHADE. ANYTHING WRONG?
YES. I QUIT!
SLAP!
I LIKE THIS SHEILA! NICE NORKS ON 'ER, TOO.
CARE TO EXPLAIN?
THE JIHAD'S LAST DEMONSTRATION USED REAL AMMO ON REAL PEOPLE!
WHY WASN'T I WARNED?
WHY DIDN'T YOU GET HERE SOONER?! YOU'VE MADE ME AN ACCESSORY TO A MASSACRE!
WE WERE TIED UP ELSEWHERE.* NOW'S NOT THE TIME TO GO INTO WHERE AND WHY.
THE SUCCESS OF THIS MISSION RIGHT NOW HINGES ON YOU.
*AS SEEN IN LEGENDS.--BOB
WITHOUT YOU, WE HAVE NO WAY INTO JOTUNHEIM. AND MORE INNOCENTS WILL DIE WHEN THE JIHAD ACTUALLY STRIKES.
SO ARE YOU COMING DOWN OFF YOUR MORAL HIGH HORSE TO GO TO WORK OR ARE WE GOING TO JUST STAND HERE WITH OUR TONGUES FLAPPING IN THE WIND?
WE'LL GO AHEAD. BUT WE'LL FINISH THIS LATER!
3

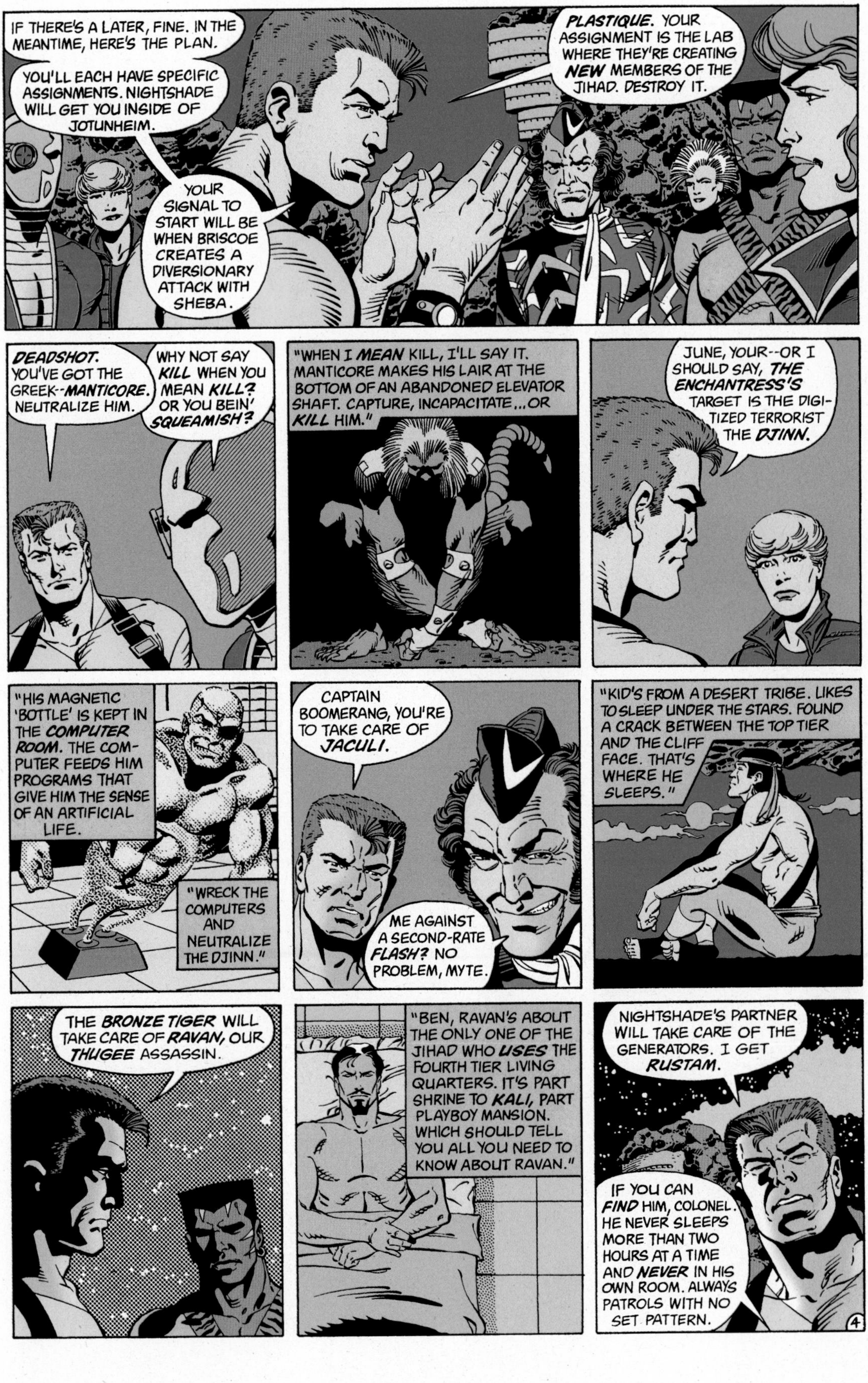
IF THERE'S A LATER, FINE. IN THE MEANTIME, HERE'S THE PLAN.
YOU'LL EACH HAVE SPECIFIC ASSIGNMENTS. NIGHTSHADE WILL GET YOU INSIDE OF JOTUNHEIM.
YOUR SIGNAL TO START WILL BE WHEN BRISCOE CREATES A DIVERSIONARY ATTACK WITH SHEBA.
PLASTIQUE. YOUR ASSIGNMENT IS THE LAB WHERE THEY'RE CREATING NEW MEMBERS OF THE JIHAD. DESTROY IT.
DEADSHOT. YOU'VE GOT THE GREEK--MANTICORE. NEUTRALIZE HIM.
WHY NOT SAY KILL WHEN YOU MEAN KILL? OR YOU BEIN' SQUEAMISH?
"WHEN I MEAN KILL, I'LL SAY IT. MANTICORE MAKES HIS LAIR AT THE BOTTOM OF AN ABANDONED ELEVATOR SHAFT. CAPTURE, INCAPACITATE...OR KILL HIM."
JUNE, YOUR--OR I SHOULD SAY, THE ENCHANTRESS'S TARGET IS THE DIGITIZED TERRORIST THE DJINN.
"HIS MAGNETIC 'BOTTLE' IS KEPT IN THE COMPUTER ROOM. THE COMPUTER FEEDS HIM PROGRAMS THAT GIVE HIM THE SENSE OF AN ARTIFICIAL LIFE.
"WRECK THE COMPUTERS AND NEUTRALIZE THE DJINN."
CAPTAIN BOOMERANG, YOU'RE TO TAKE CARE OF JACULI.
ME AGAINST A SECOND-RATE FLASH? NO PROBLEM, MYTE.
"KID'S FROM A DESERT TRIBE. LIKES TO SLEEP UNDER THE STARS. FOUND A CRACK BETWEEN THE TOP TIER AND THE CLIFF FACE. THAT'S WHERE HE SLEEPS."
THE BRONZE TIGER WILL TAKE CARE OF RAVAN, OUR THUGEE ASSASSIN.
"BEN, RAVAN'S ABOUT THE ONLY ONE OF THE JIHAD WHO USES THE FOURTH TIER LIVING QUARTERS. IT'S PART SHRINE TO KALI, PART PLAYBOY MANSION. WHICH SHOULD TELL YOU ALL YOU NEED TO KNOW ABOUT RAVAN."
NIGHTSHADE'S PARTNER WILL TAKE CARE OF THE GENERATORS. I GET RUSTAM.
IF YOU CAN FIND HIM, COLONEL. HE NEVER SLEEPS MORE THAN TWO HOURS AT A TIME AND NEVER IN HIS OWN ROOM. ALWAYS PATROLS WITH NO SET PATTERN.
4

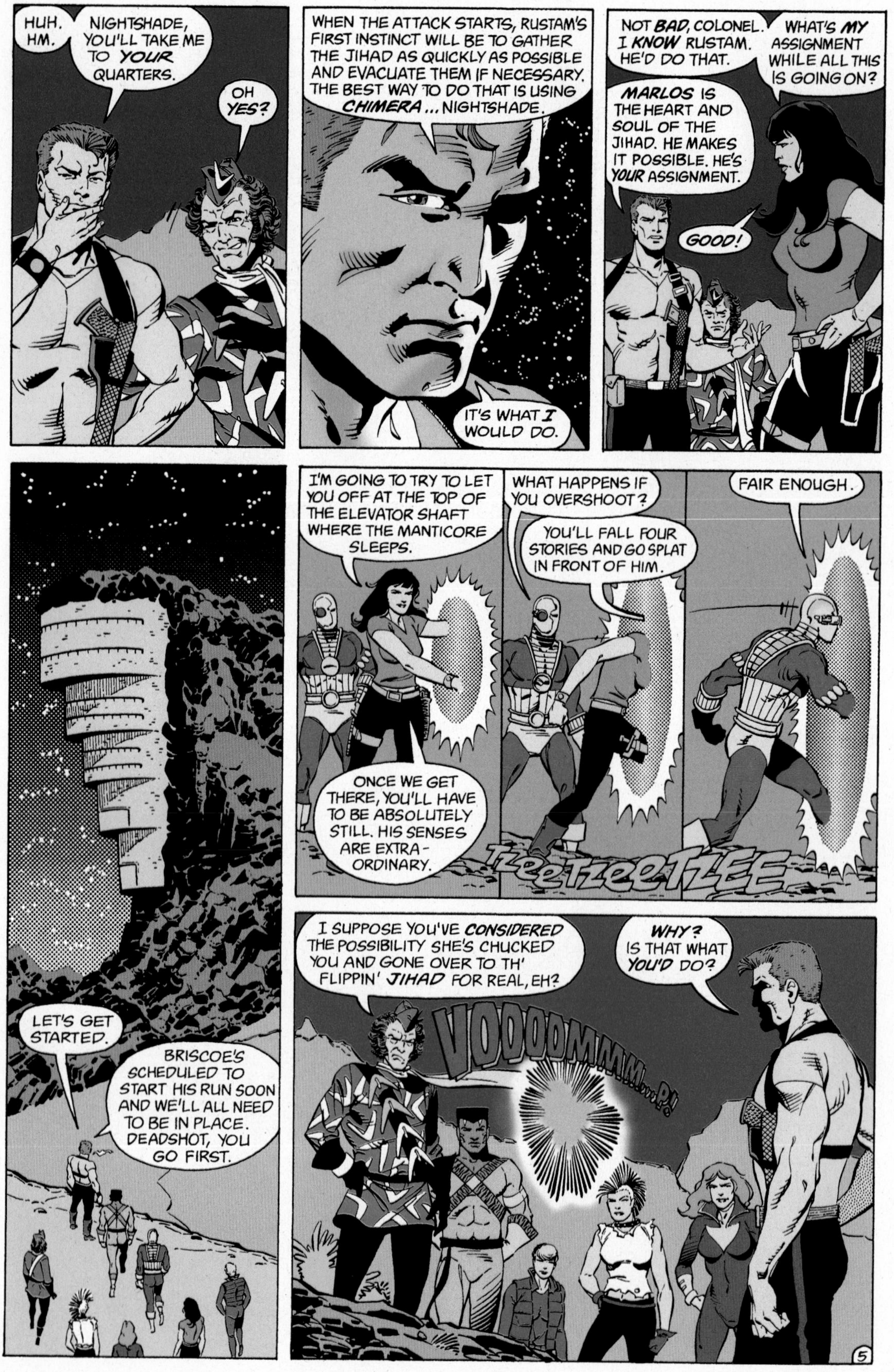

HUH. HM.
NIGHTSHADE, YOU'LL TAKE ME TO YOUR QUARTERS.
OH YES?
WHEN THE ATTACK STARTS, RUSTAM'S FIRST INSTINCT WILL BE TO GATHER THE JIHAD AS QUICKLY AS POSSIBLE AND EVACUATE THEM IF NECESSARY. THE BEST WAY TO DO THAT IS USING CHIMERA ... NIGHTSHADE.
IT'S WHAT I WOULD DO.
NOT BAD, COLONEL. I KNOW RUSTAM. HE'D DO THAT.
WHAT'S MY ASSIGNMENT WHILE ALL THIS IS GOING ON?
MARLOS IS THE HEART AND SOUL OF THE JIHAD. HE MAKES IT POSSIBLE. HE'S YOUR ASSIGNMENT.
GOOD!
LET'S GET STARTED.
BRISCOE'S SCHEDULED TO START HIS RUN SOON AND WE'LL ALL NEED TO BE IN PLACE. DEADSHOT, YOU GO FIRST.
I'M GOING TO TRY TO LET YOU OFF AT THE TOP OF THE ELEVATOR SHAFT WHERE THE MANTICORE SLEEPS.
ONCE WE GET THERE, YOU'LL HAVE TO BE ABSOLUTELY STILL. HIS SENSES ARE EXTRA-ORDINARY.
WHAT HAPPENS IF YOU OVERSHOOT?
YOU'LL FALL FOUR STORIES AND GO SPLAT IN FRONT OF HIM.
FAIR ENOUGH.
TZEETZEETZEE
I SUPPOSE YOU'VE CONSIDERED THE POSSIBILITY SHE'S CHUCKED YOU AND GONE OVER TO TH' FLIPPIN' JIHAD FOR REAL, EH?
WHY? IS THAT WHAT YOU'D DO?
VOOOOMMMM...P!
5

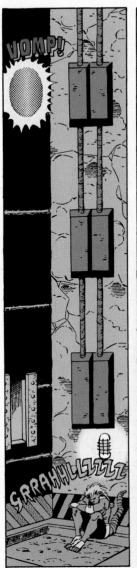

VOMP!

GRRAHLLZZZ

GRRAHLLZZZ

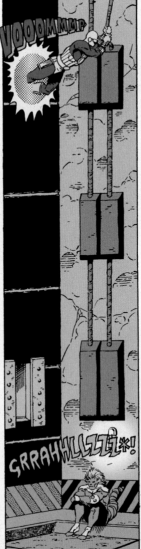

VOOOMMM!

GRRAHLLZZZ*!

Shuffle

Shuff

VOMP!

GO!

STAY IN THE LAB AND KEEP TO THE SHADOWS AND YOU SHOULD BE FINE. JUST KEEP AN EYE OUT FOR RUSTAM.

YEAH OKAY FINE. GET GOING.

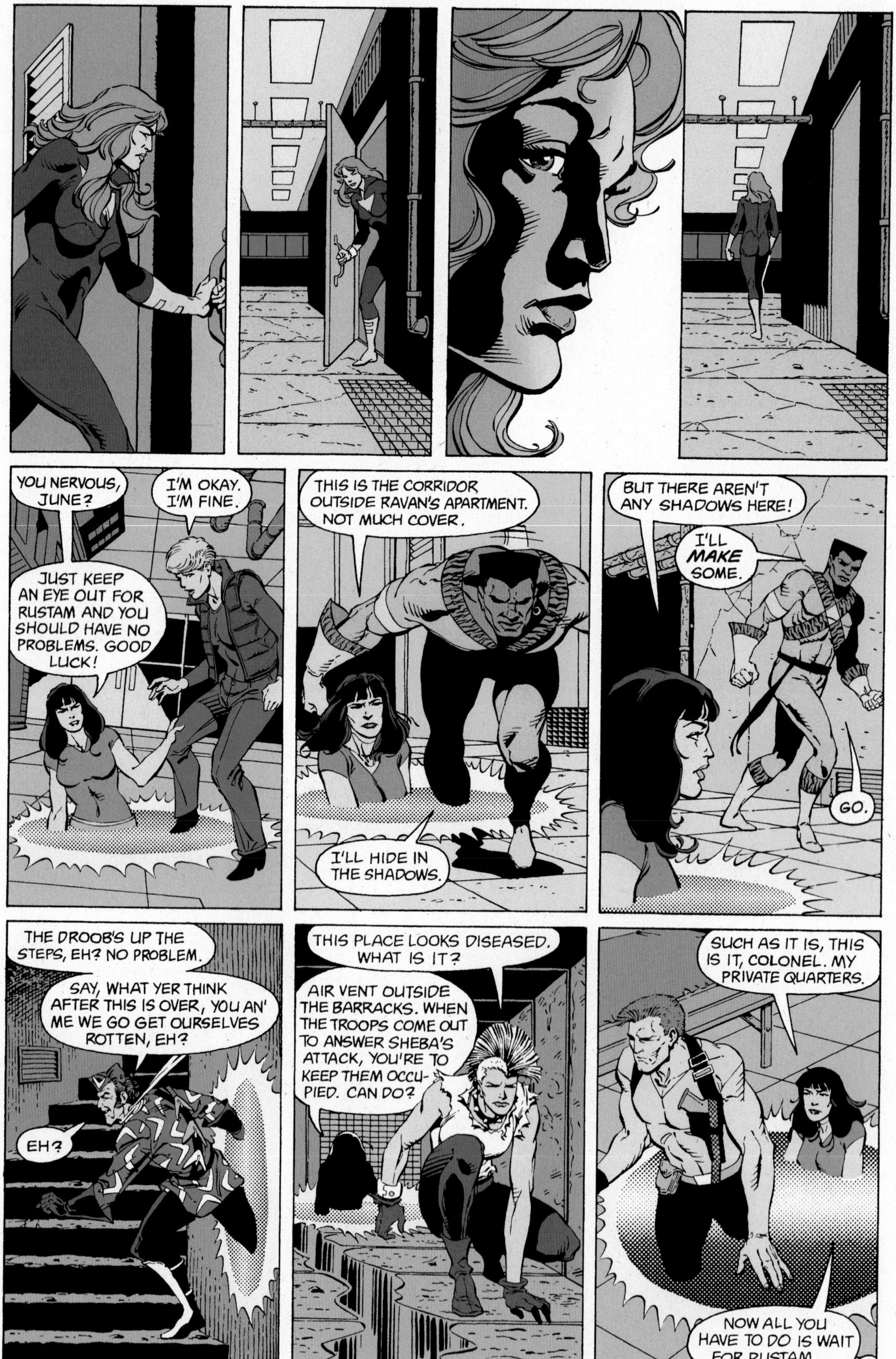
YOU NERVOUS, JUNE?
I'M OKAY. I'M FINE.
JUST KEEP AN EYE OUT FOR RUSTAM AND YOU SHOULD HAVE NO PROBLEMS. GOOD LUCK!
THIS IS THE CORRIDOR OUTSIDE RAVAN'S APARTMENT. NOT MUCH COVER.
I'LL HIDE IN THE SHADOWS.
BUT THERE AREN'T ANY SHADOWS HERE!
I'LL MAKE SOME.
GO.
THE DROOB'S UP THE STEPS, EH? NO PROBLEM.
SAY, WHAT YER THINK AFTER THIS IS OVER, YOU AN' ME WE GO GET OURSELVES ROTTEN, EH?
EH?
THIS PLACE LOOKS DISEASED. WHAT IS IT?
AIR VENT OUTSIDE THE BARRACKS. WHEN THE TROOPS COME OUT TO ANSWER SHEBA'S ATTACK, YOU'RE TO KEEP THEM OCCUPIED. CAN DO?
SUCH AS IT IS, THIS IS IT, COLONEL. MY PRIVATE QUARTERS.
NOW ALL YOU HAVE TO DO IS WAIT FOR RUSTAM.
7

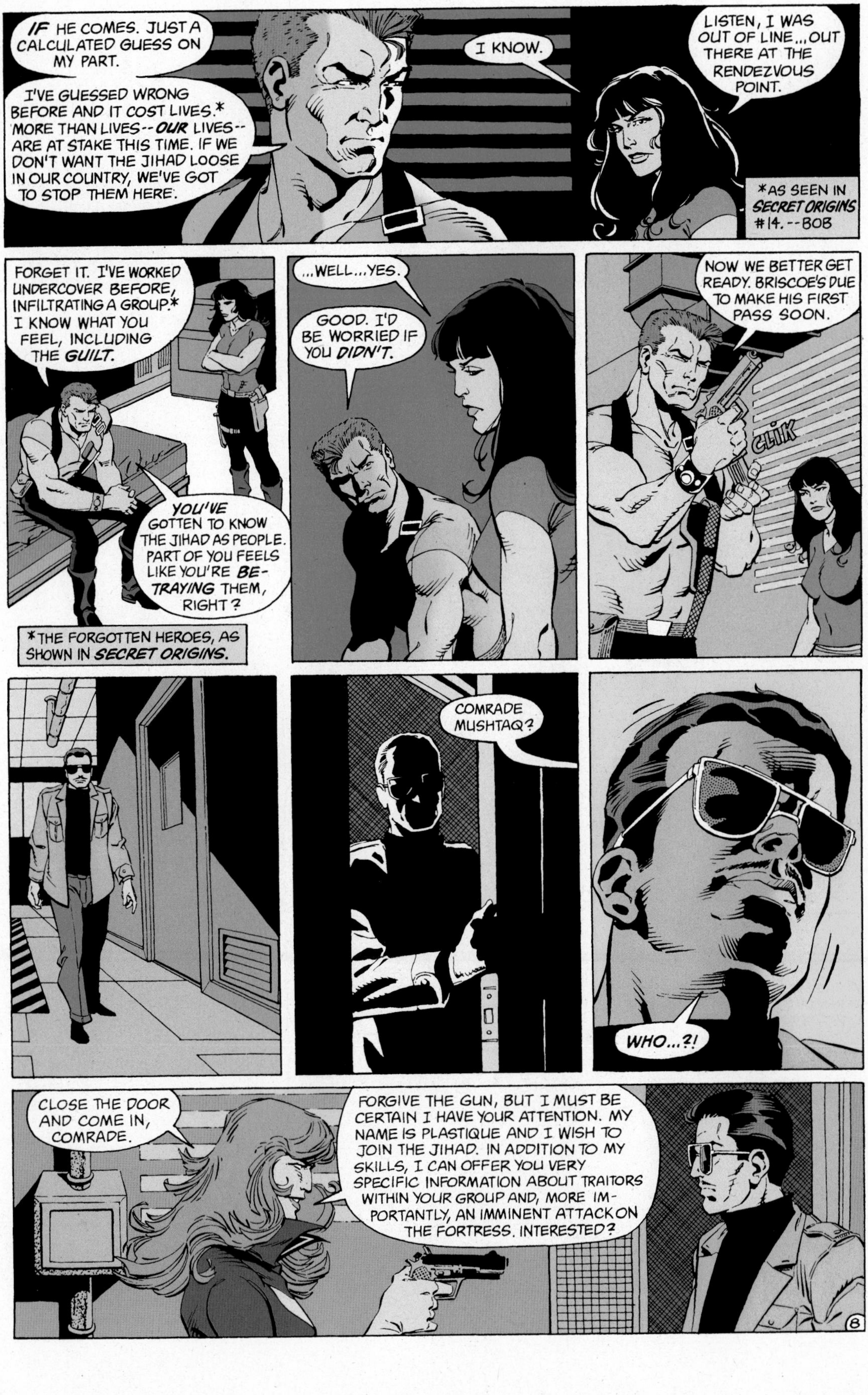
IF HE COMES. JUST A CALCULATED GUESS ON MY PART.
I'VE GUESSED WRONG BEFORE AND IT COST LIVES.* MORE THAN LIVES--OUR LIVES--ARE AT STAKE THIS TIME. IF WE DON'T WANT THE JIHAD LOOSE IN OUR COUNTRY, WE'VE GOT TO STOP THEM HERE.
I KNOW.
LISTEN, I WAS OUT OF LINE... OUT THERE AT THE RENDEZVOUS POINT.
*AS SEEN IN SECRET ORIGINS #14.--BOB
FORGET IT. I'VE WORKED UNDERCOVER BEFORE, INFILTRATING A GROUP.* I KNOW WHAT YOU FEEL, INCLUDING THE GUILT.
YOU'VE GOTTEN TO KNOW THE JIHAD AS PEOPLE. PART OF YOU FEELS LIKE YOU'RE BE-TRAYING THEM, RIGHT?
*THE FORGOTTEN HEROES, AS SHOWN IN SECRET ORIGINS.
...WELL...YES.
GOOD. I'D BE WORRIED IF YOU DIDN'T.
NOW WE BETTER GET READY. BRISCOE'S DUE TO MAKE HIS FIRST PASS SOON.
CLIK
COMRADE MUSHTAQ?
WHO...?!
CLOSE THE DOOR AND COME IN, COMRADE.
FORGIVE THE GUN, BUT I MUST BE CERTAIN I HAVE YOUR ATTENTION. MY NAME IS PLASTIQUE AND I WISH TO JOIN THE JIHAD. IN ADDITION TO MY SKILLS, I CAN OFFER YOU VERY SPECIFIC INFORMATION ABOUT TRAITORS WITHIN YOUR GROUP AND, MORE IM-PORTANTLY, AN IMMINENT ATTACK ON THE FORTRESS. INTERESTED?
8

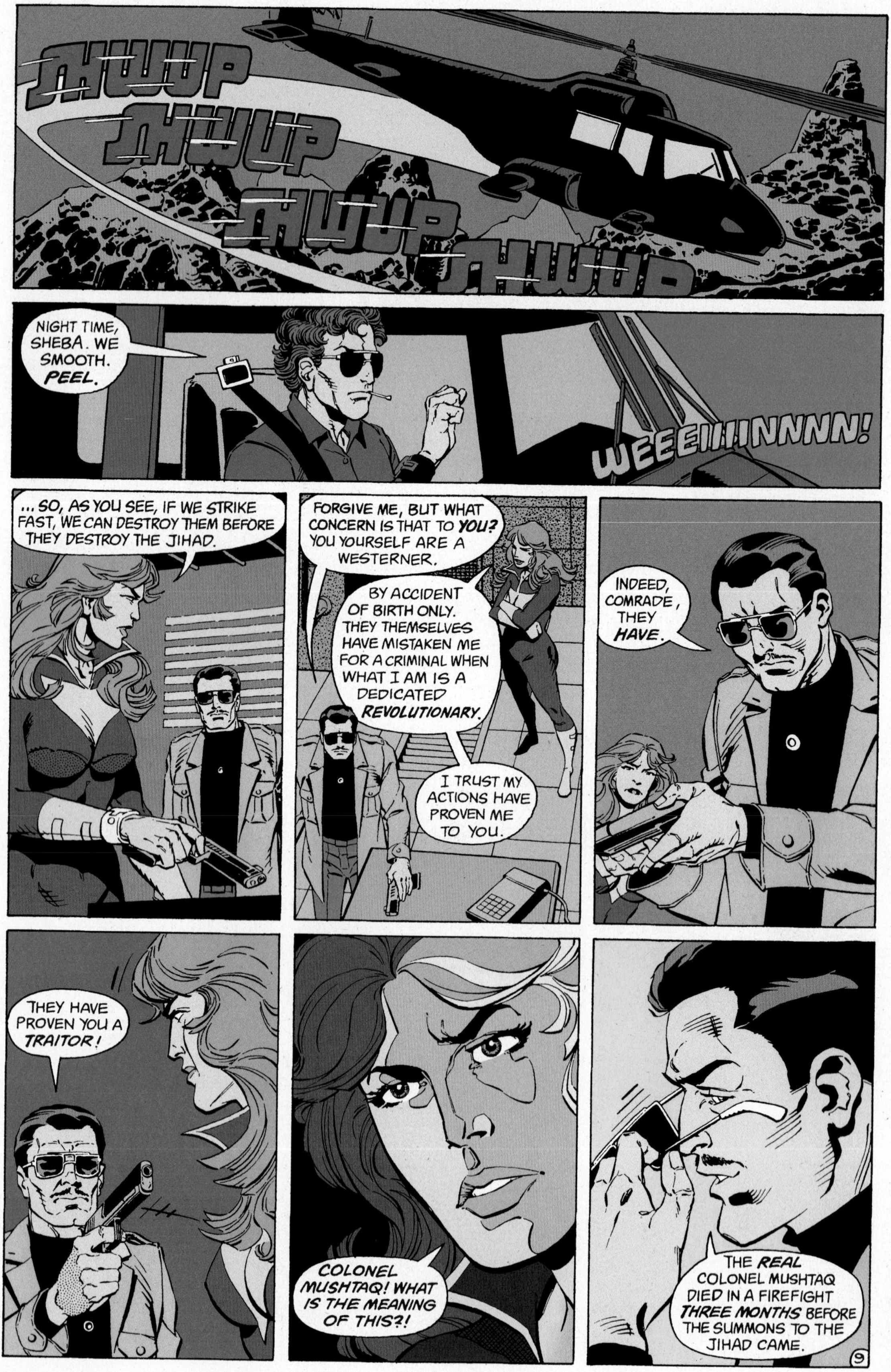
THWUP
THWUP
THWUP
THWUP
NIGHT TIME, SHEBA. WE SMOOTH. PEEL.
WEEEIIIIINNNNN!
...SO, AS YOU SEE, IF WE STRIKE FAST, WE CAN DESTROY THEM BEFORE THEY DESTROY THE JIHAD.
FORGIVE ME, BUT WHAT CONCERN IS THAT TO YOU? YOU YOURSELF ARE A WESTERNER.
BY ACCIDENT OF BIRTH ONLY. THEY THEMSELVES HAVE MISTAKEN ME FOR A CRIMINAL WHEN WHAT I AM IS A DEDICATED REVOLUTIONARY.
I TRUST MY ACTIONS HAVE PROVEN ME TO YOU.
INDEED, COMRADE, THEY HAVE.
THEY HAVE PROVEN YOU A TRAITOR!
COLONEL MUSHTAQ! WHAT IS THE MEANING OF THIS?!
THE REAL COLONEL MUSHTAQ DIED IN A FIREFIGHT THREE MONTHS BEFORE THE SUMMONS TO THE JIHAD CAME.
9

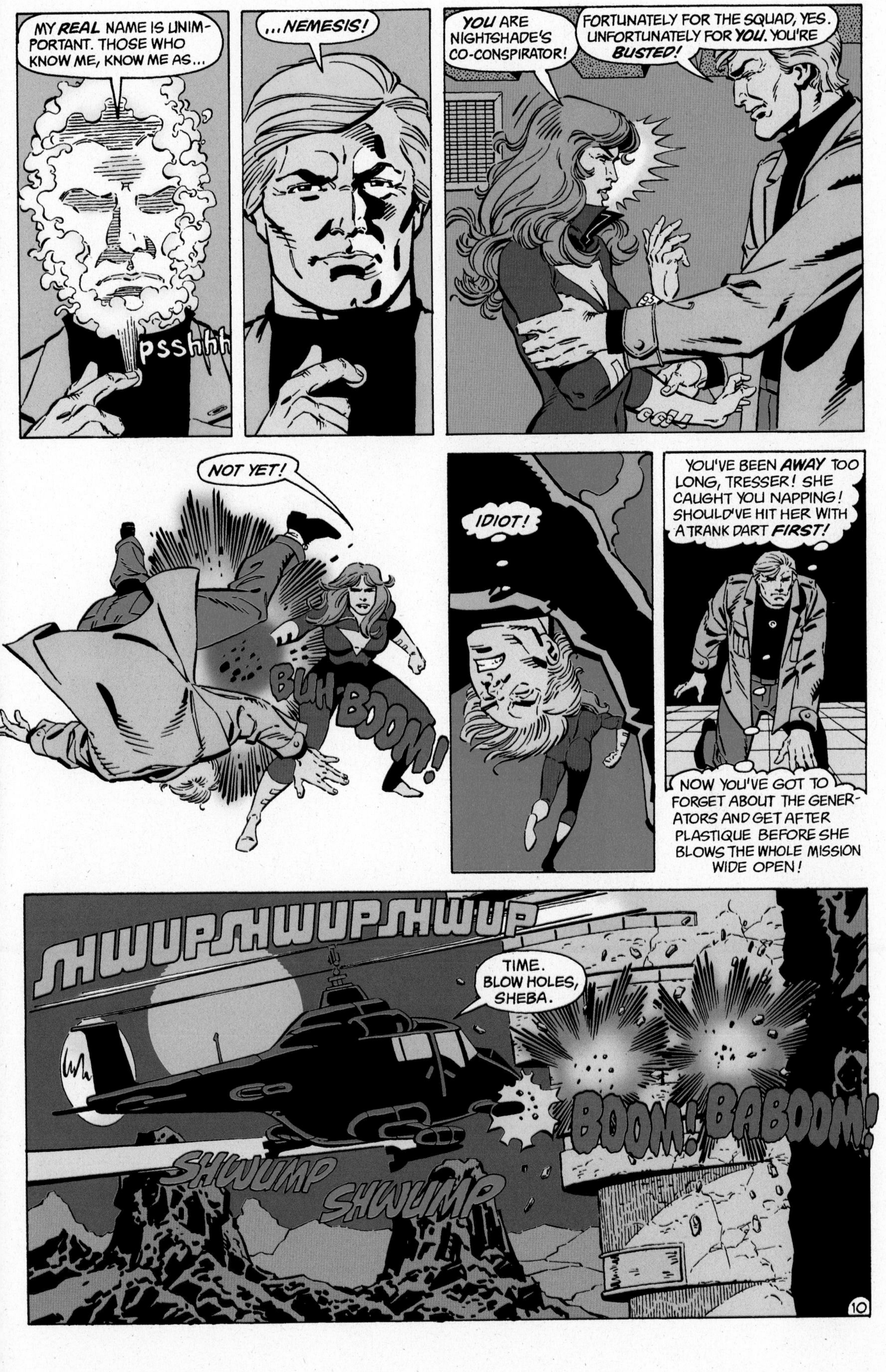
MY REAL NAME IS UNIMPORTANT. THOSE WHO KNOW ME, KNOW ME AS...
psshhh
...NEMESIS!
YOU ARE NIGHTSHADE'S CO-CONSPIRATOR!
FORTUNATELY FOR THE SQUAD, YES. UNFORTUNATELY FOR YOU. YOU'RE BUSTED!
NOT YET!
BUH-BOOM!
IDIOT!
YOU'VE BEEN AWAY TOO LONG, TRESSER! SHE CAUGHT YOU NAPPING! SHOULD'VE HIT HER WITH A TRANK DART FIRST!
NOW YOU'VE GOT TO FORGET ABOUT THE GENERATORS AND GET AFTER PLASTIQUE BEFORE SHE BLOWS THE WHOLE MISSION WIDE OPEN!
SHWUPSHWUPSHWUP
TIME. BLOW HOLES, SHEBA.
BOOM! BABOOM!
SHWUMP
SHWUMP
10

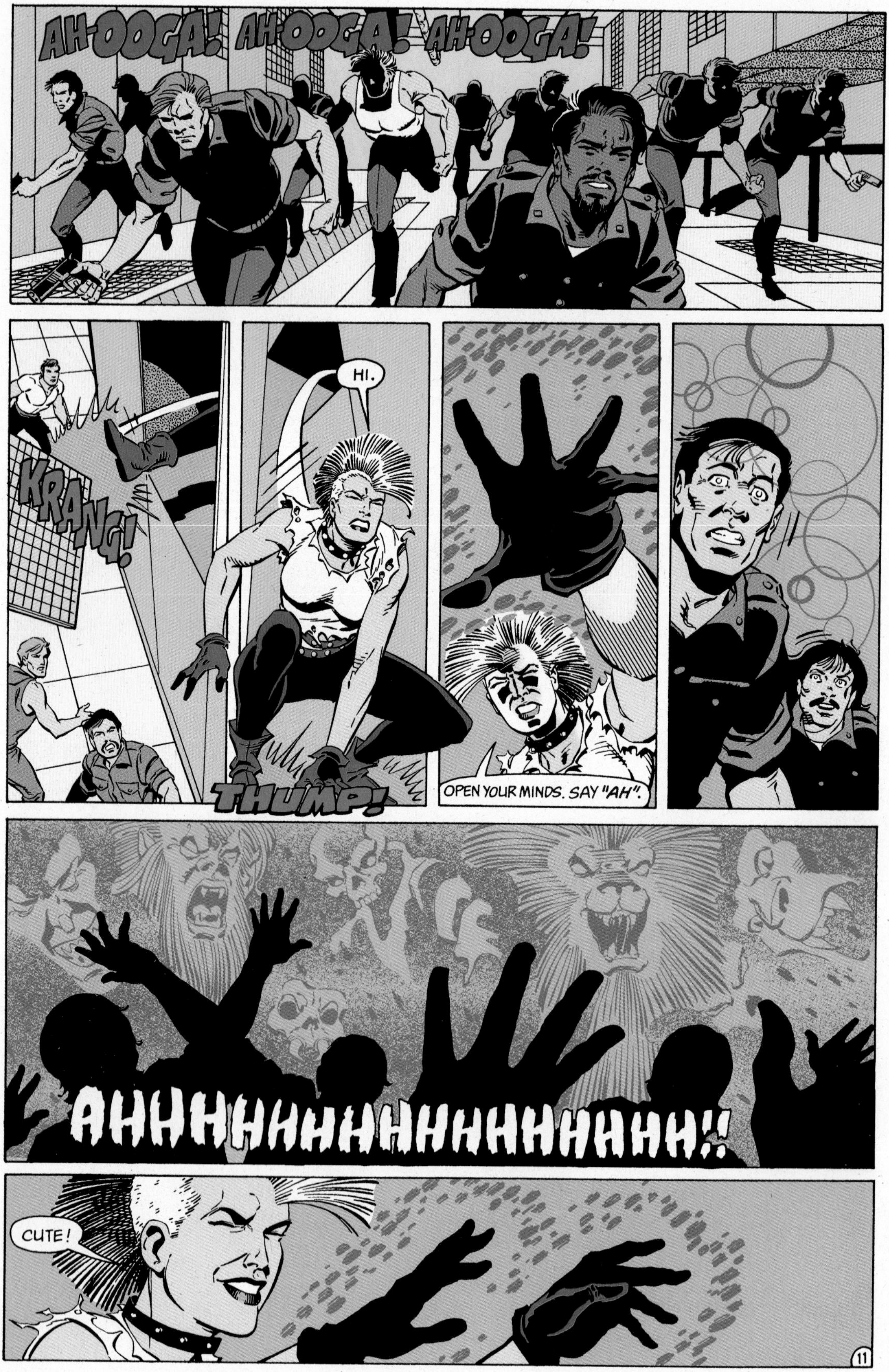
AH-OOGA! AH-OOGA! AH-OOGA!
KRANG!
HI.
THUMP!
OPEN YOUR MINDS. SAY "AH".
AHHHHHHHHHHHHHHHHHH!!
CUTE!
11

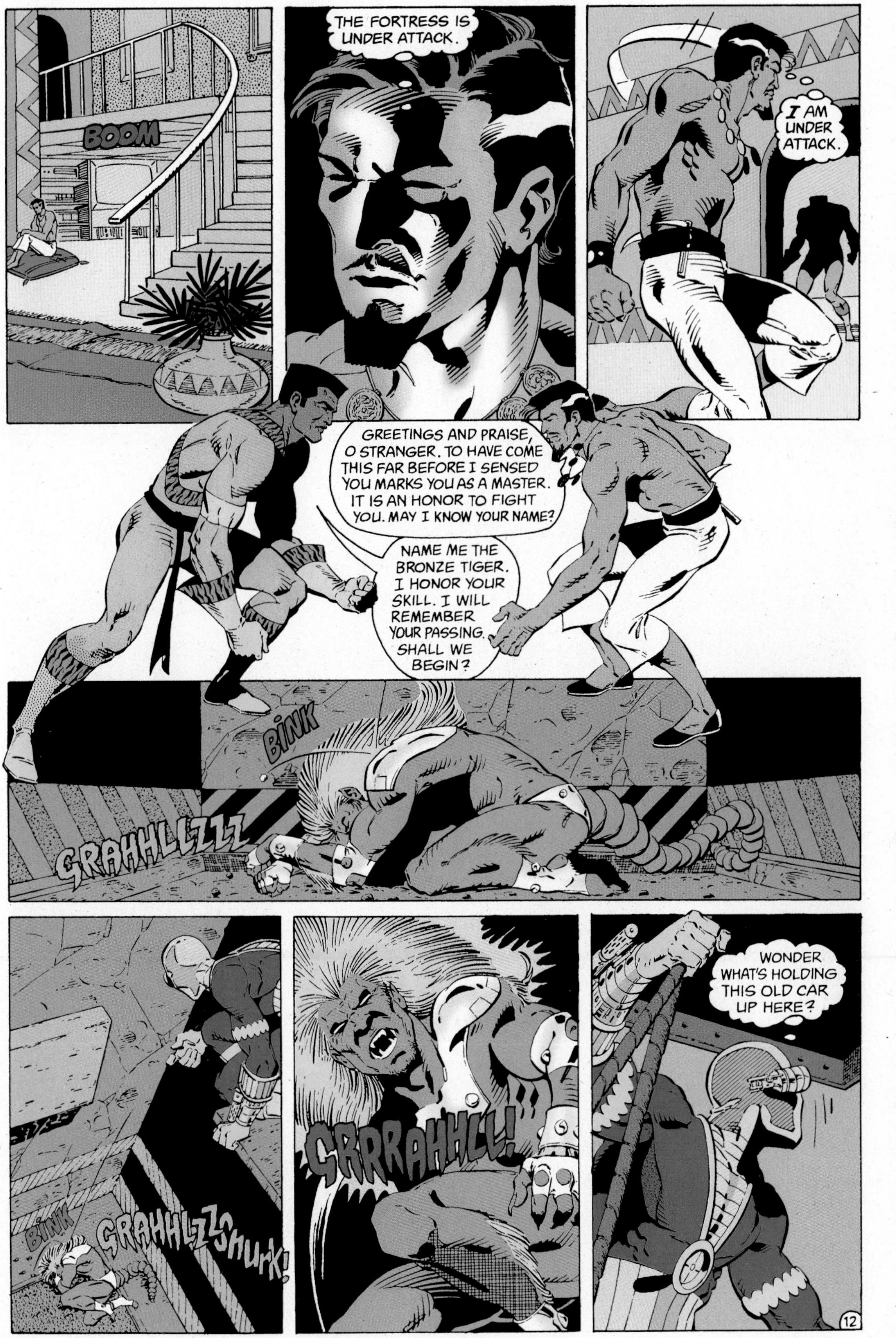
BOOM
THE FORTRESS IS UNDER ATTACK.
I AM UNDER ATTACK.
GREETINGS AND PRAISE, O STRANGER. TO HAVE COME THIS FAR BEFORE I SENSED YOU MARKS YOU AS A MASTER. IT IS AN HONOR TO FIGHT YOU. MAY I KNOW YOUR NAME?
NAME ME THE BRONZE TIGER. I HONOR YOUR SKILL. I WILL REMEMBER YOUR PASSING. SHALL WE BEGIN?
BINK
GRAHHLZZZZ
BINK
GRAHHLZZZ
Shurk!
GRRRAHHLL!
WONDER WHAT'S HOLDING THIS OLD CAR UP HERE?
12

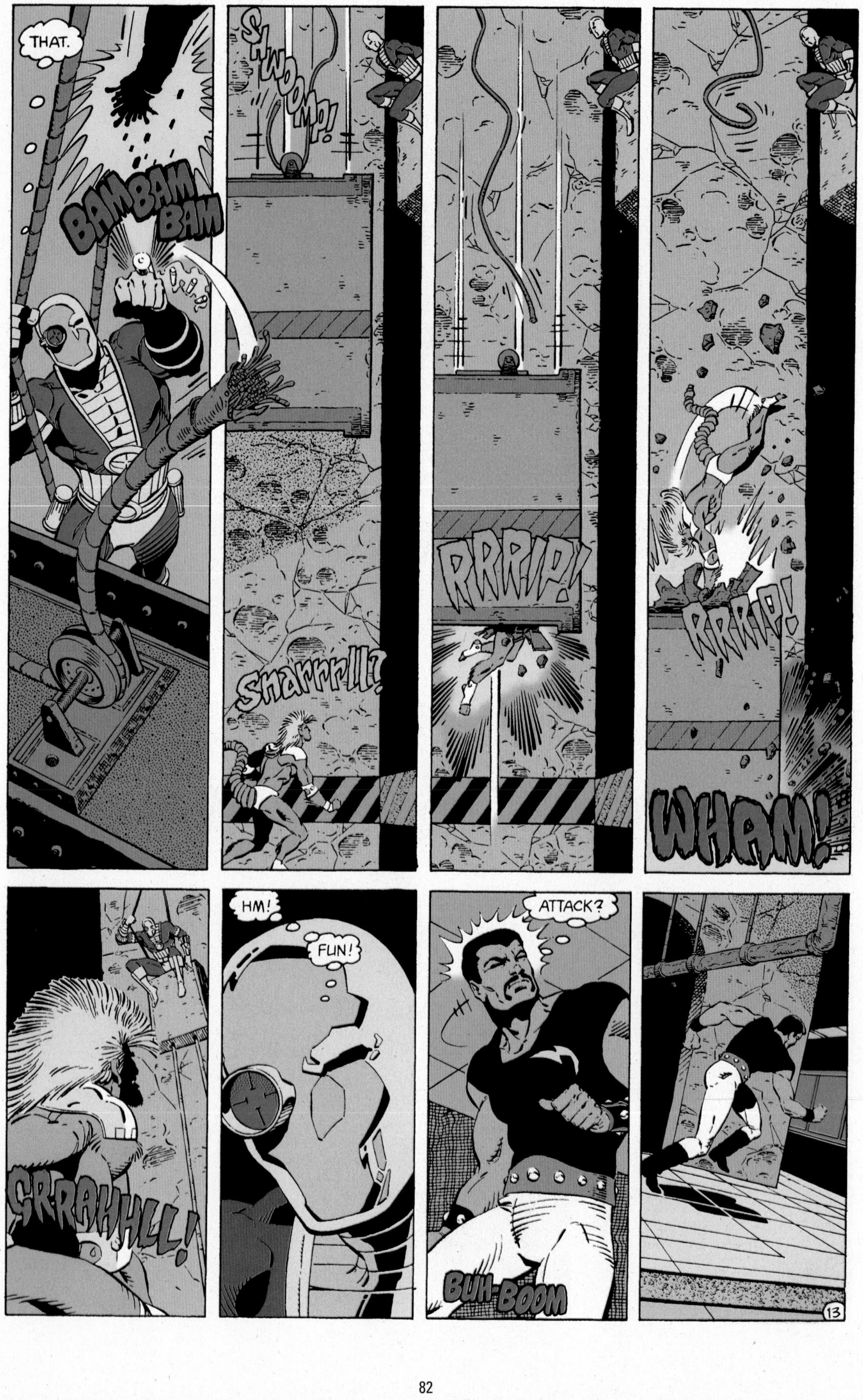
THAT.
BAMBAM
BAM
SHWOOMP!
SNARRRLLL?
RRRIP!
RRRIP!
WHAM!
GRRAHHLL!
HM!
FUN!
ATTACK?
BUH-BOOM
13

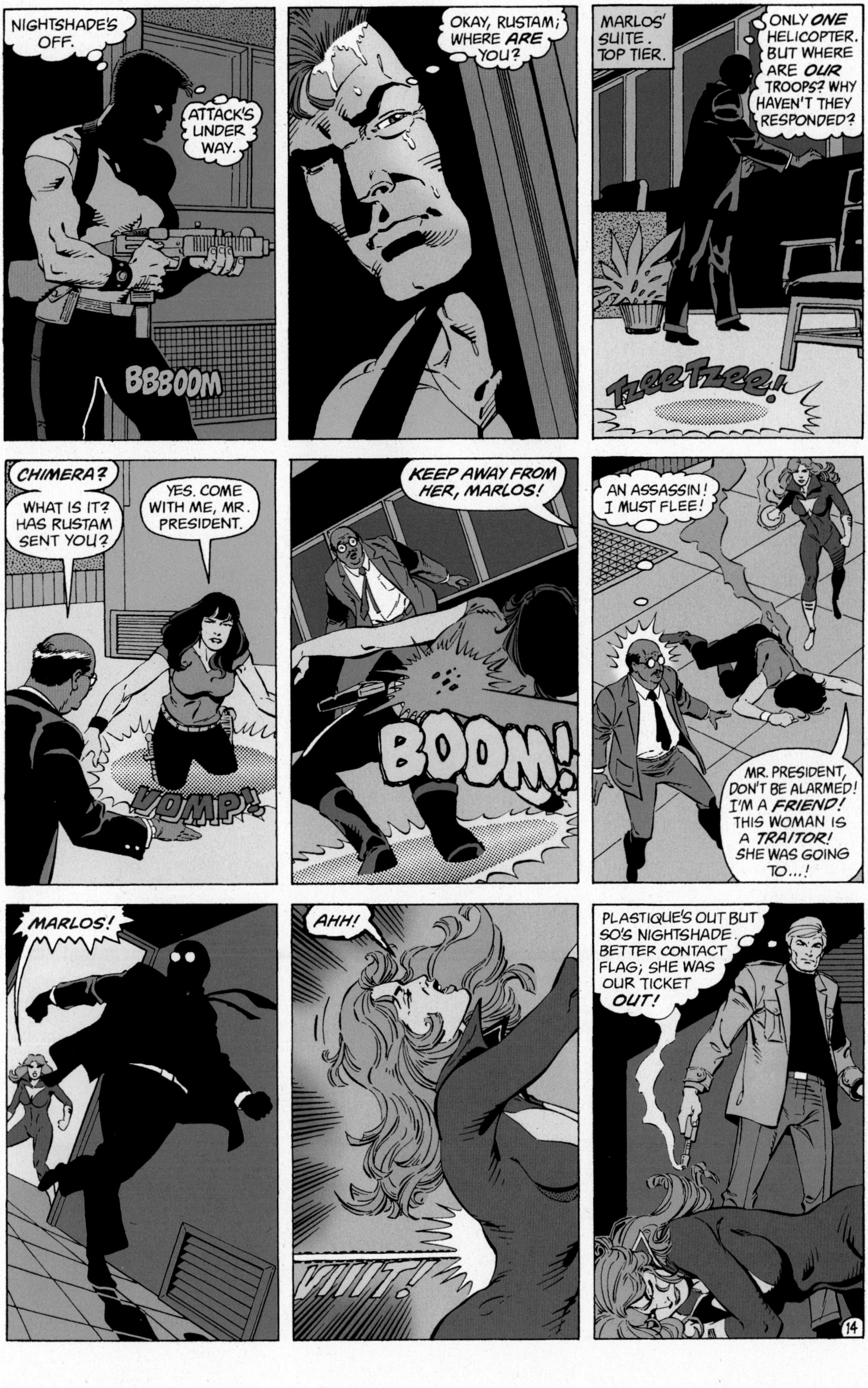
NIGHTSHADE'S OFF.
ATTACK'S UNDER WAY.
BBBOOM
OKAY, RUSTAM; WHERE ARE YOU?
MARLOS' SUITE. TOP TIER.
ONLY ONE HELICOPTER. BUT WHERE ARE OUR TROOPS? WHY HAVEN'T THEY RESPONDED?
TZEETZEE!
CHIMERA?
WHAT IS IT? HAS RUSTAM SENT YOU?
YES. COME WITH ME, MR. PRESIDENT.
VOMP!
KEEP AWAY FROM HER, MARLOS!
BOOM!
AN ASSASSIN! I MUST FLEE!
MR. PRESIDENT, DON'T BE ALARMED! I'M A FRIEND! THIS WOMAN IS A TRAITOR! SHE WAS GOING TO...!
MARLOS!
AHH!
VIIIT!
PLASTIQUE'S OUT BUT SO'S NIGHTSHADE. BETTER CONTACT FLAG; SHE WAS OUR TICKET OUT!
14

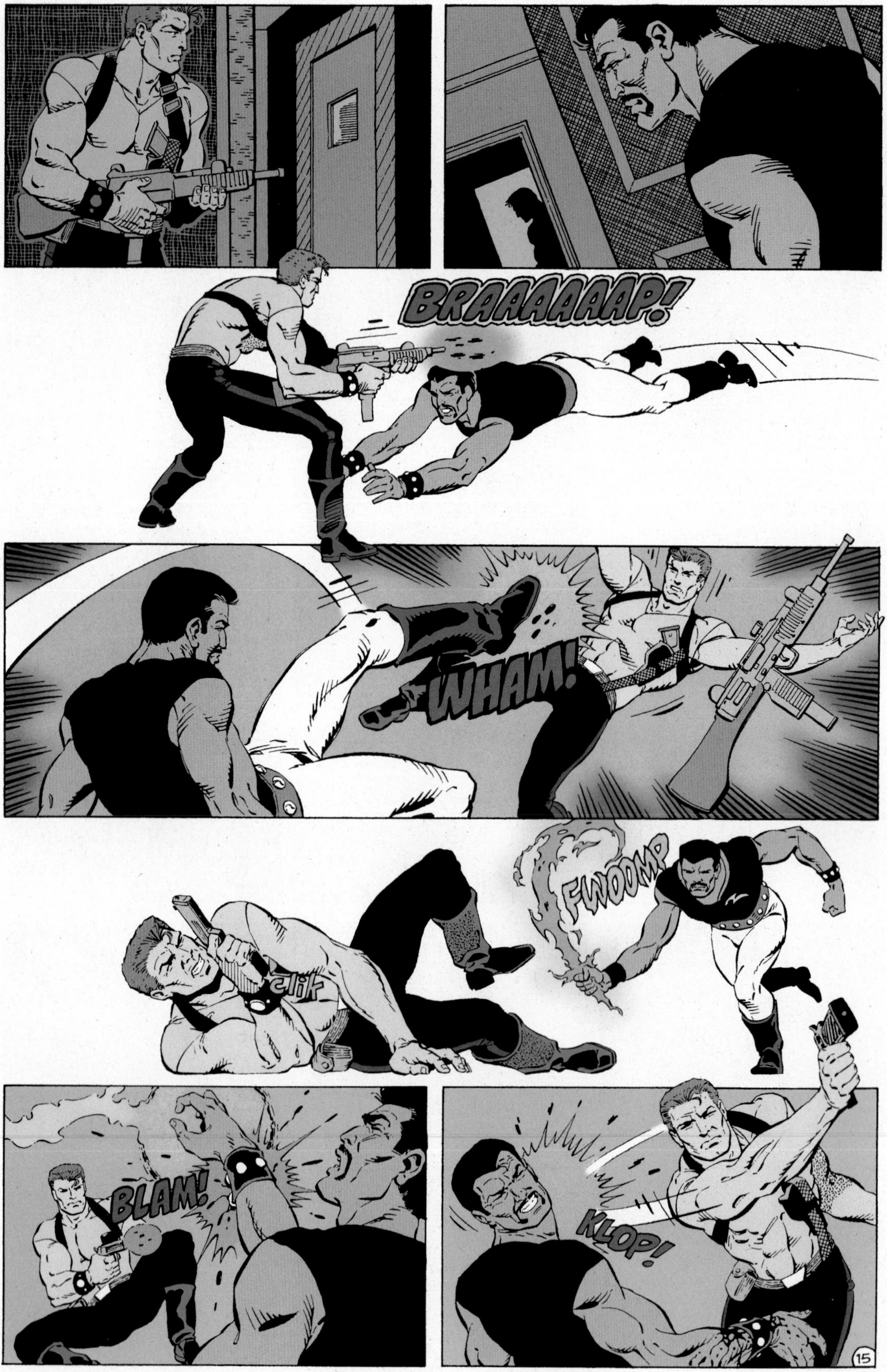
BRAAAAAAP!
WHAM!
FWOOMP
clik
BLAM!
KLOP!
15

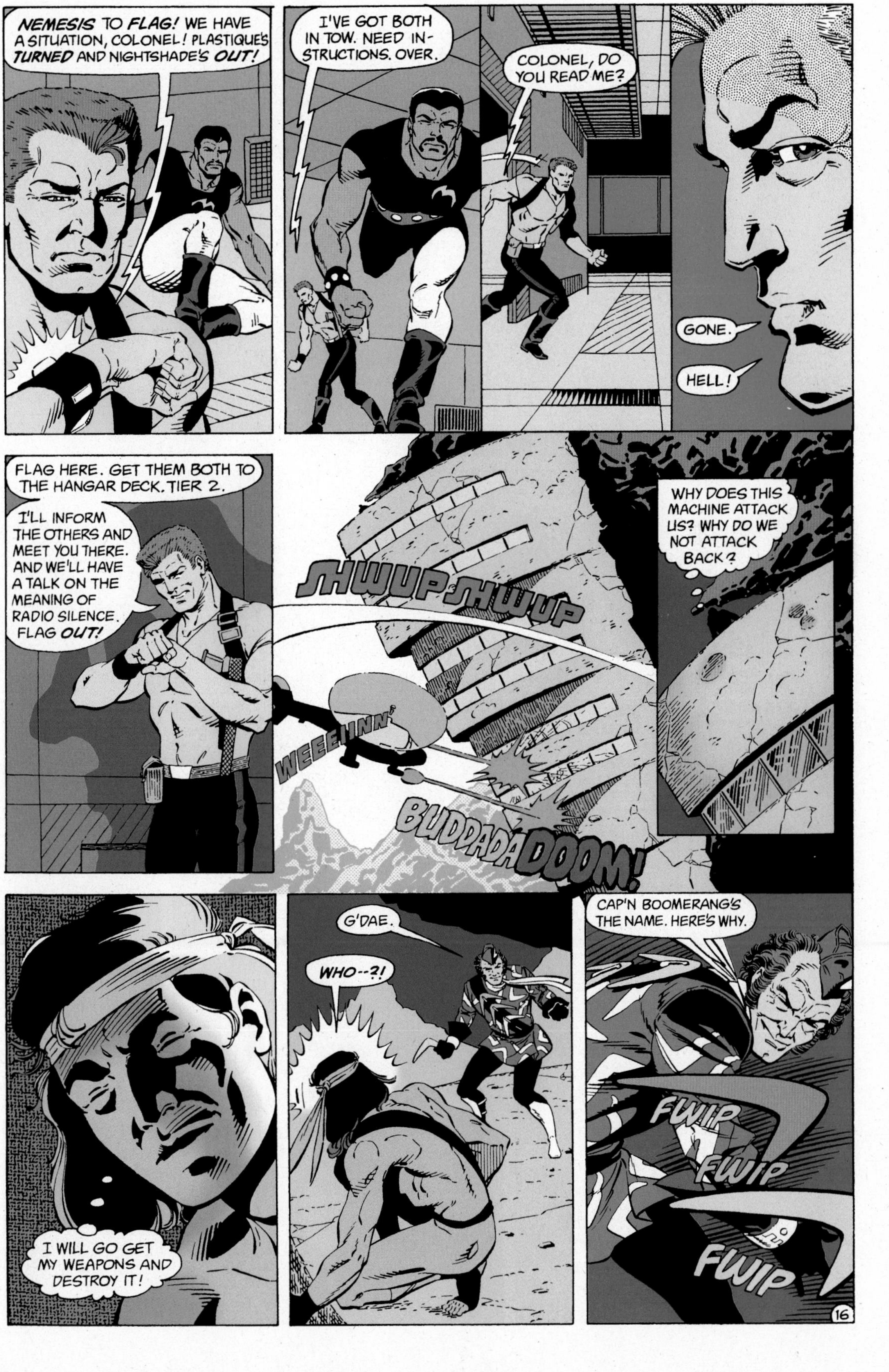
NEMESIS TO FLAG! WE HAVE A SITUATION, COLONEL! PLASTIQUE'S TURNED AND NIGHTSHADE'S OUT!
I'VE GOT BOTH IN TOW. NEED INSTRUCTIONS. OVER.
COLONEL, DO YOU READ ME?
GONE.
HELL!
FLAG HERE. GET THEM BOTH TO THE HANGAR DECK. TIER 2.
I'LL INFORM THE OTHERS AND MEET YOU THERE. AND WE'LL HAVE A TALK ON THE MEANING OF RADIO SILENCE. FLAG OUT!
SHWUP SHWUP
WEEEHNN
BUDDADADOOM!
WHY DOES THIS MACHINE ATTACK US? WHY DO WE NOT ATTACK BACK?
I WILL GO GET MY WEAPONS AND DESTROY IT!
G'DAE.
WHO--?!
CAP'N BOOMERANG'S THE NAME. HERE'S WHY.
FWIP
FWIP
FWIP
16

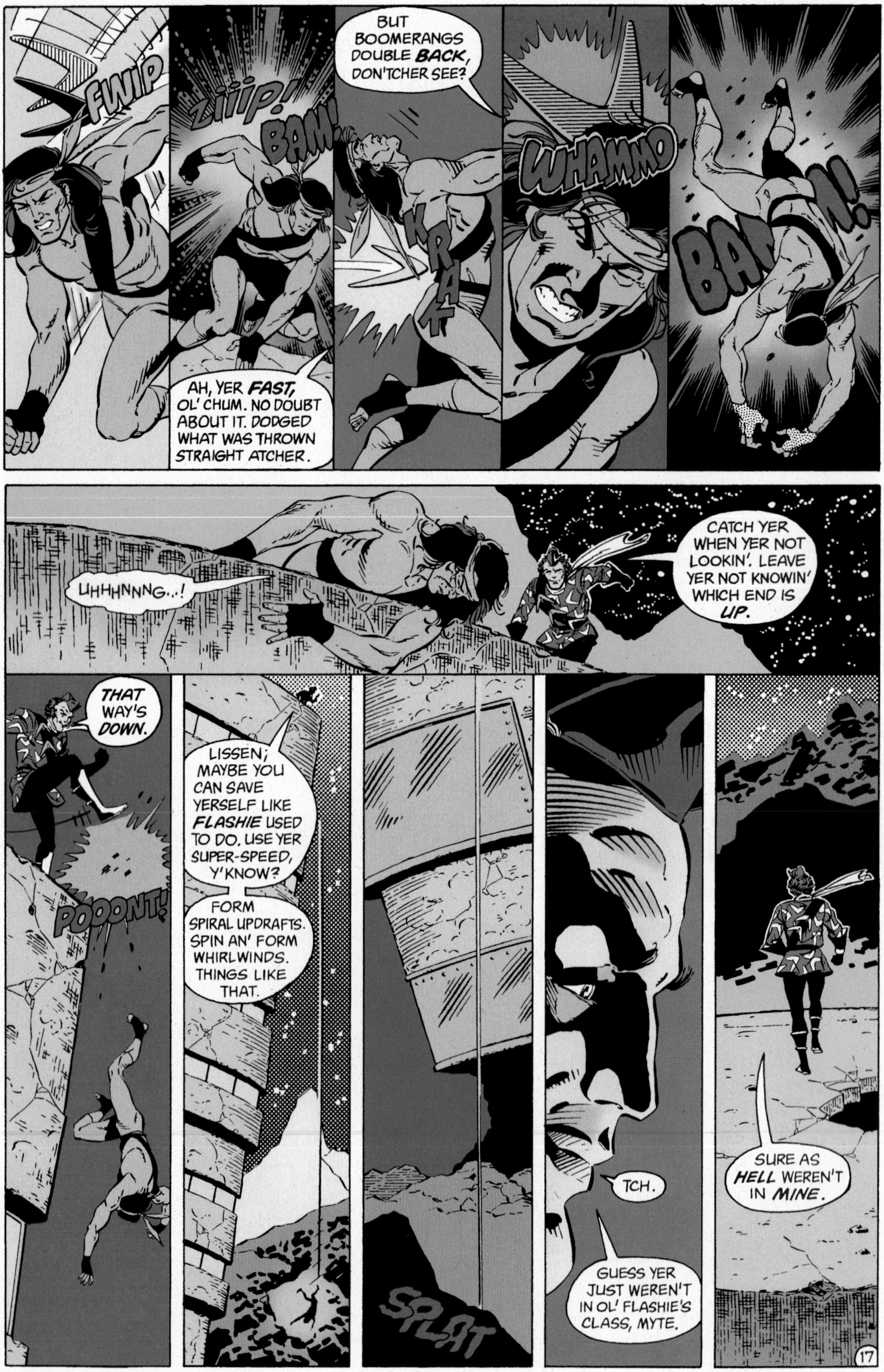
FWIP
ZIIIP!
BAM!
AH, YER **FAST,** OL' CHUM. NO DOUBT ABOUT IT. DODGED WHAT WAS THROWN STRAIGHT ATCHER.
BUT BOOMERANGS DOUBLE **BACK,** DON'TCHER SEE?
KRAK
WHAMMO
UHHHNNNG..!
CATCH YER WHEN YER NOT LOOKIN'. LEAVE YER NOT KNOWIN' WHICH END IS **UP.**
THAT WAY'S DOWN.
POOOONT!
LISSEN; MAYBE YOU CAN SAVE YERSELF LIKE **FLASHIE** USED TO DO. USE YER SUPER-SPEED, Y'KNOW?
FORM SPIRAL UPDRAFTS. SPIN AN' FORM WHIRLWINDS. THINGS LIKE THAT.
SPLAT
TCH.
GUESS YER JUST WEREN'T IN OL' FLASHIE'S CLASS, MYTE.
SURE AS **HELL** WEREN'T IN **MINE.**
17

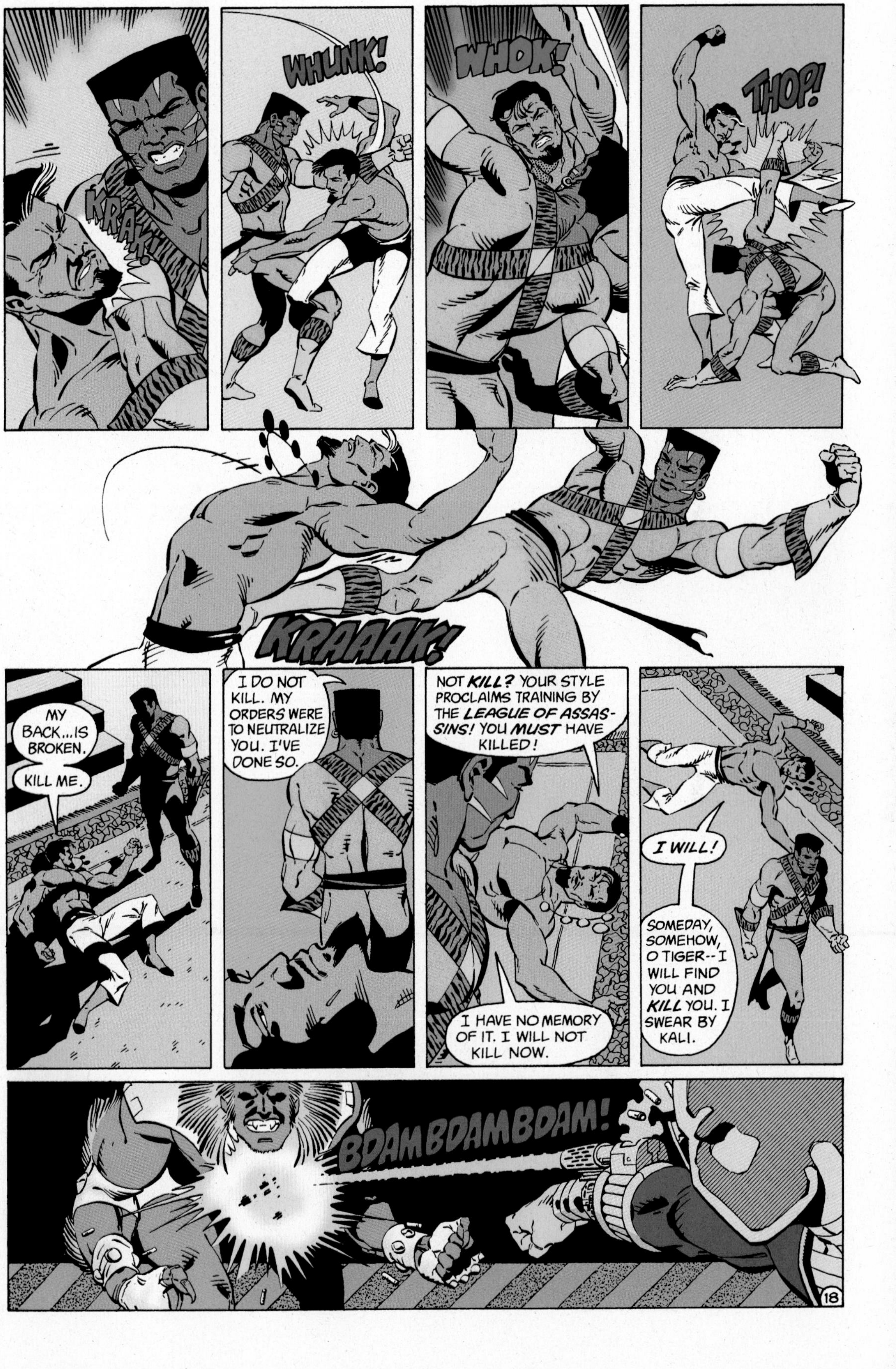
KRAK!
WHUNK!
WHOK!
THOP!
KRAAAK!
MY BACK...IS BROKEN.
KILL ME.
I DO NOT KILL. MY ORDERS WERE TO NEUTRALIZE YOU. I'VE DONE SO.
NOT KILL? YOUR STYLE PROCLAIMS TRAINING BY THE LEAGUE OF ASSAS-SINS! YOU MUST HAVE KILLED!
I HAVE NO MEMORY OF IT. I WILL NOT KILL NOW.
I WILL!
SOMEDAY, SOMEHOW, O TIGER--I WILL FIND YOU AND KILL YOU. I SWEAR BY KALI.
BDAMBDAMBDAM!
18

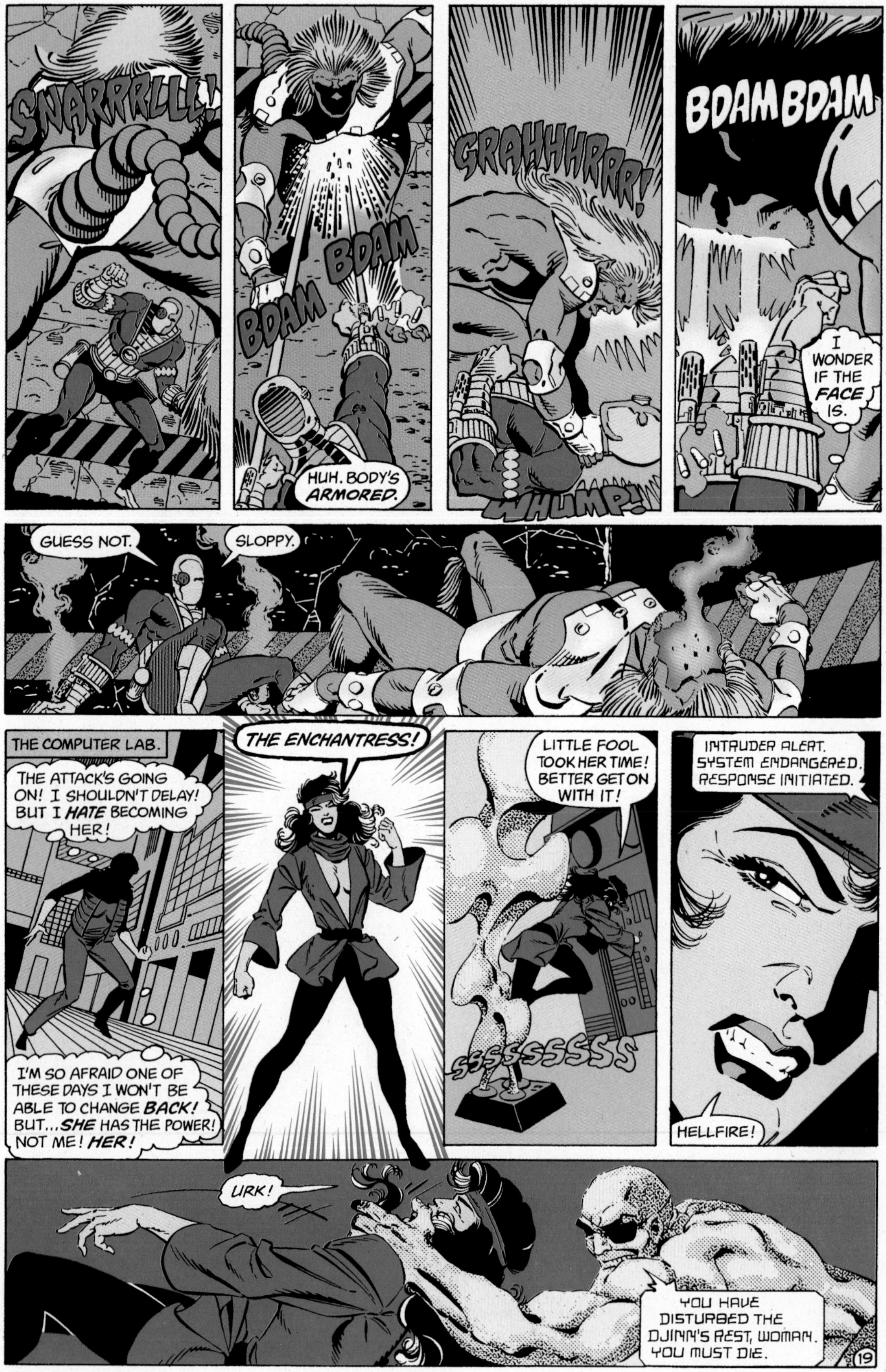

SNARRRLLL!
BDAM
BDAM
HUH. BODY'S ARMORED.
GRAHHHRRRR!
WHUMP!
BDAM BDAM
I WONDER IF THE FACE IS.
GUESS NOT.
SLOPPY.
THE COMPUTER LAB.
THE ATTACK'S GOING ON! I SHOULDN'T DELAY! BUT I HATE BECOMING HER!
I'M SO AFRAID ONE OF THESE DAYS I WON'T BE ABLE TO CHANGE BACK! BUT... SHE HAS THE POWER! NOT ME! HER!
THE ENCHANTRESS!
LITTLE FOOL TOOK HER TIME! BETTER GET ON WITH IT!
SSSSSSSSSS
INTRUDER ALERT. SYSTEM ENDANGERED. RESPONSE INITIATED.
HELLFIRE!
URK!
YOU HAVE DISTURBED THE DJINN'S REST, WOMAN. YOU MUST DIE.
19

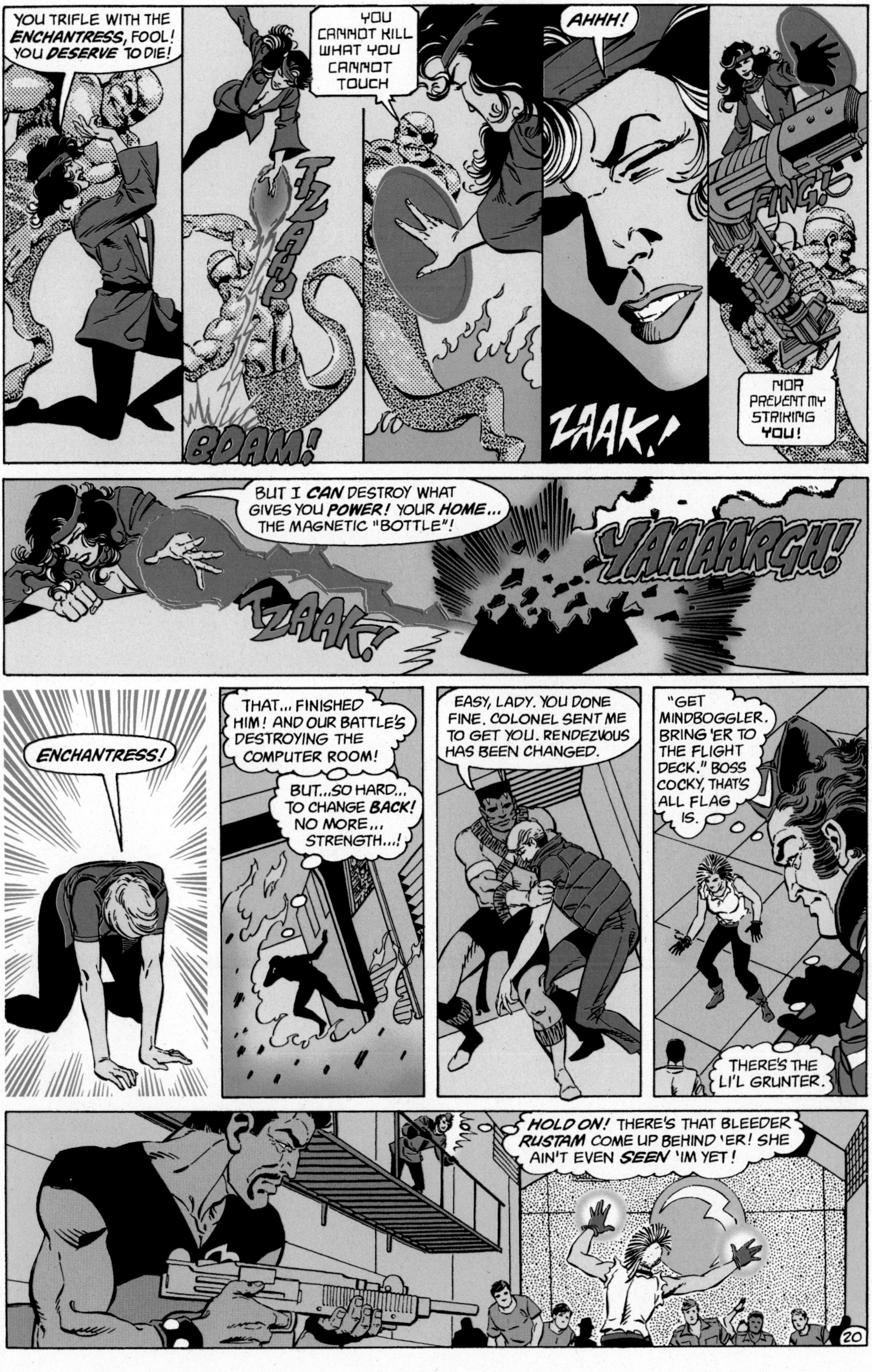

YOU TRIFLE WITH THE ENCHANTRESS, FOOL! YOU DESERVE TO DIE!
TZAAAP
BOAM!
YOU CANNOT KILL WHAT YOU CANNOT TOUCH
AHHH!
ZAAK!
FING!
NOR PREVENT MY STRIKING YOU!
BUT I CAN DESTROY WHAT GIVES YOU POWER! YOUR HOME... THE MAGNETIC "BOTTLE"!
TZAAK!
YAAAARGH!
ENCHANTRESS!
THAT... FINISHED HIM! AND OUR BATTLE'S DESTROYING THE COMPUTER ROOM!
BUT...SO HARD... TO CHANGE BACK! NO MORE... STRENGTH...!
EASY, LADY. YOU DONE FINE. COLONEL SENT ME TO GET YOU. RENDEZVOUS HAS BEEN CHANGED.
"GET MINDBOGGLER. BRING 'ER TO THE FLIGHT DECK." BOSS COCKY, THAT'S ALL FLAG IS.
THERE'S THE LI'L GRUNTER.
HOLD ON! THERE'S THAT BLEEDER RUSTAM COME UP BEHIND 'ER! SHE AIN'T EVEN SEEN 'IM YET!
20

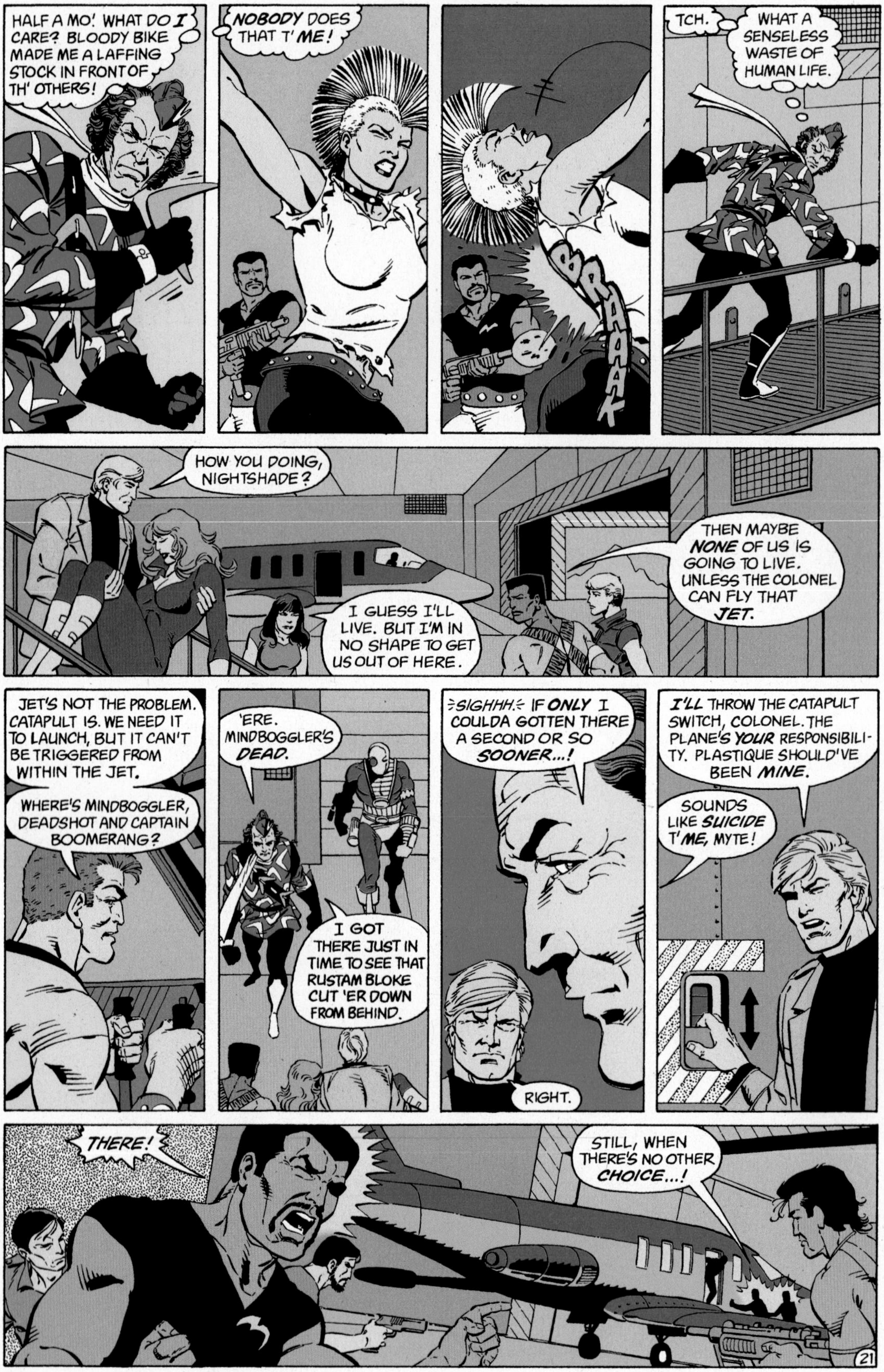

HALF A MO! WHAT DO I CARE? BLOODY BIKE MADE ME A LAFFING STOCK IN FRONT OF TH' OTHERS!
NOBODY DOES THAT T' ME!
BRAAAAK
TCH.
WHAT A SENSELESS WASTE OF HUMAN LIFE.
HOW YOU DOING, NIGHTSHADE?
I GUESS I'LL LIVE. BUT I'M IN NO SHAPE TO GET US OUT OF HERE.
THEN MAYBE NONE OF US IS GOING TO LIVE. UNLESS THE COLONEL CAN FLY THAT JET.
JET'S NOT THE PROBLEM. CATAPULT IS. WE NEED IT TO LAUNCH, BUT IT CAN'T BE TRIGGERED FROM WITHIN THE JET.
WHERE'S MINDBOGGLER, DEADSHOT AND CAPTAIN BOOMERANG?
'ERE. MINDBOGGLER'S DEAD.
I GOT THERE JUST IN TIME TO SEE THAT RUSTAM BLOKE CUT 'ER DOWN FROM BEHIND.
SIGHHH. IF ONLY I COULDA GOTTEN THERE A SECOND OR SO SOONER...!
RIGHT.
I'LL THROW THE CATAPULT SWITCH, COLONEL. THE PLANE'S YOUR RESPONSIBILITY. PLASTIQUE SHOULD'VE BEEN MINE.
SOUNDS LIKE SUICIDE T'ME, MYTE!
THERE!
STILL, WHEN THERE'S NO OTHER CHOICE...!
21

BRING THEM DOWN!

SWOOSH

WE'RE AWAY! BUT WHAT ABOUT *NEMESIS*?

SHWUP.SHWUP.SHWUP!

HEADS UP. INCOMING.

LADDER'S OUT.

BOOOM!

BRUDDABRUDDA

EVERYTHING JAKE?

UHHH... JUST MEMORIES OF MY LAST TRIP BY 'COPTER. I'M FINE.

OKAY. HANG ON. WE GONE.

HWUP.SHW

WEEEIIIN!

WE MUST REBUILD, MR. PRESIDENT. HOWEVER LONG IT TAKES.

THEN WE WILL FIND OUT WHO DID THIS AND WE WILL DESTROY THEM. THIS I PROMISE YOU.

WE GOT ONE DEAD AND ONE WHO CAN GO BACK TO JAIL AND LOSE THE KEY, MRS. WALLER. AND SOME TALKING TO DO ABOUT *SURPRISES*.

FINE. NOTHING I LIKE BETTER THAN A *GOOD CHAT*.

THE TWO AIRCRAFT TURN WEST, AWAY FROM THE DAWNING DAY, HEADING BACK INTO THE NIGHT.

FIN.

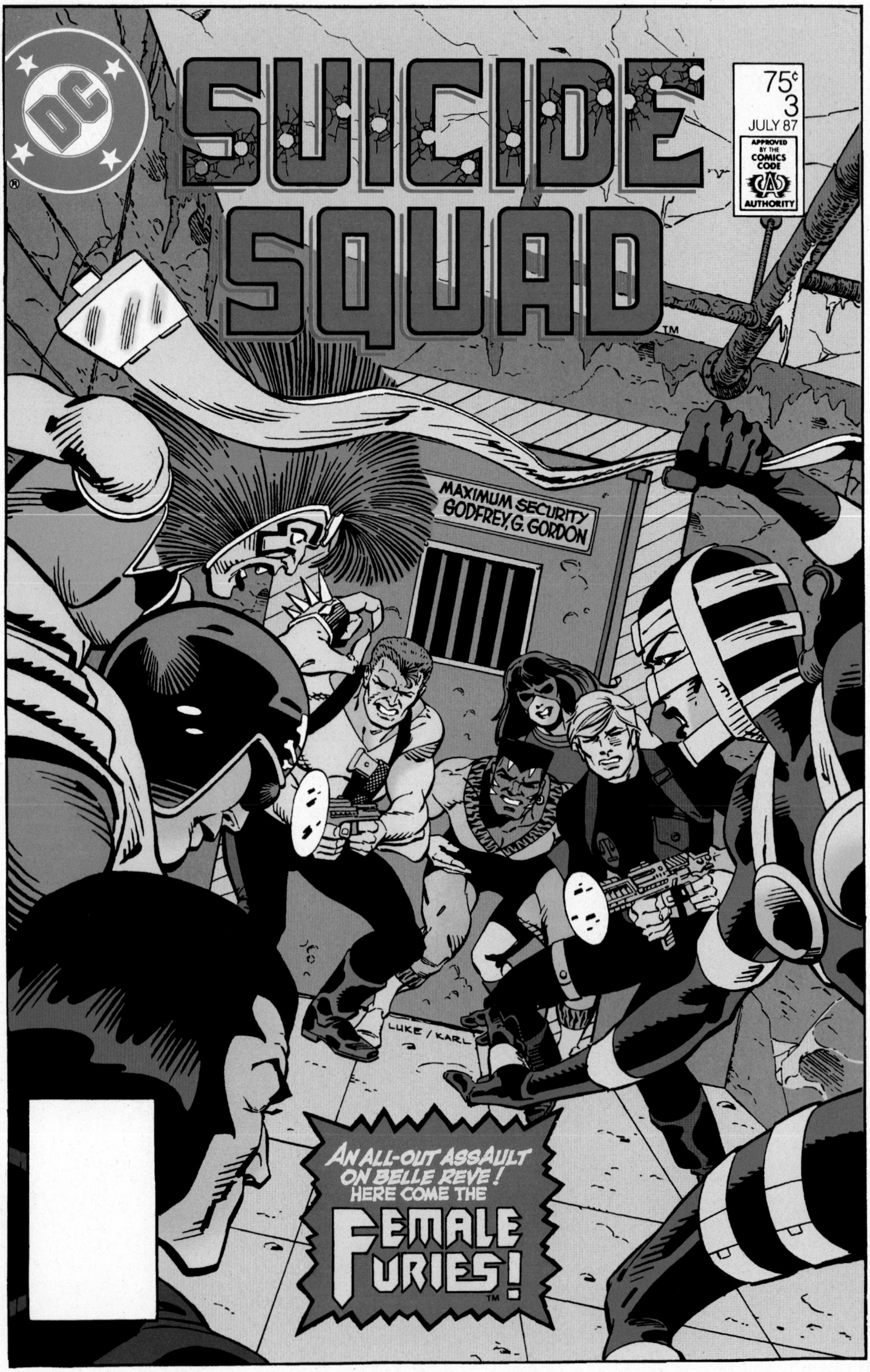

DC
SUICIDE SQUAD
75¢
3
JULY 87
APPROVED BY THE COMICS CODE AUTHORITY
MAXIMUM SECURITY
GODFREY, G. GORDON
LUKE / KARL
AN ALL-OUT ASSAULT ON BELLE REVE!
HERE COME THE
FEMALE FURIES!

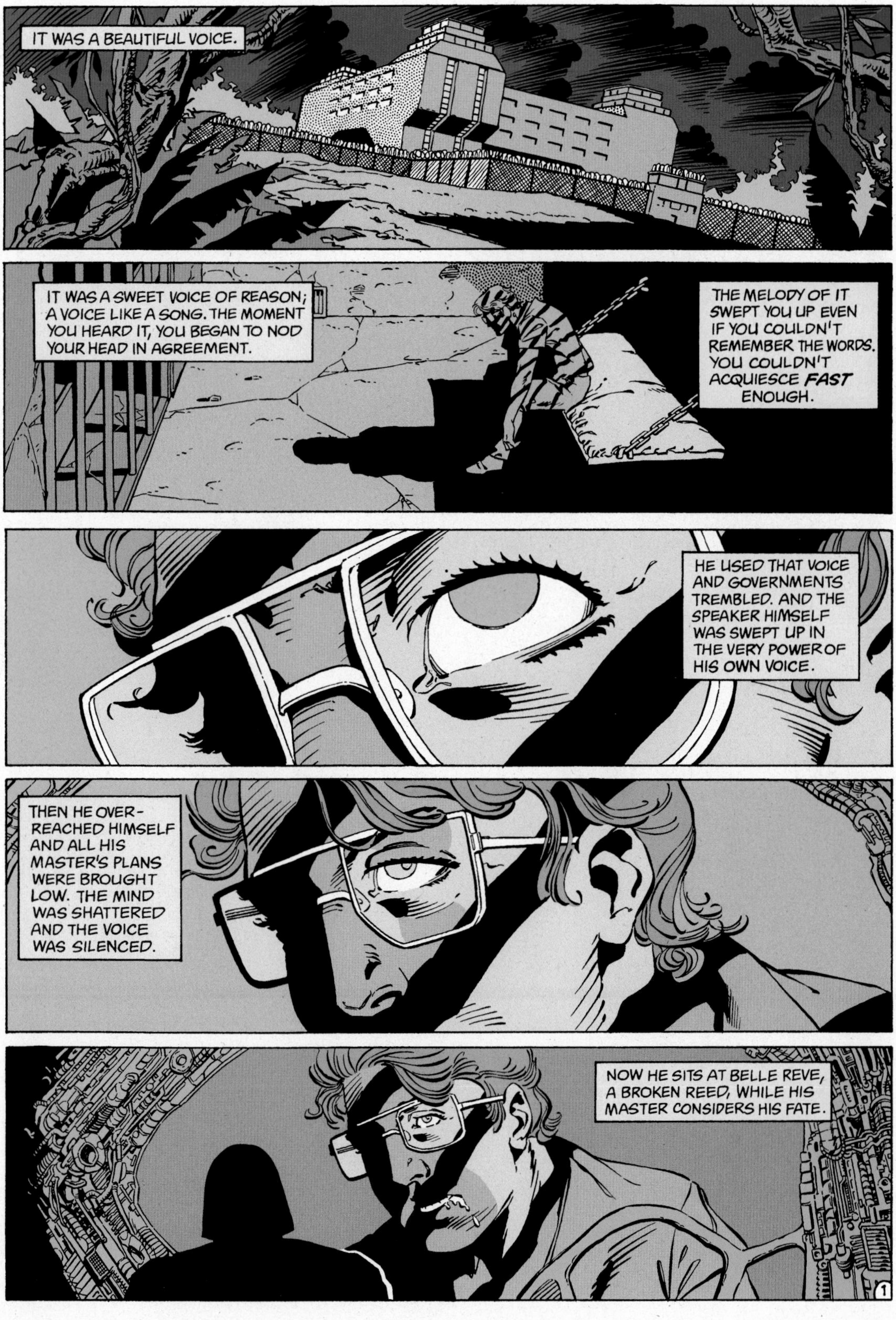
IT WAS A BEAUTIFUL VOICE.
IT WAS A SWEET VOICE OF REASON; A VOICE LIKE A SONG. THE MOMENT YOU HEARD IT, YOU BEGAN TO NOD YOUR HEAD IN AGREEMENT.
THE MELODY OF IT SWEPT YOU UP EVEN IF YOU COULDN'T REMEMBER THE WORDS. YOU COULDN'T ACQUIESCE FAST ENOUGH.
HE USED THAT VOICE AND GOVERNMENTS TREMBLED. AND THE SPEAKER HIMSELF WAS SWEPT UP IN THE VERY POWER OF HIS OWN VOICE.
THEN HE OVER-REACHED HIMSELF AND ALL HIS MASTER'S PLANS WERE BROUGHT LOW. THE MIND WAS SHATTERED AND THE VOICE WAS SILENCED.
NOW HE SITS AT BELLE REVE, A BROKEN REED, WHILE HIS MASTER CONSIDERS HIS FATE.
1

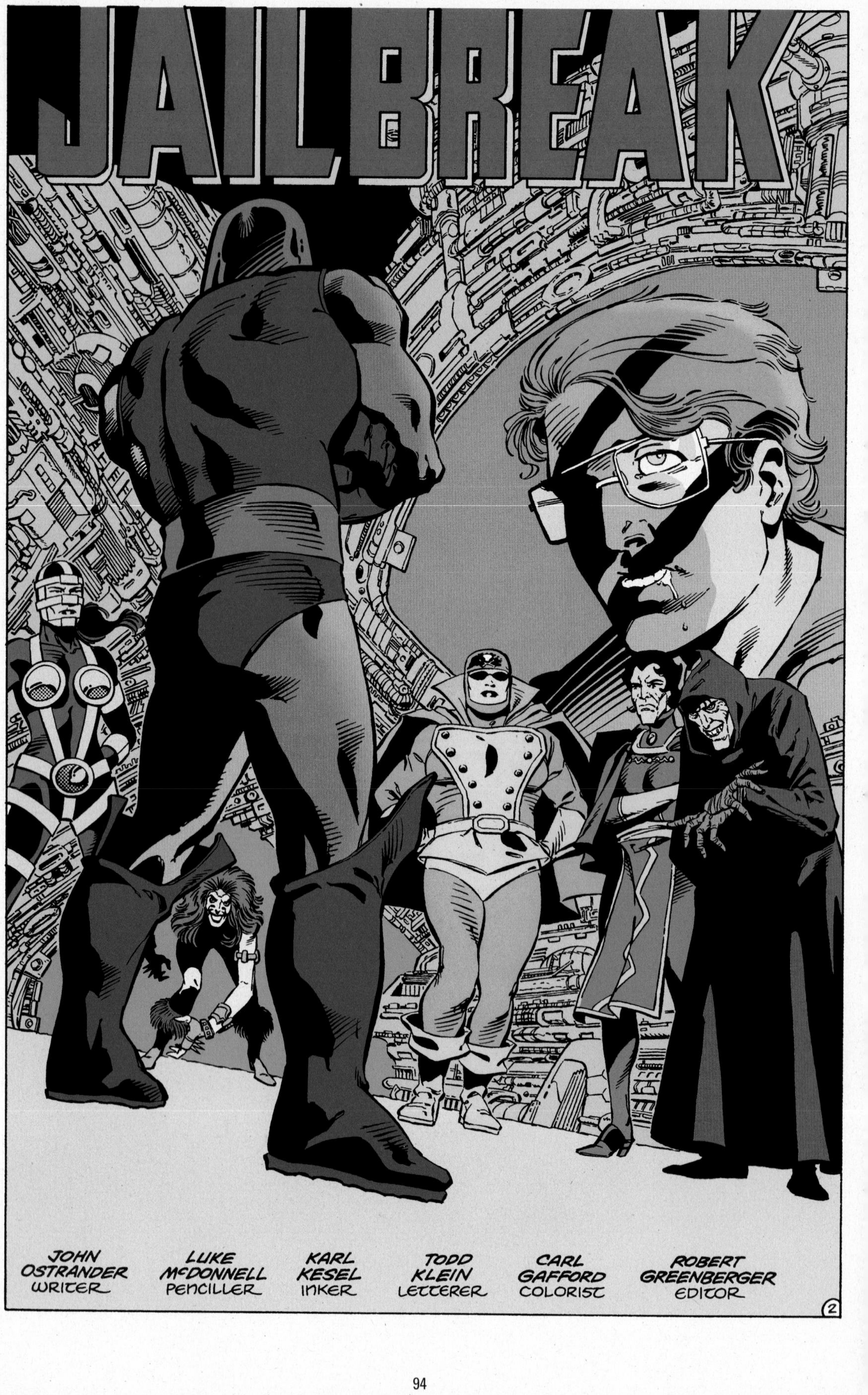
JAILBREAK
JOHN OSTRANDER WRITER
LUKE McDONNELL PENCILLER
KARL KESEL INKER
TODD KLEIN LETTERER
CARL GAFFORD COLORIST
ROBERT GREENBERGER EDITOR
2

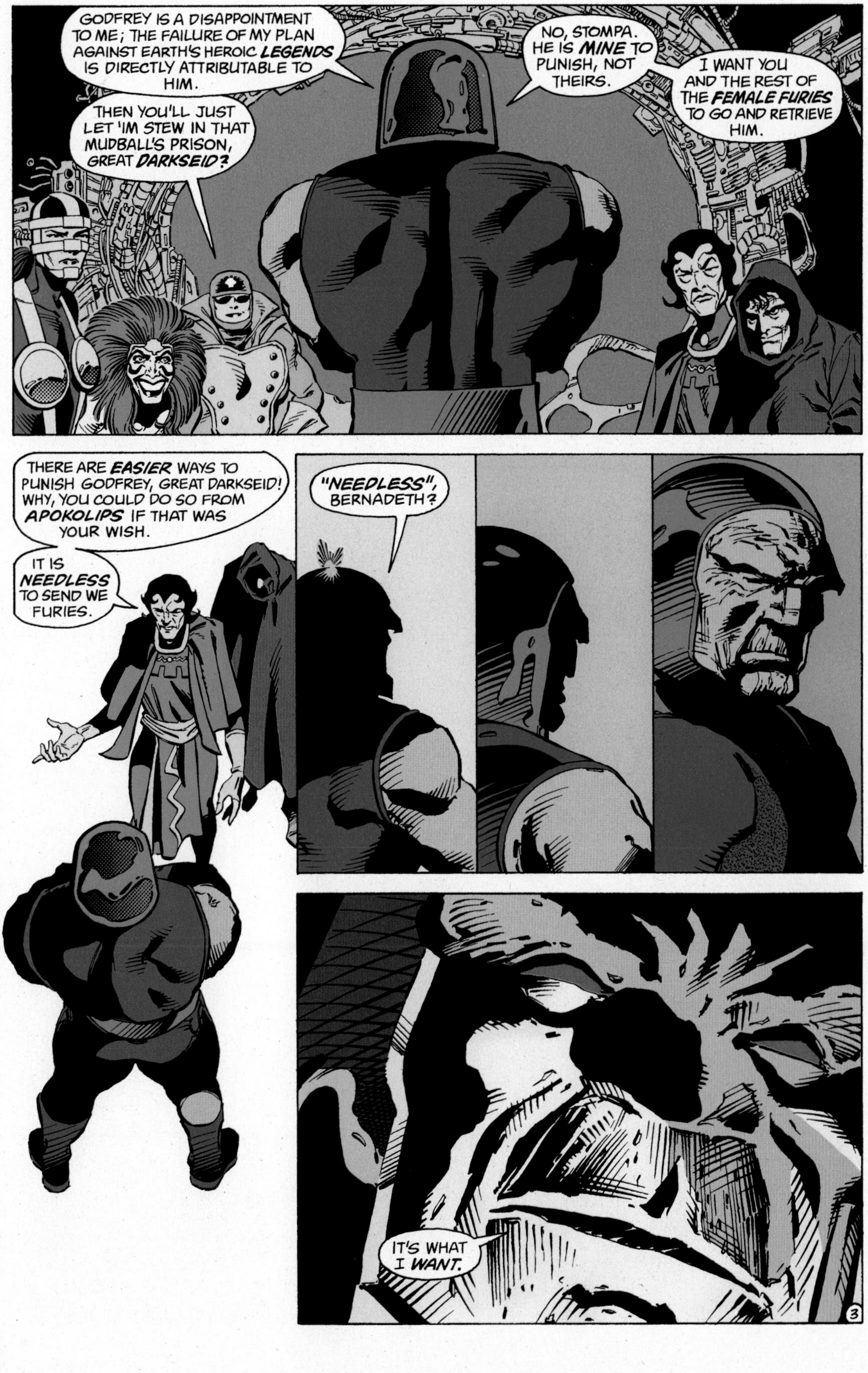
GODFREY IS A DISAPPOINTMENT TO ME; THE FAILURE OF MY PLAN AGAINST EARTH'S HEROIC LEGENDS IS DIRECTLY ATTRIBUTABLE TO HIM.
THEN YOU'LL JUST LET 'IM STEW IN THAT MUDBALL'S PRISON, GREAT DARKSEID?
NO, STOMPA. HE IS MINE TO PUNISH, NOT THEIRS.
I WANT YOU AND THE REST OF THE FEMALE FURIES TO GO AND RETRIEVE HIM.
THERE ARE EASIER WAYS TO PUNISH GODFREY, GREAT DARKSEID! WHY, YOU COULD DO SO FROM APOKOLIPS IF THAT WAS YOUR WISH.
IT IS NEEDLESS TO SEND WE FURIES.
"NEEDLESS", BERNADETH?
IT'S WHAT I WANT.
3

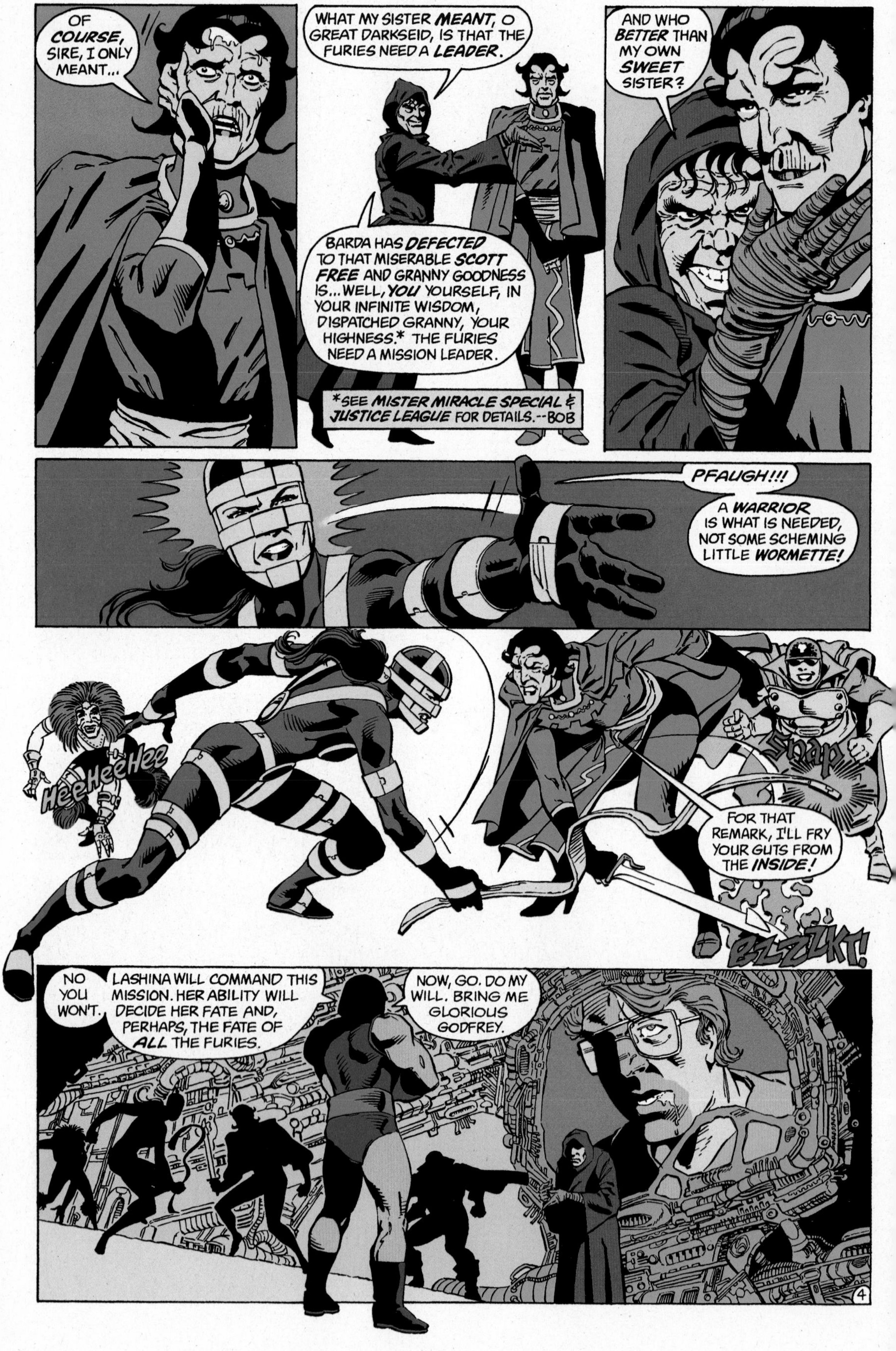
OF COURSE, SIRE, I ONLY MEANT...
WHAT MY SISTER MEANT, O GREAT DARKSEID, IS THAT THE FURIES NEED A LEADER.
BARDA HAS DEFECTED TO THAT MISERABLE SCOTT FREE AND GRANNY GOODNESS IS...WELL, YOU YOURSELF, IN YOUR INFINITE WISDOM, DISPATCHED GRANNY, YOUR HIGHNESS.* THE FURIES NEED A MISSION LEADER.
*SEE MISTER MIRACLE SPECIAL & JUSTICE LEAGUE FOR DETAILS.--BOB
AND WHO BETTER THAN MY OWN SWEET SISTER?
PFAUGH!!!
A WARRIOR IS WHAT IS NEEDED, NOT SOME SCHEMING LITTLE WORMETTE!
HeeHeeHee
SNAP
FOR THAT REMARK, I'LL FRY YOUR GUTS FROM THE INSIDE!
BZZZKT!
NO YOU WON'T.
LASHINA WILL COMMAND THIS MISSION. HER ABILITY WILL DECIDE HER FATE AND, PERHAPS, THE FATE OF ALL THE FURIES.
NOW, GO. DO MY WILL. BRING ME GLORIOUS GODFREY.
4

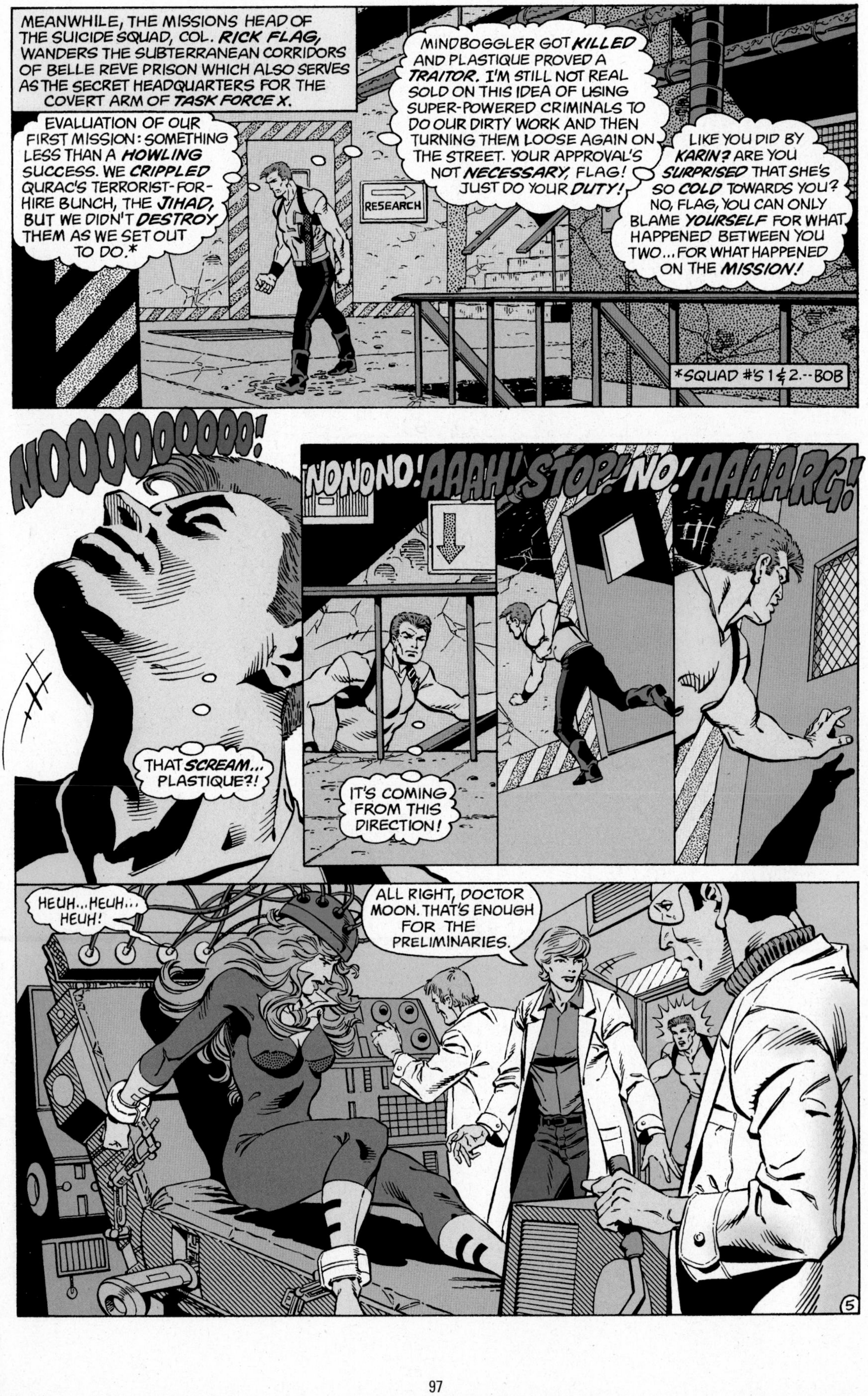
MEANWHILE, THE MISSIONS HEAD OF THE SUICIDE SQUAD, COL. RICK FLAG, WANDERS THE SUBTERRANEAN CORRIDORS OF BELLE REVE PRISON WHICH ALSO SERVES AS THE SECRET HEADQUARTERS FOR THE COVERT ARM OF TASK FORCE X.
EVALUATION OF OUR FIRST MISSION: SOMETHING LESS THAN A HOWLING SUCCESS. WE CRIPPLED QURAC'S TERRORIST-FOR-HIRE BUNCH, THE JIHAD, BUT WE DIDN'T DESTROY THEM AS WE SET OUT TO DO.*
RESEARCH
MINDBOGGLER GOT KILLED AND PLASTIQUE PROVED A TRAITOR. I'M STILL NOT REAL SOLD ON THIS IDEA OF USING SUPER-POWERED CRIMINALS TO DO OUR DIRTY WORK AND THEN TURNING THEM LOOSE AGAIN ON THE STREET. YOUR APPROVAL'S NOT NECESSARY, FLAG! JUST DO YOUR DUTY!
LIKE YOU DID BY KARIN? ARE YOU SURPRISED THAT SHE'S SO COLD TOWARDS YOU? NO, FLAG, YOU CAN ONLY BLAME YOURSELF FOR WHAT HAPPENED BETWEEN YOU TWO... FOR WHAT HAPPENED ON THE MISSION!
*SQUAD #'S 1 & 2.--BOB
NOOOOOOOOO!
THAT SCREAM... PLASTIQUE?!
NONONO! AAAH! STOP! NO! AAAARG!
IT'S COMING FROM THIS DIRECTION!
HEUH... HEUH... HEUH!
ALL RIGHT, DOCTOR MOON. THAT'S ENOUGH FOR THE PRELIMINARIES.
5

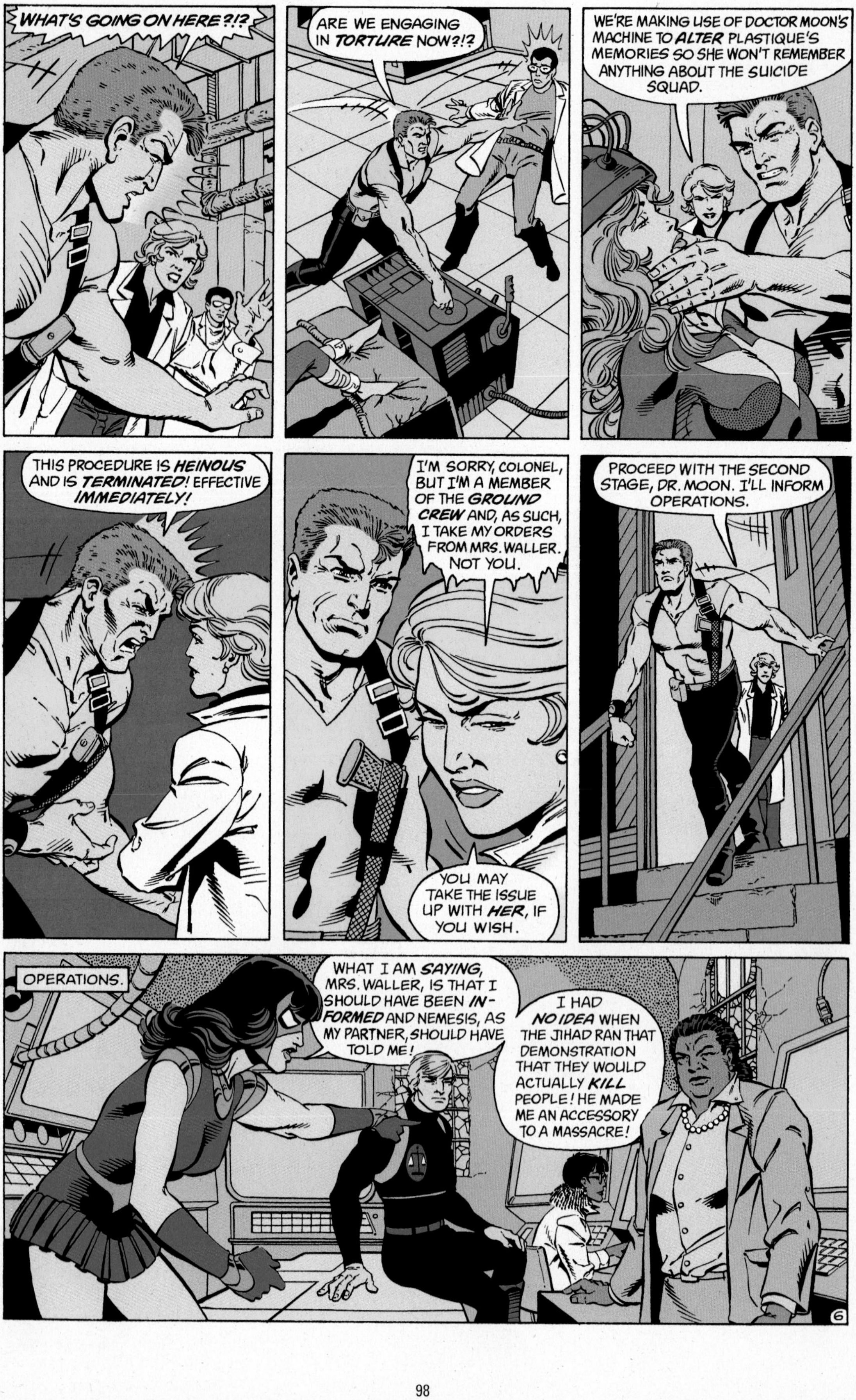
WHAT'S GOING ON HERE?!?
ARE WE ENGAGING IN TORTURE NOW?!?
WE'RE MAKING USE OF DOCTOR MOON'S MACHINE TO ALTER PLASTIQUE'S MEMORIES SO SHE WON'T REMEMBER ANYTHING ABOUT THE SUICIDE SQUAD.
THIS PROCEDURE IS HEINOUS AND IS TERMINATED! EFFECTIVE IMMEDIATELY!
I'M SORRY, COLONEL, BUT I'M A MEMBER OF THE GROUND CREW AND, AS SUCH, I TAKE MY ORDERS FROM MRS. WALLER. NOT YOU.
YOU MAY TAKE THE ISSUE UP WITH HER, IF YOU WISH.
PROCEED WITH THE SECOND STAGE, DR. MOON. I'LL INFORM OPERATIONS.
OPERATIONS.
WHAT I AM SAYING, MRS. WALLER, IS THAT I SHOULD HAVE BEEN INFORMED AND NEMESIS, AS MY PARTNER, SHOULD HAVE TOLD ME!
I HAD NO IDEA WHEN THE JIHAD RAN THAT DEMONSTRATION THAT THEY WOULD ACTUALLY KILL PEOPLE! HE MADE ME AN ACCESSORY TO A MASSACRE!
6

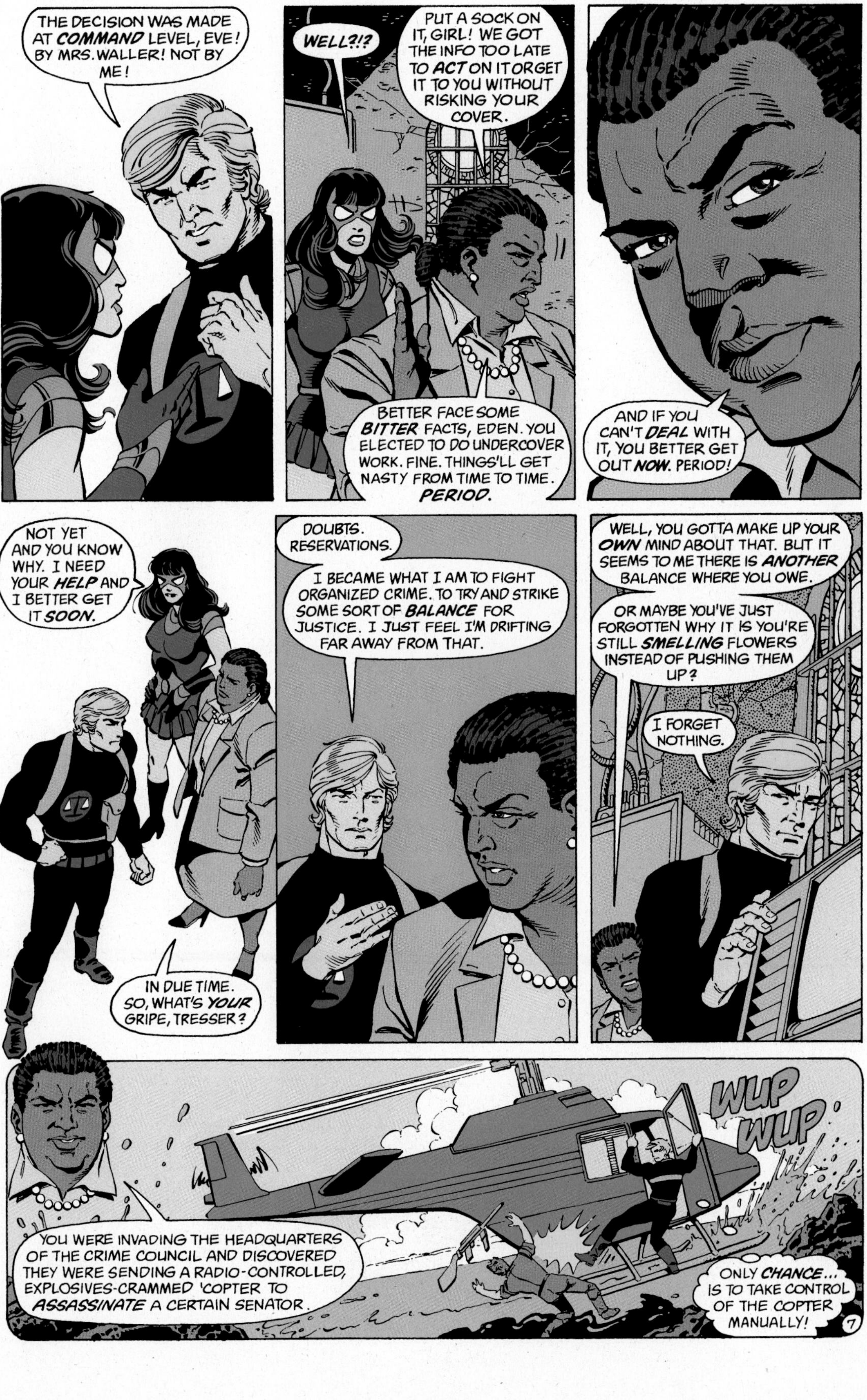

THE DECISION WAS MADE AT COMMAND LEVEL, EVE! BY MRS. WALLER! NOT BY ME!
WELL?!?
PUT A SOCK ON IT, GIRL! WE GOT THE INFO TOO LATE TO ACT ON IT OR GET IT TO YOU WITHOUT RISKING YOUR COVER.
BETTER FACE SOME BITTER FACTS, EDEN. YOU ELECTED TO DO UNDERCOVER WORK. FINE. THINGS'LL GET NASTY FROM TIME TO TIME. PERIOD.
AND IF YOU CAN'T DEAL WITH IT, YOU BETTER GET OUT NOW. PERIOD!
NOT YET AND YOU KNOW WHY. I NEED YOUR HELP AND I BETTER GET IT SOON.
IN DUE TIME. SO, WHAT'S YOUR GRIPE, TRESSER?
DOUBTS. RESERVATIONS.
I BECAME WHAT I AM TO FIGHT ORGANIZED CRIME. TO TRY AND STRIKE SOME SORT OF BALANCE FOR JUSTICE. I JUST FEEL I'M DRIFTING FAR AWAY FROM THAT.
WELL, YOU GOTTA MAKE UP YOUR OWN MIND ABOUT THAT. BUT IT SEEMS TO ME THERE IS ANOTHER BALANCE WHERE YOU OWE.
OR MAYBE YOU'VE JUST FORGOTTEN WHY IT IS YOU'RE STILL SMELLING FLOWERS INSTEAD OF PUSHING THEM UP?
I FORGET NOTHING.
YOU WERE INVADING THE HEADQUARTERS OF THE CRIME COUNCIL AND DISCOVERED THEY WERE SENDING A RADIO-CONTROLLED, EXPLOSIVES-CRAMMED 'COPTER TO ASSASSINATE A CERTAIN SENATOR.
WUP WUP
ONLY CHANCE... IS TO TAKE CONTROL OF THE COPTER MANUALLY!
7

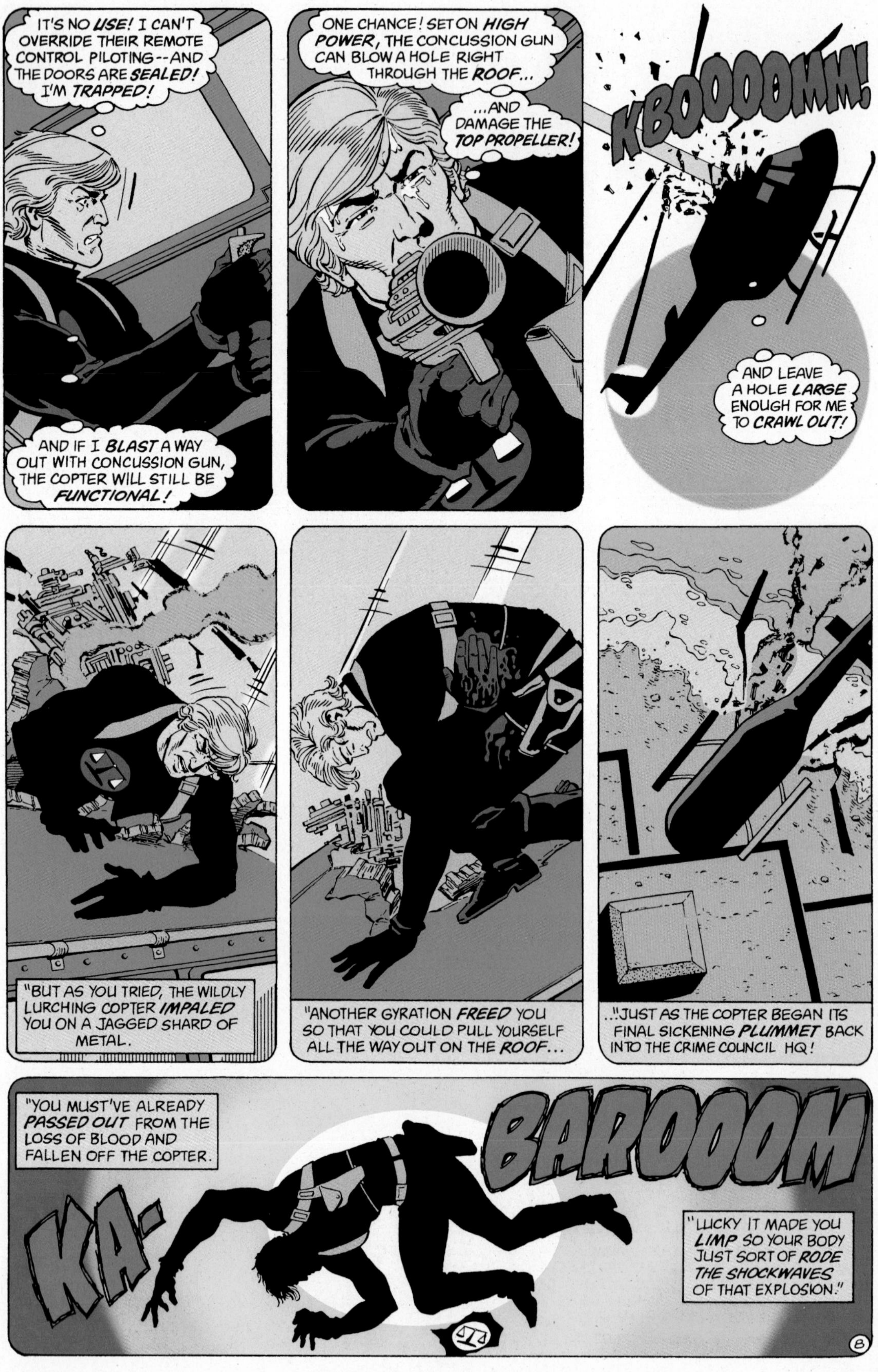
IT'S NO USE! I CAN'T OVERRIDE THEIR REMOTE CONTROL PILOTING--AND THE DOORS ARE SEALED! I'M TRAPPED!
AND IF I BLAST A WAY OUT WITH CONCUSSION GUN, THE COPTER WILL STILL BE FUNCTIONAL!
ONE CHANCE! SET ON HIGH POWER, THE CONCUSSION GUN CAN BLOW A HOLE RIGHT THROUGH THE ROOF...
...AND DAMAGE THE TOP PROPELLER!
KBOOOOOMM!
AND LEAVE A HOLE LARGE ENOUGH FOR ME TO CRAWL OUT!
"BUT AS YOU TRIED, THE WILDLY LURCHING COPTER IMPALED YOU ON A JAGGED SHARD OF METAL.
"ANOTHER GYRATION FREED YOU SO THAT YOU COULD PULL YOURSELF ALL THE WAY OUT ON THE ROOF...
..."JUST AS THE COPTER BEGAN ITS FINAL SICKENING PLUMMET BACK INTO THE CRIME COUNCIL HQ!
"YOU MUST'VE ALREADY PASSED OUT FROM THE LOSS OF BLOOD AND FALLEN OFF THE COPTER.
KA-BAROOOM
"LUCKY IT MADE YOU LIMP SO YOUR BODY JUST SORT OF RODE THE SHOCKWAVES OF THAT EXPLOSION."
8

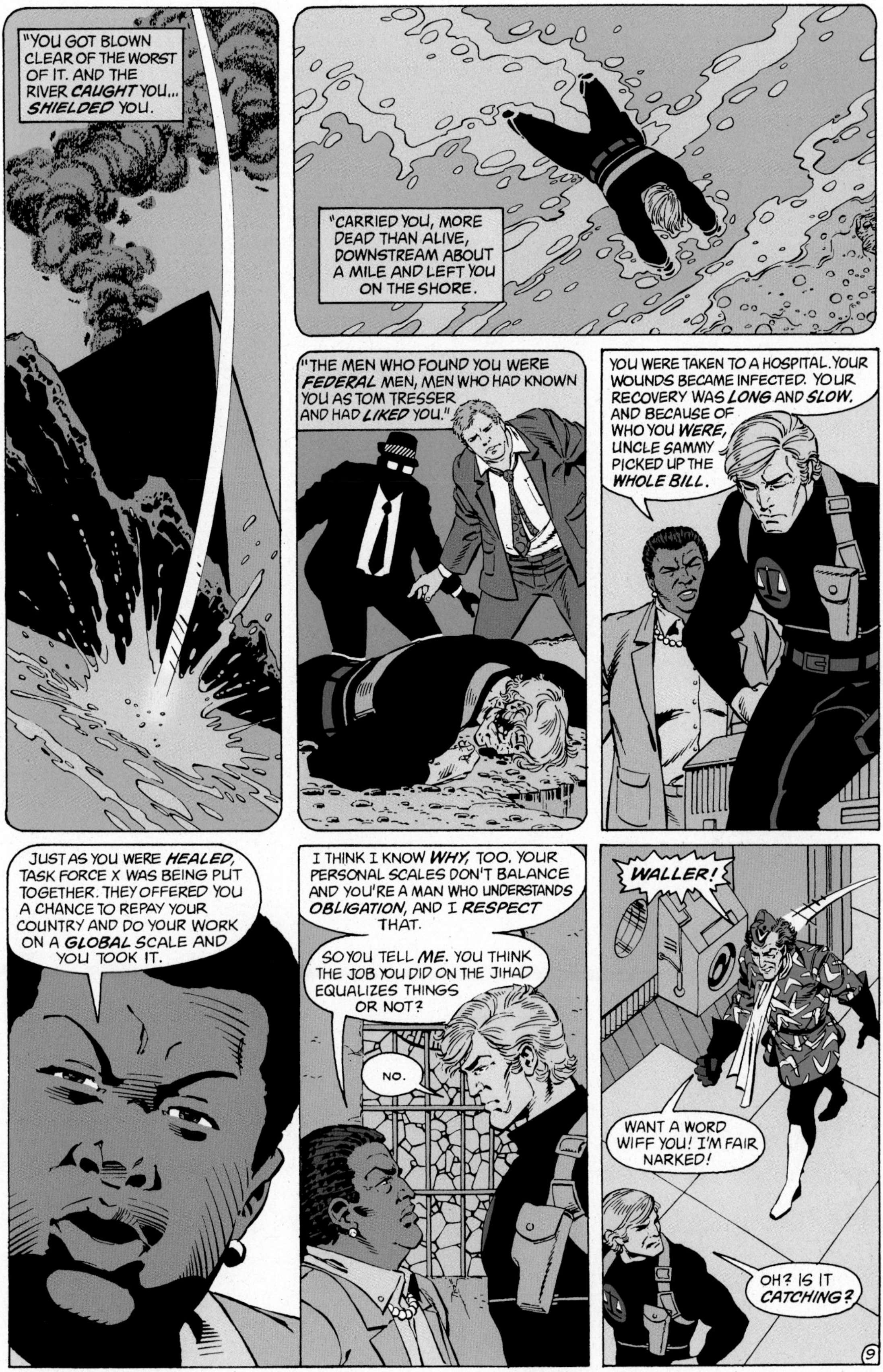
"YOU GOT BLOWN CLEAR OF THE WORST OF IT. AND THE RIVER CAUGHT YOU... SHIELDED YOU.
"CARRIED YOU, MORE DEAD THAN ALIVE, DOWNSTREAM ABOUT A MILE AND LEFT YOU ON THE SHORE.
"THE MEN WHO FOUND YOU WERE FEDERAL MEN, MEN WHO HAD KNOWN YOU AS TOM TRESSER AND HAD LIKED YOU."
YOU WERE TAKEN TO A HOSPITAL. YOUR WOUNDS BECAME INFECTED. YOUR RECOVERY WAS LONG AND SLOW. AND BECAUSE OF WHO YOU WERE, UNCLE SAMMY PICKED UP THE WHOLE BILL.
JUST AS YOU WERE HEALED, TASK FORCE X WAS BEING PUT TOGETHER. THEY OFFERED YOU A CHANCE TO REPAY YOUR COUNTRY AND DO YOUR WORK ON A GLOBAL SCALE AND YOU TOOK IT.
I THINK I KNOW WHY, TOO. YOUR PERSONAL SCALES DON'T BALANCE AND YOU'RE A MAN WHO UNDERSTANDS OBLIGATION, AND I RESPECT THAT.
SO YOU TELL ME. YOU THINK THE JOB YOU DID ON THE JIHAD EQUALIZES THINGS OR NOT?
NO.
WALLER!
WANT A WORD WIFF YOU! I'M FAIR NARKED!
OH? IS IT CATCHING?
9

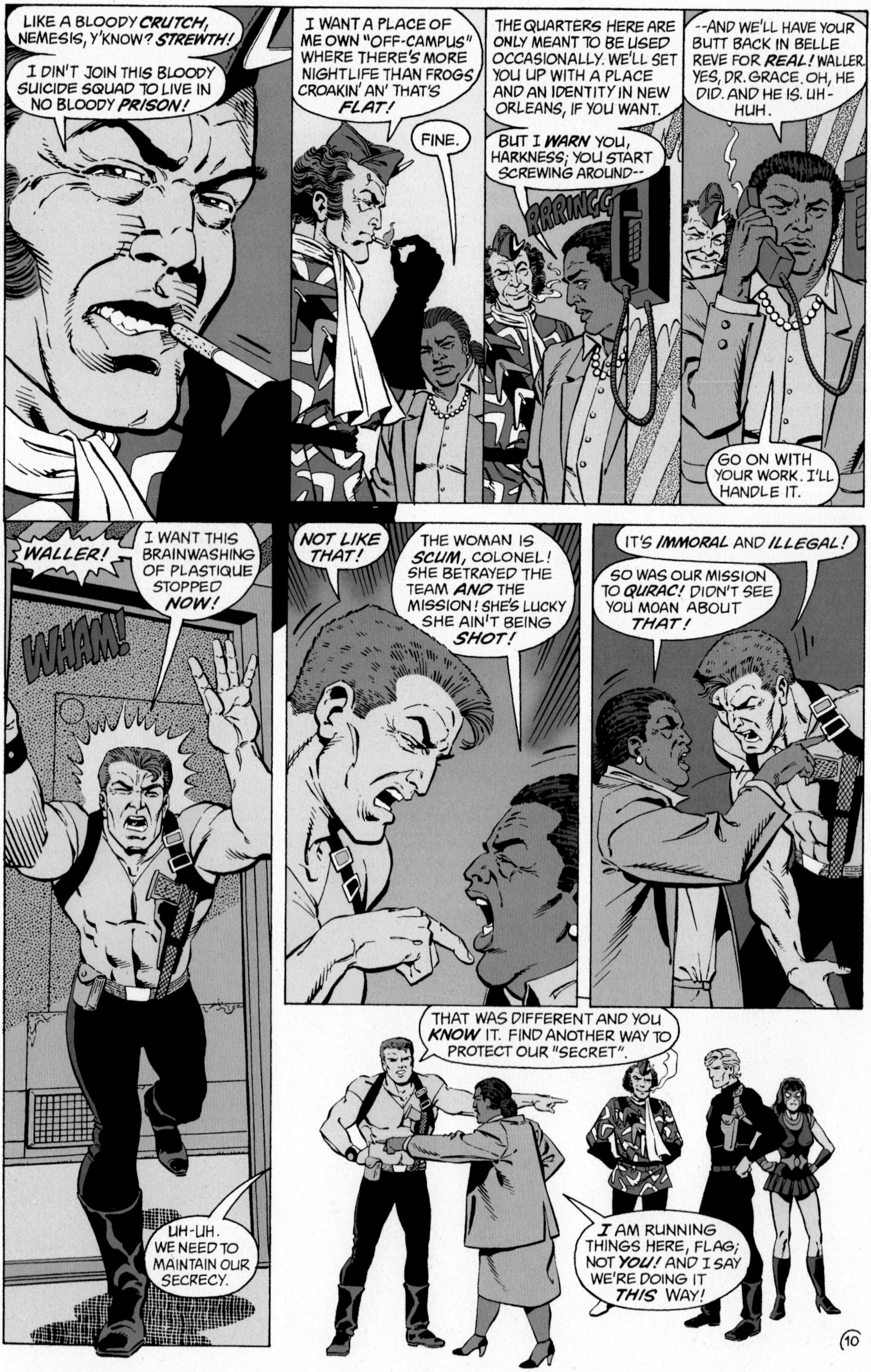
LIKE A BLOODY CRUTCH, NEMESIS, Y'KNOW? STREWTH!
I DIN'T JOIN THIS BLOODY SUICIDE SQUAD TO LIVE IN NO BLOODY PRISON!
I WANT A PLACE OF ME OWN "OFF-CAMPUS" WHERE THERE'S MORE NIGHTLIFE THAN FROGS CROAKIN' AN' THAT'S FLAT!
FINE.
THE QUARTERS HERE ARE ONLY MEANT TO BE USED OCCASIONALLY. WE'LL SET YOU UP WITH A PLACE AND AN IDENTITY IN NEW ORLEANS, IF YOU WANT.
BUT I WARN YOU, HARKNESS; YOU START SCREWING AROUND--
RRRINGG
--AND WE'LL HAVE YOUR BUTT BACK IN BELLE REVE FOR REAL! WALLER. YES, DR. GRACE. OH, HE DID. AND HE IS. UH-HUH.
GO ON WITH YOUR WORK. I'LL HANDLE IT.
WALLER!
I WANT THIS BRAINWASHING OF PLASTIQUE STOPPED NOW!
WHAM!
UH-UH. WE NEED TO MAINTAIN OUR SECRECY.
NOT LIKE THAT!
THE WOMAN IS SCUM, COLONEL! SHE BETRAYED THE TEAM AND THE MISSION! SHE'S LUCKY SHE AIN'T BEING SHOT!
IT'S IMMORAL AND ILLEGAL!
SO WAS OUR MISSION TO QURAC! DIDN'T SEE YOU MOAN ABOUT THAT!
THAT WAS DIFFERENT AND YOU KNOW IT. FIND ANOTHER WAY TO PROTECT OUR "SECRET".
I AM RUNNING THINGS HERE, FLAG; NOT YOU! AND I SAY WE'RE DOING IT THIS WAY!
10

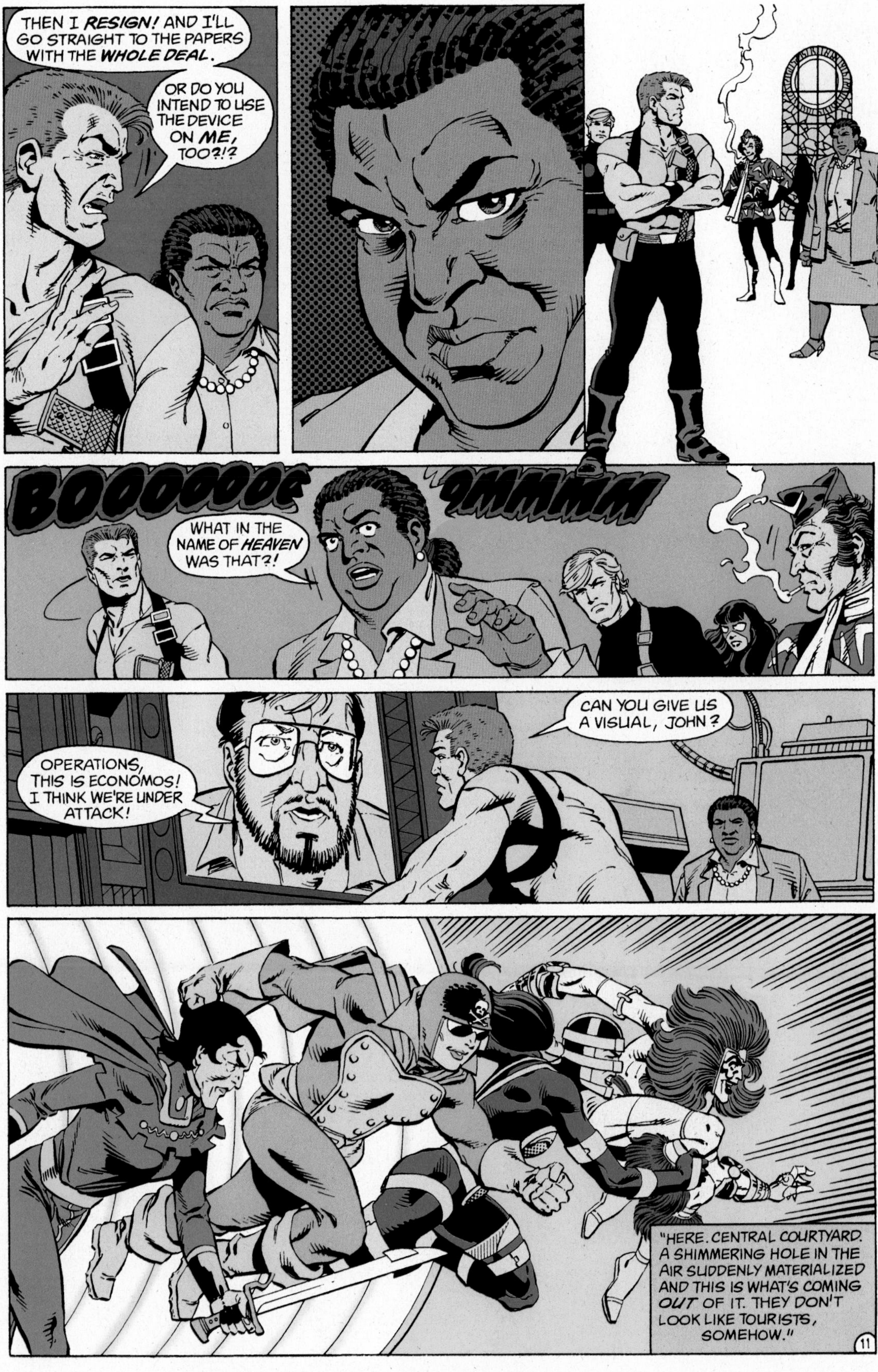
THEN I *RESIGN!* AND I'LL GO STRAIGHT TO THE PAPERS WITH THE *WHOLE DEAL*.
OR DO YOU INTEND TO USE THE DEVICE ON *ME*, TOO?!?
BOOOOOOOOMMMMM
WHAT IN THE NAME OF *HEAVEN* WAS THAT?!
OPERATIONS, THIS IS ECONOMOS! I THINK WE'RE UNDER ATTACK!
CAN YOU GIVE US A VISUAL, JOHN?
"HERE. CENTRAL COURTYARD. A SHIMMERING HOLE IN THE AIR SUDDENLY MATERIALIZED AND THIS IS WHAT'S COMING *OUT* OF IT. THEY DON'T LOOK LIKE TOURISTS, SOMEHOW."
11

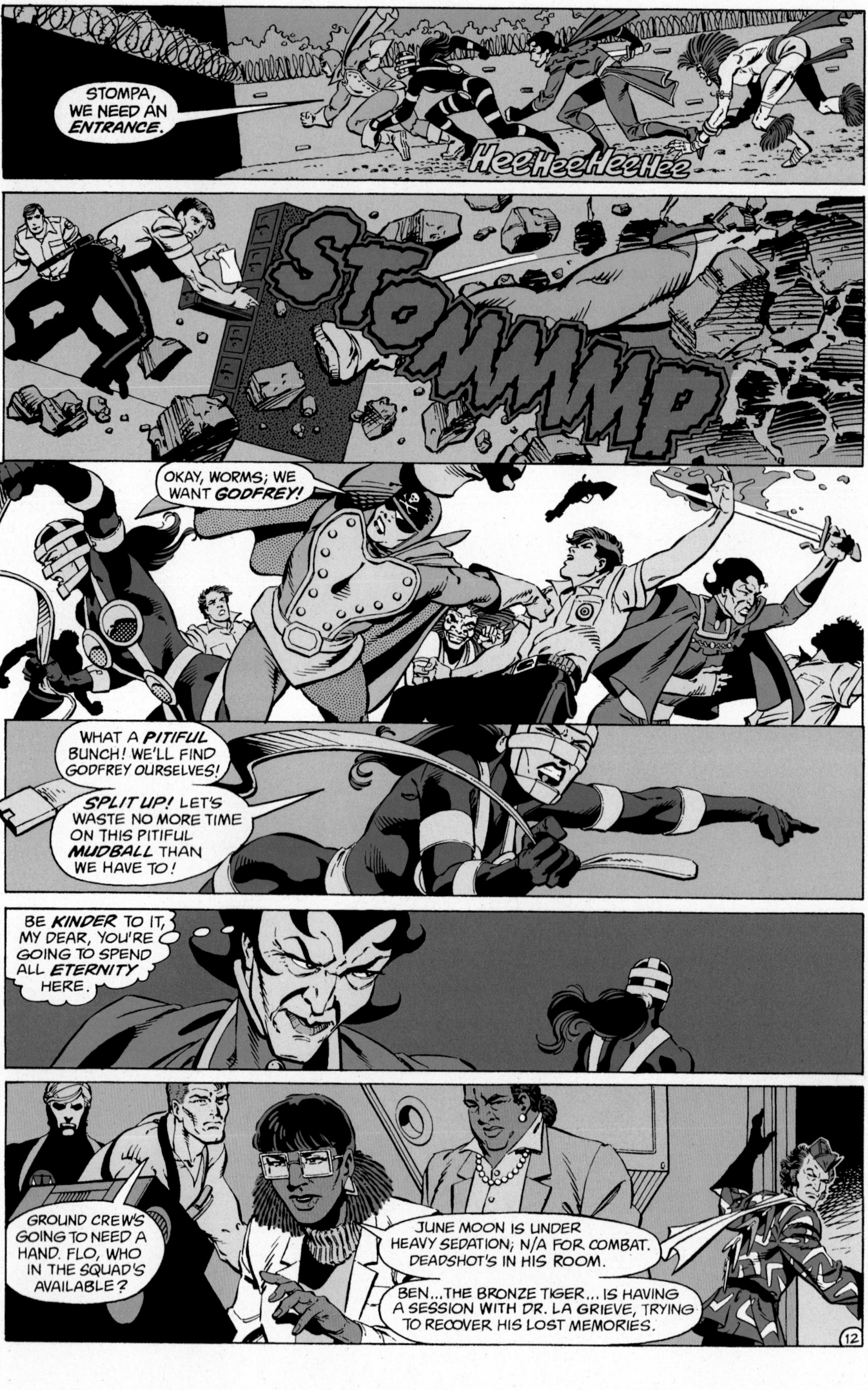
STOMPA, WE NEED AN ENTRANCE.
HEEHEEHEEHEE
STOMMMMP
OKAY, WORMS; WE WANT GODFREY!
WHAT A PITIFUL BUNCH! WE'LL FIND GODFREY OURSELVES!
SPLIT UP! LET'S WASTE NO MORE TIME ON THIS PITIFUL MUDBALL THAN WE HAVE TO!
BE KINDER TO IT, MY DEAR, YOU'RE GOING TO SPEND ALL ETERNITY HERE.
GROUND CREW'S GOING TO NEED A HAND. FLO, WHO IN THE SQUAD'S AVAILABLE?
JUNE MOON IS UNDER HEAVY SEDATION; N/A FOR COMBAT. DEADSHOT'S IN HIS ROOM.
BEN... THE BRONZE TIGER... IS HAVING A SESSION WITH DR. LA GRIEVE, TRYING TO RECOVER HIS LOST MEMORIES.
12

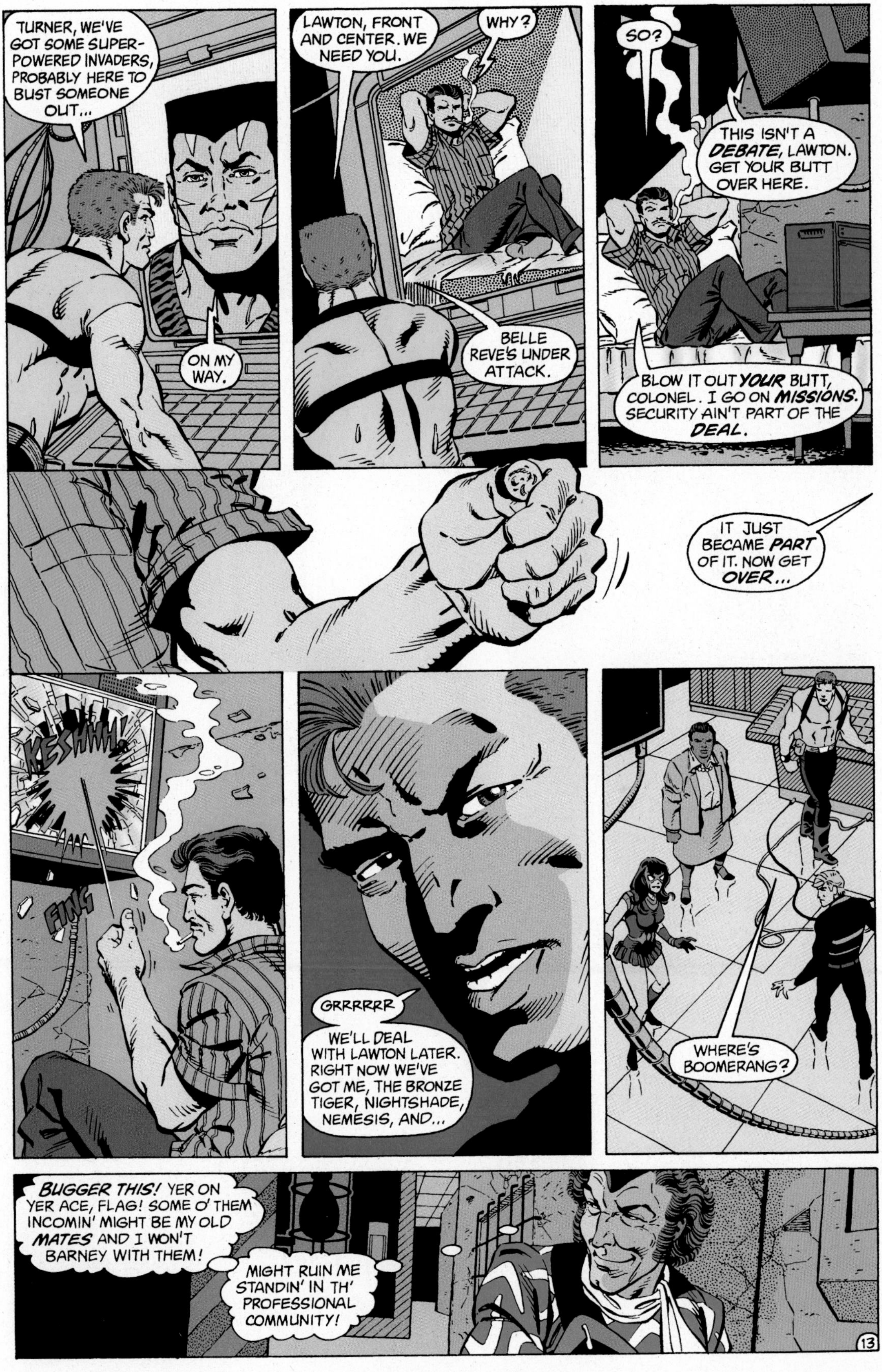

TURNER, WE'VE GOT SOME SUPER-POWERED INVADERS, PROBABLY HERE TO BUST SOMEONE OUT...
ON MY WAY.
LAWTON, FRONT AND CENTER. WE NEED YOU.
WHY?
BELLE REVE'S UNDER ATTACK.
SO?
THIS ISN'T A DEBATE, LAWTON. GET YOUR BUTT OVER HERE.
BLOW IT OUT YOUR BUTT, COLONEL. I GO ON MISSIONS. SECURITY AIN'T PART OF THE DEAL.
IT JUST BECAME PART OF IT. NOW GET OVER...
KESHHH!
FING
GRRRRRR
WE'LL DEAL WITH LAWTON LATER. RIGHT NOW WE'VE GOT ME, THE BRONZE TIGER, NIGHTSHADE, NEMESIS, AND...
WHERE'S BOOMERANG?
BUGGER THIS! YER ON YER ACE, FLAG! SOME O' THEM INCOMIN' MIGHT BE MY OLD MATES AND I WON'T BARNEY WITH THEM!
MIGHT RUIN ME STANDIN' IN TH' PROFESSIONAL COMMUNITY!
13

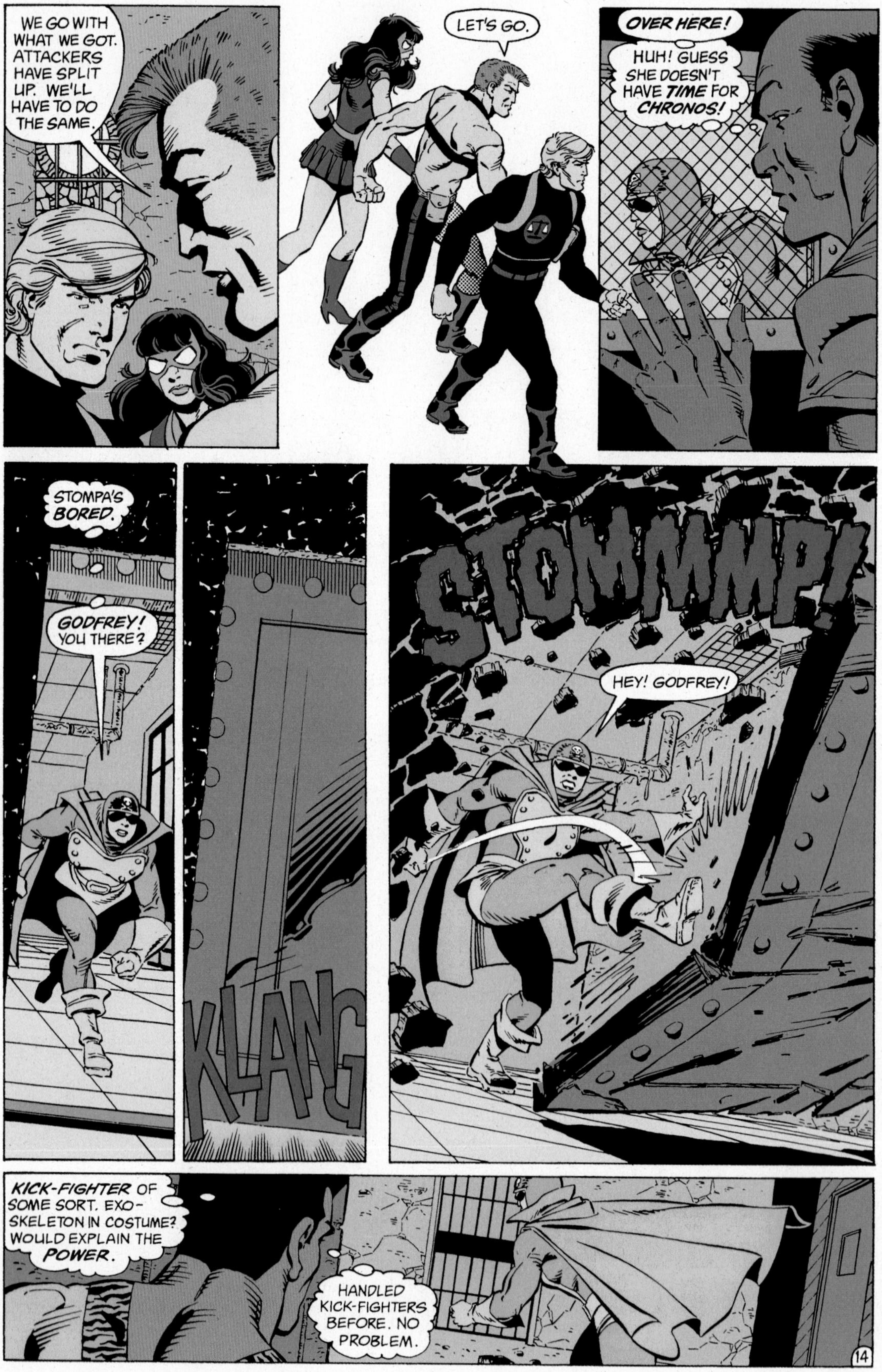

WE GO WITH WHAT WE GOT. ATTACKERS HAVE SPLIT UP. WE'LL HAVE TO DO THE SAME.
LET'S GO.
OVER HERE!
HUH! GUESS SHE DOESN'T HAVE TIME FOR CHRONOS!
STOMPA'S BORED.
GODFREY! YOU THERE?
KLANG
STOMMMP!
HEY! GODFREY!
KICK-FIGHTER OF SOME SORT. EXO-SKELETON IN COSTUME? WOULD EXPLAIN THE POWER.
HANDLED KICK-FIGHTERS BEFORE. NO PROBLEM.
14

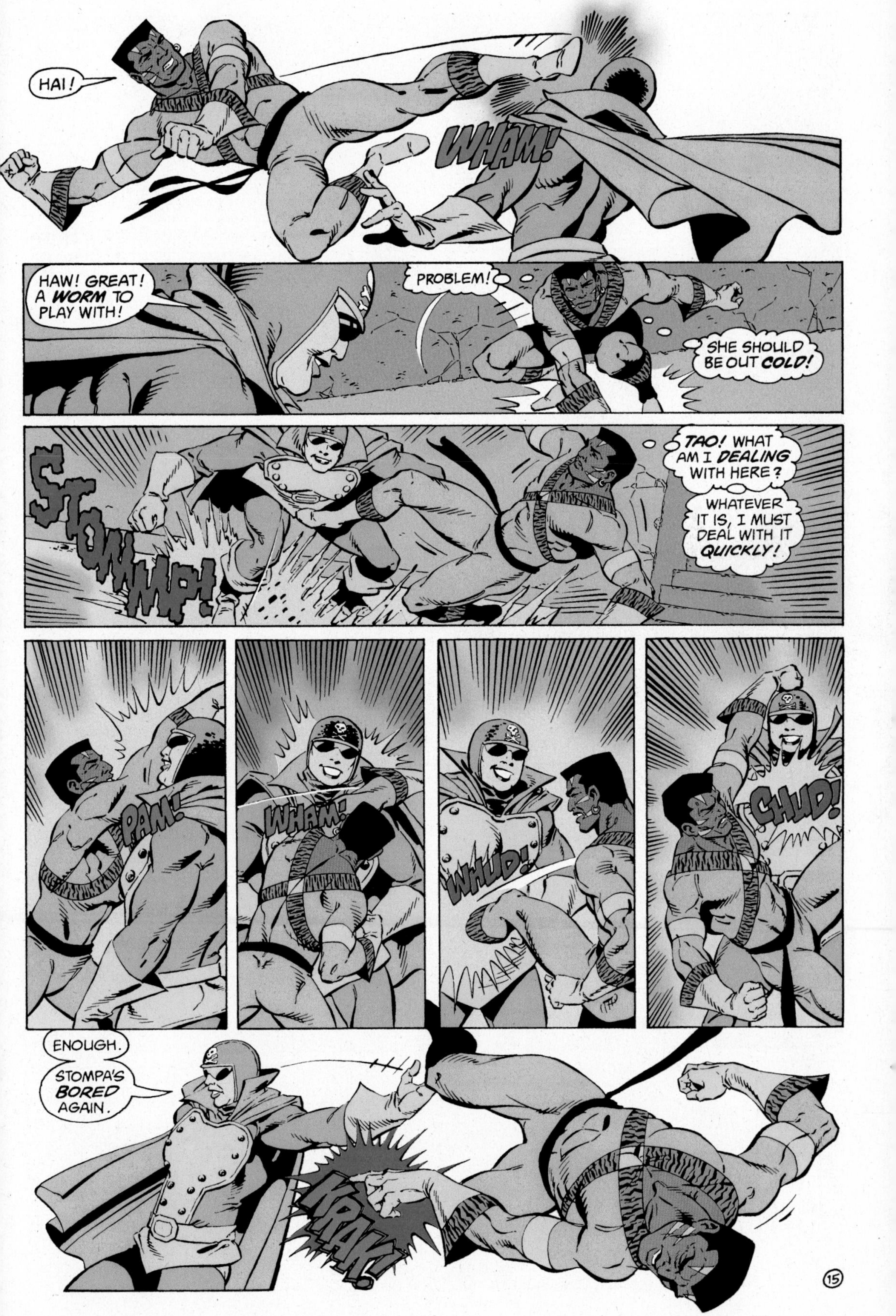
HAI!
WHAM!
HAW! GREAT! A WORM TO PLAY WITH!
PROBLEM!
SHE SHOULD BE OUT COLD!
STOMMMP!
TAO! WHAT AM I DEALING WITH HERE?
WHATEVER IT IS, I MUST DEAL WITH IT QUICKLY!
PAM!
WHAM!
WHUD!
CHUD!
ENOUGH.
STOMPA'S BORED AGAIN.
KRAK!
15

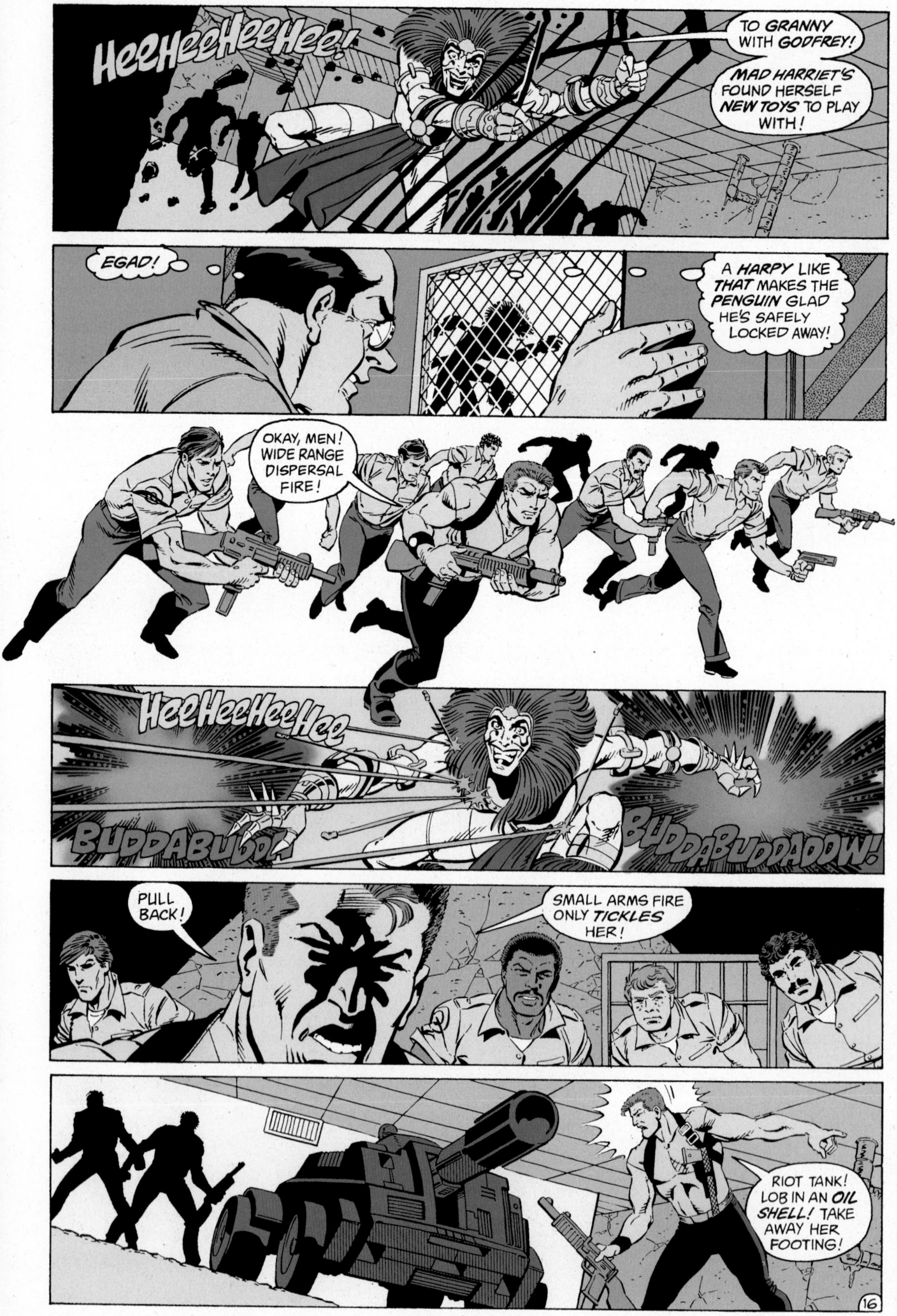
HEEHEEHEEHEE!
TO GRANNY WITH GODFREY!
MAD HARRIET'S FOUND HERSELF NEW TOYS TO PLAY WITH!
EGAD!
A HARPY LIKE THAT MAKES THE PENGUIN GLAD HE'S SAFELY LOCKED AWAY!
OKAY, MEN! WIDE RANGE DISPERSAL FIRE!
HEEHEEHEEHEE
BUDDABUDDA
BUDDABUDDADOW!
PULL BACK!
SMALL ARMS FIRE ONLY TICKLES HER!
RIOT TANK! LOB IN AN OIL SHELL! TAKE AWAY HER FOOTING!
16

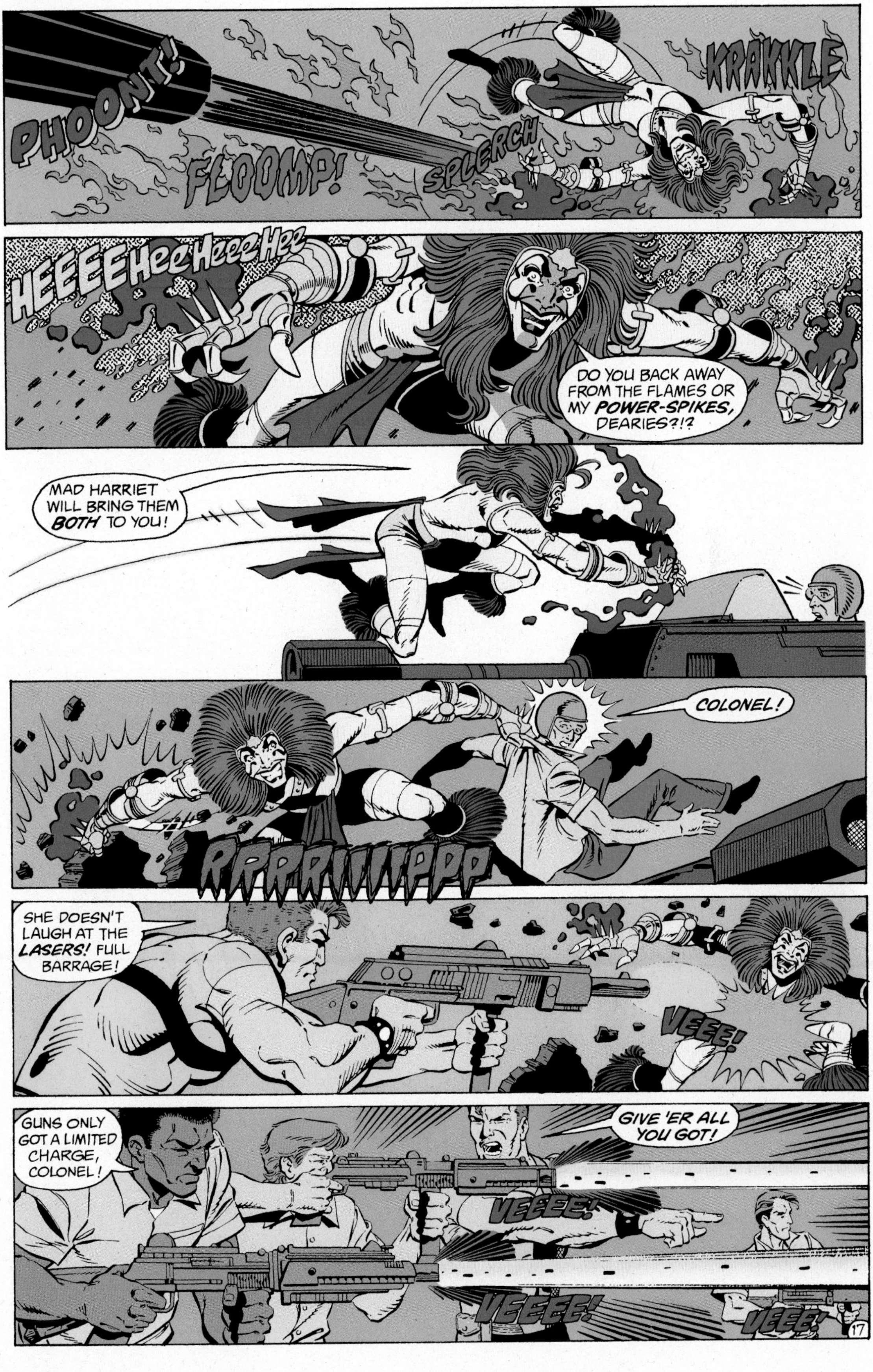
PHOONT!
FLOOMP!
SPLERCH
KRAKKLE
HEEEEHeeHeeeHee
DO YOU BACK AWAY FROM THE FLAMES OR MY POWER-SPIKES, DEARIES?!?
MAD HARRIET WILL BRING THEM BOTH TO YOU!
COLONEL!
RRRRIIIIPPP
SHE DOESN'T LAUGH AT THE LASERS! FULL BARRAGE!
VEEE!
GUNS ONLY GOT A LIMITED CHARGE, COLONEL!
GIVE 'ER ALL YOU GOT!
VEEEE!
VEEEE!
VEEE!
17

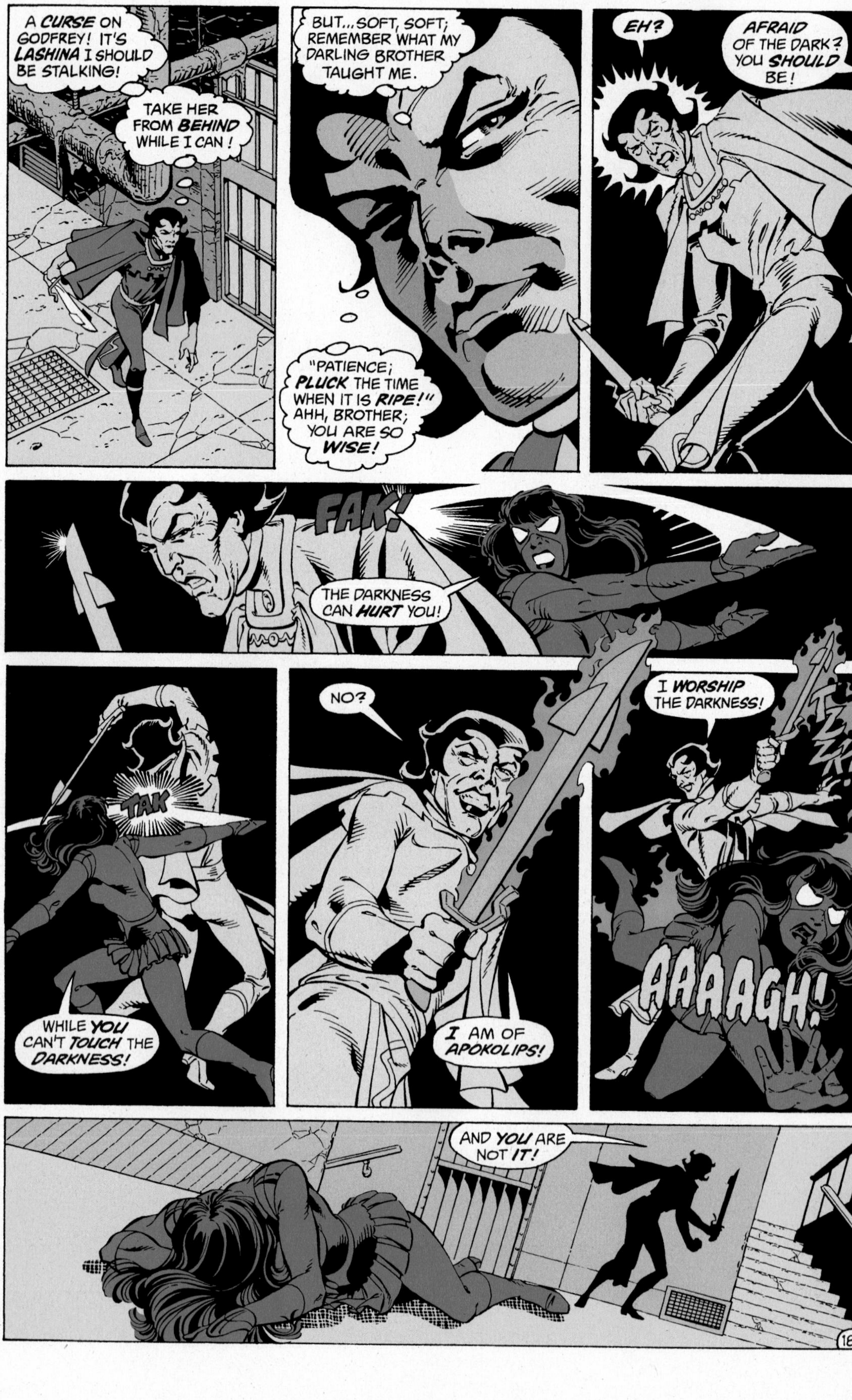
A CURSE ON GODFREY! IT'S LASHINA I SHOULD BE STALKING!
TAKE HER FROM BEHIND WHILE I CAN!
BUT... SOFT, SOFT; REMEMBER WHAT MY DARLING BROTHER TAUGHT ME.
"PATIENCE; PLUCK THE TIME WHEN IT IS RIPE!" AHH, BROTHER; YOU ARE SO WISE!
EH?
AFRAID OF THE DARK? YOU SHOULD BE!
FAK!
THE DARKNESS CAN HURT YOU!
TAK
WHILE YOU CAN'T TOUCH THE DARKNESS!
NO?
I AM OF APOKOLIPS!
I WORSHIP THE DARKNESS!
AAAAGH!
AND YOU ARE NOT IT!
18

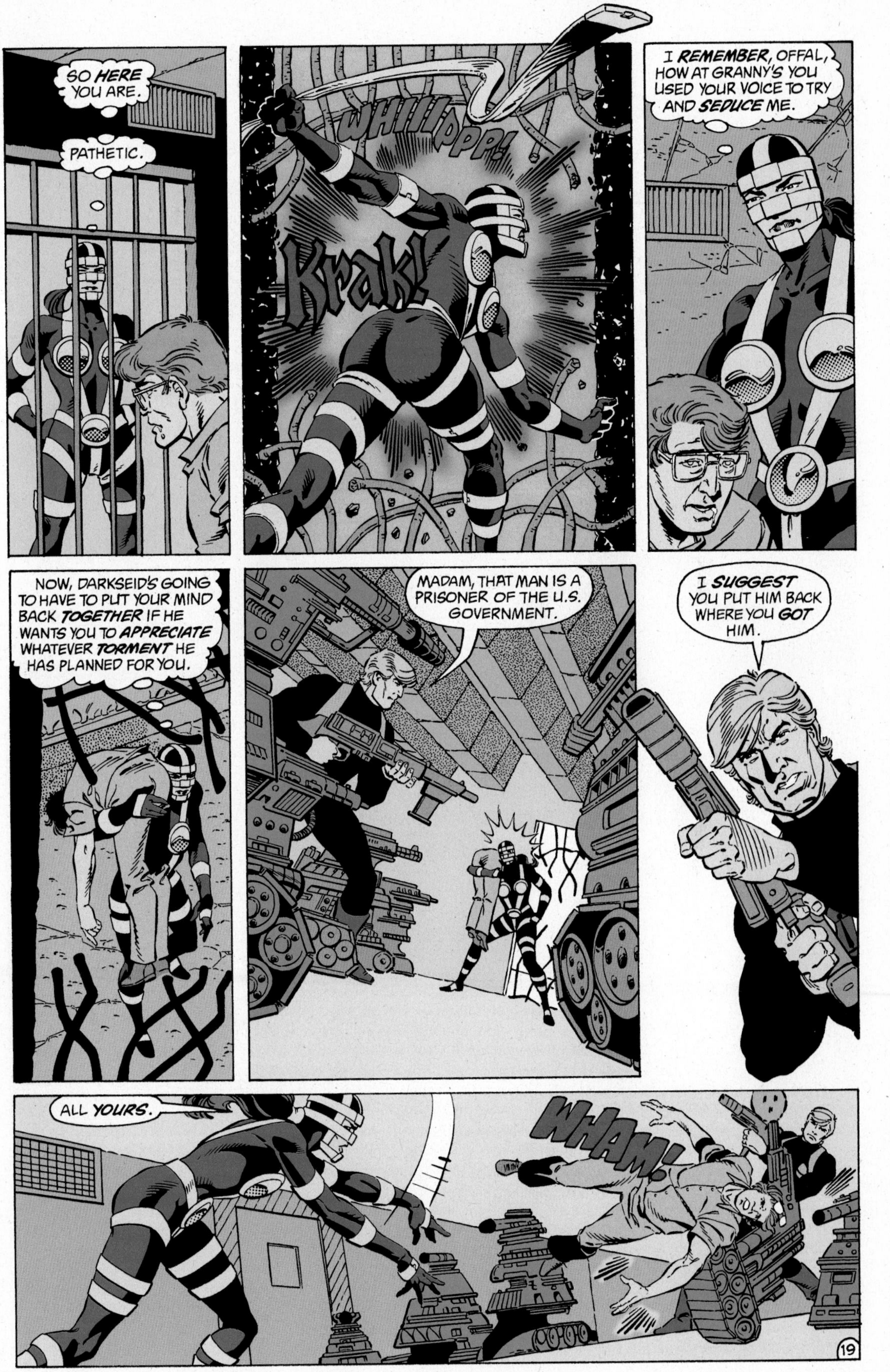
SO HERE YOU ARE.
PATHETIC.
WHIIIIPPP!
KRAK!
I REMEMBER, OFFAL, HOW AT GRANNY'S YOU USED YOUR VOICE TO TRY AND SEDUCE ME.
NOW, DARKSEID'S GOING TO HAVE TO PUT YOUR MIND BACK TOGETHER IF HE WANTS YOU TO APPRECIATE WHATEVER TORMENT HE HAS PLANNED FOR YOU.
MADAM, THAT MAN IS A PRISONER OF THE U.S. GOVERNMENT.
I SUGGEST YOU PUT HIM BACK WHERE YOU GOT HIM.
ALL YOURS.
WHAM!
19

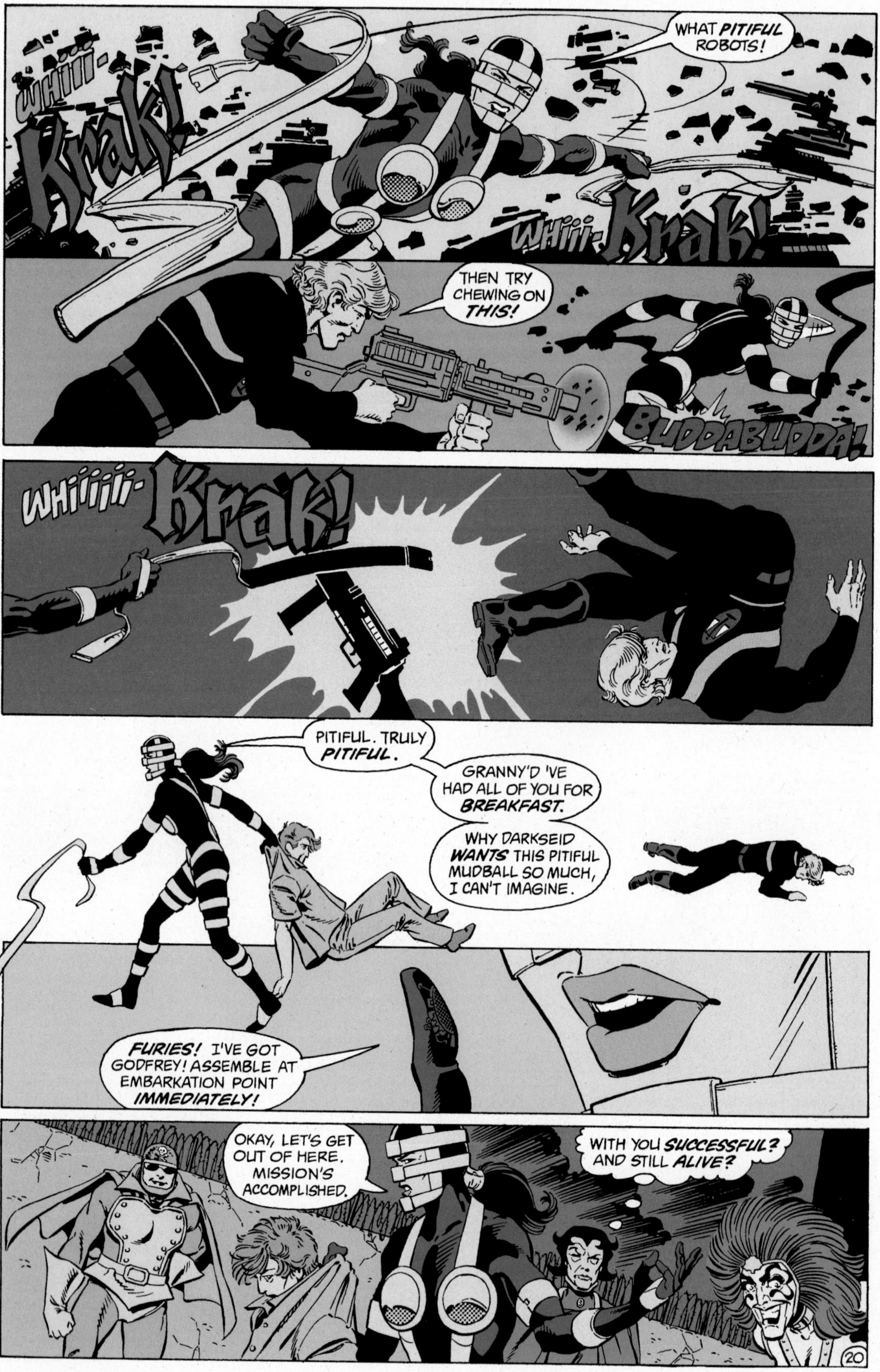
WHIIII-KRAK!
WHAT PITIFUL ROBOTS!
WHIIII-KRAK!
THEN TRY CHEWING ON THIS!
BUDDABUDDA!
WHIIIIII-KRAK!
PITIFUL. TRULY PITIFUL.
GRANNY'D 'VE HAD ALL OF YOU FOR BREAKFAST.
WHY DARKSEID WANTS THIS PITIFUL MUDBALL SO MUCH, I CAN'T IMAGINE.
FURIES! I'VE GOT GODFREY! ASSEMBLE AT EMBARKATION POINT IMMEDIATELY!
OKAY, LET'S GET OUT OF HERE. MISSION'S ACCOMPLISHED.
WITH YOU SUCCESSFUL? AND STILL ALIVE?
20

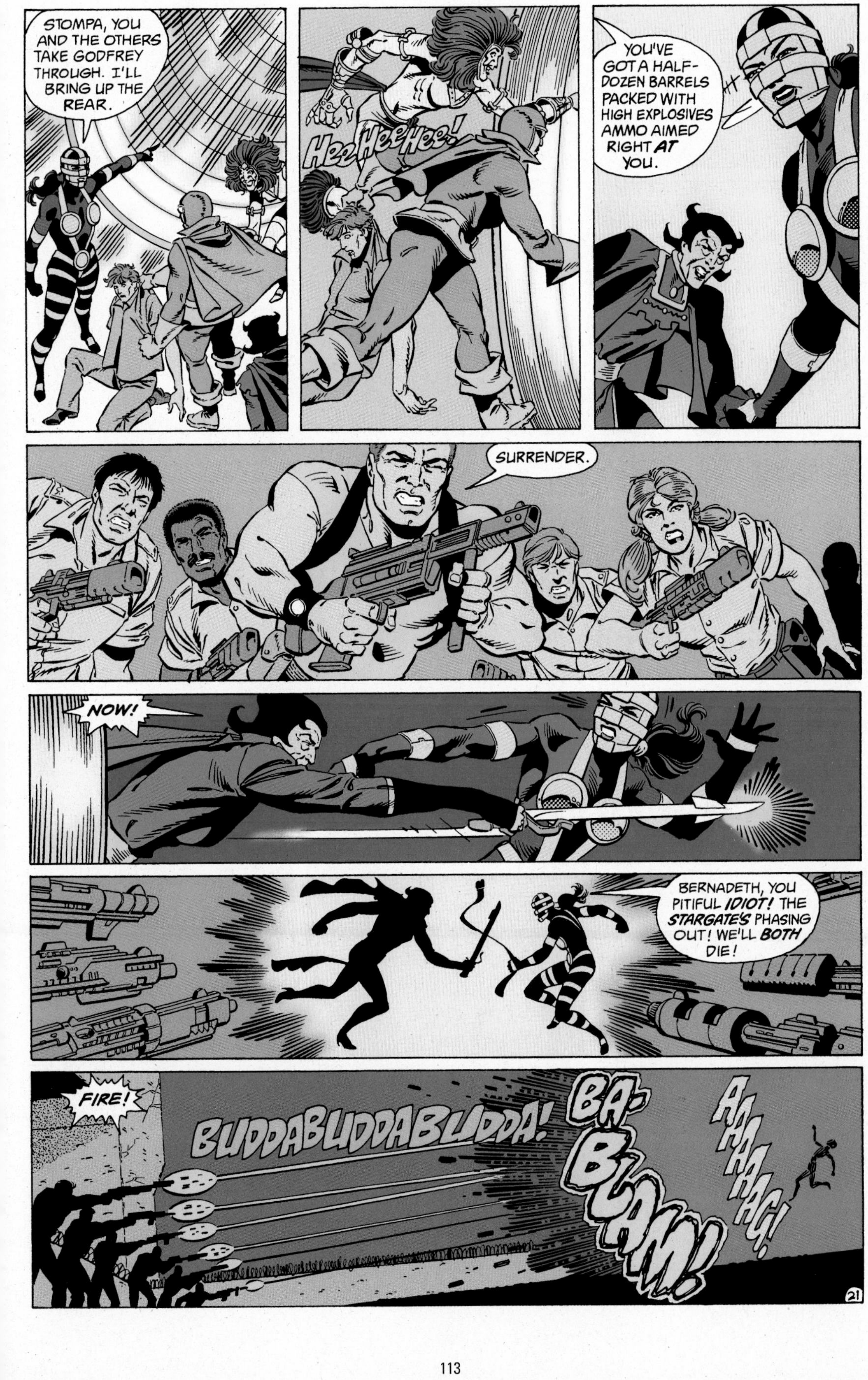
STOMPA, YOU AND THE OTHERS TAKE GODFREY THROUGH. I'LL BRING UP THE REAR.
HEE HEE HEE!
YOU'VE GOT A HALF-DOZEN BARRELS PACKED WITH HIGH EXPLOSIVES AMMO AIMED RIGHT *AT* YOU.
SURRENDER.
NOW!
BERNADETH, YOU PITIFUL *IDIOT!* THE *STARGATE'S* PHASING OUT! WE'LL *BOTH* DIE!
FIRE!
BUDDABUDDABUDDA!
BA-BLAM!
AAAAAG!
21

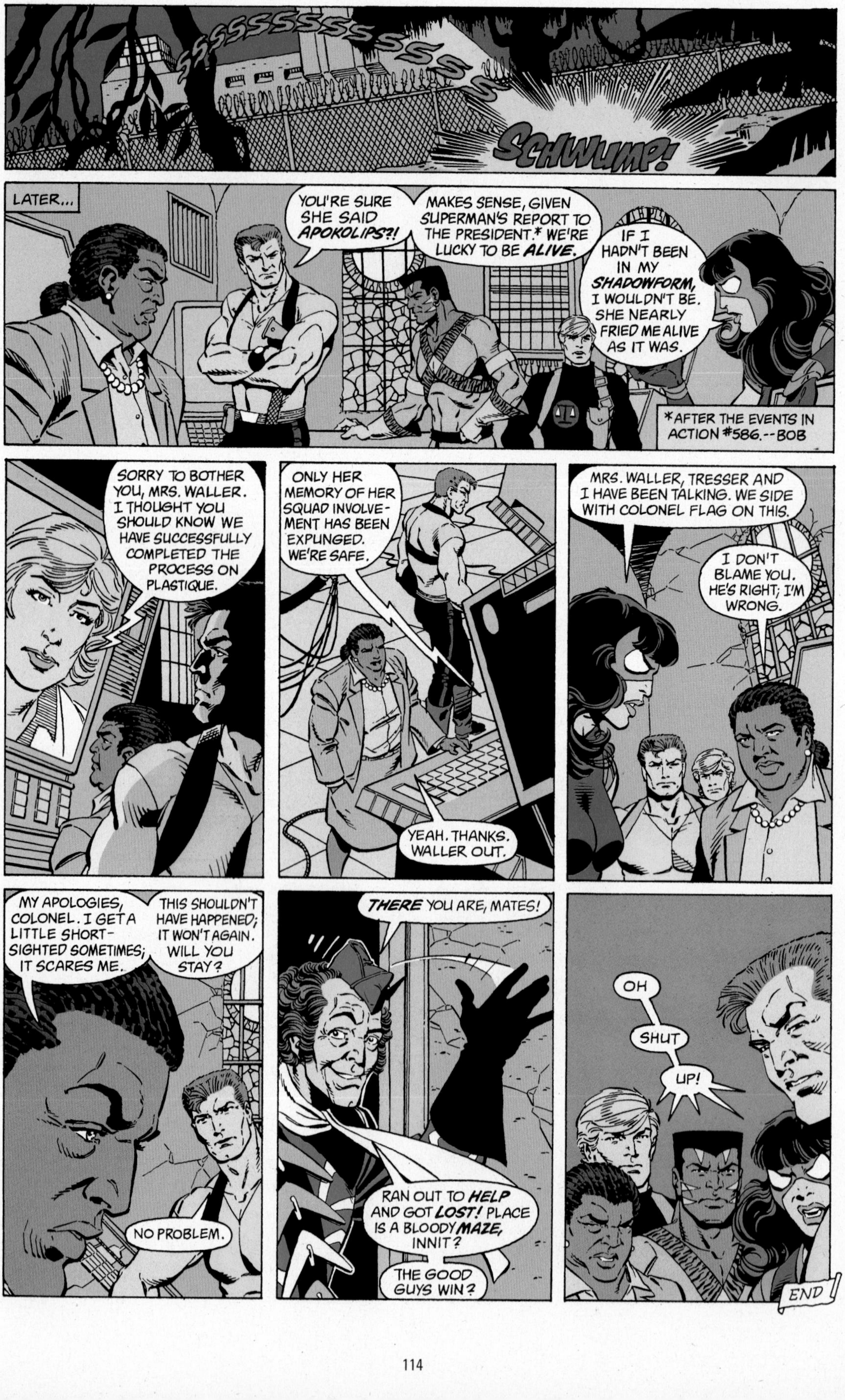
SSSSSSSSSSSSSSSSS
SCHWUMP!
LATER...
YOU'RE SURE SHE SAID APOKOLIPS?!
MAKES SENSE, GIVEN SUPERMAN'S REPORT TO THE PRESIDENT.* WE'RE LUCKY TO BE ALIVE.
IF I HADN'T BEEN IN MY SHADOWFORM, I WOULDN'T BE. SHE NEARLY FRIED ME ALIVE AS IT WAS.
*AFTER THE EVENTS IN ACTION #586.--BOB
SORRY TO BOTHER YOU, MRS. WALLER. I THOUGHT YOU SHOULD KNOW WE HAVE SUCCESSFULLY COMPLETED THE PROCESS ON PLASTIQUE.
ONLY HER MEMORY OF HER SQUAD INVOLVE-MENT HAS BEEN EXPUNGED. WE'RE SAFE.
YEAH. THANKS. WALLER OUT.
MRS. WALLER, TRESSER AND I HAVE BEEN TALKING. WE SIDE WITH COLONEL FLAG ON THIS.
I DON'T BLAME YOU. HE'S RIGHT; I'M WRONG.
MY APOLOGIES, COLONEL. I GET A LITTLE SHORT-SIGHTED SOMETIMES; IT SCARES ME.
THIS SHOULDN'T HAVE HAPPENED; IT WON'T AGAIN. WILL YOU STAY?
NO PROBLEM.
THERE YOU ARE, MATES!
RAN OUT TO HELP AND GOT LOST! PLACE IS A BLOODY MAZE, INNIT?
THE GOOD GUYS WIN?
OH
SHUT
UP!
END

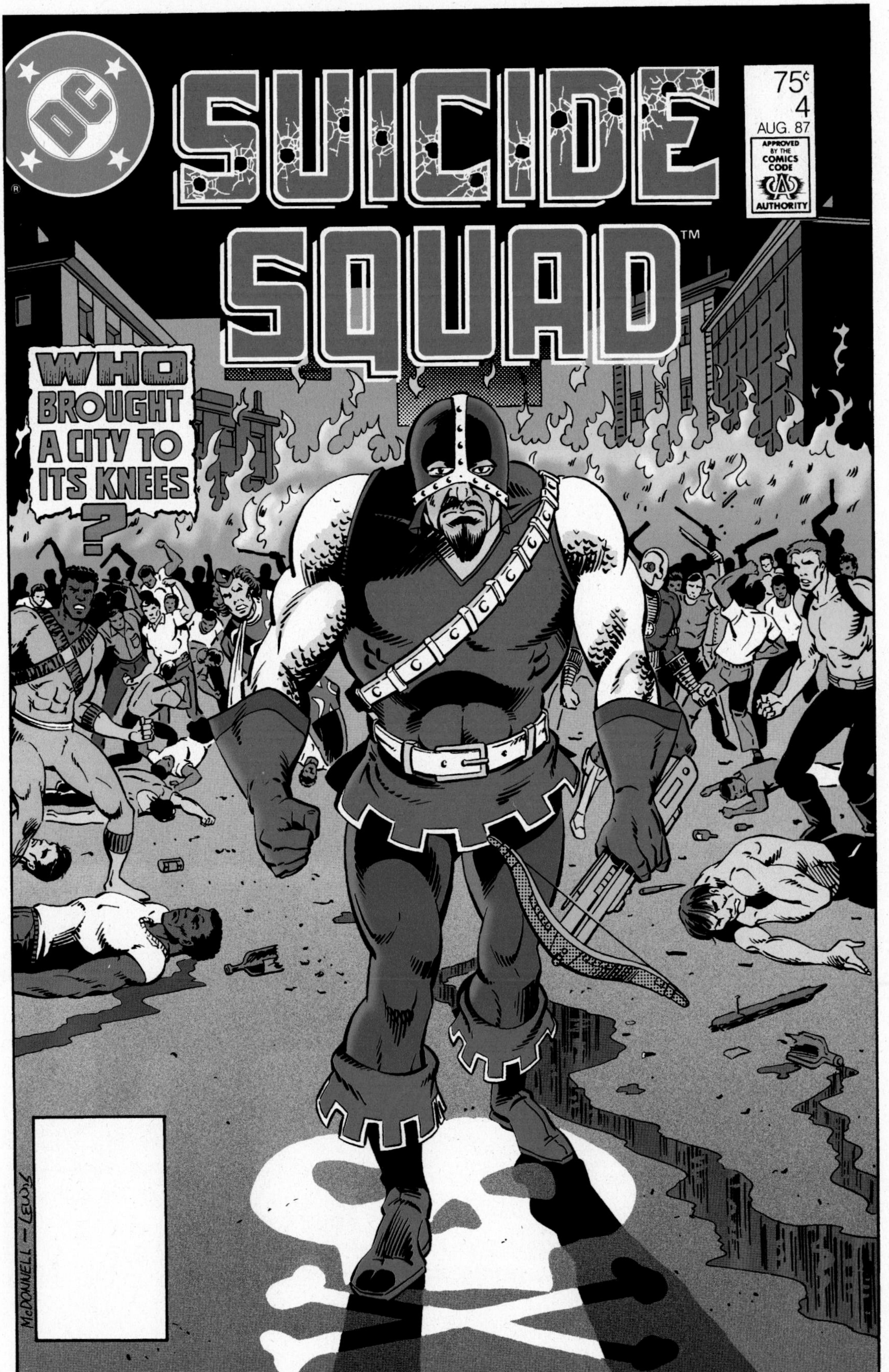
SUICIDE SQUAD™
75¢
4
AUG. 87
APPROVED BY THE COMICS CODE AUTHORITY
WHO BROUGHT A CITY TO ITS KNEES ?
McDONNELL - LEWIS

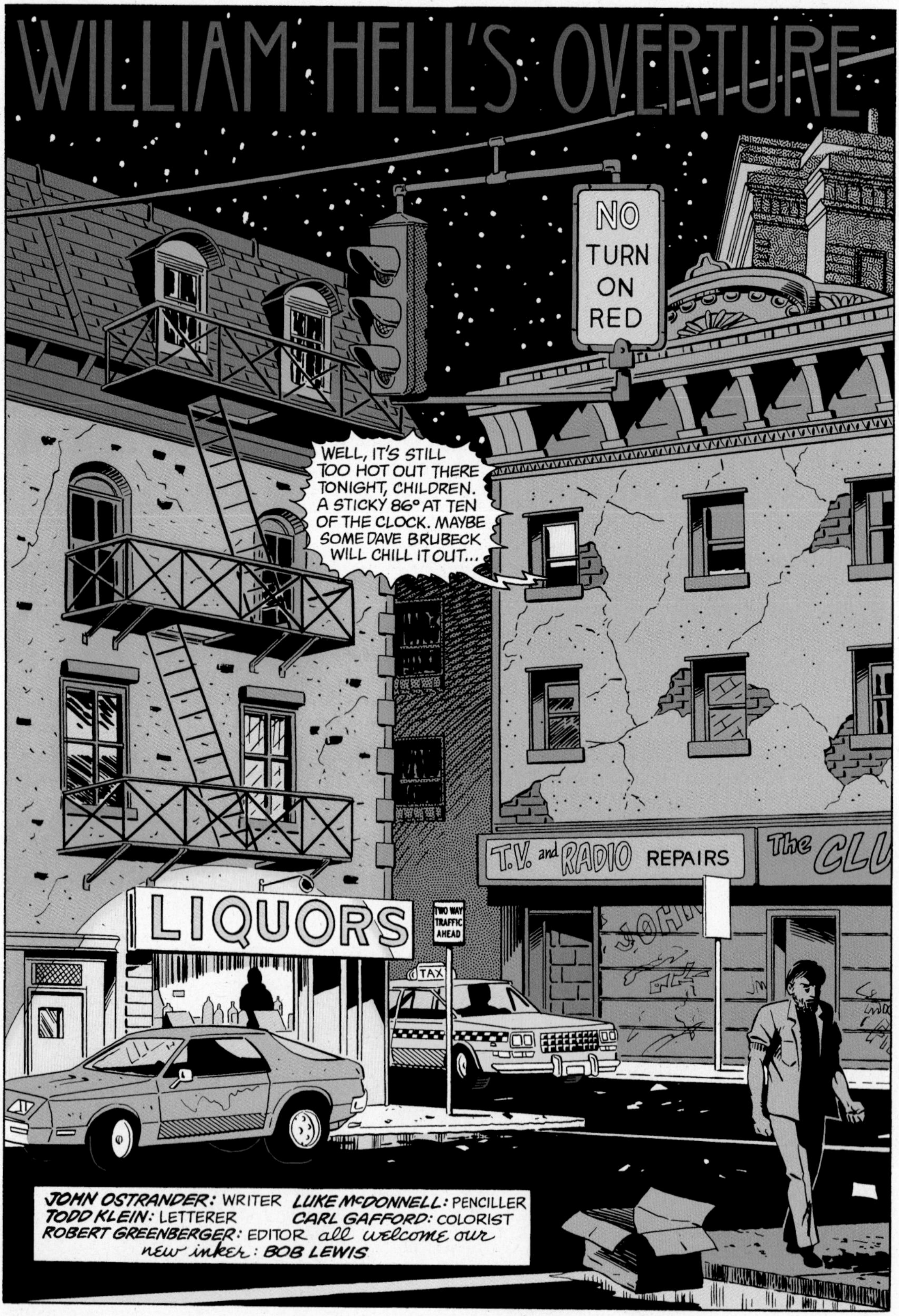

WILLIAM HELL'S OVERTURE
NO TURN ON RED
WELL, IT'S STILL TOO HOT OUT THERE TONIGHT, CHILDREN. A STICKY 86° AT TEN OF THE CLOCK. MAYBE SOME DAVE BRUBECK WILL CHILL IT OUT...
T.V. and RADIO REPAIRS
LIQUORS
TWO WAY TRAFFIC AHEAD
TAXI
JOHN OSTRANDER: WRITER LUKE McDONNELL: PENCILLER
TODD KLEIN: LETTERER CARL GAFFORD: COLORIST
ROBERT GREENBERGER: EDITOR all welcome our new inker: BOB LEWIS

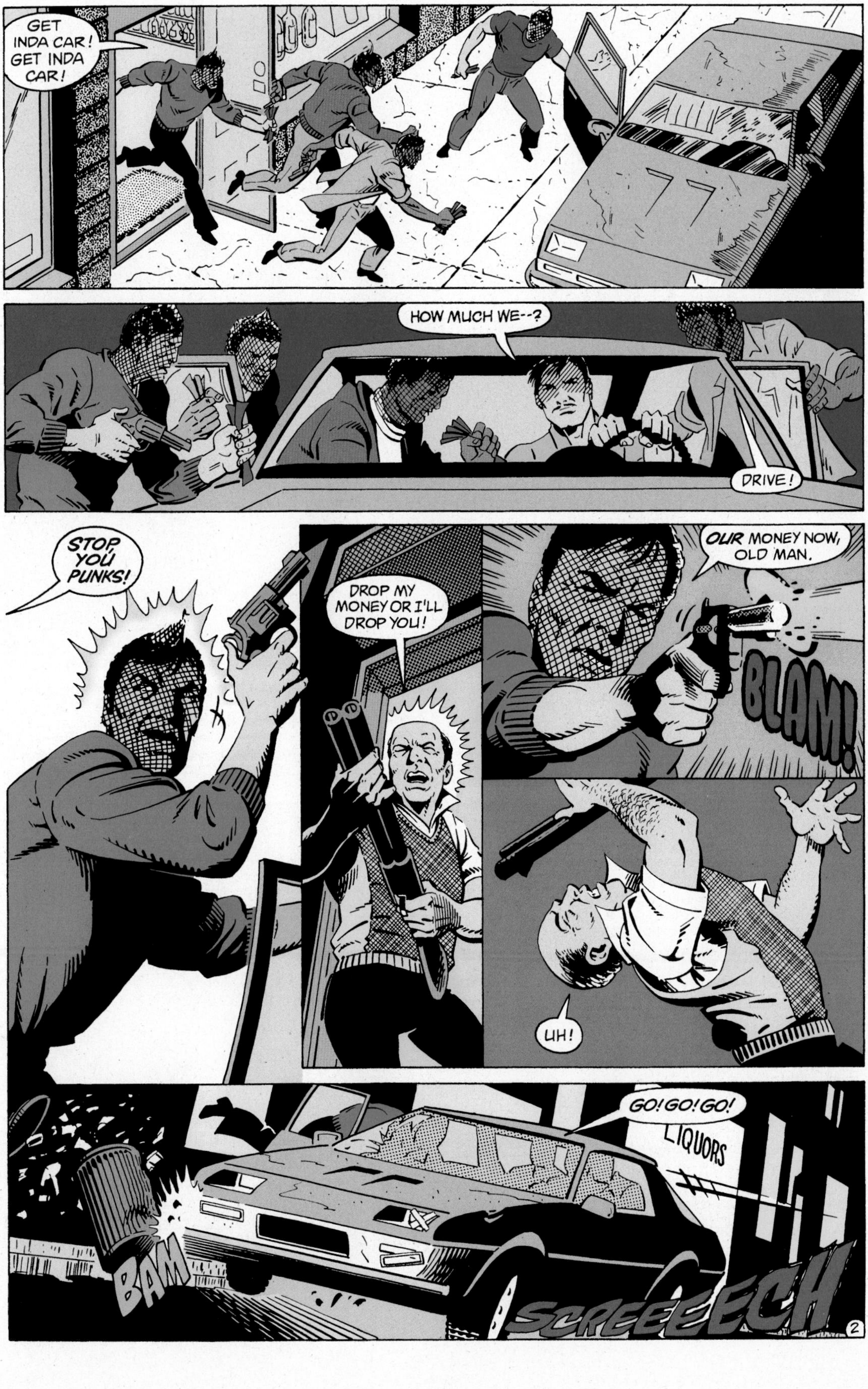
GET INDA CAR! GET INDA CAR!
HOW MUCH WE--?
DRIVE!
STOP YOU PUNKS!
DROP MY MONEY OR I'LL DROP YOU!
OUR MONEY NOW, OLD MAN.
BLAM!
UH!
GO! GO! GO!
LIQUORS
BAM
SCREEEEECH
2

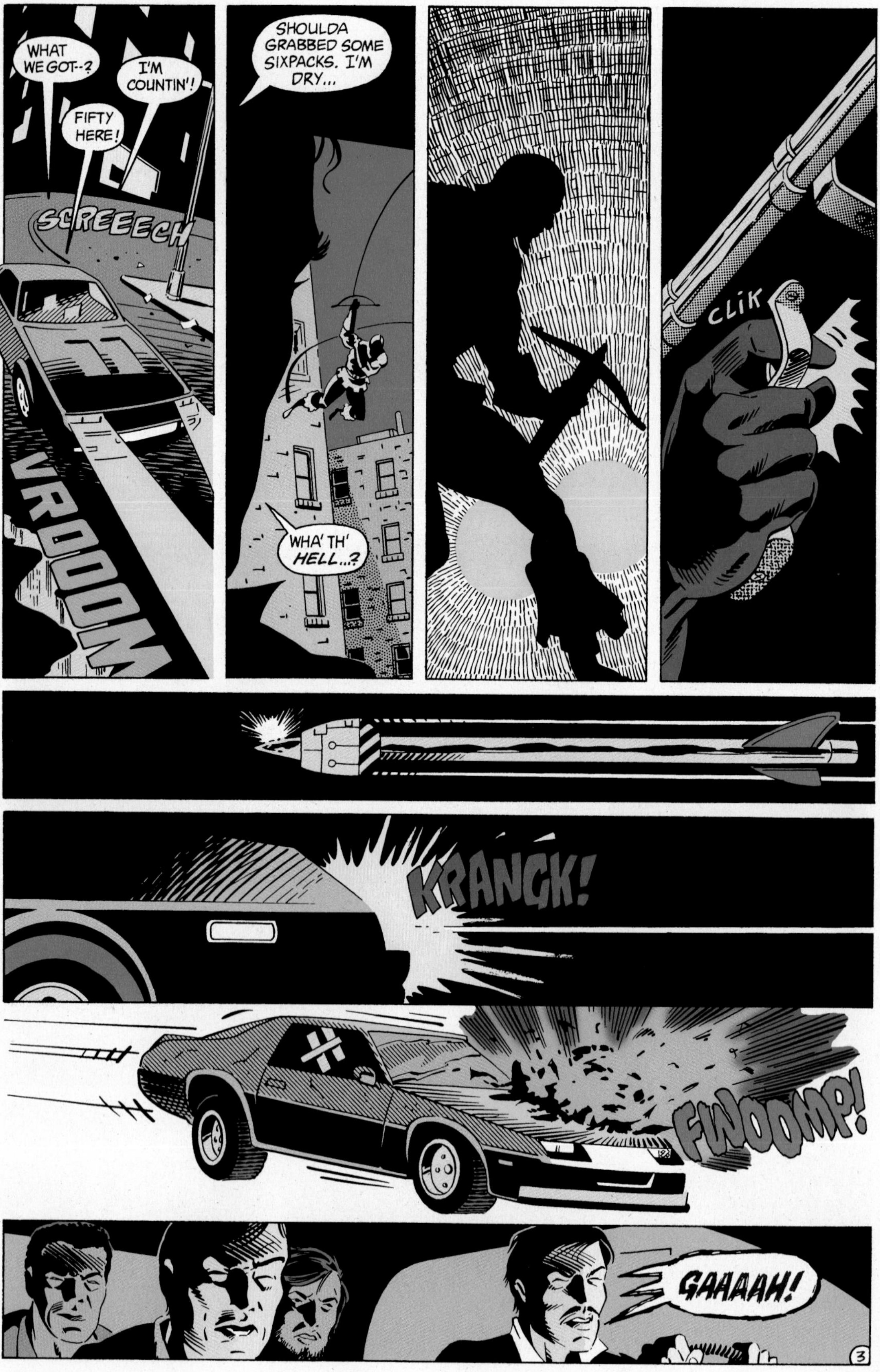
WHAT WE GOT--?
I'M COUNTIN'!
FIFTY HERE!
SCREEECH
VROOOM
SHOULDA GRABBED SOME SIXPACKS. I'M DRY...
WHA' TH' HELL...?
CLIK
KRANGK!
FWOOMP!
GAAAAH!
3

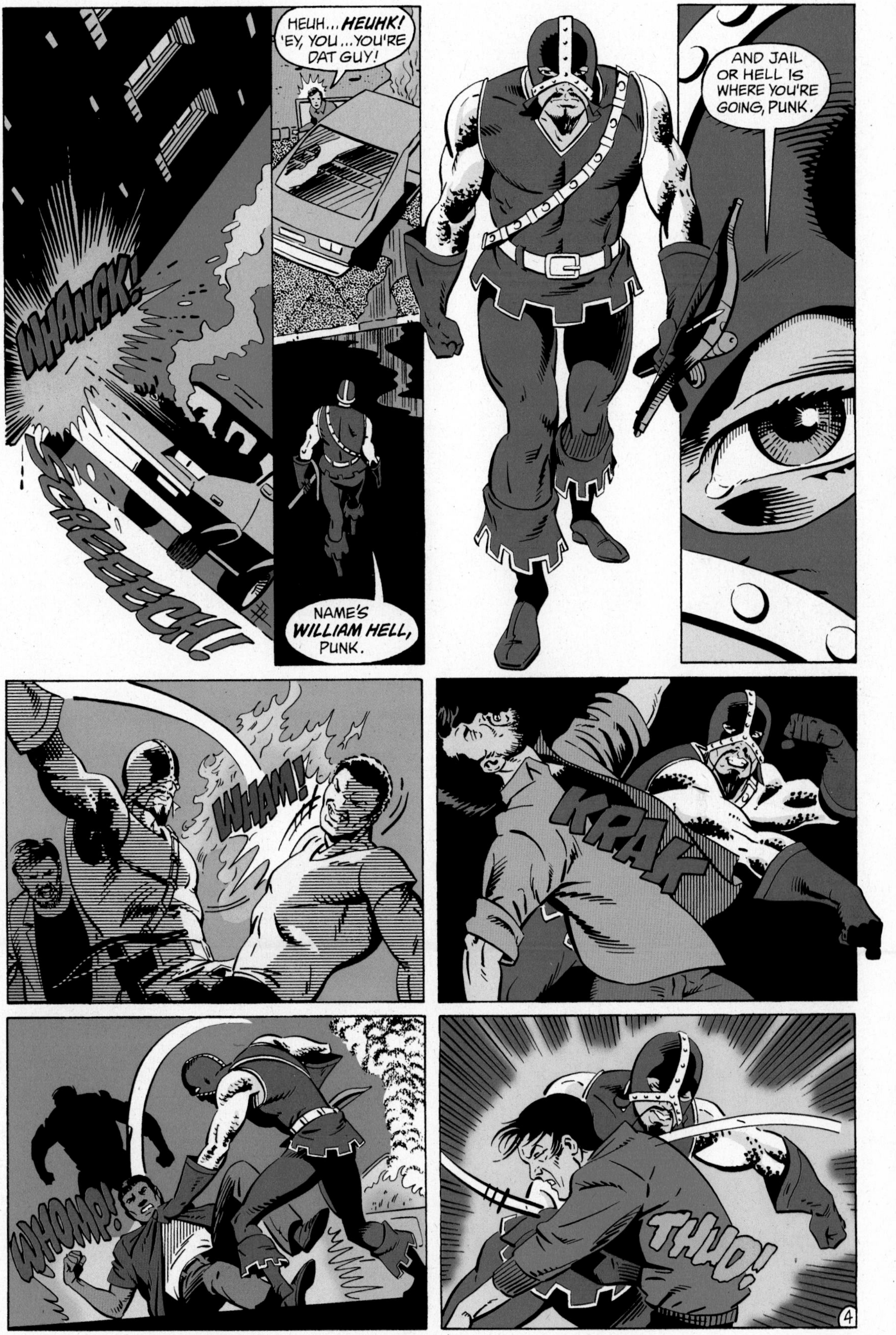
WHANGK!
SCREEECH!
HEUH... HEUHK! 'EY, YOU... YOU'RE DAT GUY!
NAME'S WILLIAM HELL, PUNK.
AND JAIL OR HELL IS WHERE YOU'RE GOING, PUNK.
WHAM!
KRAK
WHOMP!
THUD!
4

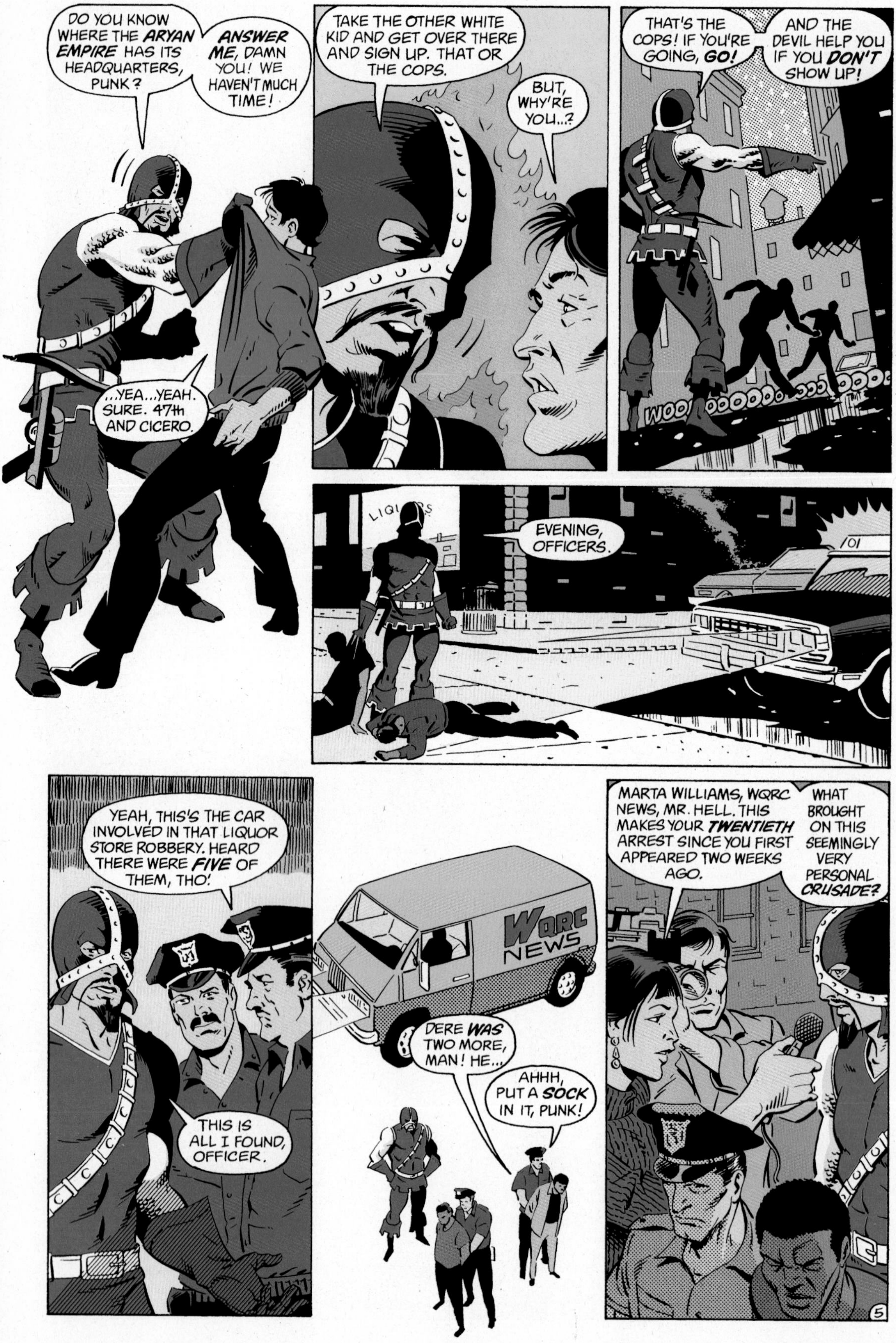
DO YOU KNOW WHERE THE ARYAN EMPIRE HAS ITS HEADQUARTERS, PUNK?
ANSWER ME, DAMN YOU! WE HAVEN'T MUCH TIME!
...YEA...YEAH. SURE. 47th AND CICERO.
TAKE THE OTHER WHITE KID AND GET OVER THERE AND SIGN UP. THAT OR THE COPS.
BUT, WHY'RE YOU...?
THAT'S THE COPS! IF YOU'RE GOING, GO!
AND THE DEVIL HELP YOU IF YOU DON'T SHOW UP!
WOOOOOOOOOOOO
LIQUORS
EVENING, OFFICERS.
101
YEAH, THIS'S THE CAR INVOLVED IN THAT LIQUOR STORE ROBBERY. HEARD THERE WERE FIVE OF THEM, THO!
THIS IS ALL I FOUND, OFFICER.
WQRC NEWS
DERE WAS TWO MORE, MAN! HE...
AHHH, PUT A SOCK IN IT, PUNK!
MARTA WILLIAMS, WQRC NEWS, MR. HELL. THIS MAKES YOUR TWENTIETH ARREST SINCE YOU FIRST APPEARED TWO WEEKS AGO.
WHAT BROUGHT ON THIS SEEMINGLY VERY PERSONAL CRUSADE?
5

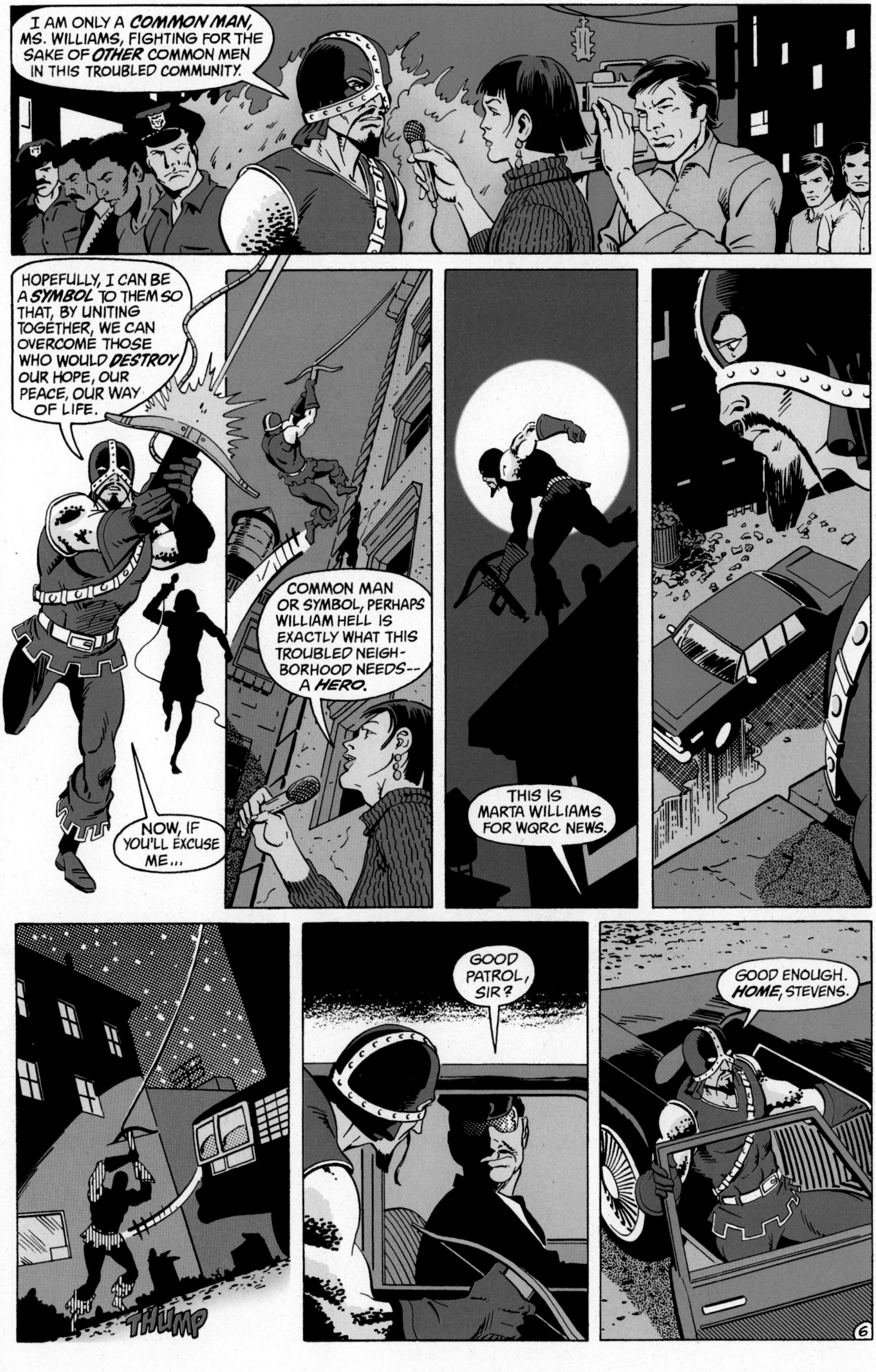

I AM ONLY A COMMON MAN, MS. WILLIAMS, FIGHTING FOR THE SAKE OF OTHER COMMON MEN IN THIS TROUBLED COMMUNITY.
HOPEFULLY, I CAN BE A SYMBOL TO THEM SO THAT, BY UNITING TOGETHER, WE CAN OVERCOME THOSE WHO WOULD DESTROY OUR HOPE, OUR PEACE, OUR WAY OF LIFE.
NOW, IF YOU'LL EXCUSE ME...
COMMON MAN OR SYMBOL, PERHAPS WILLIAM HELL IS EXACTLY WHAT THIS TROUBLED NEIGH-BORHOOD NEEDS-- A HERO.
THIS IS MARTA WILLIAMS FOR WQRC NEWS.
THUMP
GOOD PATROL, SIR?
GOOD ENOUGH. HOME, STEVENS.
6

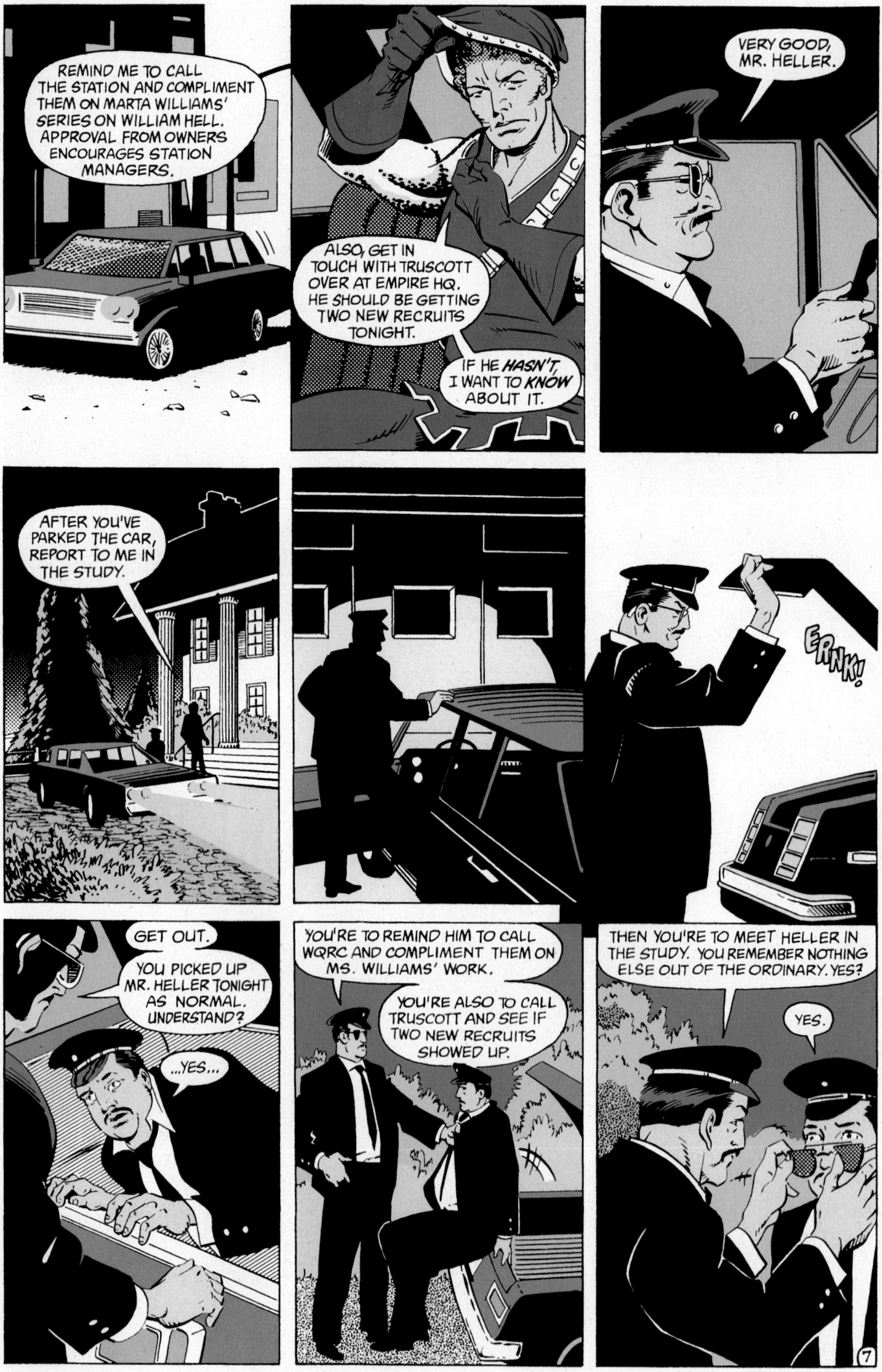
REMIND ME TO CALL THE STATION AND COMPLIMENT THEM ON MARTA WILLIAMS' SERIES ON WILLIAM HELL. APPROVAL FROM OWNERS ENCOURAGES STATION MANAGERS.
ALSO, GET IN TOUCH WITH TRUSCOTT OVER AT EMPIRE HQ. HE SHOULD BE GETTING TWO NEW RECRUITS TONIGHT.
IF HE HASN'T, I WANT TO KNOW ABOUT IT.
VERY GOOD, MR. HELLER.
AFTER YOU'VE PARKED THE CAR, REPORT TO ME IN THE STUDY.
ERNK!
GET OUT.
YOU PICKED UP MR. HELLER TONIGHT AS NORMAL. UNDERSTAND?
...YES...
YOU'RE TO REMIND HIM TO CALL WQRC AND COMPLIMENT THEM ON MS. WILLIAMS' WORK.
YOU'RE ALSO TO CALL TRUSCOTT AND SEE IF TWO NEW RECRUITS SHOWED UP.
THEN YOU'RE TO MEET HELLER IN THE STUDY. YOU REMEMBER NOTHING ELSE OUT OF THE ORDINARY. YES?
YES.
7

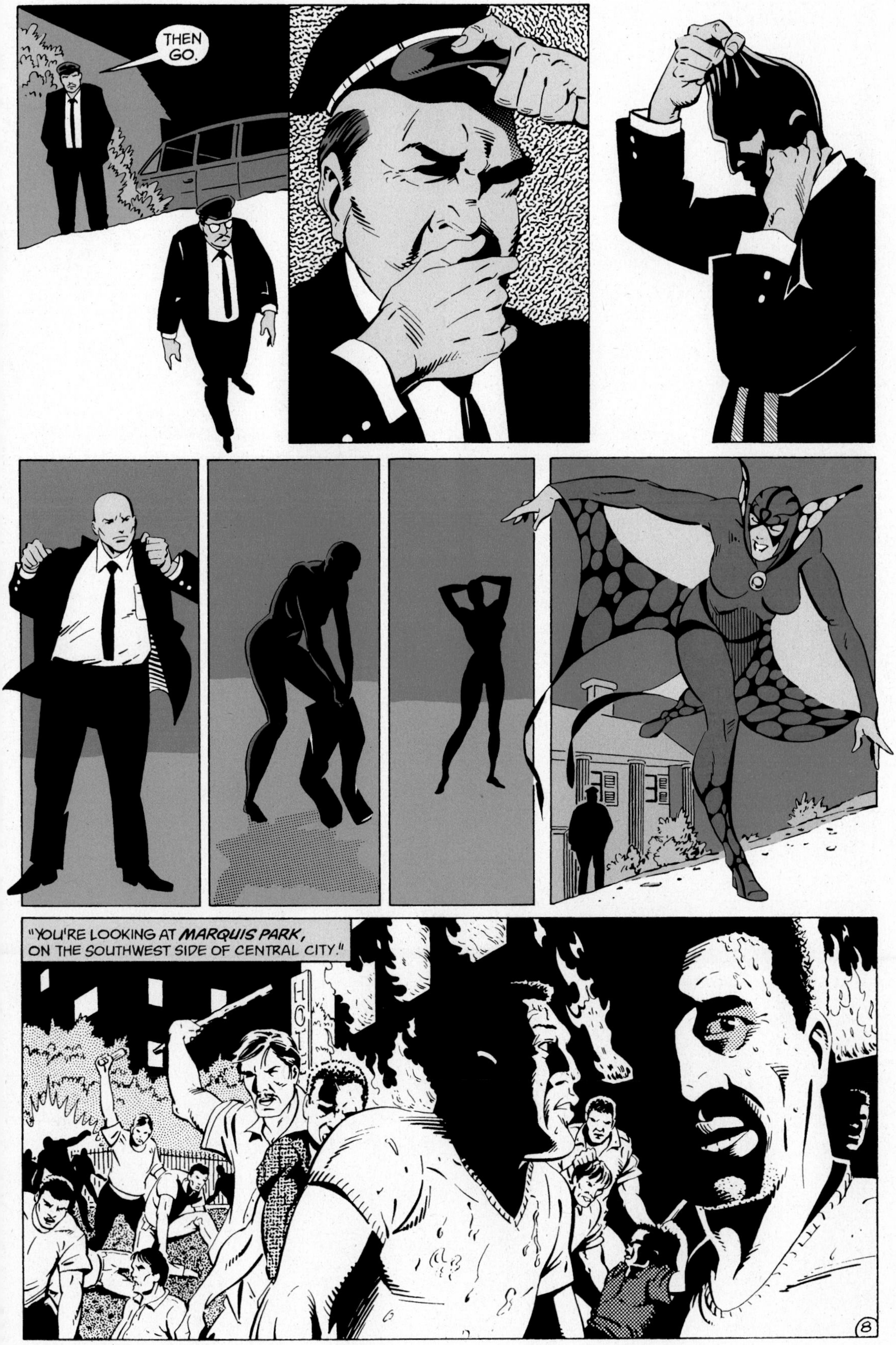
THEN GO.
"YOU'RE LOOKING AT MARQUIS PARK, ON THE SOUTHWEST SIDE OF CENTRAL CITY."
HOT
8

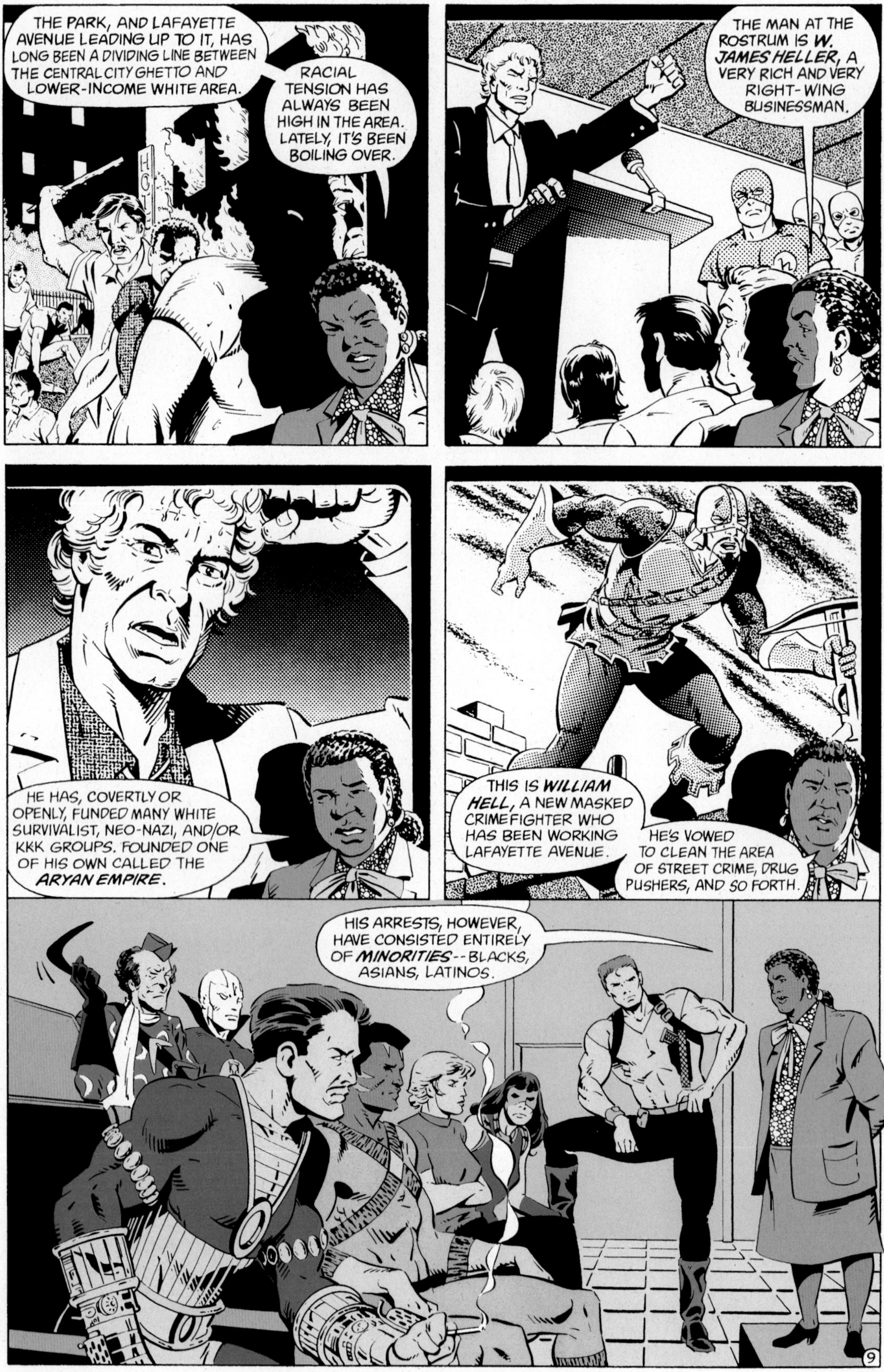
THE PARK, AND LAFAYETTE AVENUE LEADING UP TO IT, HAS LONG BEEN A DIVIDING LINE BETWEEN THE CENTRAL CITY GHETTO AND LOWER-INCOME WHITE AREA.
RACIAL TENSION HAS ALWAYS BEEN HIGH IN THE AREA. LATELY, IT'S BEEN BOILING OVER.
HOT
THE MAN AT THE ROSTRUM IS W. JAMES HELLER, A VERY RICH AND VERY RIGHT-WING BUSINESSMAN.
HE HAS, COVERTLY OR OPENLY, FUNDED MANY WHITE SURVIVALIST, NEO-NAZI, AND/OR KKK GROUPS. FOUNDED ONE OF HIS OWN CALLED THE ARYAN EMPIRE.
THIS IS WILLIAM HELL, A NEW MASKED CRIMEFIGHTER WHO HAS BEEN WORKING LAFAYETTE AVENUE.
HE'S VOWED TO CLEAN THE AREA OF STREET CRIME, DRUG PUSHERS, AND SO FORTH.
HIS ARRESTS, HOWEVER, HAVE CONSISTED ENTIRELY OF MINORITIES--BLACKS, ASIANS, LATINOS.
9

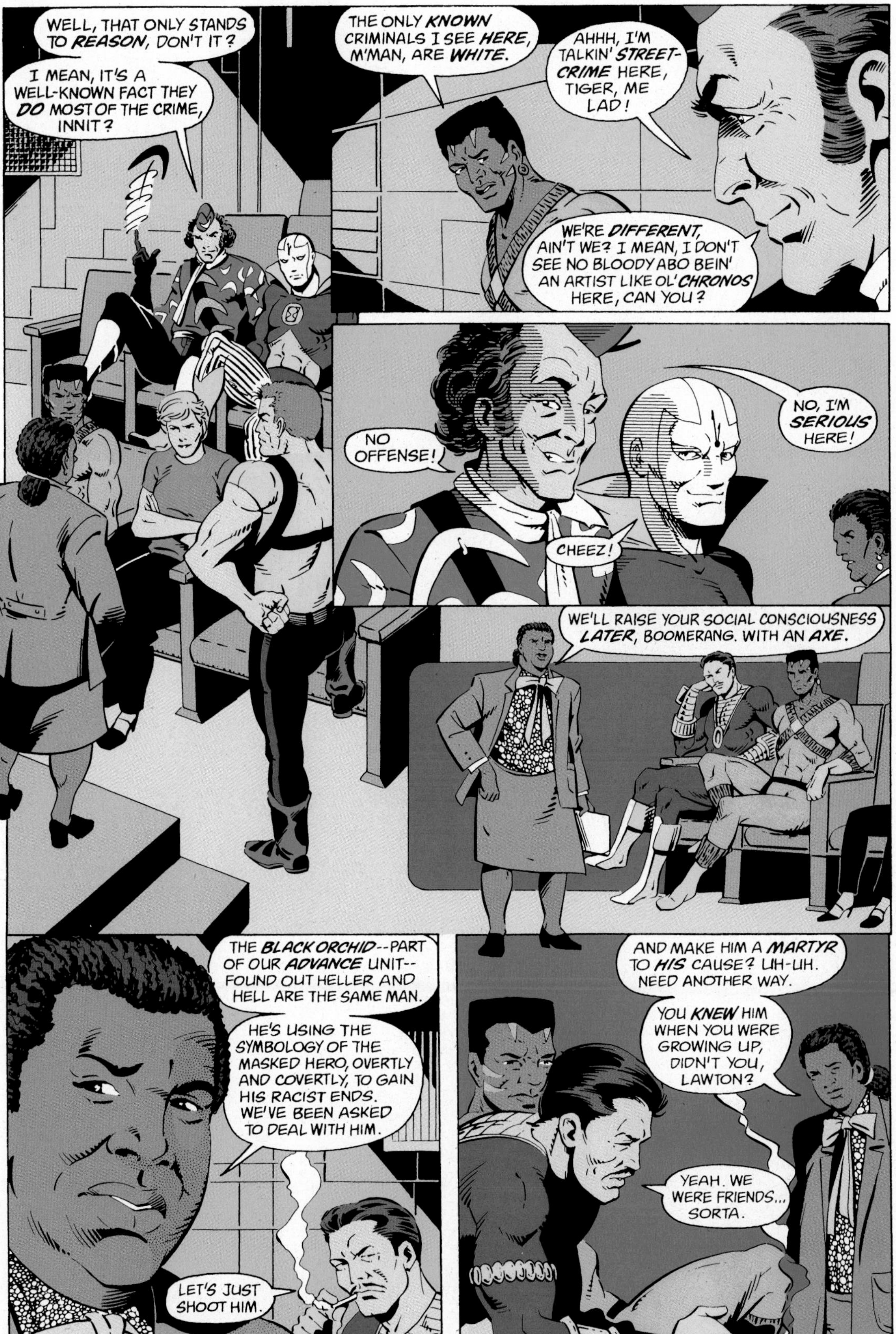
WELL, THAT ONLY STANDS TO REASON, DON'T IT?
I MEAN, IT'S A WELL-KNOWN FACT THEY DO MOST OF THE CRIME, INNIT?
THE ONLY KNOWN CRIMINALS I SEE HERE, M'MAN, ARE WHITE.
AHHH, I'M TALKIN' STREET-CRIME HERE, TIGER, ME LAD!
WE'RE DIFFERENT, AIN'T WE? I MEAN, I DON'T SEE NO BLOODY ABO BEIN' AN ARTIST LIKE OL' CHRONOS HERE, CAN YOU?
NO OFFENSE!
NO, I'M SERIOUS HERE!
CHEEZ!
WE'LL RAISE YOUR SOCIAL CONSCIOUSNESS LATER, BOOMERANG. WITH AN AXE.
THE BLACK ORCHID--PART OF OUR ADVANCE UNIT--FOUND OUT HELLER AND HELL ARE THE SAME MAN.
HE'S USING THE SYMBOLOGY OF THE MASKED HERO, OVERTLY AND COVERTLY, TO GAIN HIS RACIST ENDS. WE'VE BEEN ASKED TO DEAL WITH HIM.
LET'S JUST SHOOT HIM.
AND MAKE HIM A MARTYR TO HIS CAUSE? UH-UH. NEED ANOTHER WAY.
YOU KNEW HIM WHEN YOU WERE GROWING UP, DIDN'T YOU, LAWTON?
YEAH. WE WERE FRIENDS... SORTA.
10

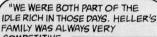

"WE WERE BOTH PART OF THE IDLE RICH IN THOSE DAYS. HELLER'S FAMILY WAS ALWAYS VERY COMPETITIVE.

"ALWAYS HAD TO *WIN*, NO MATTER THE MEANS.

"I COULD GET BEHIND THAT. DAMN FEW OTHERS COULD, THOUGH. WHEN YOU'RE LEFT ALONE PRETTY MUCH YOU TEND TO BECOME A LONER. HE *GOT* WHAT HE *WANTED.*

"ON A FAMILY OUTING, THEY TOOK A WRONG TURN AND RAN INTO A RACE RIOT.

"BILLY'S THE ONLY ONE SURVIVED THE ATTACK.

"JAMES HELLER, THE ELDER, BILLY'S GRANDFATHER, BECAME HIS GUARDIAN. FAMILY ALWAYS *WAS* CONSERVATIVE BUT THE OLD MAN WAS *REACTIONARY.*

"IT WAS THOUGHT HE SOLD STUFF TO THE NAZIS DURING THE WAR BUT NOBODY EVER *PINNED* ANYTHING ON HIM. FOXY OLD BASTARD.

"LOST CONTACT WITH BILL AFTER THIS, THOUGH I *HEARD* THAT WHEN THE OLD MAN DIED HE LEFT ALL HIS HOLDINGS TO BILL. THAT'S ALL I KNOW."

CAN'T JUST DEFEAT OR UNMASK HELLER. GOT TO *DISCREDIT* HIM.

HIS ARYAN EMPIRE'S HOLDING A RALLY IN MARQUIS PARK IN A FEW DAYS. SOME BLACK GROUPS HAVE THREATENED A COUNTER-DEMONSTRATION. PLACE'LL BE A *TINDERBOX.* THAT'S WHEN WE'LL MAKE *OUR* MOVE.

I HELP, IT WORKS, I KEEP MY TRAP SHUT, AND MY SENTENCE IS COMMUTED TO TIME SERVED, RIGHT ?

WHICH IS WHY YOU NEED *ME* AND MY DEVICE.

THAT'S THE *DEAL,* CHRONOS.

NOW, YOU ALL LISTEN *CLOSE.* HERE'S THE *PLAN.*

11

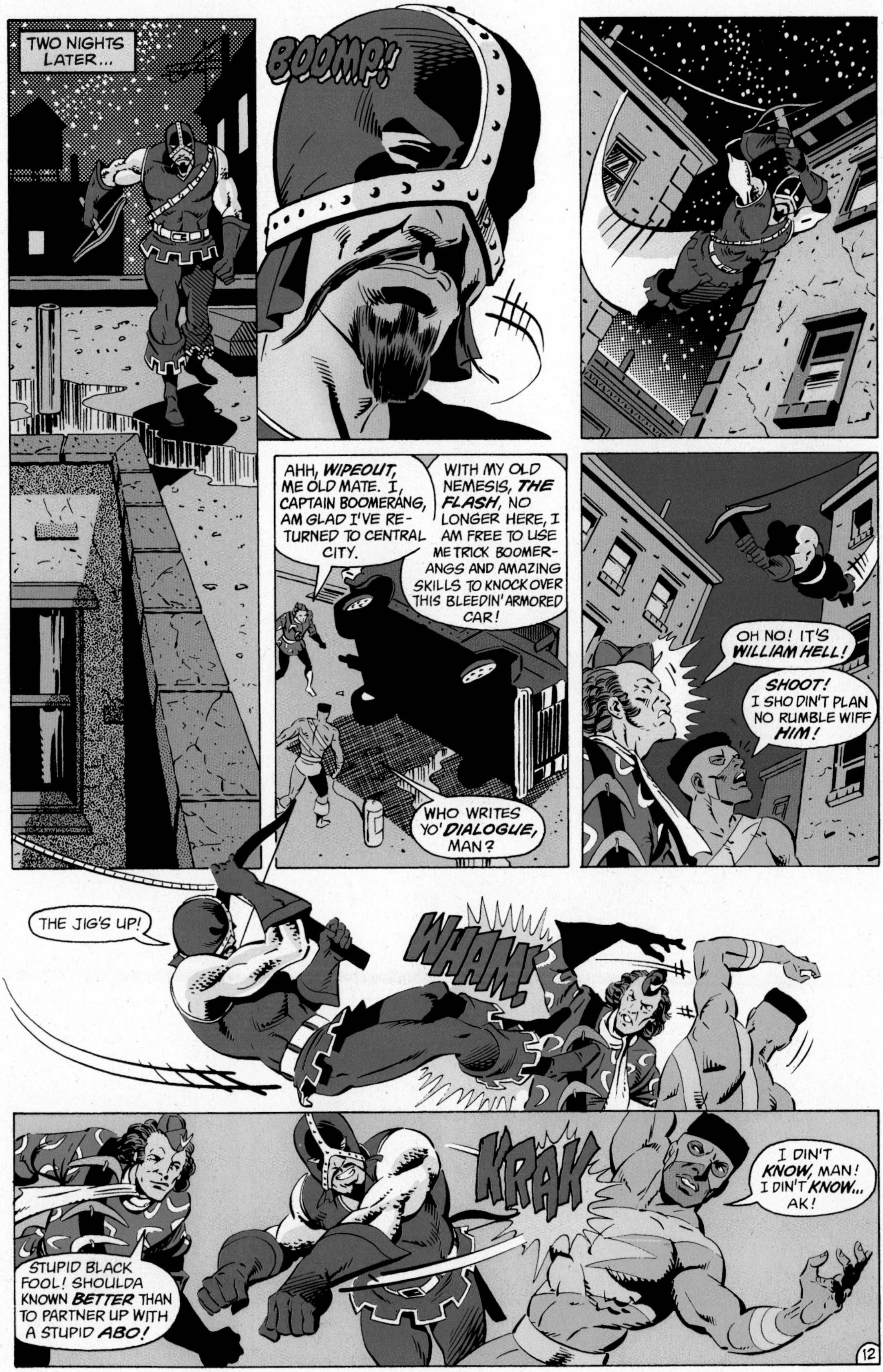
TWO NIGHTS LATER...
BOOMP!
AHH, WIPEOUT, ME OLD MATE. I, CAPTAIN BOOMERANG, AM GLAD I'VE RE-TURNED TO CENTRAL CITY.
WITH MY OLD NEMESIS, THE FLASH, NO LONGER HERE, I AM FREE TO USE ME TRICK BOOMER-ANGS AND AMAZING SKILLS TO KNOCK OVER THIS BLEEDIN' ARMORED CAR!
WHO WRITES YO' DIALOGUE, MAN?
OH NO! IT'S WILLIAM HELL!
SHOOT! I SHO DIN'T PLAN NO RUMBLE WIFF HIM!
THE JIG'S UP!
WHAM!
KRAK
I DIN'T KNOW, MAN! I DIN'T KNOW... AK!
STUPID BLACK FOOL! SHOULDA KNOWN BETTER THAN TO PARTNER UP WITH A STUPID ABO!
12

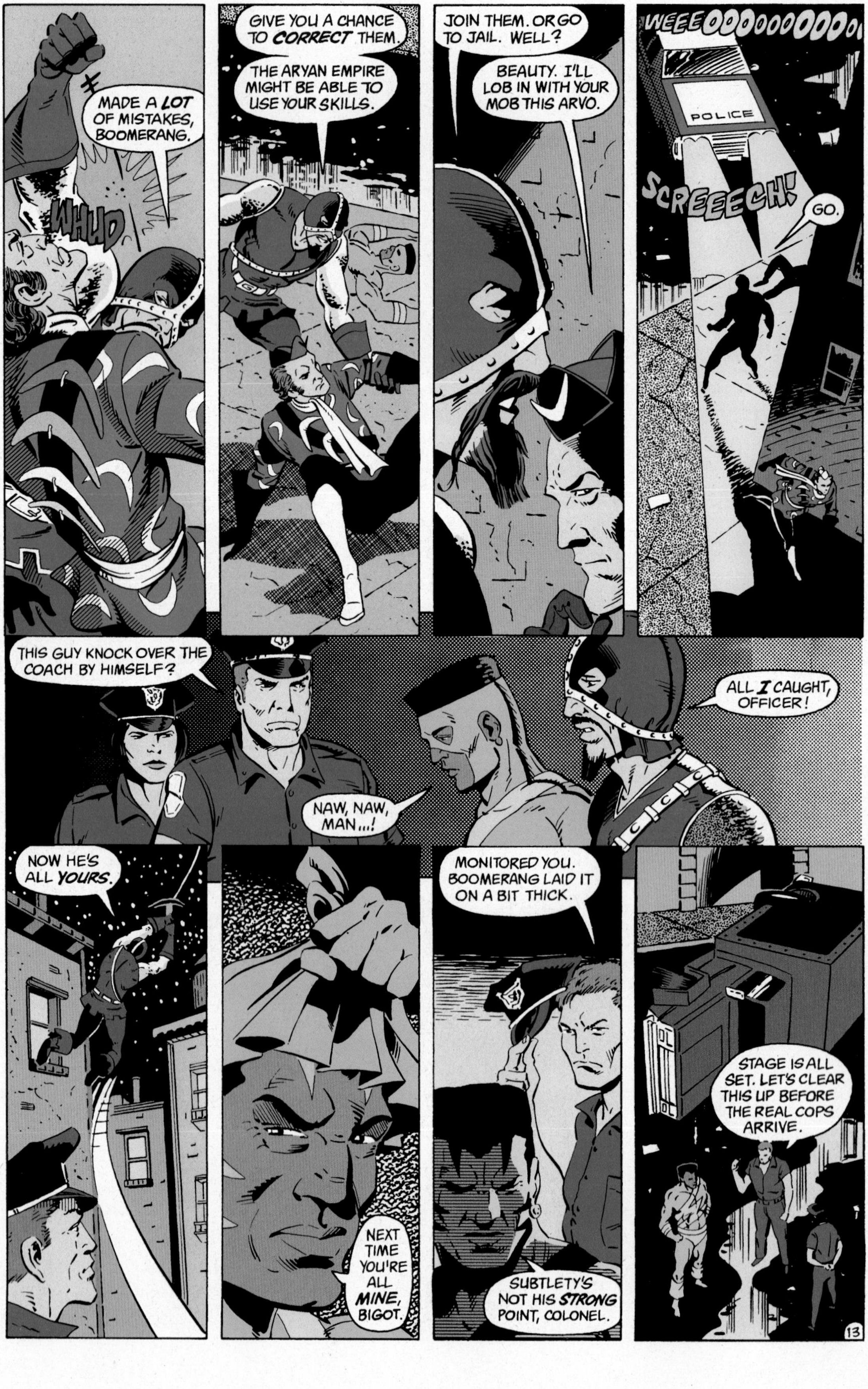
MADE A LOT OF MISTAKES, BOOMERANG.
WHUD
GIVE YOU A CHANCE TO CORRECT THEM.
THE ARYAN EMPIRE MIGHT BE ABLE TO USE YOUR SKILLS.
JOIN THEM. OR GO TO JAIL. WELL?
BEAUTY. I'LL LOB IN WITH YOUR MOB THIS ARVO.
POLICE
SCREEECH!
GO.
THIS GUY KNOCK OVER THE COACH BY HIMSELF?
ALL I CAUGHT, OFFICER!
NAW, NAW, MAN...!
NOW HE'S ALL YOURS.
NEXT TIME YOU'RE ALL MINE, BIGOT.
MONITORED YOU. BOOMERANG LAID IT ON A BIT THICK.
SUBTLETY'S NOT HIS STRONG POINT, COLONEL.
STAGE IS ALL SET. LET'S CLEAR THIS UP BEFORE THE REAL COPS ARRIVE.
13

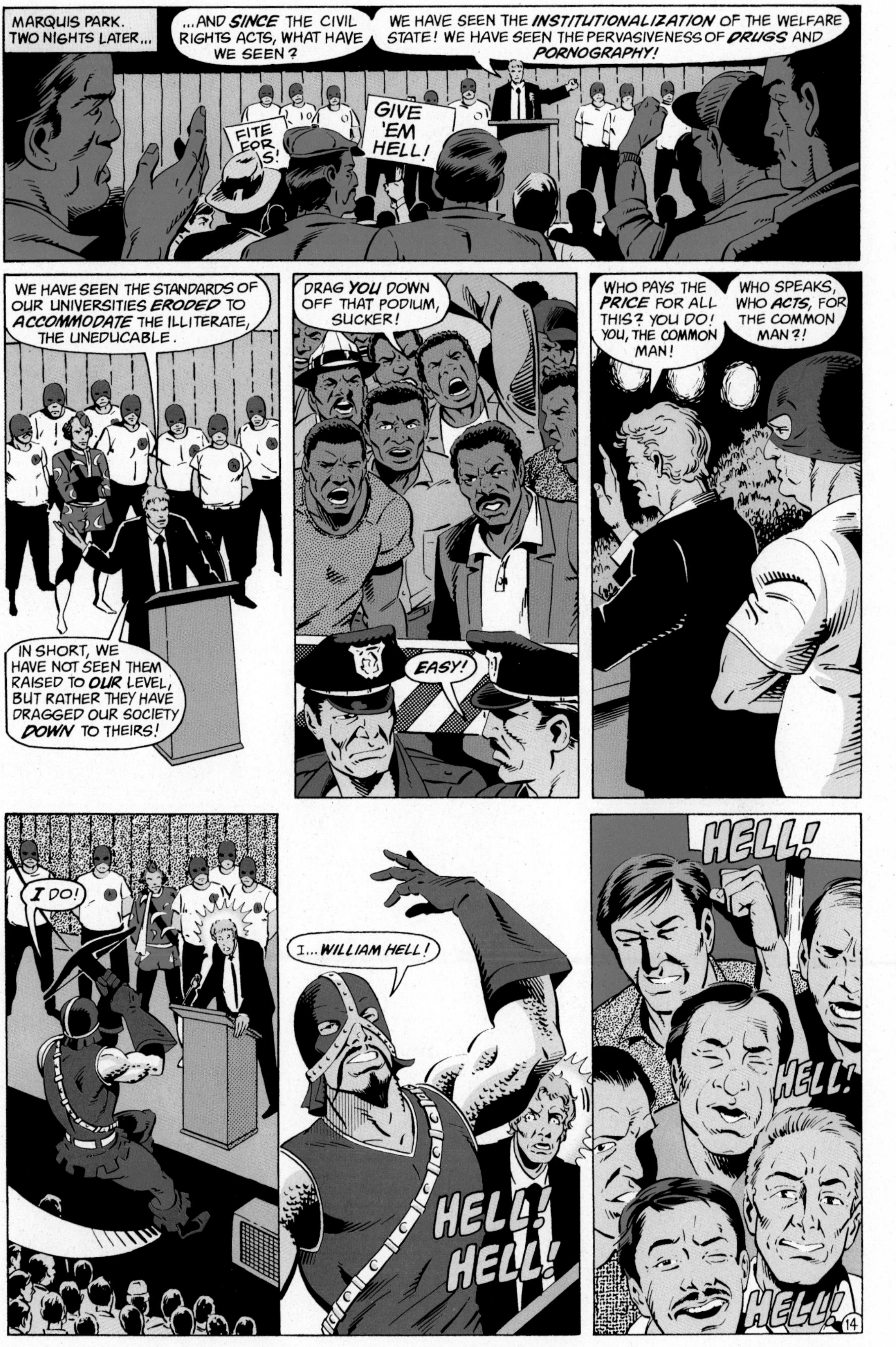
MARQUIS PARK. TWO NIGHTS LATER...
...AND SINCE THE CIVIL RIGHTS ACTS, WHAT HAVE WE SEEN?
WE HAVE SEEN THE INSTITUTIONALIZATION OF THE WELFARE STATE! WE HAVE SEEN THE PERVASIVENESS OF DRUGS AND PORNOGRAPHY!
GIVE 'EM HELL!
WE HAVE SEEN THE STANDARDS OF OUR UNIVERSITIES ERODED TO ACCOMMODATE THE ILLITERATE, THE UNEDUCABLE.
IN SHORT, WE HAVE NOT SEEN THEM RAISED TO OUR LEVEL, BUT RATHER THEY HAVE DRAGGED OUR SOCIETY DOWN TO THEIRS!
DRAG YOU DOWN OFF THAT PODIUM, SUCKER!
EASY!
WHO PAYS THE PRICE FOR ALL THIS? YOU DO! YOU, THE COMMON MAN!
WHO SPEAKS, WHO ACTS, FOR THE COMMON MAN?!
I DO!
I... WILLIAM HELL!
HELL! HELL!
HELL!
HELL!
HELL!
14

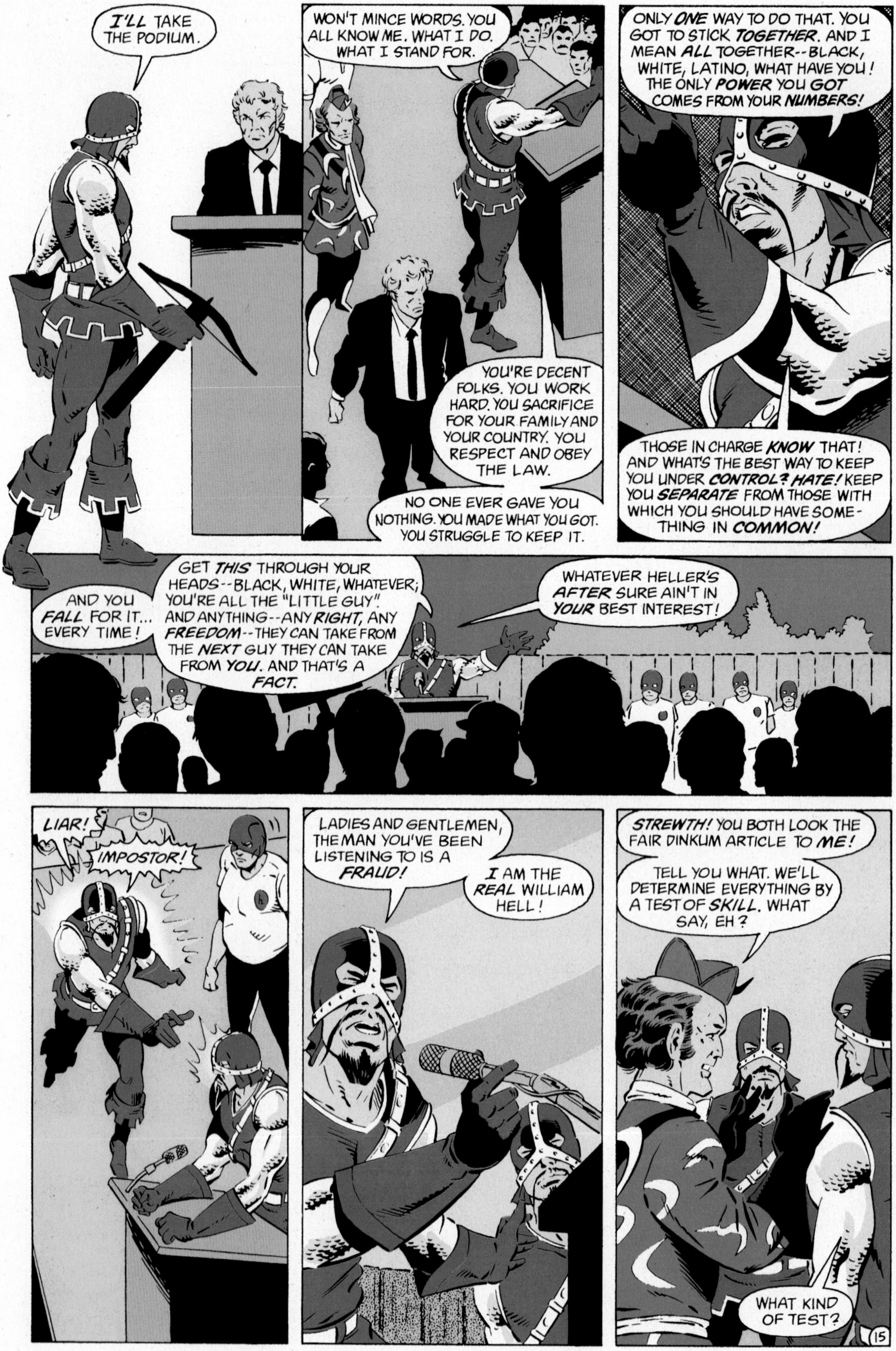
I'LL TAKE THE PODIUM.
WON'T MINCE WORDS. YOU ALL KNOW ME. WHAT I DO. WHAT I STAND FOR.
YOU'RE DECENT FOLKS. YOU WORK HARD. YOU SACRIFICE FOR YOUR FAMILY AND YOUR COUNTRY. YOU RESPECT AND OBEY THE LAW.
NO ONE EVER GAVE YOU NOTHING. YOU MADE WHAT YOU GOT. YOU STRUGGLE TO KEEP IT.
ONLY ONE WAY TO DO THAT. YOU GOT TO STICK TOGETHER. AND I MEAN ALL TOGETHER--BLACK, WHITE, LATINO, WHAT HAVE YOU! THE ONLY POWER YOU GOT COMES FROM YOUR NUMBERS!
THOSE IN CHARGE KNOW THAT! AND WHAT'S THE BEST WAY TO KEEP YOU UNDER CONTROL? HATE! KEEP YOU SEPARATE FROM THOSE WITH WHICH YOU SHOULD HAVE SOME-THING IN COMMON!
AND YOU FALL FOR IT... EVERY TIME!
GET THIS THROUGH YOUR HEADS--BLACK, WHITE, WHATEVER; YOU'RE ALL THE "LITTLE GUY." AND ANYTHING--ANY RIGHT, ANY FREEDOM--THEY CAN TAKE FROM THE NEXT GUY THEY CAN TAKE FROM YOU. AND THAT'S A FACT.
WHATEVER HELLER'S AFTER SURE AIN'T IN YOUR BEST INTEREST!
LIAR!
IMPOSTOR!
LADIES AND GENTLEMEN, THE MAN YOU'VE BEEN LISTENING TO IS A FRAUD!
I AM THE REAL WILLIAM HELL!
STREWTH! YOU BOTH LOOK THE FAIR DINKUM ARTICLE TO ME!
TELL YOU WHAT. WE'LL DETERMINE EVERYTHING BY A TEST OF SKILL. WHAT SAY, EH?
WHAT KIND OF TEST?
15

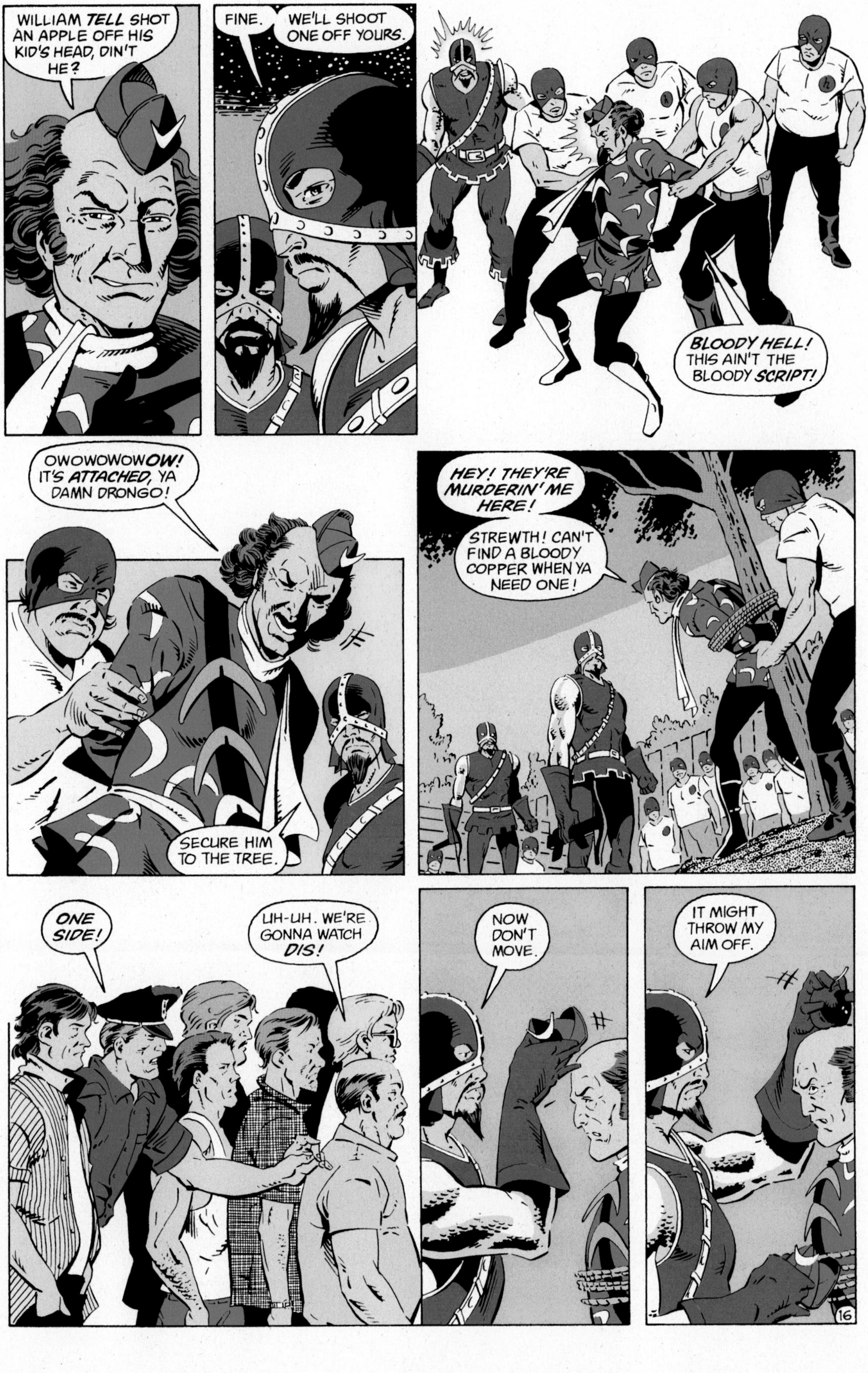
WILLIAM TELL SHOT AN APPLE OFF HIS KID'S HEAD, DIN'T HE?
FINE.
WE'LL SHOOT ONE OFF YOURS.
BLOODY HELL! THIS AIN'T THE BLOODY SCRIPT!
OWOWOWOWOW! IT'S ATTACHED, YA DAMN DRONGO!
SECURE HIM TO THE TREE.
HEY! THEY'RE MURDERIN' ME HERE!
STREWTH! CAN'T FIND A BLOODY COPPER WHEN YA NEED ONE!
ONE SIDE!
UH-UH. WE'RE GONNA WATCH DIS!
NOW DON'T MOVE.
IT MIGHT THROW MY AIM OFF.
16

FIRST *COME*, FIRST *SHOOT*... IMPOSTOR.

TWANGG!

HELL!
HELL!
HELL!

MAKE OR BREAK, BOZO.

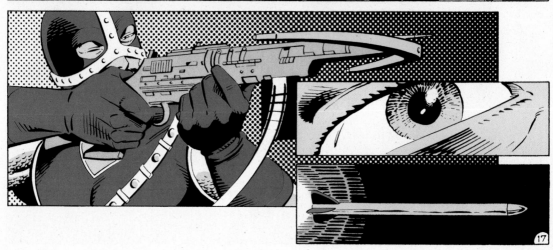

17

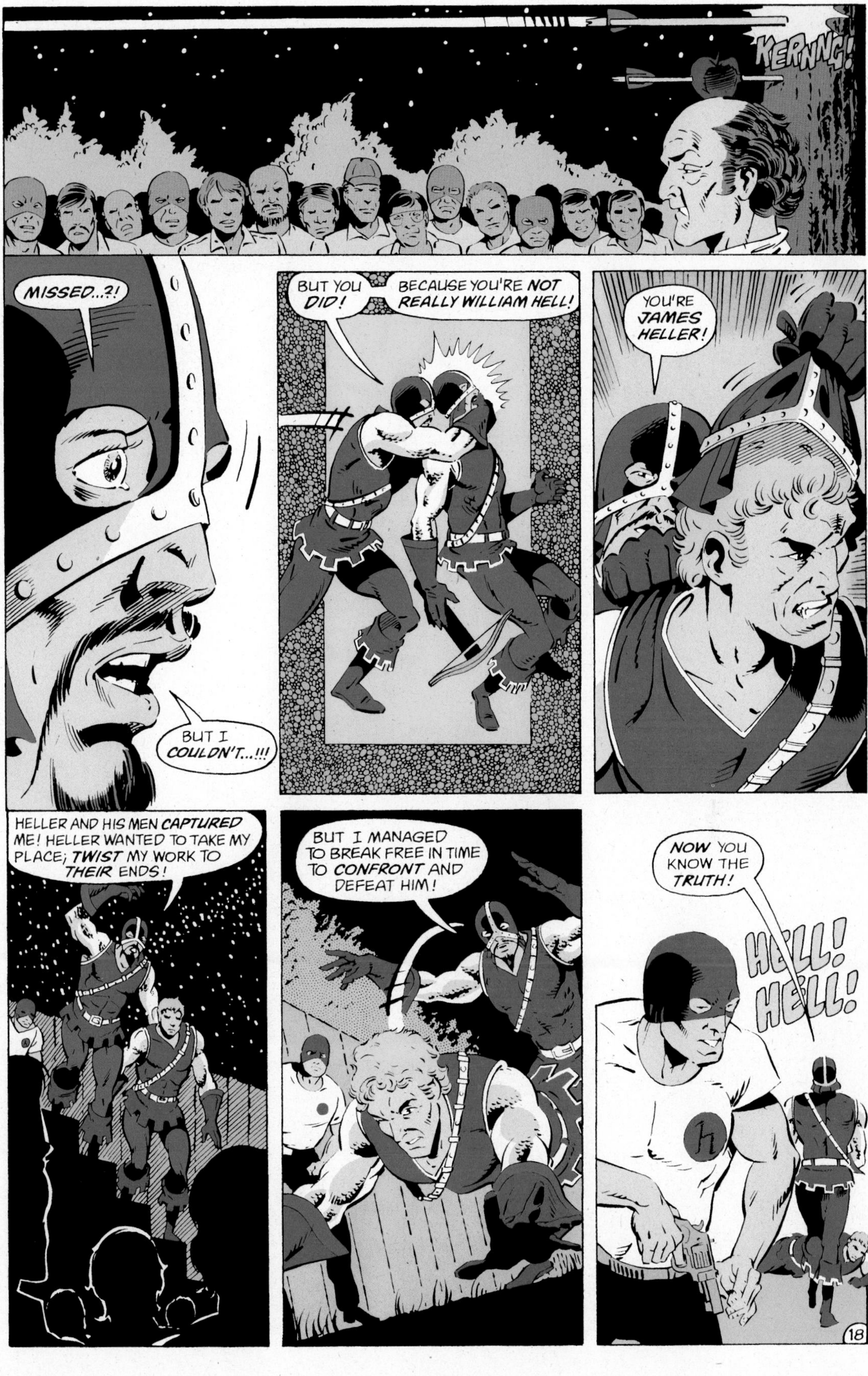
KERNNG!
MISSED...?!
BUT I COULDN'T...!!!
BUT YOU DID!
BECAUSE YOU'RE NOT REALLY WILLIAM HELL!
YOU'RE JAMES HELLER!
HELLER AND HIS MEN CAPTURED ME! HELLER WANTED TO TAKE MY PLACE; TWIST MY WORK TO THEIR ENDS!
BUT I MANAGED TO BREAK FREE IN TIME TO CONFRONT AND DEFEAT HIM!
NOW YOU KNOW THE TRUTH!
HELL! HELL!
18

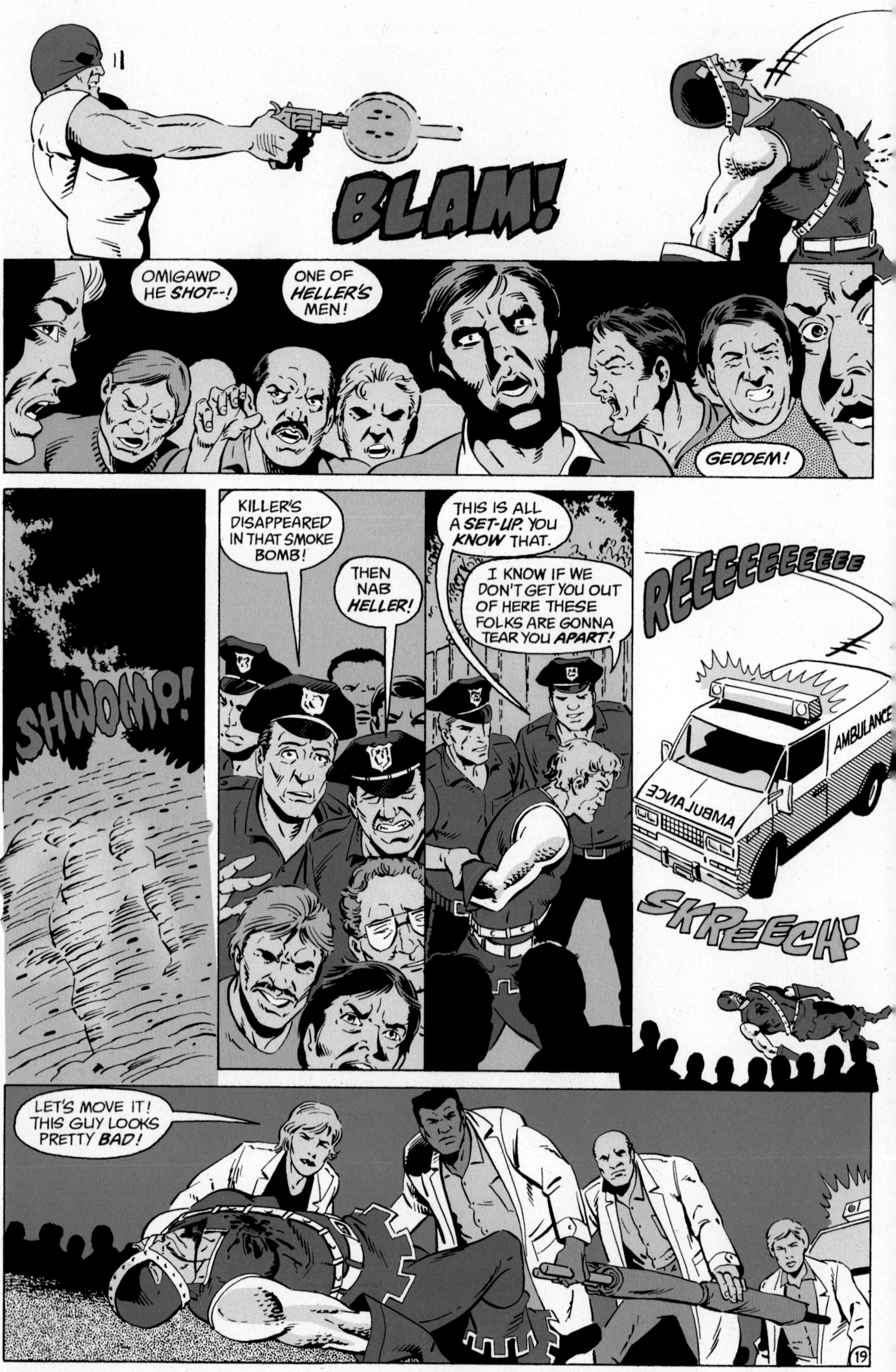
BLAM!
OMIGAWD HE SHOT--!
ONE OF HELLER'S MEN!
GEDDEM!
SHWOMP!
KILLER'S DISAPPEARED IN THAT SMOKE BOMB!
THEN NAB HELLER!
THIS IS ALL A SET-UP. YOU KNOW THAT.
I KNOW IF WE DON'T GET YOU OUT OF HERE THESE FOLKS ARE GONNA TEAR YOU APART!
REEEEEEEEEEE
AMBULANCE
AMBULANCE
SKREECH!
LET'S MOVE IT! THIS GUY LOOKS PRETTY BAD!
19

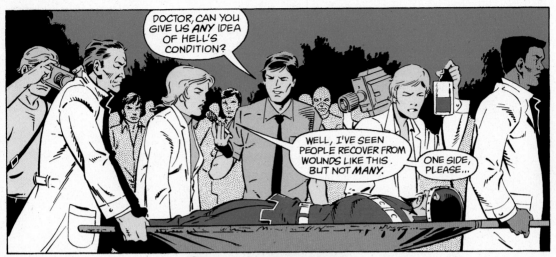

DOCTOR, CAN YOU GIVE US *ANY* IDEA OF HELL'S CONDITION?

WELL, I'VE SEEN PEOPLE RECOVER FROM WOUNDS LIKE THIS. BUT NOT *MANY*.

ONE SIDE, PLEASE...

ALL PACKED?

LET'S GO.

AMBULANCE

AMBULANCE

REEEEEEEEEEEEEEE

UHN!

THAT EXPLOSIVE CHARGE ON THE FRONT OF THE COSTUME SINGED MY SKIN. MAKING ME *NUTS*.

GOT SOME *SALVE*?

20

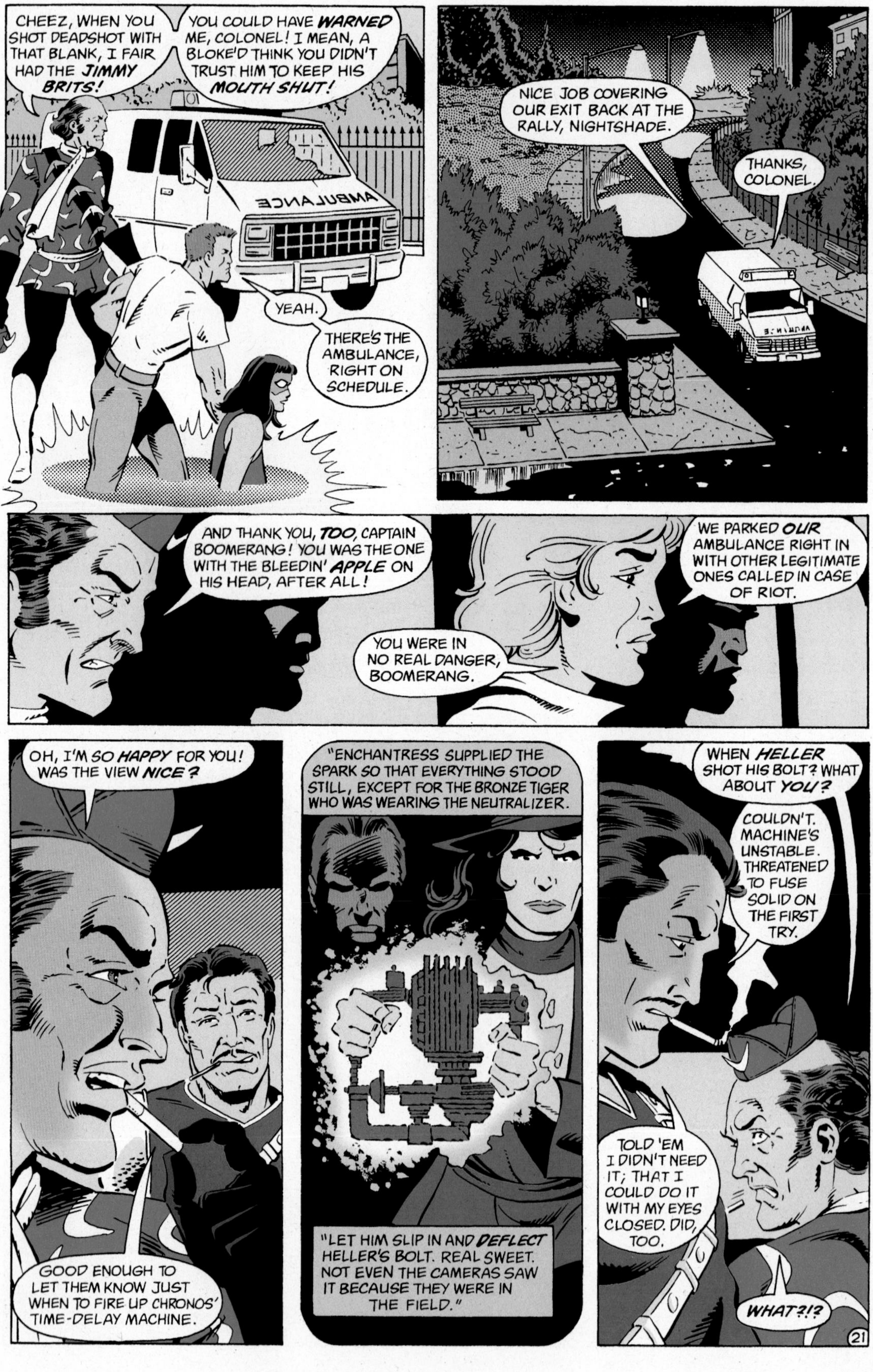

CHEEZ, WHEN YOU SHOT DEADSHOT WITH THAT BLANK, I FAIR HAD THE JIMMY BRITS!
YOU COULD HAVE WARNED ME, COLONEL! I MEAN, A BLOKE'D THINK YOU DIDN'T TRUST HIM TO KEEP HIS MOUTH SHUT!
AMBULANCE
YEAH.
THERE'S THE AMBULANCE, RIGHT ON SCHEDULE.
NICE JOB COVERING OUR EXIT BACK AT THE RALLY, NIGHTSHADE.
THANKS, COLONEL.
AND THANK YOU, TOO, CAPTAIN BOOMERANG! YOU WAS THE ONE WITH THE BLEEDIN' APPLE ON HIS HEAD, AFTER ALL!
YOU WERE IN NO REAL DANGER, BOOMERANG.
WE PARKED OUR AMBULANCE RIGHT IN WITH OTHER LEGITIMATE ONES CALLED IN CASE OF RIOT.
OH, I'M SO HAPPY FOR YOU! WAS THE VIEW NICE?
GOOD ENOUGH TO LET THEM KNOW JUST WHEN TO FIRE UP CHRONOS' TIME-DELAY MACHINE.
"ENCHANTRESS SUPPLIED THE SPARK SO THAT EVERYTHING STOOD STILL, EXCEPT FOR THE BRONZE TIGER WHO WAS WEARING THE NEUTRALIZER.
"LET HIM SLIP IN AND DEFLECT HELLER'S BOLT. REAL SWEET. NOT EVEN THE CAMERAS SAW IT BECAUSE THEY WERE IN THE FIELD."
WHEN HELLER SHOT HIS BOLT? WHAT ABOUT YOU?
COULDN'T. MACHINE'S UNSTABLE. THREATENED TO FUSE SOLID ON THE FIRST TRY.
TOLD 'EM I DIDN'T NEED IT; THAT I COULD DO IT WITH MY EYES CLOSED. DID, TOO.
WHAT?!?
21

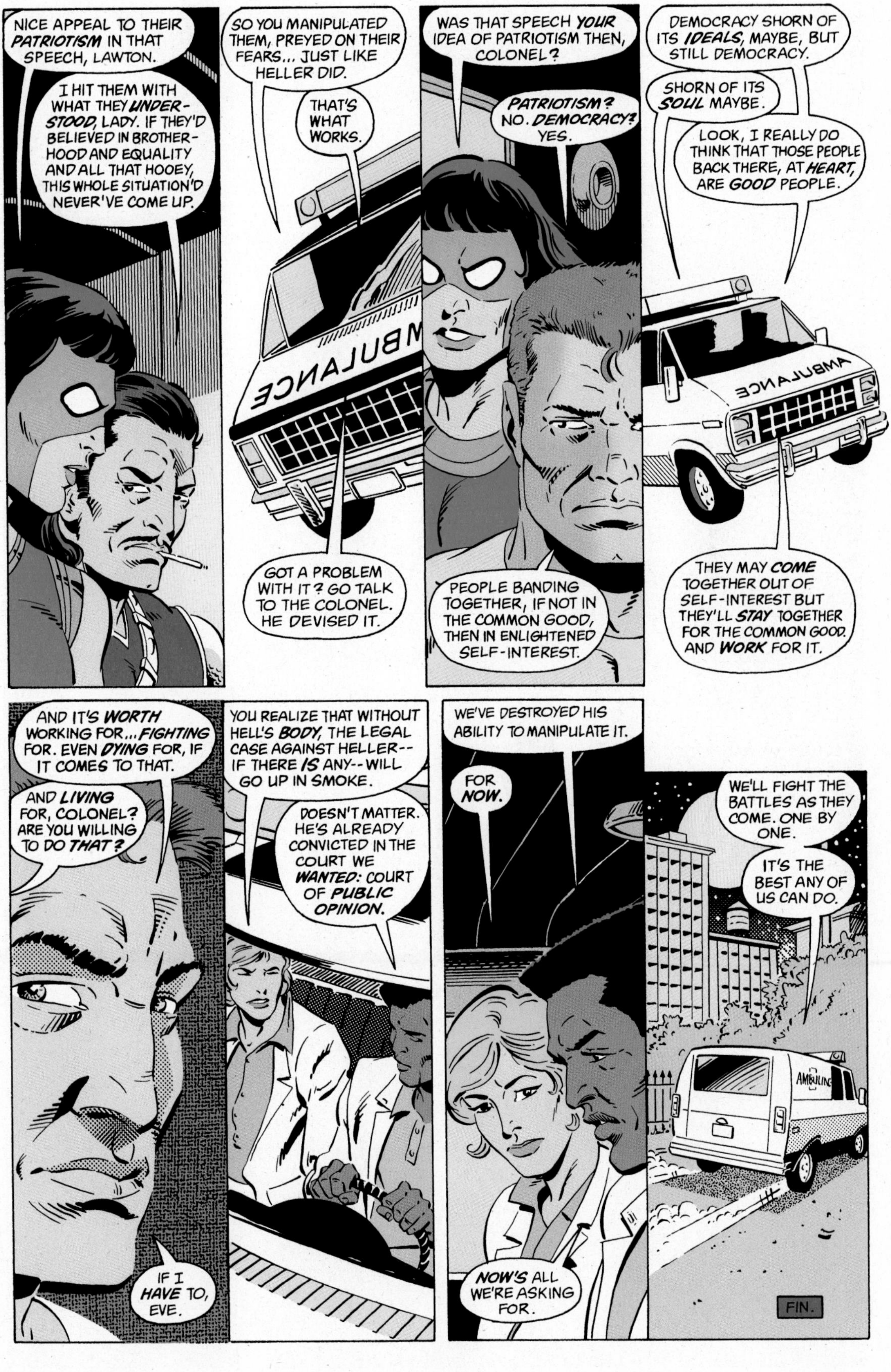
NICE APPEAL TO THEIR PATRIOTISM IN THAT SPEECH, LAWTON.
I HIT THEM WITH WHAT THEY UNDERSTOOD, LADY. IF THEY'D BELIEVED IN BROTHERHOOD AND EQUALITY AND ALL THAT HOOEY, THIS WHOLE SITUATION'D NEVER'VE COME UP.
SO YOU MANIPULATED THEM, PREYED ON THEIR FEARS... JUST LIKE HELLER DID.
THAT'S WHAT WORKS.
AMBULANCE
GOT A PROBLEM WITH IT? GO TALK TO THE COLONEL. HE DEVISED IT.
WAS THAT SPEECH YOUR IDEA OF PATRIOTISM THEN, COLONEL?
PATRIOTISM? NO. DEMOCRACY? YES.
PEOPLE BANDING TOGETHER, IF NOT IN THE COMMON GOOD, THEN IN ENLIGHTENED SELF-INTEREST.
DEMOCRACY SHORN OF ITS IDEALS, MAYBE, BUT STILL DEMOCRACY.
SHORN OF ITS SOUL MAYBE.
LOOK, I REALLY DO THINK THAT THOSE PEOPLE BACK THERE, AT HEART, ARE GOOD PEOPLE.
AMBULANCE
THEY MAY COME TOGETHER OUT OF SELF-INTEREST BUT THEY'LL STAY TOGETHER FOR THE COMMON GOOD. AND WORK FOR IT.
AND IT'S WORTH WORKING FOR... FIGHTING FOR. EVEN DYING FOR, IF IT COMES TO THAT.
AND LIVING FOR, COLONEL? ARE YOU WILLING TO DO THAT?
IF I HAVE TO, EVE.
YOU REALIZE THAT WITHOUT HELL'S BODY, THE LEGAL CASE AGAINST HELLER-- IF THERE IS ANY-- WILL GO UP IN SMOKE.
DOESN'T MATTER. HE'S ALREADY CONVICTED IN THE COURT WE WANTED: COURT OF PUBLIC OPINION.
WE'VE DESTROYED HIS ABILITY TO MANIPULATE IT.
FOR NOW.
NOW'S ALL WE'RE ASKING FOR.
WE'LL FIGHT THE BATTLES AS THEY COME. ONE BY ONE.
IT'S THE BEST ANY OF US CAN DO.
FIN.

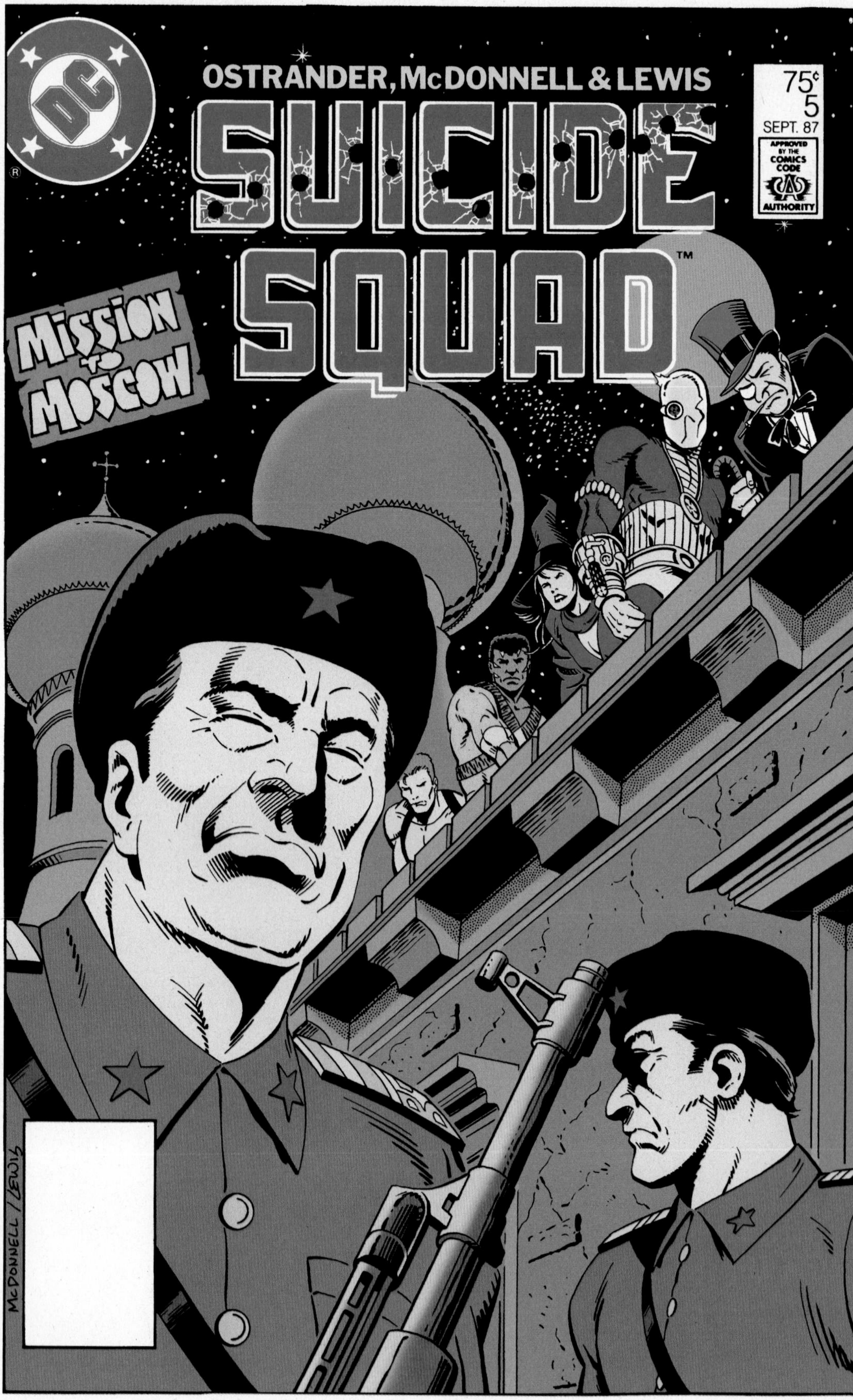
OSTRANDER, McDONNELL & LEWIS
SUICIDE SQUAD
75¢
5
SEPT. 87
APPROVED BY THE COMICS CODE AUTHORITY
MISSION TO MOSCOW
McDONNELL / LEWIS

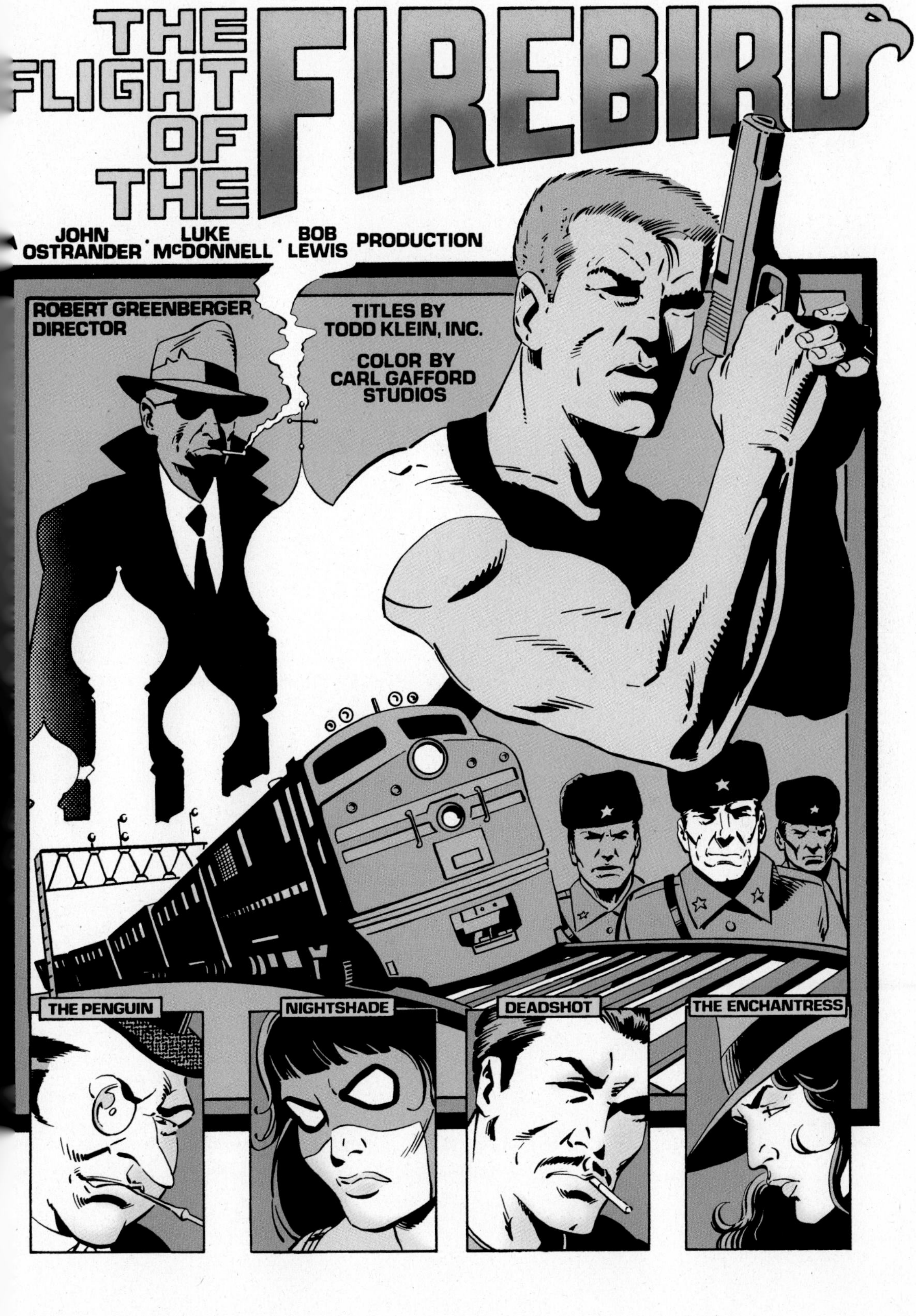

THE FLIGHT OF THE FIREBIRD
A JOHN OSTRANDER · LUKE McDONNELL · BOB LEWIS PRODUCTION
ROBERT GREENBERGER DIRECTOR
TITLES BY TODD KLEIN, INC.
COLOR BY CARL GAFFORD STUDIOS
THE PENGUIN
NIGHTSHADE
DEADSHOT
THE ENCHANTRESS

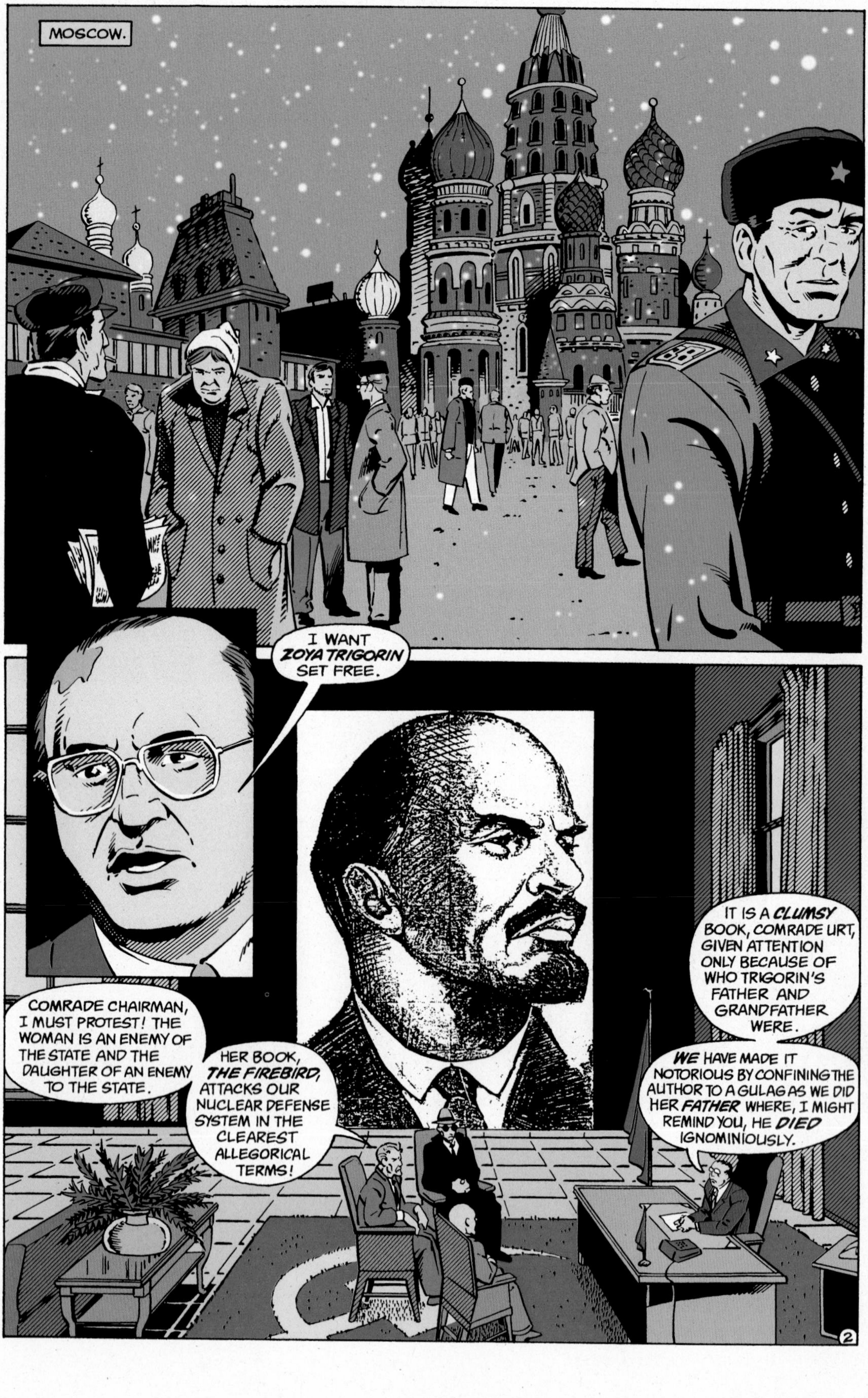
MOSCOW.
I WANT ZOYA TRIGORIN SET FREE.
COMRADE CHAIRMAN, I MUST PROTEST! THE WOMAN IS AN ENEMY OF THE STATE AND THE DAUGHTER OF AN ENEMY TO THE STATE.
HER BOOK, THE FIREBIRD, ATTACKS OUR NUCLEAR DEFENSE SYSTEM IN THE CLEAREST ALLEGORICAL TERMS!
IT IS A CLUMSY BOOK, COMRADE URT, GIVEN ATTENTION ONLY BECAUSE OF WHO TRIGORIN'S FATHER AND GRANDFATHER WERE.
WE HAVE MADE IT NOTORIOUS BY CONFINING THE AUTHOR TO A GULAG AS WE DID HER FATHER WHERE, I MIGHT REMIND YOU, HE DIED IGNOMINIOUSLY.
2

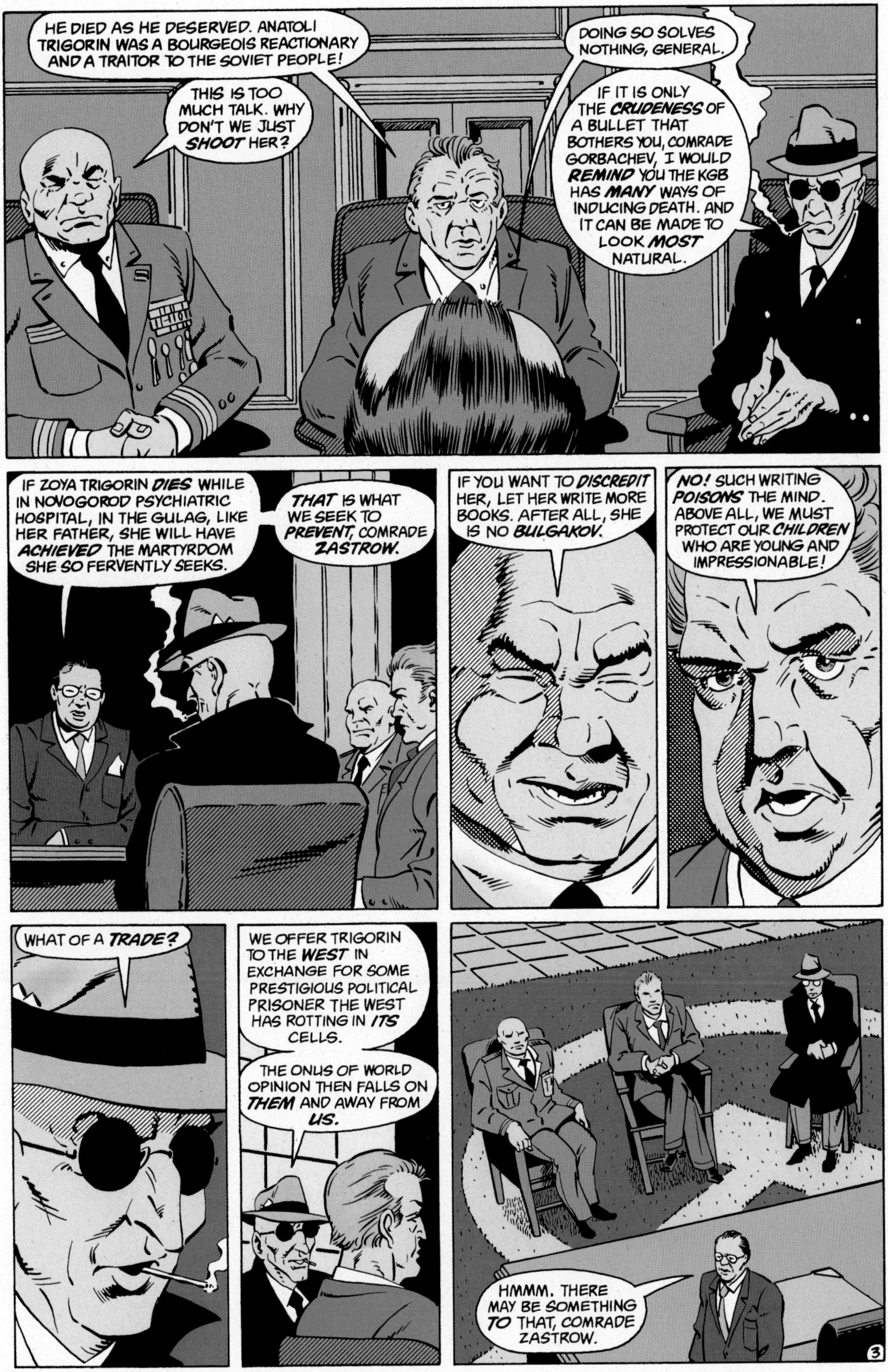
HE DIED AS HE DESERVED. ANATOLI TRIGORIN WAS A BOURGEOIS REACTIONARY AND A TRAITOR TO THE SOVIET PEOPLE!
THIS IS TOO MUCH TALK. WHY DON'T WE JUST SHOOT HER?
DOING SO SOLVES NOTHING, GENERAL.
IF IT IS ONLY THE CRUDENESS OF A BULLET THAT BOTHERS YOU, COMRADE GORBACHEV, I WOULD REMIND YOU THE KGB HAS MANY WAYS OF INDUCING DEATH. AND IT CAN BE MADE TO LOOK MOST NATURAL.
IF ZOYA TRIGORIN DIES WHILE IN NOVOGOROD PSYCHIATRIC HOSPITAL, IN THE GULAG, LIKE HER FATHER, SHE WILL HAVE ACHIEVED THE MARTYRDOM SHE SO FERVENTLY SEEKS.
THAT IS WHAT WE SEEK TO PREVENT, COMRADE ZASTROW.
IF YOU WANT TO DISCREDIT HER, LET HER WRITE MORE BOOKS. AFTER ALL, SHE IS NO BULGAKOV.
NO! SUCH WRITING POISONS THE MIND. ABOVE ALL, WE MUST PROTECT OUR CHILDREN WHO ARE YOUNG AND IMPRESSIONABLE!
WHAT OF A TRADE?
WE OFFER TRIGORIN TO THE WEST IN EXCHANGE FOR SOME PRESTIGIOUS POLITICAL PRISONER THE WEST HAS ROTTING IN ITS CELLS.
THE ONUS OF WORLD OPINION THEN FALLS ON THEM AND AWAY FROM US.
HMMM. THERE MAY BE SOMETHING TO THAT, COMRADE ZASTROW.
3

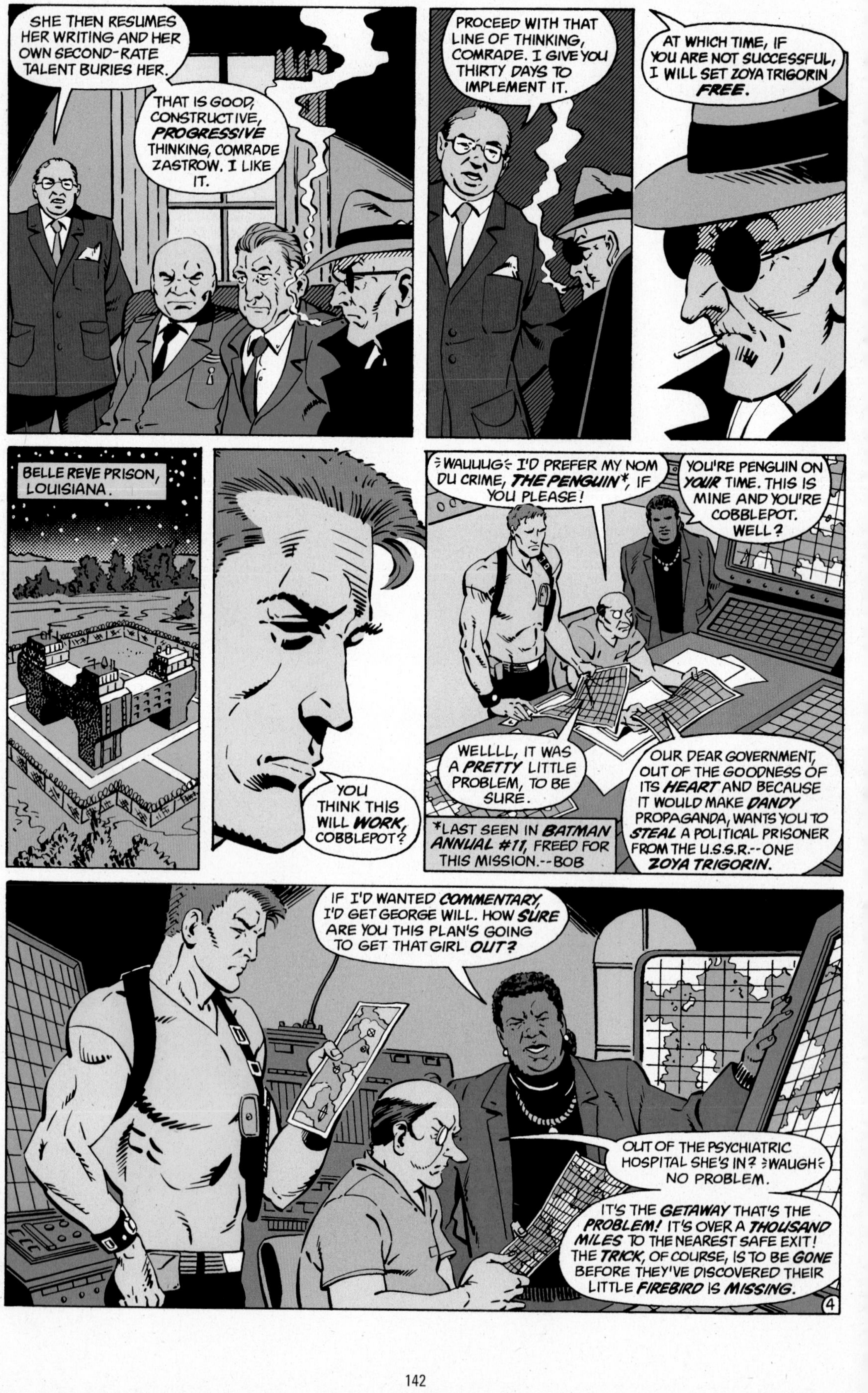

SHE THEN RESUMES HER WRITING AND HER OWN SECOND-RATE TALENT BURIES HER.
THAT IS GOOD, CONSTRUCTIVE, PROGRESSIVE THINKING, COMRADE ZASTROW. I LIKE IT.
PROCEED WITH THAT LINE OF THINKING, COMRADE. I GIVE YOU THIRTY DAYS TO IMPLEMENT IT.
AT WHICH TIME, IF YOU ARE NOT SUCCESSFUL, I WILL SET ZOYA TRIGORIN FREE.
BELLE REVE PRISON, LOUISIANA.
YOU THINK THIS WILL WORK, COBBLEPOT?
WAUUUG I'D PREFER MY NOM DU CRIME, THE PENGUIN*, IF YOU PLEASE!
YOU'RE PENGUIN ON YOUR TIME. THIS IS MINE AND YOU'RE COBBLEPOT. WELL?
WELLLL, IT WAS A PRETTY LITTLE PROBLEM, TO BE SURE.
OUR DEAR GOVERNMENT, OUT OF THE GOODNESS OF ITS HEART AND BECAUSE IT WOULD MAKE DANDY PROPAGANDA, WANTS YOU TO STEAL A POLITICAL PRISONER FROM THE U.S.S.R.--ONE ZOYA TRIGORIN.
*LAST SEEN IN BATMAN ANNUAL #11, FREED FOR THIS MISSION.--BOB
IF I'D WANTED COMMENTARY, I'D GET GEORGE WILL. HOW SURE ARE YOU THIS PLAN'S GOING TO GET THAT GIRL OUT?
OUT OF THE PSYCHIATRIC HOSPITAL SHE'S IN? WAUGH NO PROBLEM.
IT'S THE GETAWAY THAT'S THE PROBLEM! IT'S OVER A THOUSAND MILES TO THE NEAREST SAFE EXIT! THE TRICK, OF COURSE, IS TO BE GONE BEFORE THEY'VE DISCOVERED THEIR LITTLE FIREBIRD IS MISSING.
4

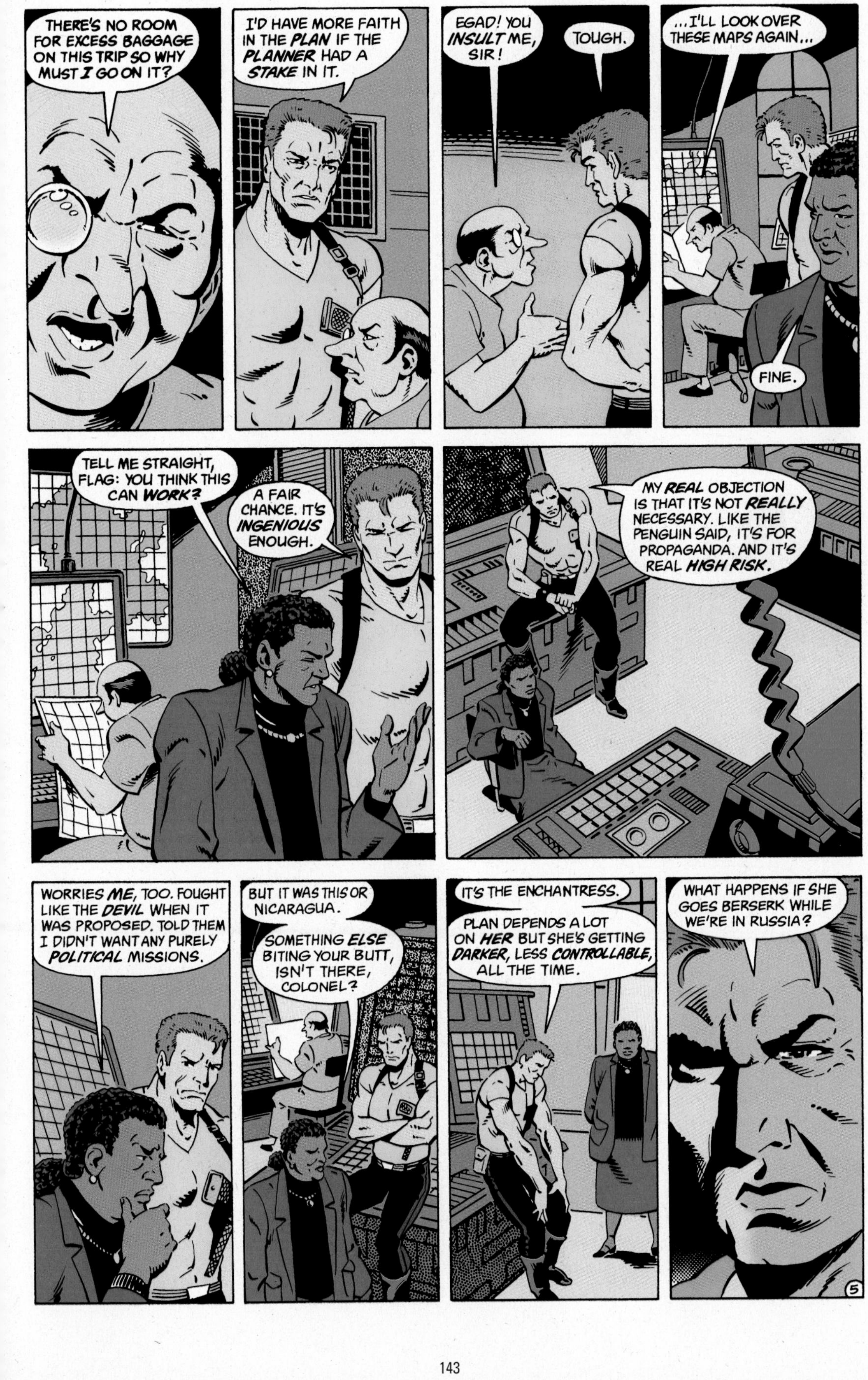
THERE'S NO ROOM FOR EXCESS BAGGAGE ON THIS TRIP SO WHY MUST I GO ON IT?
I'D HAVE MORE FAITH IN THE PLAN IF THE PLANNER HAD A STAKE IN IT.
EGAD! YOU INSULT ME, SIR!
TOUGH.
...I'LL LOOK OVER THESE MAPS AGAIN...
FINE.
TELL ME STRAIGHT, FLAG: YOU THINK THIS CAN WORK?
A FAIR CHANCE. IT'S INGENIOUS ENOUGH.
MY REAL OBJECTION IS THAT IT'S NOT REALLY NECESSARY. LIKE THE PENGUIN SAID, IT'S FOR PROPAGANDA. AND IT'S REAL HIGH RISK.
WORRIES ME, TOO. FOUGHT LIKE THE DEVIL WHEN IT WAS PROPOSED. TOLD THEM I DIDN'T WANT ANY PURELY POLITICAL MISSIONS.
BUT IT WAS THIS OR NICARAGUA.
SOMETHING ELSE BITING YOUR BUTT, ISN'T THERE, COLONEL?
IT'S THE ENCHANTRESS.
PLAN DEPENDS A LOT ON HER BUT SHE'S GETTING DARKER, LESS CONTROLLABLE, ALL THE TIME.
WHAT HAPPENS IF SHE GOES BERSERK WHILE WE'RE IN RUSSIA?
5

≶WAUUUUG≶ IT'S THE BEST I CAN DO. IT *HAS* TO WORK! AND IF... *WHEN* IT DOES, I GO *FREE*, RIGHT? SENTENCE COMMUTED TO TIME SERVED? NO CATCH? NO *TRICK*?

ONLY TRICK IS *SURVIVING*, COBBLEPOT. THAT'S THE ONLY TRICK THERE *EVER* IS.

THE OFFICE OF SIMON LAGRIEVE, RESIDENT PSYCHIATRIST TO THE SUICIDE SQUAD...

EVERYTHING YOU'VE TOLD ME, JUNE, ARGUES A DESIRE FOR *WELLNESS*, A WISH TO BE *HEALED* AND *WHOLE*.

EXAMINE THE FACTS YOURSELF.

YOU SAY IT WAS AN ENCOUNTER WITH THIS CREATURE CALLED *DZAMOR* THAT GAVE YOU YOUR POWERS.

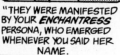

"THEY WERE MANIFESTED BY YOUR *ENCHANTRESS* PERSONA, WHO EMERGED WHENEVER YOU SAID HER NAME.

"WHILE ORIGINALLY A FORCE FOR *GOOD*, THE ENCHANTRESS PERSONA BECAME EVIL, ULTIMATELY JOINING A GROUP CALLED THE FORGOTTEN VILLAINS."

YES..., *YES!* SHE JUST TOOK OVER AND WOULDN'T CHANGE *BACK!* I FELT *TRAPPED!*

BUT EVENTUALLY YOU *WERE* ABLE TO *RE-ASSERT* YOUR OWN PERSONALITY. YOU SOUGHT *HELP* AND THE TRAIL LED YOU TO *TASK FORCE X*.

≶SNIFF!≶ THEY SAID THEY WOULD HELP ME FIND A WAY TO CURE THE ENCHANTRESS OR MAKE ME *GOOD* AGAIN IF I HELPED THEM!

WHICH IS WHAT WE'RE TRYING TO DO HERE, JUNE.

WOULDN'T THE PROBLEM BE MOST SIMPLY SOLVED IF YOU SIMPLY DIDN'T *BECOME* THE ENCHANTRESS AGAIN?

IT'S NOT THAT *EASY*, DOCTOR!

6

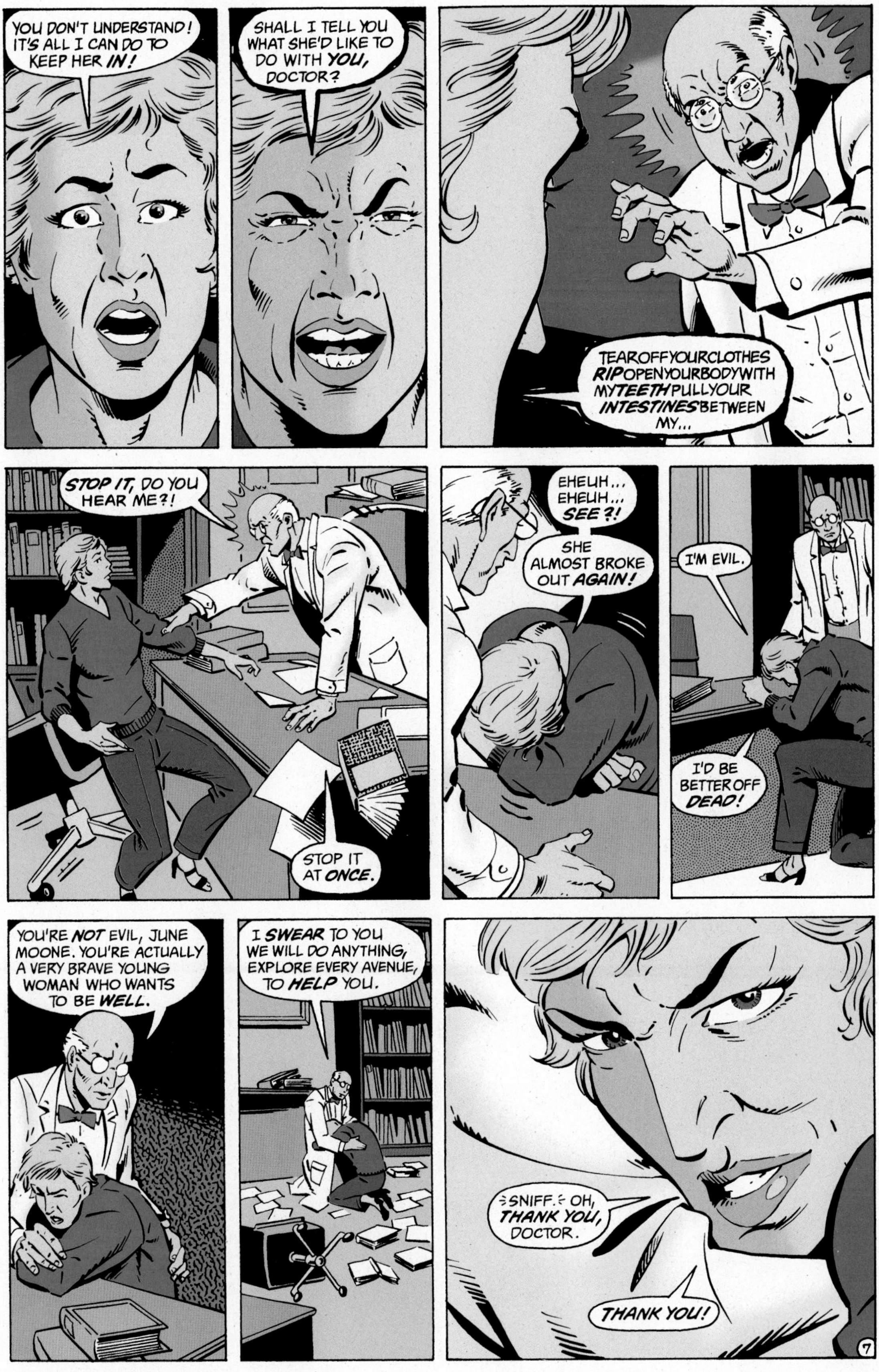
YOU DON'T UNDERSTAND! IT'S ALL I CAN DO TO KEEP HER IN!
SHALL I TELL YOU WHAT SHE'D LIKE TO DO WITH YOU, DOCTOR?
TEAROFFYOURCLOTHES RIPOPENYOURBODYWITH MYTEETHPULLYOUR INTESTINESBETWEEN MY...
STOP IT, DO YOU HEAR ME?!
STOP IT AT ONCE.
EHEUH... EHEUH... SEE?!
SHE ALMOST BROKE OUT AGAIN!
I'M EVIL.
I'D BE BETTER OFF DEAD!
YOU'RE NOT EVIL, JUNE MOONE. YOU'RE ACTUALLY A VERY BRAVE YOUNG WOMAN WHO WANTS TO BE WELL.
I SWEAR TO YOU WE WILL DO ANYTHING, EXPLORE EVERY AVENUE, TO HELP YOU.
SNIFF. OH, THANK YOU, DOCTOR.
THANK YOU!
7

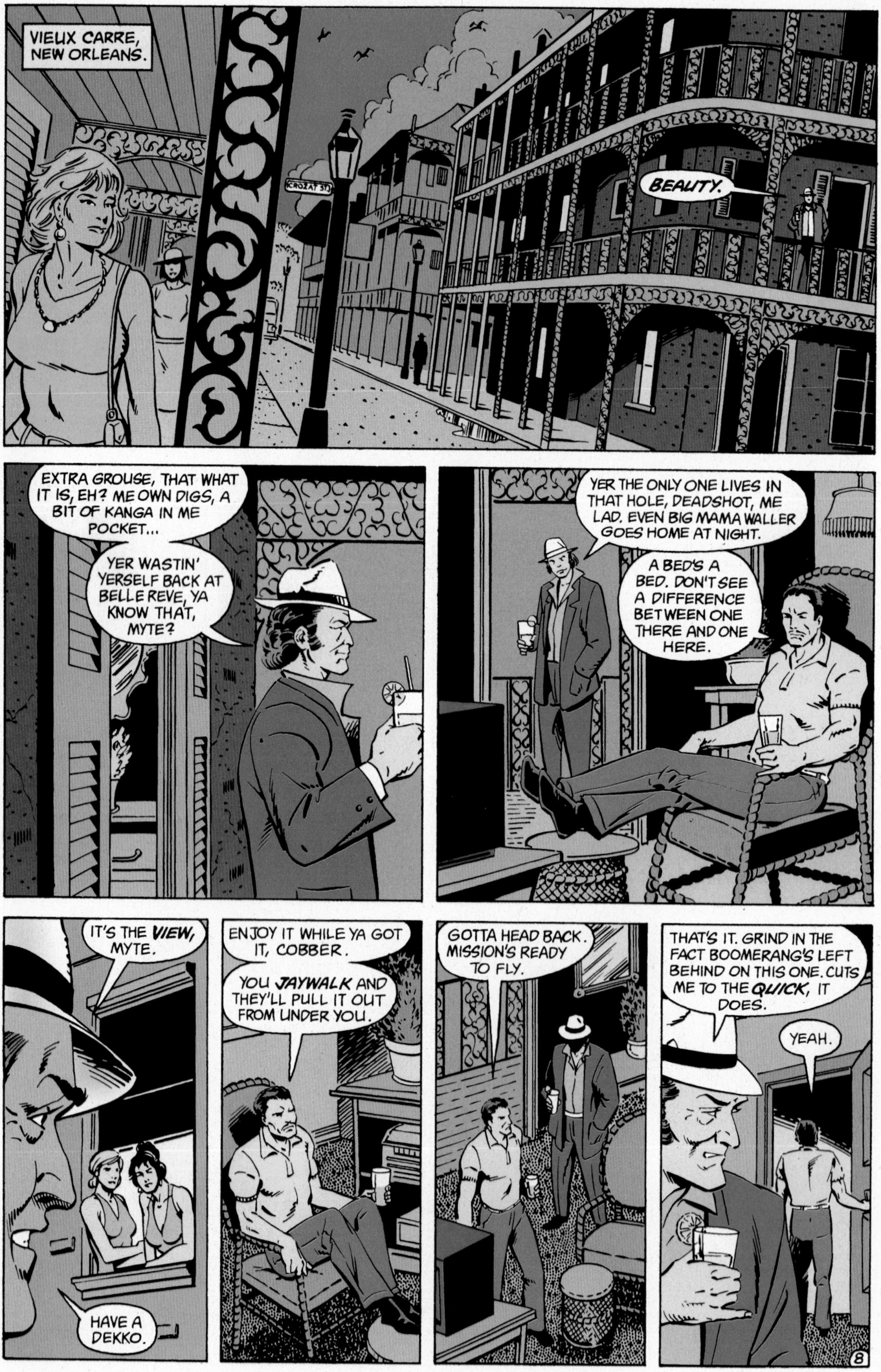
VIEUX CARRE, NEW ORLEANS.
CROZAT ST.
BEAUTY.
EXTRA GROUSE, THAT WHAT IT IS, EH? ME OWN DIGS, A BIT OF KANGA IN ME POCKET...
YER WASTIN' YERSELF BACK AT BELLE REVE, YA KNOW THAT, MYTE?
YER THE ONLY ONE LIVES IN THAT HOLE, DEADSHOT, ME LAD. EVEN BIG MAMA WALLER GOES HOME AT NIGHT.
A BED'S A BED. DON'T SEE A DIFFERENCE BETWEEN ONE THERE AND ONE HERE.
IT'S THE VIEW, MYTE.
HAVE A DEKKO.
ENJOY IT WHILE YA GOT IT, COBBER.
YOU JAYWALK AND THEY'LL PULL IT OUT FROM UNDER YOU.
GOTTA HEAD BACK. MISSION'S READY TO FLY.
THAT'S IT. GRIND IN THE FACT BOOMERANG'S LEFT BEHIND ON THIS ONE. CUTS ME TO THE QUICK, IT DOES.
YEAH.
8

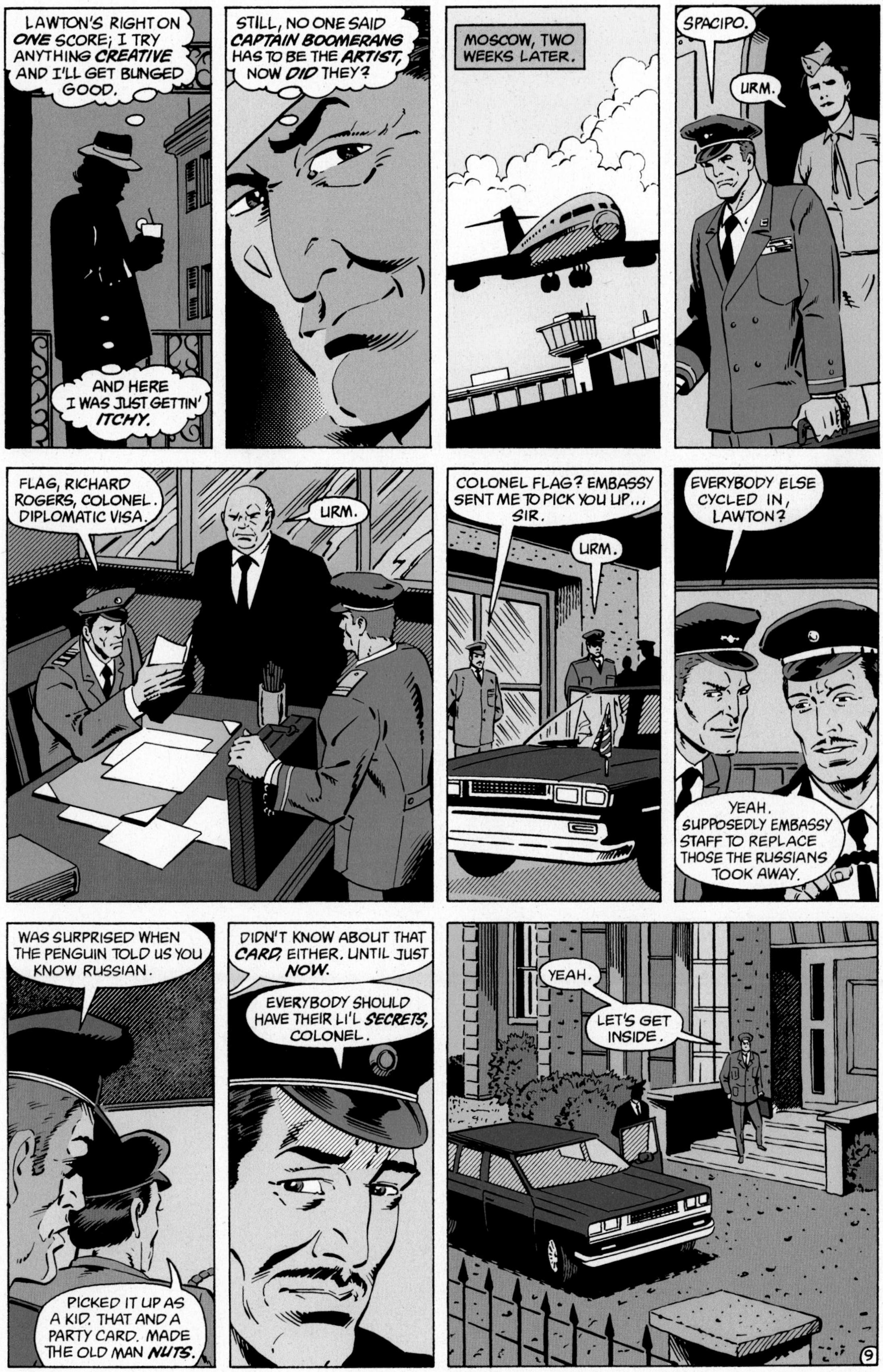

LAWTON'S RIGHT ON ONE SCORE; I TRY ANYTHING CREATIVE AND I'LL GET BUNGED GOOD.
AND HERE I WAS JUST GETTIN' ITCHY.
STILL, NO ONE SAID CAPTAIN BOOMERANG HAS TO BE THE ARTIST, NOW DID THEY?
MOSCOW, TWO WEEKS LATER.
SPACIPO.
URM.
FLAG, RICHARD ROGERS, COLONEL. DIPLOMATIC VISA.
URM.
COLONEL FLAG? EMBASSY SENT ME TO PICK YOU UP... SIR.
URM.
EVERYBODY ELSE CYCLED IN, LAWTON?
YEAH. SUPPOSEDLY EMBASSY STAFF TO REPLACE THOSE THE RUSSIANS TOOK AWAY.
WAS SURPRISED WHEN THE PENGUIN TOLD US YOU KNOW RUSSIAN.
PICKED IT UP AS A KID. THAT AND A PARTY CARD. MADE THE OLD MAN NUTS.
DIDN'T KNOW ABOUT THAT CARD, EITHER. UNTIL JUST NOW.
EVERYBODY SHOULD HAVE THEIR LI'L SECRETS, COLONEL.
YEAH.
LET'S GET INSIDE.
9

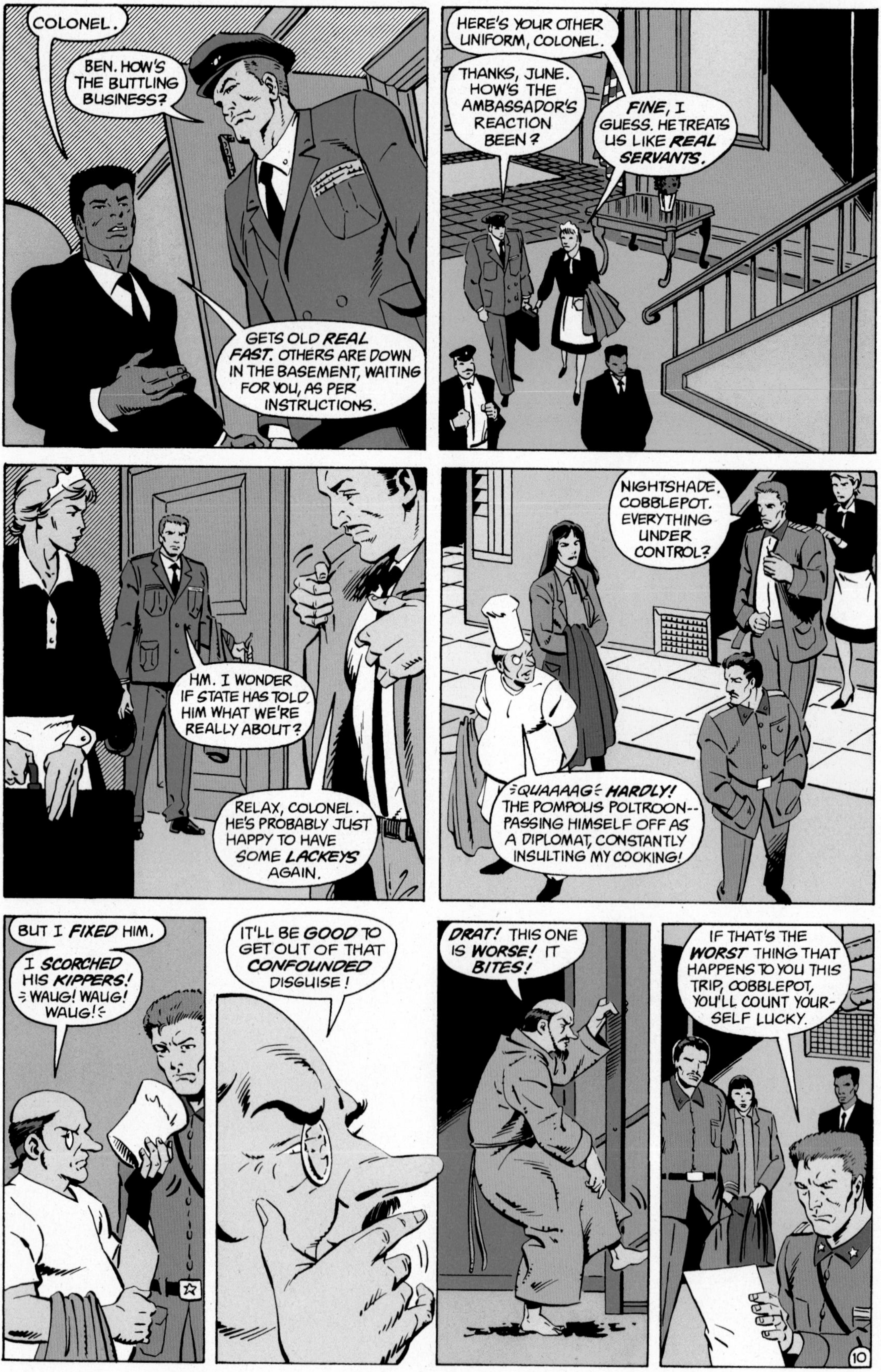
COLONEL.
BEN. HOW'S THE BUTTLING BUSINESS?
GETS OLD REAL FAST. OTHERS ARE DOWN IN THE BASEMENT, WAITING FOR YOU, AS PER INSTRUCTIONS.
HERE'S YOUR OTHER UNIFORM, COLONEL.
THANKS, JUNE. HOW'S THE AMBASSADOR'S REACTION BEEN?
FINE, I GUESS. HE TREATS US LIKE REAL SERVANTS.
HM. I WONDER IF STATE HAS TOLD HIM WHAT WE'RE REALLY ABOUT?
RELAX, COLONEL. HE'S PROBABLY JUST HAPPY TO HAVE SOME LACKEYS AGAIN.
NIGHTSHADE. COBBLEPOT. EVERYTHING UNDER CONTROL?
QUAAAAG HARDLY! THE POMPOUS POLTROON-- PASSING HIMSELF OFF AS A DIPLOMAT, CONSTANTLY INSULTING MY COOKING!
BUT I FIXED HIM.
I SCORCHED HIS KIPPERS! WAUG! WAUG! WAUG!
IT'LL BE GOOD TO GET OUT OF THAT CONFOUNDED DISGUISE!
DRAT! THIS ONE IS WORSE! IT BITES!
IF THAT'S THE WORST THING THAT HAPPENS TO YOU THIS TRIP, COBBLEPOT, YOU'LL COUNT YOURSELF LUCKY.
10

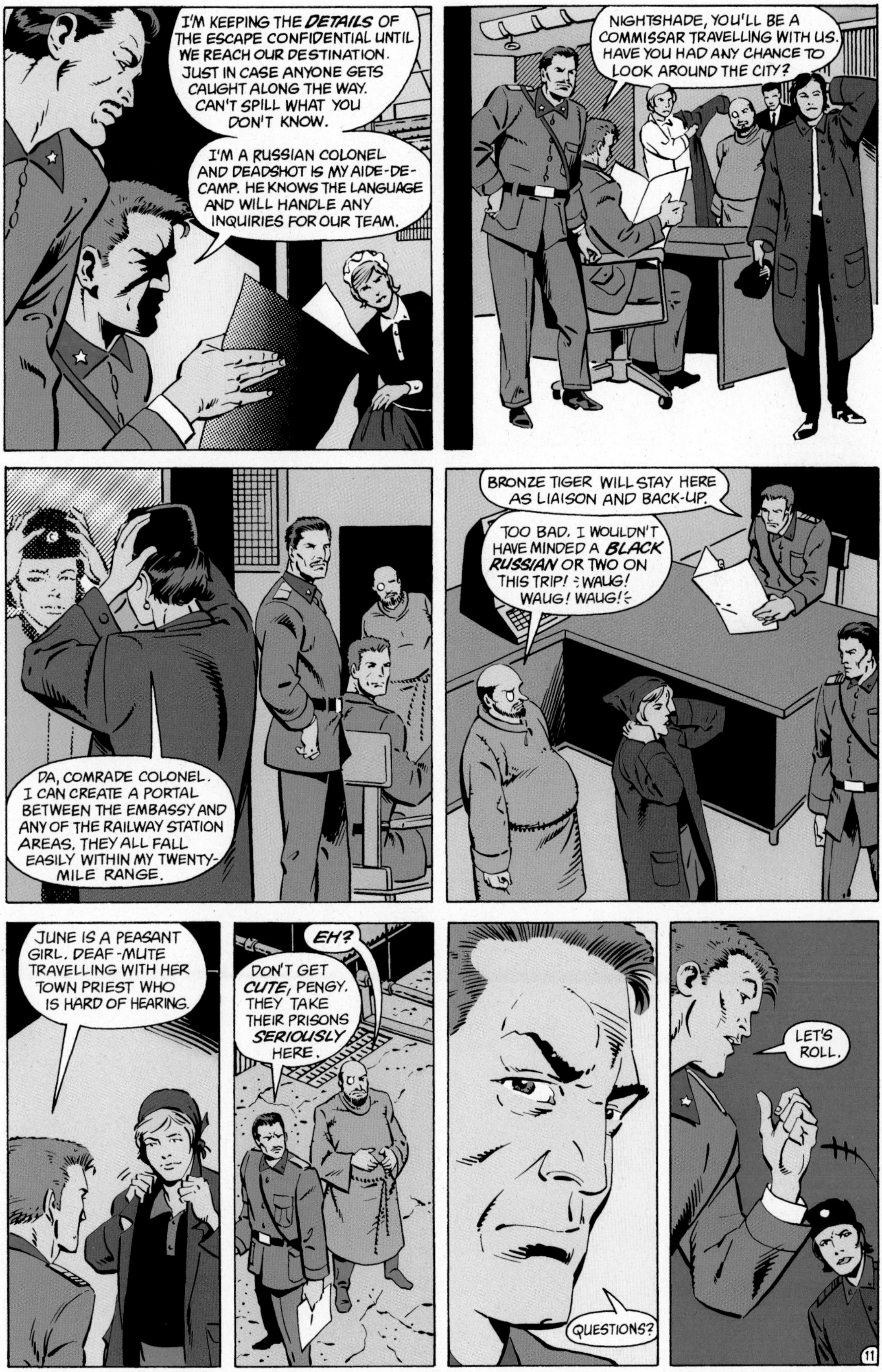

I'M KEEPING THE DETAILS OF THE ESCAPE CONFIDENTIAL UNTIL WE REACH OUR DESTINATION. JUST IN CASE ANYONE GETS CAUGHT ALONG THE WAY. CAN'T SPILL WHAT YOU DON'T KNOW.
I'M A RUSSIAN COLONEL AND DEADSHOT IS MY AIDE-DE-CAMP. HE KNOWS THE LANGUAGE AND WILL HANDLE ANY INQUIRIES FOR OUR TEAM.
NIGHTSHADE, YOU'LL BE A COMMISSAR TRAVELLING WITH US. HAVE YOU HAD ANY CHANCE TO LOOK AROUND THE CITY?
DA, COMRADE COLONEL. I CAN CREATE A PORTAL BETWEEN THE EMBASSY AND ANY OF THE RAILWAY STATION AREAS. THEY ALL FALL EASILY WITHIN MY TWENTY-MILE RANGE.
BRONZE TIGER WILL STAY HERE AS LIAISON AND BACK-UP.
TOO BAD. I WOULDN'T HAVE MINDED A BLACK RUSSIAN OR TWO ON THIS TRIP! WAUG! WAUG! WAUG!
JUNE IS A PEASANT GIRL. DEAF-MUTE TRAVELLING WITH HER TOWN PRIEST WHO IS HARD OF HEARING.
EH?
DON'T GET CUTE, PENGY. THEY TAKE THEIR PRISONS SERIOUSLY HERE.
QUESTIONS?
LET'S ROLL.
11

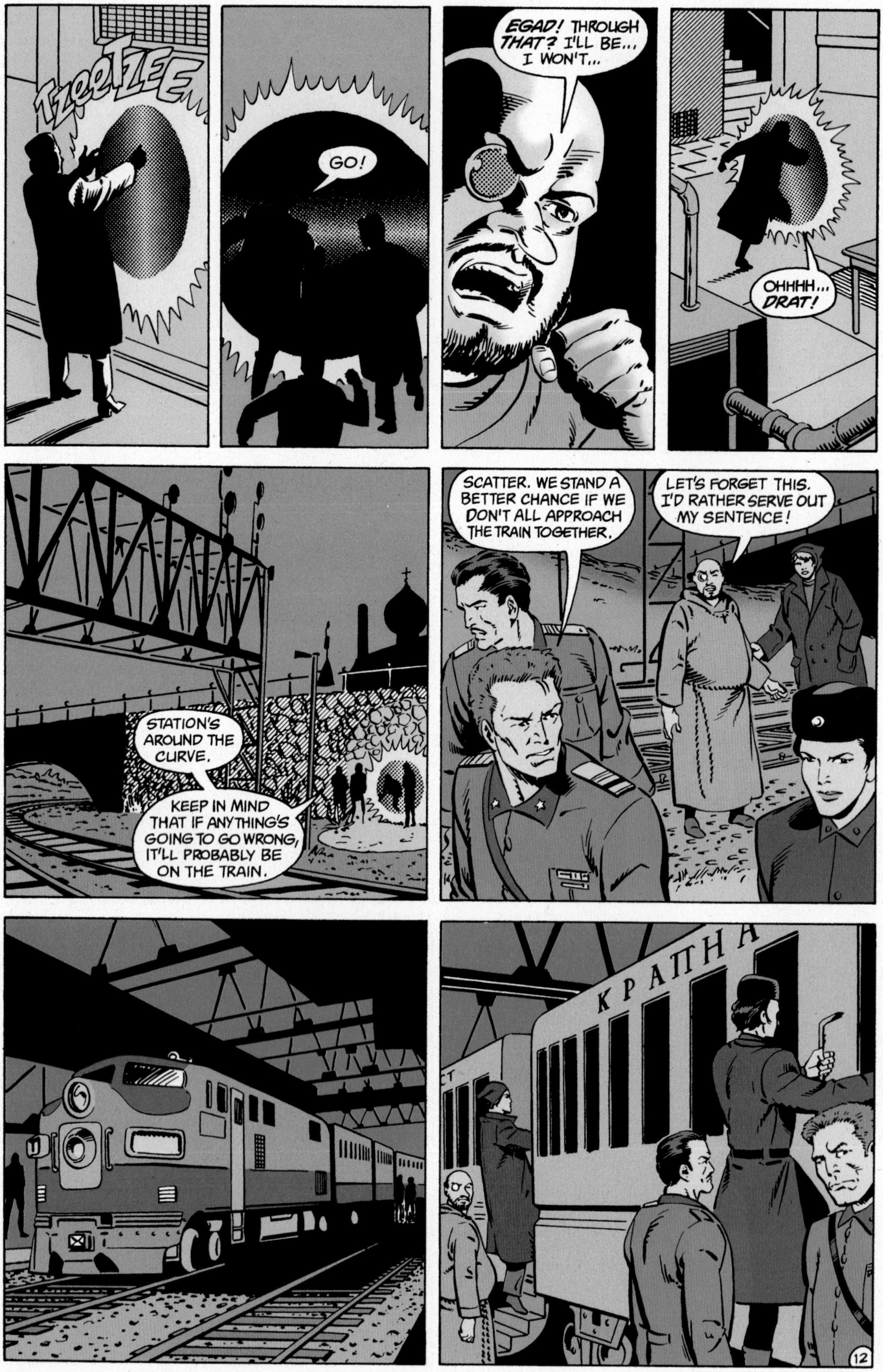
TZEETZEE
GO!
EGAD! THROUGH THAT? I'LL BE... I WON'T...
OHHHH... DRAT!
STATION'S AROUND THE CURVE.
KEEP IN MIND THAT IF ANYTHING'S GOING TO GO WRONG, IT'LL PROBABLY BE ON THE TRAIN.
SCATTER. WE STAND A BETTER CHANCE IF WE DON'T ALL APPROACH THE TRAIN TOGETHER.
LET'S FORGET THIS. I'D RATHER SERVE OUT MY SENTENCE!
КРАПНА
12

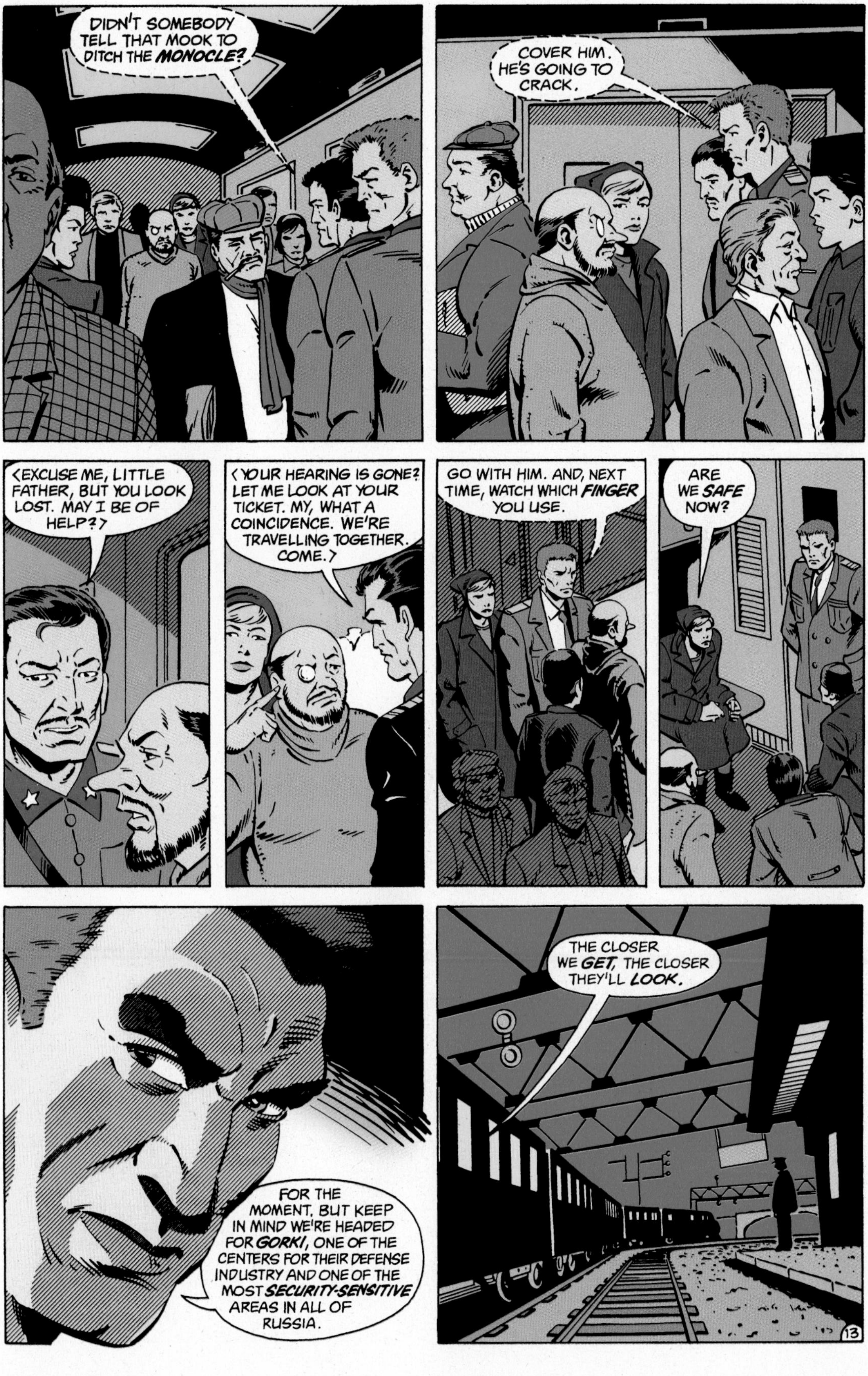
DIDN'T SOMEBODY TELL THAT MOOK TO DITCH THE MONOCLE?
COVER HIM. HE'S GOING TO CRACK.
<EXCUSE ME, LITTLE FATHER, BUT YOU LOOK LOST. MAY I BE OF HELP?>
<YOUR HEARING IS GONE? LET ME LOOK AT YOUR TICKET. MY, WHAT A COINCIDENCE. WE'RE TRAVELLING TOGETHER. COME.>
GO WITH HIM. AND, NEXT TIME, WATCH WHICH FINGER YOU USE.
ARE WE SAFE NOW?
FOR THE MOMENT, BUT KEEP IN MIND WE'RE HEADED FOR GORKI, ONE OF THE CENTERS FOR THEIR DEFENSE INDUSTRY AND ONE OF THE MOST SECURITY-SENSITIVE AREAS IN ALL OF RUSSIA.
THE CLOSER WE GET, THE CLOSER THEY'LL LOOK.
13

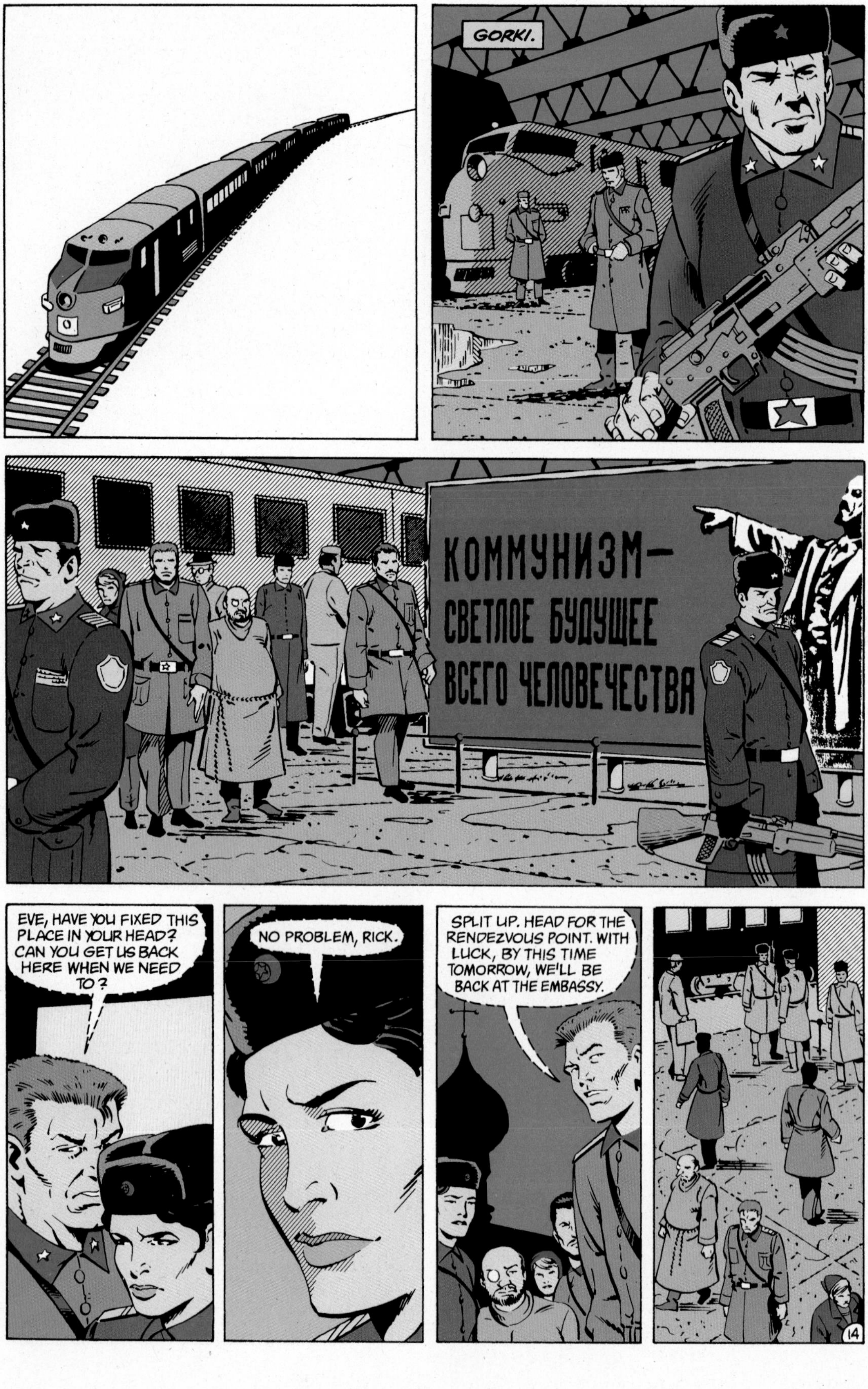
GORKI.
КОММУНИЗМ—
СВЕТЛОЕ БУДУЩЕЕ
ВСЕГО ЧЕЛОВЕЧЕСТВА
EVE, HAVE YOU FIXED THIS PLACE IN YOUR HEAD? CAN YOU GET US BACK HERE WHEN WE NEED TO?
NO PROBLEM, RICK.
SPLIT UP. HEAD FOR THE RENDEZVOUS POINT. WITH LUCK, BY THIS TIME TOMORROW, WE'LL BE BACK AT THE EMBASSY.
14

NOVOGOROD PSYCHIATRIC HOSPITAL, JUST OUTSIDE GORKI.

THERE'S THE TARGET. GLAD YOU ALL MADE IT.

IT'S *YOUR* PLAN, PENGUIN, SO WHY DON'T YOU BRIEF THE OTHERS.

≥QUAAAG!≤ PLEASE HOLD YOUR *APPLAUSE* UNTIL I'M *FINISHED.* GETTING THE FIREBIRD OUT OF HER CAGE WAS NEVER THE *PROBLEM!*

SECURITY IS *NOTHING* IN THAT TINDERBOX! THE *PROBLEM* HAS ALWAYS BEEN GETTING TRIGORIN OUT OF *RUSSIA* ONCE WE *HAD* HER!

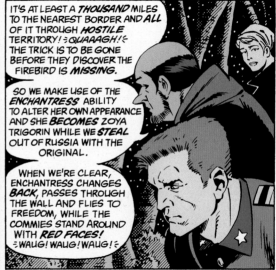

IT'S AT LEAST A *THOUSAND* MILES TO THE NEAREST BORDER AND *ALL* OF IT THROUGH *HOSTILE* TERRITORY! ≥QUAAAGH!≤ THE TRICK IS TO BE GONE BEFORE THEY DISCOVER THE FIREBIRD IS *MISSING.*

SO WE MAKE USE OF THE *ENCHANTRESS'* ABILITY TO ALTER HER OWN APPEARANCE AND SHE *BECOMES* ZOYA TRIGORIN WHILE WE *STEAL* OUT OF RUSSIA WITH THE ORIGINAL.

WHEN WE'RE CLEAR, ENCHANTRESS CHANGES *BACK,* PASSES THROUGH THE WALL AND FLIES TO FREEDOM, WHILE THE COMMIES STAND AROUND WITH *RED FACES!* ≥WAUG! WAUG! WAUG!≤

THERE'S THE SIGNAL. LET'S GO, JUNE.

COLONEL, I...

LET'S GO, JUNE!

ENCHANTRESS!

15

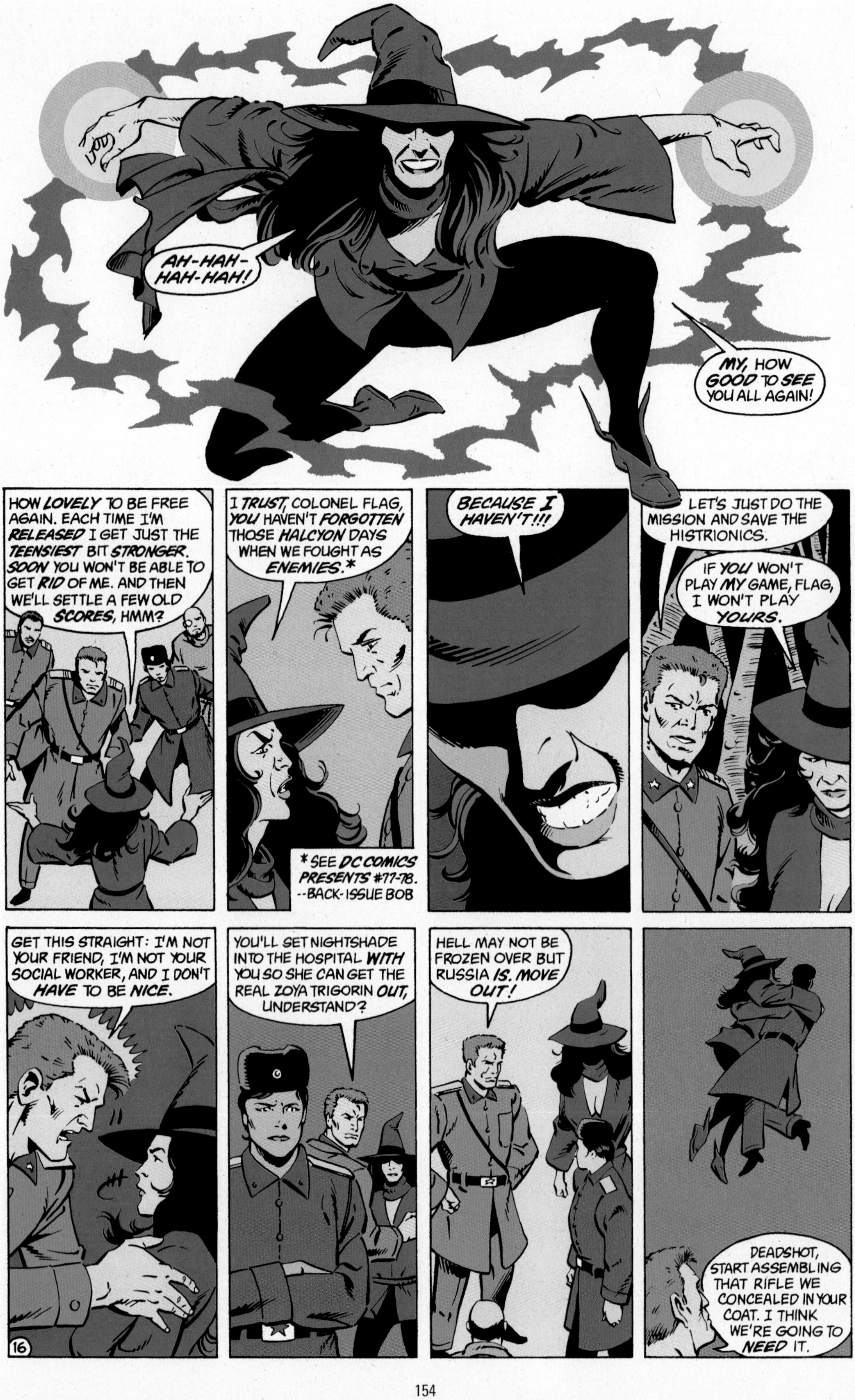
AH-HAH-HAH-HAH!
MY, HOW GOOD TO SEE YOU ALL AGAIN!
HOW LOVELY TO BE FREE AGAIN. EACH TIME I'M RELEASED I GET JUST THE TEENSIEST BIT STRONGER. SOON YOU WON'T BE ABLE TO GET RID OF ME. AND THEN WE'LL SETTLE A FEW OLD SCORES, HMM?
I TRUST, COLONEL FLAG, YOU HAVEN'T FORGOTTEN THOSE HALCYON DAYS WHEN WE FOUGHT AS ENEMIES.*
* SEE DC COMICS PRESENTS #77-78. --BACK-ISSUE BOB
BECAUSE I HAVEN'T!!!
LET'S JUST DO THE MISSION AND SAVE THE HISTRIONICS.
IF YOU WON'T PLAY MY GAME, FLAG, I WON'T PLAY YOURS.
GET THIS STRAIGHT: I'M NOT YOUR FRIEND, I'M NOT YOUR SOCIAL WORKER, AND I DON'T HAVE TO BE NICE.
16
YOU'LL GET NIGHTSHADE INTO THE HOSPITAL WITH YOU SO SHE CAN GET THE REAL ZOYA TRIGORIN OUT, UNDERSTAND?
HELL MAY NOT BE FROZEN OVER BUT RUSSIA IS. MOVE OUT!
DEADSHOT, START ASSEMBLING THAT RIFLE WE CONCEALED IN YOUR COAT. I THINK WE'RE GOING TO NEED IT.

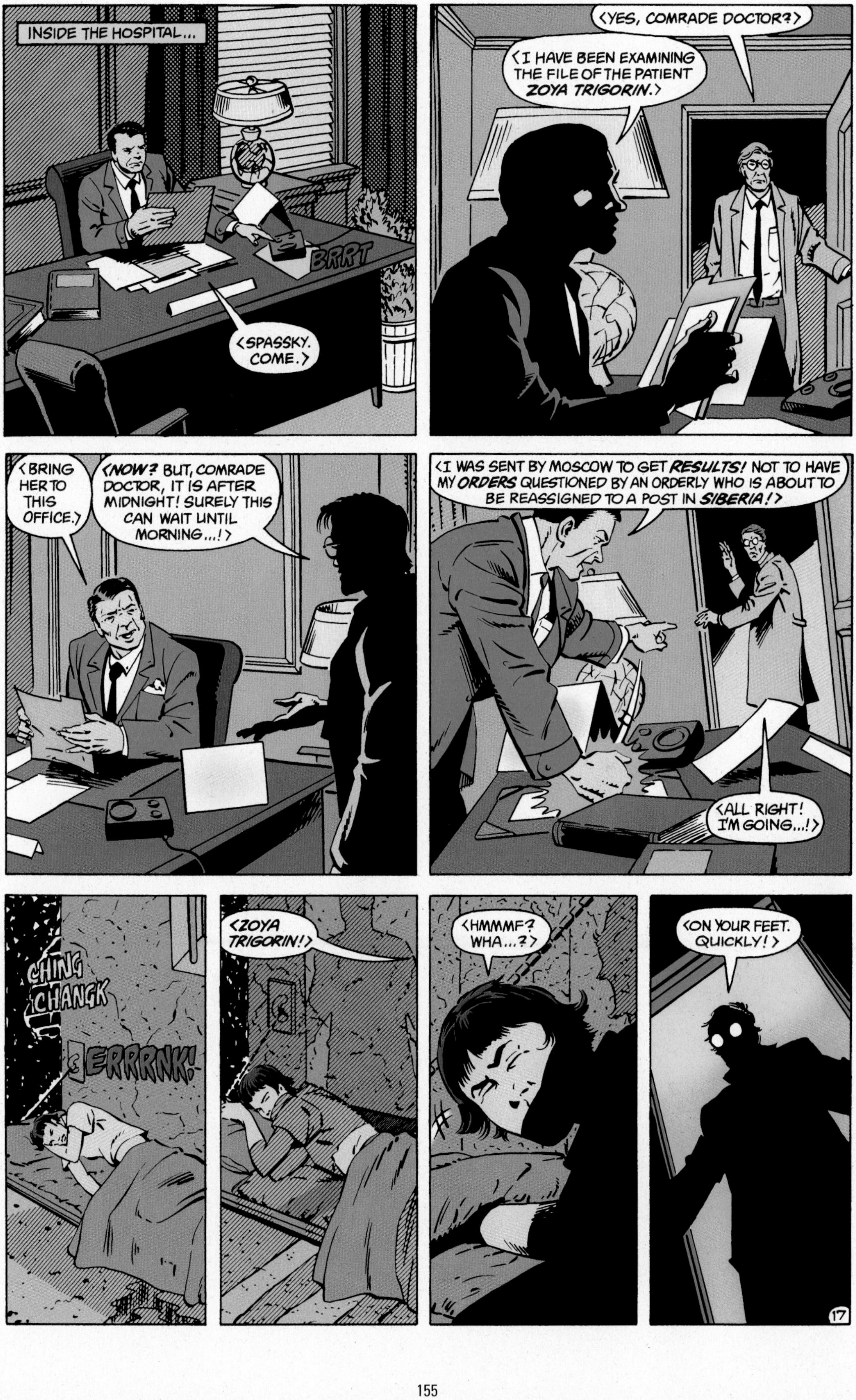
INSIDE THE HOSPITAL...
BRRT
<SPASSKY. COME.>
<YES, COMRADE DOCTOR?>
<I HAVE BEEN EXAMINING THE FILE OF THE PATIENT ZOYA TRIGORIN.>
<BRING HER TO THIS OFFICE.>
<NOW? BUT, COMRADE DOCTOR, IT IS AFTER MIDNIGHT! SURELY THIS CAN WAIT UNTIL MORNING...!>
<I WAS SENT BY MOSCOW TO GET RESULTS! NOT TO HAVE MY ORDERS QUESTIONED BY AN ORDERLY WHO IS ABOUT TO BE REASSIGNED TO A POST IN SIBERIA!>
<ALL RIGHT! I'M GOING...!>
CHING CHANGK
ERRRNK!
<ZOYA TRIGORIN!>
<HMMMF? WHA...?>
<ON YOUR FEET. QUICKLY!>
17

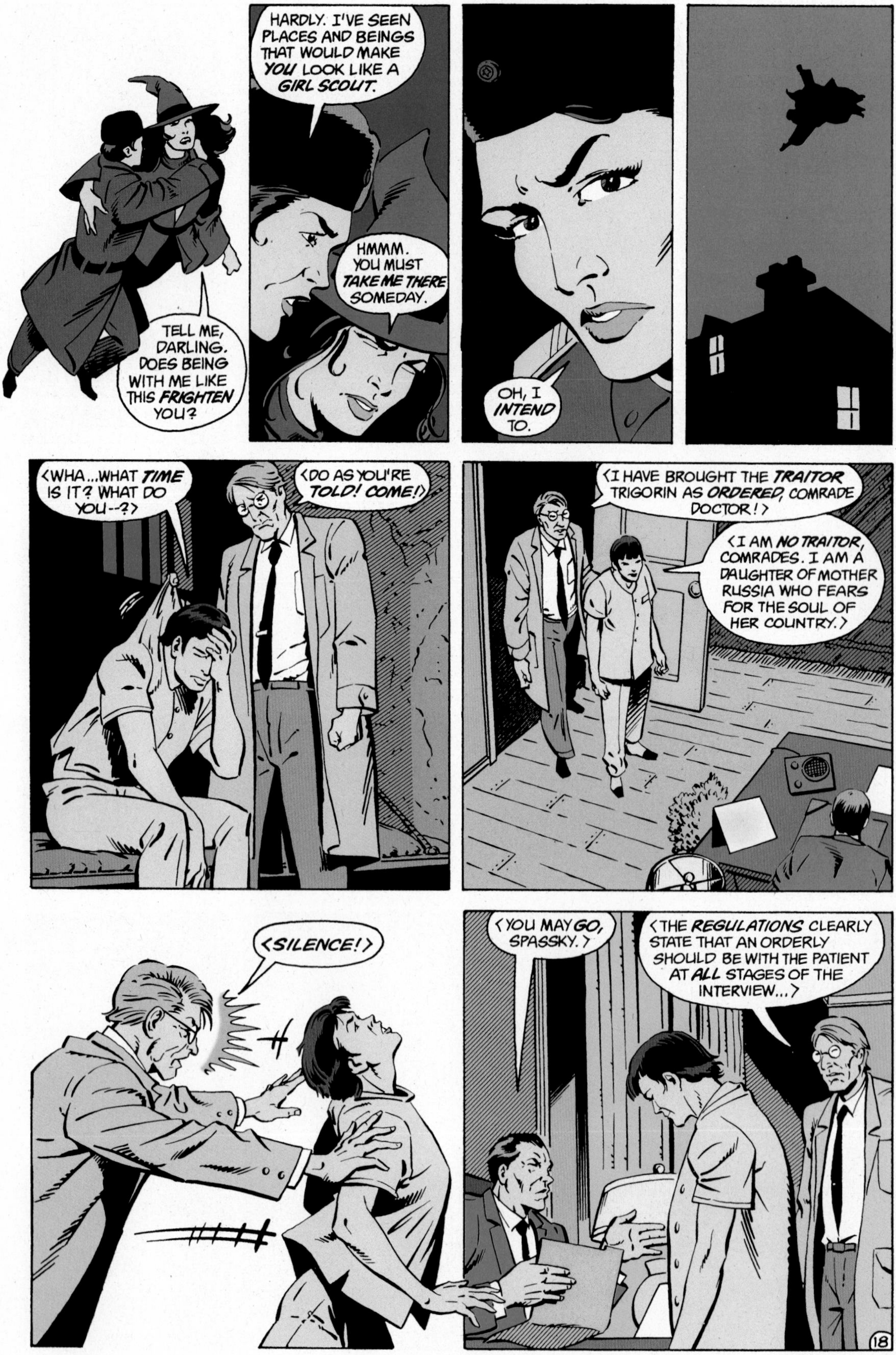
TELL ME, DARLING. DOES BEING WITH ME LIKE THIS FRIGHTEN YOU?
HARDLY. I'VE SEEN PLACES AND BEINGS THAT WOULD MAKE YOU LOOK LIKE A GIRL SCOUT.
HMMM. YOU MUST TAKE ME THERE SOMEDAY.
OH, I INTEND TO.
<WHA...WHAT TIME IS IT? WHAT DO YOU--?>
<DO AS YOU'RE TOLD! COME!>
<I HAVE BROUGHT THE TRAITOR TRIGORIN AS ORDERED, COMRADE DOCTOR!>
<I AM NO TRAITOR, COMRADES. I AM A DAUGHTER OF MOTHER RUSSIA WHO FEARS FOR THE SOUL OF HER COUNTRY.>
<SILENCE!>
<YOU MAY GO, SPASSKY.>
<THE REGULATIONS CLEARLY STATE THAT AN ORDERLY SHOULD BE WITH THE PATIENT AT ALL STAGES OF THE INTERVIEW...>
18

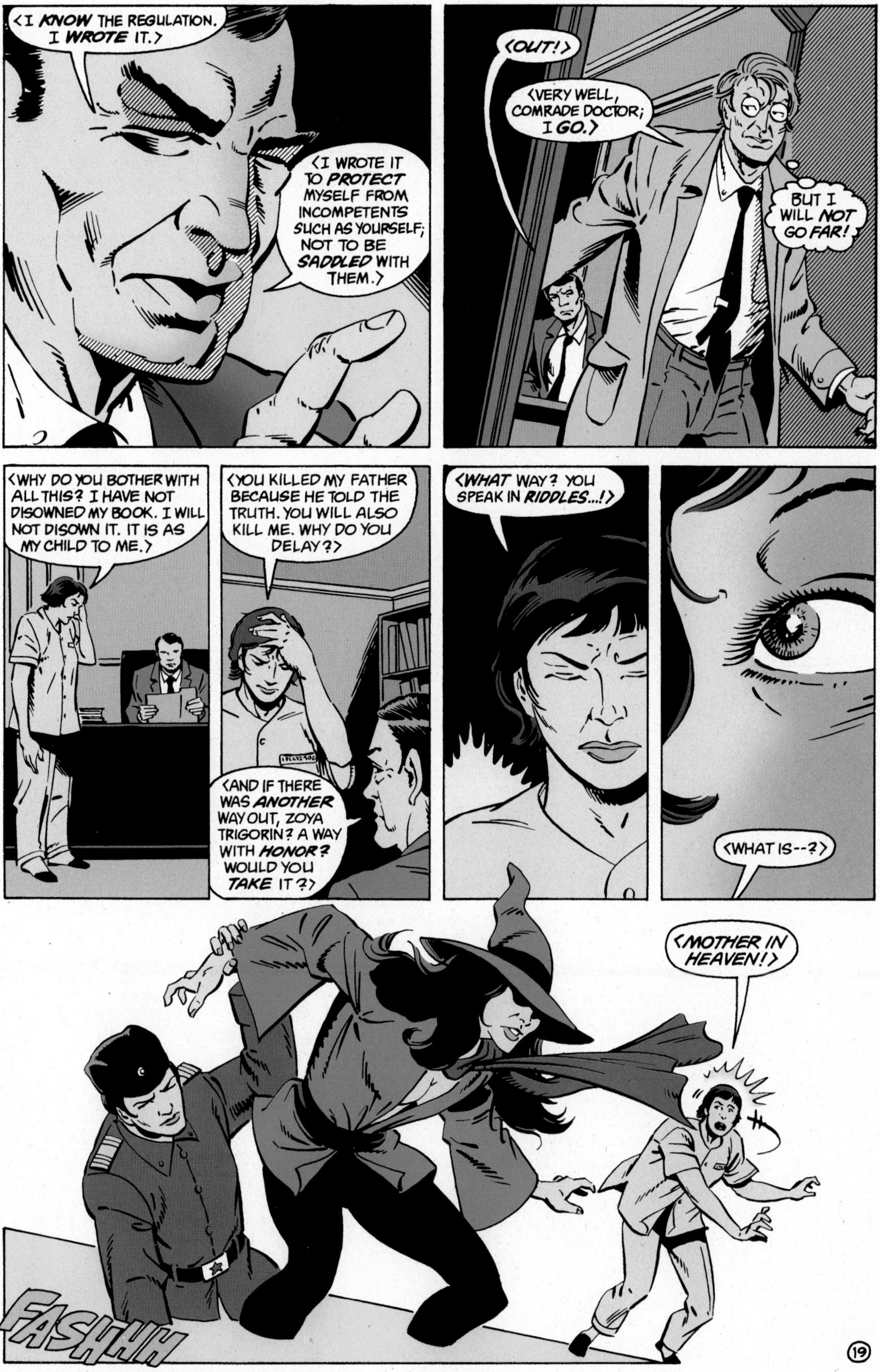
<I KNOW THE REGULATION. I WROTE IT.>
<I WROTE IT TO PROTECT MYSELF FROM INCOMPETENTS SUCH AS YOURSELF; NOT TO BE SADDLED WITH THEM.>
<OUT!>
<VERY WELL, COMRADE DOCTOR; I GO.>
BUT I WILL NOT GO FAR!
<WHY DO YOU BOTHER WITH ALL THIS? I HAVE NOT DISOWNED MY BOOK. I WILL NOT DISOWN IT. IT IS AS MY CHILD TO ME.>
<YOU KILLED MY FATHER BECAUSE HE TOLD THE TRUTH. YOU WILL ALSO KILL ME. WHY DO YOU DELAY?>
<AND IF THERE WAS ANOTHER WAY OUT, ZOYA TRIGORIN? A WAY WITH HONOR? WOULD YOU TAKE IT?>
<WHAT WAY? YOU SPEAK IN RIDDLES...!>
<WHAT IS--?>
<MOTHER IN HEAVEN!>
FASHHH
19

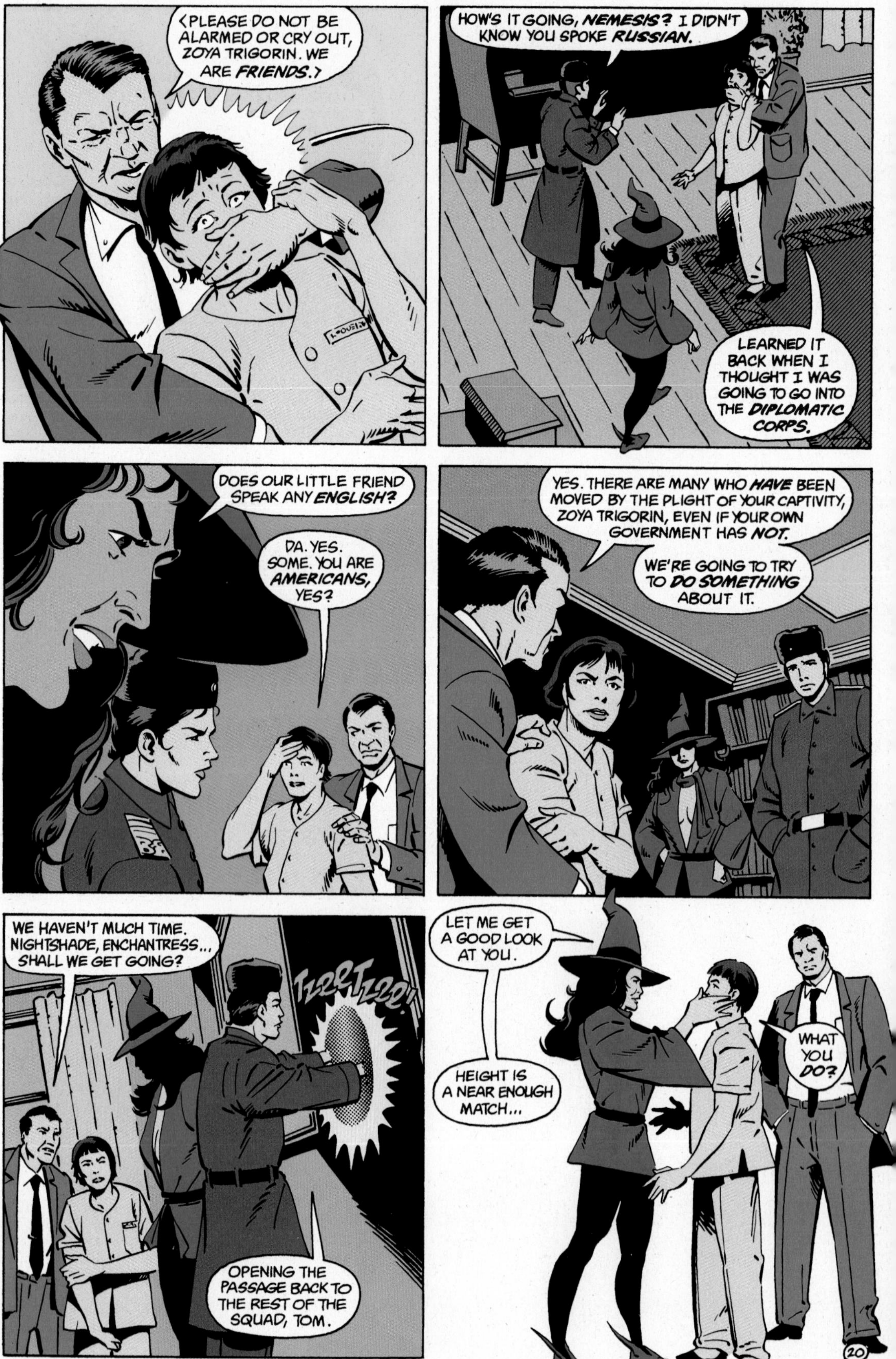

<PLEASE DO NOT BE ALARMED OR CRY OUT, ZOYA TRIGORIN. WE ARE FRIENDS.>
HOW'S IT GOING, NEMESIS? I DIDN'T KNOW YOU SPOKE RUSSIAN.
LEARNED IT BACK WHEN I THOUGHT I WAS GOING TO GO INTO THE DIPLOMATIC CORPS.
DOES OUR LITTLE FRIEND SPEAK ANY ENGLISH?
DA. YES. SOME. YOU ARE AMERICANS, YES?
YES. THERE ARE MANY WHO HAVE BEEN MOVED BY THE PLIGHT OF YOUR CAPTIVITY, ZOYA TRIGORIN, EVEN IF YOUR OWN GOVERNMENT HAS NOT.
WE'RE GOING TO TRY TO DO SOMETHING ABOUT IT.
WE HAVEN'T MUCH TIME. NIGHTSHADE, ENCHANTRESS... SHALL WE GET GOING?
TZZZRT TZZZ
OPENING THE PASSAGE BACK TO THE REST OF THE SQUAD, TOM.
LET ME GET A GOOD LOOK AT YOU.
HEIGHT IS A NEAR ENOUGH MATCH...
WHAT YOU DO?
20

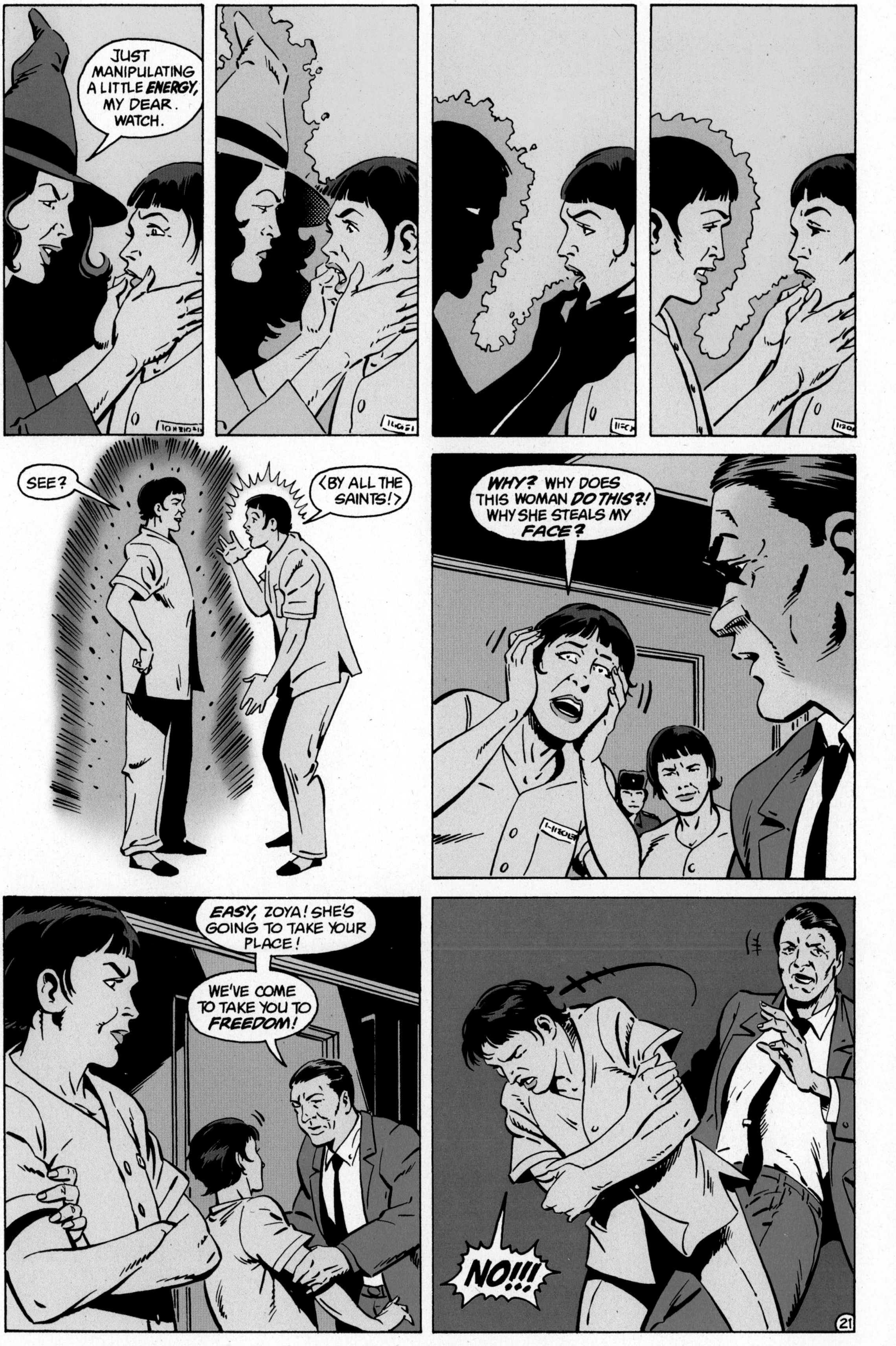
JUST MANIPULATING A LITTLE ENERGY, MY DEAR. WATCH.
SEE?
<BY ALL THE SAINTS!>
WHY? WHY DOES THIS WOMAN DO THIS?! WHY SHE STEALS MY FACE?
EASY, ZOYA! SHE'S GOING TO TAKE YOUR PLACE!
WE'VE COME TO TAKE YOU TO FREEDOM!
NO!!!
21

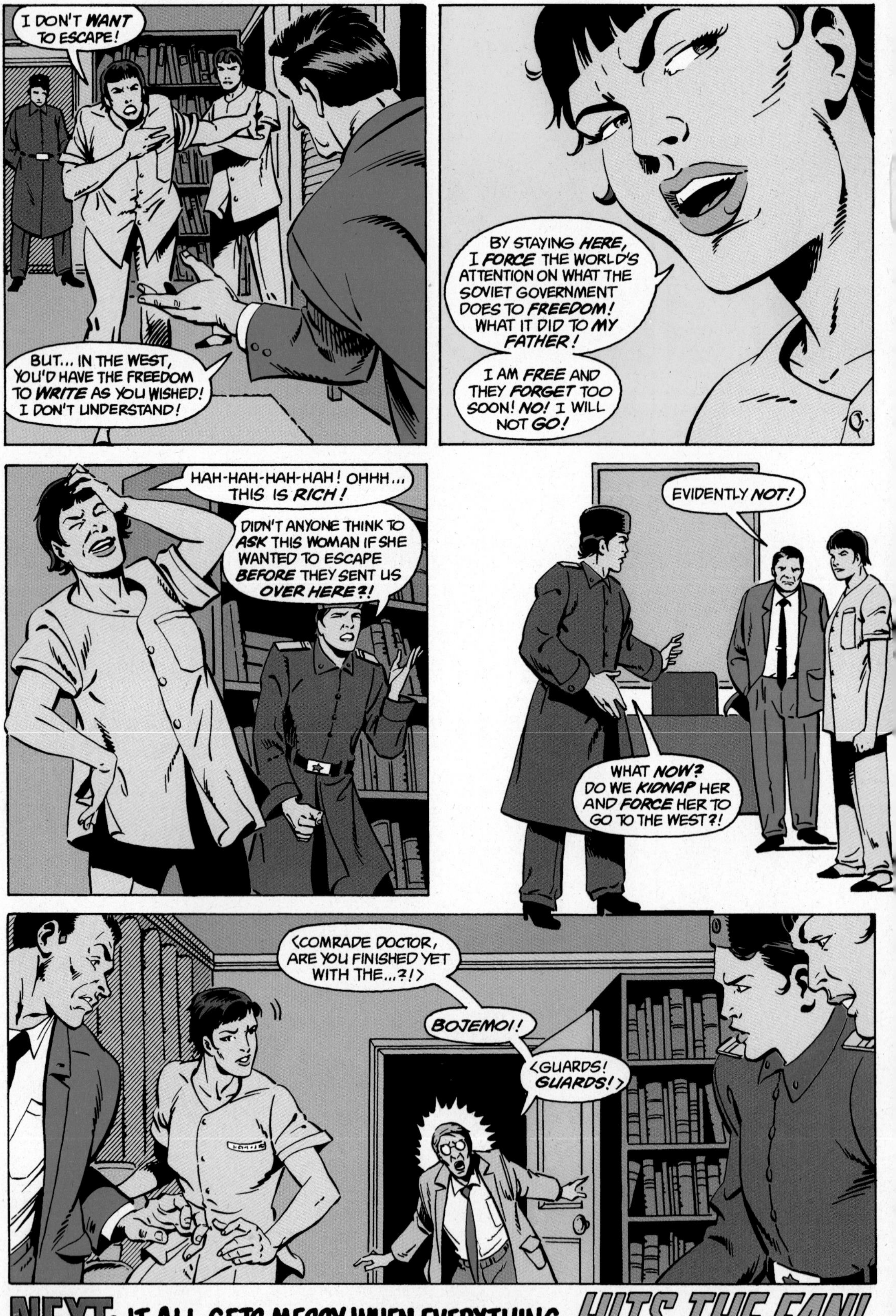
I DON'T WANT TO ESCAPE!
BUT... IN THE WEST, YOU'D HAVE THE FREEDOM TO WRITE AS YOU WISHED! I DON'T UNDERSTAND!
BY STAYING HERE, I FORCE THE WORLD'S ATTENTION ON WHAT THE SOVIET GOVERNMENT DOES TO FREEDOM! WHAT IT DID TO MY FATHER!
I AM FREE AND THEY FORGET TOO SOON! NO! I WILL NOT GO!
HAH-HAH-HAH-HAH! OHHH... THIS IS RICH!
DIDN'T ANYONE THINK TO ASK THIS WOMAN IF SHE WANTED TO ESCAPE BEFORE THEY SENT US OVER HERE?!
EVIDENTLY NOT!
WHAT NOW? DO WE KIDNAP HER AND FORCE HER TO GO TO THE WEST?!
<COMRADE DOCTOR, ARE YOU FINISHED YET WITH THE...?!>
BOJEMOI!
<GUARDS! GUARDS!>

NEXT: IT ALL GETS MESSY WHEN EVERYTHING HITS THE FAN!

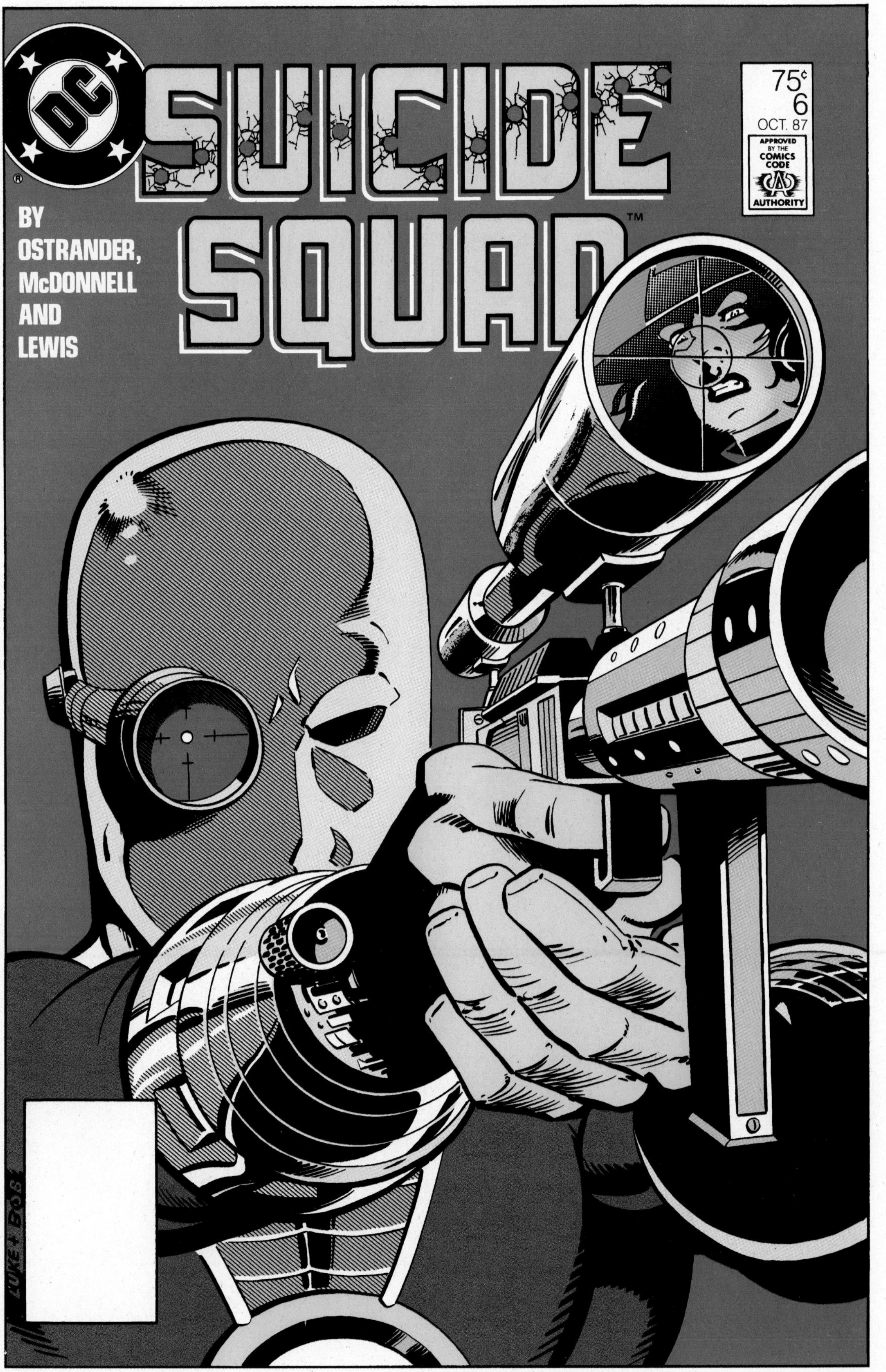

SUICIDE SQUAD
75¢
6
OCT. 87
APPROVED BY THE COMICS CODE AUTHORITY
BY OSTRANDER, McDONNELL AND LEWIS
LUKE + BOB

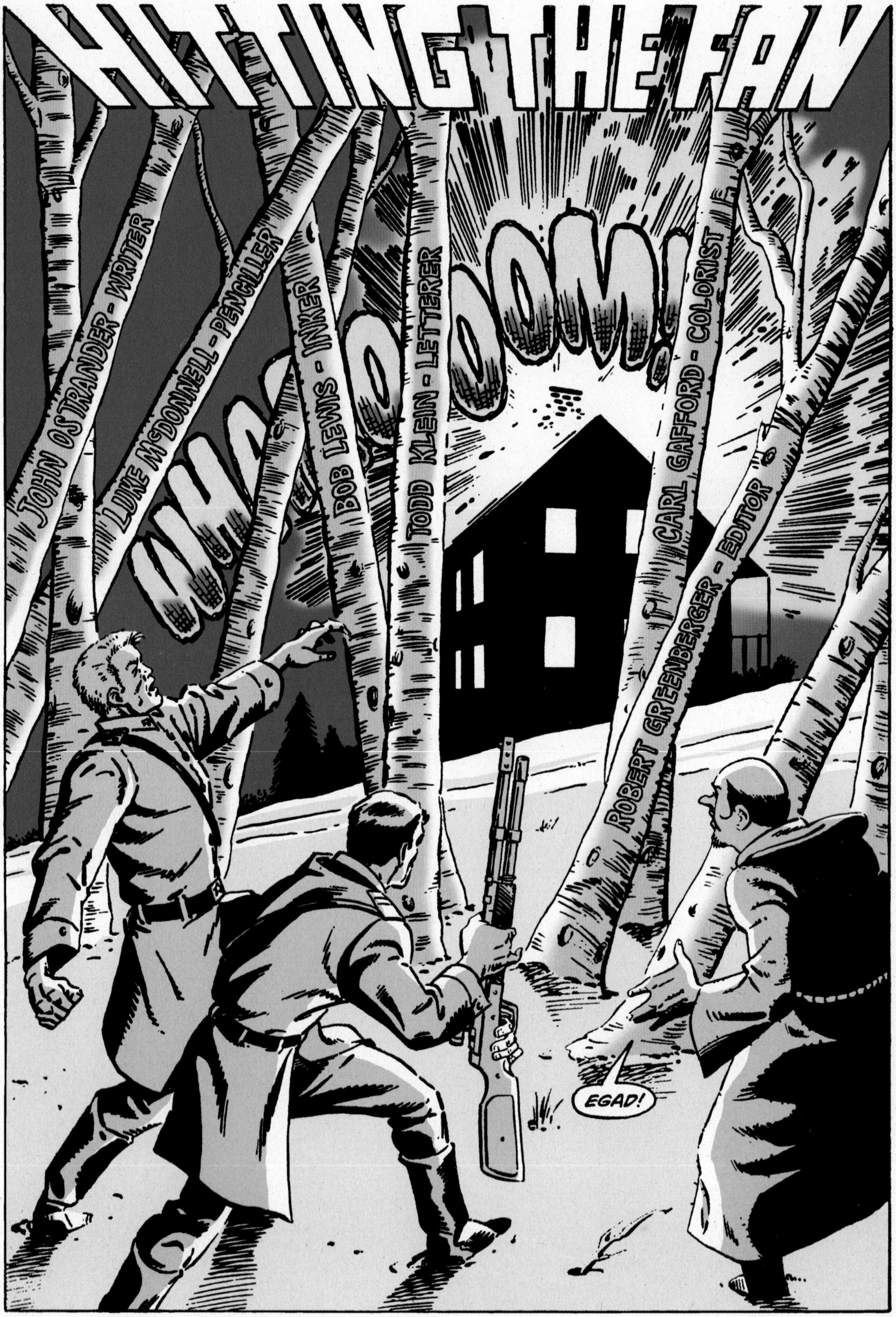
HITTING THE FAN
JOHN OSTRANDER - WRITER
LUKE McDONNELL - PENCILLER
BOB LEWIS - INKER
TODD KLEIN - LETTERER
CARL GAFFORD - COLORIST
ROBERT GREENBERGER - EDITOR
EGAD!

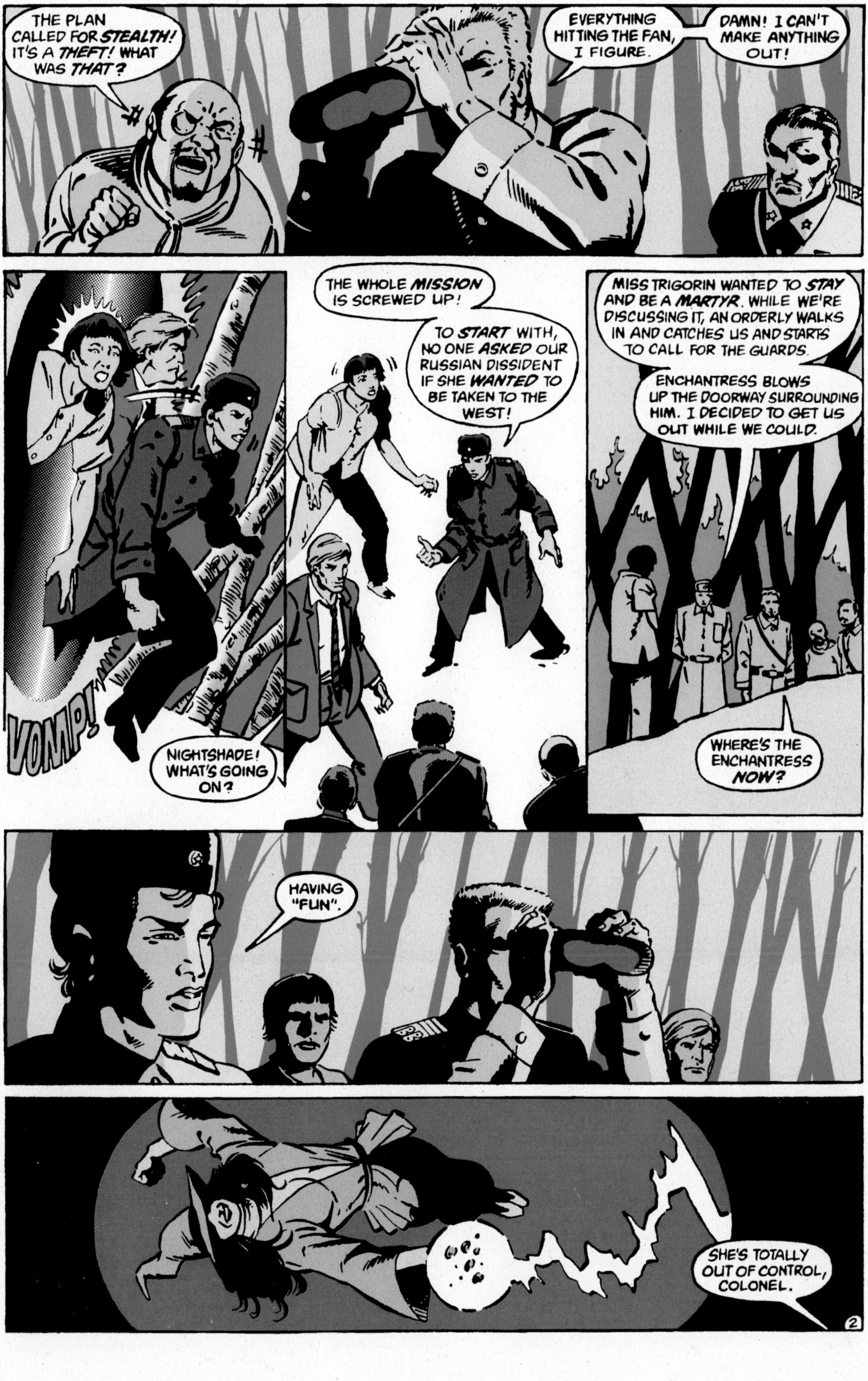
THE PLAN CALLED FOR STEALTH! IT'S A THEFT! WHAT WAS THAT?
EVERYTHING HITTING THE FAN, I FIGURE.
DAMN! I CAN'T MAKE ANYTHING OUT!
VOMP!
NIGHTSHADE! WHAT'S GOING ON?
THE WHOLE MISSION IS SCREWED UP!
TO START WITH, NO ONE ASKED OUR RUSSIAN DISSIDENT IF SHE WANTED TO BE TAKEN TO THE WEST!
MISS TRIGORIN WANTED TO STAY AND BE A MARTYR. WHILE WE'RE DISCUSSING IT, AN ORDERLY WALKS IN AND CATCHES US AND STARTS TO CALL FOR THE GUARDS.
ENCHANTRESS BLOWS UP THE DOORWAY SURROUNDING HIM. I DECIDED TO GET US OUT WHILE WE COULD.
WHERE'S THE ENCHANTRESS NOW?
HAVING "FUN".
SHE'S TOTALLY OUT OF CONTROL, COLONEL.
2

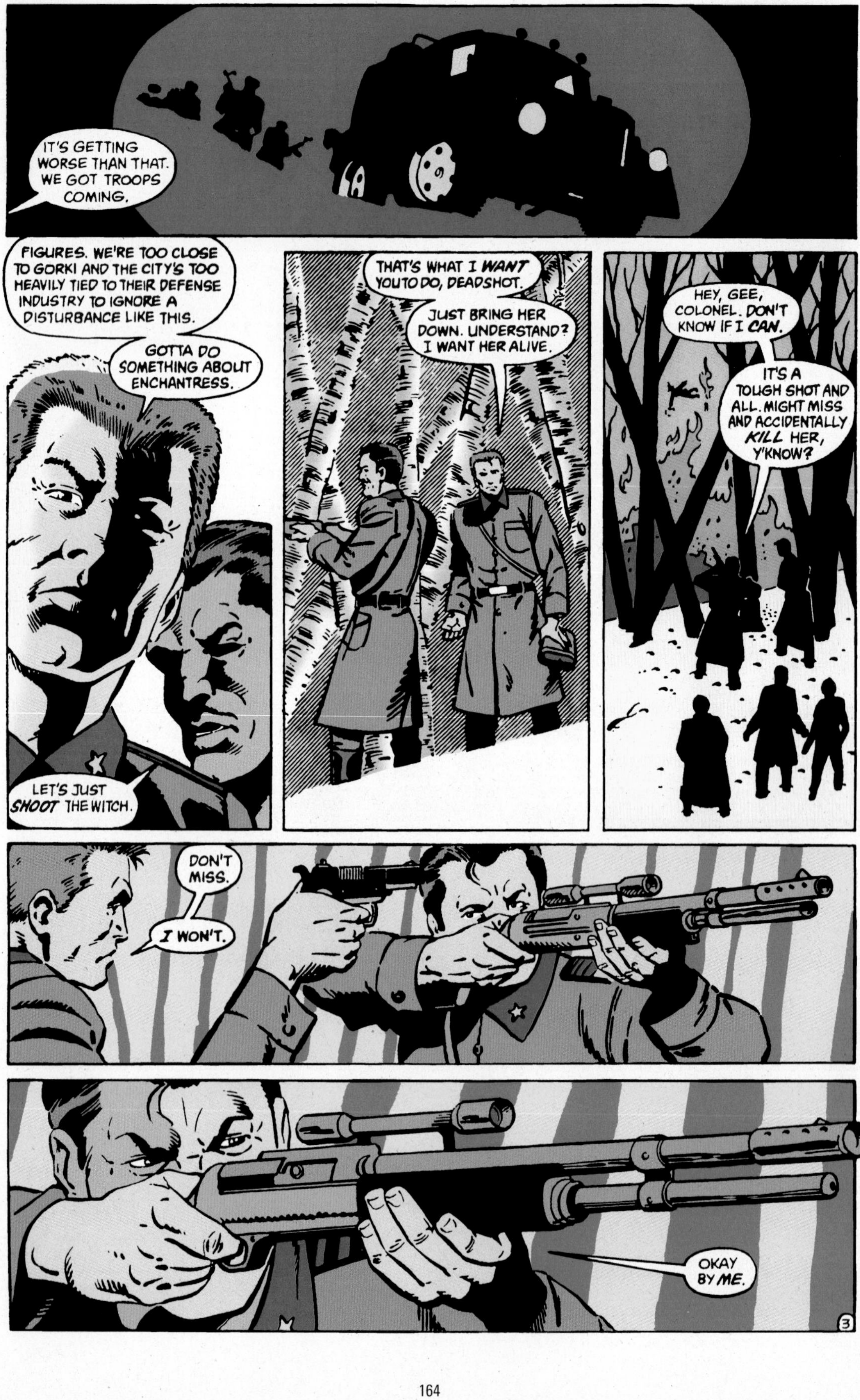
IT'S GETTING WORSE THAN THAT. WE GOT TROOPS COMING.
FIGURES. WE'RE TOO CLOSE TO GORKI AND THE CITY'S TOO HEAVILY TIED TO THEIR DEFENSE INDUSTRY TO IGNORE A DISTURBANCE LIKE THIS.
GOTTA DO SOMETHING ABOUT ENCHANTRESS.
LET'S JUST SHOOT THE WITCH.
THAT'S WHAT I WANT YOU TO DO, DEADSHOT.
JUST BRING HER DOWN. UNDERSTAND? I WANT HER ALIVE.
HEY, GEE, COLONEL. DON'T KNOW IF I CAN.
IT'S A TOUGH SHOT AND ALL. MIGHT MISS AND ACCIDENTALLY KILL HER, Y'KNOW?
DON'T MISS.
I WON'T.
OKAY BY ME.
3

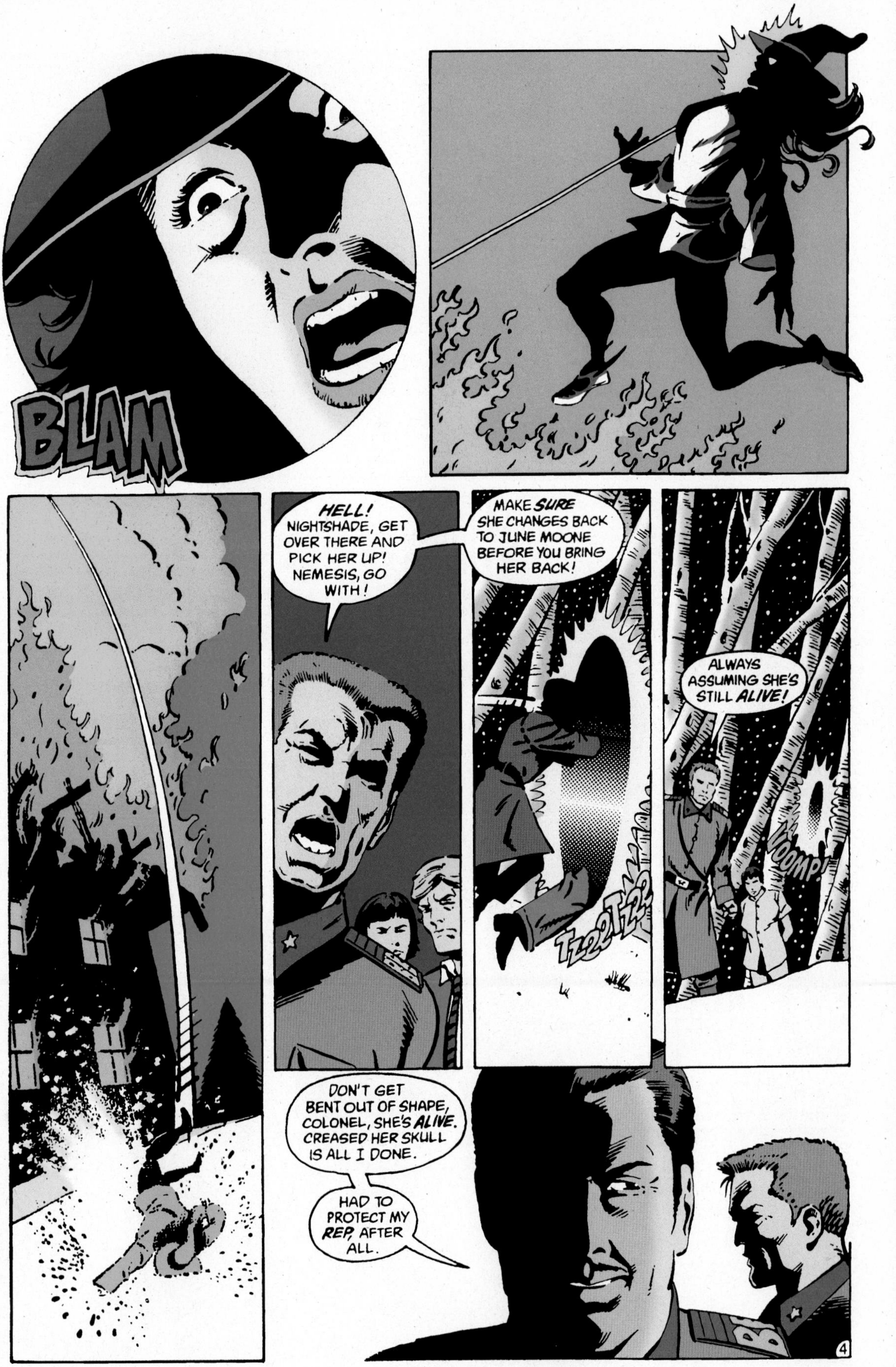
BLAM
HELL! NIGHTSHADE, GET OVER THERE AND PICK HER UP! NEMESIS, GO WITH!
MAKE SURE SHE CHANGES BACK TO JUNE MOONE BEFORE YOU BRING HER BACK!
TZZZTZZZ
ALWAYS ASSUMING SHE'S STILL ALIVE!
VOOMP!
DON'T GET BENT OUT OF SHAPE, COLONEL, SHE'S ALIVE. CREASED HER SKULL IS ALL I DONE.
HAD TO PROTECT MY REP, AFTER ALL.
4

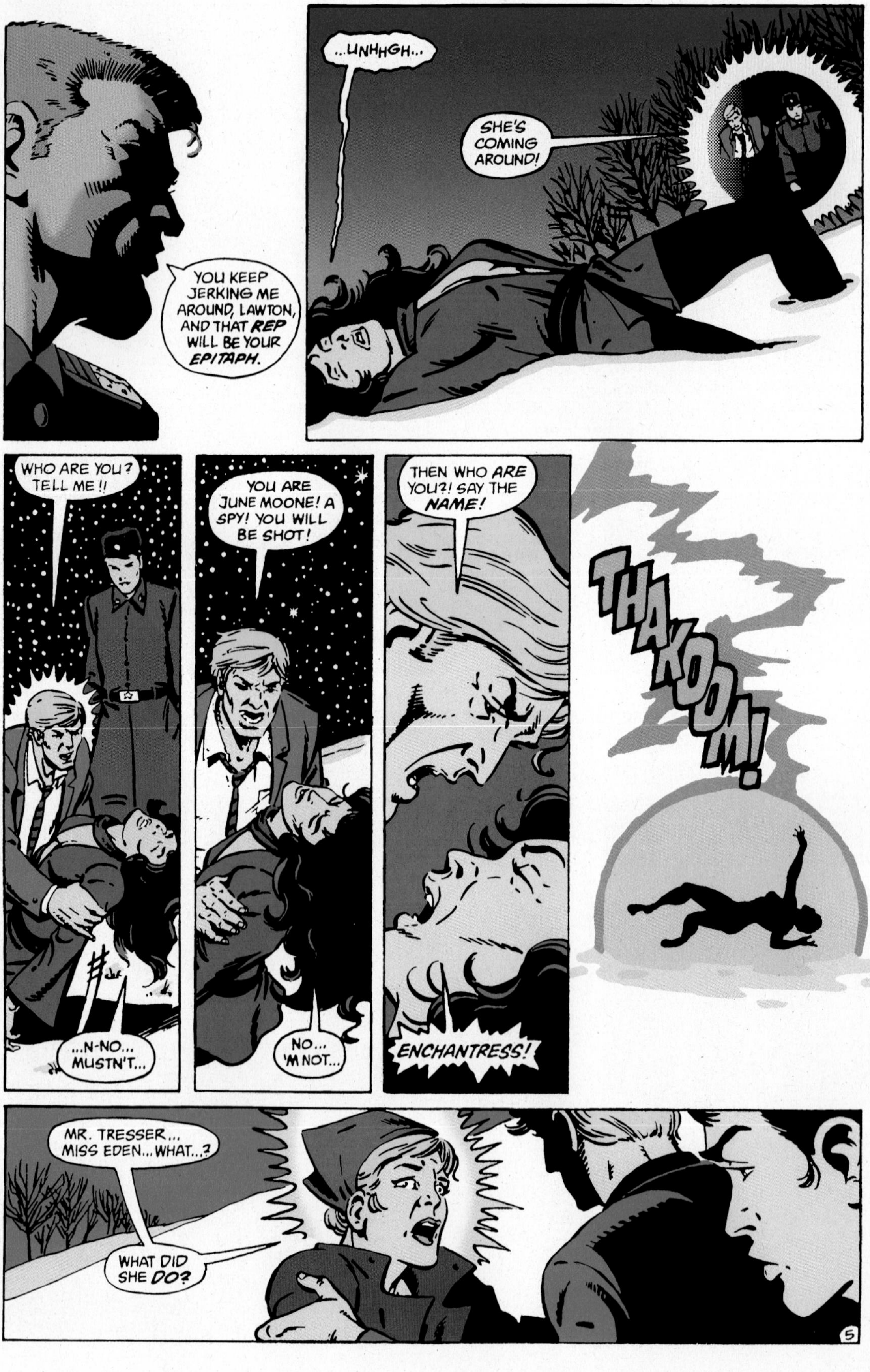
YOU KEEP JERKING ME AROUND, LAWTON, AND THAT REP WILL BE YOUR EPITAPH.
...UNHHGH...
SHE'S COMING AROUND!
WHO ARE YOU? TELL ME!!
...N-NO... MUSTN'T...
YOU ARE JUNE MOONE! A SPY! YOU WILL BE SHOT!
NO... 'M NOT...
THEN WHO ARE YOU?! SAY THE NAME!
ENCHANTRESS!
THAKOOOM!
MR. TRESSER... MISS EDEN... WHAT...?
WHAT DID SHE DO?
5

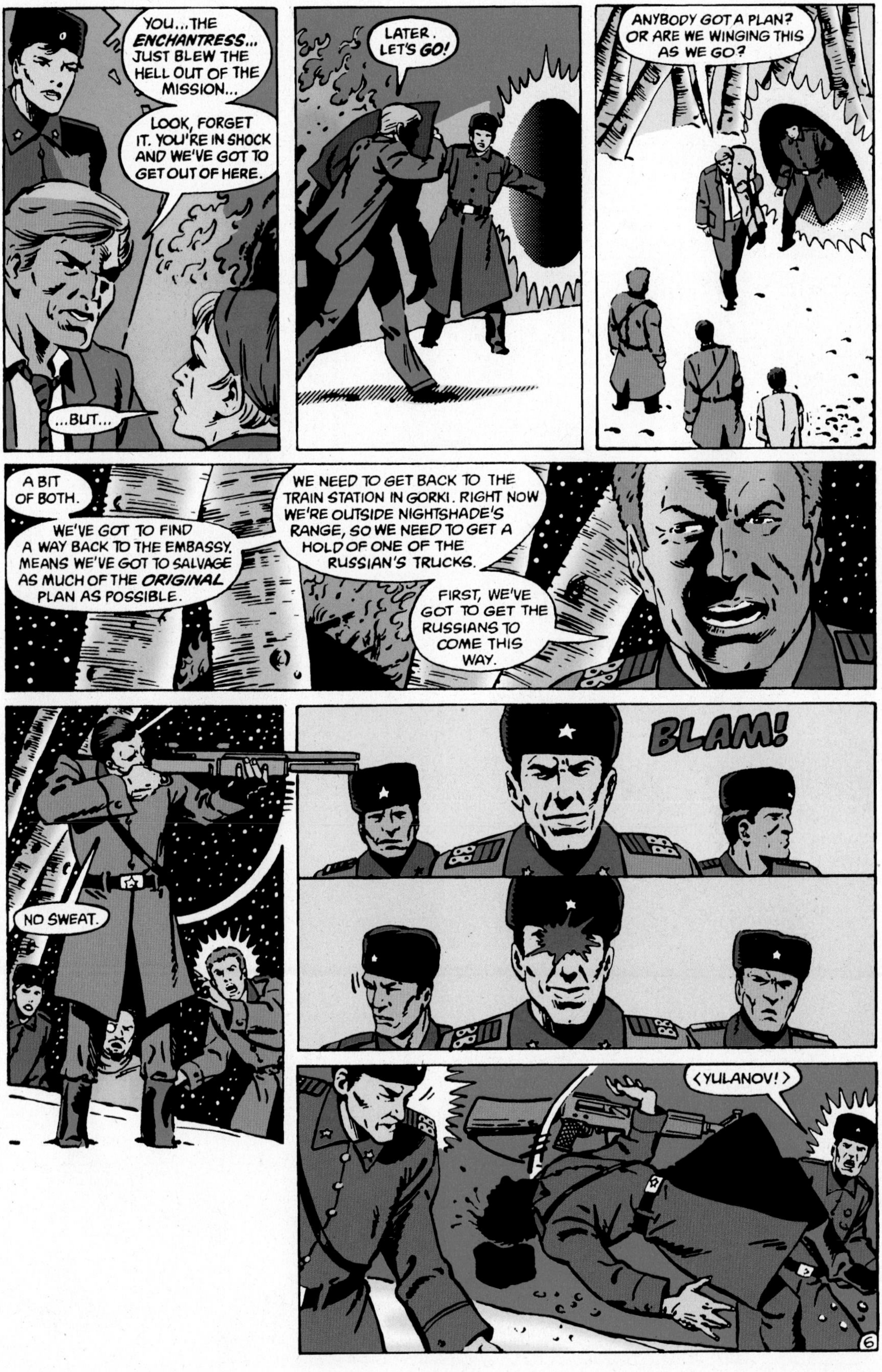
YOU...THE ENCHANTRESS... JUST BLEW THE HELL OUT OF THE MISSION...
LOOK, FORGET IT. YOU'RE IN SHOCK AND WE'VE GOT TO GET OUT OF HERE.
...BUT...
LATER. LET'S GO!
ANYBODY GOT A PLAN? OR ARE WE WINGING THIS AS WE GO?
A BIT OF BOTH.
WE'VE GOT TO FIND A WAY BACK TO THE EMBASSY. MEANS WE'VE GOT TO SALVAGE AS MUCH OF THE ORIGINAL PLAN AS POSSIBLE.
WE NEED TO GET BACK TO THE TRAIN STATION IN GORKI. RIGHT NOW WE'RE OUTSIDE NIGHTSHADE'S RANGE, SO WE NEED TO GET A HOLD OF ONE OF THE RUSSIAN'S TRUCKS.
FIRST, WE'VE GOT TO GET THE RUSSIANS TO COME THIS WAY.
NO SWEAT.
BLAM!
‹YULANOV!›
6

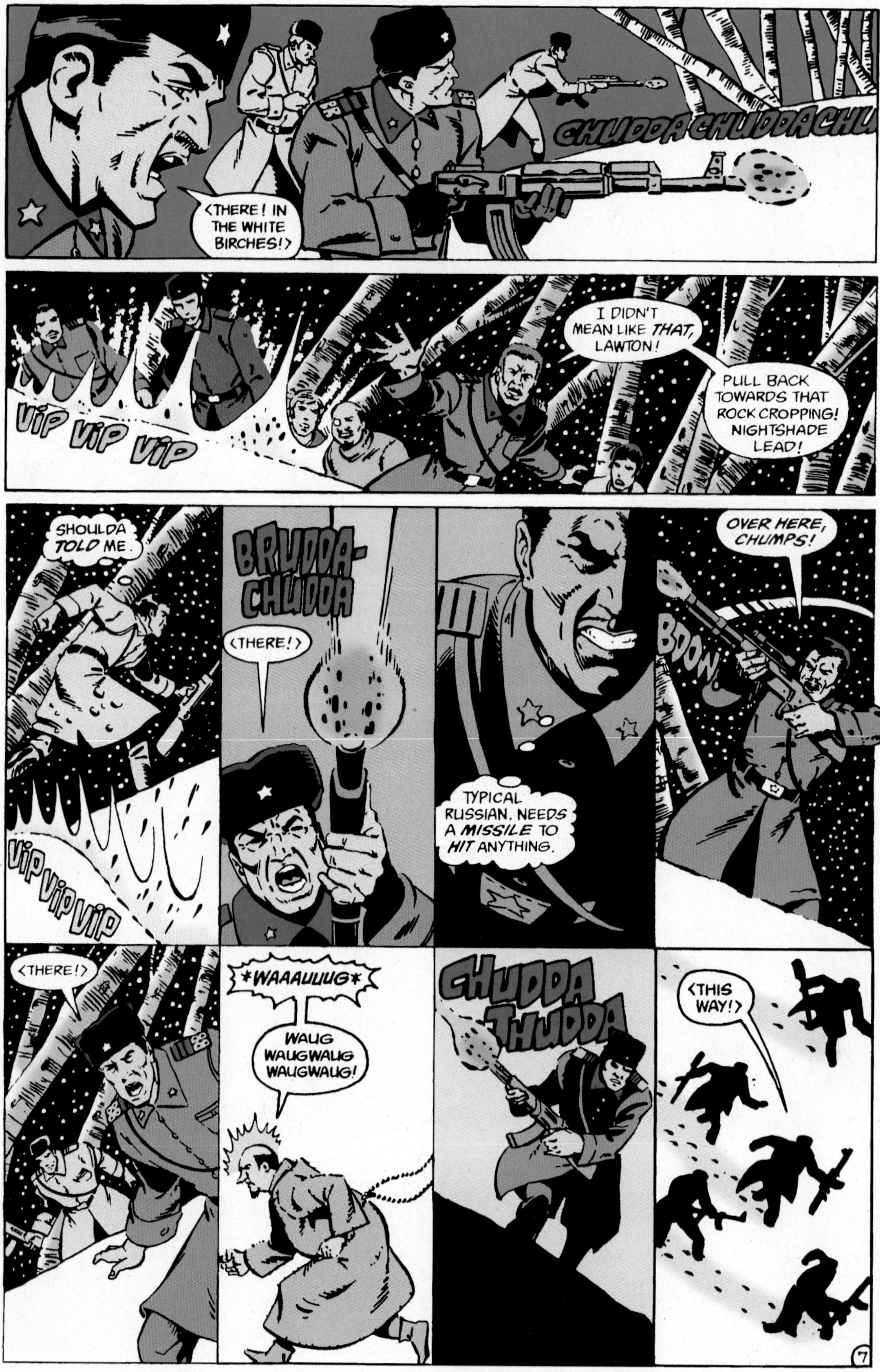
CHUDDA CHUDDA CHU
<THERE! IN THE WHITE BIRCHES!>
I DIDN'T MEAN LIKE THAT, LAWTON!
PULL BACK TOWARDS THAT ROCK CROPPING! NIGHTSHADE LEAD!
VIP VIP VIP
SHOULDA TOLD ME.
VIP VIP VIP
BRUDDA-CHUDDA
<THERE!>
TYPICAL RUSSIAN. NEEDS A MISSILE TO HIT ANYTHING.
OVER HERE, CHUMPS!
BOOM
<THERE!>
WAAAUUUG
WAUG WAUGWAUG WAUGWAUG!
CHUDDA THUDDA
<THIS WAY!>
7

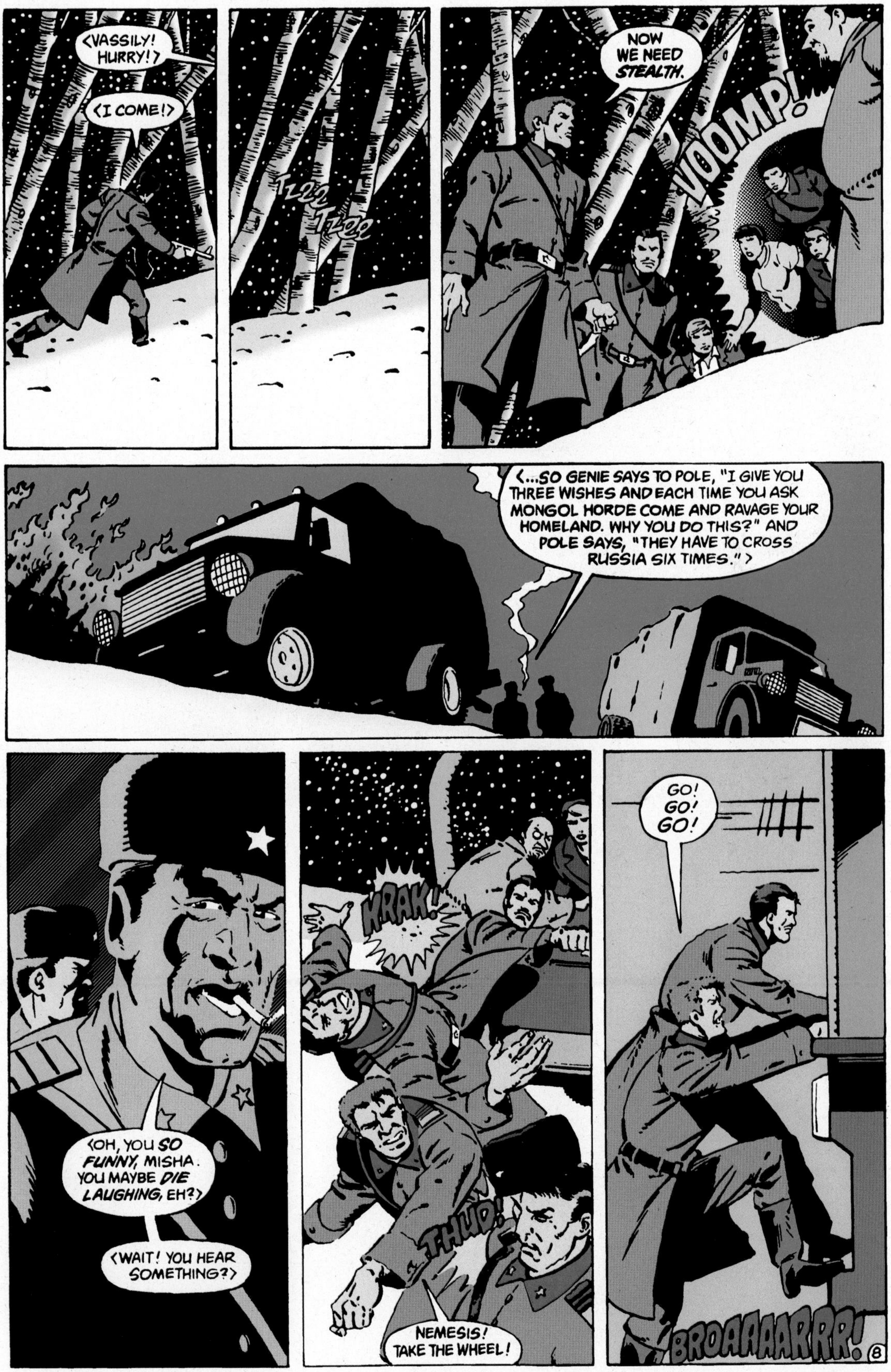

<VASSILY! HURRY!>
<I COME!>
TZZZ TZZZ
NOW WE NEED STEALTH.
VOOMP!
<...SO GENIE SAYS TO POLE, "I GIVE YOU THREE WISHES AND EACH TIME YOU ASK MONGOL HORDE COME AND RAVAGE YOUR HOMELAND. WHY YOU DO THIS?" AND POLE SAYS, "THEY HAVE TO CROSS RUSSIA SIX TIMES.">
<OH, YOU SO FUNNY, MISHA. YOU MAYBE DIE LAUGHING, EH?>
<WAIT! YOU HEAR SOMETHING?>
KRAK!
THUD!
NEMESIS! TAKE THE WHEEL!
GO! GO! GO!
BROAAAARRR!
8

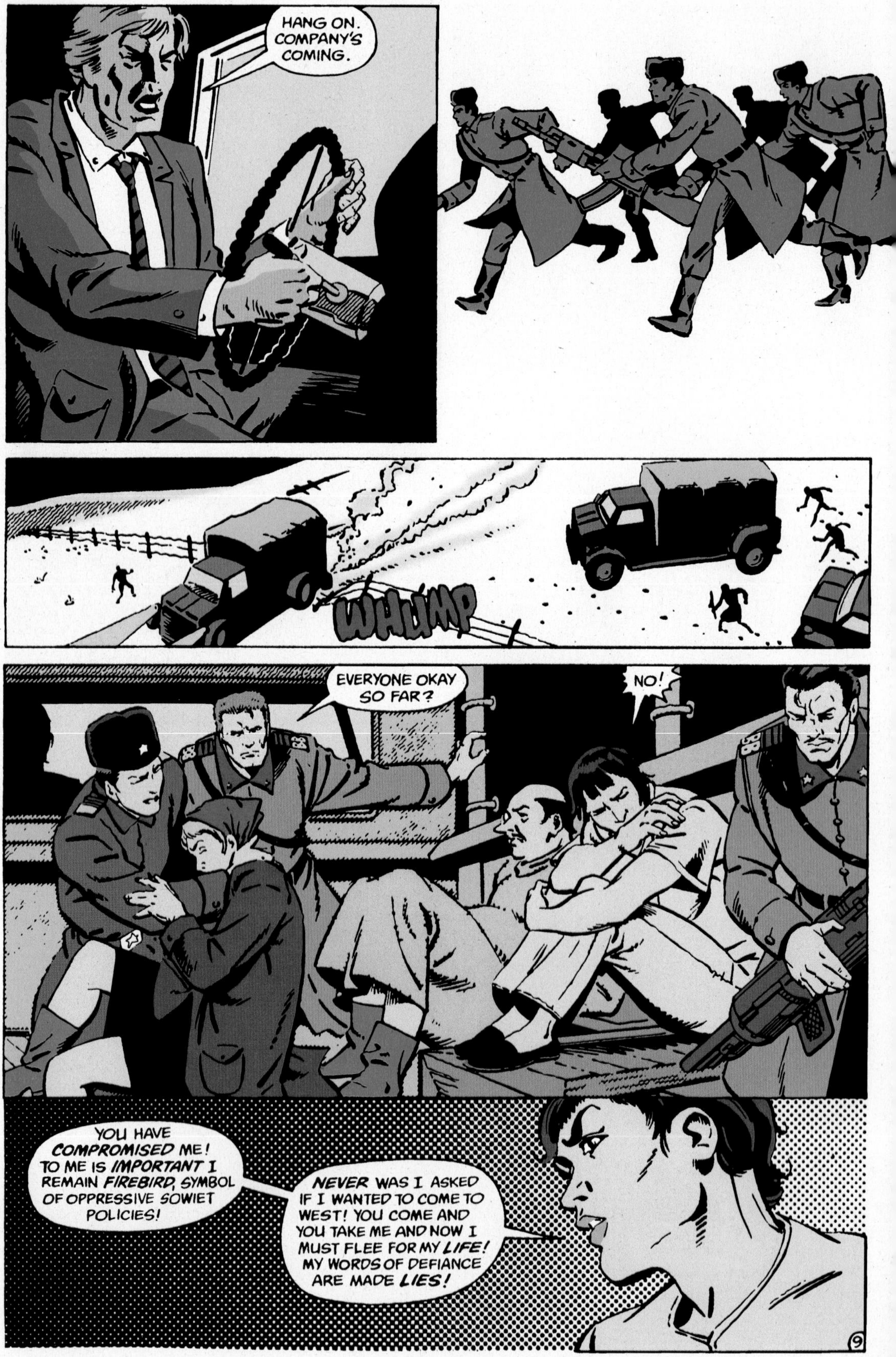
HANG ON. COMPANY'S COMING.
WHUMP
EVERYONE OKAY SO FAR?
NO!
YOU HAVE COMPROMISED ME! TO ME IS IMPORTANT I REMAIN FIREBIRD, SYMBOL OF OPPRESSIVE SOWIET POLICIES!
NEVER WAS I ASKED IF I WANTED TO COME TO WEST! YOU COME AND YOU TAKE ME AND NOW I MUST FLEE FOR MY LIFE! MY WORDS OF DEFIANCE ARE MADE LIES!
9

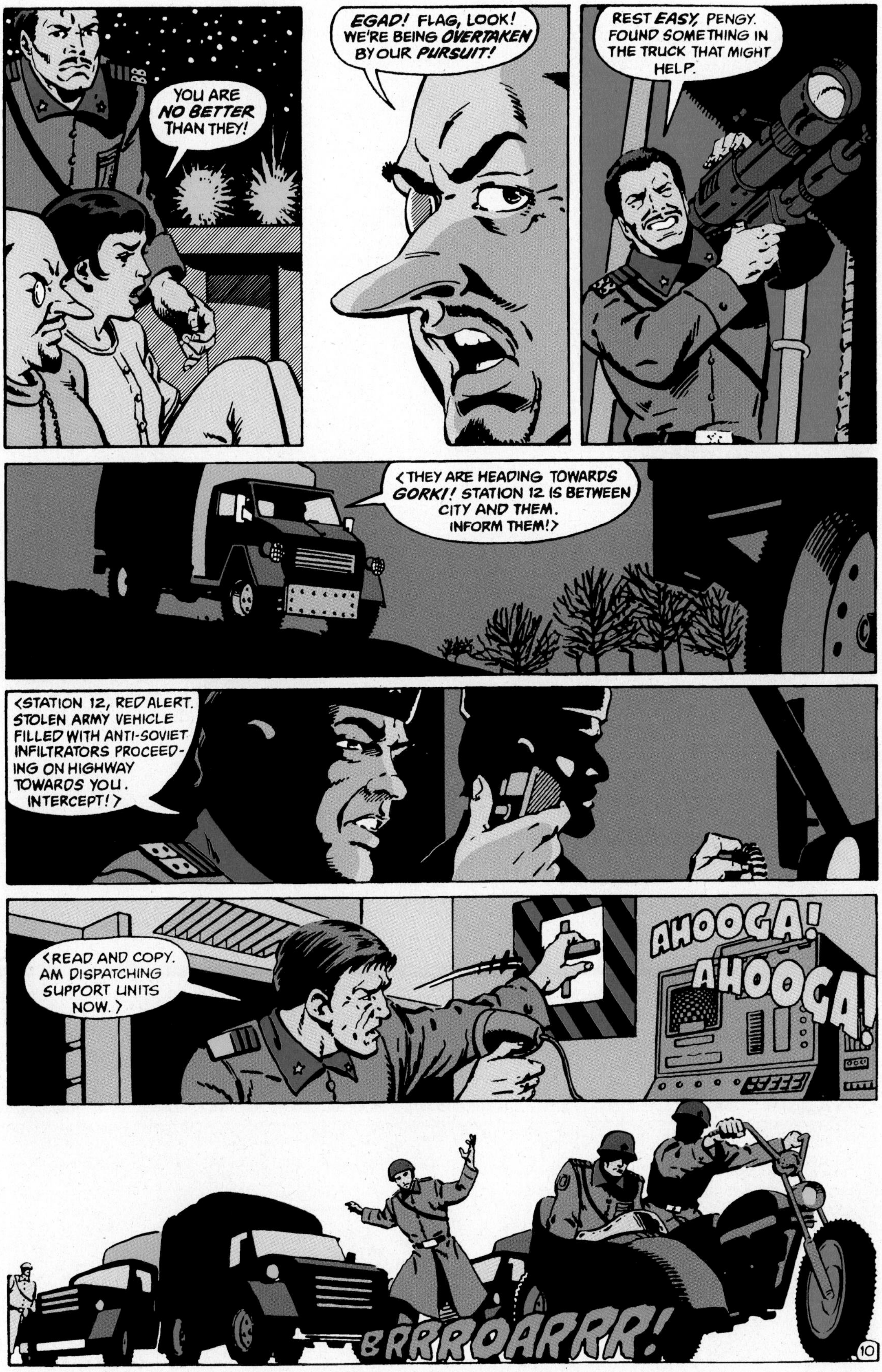
YOU ARE NO BETTER THAN THEY!
EGAD! FLAG, LOOK! WE'RE BEING OVERTAKEN BY OUR PURSUIT!
REST EASY, PENGY. FOUND SOMETHING IN THE TRUCK THAT MIGHT HELP.
<THEY ARE HEADING TOWARDS GORKI! STATION 12 IS BETWEEN CITY AND THEM. INFORM THEM!>
<STATION 12, RED ALERT. STOLEN ARMY VEHICLE FILLED WITH ANTI-SOVIET INFILTRATORS PROCEEDING ON HIGHWAY TOWARDS YOU. INTERCEPT!>
<READ AND COPY. AM DISPATCHING SUPPORT UNITS NOW.>
AHOOGA!
AHOOGA!
BRRROARRR!
10

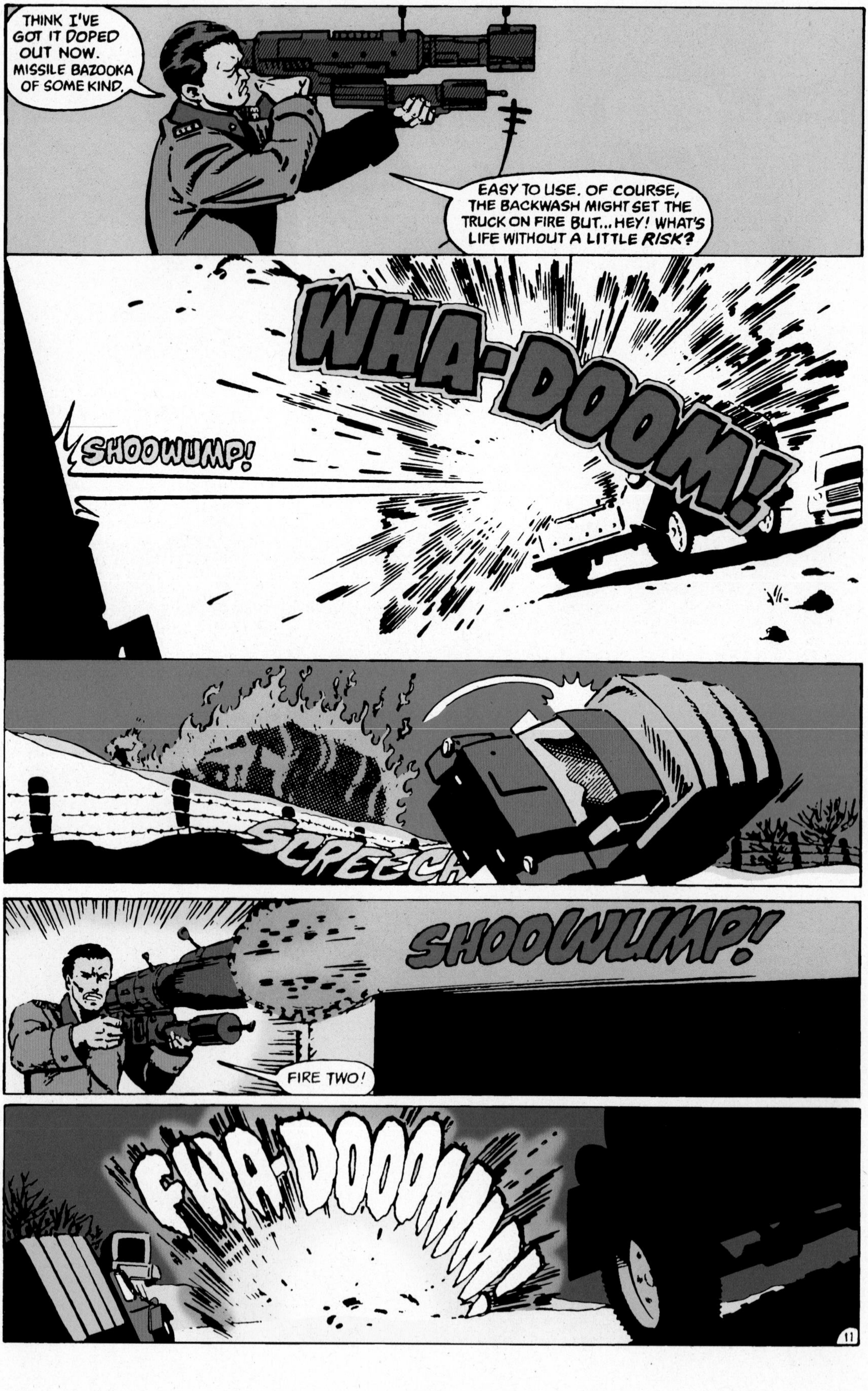
THINK I'VE GOT IT DOPED OUT NOW. MISSILE BAZOOKA OF SOME KIND.
EASY TO USE. OF COURSE, THE BACKWASH MIGHT SET THE TRUCK ON FIRE BUT... HEY! WHAT'S LIFE WITHOUT A LITTLE RISK?
WHA-DOOM!
SHOOWUMP!
SCREECH
SHOOWUMP!
FIRE TWO!
FWA-DOOOMM!
11

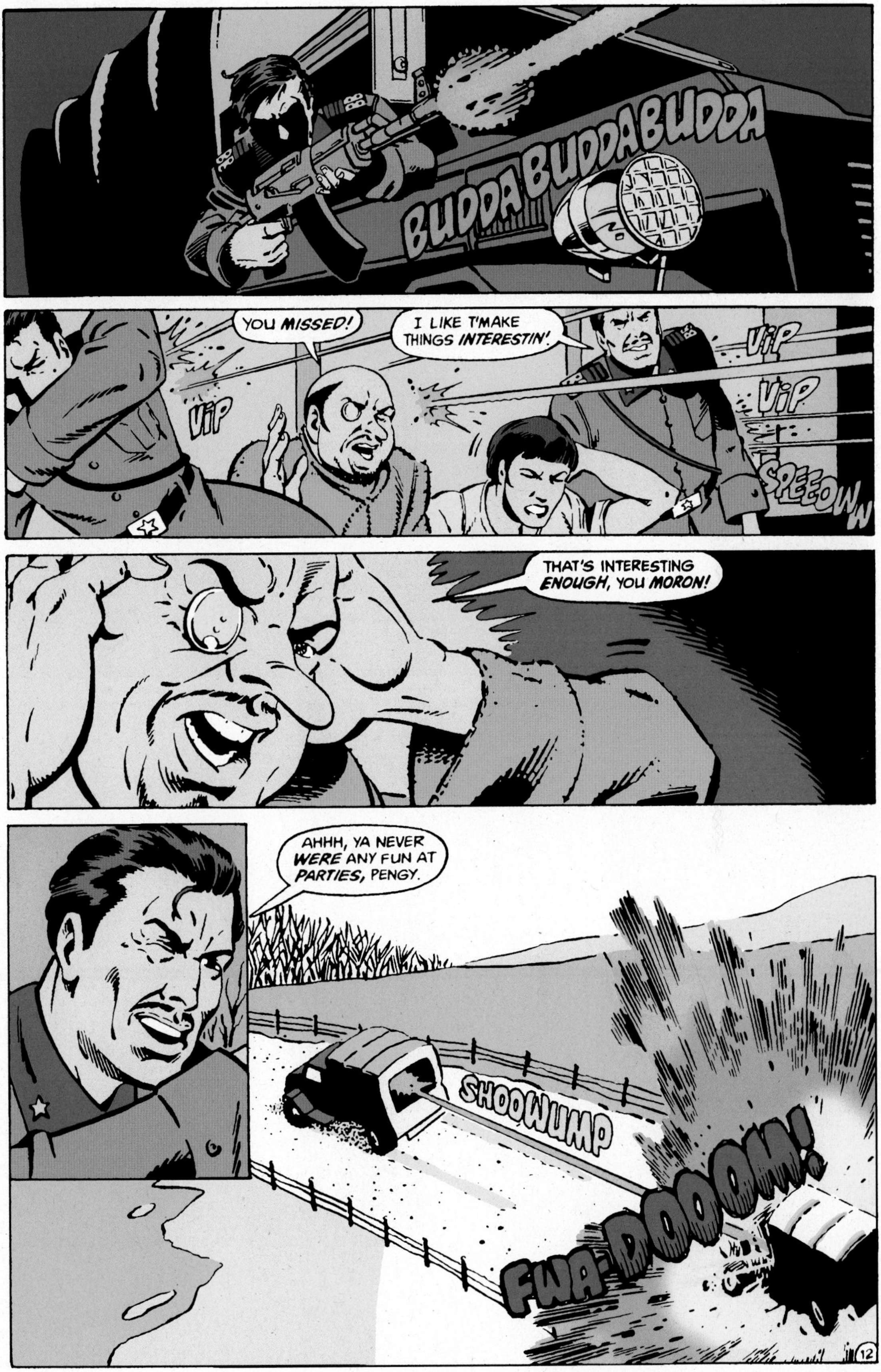
BUDDA BUDDA BUDDA
YOU MISSED!
I LIKE T'MAKE THINGS INTERESTIN'.
VIP
VIP
VIP
SPEEOWW
THAT'S INTERESTING ENOUGH, YOU MORON!
AHHH, YA NEVER WERE ANY FUN AT PARTIES, PENGY.
SHOOWUMP
FWA-DOOOM!
12

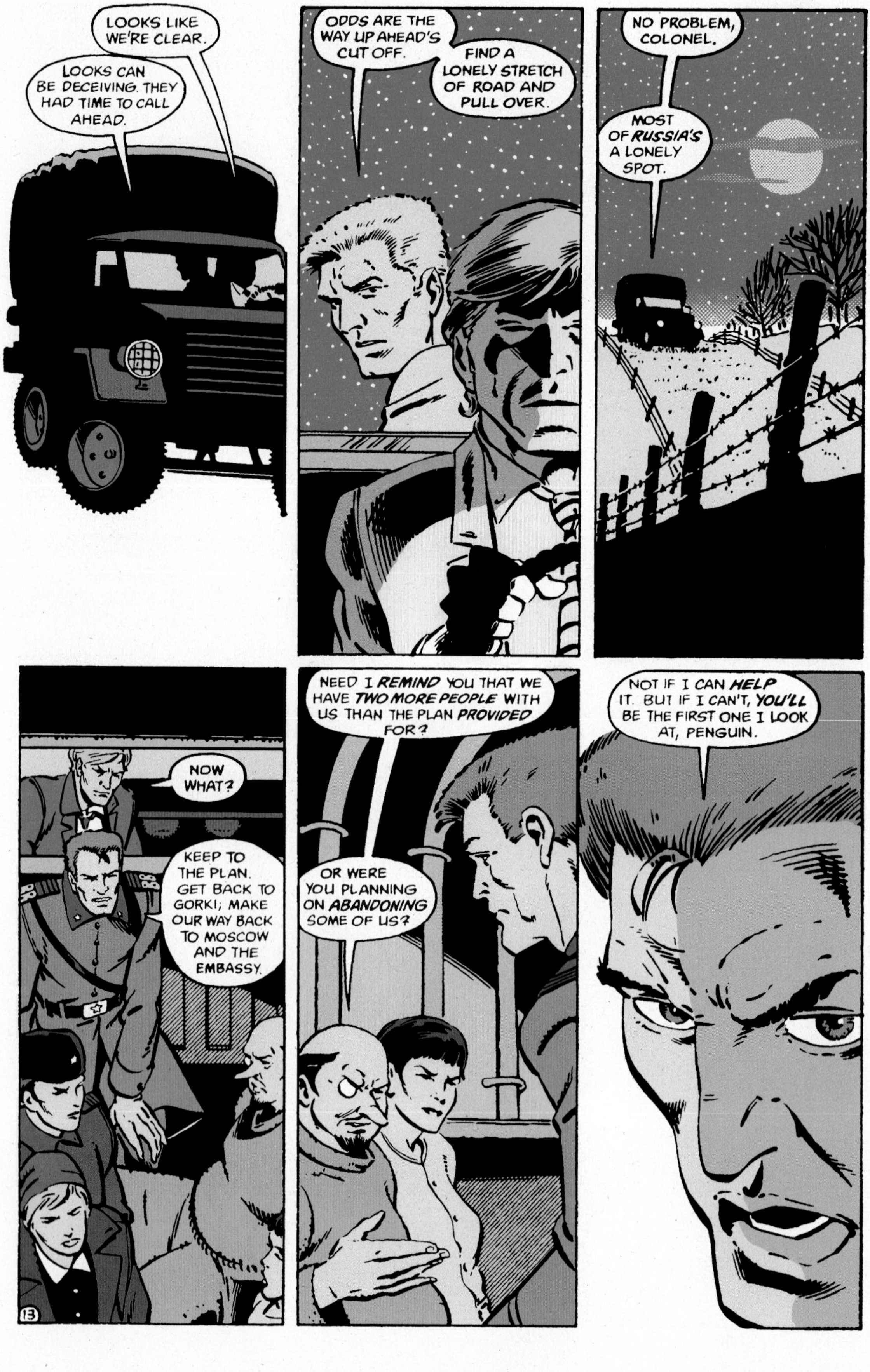
LOOKS LIKE WE'RE CLEAR.
LOOKS CAN BE DECEIVING. THEY HAD TIME TO CALL AHEAD.
ODDS ARE THE WAY UP AHEAD'S CUT OFF.
FIND A LONELY STRETCH OF ROAD AND PULL OVER.
NO PROBLEM, COLONEL.
MOST OF RUSSIA'S A LONELY SPOT.
NOW WHAT?
KEEP TO THE PLAN. GET BACK TO GORKI; MAKE OUR WAY BACK TO MOSCOW AND THE EMBASSY.
13
NEED I REMIND YOU THAT WE HAVE TWO MORE PEOPLE WITH US THAN THE PLAN PROVIDED FOR?
OR WERE YOU PLANNING ON ABANDONING SOME OF US?
NOT IF I CAN HELP IT. BUT IF I CAN'T, YOU'LL BE THE FIRST ONE I LOOK AT, PENGUIN.

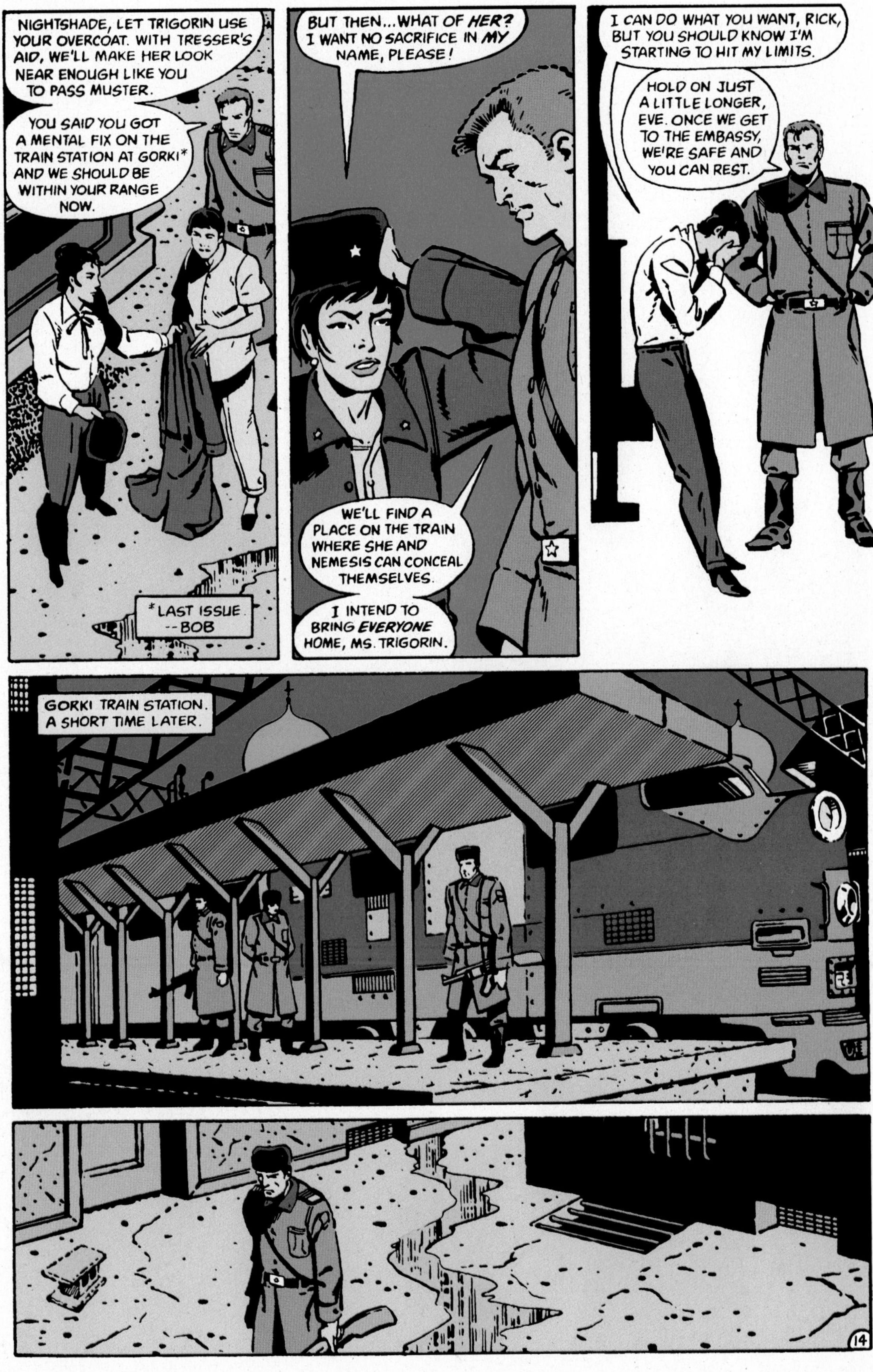
NIGHTSHADE, LET TRIGORIN USE YOUR OVERCOAT. WITH TRESSER'S AID, WE'LL MAKE HER LOOK NEAR ENOUGH LIKE YOU TO PASS MUSTER.
YOU SAID YOU GOT A MENTAL FIX ON THE TRAIN STATION AT GORKI* AND WE SHOULD BE WITHIN YOUR RANGE NOW.
*LAST ISSUE. --BOB
BUT THEN...WHAT OF HER? I WANT NO SACRIFICE IN MY NAME, PLEASE!
WE'LL FIND A PLACE ON THE TRAIN WHERE SHE AND NEMESIS CAN CONCEAL THEMSELVES.
I INTEND TO BRING EVERYONE HOME, MS. TRIGORIN.
I CAN DO WHAT YOU WANT, RICK, BUT YOU SHOULD KNOW I'M STARTING TO HIT MY LIMITS.
HOLD ON JUST A LITTLE LONGER, EVE. ONCE WE GET TO THE EMBASSY, WE'RE SAFE AND YOU CAN REST.
GORKI TRAIN STATION. A SHORT TIME LATER.
14

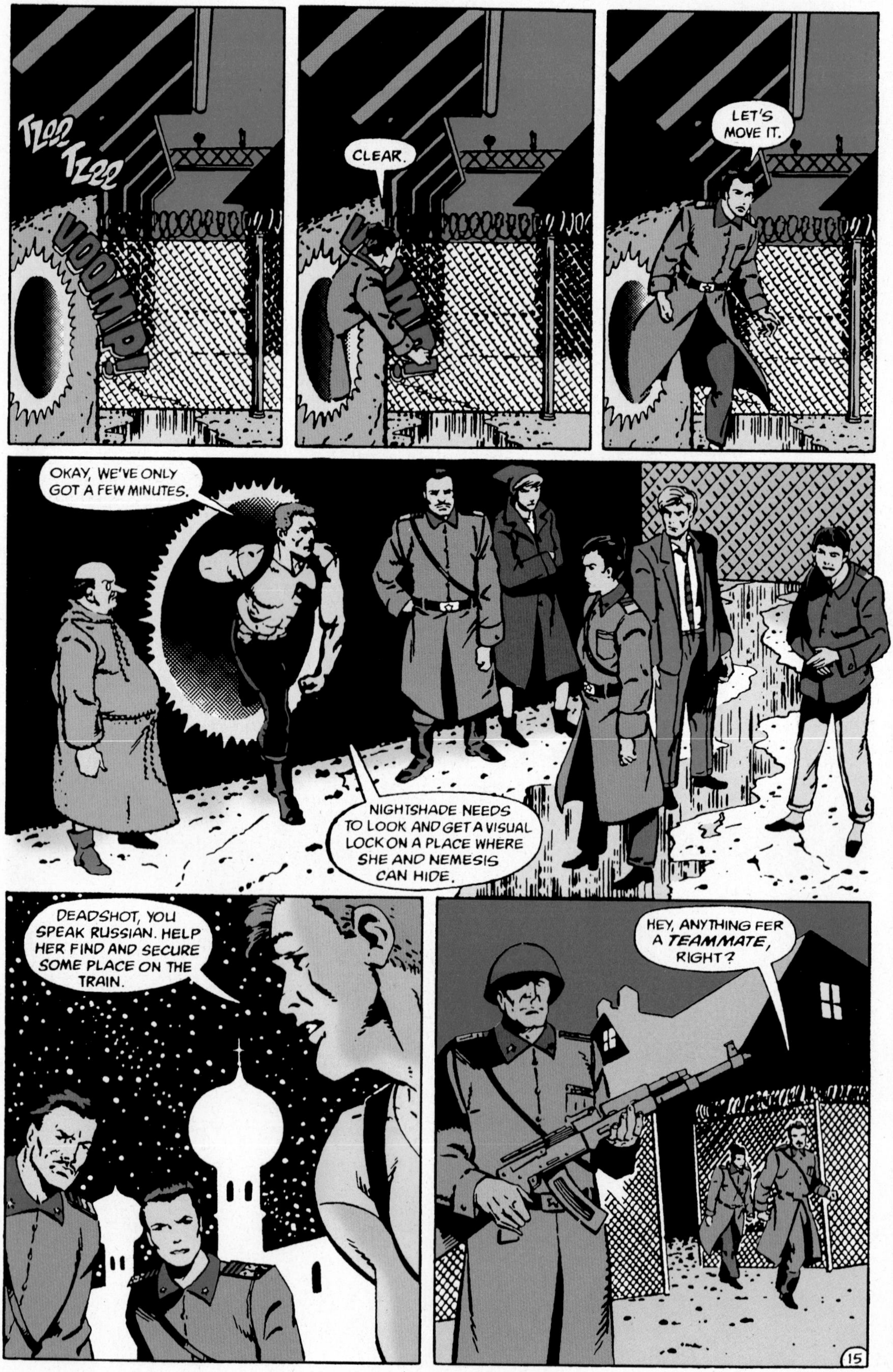
TZZZ TZZZ
VOOMP!
CLEAR.
LET'S MOVE IT.
OKAY, WE'VE ONLY GOT A FEW MINUTES.
NIGHTSHADE NEEDS TO LOOK AND GET A VISUAL LOCK ON A PLACE WHERE SHE AND NEMESIS CAN HIDE.
DEADSHOT, YOU SPEAK RUSSIAN. HELP HER FIND AND SECURE SOME PLACE ON THE TRAIN.
HEY, ANYTHING FER A *TEAMMATE*, RIGHT?
15

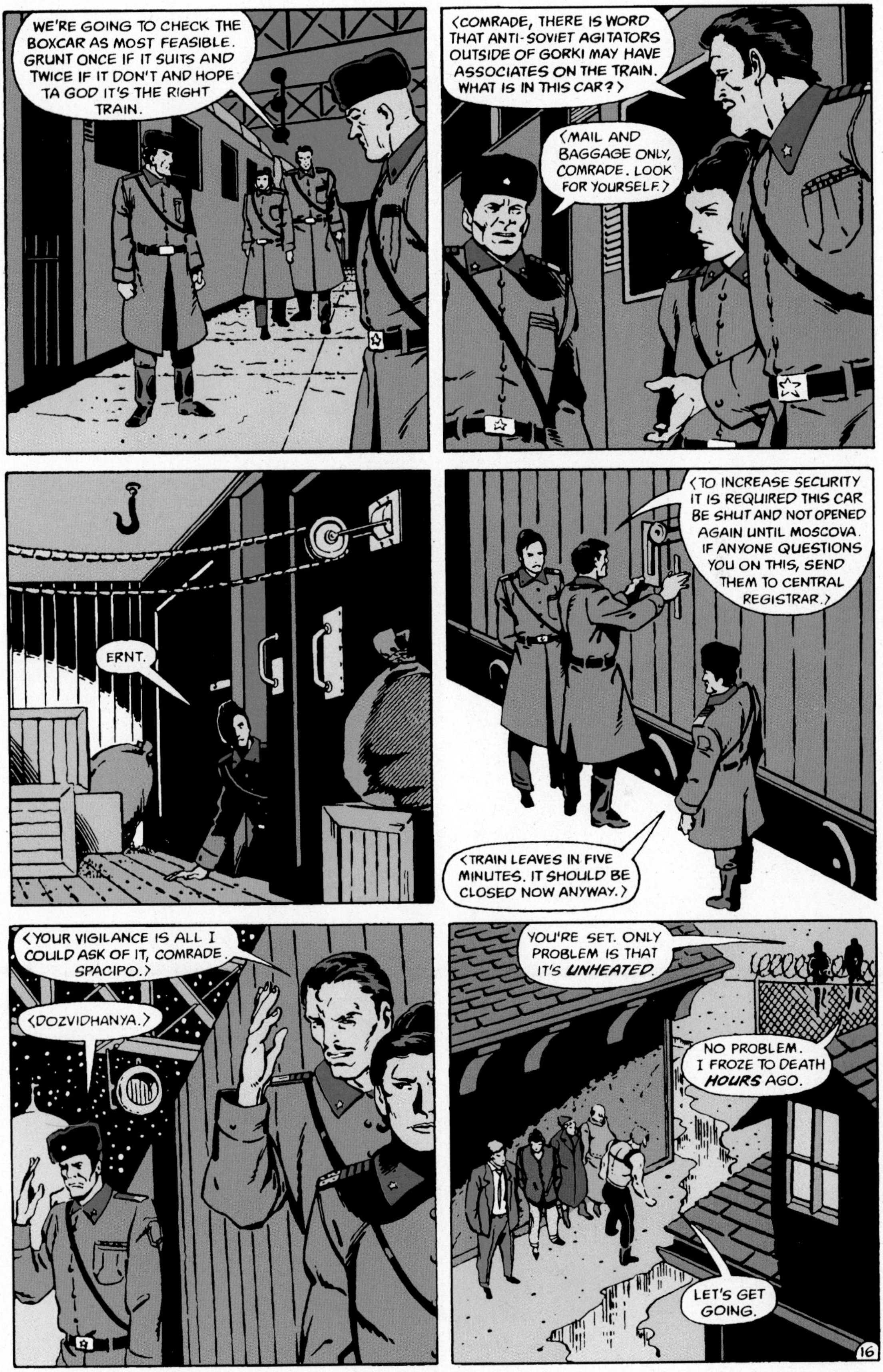
WE'RE GOING TO CHECK THE BOXCAR AS MOST FEASIBLE. GRUNT ONCE IF IT SUITS AND TWICE IF IT DON'T AND HOPE TA GOD IT'S THE RIGHT TRAIN.
<COMRADE, THERE IS WORD THAT ANTI-SOVIET AGITATORS OUTSIDE OF GORKI MAY HAVE ASSOCIATES ON THE TRAIN. WHAT IS IN THIS CAR?>
<MAIL AND BAGGAGE ONLY, COMRADE. LOOK FOR YOURSELF.>
ERNT.
<TO INCREASE SECURITY IT IS REQUIRED THIS CAR BE SHUT AND NOT OPENED AGAIN UNTIL MOSCOVA. IF ANYONE QUESTIONS YOU ON THIS, SEND THEM TO CENTRAL REGISTRAR.>
<TRAIN LEAVES IN FIVE MINUTES. IT SHOULD BE CLOSED NOW ANYWAY.>
<YOUR VIGILANCE IS ALL I COULD ASK OF IT, COMRADE. SPACIPO.>
<DOZVIDHANYA.>
YOU'RE SET. ONLY PROBLEM IS THAT IT'S UNHEATED.
NO PROBLEM. I FROZE TO DEATH HOURS AGO.
LET'S GET GOING.
16

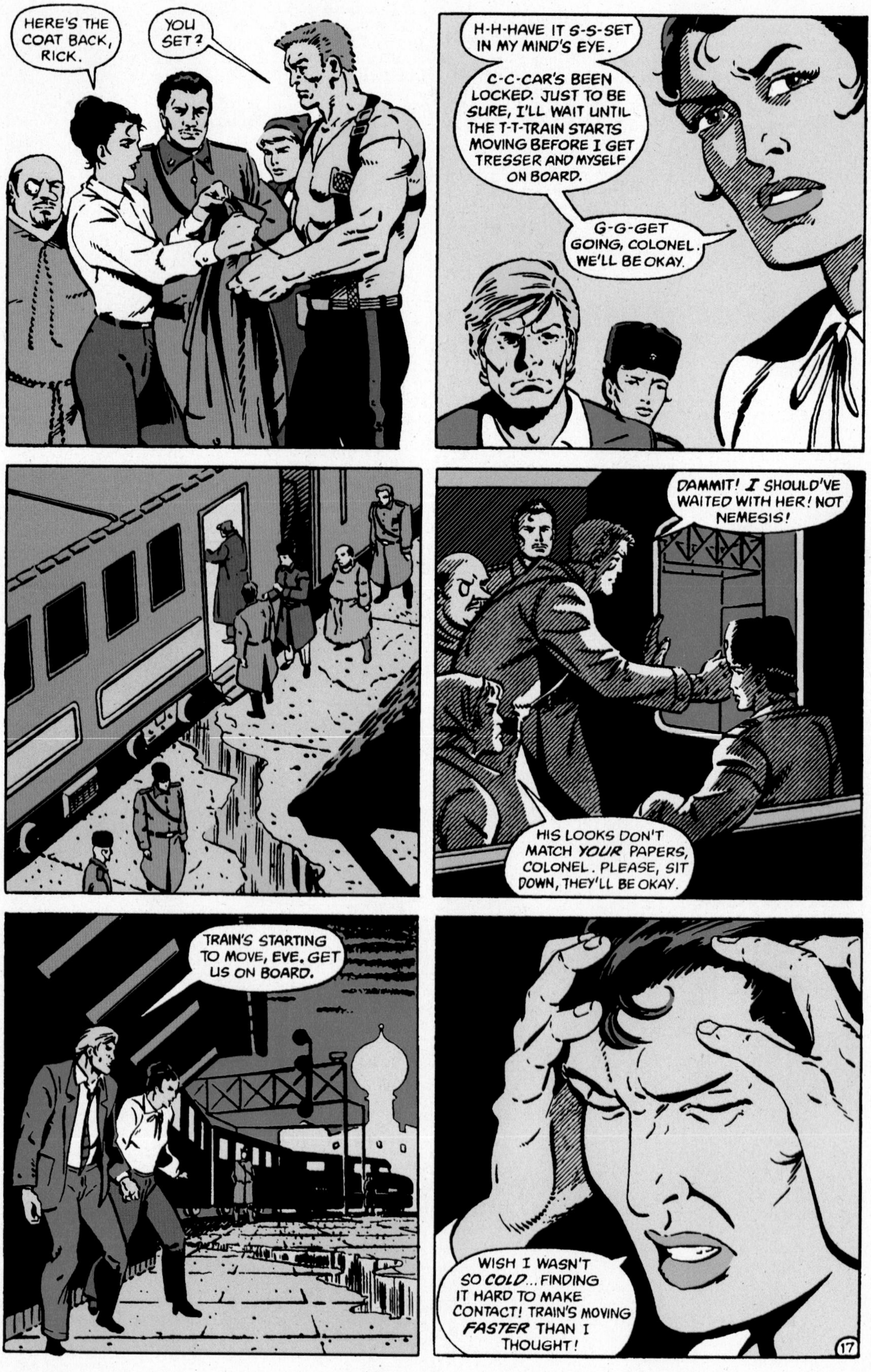
HERE'S THE COAT BACK, RICK.
YOU SET?
H-H-HAVE IT S-S-SET IN MY MIND'S EYE.
C-C-CAR'S BEEN LOCKED. JUST TO BE SURE, I'LL WAIT UNTIL THE T-T-TRAIN STARTS MOVING BEFORE I GET TRESSER AND MYSELF ON BOARD.
G-G-GET GOING, COLONEL. WE'LL BE OKAY.
DAMMIT! I SHOULD'VE WAITED WITH HER! NOT NEMESIS!
HIS LOOKS DON'T MATCH YOUR PAPERS, COLONEL. PLEASE, SIT DOWN, THEY'LL BE OKAY.
TRAIN'S STARTING TO MOVE, EVE. GET US ON BOARD.
WISH I WASN'T SO COLD... FINDING IT HARD TO MAKE CONTACT! TRAIN'S MOVING FASTER THAN I THOUGHT!
17

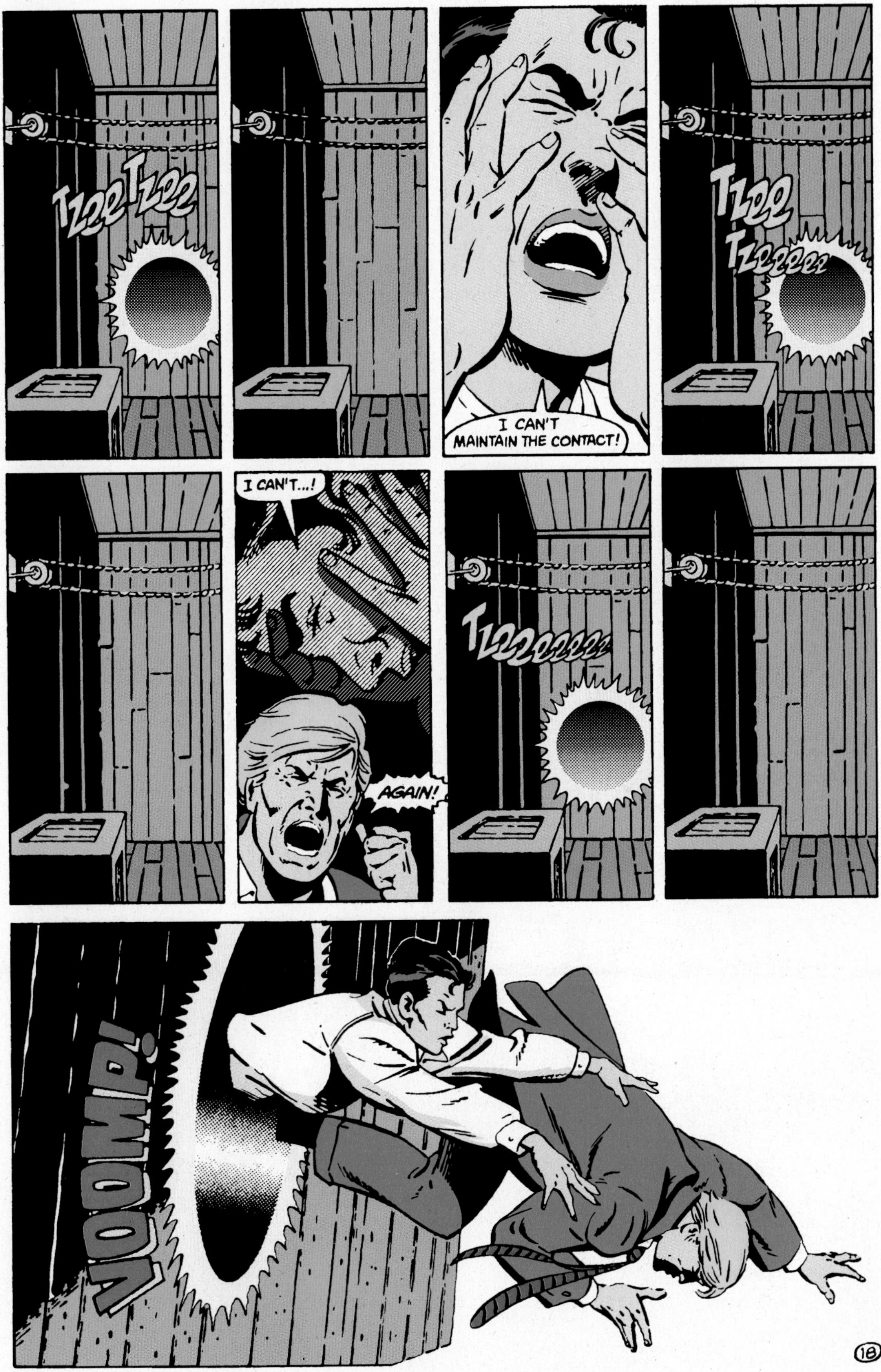
TZZEE TZZEE
TZZEE
TZZEEEEEE
I CAN'T MAINTAIN THE CONTACT!
I CAN'T...!
AGAIN!
TZZZZZZZZZZ
VOOMP!
18

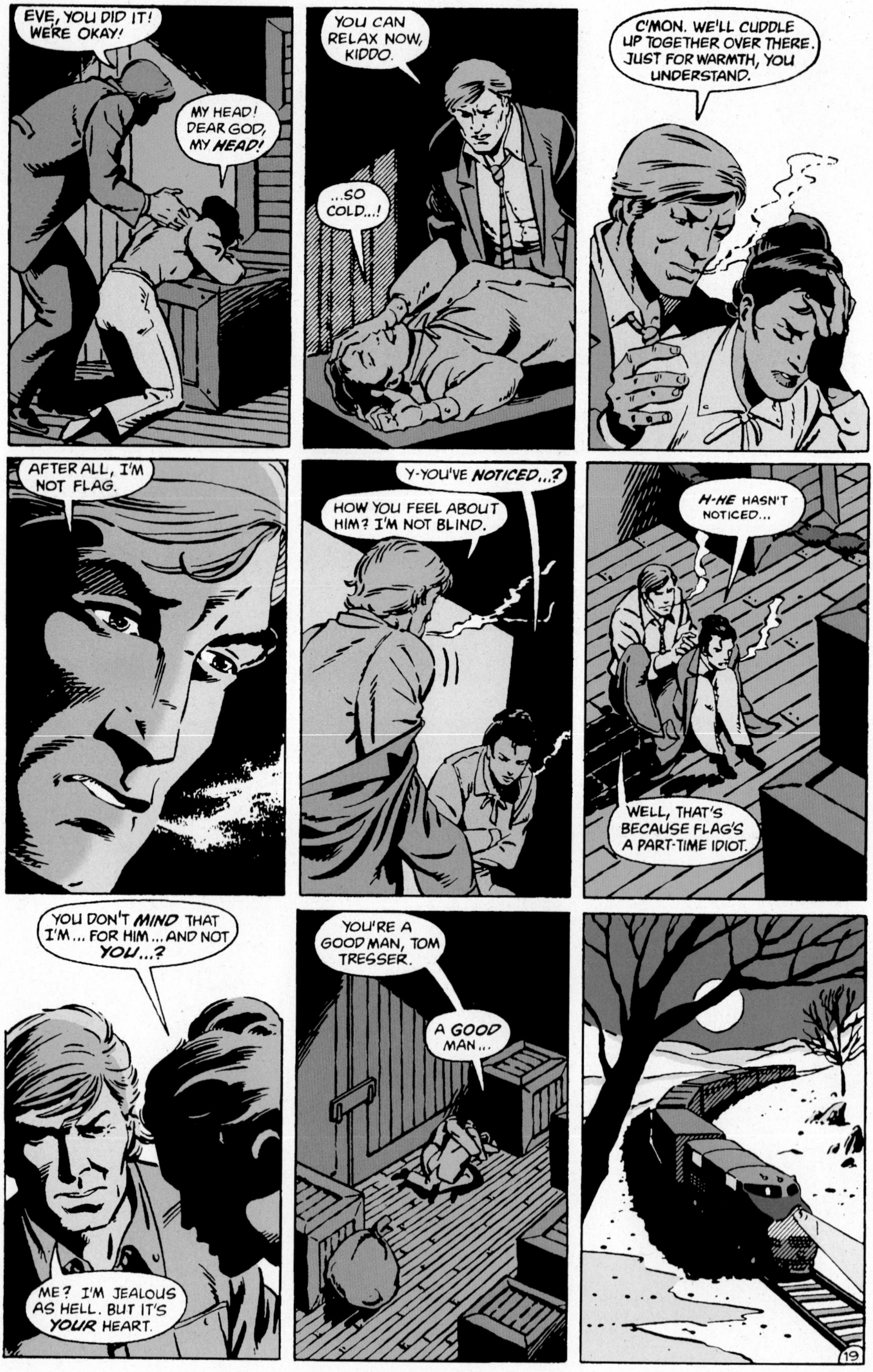
EVE, YOU DID IT! WE'RE OKAY!
MY HEAD! DEAR GOD, MY HEAD!
YOU CAN RELAX NOW, KIDDO.
...SO COLD...!
C'MON. WE'LL CUDDLE UP TOGETHER OVER THERE. JUST FOR WARMTH, YOU UNDERSTAND.
AFTER ALL, I'M NOT FLAG.
Y-YOU'VE NOTICED...?
HOW YOU FEEL ABOUT HIM? I'M NOT BLIND.
H-HE HASN'T NOTICED...
WELL, THAT'S BECAUSE FLAG'S A PART-TIME IDIOT.
YOU DON'T MIND THAT I'M... FOR HIM... AND NOT YOU...?
ME? I'M JEALOUS AS HELL. BUT IT'S YOUR HEART.
YOU'RE A GOOD MAN, TOM TRESSER.
A GOOD MAN...
19

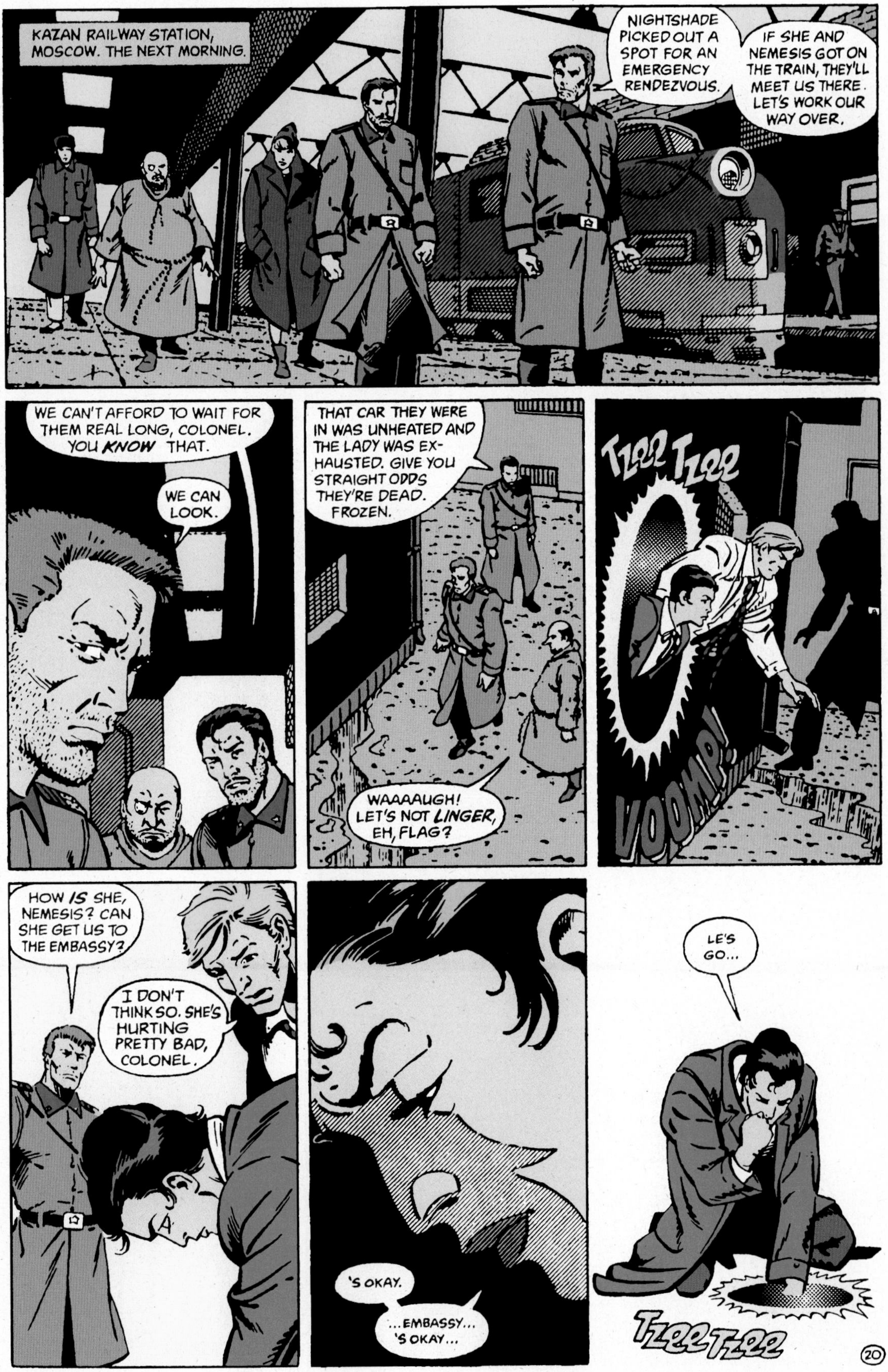
KAZAN RAILWAY STATION, MOSCOW. THE NEXT MORNING.
NIGHTSHADE PICKED OUT A SPOT FOR AN EMERGENCY RENDEZVOUS.
IF SHE AND NEMESIS GOT ON THE TRAIN, THEY'LL MEET US THERE. LET'S WORK OUR WAY OVER.
WE CAN'T AFFORD TO WAIT FOR THEM REAL LONG, COLONEL. YOU KNOW THAT.
WE CAN LOOK.
THAT CAR THEY WERE IN WAS UNHEATED AND THE LADY WAS EX-HAUSTED. GIVE YOU STRAIGHT ODDS THEY'RE DEAD. FROZEN.
WAAAAUGH! LET'S NOT LINGER, EH, FLAG?
TZEE TZEE
VOOMP!
HOW IS SHE, NEMESIS? CAN SHE GET US TO THE EMBASSY?
I DON'T THINK SO. SHE'S HURTING PRETTY BAD, COLONEL.
'S OKAY.
...EMBASSY... 'S OKAY...
LE'S GO...
TZEE TZEE
20

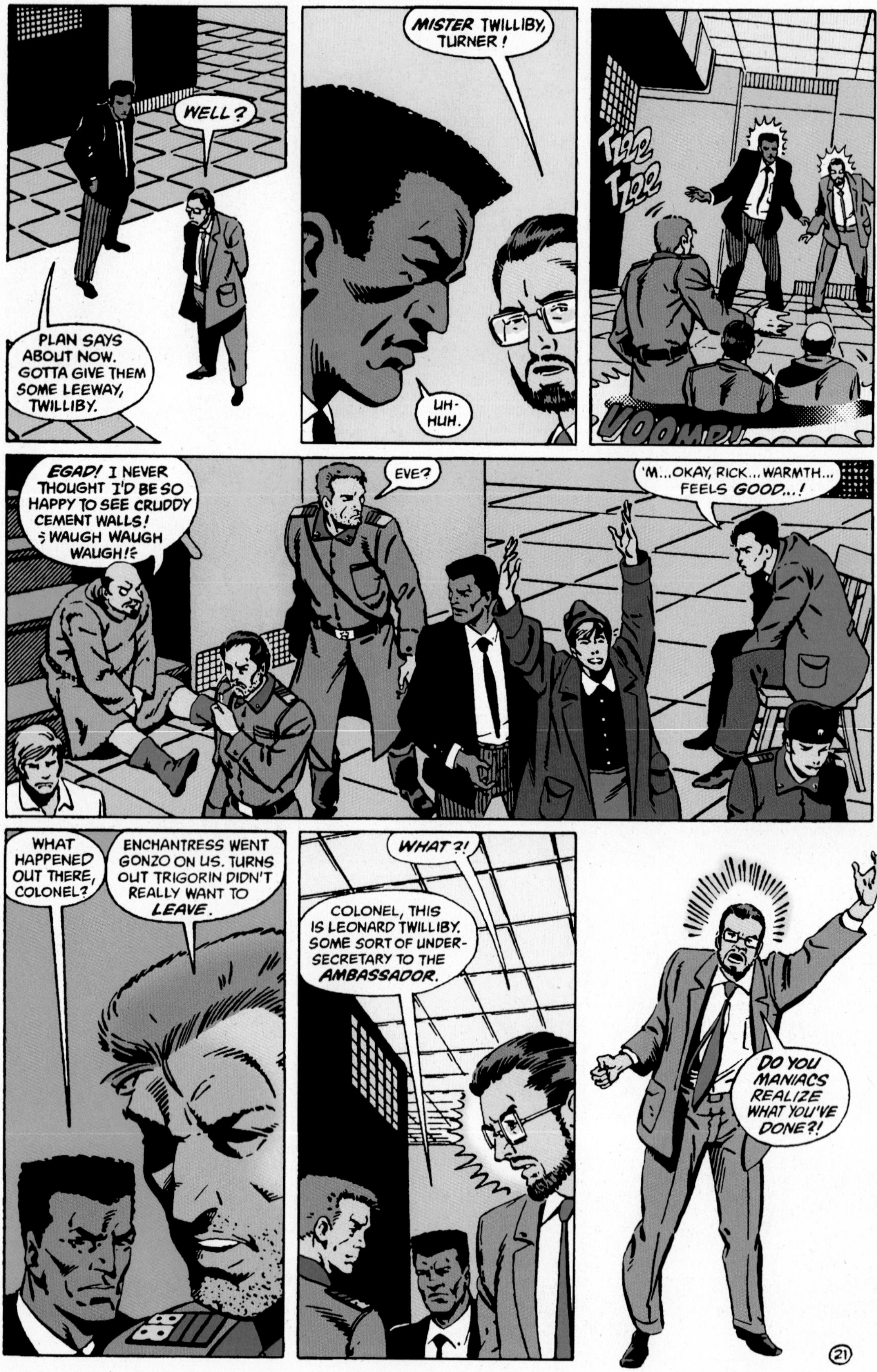
WELL?
PLAN SAYS ABOUT NOW. GOTTA GIVE THEM SOME LEEWAY, TWILLIBY.
MISTER TWILLIBY, TURNER!
UH-HUH.
TZZZ TZZZ
VOOMP!
EGAD! I NEVER THOUGHT I'D BE SO HAPPY TO SEE CRUDDY CEMENT WALLS! WAUGH WAUGH WAUGH!
EVE?
'M...OKAY, RICK...WARMTH... FEELS GOOD...!
WHAT HAPPENED OUT THERE, COLONEL?
ENCHANTRESS WENT GONZO ON US. TURNS OUT TRIGORIN DIDN'T REALLY WANT TO LEAVE.
WHAT?!
COLONEL, THIS IS LEONARD TWILLIBY. SOME SORT OF UNDER-SECRETARY TO THE AMBASSADOR.
DO YOU MANIACS REALIZE WHAT YOU'VE DONE?!
21

YOU'VE CREATED AN *INTERNATIONAL SITUATION!*

THE SOVIETS ARE FORMALLY PROTESTING THE KIDNAPPING OF AN ILL SOVIET CITIZEN!

THE AMERICAN GOVERNMENT HAS *DISOWNED* THE MISSION AS AN ACT BY INTERNATIONAL ADVENTURERS!

PLUS, SOMEONE IN YOUR ORGANIZATION EVIDENTLY *FAILED* TO NOTIFY THE STATE DEPARTMENT OF WHAT YOU WERE REALLY DOING HERE!

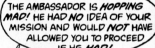

THE AMBASSADOR IS *HOPPING MAD!* HE HAD *NO* IDEA OF YOUR MISSION AND WOULD *NOT* HAVE ALLOWED YOU TO PROCEED IF HE *HAD!*

IF YOU DO NOT *SURRENDER* YOURSELVES TO THE RUSSIAN AUTHORITIES...

...HE WILL TURN YOU OVER TO THEM *HIMSELF.*

YOU HAVE THIRTY MINUTES TO THINK IT OVER.

NICE BUNCH. SO, TELL ME, FLAG.

WHAT DO YOU WANT TO DO *NOW?*

NEXT: THE CONCLUSION! THE SQUAD VS. THE PEOPLE'S HEROES!
"THROWN TO THE WOLVES!"

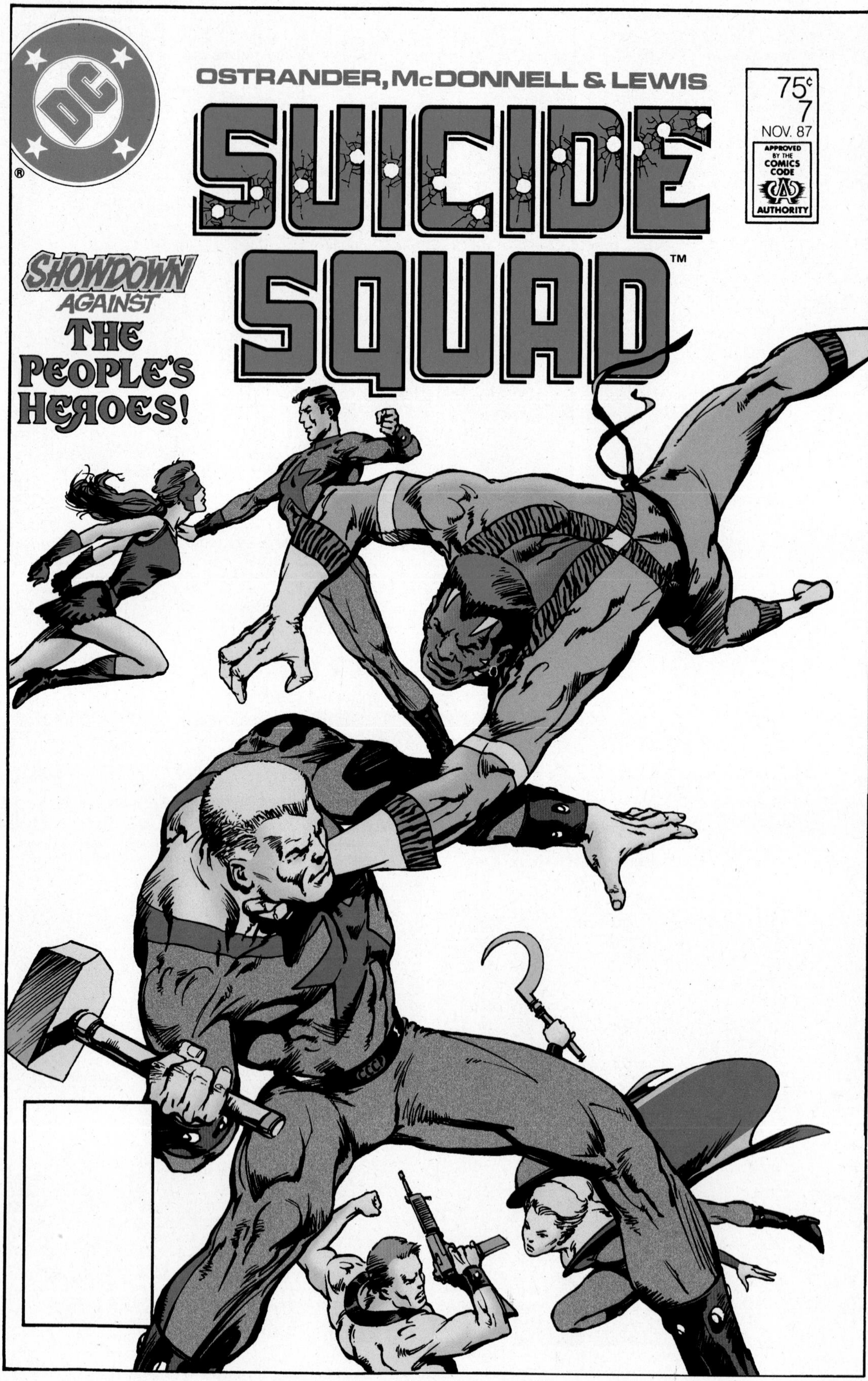
OSTRANDER, McDONNELL & LEWIS
SUICIDE SQUAD™
75¢
7
NOV. 87
APPROVED BY THE COMICS CODE AUTHORITY
SHOWDOWN AGAINST THE PEOPLE'S HEROES!

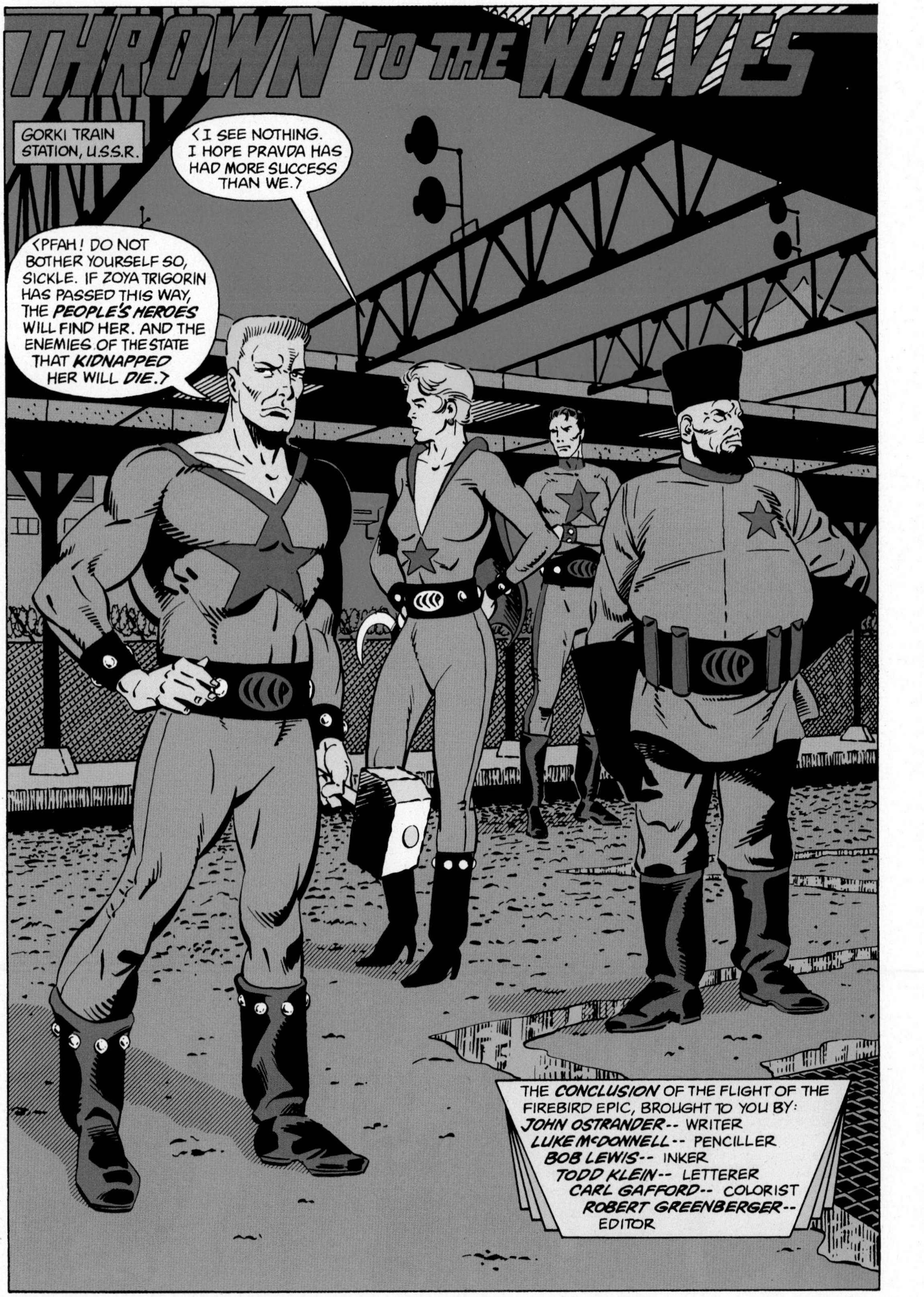
THROWN TO THE WOLVES
GORKI TRAIN STATION, U.S.S.R.
<I SEE NOTHING. I HOPE PRAVDA HAS HAD MORE SUCCESS THAN WE.>
<PFAH! DO NOT BOTHER YOURSELF SO, SICKLE. IF ZOYA TRIGORIN HAS PASSED THIS WAY, THE PEOPLE'S HEROES WILL FIND HER. AND THE ENEMIES OF THE STATE THAT KIDNAPPED HER WILL DIE.>
THE CONCLUSION OF THE FLIGHT OF THE FIREBIRD EPIC, BROUGHT TO YOU BY:
JOHN OSTRANDER-- WRITER
LUKE McDONNELL-- PENCILLER
BOB LEWIS-- INKER
TODD KLEIN-- LETTERER
CARL GAFFORD-- COLORIST
ROBERT GREENBERGER-- EDITOR

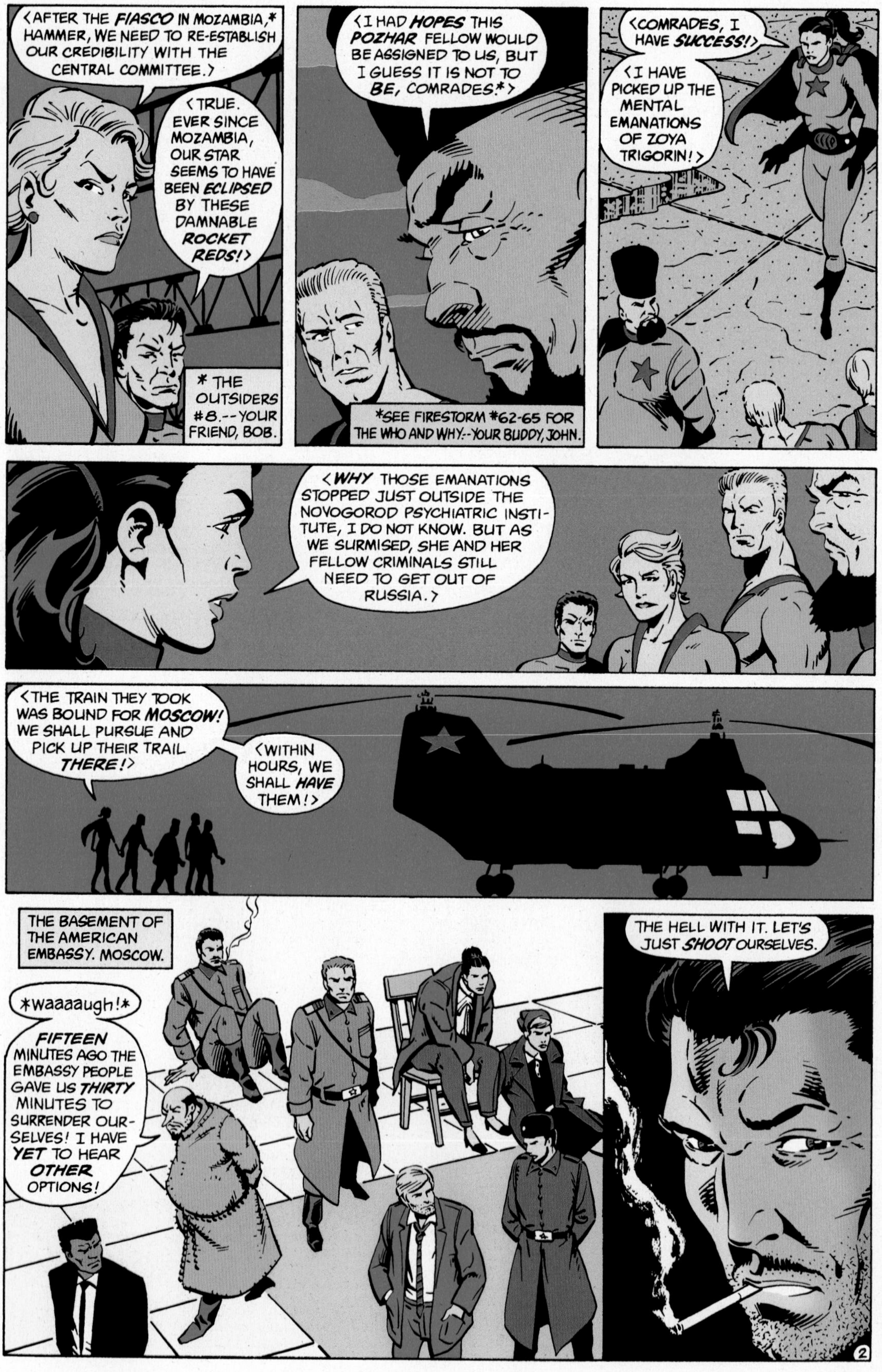

<AFTER THE FIASCO IN MOZAMBIA,* HAMMER, WE NEED TO RE-ESTABLISH OUR CREDIBILITY WITH THE CENTRAL COMMITTEE.>
<TRUE. EVER SINCE MOZAMBIA, OUR STAR SEEMS TO HAVE BEEN ECLIPSED BY THESE DAMNABLE ROCKET REDS!>
* THE OUTSIDERS #8.--YOUR FRIEND, BOB.
<I HAD HOPES THIS POZHAR FELLOW WOULD BE ASSIGNED TO US, BUT I GUESS IT IS NOT TO BE, COMRADES.*>
*SEE FIRESTORM #62-65 FOR THE WHO AND WHY.--YOUR BUDDY, JOHN.
<COMRADES, I HAVE SUCCESS!>
<I HAVE PICKED UP THE MENTAL EMANATIONS OF ZOYA TRIGORIN!>
<WHY THOSE EMANATIONS STOPPED JUST OUTSIDE THE NOVOGOROD PSYCHIATRIC INSTITUTE, I DO NOT KNOW. BUT AS WE SURMISED, SHE AND HER FELLOW CRIMINALS STILL NEED TO GET OUT OF RUSSIA.>
<THE TRAIN THEY TOOK WAS BOUND FOR MOSCOW! WE SHALL PURSUE AND PICK UP THEIR TRAIL THERE!>
<WITHIN HOURS, WE SHALL HAVE THEM!>
THE BASEMENT OF THE AMERICAN EMBASSY. MOSCOW.
waaaaugh!
FIFTEEN MINUTES AGO THE EMBASSY PEOPLE GAVE US THIRTY MINUTES TO SURRENDER OURSELVES! I HAVE YET TO HEAR OTHER OPTIONS!
THE HELL WITH IT. LET'S JUST SHOOT OURSELVES.
2

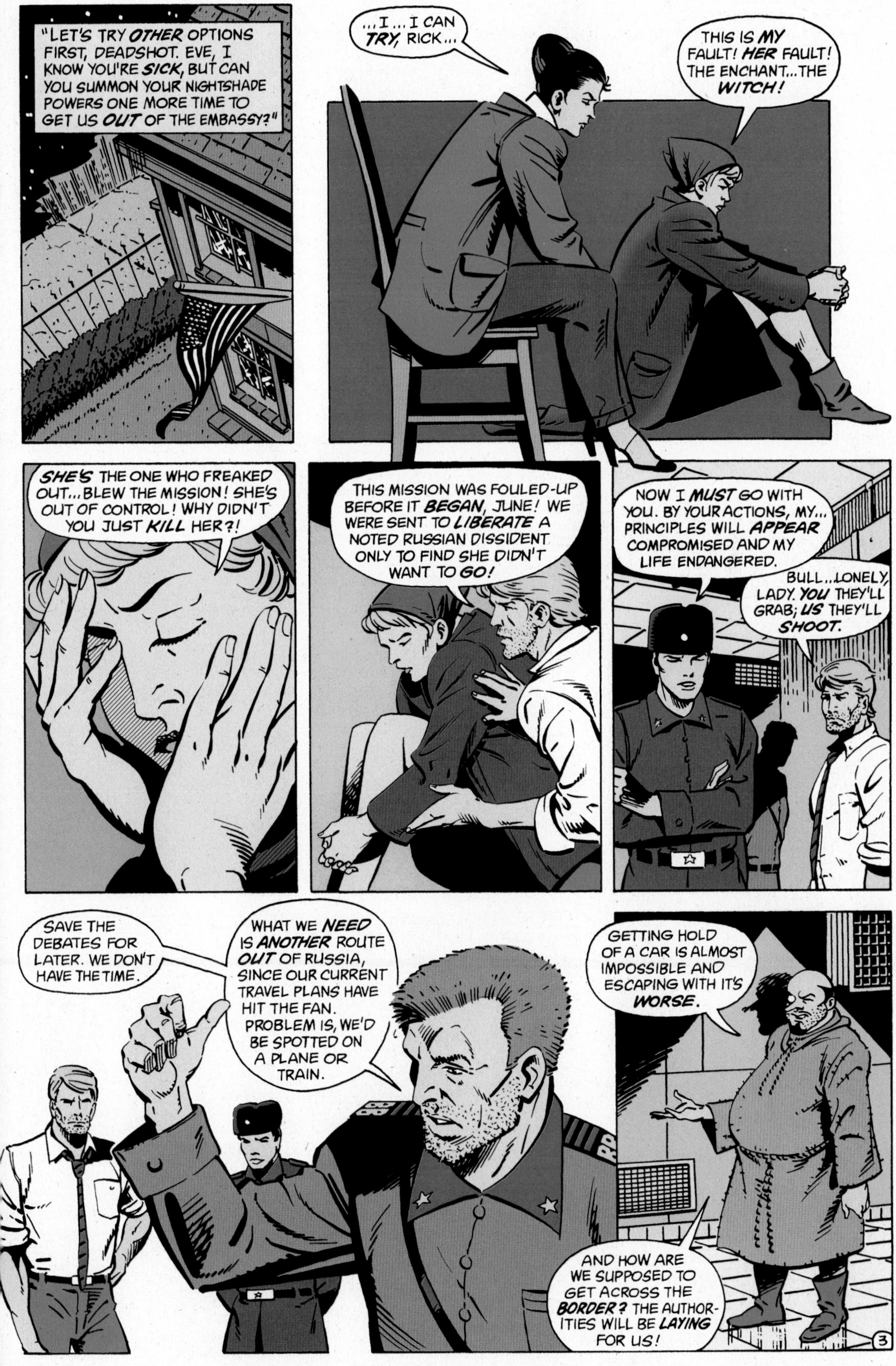
"LET'S TRY OTHER OPTIONS FIRST, DEADSHOT. EVE, I KNOW YOU'RE SICK, BUT CAN YOU SUMMON YOUR NIGHTSHADE POWERS ONE MORE TIME TO GET US OUT OF THE EMBASSY?"
...I...I CAN TRY, RICK...
THIS IS MY FAULT! HER FAULT! THE ENCHANT...THE WITCH!
SHE'S THE ONE WHO FREAKED OUT...BLEW THE MISSION! SHE'S OUT OF CONTROL! WHY DIDN'T YOU JUST KILL HER?!
THIS MISSION WAS FOULED-UP BEFORE IT BEGAN, JUNE! WE WERE SENT TO LIBERATE A NOTED RUSSIAN DISSIDENT ONLY TO FIND SHE DIDN'T WANT TO GO!
NOW I MUST GO WITH YOU. BY YOUR ACTIONS, MY... PRINCIPLES WILL APPEAR COMPROMISED AND MY LIFE ENDANGERED.
BULL...LONELY LADY. YOU THEY'LL GRAB; US THEY'LL SHOOT.
SAVE THE DEBATES FOR LATER. WE DON'T HAVE THE TIME.
WHAT WE NEED IS ANOTHER ROUTE OUT OF RUSSIA, SINCE OUR CURRENT TRAVEL PLANS HAVE HIT THE FAN. PROBLEM IS, WE'D BE SPOTTED ON A PLANE OR TRAIN.
GETTING HOLD OF A CAR IS ALMOST IMPOSSIBLE AND ESCAPING WITH IT'S WORSE.
AND HOW ARE WE SUPPOSED TO GET ACROSS THE BORDER? THE AUTHORITIES WILL BE LAYING FOR US!
3

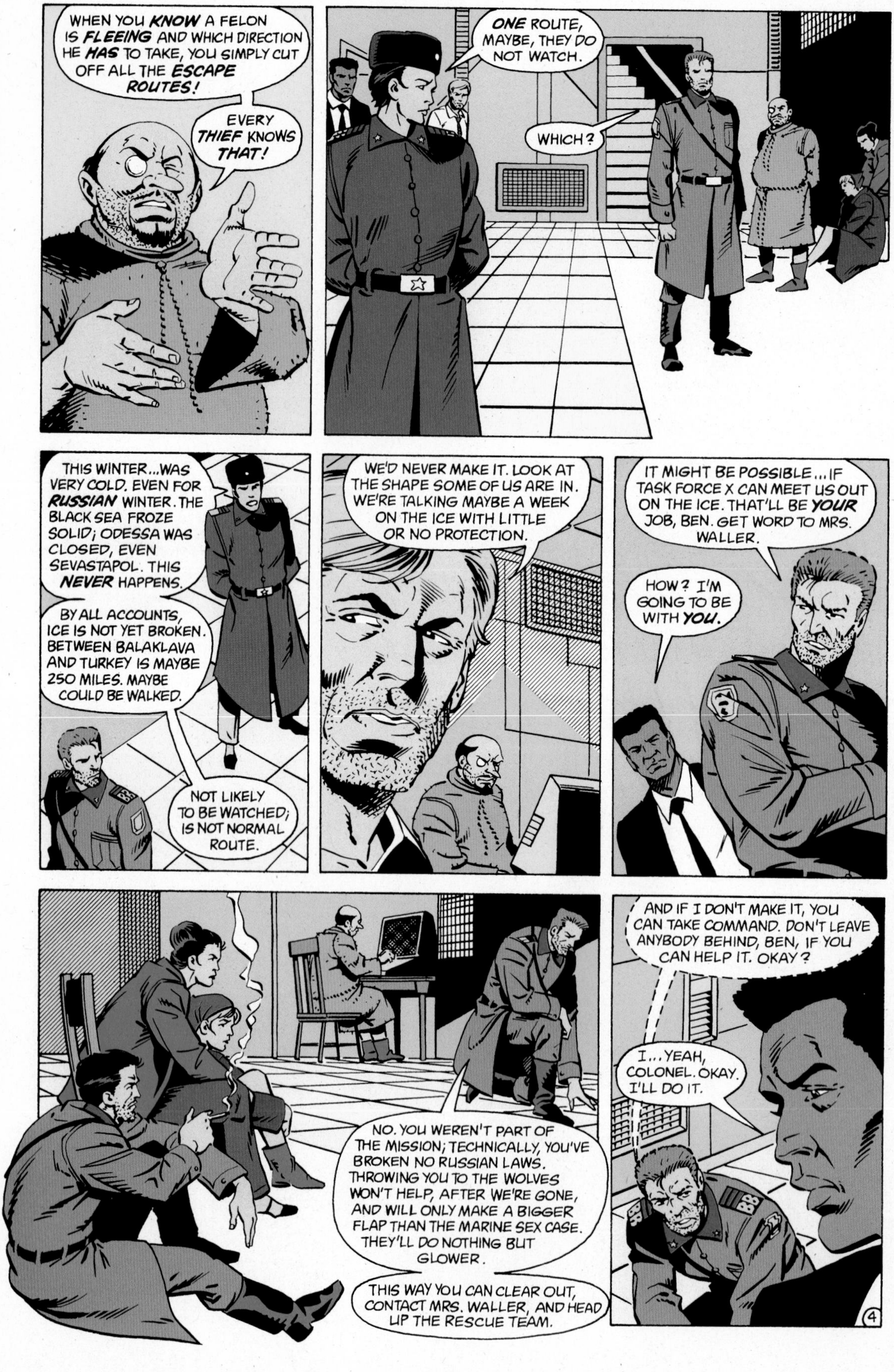

WHEN YOU KNOW A FELON IS FLEEING AND WHICH DIRECTION HE HAS TO TAKE, YOU SIMPLY CUT OFF ALL THE ESCAPE ROUTES!
EVERY THIEF KNOWS THAT!
ONE ROUTE, MAYBE, THEY DO NOT WATCH.
WHICH?
THIS WINTER...WAS VERY COLD. EVEN FOR RUSSIAN WINTER. THE BLACK SEA FROZE SOLID; ODESSA WAS CLOSED, EVEN SEVASTAPOL. THIS NEVER HAPPENS.
BY ALL ACCOUNTS, ICE IS NOT YET BROKEN. BETWEEN BALAKLAVA AND TURKEY IS MAYBE 250 MILES. MAYBE COULD BE WALKED.
NOT LIKELY TO BE WATCHED; IS NOT NORMAL ROUTE.
WE'D NEVER MAKE IT. LOOK AT THE SHAPE SOME OF US ARE IN. WE'RE TALKING MAYBE A WEEK ON THE ICE WITH LITTLE OR NO PROTECTION.
IT MIGHT BE POSSIBLE...IF TASK FORCE X CAN MEET US OUT ON THE ICE. THAT'LL BE YOUR JOB, BEN. GET WORD TO MRS. WALLER.
HOW? I'M GOING TO BE WITH YOU.
NO. YOU WEREN'T PART OF THE MISSION; TECHNICALLY, YOU'VE BROKEN NO RUSSIAN LAWS. THROWING YOU TO THE WOLVES WON'T HELP, AFTER WE'RE GONE, AND WILL ONLY MAKE A BIGGER FLAP THAN THE MARINE SEX CASE. THEY'LL DO NOTHING BUT GLOWER.
THIS WAY YOU CAN CLEAR OUT, CONTACT MRS. WALLER, AND HEAD UP THE RESCUE TEAM.
AND IF I DON'T MAKE IT, YOU CAN TAKE COMMAND. DON'T LEAVE ANYBODY BEHIND, BEN, IF YOU CAN HELP IT. OKAY?
I...YEAH, COLONEL. OKAY. I'LL DO IT.
4

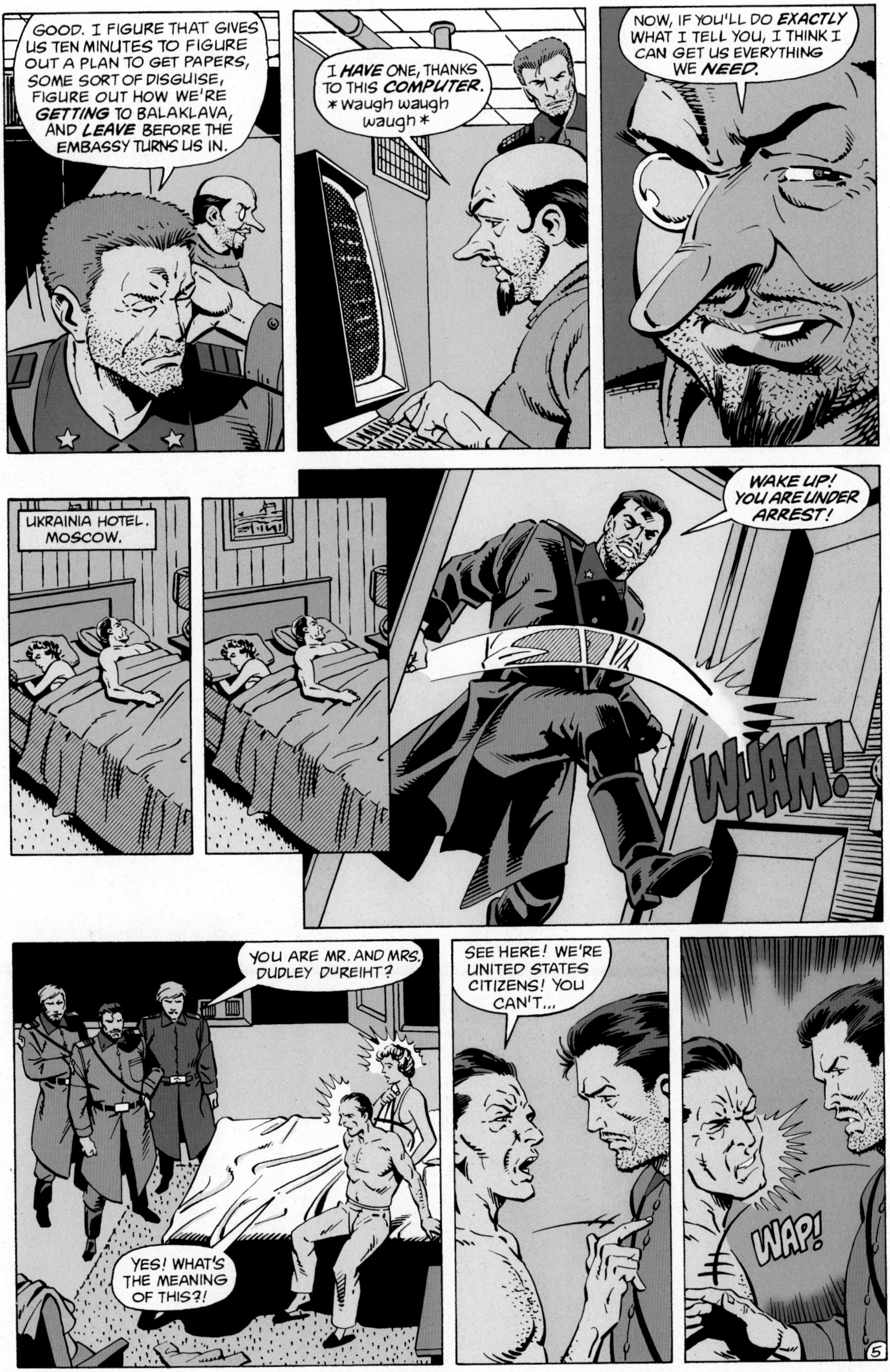
GOOD. I FIGURE THAT GIVES US TEN MINUTES TO FIGURE OUT A PLAN TO GET PAPERS, SOME SORT OF DISGUISE, FIGURE OUT HOW WE'RE GETTING TO BALAKLAVA, AND LEAVE BEFORE THE EMBASSY TURNS US IN.
I HAVE ONE, THANKS TO THIS COMPUTER. *waugh waugh waugh*
NOW, IF YOU'LL DO EXACTLY WHAT I TELL YOU, I THINK I CAN GET US EVERYTHING WE NEED.
UKRAINIA HOTEL. MOSCOW.
WAKE UP! YOU ARE UNDER ARREST!
WHAM!
YOU ARE MR. AND MRS. DUDLEY DUREIHT?
YES! WHAT'S THE MEANING OF THIS?!
SEE HERE! WE'RE UNITED STATES CITIZENS! YOU CAN'T...
WAP!
5

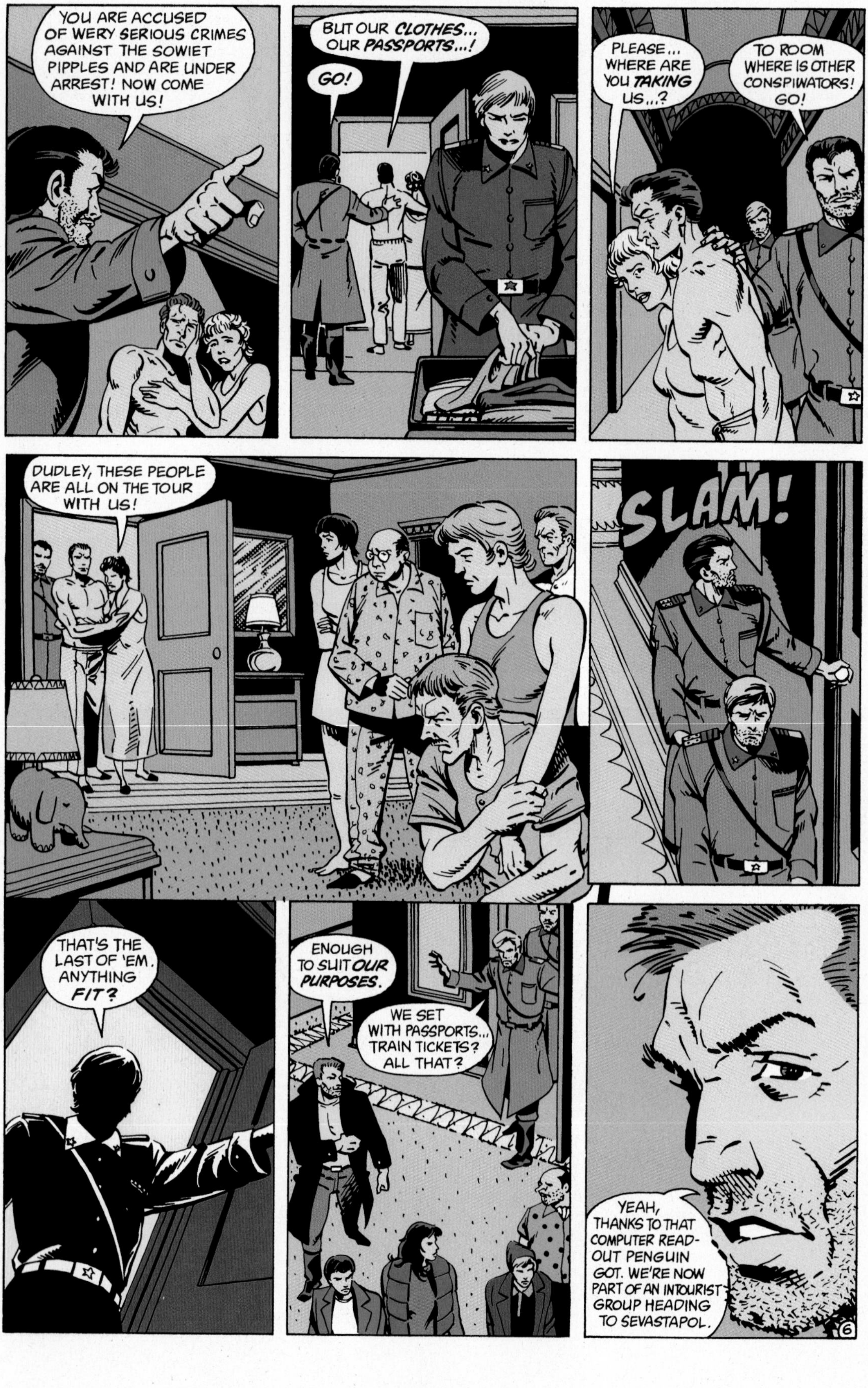
YOU ARE ACCUSED OF WERY SERIOUS CRIMES AGAINST THE SOWIET PIPPLES AND ARE UNDER ARREST! NOW COME WITH US!
BUT OUR CLOTHES... OUR PASSPORTS...!
GO!
PLEASE... WHERE ARE YOU TAKING US...?
TO ROOM WHERE IS OTHER CONSPIWATORS! GO!
DUDLEY, THESE PEOPLE ARE ALL ON THE TOUR WITH US!
SLAM!
THAT'S THE LAST OF 'EM. ANYTHING FIT?
ENOUGH TO SUIT OUR PURPOSES.
WE SET WITH PASSPORTS... TRAIN TICKETS? ALL THAT?
YEAH, THANKS TO THAT COMPUTER READ-OUT PENGUIN GOT. WE'RE NOW PART OF AN INTOURIST GROUP HEADING TO SEVASTAPOL.
6

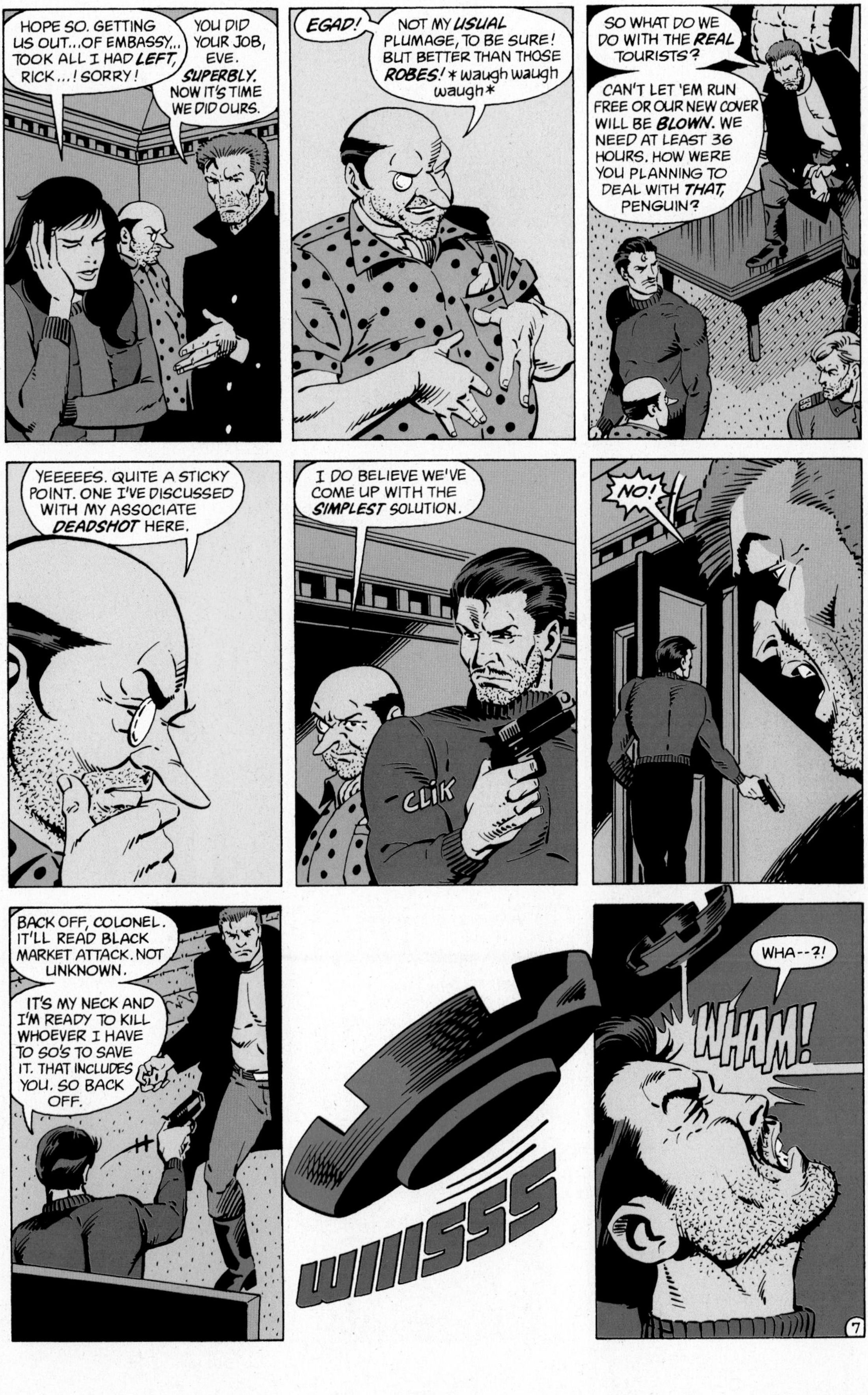

HOPE SO. GETTING US OUT...OF EMBASSY... TOOK ALL I HAD LEFT, RICK...! SORRY!
YOU DID YOUR JOB, EVE. SUPERBLY. NOW IT'S TIME WE DID OURS.
EGAD!
NOT MY USUAL PLUMAGE, TO BE SURE! BUT BETTER THAN THOSE ROBES! *waugh waugh waugh*
SO WHAT DO WE DO WITH THE REAL TOURISTS?
CAN'T LET 'EM RUN FREE OR OUR NEW COVER WILL BE BLOWN. WE NEED AT LEAST 36 HOURS. HOW WERE YOU PLANNING TO DEAL WITH THAT, PENGUIN?
YEEEEES. QUITE A STICKY POINT. ONE I'VE DISCUSSED WITH MY ASSOCIATE DEADSHOT HERE.
I DO BELIEVE WE'VE COME UP WITH THE SIMPLEST SOLUTION.
CLIK
NO!
BACK OFF, COLONEL. IT'LL READ BLACK MARKET ATTACK. NOT UNKNOWN.
IT'S MY NECK AND I'M READY TO KILL WHOEVER I HAVE TO SO'S TO SAVE IT. THAT INCLUDES YOU. SO BACK OFF.
WIIISSS
WHA--?!
WHAM!
7

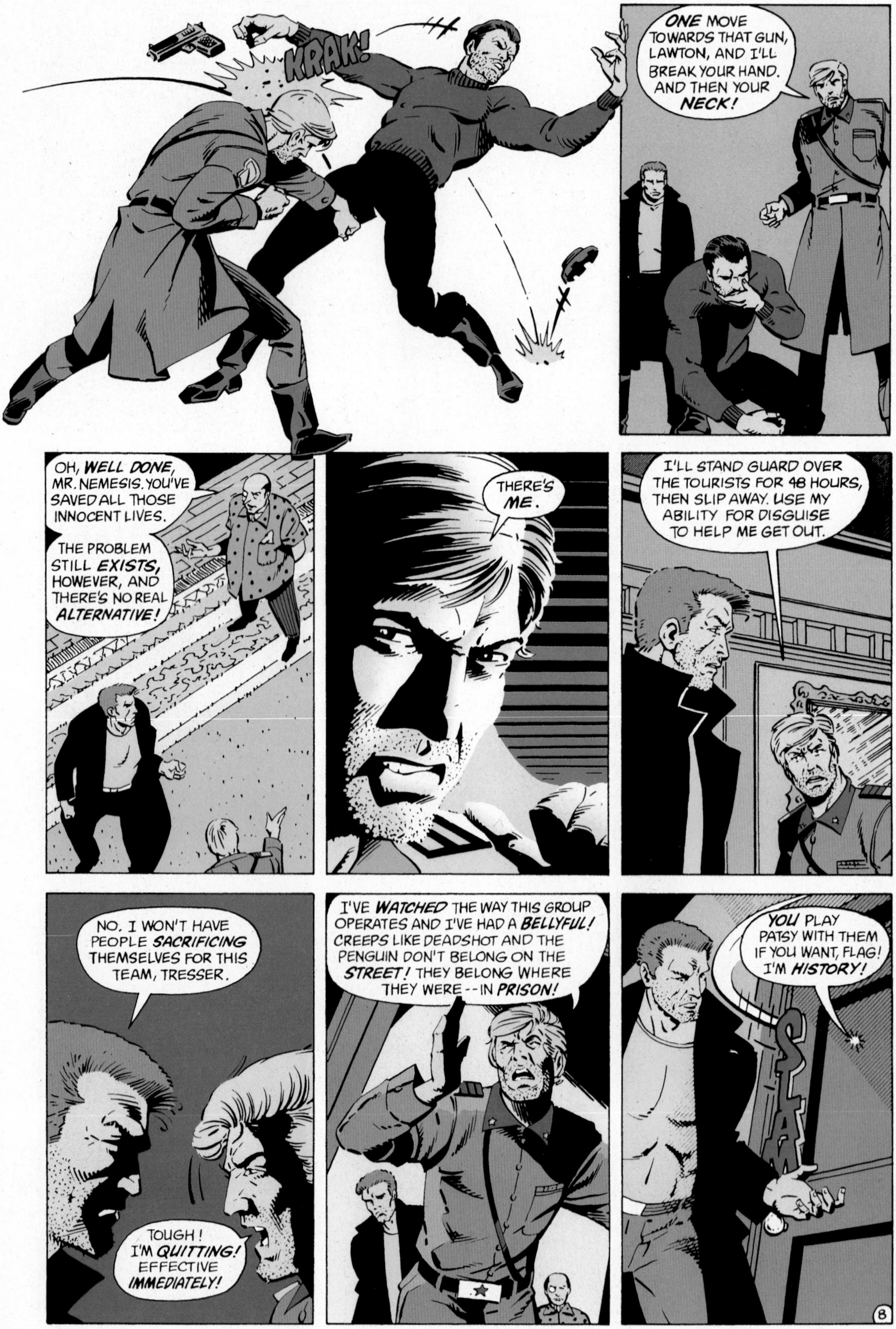
KRAK!
ONE MOVE TOWARDS THAT GUN, LAWTON, AND I'LL BREAK YOUR HAND. AND THEN YOUR NECK!
OH, WELL DONE, MR. NEMESIS. YOU'VE SAVED ALL THOSE INNOCENT LIVES.
THE PROBLEM STILL EXISTS, HOWEVER, AND THERE'S NO REAL ALTERNATIVE!
THERE'S ME.
I'LL STAND GUARD OVER THE TOURISTS FOR 48 HOURS, THEN SLIP AWAY. USE MY ABILITY FOR DISGUISE TO HELP ME GET OUT.
NO. I WON'T HAVE PEOPLE SACRIFICING THEMSELVES FOR THIS TEAM, TRESSER.
TOUGH! I'M QUITTING! EFFECTIVE IMMEDIATELY!
I'VE WATCHED THE WAY THIS GROUP OPERATES AND I'VE HAD A BELLYFUL! CREEPS LIKE DEADSHOT AND THE PENGUIN DON'T BELONG ON THE STREET! THEY BELONG WHERE THEY WERE--IN PRISON!
YOU PLAY PATSY WITH THEM IF YOU WANT, FLAG! I'M HISTORY!
SLAM
8

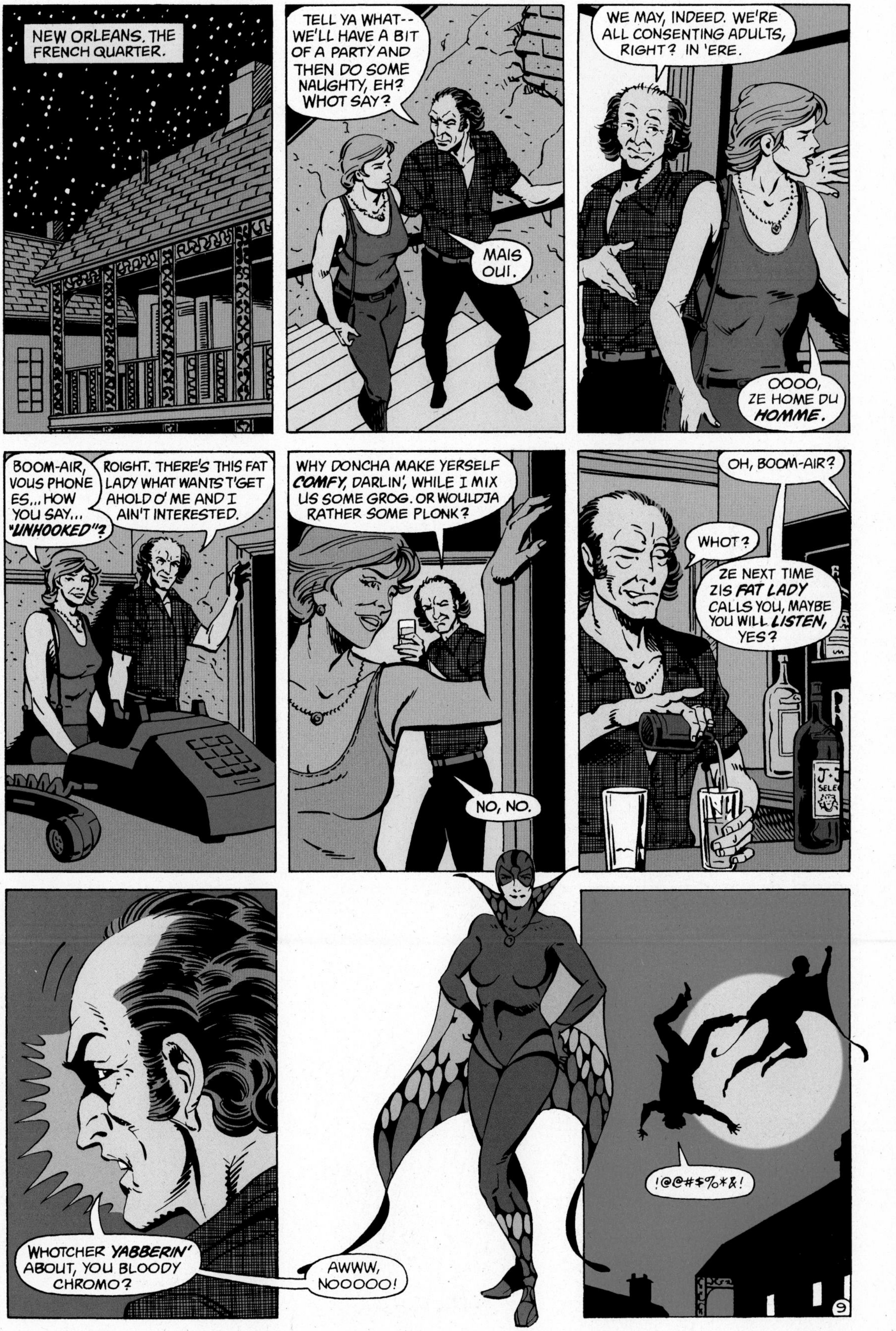
NEW ORLEANS. THE FRENCH QUARTER.
TELL YA WHAT-- WE'LL HAVE A BIT OF A PARTY AND THEN DO SOME NAUGHTY, EH? WHOT SAY?
MAIS OUI.
WE MAY, INDEED. WE'RE ALL CONSENTING ADULTS, RIGHT? IN 'ERE.
OOOO, ZE HOME DU HOMME.
BOOM-AIR, VOUS PHONE ES... HOW YOU SAY... "UNHOOKED"?
ROIGHT. THERE'S THIS FAT LADY WHAT WANTS T'GET AHOLD O' ME AND I AIN'T INTERESTED.
WHY DONCHA MAKE YERSELF COMFY, DARLIN', WHILE I MIX US SOME GROG. OR WOULDJA RATHER SOME PLONK?
NO, NO.
OH, BOOM-AIR?
WHOT?
ZE NEXT TIME ZIS FAT LADY CALLS YOU, MAYBE YOU WILL LISTEN, YES?
WHOTCHER YABBERIN' ABOUT, YOU BLOODY CHROMO?
AWWW, NOOOOO!
!@#$%*&!
9

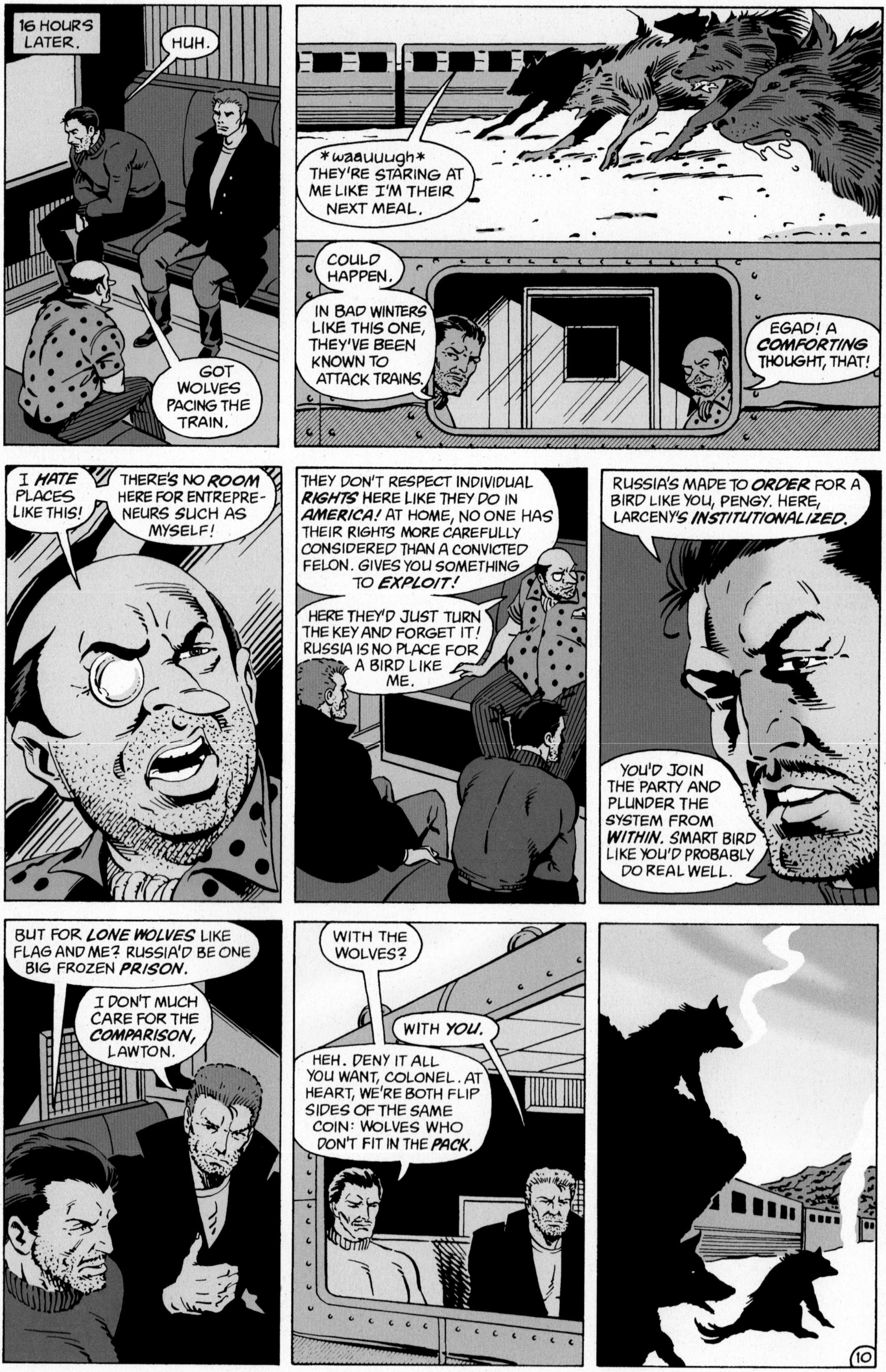
16 HOURS LATER.
HUH.
GOT WOLVES PACING THE TRAIN.
waauuugh THEY'RE STARING AT ME LIKE I'M THEIR NEXT MEAL.
COULD HAPPEN.
IN BAD WINTERS LIKE THIS ONE, THEY'VE BEEN KNOWN TO ATTACK TRAINS.
EGAD! A COMFORTING THOUGHT, THAT!
I HATE PLACES LIKE THIS!
THERE'S NO ROOM HERE FOR ENTREPRENEURS SUCH AS MYSELF!
THEY DON'T RESPECT INDIVIDUAL RIGHTS HERE LIKE THEY DO IN AMERICA! AT HOME, NO ONE HAS THEIR RIGHTS MORE CAREFULLY CONSIDERED THAN A CONVICTED FELON. GIVES YOU SOMETHING TO EXPLOIT!
HERE THEY'D JUST TURN THE KEY AND FORGET IT! RUSSIA IS NO PLACE FOR A BIRD LIKE ME.
RUSSIA'S MADE TO ORDER FOR A BIRD LIKE YOU, PENGY. HERE, LARCENY'S INSTITUTIONALIZED.
YOU'D JOIN THE PARTY AND PLUNDER THE SYSTEM FROM WITHIN. SMART BIRD LIKE YOU'D PROBABLY DO REAL WELL.
BUT FOR LONE WOLVES LIKE FLAG AND ME? RUSSIA'D BE ONE BIG FROZEN PRISON.
I DON'T MUCH CARE FOR THE COMPARISON, LAWTON.
WITH THE WOLVES?
WITH YOU.
HEH. DENY IT ALL YOU WANT, COLONEL. AT HEART, WE'RE BOTH FLIP SIDES OF THE SAME COIN: WOLVES WHO DON'T FIT IN THE PACK.
10

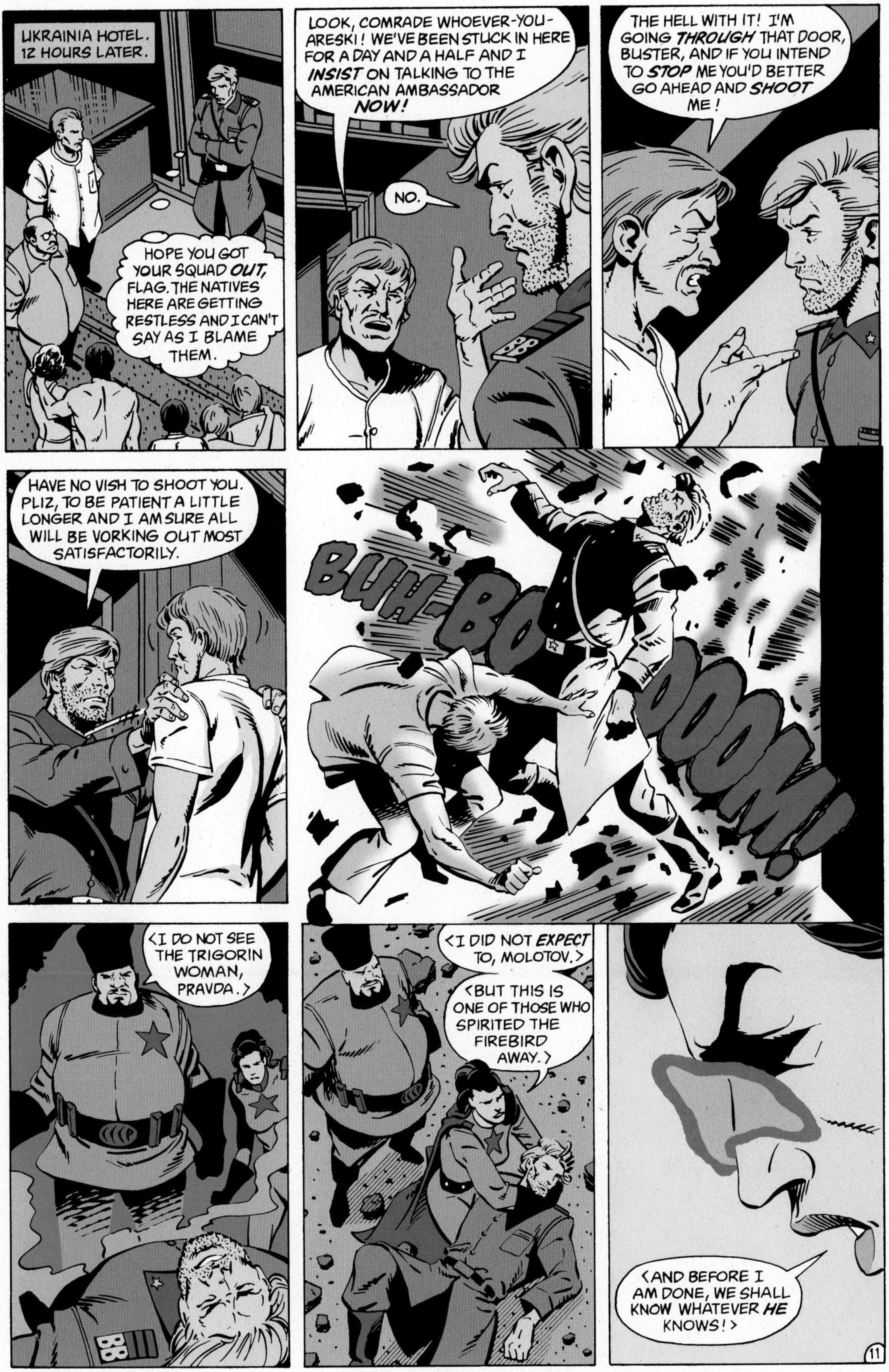
UKRAINIA HOTEL. 12 HOURS LATER.
HOPE YOU GOT YOUR SQUAD OUT, FLAG. THE NATIVES HERE ARE GETTING RESTLESS AND I CAN'T SAY AS I BLAME THEM.
LOOK, COMRADE WHOEVER-YOU-ARESKI! WE'VE BEEN STUCK IN HERE FOR A DAY AND A HALF AND I INSIST ON TALKING TO THE AMERICAN AMBASSADOR NOW!
NO.
THE HELL WITH IT! I'M GOING THROUGH THAT DOOR, BUSTER, AND IF YOU INTEND TO STOP ME YOU'D BETTER GO AHEAD AND SHOOT ME!
HAVE NO VISH TO SHOOT YOU. PLIZ, TO BE PATIENT A LITTLE LONGER AND I AM SURE ALL WILL BE VORKING OUT MOST SATISFACTORILY.
BUH-BOOOOOM!
<I DO NOT SEE THE TRIGORIN WOMAN, PRAVDA.>
<I DID NOT EXPECT TO, MOLOTOV.>
<BUT THIS IS ONE OF THOSE WHO SPIRITED THE FIREBIRD AWAY.>
<AND BEFORE I AM DONE, WE SHALL KNOW WHATEVER HE KNOWS!>
11

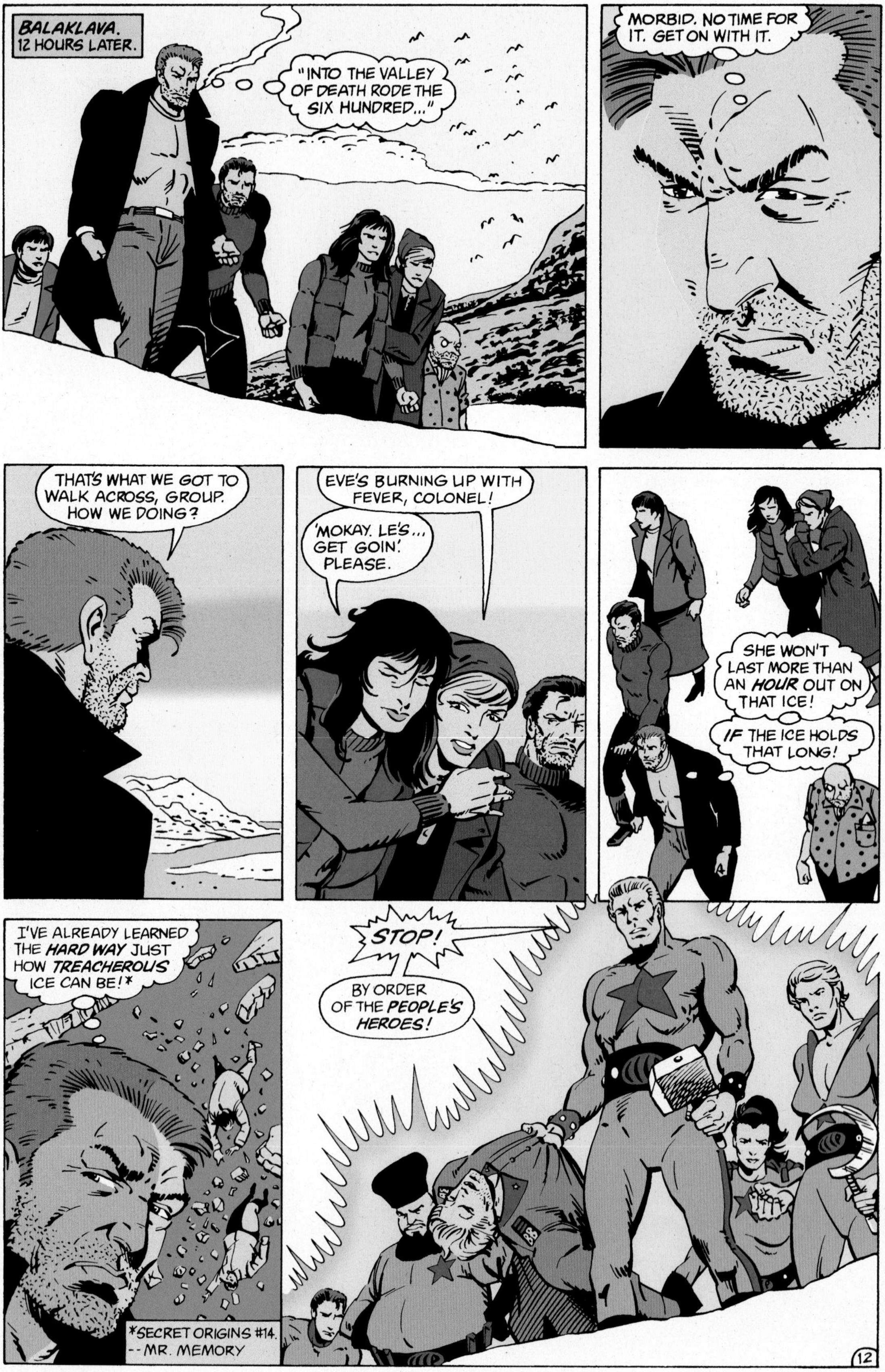
BALAKLAVA.
12 HOURS LATER.
"INTO THE VALLEY OF DEATH RODE THE SIX HUNDRED..."
MORBID. NO TIME FOR IT. GET ON WITH IT.
THAT'S WHAT WE GOT TO WALK ACROSS, GROUP. HOW WE DOING?
EVE'S BURNING UP WITH FEVER, COLONEL!
'MOKAY. LE'S... GET GOIN'. PLEASE.
SHE WON'T LAST MORE THAN AN HOUR OUT ON THAT ICE!
IF THE ICE HOLDS THAT LONG!
I'VE ALREADY LEARNED THE HARD WAY JUST HOW TREACHEROUS ICE CAN BE!*
*SECRET ORIGINS #14.
--MR. MEMORY
STOP!
BY ORDER OF THE PEOPLE'S HEROES!
12

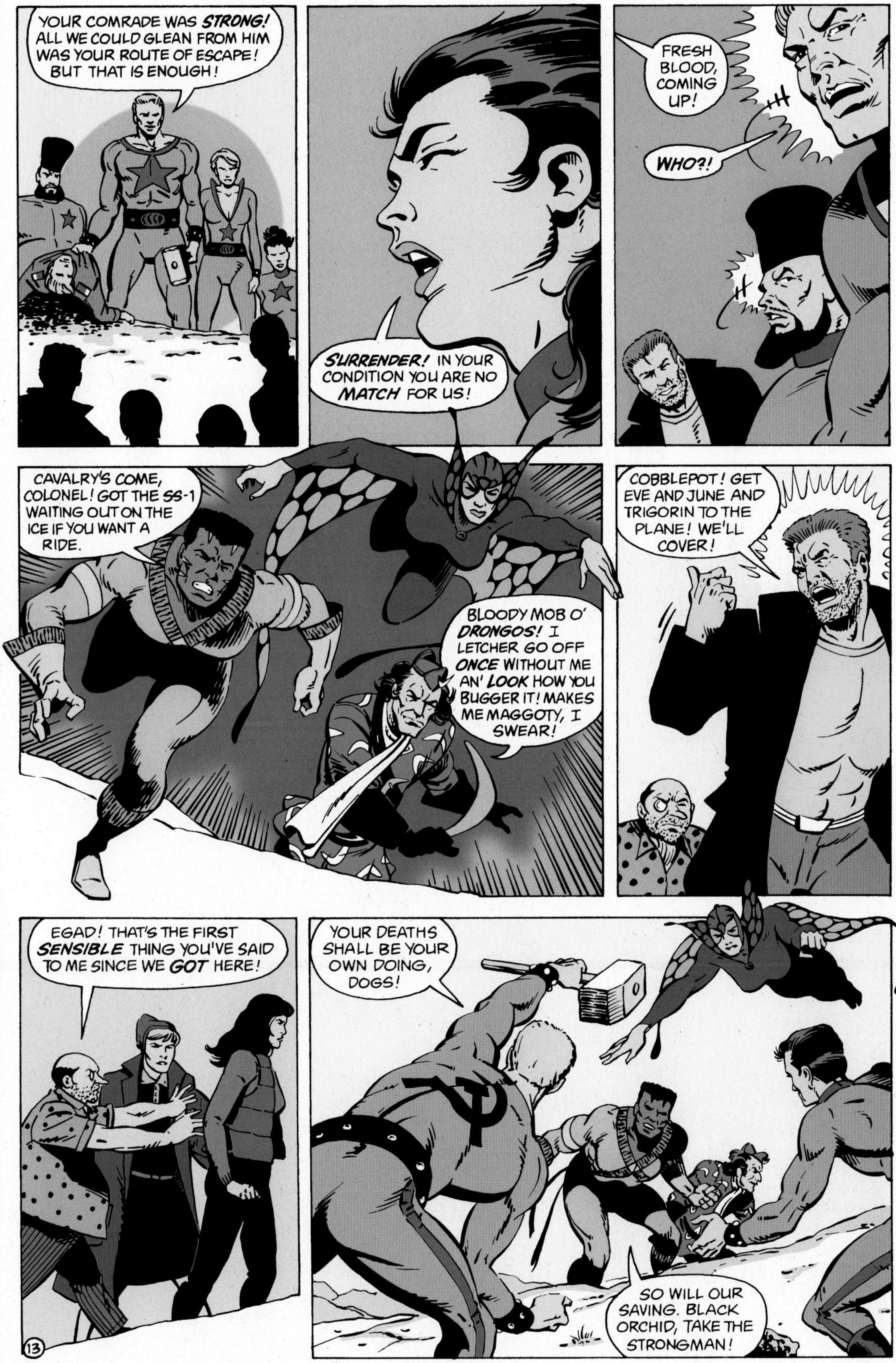
YOUR COMRADE WAS STRONG! ALL WE COULD GLEAN FROM HIM WAS YOUR ROUTE OF ESCAPE! BUT THAT IS ENOUGH!
SURRENDER! IN YOUR CONDITION YOU ARE NO MATCH FOR US!
FRESH BLOOD, COMING UP!
WHO?!
CAVALRY'S COME, COLONEL! GOT THE SS-1 WAITING OUT ON THE ICE IF YOU WANT A RIDE.
BLOODY MOB O' DRONGOS! I LETCHER GO OFF ONCE WITHOUT ME AN' LOOK HOW YOU BUGGER IT! MAKES ME MAGGOTY, I SWEAR!
COBBLEPOT! GET EVE AND JUNE AND TRIGORIN TO THE PLANE! WE'LL COVER!
EGAD! THAT'S THE FIRST SENSIBLE THING YOU'VE SAID TO ME SINCE WE GOT HERE!
YOUR DEATHS SHALL BE YOUR OWN DOING, DOGS!
SO WILL OUR SAVING. BLACK ORCHID, TAKE THE STRONGMAN!
13

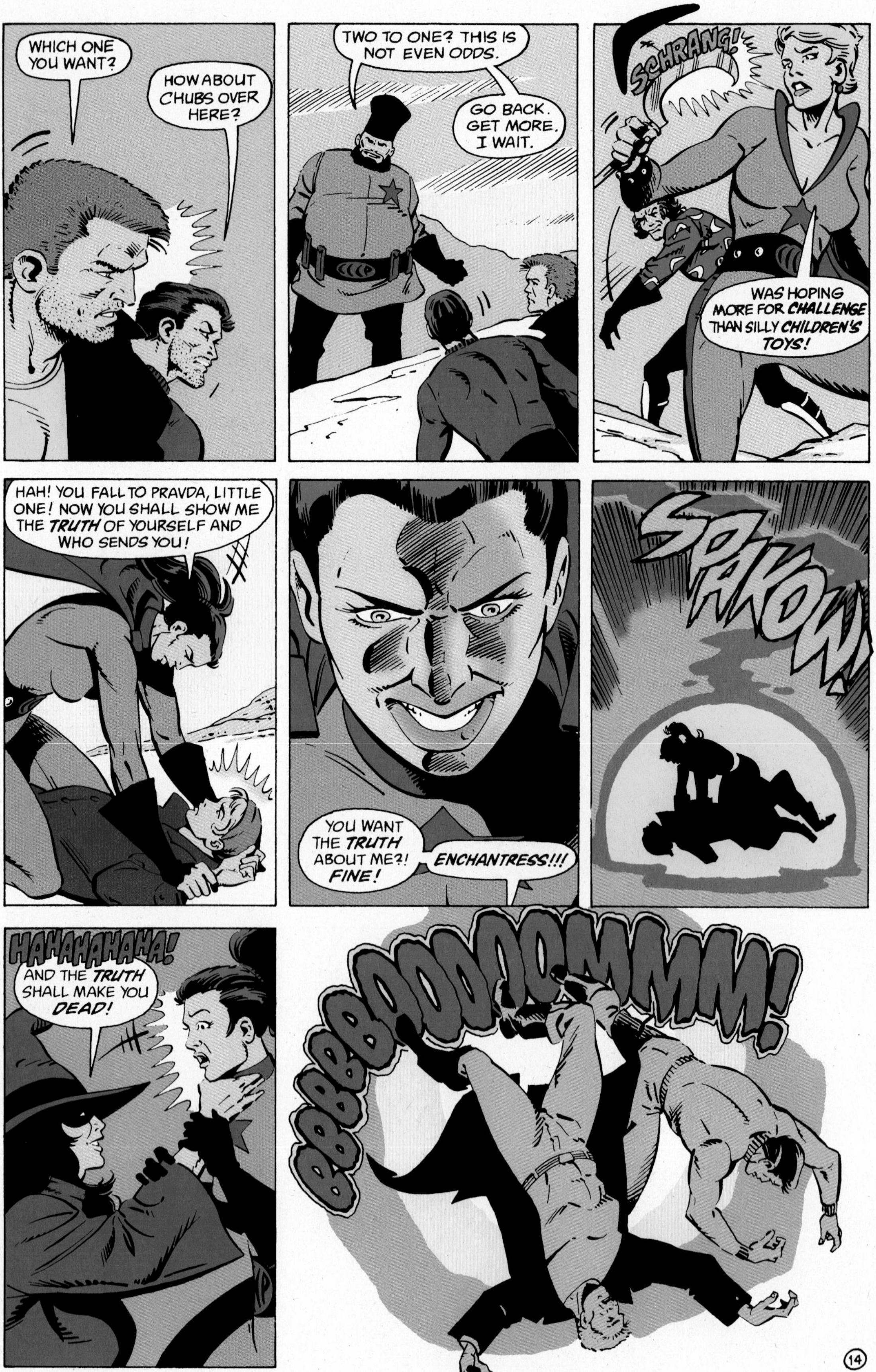
WHICH ONE YOU WANT?
HOW ABOUT CHUBS OVER HERE?
TWO TO ONE? THIS IS NOT EVEN ODDS.
GO BACK. GET MORE. I WAIT.
SCHRANG!
WAS HOPING MORE FOR CHALLENGE THAN SILLY CHILDREN'S TOYS!
HAH! YOU FALL TO PRAVDA, LITTLE ONE! NOW YOU SHALL SHOW ME THE TRUTH OF YOURSELF AND WHO SENDS YOU!
YOU WANT THE TRUTH ABOUT ME?! FINE!
ENCHANTRESS!!!
SPAKOW!
HAHAHAHAHA!
AND THE TRUTH SHALL MAKE YOU DEAD!
BBBBBOOOOOOMMMM!
14

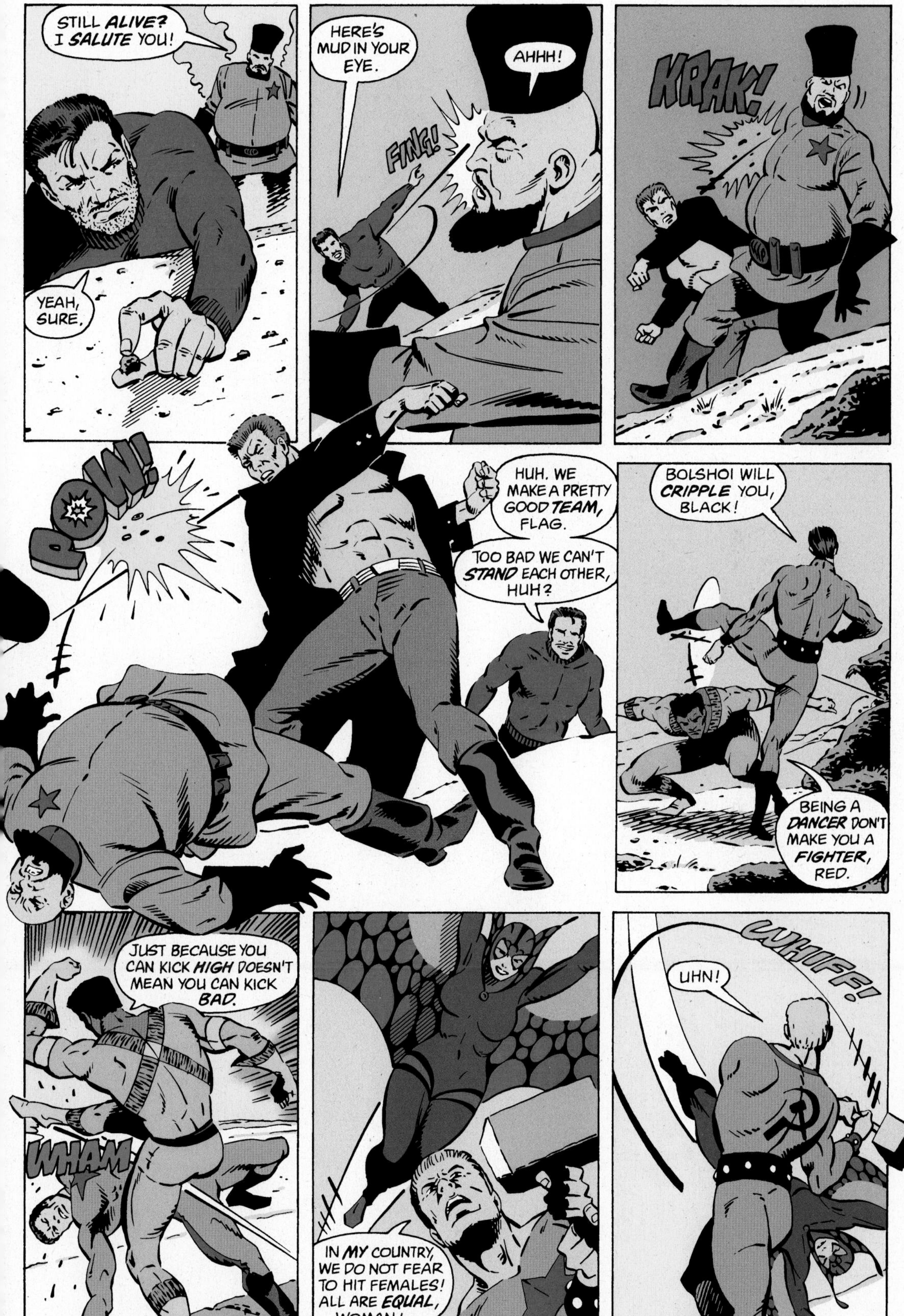
STILL ALIVE? I SALUTE YOU!
YEAH, SURE.
HERE'S MUD IN YOUR EYE.
AHHH!
FING!
KRAK!
POW!
HUH. WE MAKE A PRETTY GOOD TEAM, FLAG.
TOO BAD WE CAN'T STAND EACH OTHER, HUH?
BOLSHOI WILL CRIPPLE YOU, BLACK!
BEING A DANCER DON'T MAKE YOU A FIGHTER, RED.
JUST BECAUSE YOU CAN KICK HIGH DOESN'T MEAN YOU CAN KICK BAD.
WHAM
IN MY COUNTRY, WE DO NOT FEAR TO HIT FEMALES! ALL ARE EQUAL, WOMAN!
UHN!
UUHIFF!
15

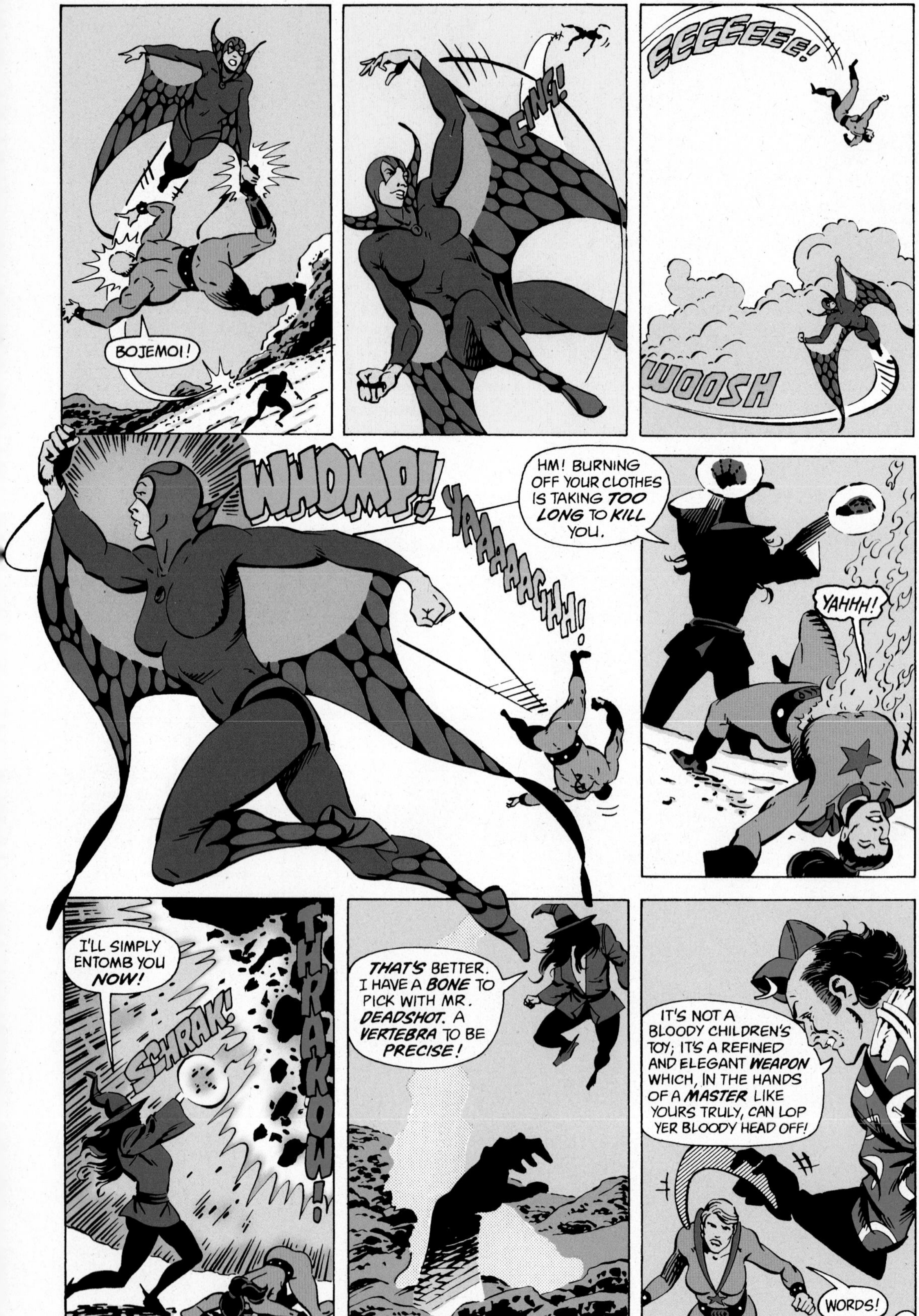
BOJEMOI!
FING!
EEEEEEE!
WOOSH
WHOMP!
YAAAAAAGHHH!
HM! BURNING OFF YOUR CLOTHES IS TAKING TOO LONG TO KILL YOU.
YAHHH!
I'LL SIMPLY ENTOMB YOU NOW!
SCHRAK!
THRAKOOW!
THAT'S BETTER. I HAVE A BONE TO PICK WITH MR. DEADSHOT. A VERTEBRA TO BE PRECISE!
IT'S NOT A BLOODY CHILDREN'S TOY; IT'S A REFINED AND ELEGANT WEAPON WHICH, IN THE HANDS OF A MASTER LIKE YOURS TRULY, CAN LOP YER BLOODY HEAD OFF!
WORDS!
16

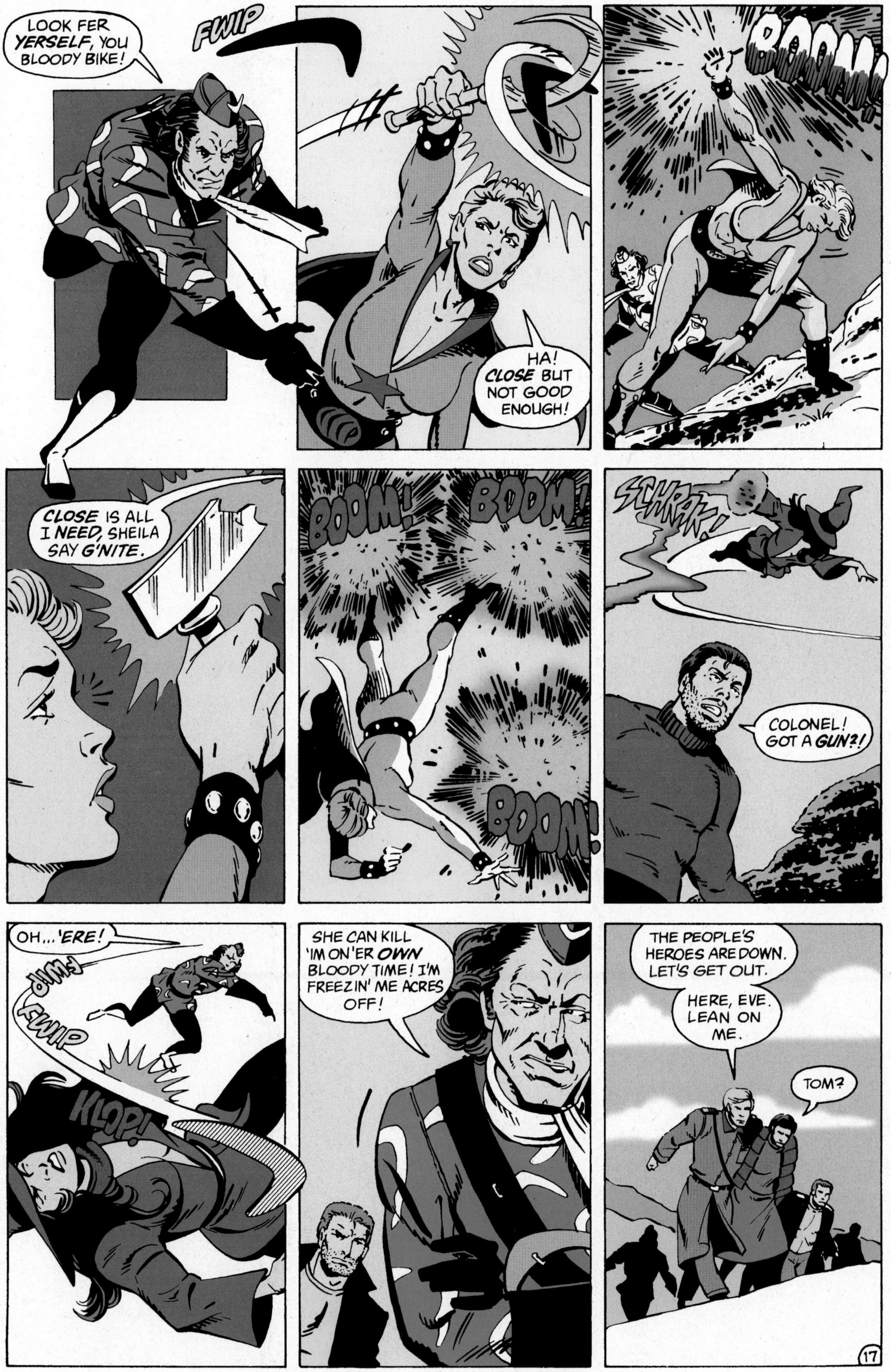
LOOK FER YERSELF, YOU BLOODY BIKE!
FWIP
HA! CLOSE BUT NOT GOOD ENOUGH!
BOOM!
CLOSE IS ALL I NEED, SHEILA SAY G'NITE.
BOOM!
BOOM!
BOOM!
SCHRAK!
COLONEL! GOT A GUN?!
OH...'ERE!
FWIP
FWIP
KLOP!
SHE CAN KILL 'IM ON 'ER OWN BLOODY TIME! I'M FREEZIN' ME ACRES OFF!
THE PEOPLE'S HEROES ARE DOWN. LET'S GET OUT.
HERE, EVE. LEAN ON ME.
TOM?
17

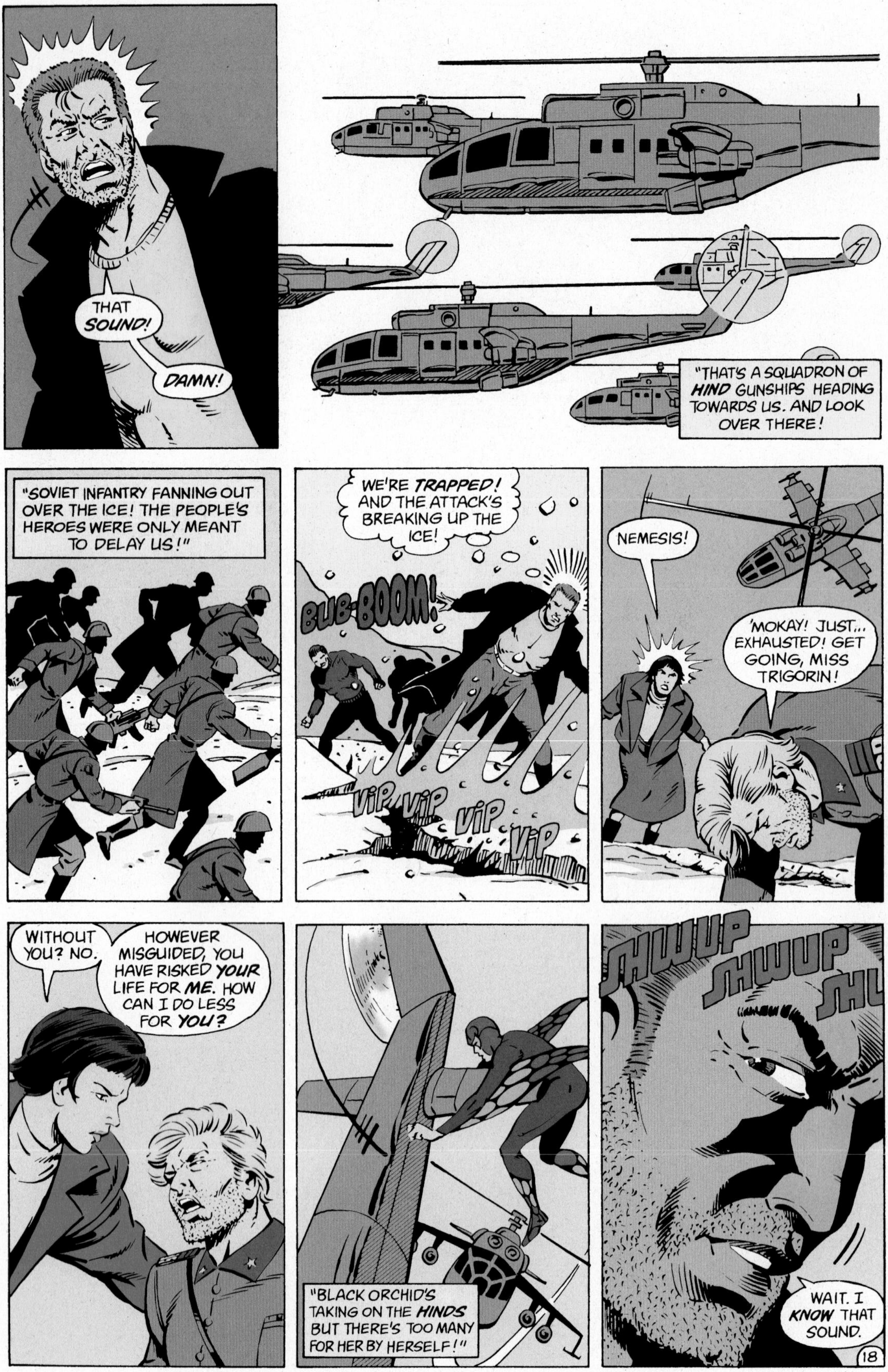
THAT SOUND!
DAMN!
"THAT'S A SQUADRON OF HIND GUNSHIPS HEADING TOWARDS US. AND LOOK OVER THERE!
"SOVIET INFANTRY FANNING OUT OVER THE ICE! THE PEOPLE'S HEROES WERE ONLY MEANT TO DELAY US!"
WE'RE TRAPPED! AND THE ATTACK'S BREAKING UP THE ICE!
BUB-BOOM!
ViP ViP ViP ViP
NEMESIS!
'MOKAY! JUST... EXHAUSTED! GET GOING, MISS TRIGORIN!
WITHOUT YOU? NO.
HOWEVER MISGUIDED, YOU HAVE RISKED YOUR LIFE FOR ME. HOW CAN I DO LESS FOR YOU?
"BLACK ORCHID'S TAKING ON THE HINDS BUT THERE'S TOO MANY FOR HER BY HERSELF!"
SHWUP SHWUP SH
WAIT. I KNOW THAT SOUND.
18

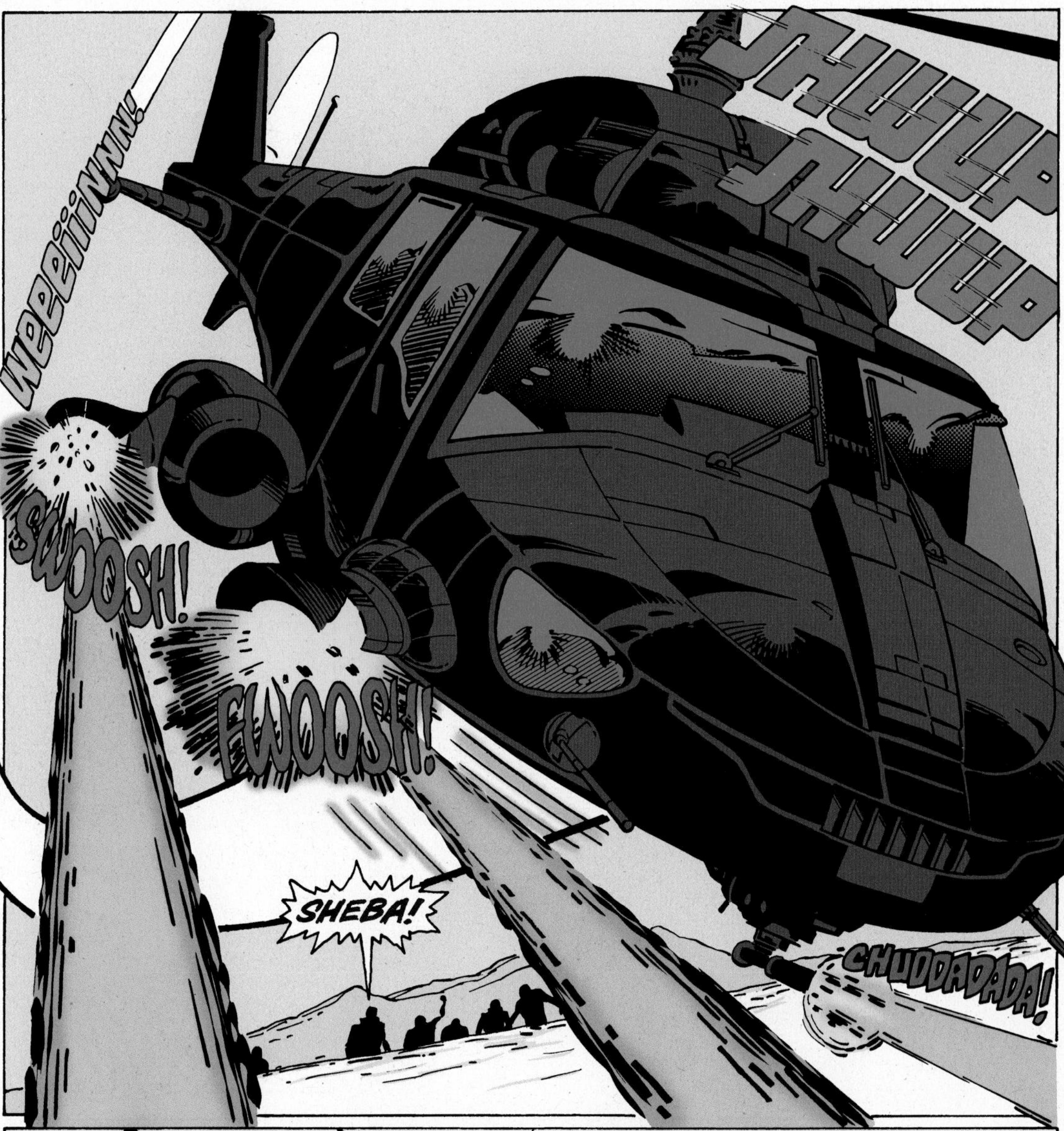
JAWUP JAWUP
WEEEIIINNN!
SWOOSH!
FWOOSH!
SHEBA!
CHUDDADADA!
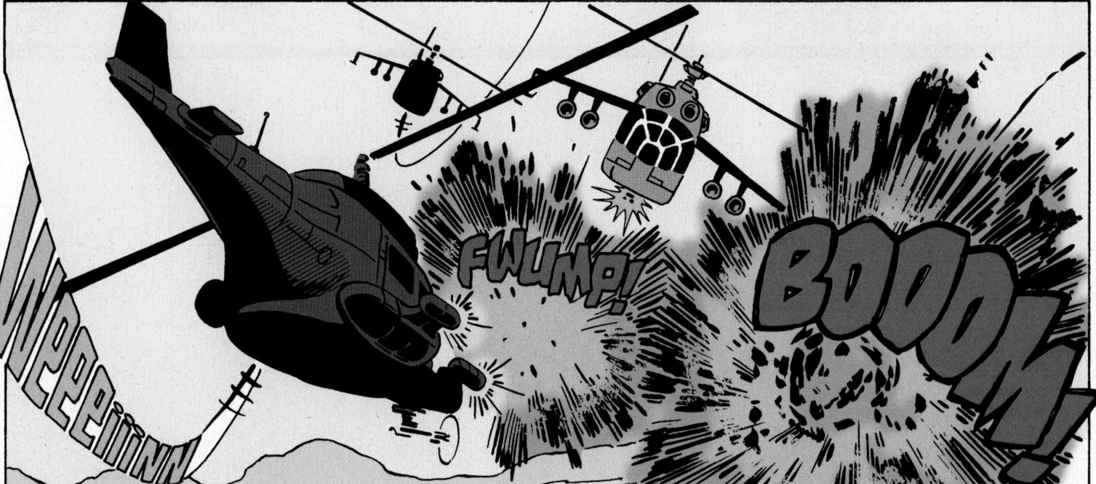
WEEEIIINN
FWUMP!
BOOOM!
19

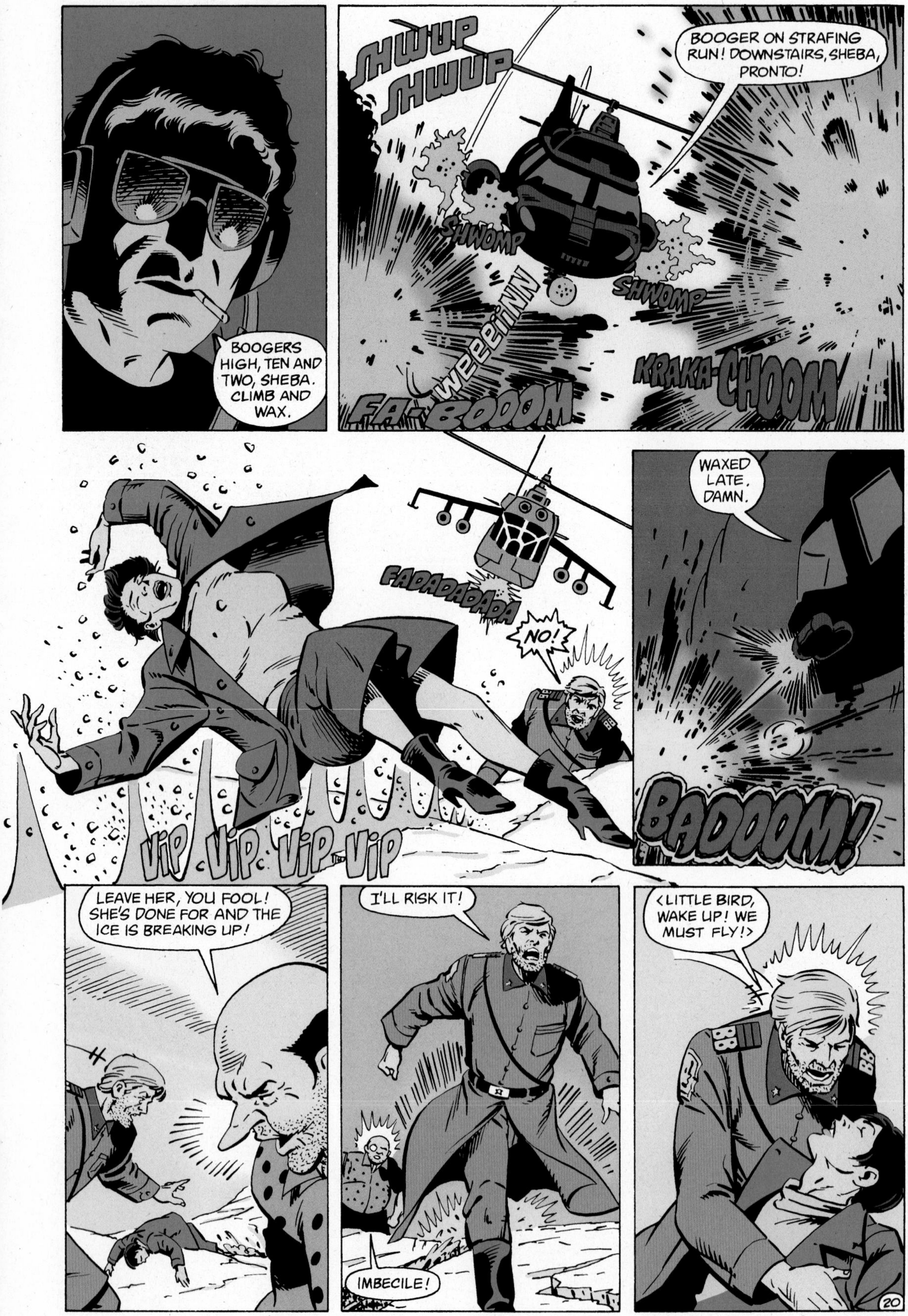
BOOGERS HIGH, TEN AND TWO, SHEBA. CLIMB AND WAX.
SHWUP SHWUP
BOOGER ON STRAFING RUN! DOWNSTAIRS, SHEBA, PRONTO!
SHWOMP
WEEEEIINN
SHWOMP
KRAKA-CHOOM
FA-BOOOM
FADADADADA
NO!
VIP VIP VIP VIP
WAXED LATE. DAMN.
BADOOOM!
LEAVE HER, YOU FOOL! SHE'S DONE FOR AND THE ICE IS BREAKING UP!
I'LL RISK IT!
IMBECILE!
<LITTLE BIRD, WAKE UP! WE MUST FLY!>
20

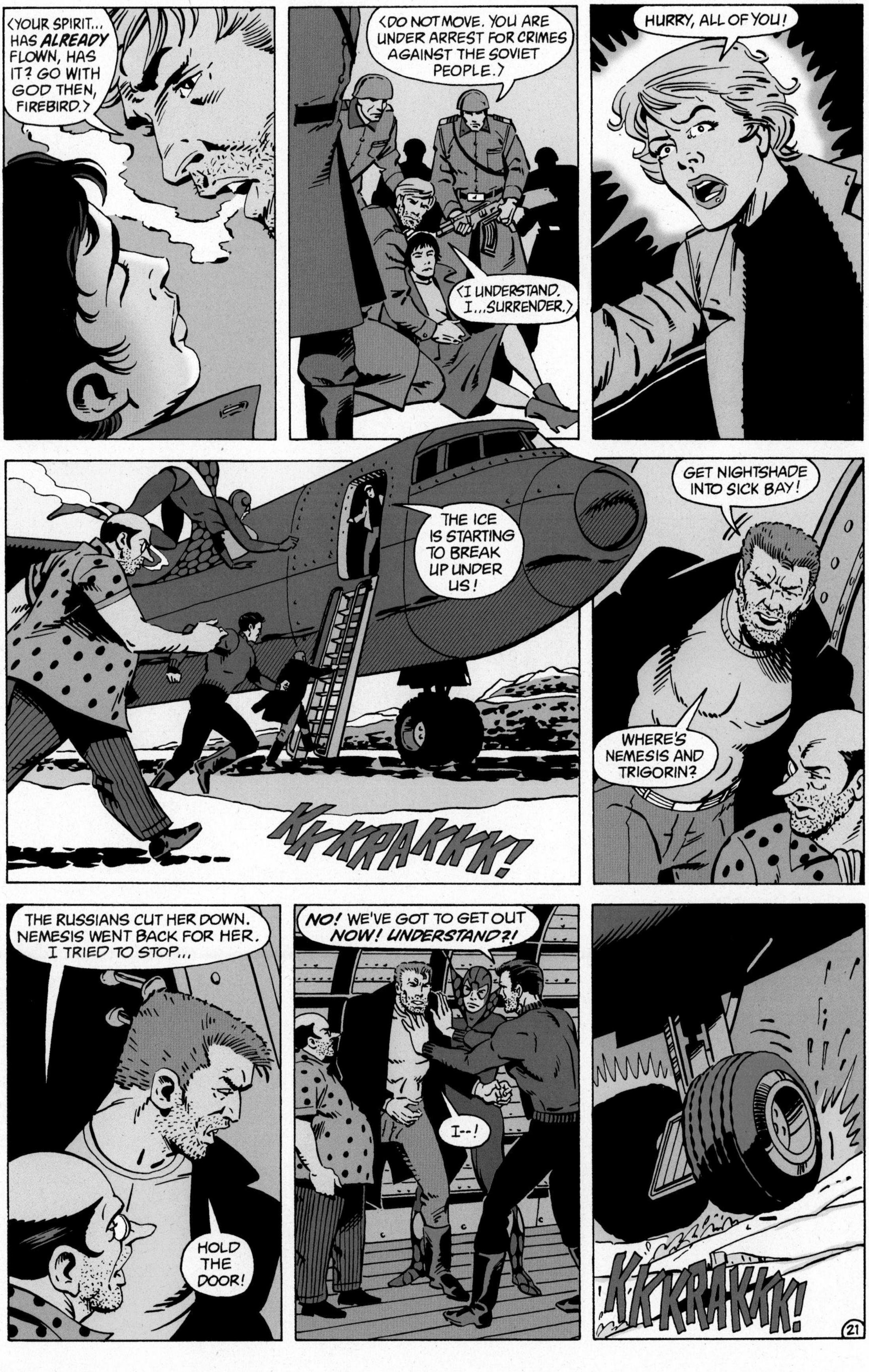

<YOUR SPIRIT... HAS ALREADY FLOWN, HAS IT? GO WITH GOD THEN, FIREBIRD.>
<DO NOT MOVE. YOU ARE UNDER ARREST FOR CRIMES AGAINST THE SOVIET PEOPLE.>
<I UNDERSTAND. I...SURRENDER.>
HURRY, ALL OF YOU!
THE ICE IS STARTING TO BREAK UP UNDER US!
KKKRAKKK!
GET NIGHTSHADE INTO SICK BAY!
WHERE'S NEMESIS AND TRIGORIN?
THE RUSSIANS CUT HER DOWN. NEMESIS WENT BACK FOR HER. I TRIED TO STOP...
HOLD THE DOOR!
NO! WE'VE GOT TO GET OUT NOW! UNDERSTAND?!
I--!
KKKRAKKK!
21

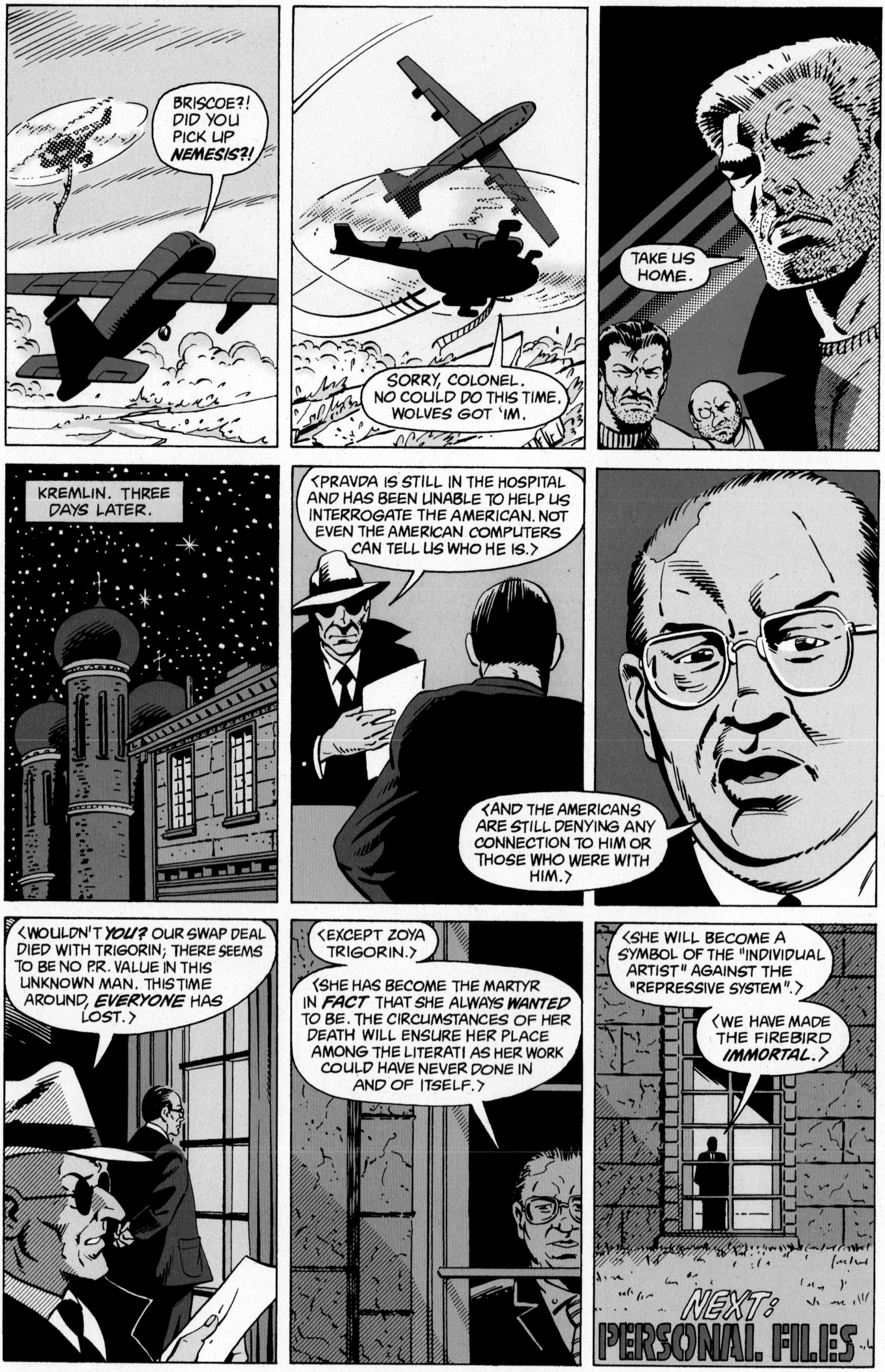
BRISCOE?! DID YOU PICK UP NEMESIS?!
SORRY, COLONEL. NO COULD DO THIS TIME. WOLVES GOT 'IM.
TAKE US HOME.
KREMLIN. THREE DAYS LATER.
<PRAVDA IS STILL IN THE HOSPITAL AND HAS BEEN UNABLE TO HELP US INTERROGATE THE AMERICAN. NOT EVEN THE AMERICAN COMPUTERS CAN TELL US WHO HE IS.>
<AND THE AMERICANS ARE STILL DENYING ANY CONNECTION TO HIM OR THOSE WHO WERE WITH HIM.>
<WOULDN'T YOU? OUR SWAP DEAL DIED WITH TRIGORIN; THERE SEEMS TO BE NO P.R. VALUE IN THIS UNKNOWN MAN. THIS TIME AROUND, EVERYONE HAS LOST.>
<EXCEPT ZOYA TRIGORIN.>
<SHE HAS BECOME THE MARTYR IN FACT THAT SHE ALWAYS WANTED TO BE. THE CIRCUMSTANCES OF HER DEATH WILL ENSURE HER PLACE AMONG THE LITERATI AS HER WORK COULD HAVE NEVER DONE IN AND OF ITSELF.>
<SHE WILL BECOME A SYMBOL OF THE "INDIVIDUAL ARTIST" AGAINST THE "REPRESSIVE SYSTEM".>
<WE HAVE MADE THE FIREBIRD IMMORTAL.>
NEXT: PERSONAL FILES

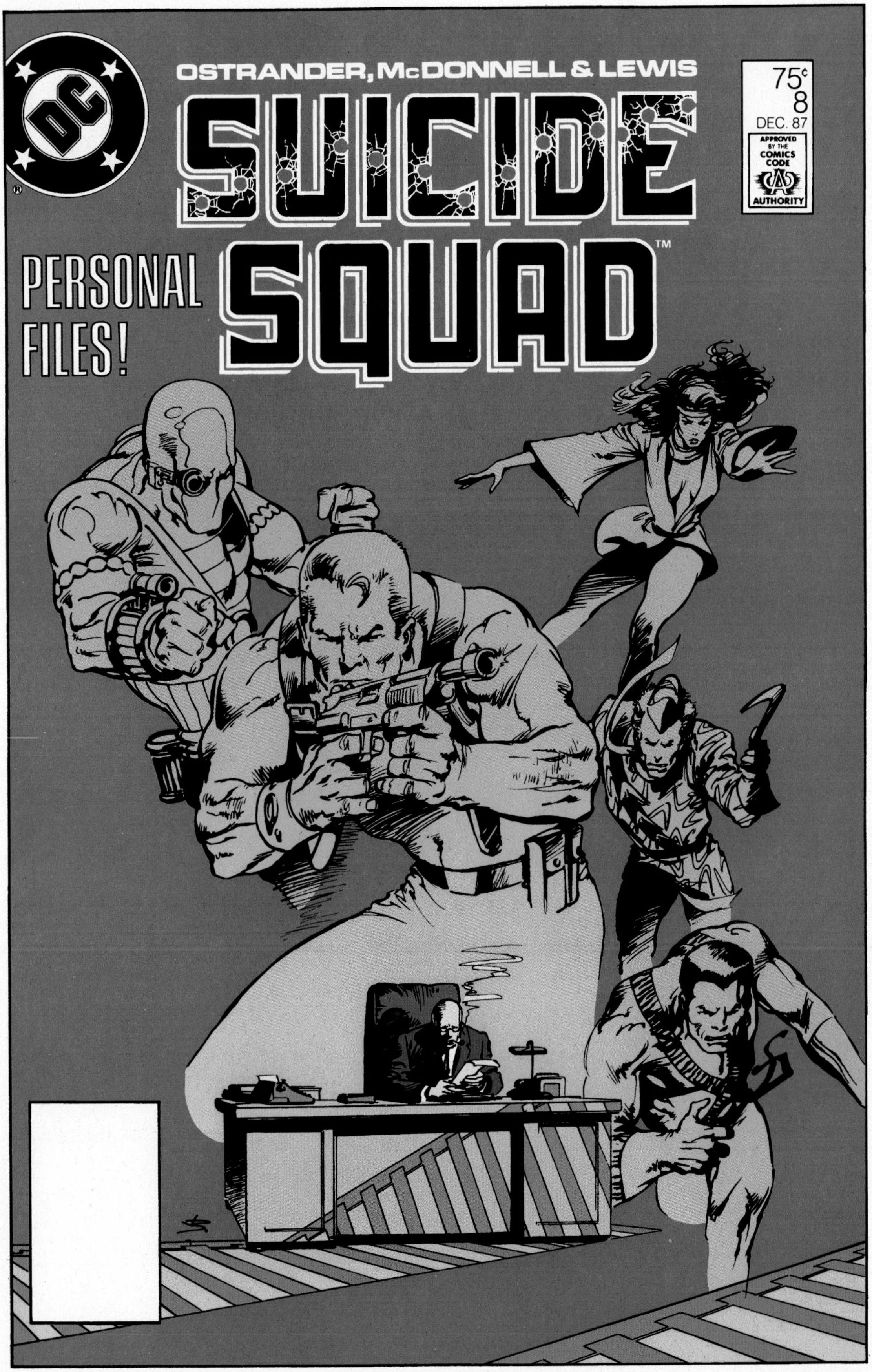

OSTRANDER, McDONNELL & LEWIS
SUICIDE SQUAD™
75¢
8
DEC. 87
APPROVED BY THE COMICS CODE AUTHORITY
PERSONAL FILES!

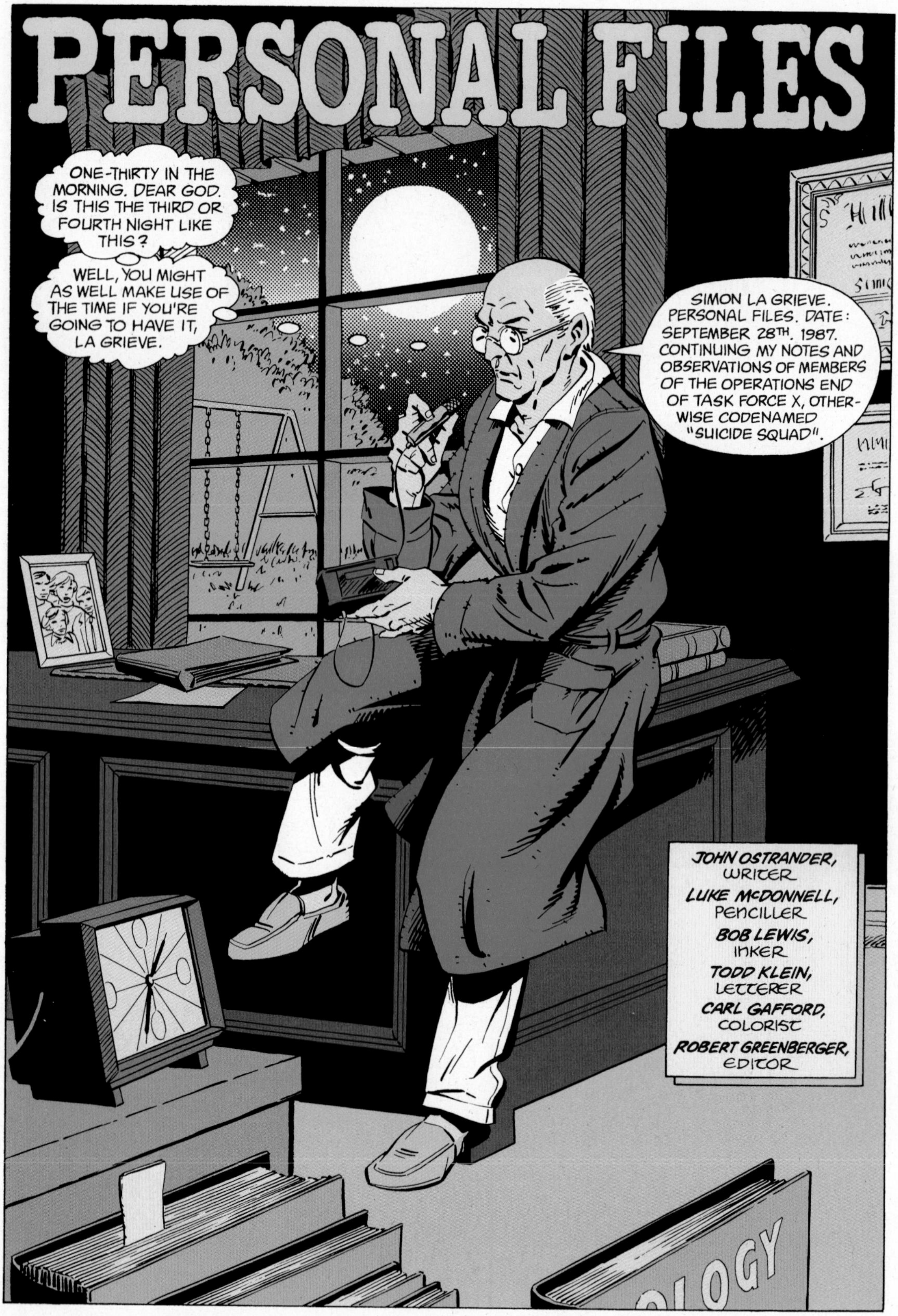
PERSONAL FILES
ONE-THIRTY IN THE MORNING. DEAR GOD. IS THIS THE THIRD OR FOURTH NIGHT LIKE THIS?
WELL, YOU MIGHT AS WELL MAKE USE OF THE TIME IF YOU'RE GOING TO HAVE IT, LA GRIEVE.
SIMON LA GRIEVE. PERSONAL FILES. DATE: SEPTEMBER 28TH. 1987. CONTINUING MY NOTES AND OBSERVATIONS OF MEMBERS OF THE OPERATIONS END OF TASK FORCE X, OTHERWISE CODENAMED "SUICIDE SQUAD".
JOHN OSTRANDER, WRITER
LUKE McDONNELL, PENCILLER
BOB LEWIS, INKER
TODD KLEIN, LETTERER
CARL GAFFORD, COLORIST
ROBERT GREENBERGER, EDITOR
OLOGY

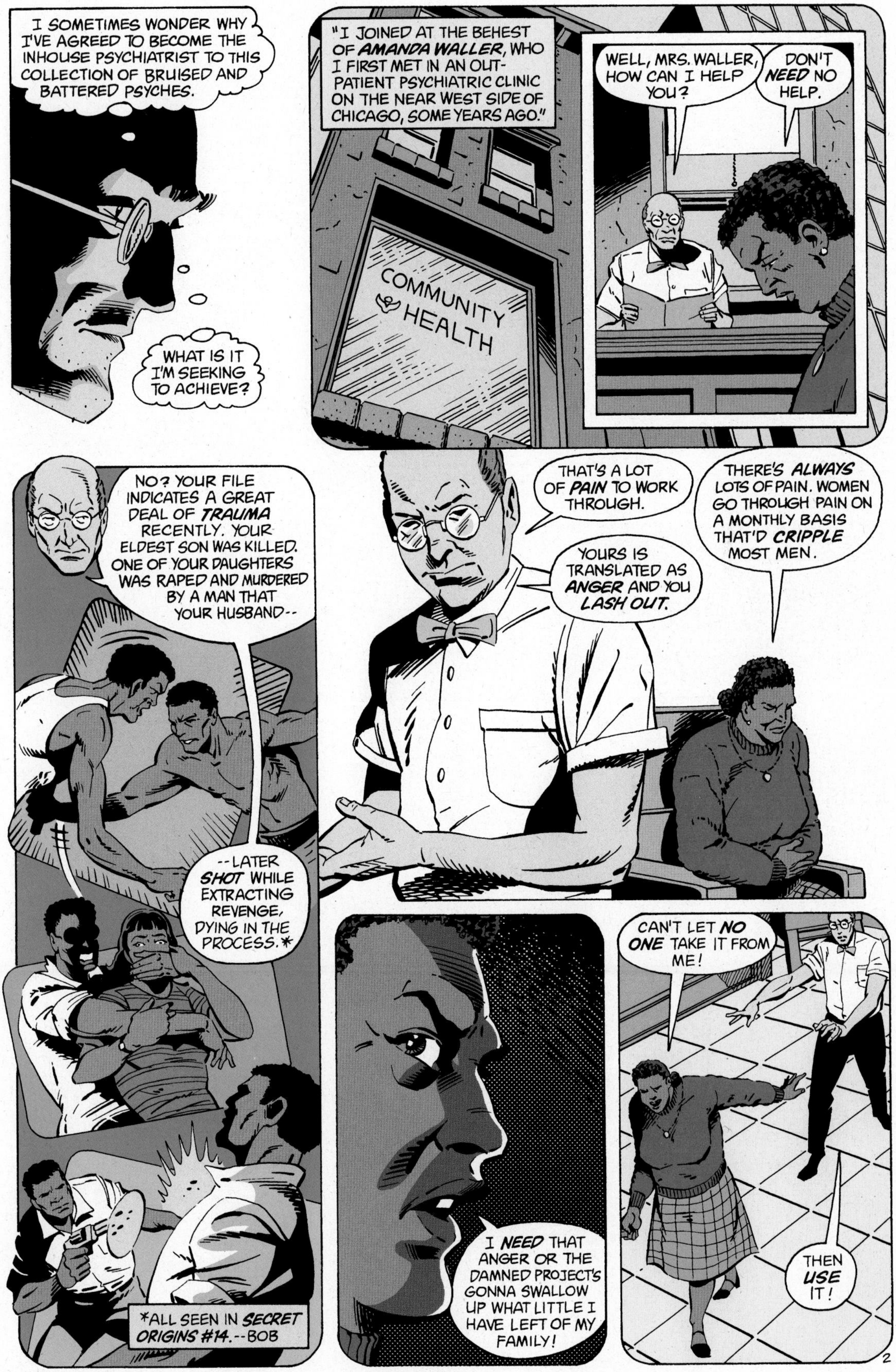

I SOMETIMES WONDER WHY I'VE AGREED TO BECOME THE INHOUSE PSYCHIATRIST TO THIS COLLECTION OF BRUISED AND BATTERED PSYCHES.
WHAT IS IT I'M SEEKING TO ACHIEVE?
"I JOINED AT THE BEHEST OF AMANDA WALLER, WHO I FIRST MET IN AN OUT-PATIENT PSYCHIATRIC CLINIC ON THE NEAR WEST SIDE OF CHICAGO, SOME YEARS AGO."
COMMUNITY HEALTH
WELL, MRS. WALLER, HOW CAN I HELP YOU?
DON'T NEED NO HELP.
NO? YOUR FILE INDICATES A GREAT DEAL OF TRAUMA RECENTLY. YOUR ELDEST SON WAS KILLED. ONE OF YOUR DAUGHTERS WAS RAPED AND MURDERED BY A MAN THAT YOUR HUSBAND--
--LATER SHOT WHILE EXTRACTING REVENGE, DYING IN THE PROCESS.*
*ALL SEEN IN SECRET ORIGINS #14.--BOB
THAT'S A LOT OF PAIN TO WORK THROUGH.
YOURS IS TRANSLATED AS ANGER AND YOU LASH OUT.
THERE'S ALWAYS LOTS OF PAIN. WOMEN GO THROUGH PAIN ON A MONTHLY BASIS THAT'D CRIPPLE MOST MEN.
I NEED THAT ANGER OR THE DAMNED PROJECT'S GONNA SWALLOW UP WHAT LITTLE I HAVE LEFT OF MY FAMILY!
CAN'T LET NO ONE TAKE IT FROM ME!
THEN USE IT!
2

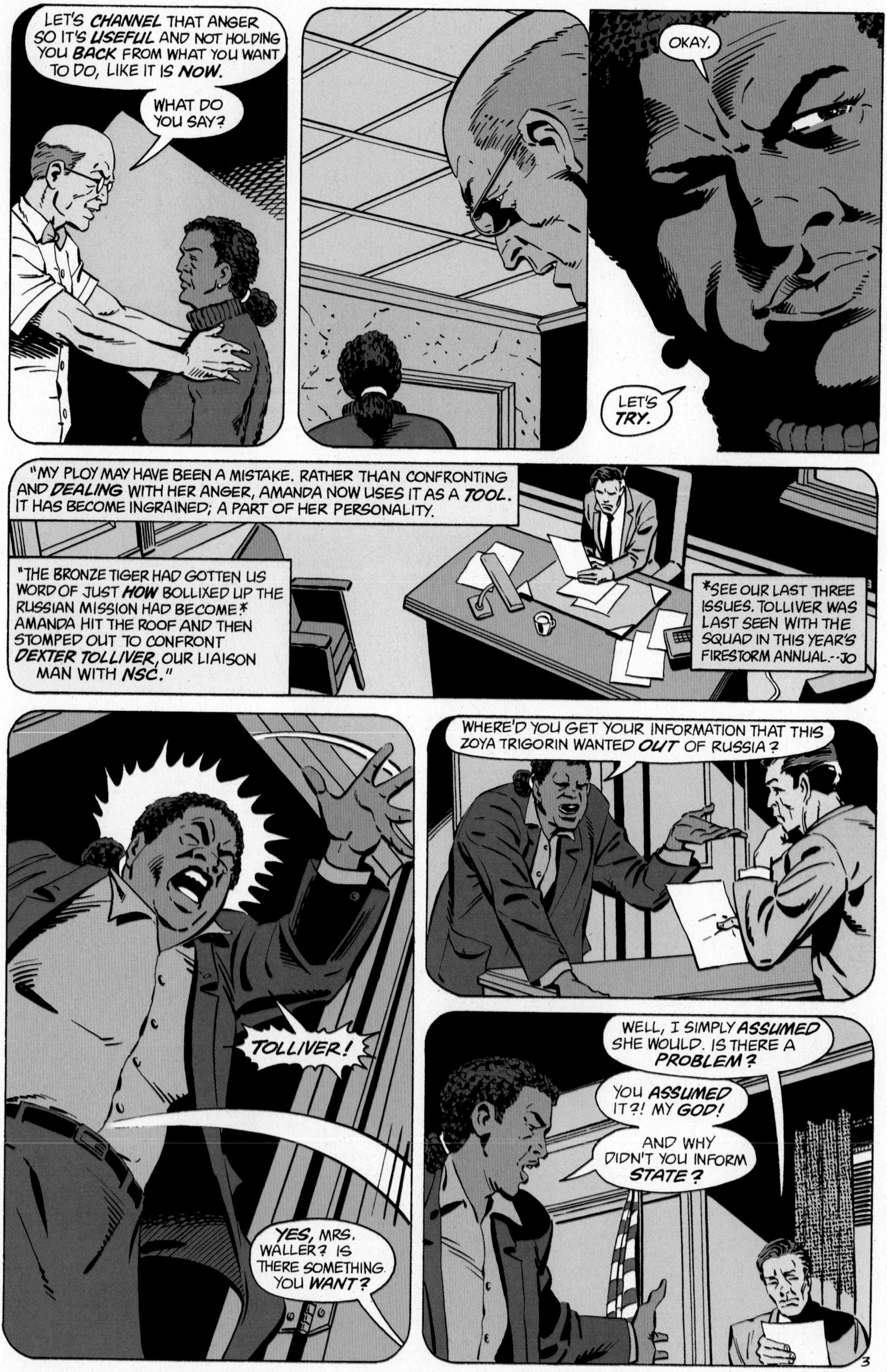

LET'S CHANNEL THAT ANGER SO IT'S USEFUL AND NOT HOLDING YOU BACK FROM WHAT YOU WANT TO DO, LIKE IT IS NOW.
WHAT DO YOU SAY?
OKAY.
LET'S TRY.
"MY PLOY MAY HAVE BEEN A MISTAKE. RATHER THAN CONFRONTING AND DEALING WITH HER ANGER, AMANDA NOW USES IT AS A TOOL. IT HAS BECOME INGRAINED; A PART OF HER PERSONALITY.
"THE BRONZE TIGER HAD GOTTEN US WORD OF JUST HOW BOLLIXED UP THE RUSSIAN MISSION HAD BECOME.* AMANDA HIT THE ROOF AND THEN STOMPED OUT TO CONFRONT DEXTER TOLLIVER, OUR LIAISON MAN WITH NSC."
*SEE OUR LAST THREE ISSUES. TOLLIVER WAS LAST SEEN WITH THE SQUAD IN THIS YEAR'S FIRESTORM ANNUAL.--JO
TOLLIVER!
YES, MRS. WALLER? IS THERE SOMETHING YOU WANT?
WHERE'D YOU GET YOUR INFORMATION THAT THIS ZOYA TRIGORIN WANTED OUT OF RUSSIA?
WELL, I SIMPLY ASSUMED SHE WOULD. IS THERE A PROBLEM?
YOU ASSUMED IT?! MY GOD!
AND WHY DIDN'T YOU INFORM STATE?
3

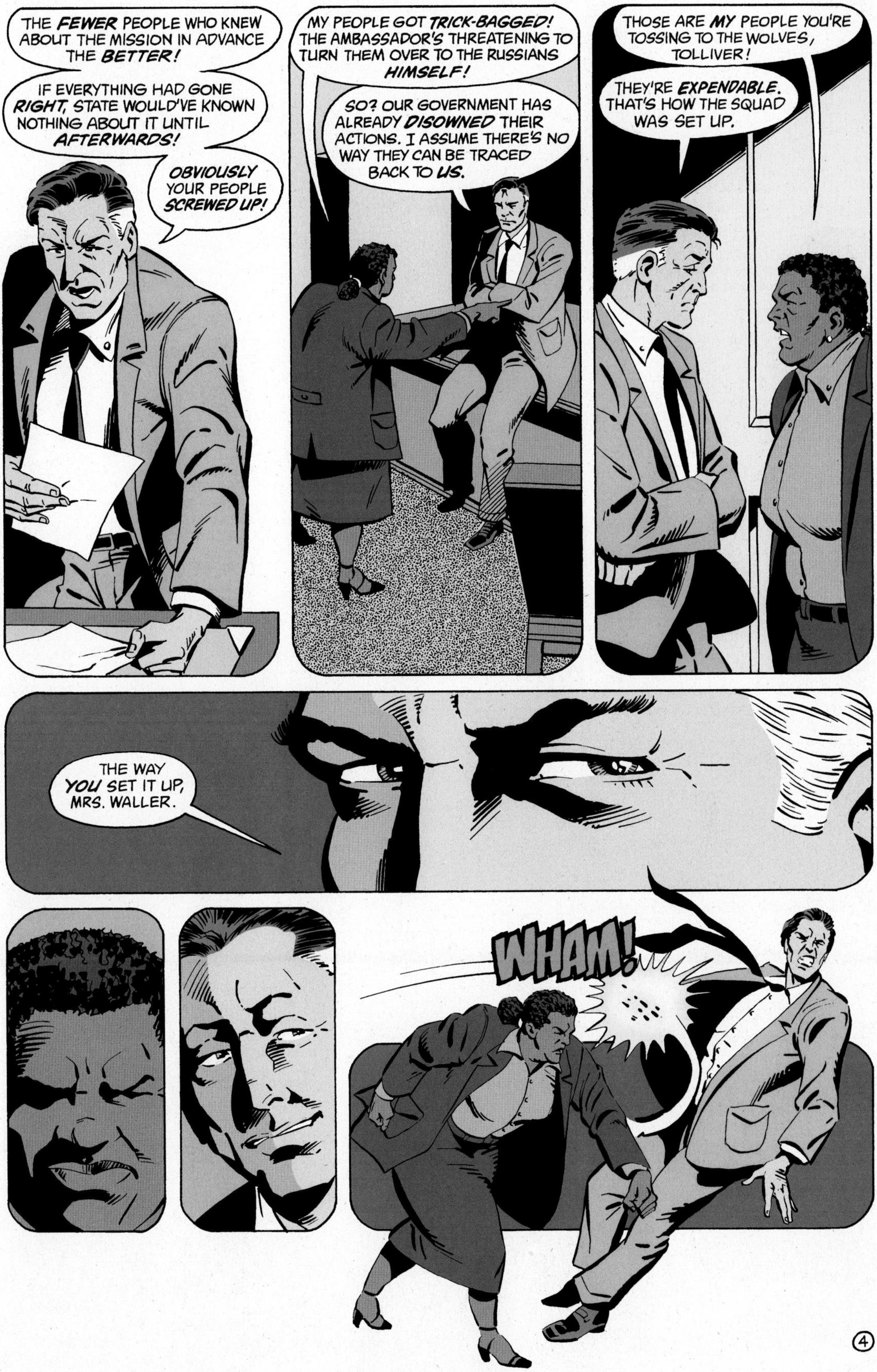
THE FEWER PEOPLE WHO KNEW ABOUT THE MISSION IN ADVANCE THE BETTER!
IF EVERYTHING HAD GONE RIGHT, STATE WOULD'VE KNOWN NOTHING ABOUT IT UNTIL AFTERWARDS!
OBVIOUSLY YOUR PEOPLE SCREWED UP!
MY PEOPLE GOT TRICK-BAGGED! THE AMBASSADOR'S THREATENING TO TURN THEM OVER TO THE RUSSIANS HIMSELF!
SO? OUR GOVERNMENT HAS ALREADY DISOWNED THEIR ACTIONS. I ASSUME THERE'S NO WAY THEY CAN BE TRACED BACK TO US.
THOSE ARE MY PEOPLE YOU'RE TOSSING TO THE WOLVES, TOLLIVER!
THEY'RE EXPENDABLE. THAT'S HOW THE SQUAD WAS SET UP.
THE WAY YOU SET IT UP, MRS. WALLER.
WHAM!
4

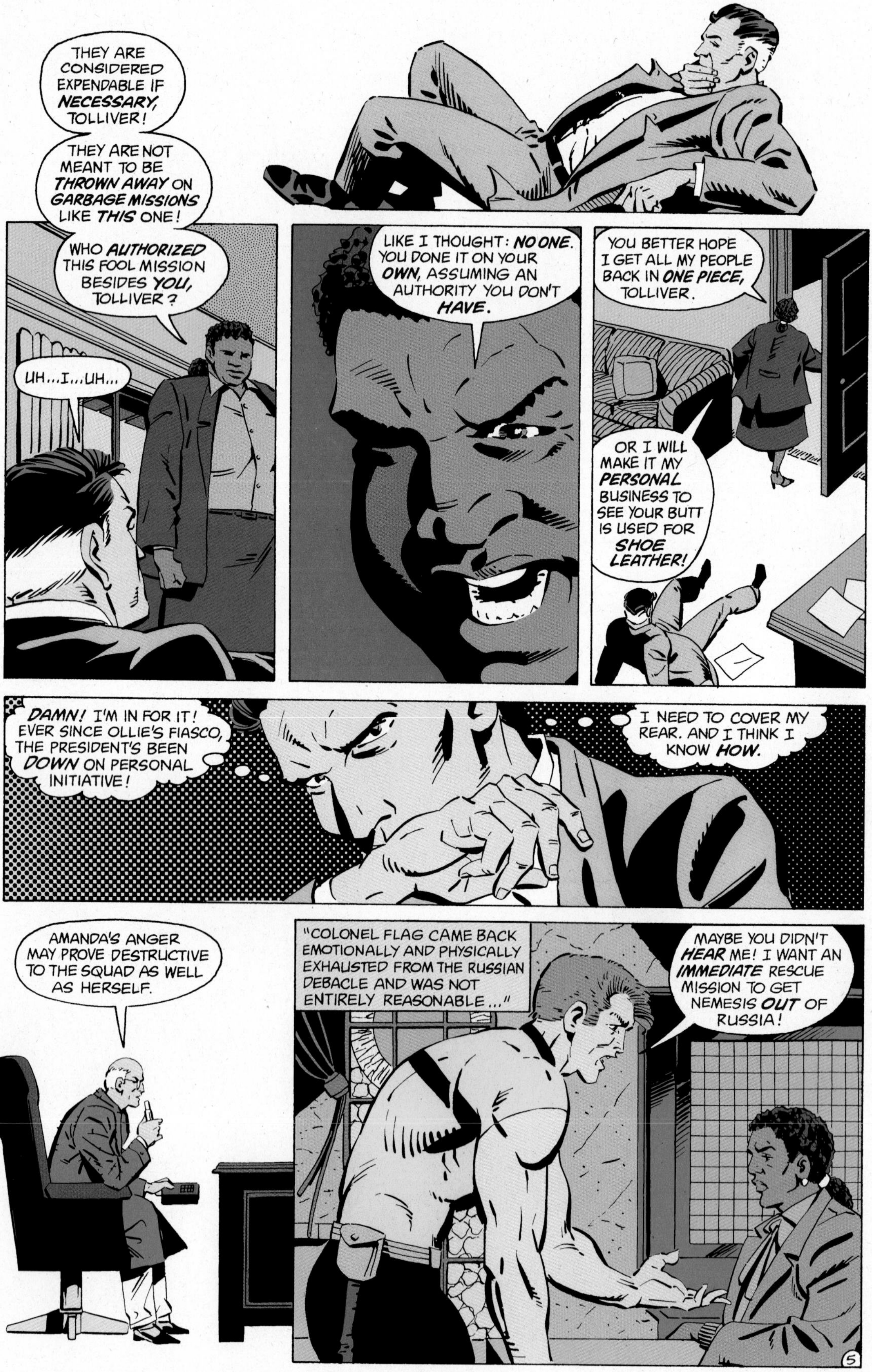
THEY ARE CONSIDERED EXPENDABLE IF NECESSARY, TOLLIVER!
THEY ARE NOT MEANT TO BE THROWN AWAY ON GARBAGE MISSIONS LIKE THIS ONE!
WHO AUTHORIZED THIS FOOL MISSION BESIDES YOU, TOLLIVER?
UH...I...UH...
LIKE I THOUGHT: NO ONE. YOU DONE IT ON YOUR OWN, ASSUMING AN AUTHORITY YOU DON'T HAVE.
YOU BETTER HOPE I GET ALL MY PEOPLE BACK IN ONE PIECE, TOLLIVER.
OR I WILL MAKE IT MY PERSONAL BUSINESS TO SEE YOUR BUTT IS USED FOR SHOE LEATHER!
DAMN! I'M IN FOR IT! EVER SINCE OLLIE'S FIASCO, THE PRESIDENT'S BEEN DOWN ON PERSONAL INITIATIVE!
I NEED TO COVER MY REAR. AND I THINK I KNOW HOW.
AMANDA'S ANGER MAY PROVE DESTRUCTIVE TO THE SQUAD AS WELL AS HERSELF.
"COLONEL FLAG CAME BACK EMOTIONALLY AND PHYSICALLY EXHAUSTED FROM THE RUSSIAN DEBACLE AND WAS NOT ENTIRELY REASONABLE..."
MAYBE YOU DIDN'T HEAR ME! I WANT AN IMMEDIATE RESCUE MISSION TO GET NEMESIS OUT OF RUSSIA!
5

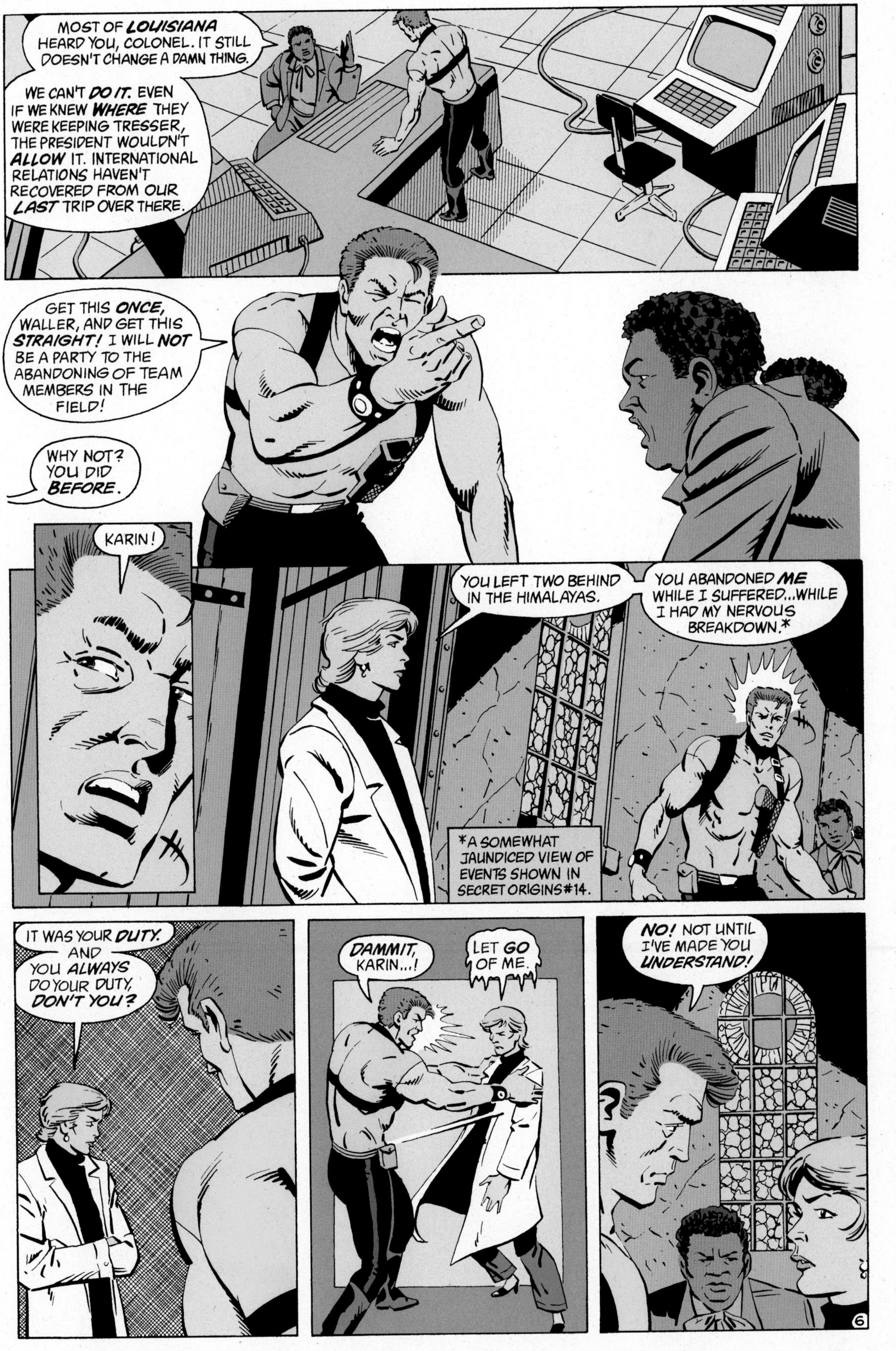
MOST OF LOUISIANA HEARD YOU, COLONEL. IT STILL DOESN'T CHANGE A DAMN THING.
WE CAN'T DO IT. EVEN IF WE KNEW WHERE THEY WERE KEEPING TRESSER, THE PRESIDENT WOULDN'T ALLOW IT. INTERNATIONAL RELATIONS HAVEN'T RECOVERED FROM OUR LAST TRIP OVER THERE.
GET THIS ONCE, WALLER, AND GET THIS STRAIGHT! I WILL NOT BE A PARTY TO THE ABANDONING OF TEAM MEMBERS IN THE FIELD!
WHY NOT? YOU DID BEFORE.
KARIN!
YOU LEFT TWO BEHIND IN THE HIMALAYAS.
YOU ABANDONED ME WHILE I SUFFERED...WHILE I HAD MY NERVOUS BREAKDOWN.*
*A SOMEWHAT JAUNDICED VIEW OF EVENTS SHOWN IN SECRET ORIGINS #14.
IT WAS YOUR DUTY. AND YOU ALWAYS DO YOUR DUTY, DON'T YOU?
DAMMIT, KARIN...!
LET GO OF ME.
NO! NOT UNTIL I'VE MADE YOU UNDERSTAND!
6

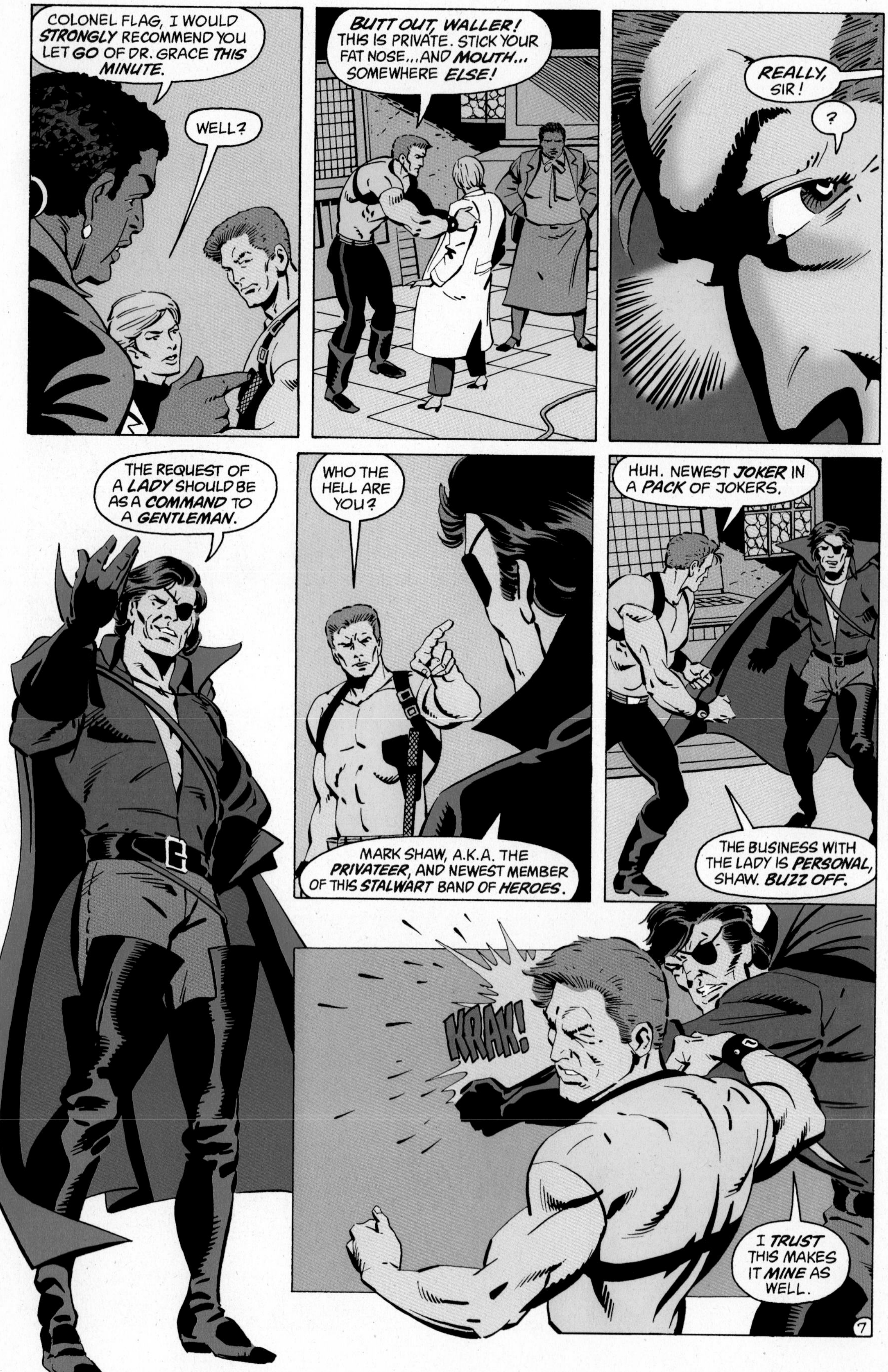
COLONEL FLAG, I WOULD STRONGLY RECOMMEND YOU LET GO OF DR. GRACE THIS MINUTE.
WELL?
BUTT OUT, WALLER! THIS IS PRIVATE. STICK YOUR FAT NOSE... AND MOUTH... SOMEWHERE ELSE!
REALLY, SIR!
?
THE REQUEST OF A LADY SHOULD BE AS A COMMAND TO A GENTLEMAN.
WHO THE HELL ARE YOU?
MARK SHAW, A.K.A. THE PRIVATEER, AND NEWEST MEMBER OF THIS STALWART BAND OF HEROES.
HUH. NEWEST JOKER IN A PACK OF JOKERS.
THE BUSINESS WITH THE LADY IS PERSONAL, SHAW. BUZZ OFF.
KRAK!
I TRUST THIS MAKES IT MINE AS WELL.
7

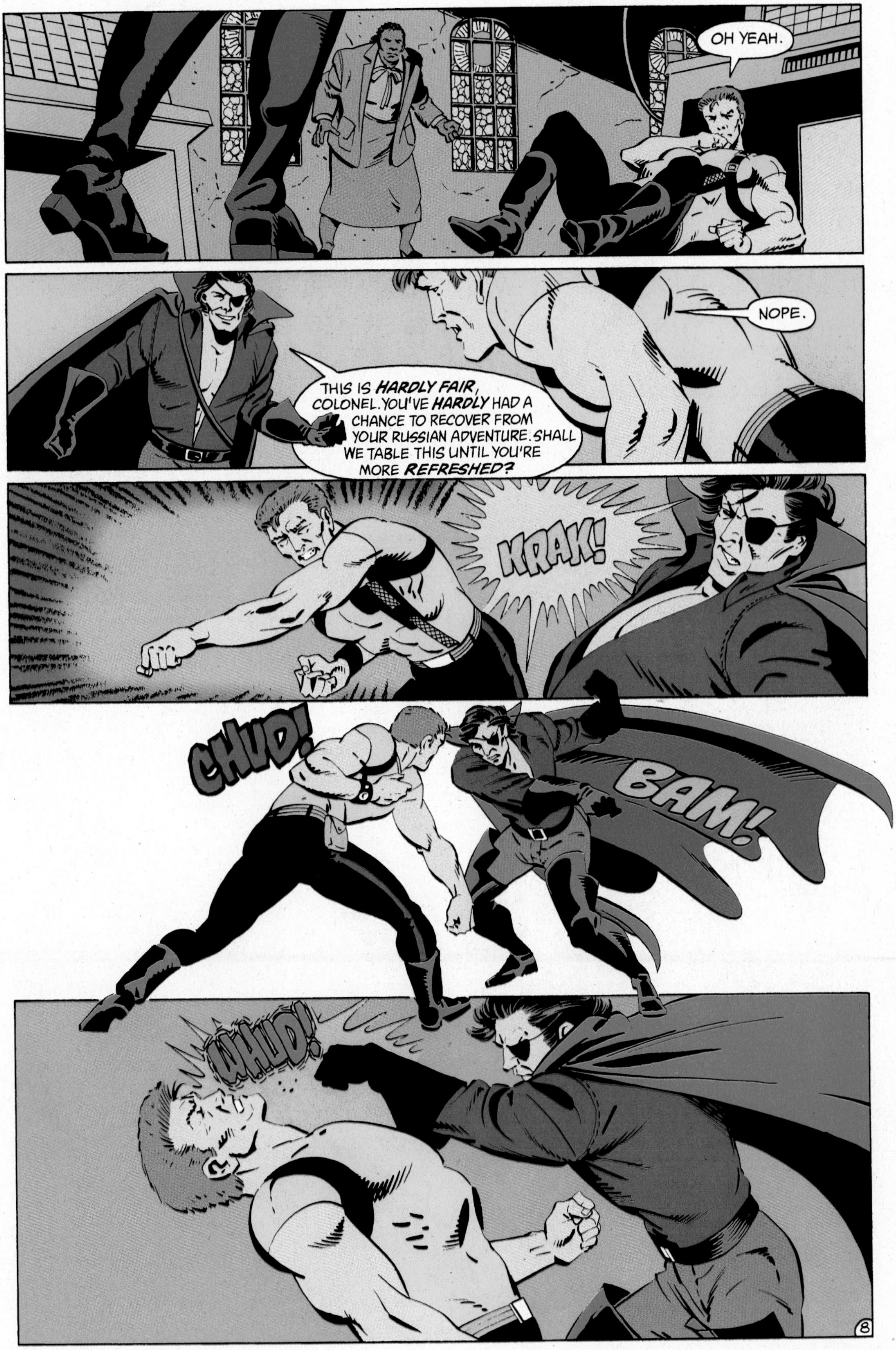
OH YEAH.
NOPE.
THIS IS HARDLY FAIR, COLONEL. YOU'VE HARDLY HAD A CHANCE TO RECOVER FROM YOUR RUSSIAN ADVENTURE. SHALL WE TABLE THIS UNTIL YOU'RE MORE REFRESHED?
KRAK!
CHUD!
BAM!
WHUD!
8

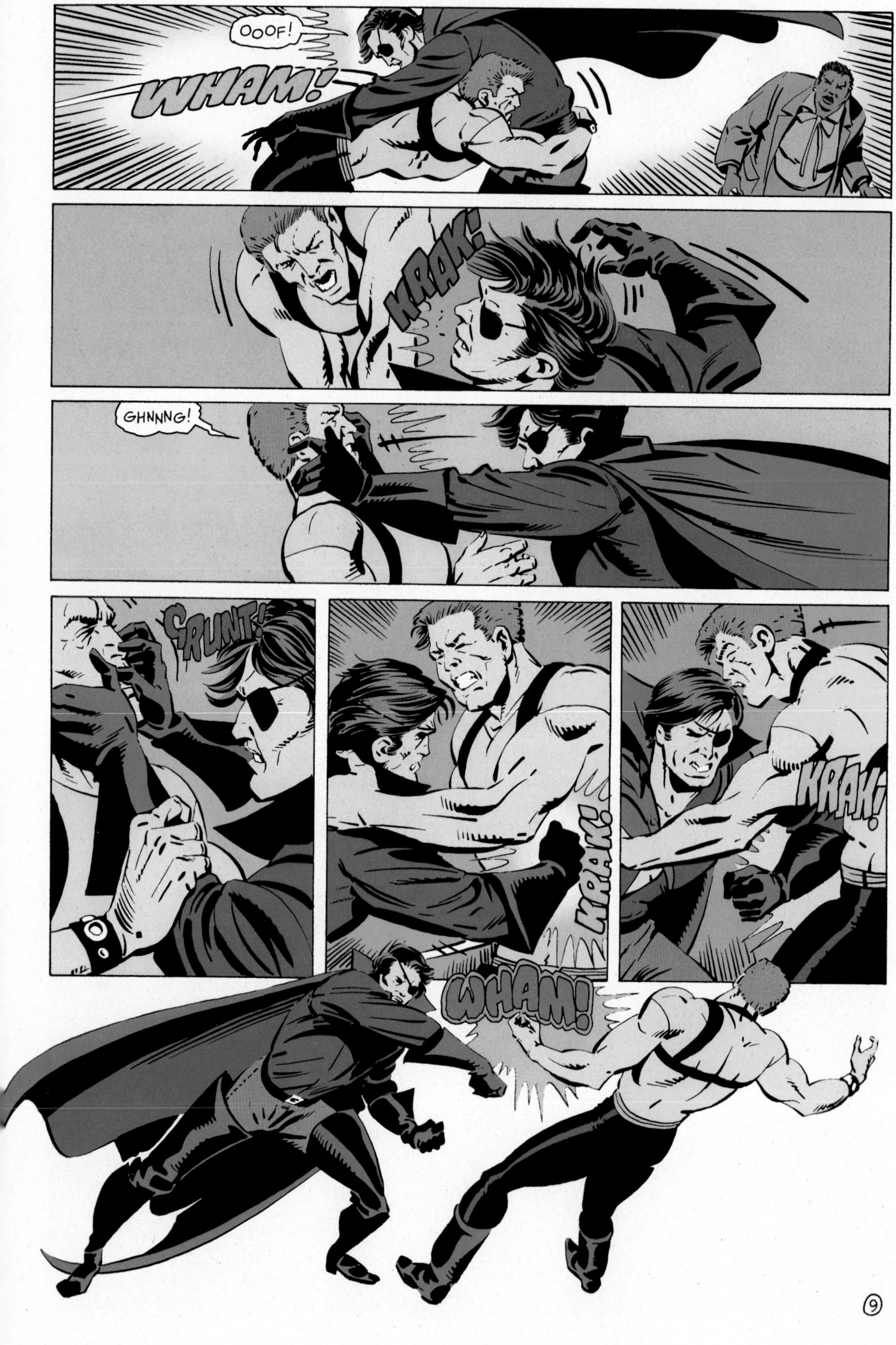
OOOF!
WHAM!
KRAK!
GHNNNG!
GRUNT!
KRAK!
KRAK!
WHAM!
9

BRAVELY FOUGHT, COLONEL, BUT IT'S OVER. LET US SAY YOU WERE NOT AT YOUR BEST, HM?

AND YOU NEED TO BE AT YOUR BEST IF YOU'RE TO FACE ONE WHO WAS TRAINED BY THE *MANHUNTERS*.*

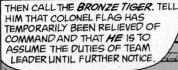

*SEE *FIRST ISSUE SPECIAL* #5. -- BACK-ISSUE BOB.

FLO, GIVE *DR. LA GRIEVE* A CALL. TELL HIM THAT COLONEL FLAG IS SUFFERING COMPLETE MENTAL AND PHYSICAL EXHAUSTION FROM THE RUSSIAN MISSION AND IS BEING CHECKED INTO THE INFIRMARY.

THEN CALL THE *BRONZE TIGER*. TELL HIM THAT COLONEL FLAG HAS TEMPORARILY BEEN RELIEVED OF *COMMAND* AND THAT *HE* IS TO ASSUME THE DUTIES OF TEAM LEADER UNTIL FURTHER NOTICE.

THANK YOU, MR. SHAW... MAY I CALL YOU MARK?

I SHALL *INSIST* UPON IT... KARIN.

KARIN, I.... I'M...

THUMP!

10

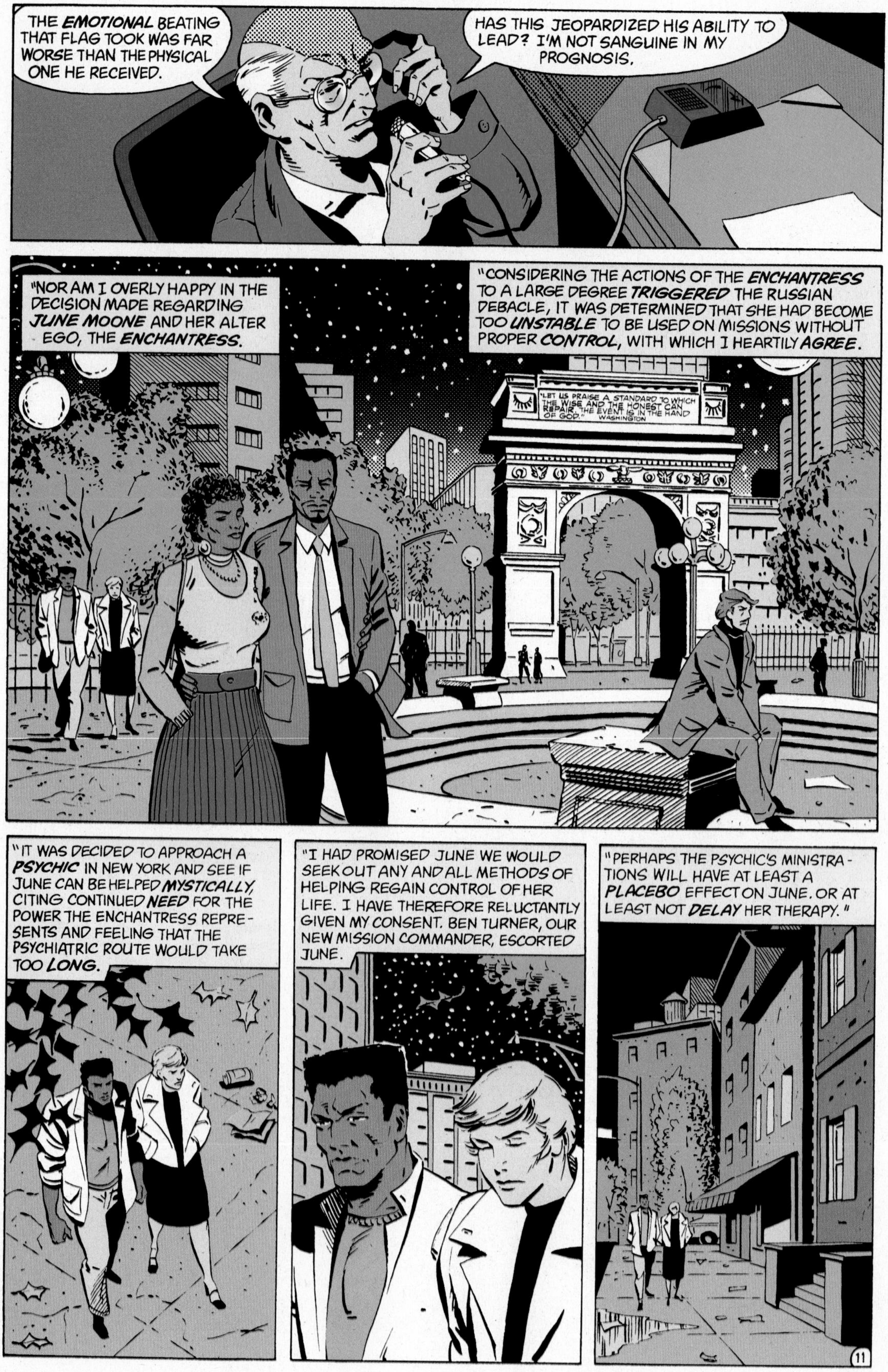
THE EMOTIONAL BEATING THAT FLAG TOOK WAS FAR WORSE THAN THE PHYSICAL ONE HE RECEIVED.
HAS THIS JEOPARDIZED HIS ABILITY TO LEAD? I'M NOT SANGUINE IN MY PROGNOSIS.
"NOR AM I OVERLY HAPPY IN THE DECISION MADE REGARDING JUNE MOONE AND HER ALTER EGO, THE ENCHANTRESS.
"CONSIDERING THE ACTIONS OF THE ENCHANTRESS TO A LARGE DEGREE TRIGGERED THE RUSSIAN DEBACLE, IT WAS DETERMINED THAT SHE HAD BECOME TOO UNSTABLE TO BE USED ON MISSIONS WITHOUT PROPER CONTROL, WITH WHICH I HEARTILY AGREE.
"LET US PRAISE A STANDARD TO WHICH THE WISE AND THE HONEST CAN REPAIR. THE EVENT IS IN THE HAND OF GOD." WASHINGTON
"IT WAS DECIDED TO APPROACH A PSYCHIC IN NEW YORK AND SEE IF JUNE CAN BE HELPED MYSTICALLY, CITING CONTINUED NEED FOR THE POWER THE ENCHANTRESS REPRESENTS AND FEELING THAT THE PSYCHIATRIC ROUTE WOULD TAKE TOO LONG.
"I HAD PROMISED JUNE WE WOULD SEEK OUT ANY AND ALL METHODS OF HELPING REGAIN CONTROL OF HER LIFE. I HAVE THEREFORE RELUCTANTLY GIVEN MY CONSENT. BEN TURNER, OUR NEW MISSION COMMANDER, ESCORTED JUNE.
"PERHAPS THE PSYCHIC'S MINISTRATIONS WILL HAVE AT LEAST A PLACEBO EFFECT ON JUNE. OR AT LEAST NOT DELAY HER THERAPY."
11

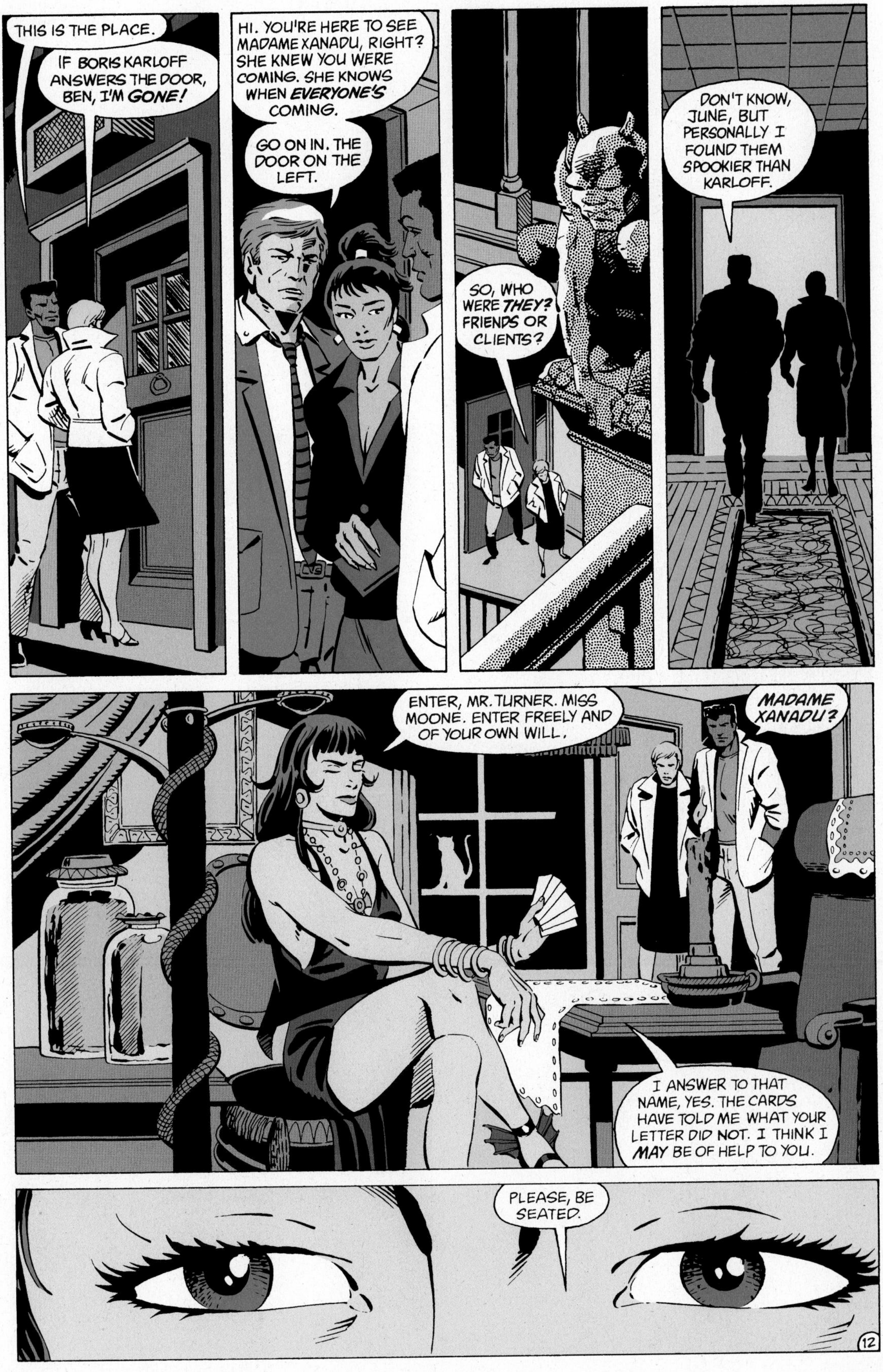
THIS IS THE PLACE.
IF BORIS KARLOFF ANSWERS THE DOOR, BEN, I'M GONE!
HI. YOU'RE HERE TO SEE MADAME XANADU, RIGHT? SHE KNEW YOU WERE COMING. SHE KNOWS WHEN EVERYONE'S COMING.
GO ON IN. THE DOOR ON THE LEFT.
SO, WHO WERE THEY? FRIENDS OR CLIENTS?
DON'T KNOW, JUNE, BUT PERSONALLY I FOUND THEM SPOOKIER THAN KARLOFF.
ENTER, MR. TURNER. MISS MOONE. ENTER FREELY AND OF YOUR OWN WILL.
MADAME XANADU?
I ANSWER TO THAT NAME, YES. THE CARDS HAVE TOLD ME WHAT YOUR LETTER DID NOT. I THINK I MAY BE OF HELP TO YOU.
PLEASE, BE SEATED.
12

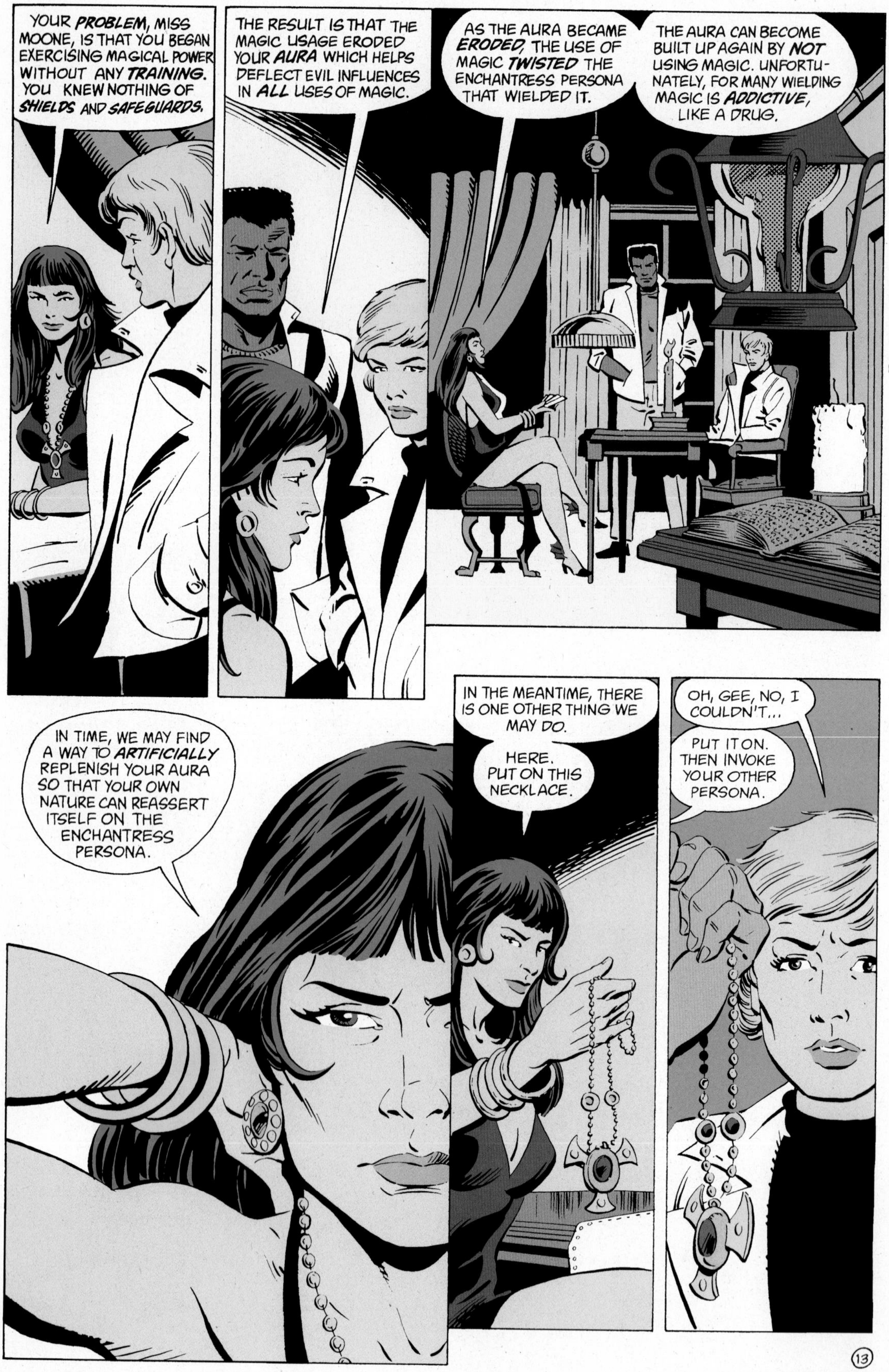
YOUR PROBLEM, MISS MOONE, IS THAT YOU BEGAN EXERCISING MAGICAL POWER WITHOUT ANY TRAINING. YOU KNEW NOTHING OF SHIELDS AND SAFEGUARDS.
THE RESULT IS THAT THE MAGIC USAGE ERODED YOUR AURA WHICH HELPS DEFLECT EVIL INFLUENCES IN ALL USES OF MAGIC.
AS THE AURA BECAME ERODED, THE USE OF MAGIC TWISTED THE ENCHANTRESS PERSONA THAT WIELDED IT.
THE AURA CAN BECOME BUILT UP AGAIN BY NOT USING MAGIC. UNFORTU-NATELY, FOR MANY WIELDING MAGIC IS ADDICTIVE, LIKE A DRUG.
IN TIME, WE MAY FIND A WAY TO ARTIFICIALLY REPLENISH YOUR AURA SO THAT YOUR OWN NATURE CAN REASSERT ITSELF ON THE ENCHANTRESS PERSONA.
IN THE MEANTIME, THERE IS ONE OTHER THING WE MAY DO.
HERE. PUT ON THIS NECKLACE.
OH, GEE, NO, I COULDN'T...
PUT IT ON. THEN INVOKE YOUR OTHER PERSONA.
13

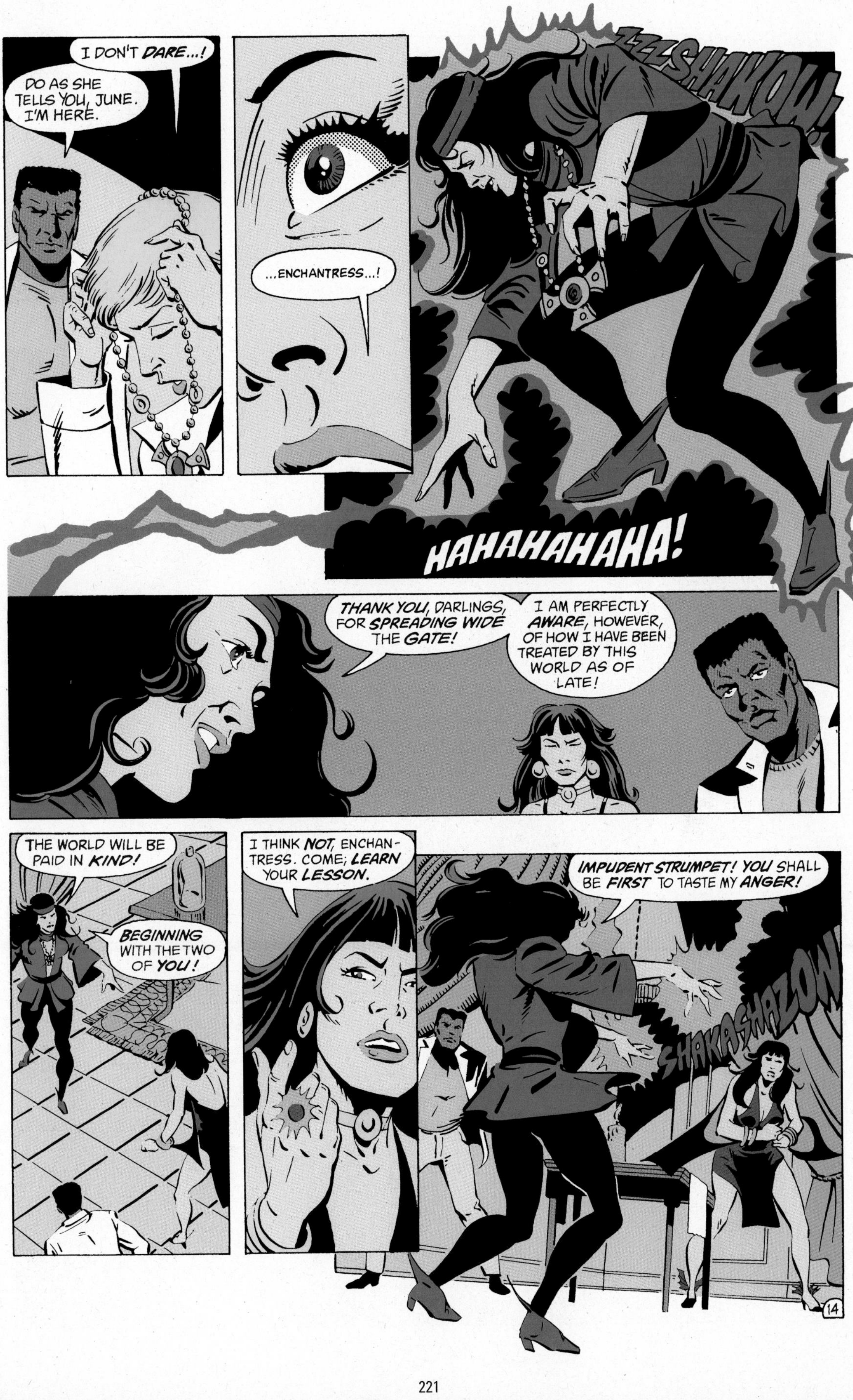
I DON'T DARE...!
DO AS SHE TELLS YOU, JUNE. I'M HERE.
...ENCHANTRESS...!
ZZZSHAKOW!
HAHAHAHAHAHA!
THANK YOU, DARLINGS, FOR SPREADING WIDE THE GATE!
I AM PERFECTLY AWARE, HOWEVER, OF HOW I HAVE BEEN TREATED BY THIS WORLD AS OF LATE!
THE WORLD WILL BE PAID IN KIND!
BEGINNING WITH THE TWO OF YOU!
I THINK NOT, ENCHANTRESS. COME; LEARN YOUR LESSON.
IMPUDENT STRUMPET! YOU SHALL BE FIRST TO TASTE MY ANGER!
SHAKASHAZOW
14

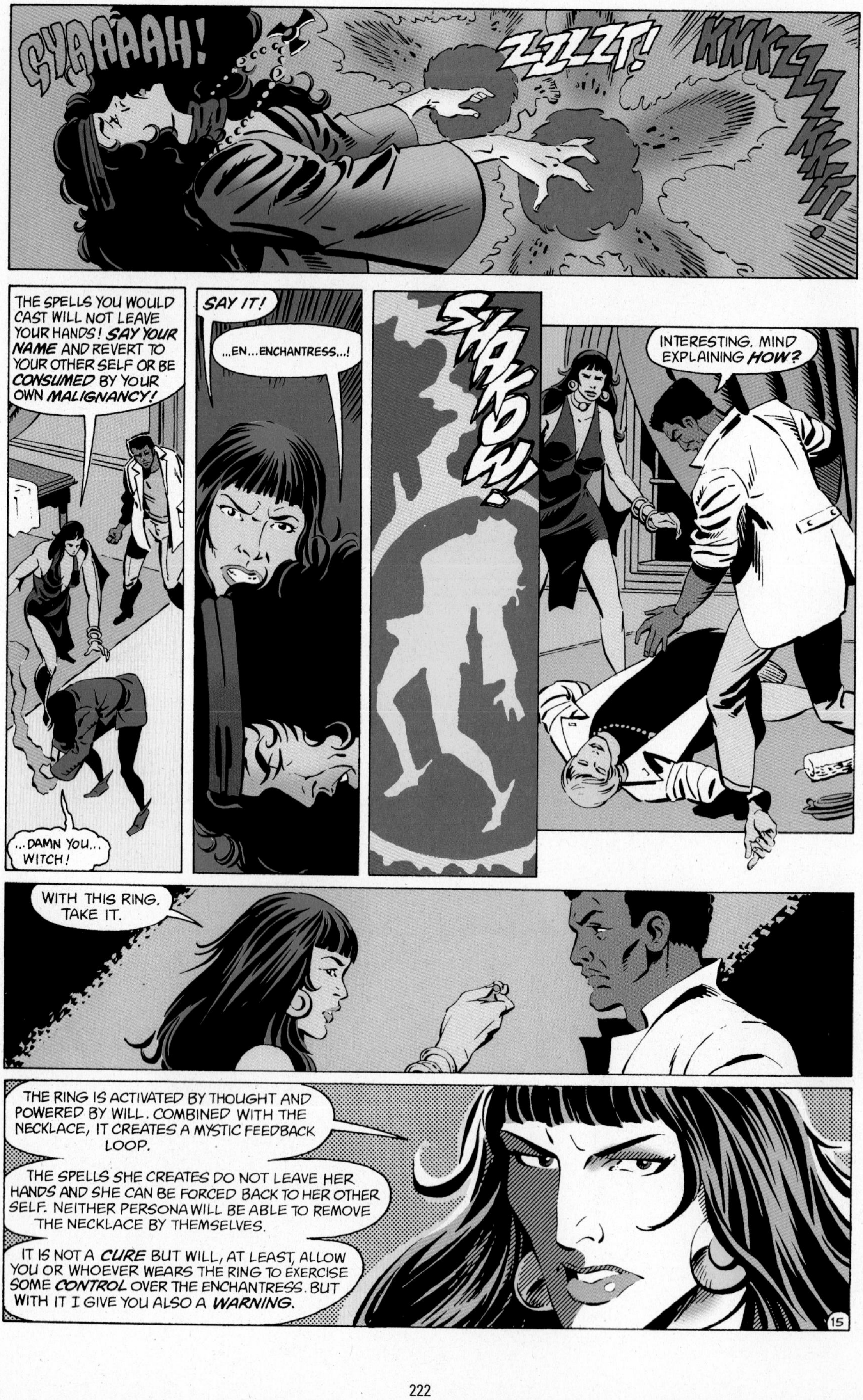
GYAAAAH!
ZZZZT!
KKKZZZZKKKT!
THE SPELLS YOU WOULD CAST WILL NOT LEAVE YOUR HANDS! SAY YOUR NAME AND REVERT TO YOUR OTHER SELF OR BE CONSUMED BY YOUR OWN MALIGNANCY!
...DAMN YOU... WITCH!
SAY IT!
...EN...ENCHANTRESS...!
SHAKOW!
INTERESTING. MIND EXPLAINING HOW?
WITH THIS RING. TAKE IT.
THE RING IS ACTIVATED BY THOUGHT AND POWERED BY WILL. COMBINED WITH THE NECKLACE, IT CREATES A MYSTIC FEEDBACK LOOP.
THE SPELLS SHE CREATES DO NOT LEAVE HER HANDS AND SHE CAN BE FORCED BACK TO HER OTHER SELF. NEITHER PERSONA WILL BE ABLE TO REMOVE THE NECKLACE BY THEMSELVES.
IT IS NOT A CURE BUT WILL, AT LEAST, ALLOW YOU OR WHOEVER WEARS THE RING TO EXERCISE SOME CONTROL OVER THE ENCHANTRESS. BUT WITH IT I GIVE YOU ALSO A WARNING.
15

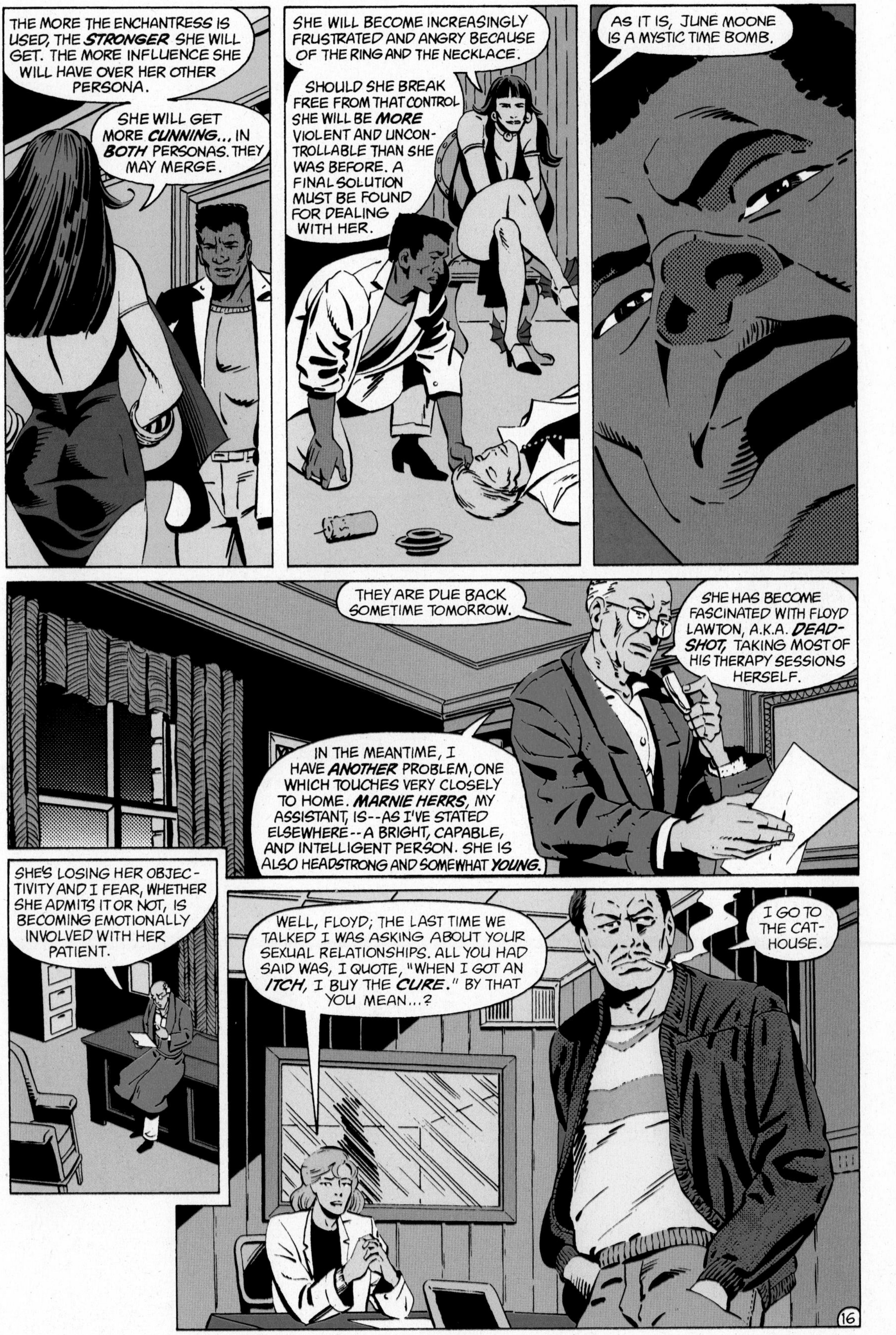
THE MORE THE ENCHANTRESS IS USED, THE STRONGER SHE WILL GET. THE MORE INFLUENCE SHE WILL HAVE OVER HER OTHER PERSONA.
SHE WILL GET MORE CUNNING... IN BOTH PERSONAS. THEY MAY MERGE.
SHE WILL BECOME INCREASINGLY FRUSTRATED AND ANGRY BECAUSE OF THE RING AND THE NECKLACE.
SHOULD SHE BREAK FREE FROM THAT CONTROL SHE WILL BE MORE VIOLENT AND UNCONTROLLABLE THAN SHE WAS BEFORE. A FINAL SOLUTION MUST BE FOUND FOR DEALING WITH HER.
AS IT IS, JUNE MOONE IS A MYSTIC TIME BOMB.
THEY ARE DUE BACK SOMETIME TOMORROW.
SHE HAS BECOME FASCINATED WITH FLOYD LAWTON, A.K.A. DEADSHOT, TAKING MOST OF HIS THERAPY SESSIONS HERSELF.
IN THE MEANTIME, I HAVE ANOTHER PROBLEM, ONE WHICH TOUCHES VERY CLOSELY TO HOME. MARNIE HERRS, MY ASSISTANT, IS--AS I'VE STATED ELSEWHERE--A BRIGHT, CAPABLE, AND INTELLIGENT PERSON. SHE IS ALSO HEADSTRONG AND SOMEWHAT YOUNG.
SHE'S LOSING HER OBJECTIVITY AND I FEAR, WHETHER SHE ADMITS IT OR NOT, IS BECOMING EMOTIONALLY INVOLVED WITH HER PATIENT.
WELL, FLOYD; THE LAST TIME WE TALKED I WAS ASKING ABOUT YOUR SEXUAL RELATIONSHIPS. ALL YOU HAD SAID WAS, I QUOTE, "WHEN I GOT AN ITCH, I BUY THE CURE." BY THAT YOU MEAN...?
I GO TO THE CATHOUSE.
16

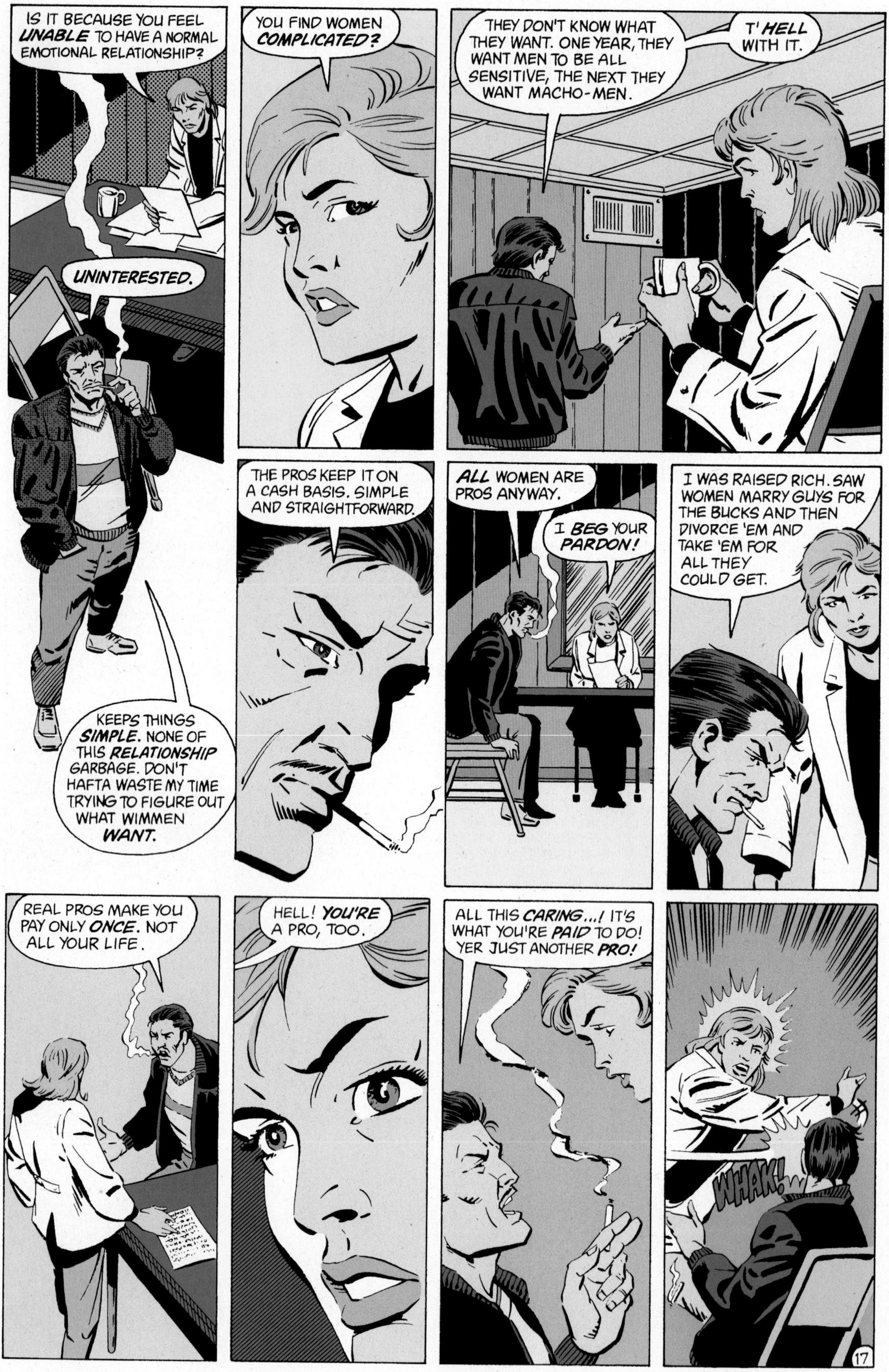
IS IT BECAUSE YOU FEEL UNABLE TO HAVE A NORMAL EMOTIONAL RELATIONSHIP?
UNINTERESTED.
KEEPS THINGS SIMPLE. NONE OF THIS RELATIONSHIP GARBAGE. DON'T HAFTA WASTE MY TIME TRYING TO FIGURE OUT WHAT WIMMEN WANT.
YOU FIND WOMEN COMPLICATED?
THEY DON'T KNOW WHAT THEY WANT. ONE YEAR, THEY WANT MEN TO BE ALL SENSITIVE, THE NEXT THEY WANT MACHO-MEN.
T' HELL WITH IT.
THE PROS KEEP IT ON A CASH BASIS. SIMPLE AND STRAIGHTFORWARD.
ALL WOMEN ARE PROS ANYWAY.
I BEG YOUR PARDON!
I WAS RAISED RICH. SAW WOMEN MARRY GUYS FOR THE BUCKS AND THEN DIVORCE 'EM AND TAKE 'EM FOR ALL THEY COULD GET.
REAL PROS MAKE YOU PAY ONLY ONCE. NOT ALL YOUR LIFE.
HELL! YOU'RE A PRO, TOO.
ALL THIS CARING...! IT'S WHAT YOU'RE PAID TO DO! YER JUST ANOTHER PRO!
WHAK!
17

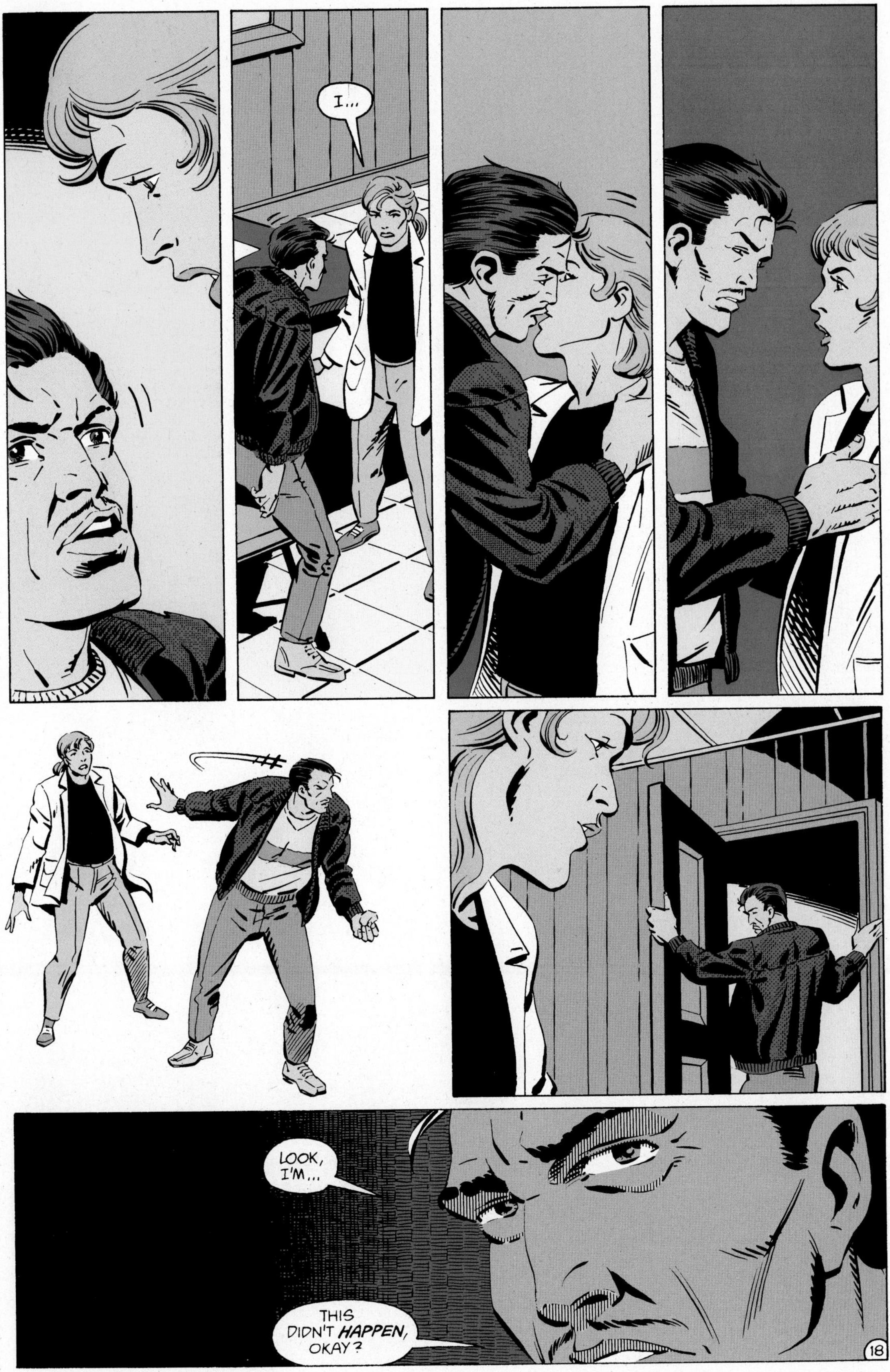
I...
LOOK, I'M...
THIS DIDN'T HAPPEN, OKAY?
18

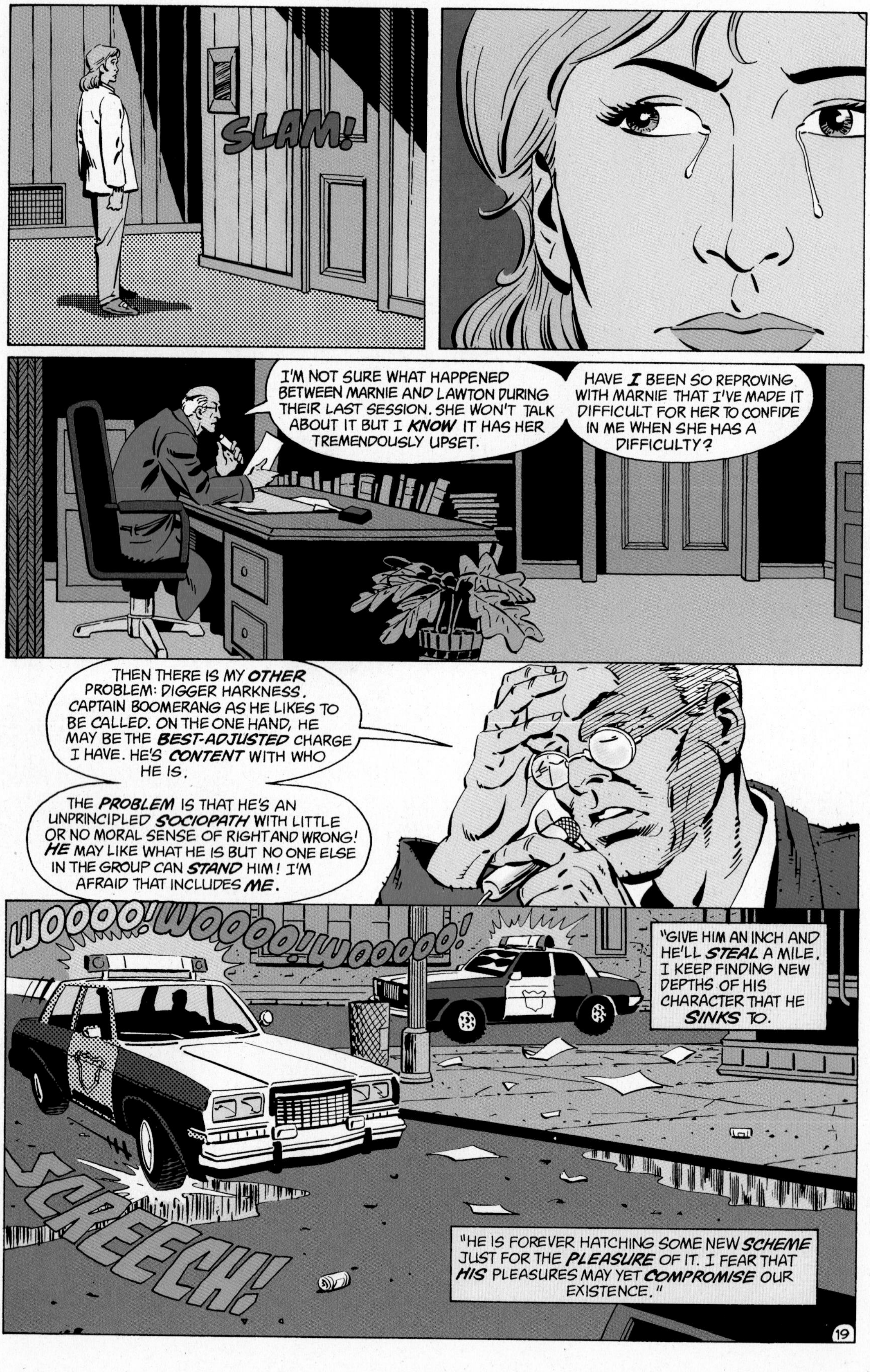

SLAM!
I'M NOT SURE WHAT HAPPENED BETWEEN MARNIE AND LAWTON DURING THEIR LAST SESSION. SHE WON'T TALK ABOUT IT BUT I KNOW IT HAS HER TREMENDOUSLY UPSET.
HAVE I BEEN SO REPROVING WITH MARNIE THAT I'VE MADE IT DIFFICULT FOR HER TO CONFIDE IN ME WHEN SHE HAS A DIFFICULTY?
THEN THERE IS MY OTHER PROBLEM: DIGGER HARKNESS. CAPTAIN BOOMERANG AS HE LIKES TO BE CALLED. ON THE ONE HAND, HE MAY BE THE BEST-ADJUSTED CHARGE I HAVE. HE'S CONTENT WITH WHO HE IS.
THE PROBLEM IS THAT HE'S AN UNPRINCIPLED SOCIOPATH WITH LITTLE OR NO MORAL SENSE OF RIGHT AND WRONG! HE MAY LIKE WHAT HE IS BUT NO ONE ELSE IN THE GROUP CAN STAND HIM! I'M AFRAID THAT INCLUDES ME.
WOOOO! WOOOO! WOOOOO!
"GIVE HIM AN INCH AND HE'LL STEAL A MILE. I KEEP FINDING NEW DEPTHS OF HIS CHARACTER THAT HE SINKS TO.
SCREECH!
"HE IS FOREVER HATCHING SOME NEW SCHEME JUST FOR THE PLEASURE OF IT. I FEAR THAT HIS PLEASURES MAY YET COMPROMISE OUR EXISTENCE."
19

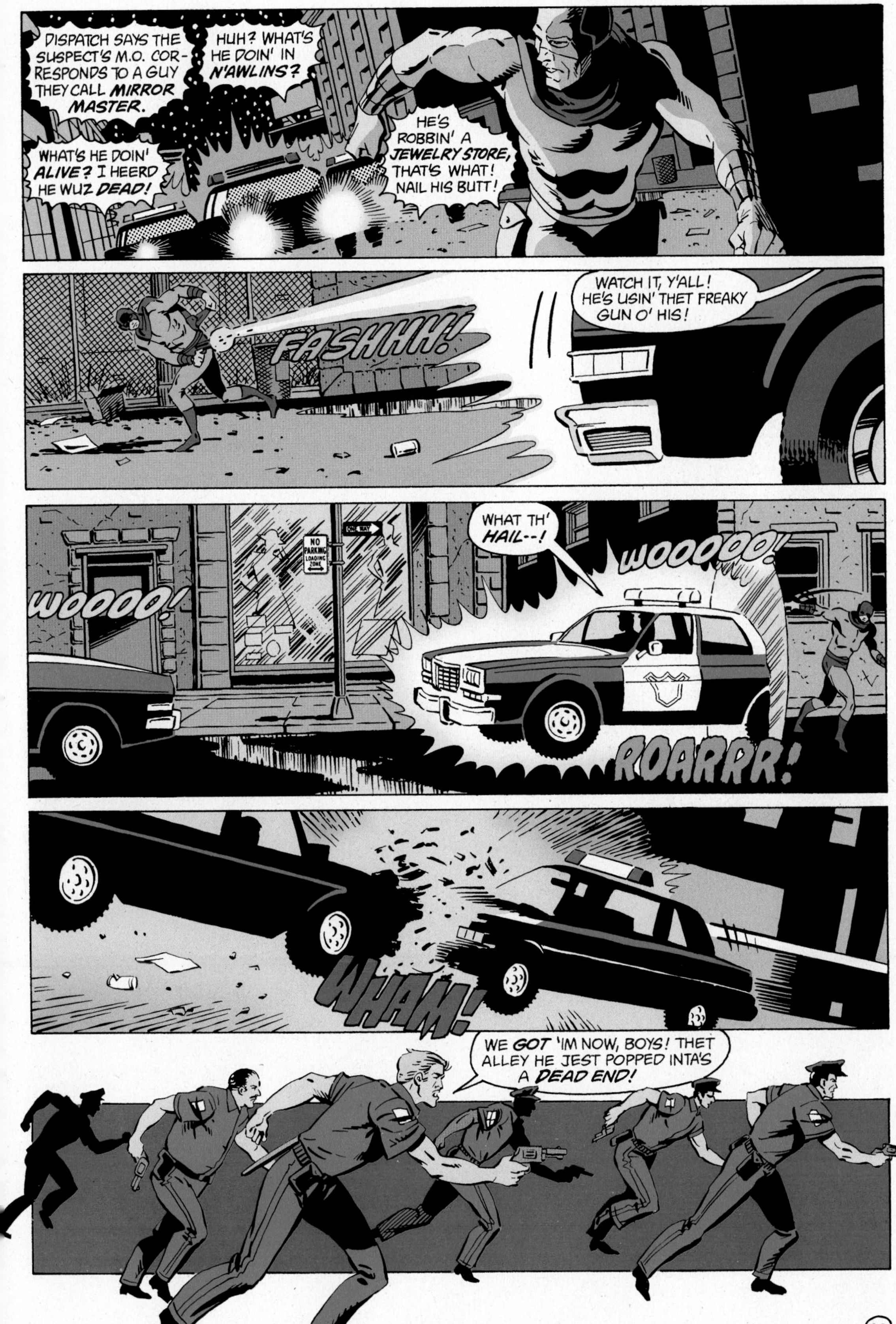
DISPATCH SAYS THE SUSPECT'S M.O. CORRESPONDS TO A GUY THEY CALL MIRROR MASTER.
HUH? WHAT'S HE DOIN' IN N'AWLINS?
WHAT'S HE DOIN' ALIVE? I HEERD HE WUZ DEAD!
HE'S ROBBIN' A JEWELRY STORE, THAT'S WHAT! NAIL HIS BUTT!
FASHHH!
WATCH IT, Y'ALL! HE'S USIN' THET FREAKY GUN O' HIS!
WHAT TH' HAIL--!
WOOOOO!
WOOOOO!
NO PARKING LOADING ZONE
ONE WAY
ROARRRR!
WHAM!
WE GOT 'IM NOW, BOYS! THET ALLEY HE JEST POPPED INTA'S A DEAD END!
20

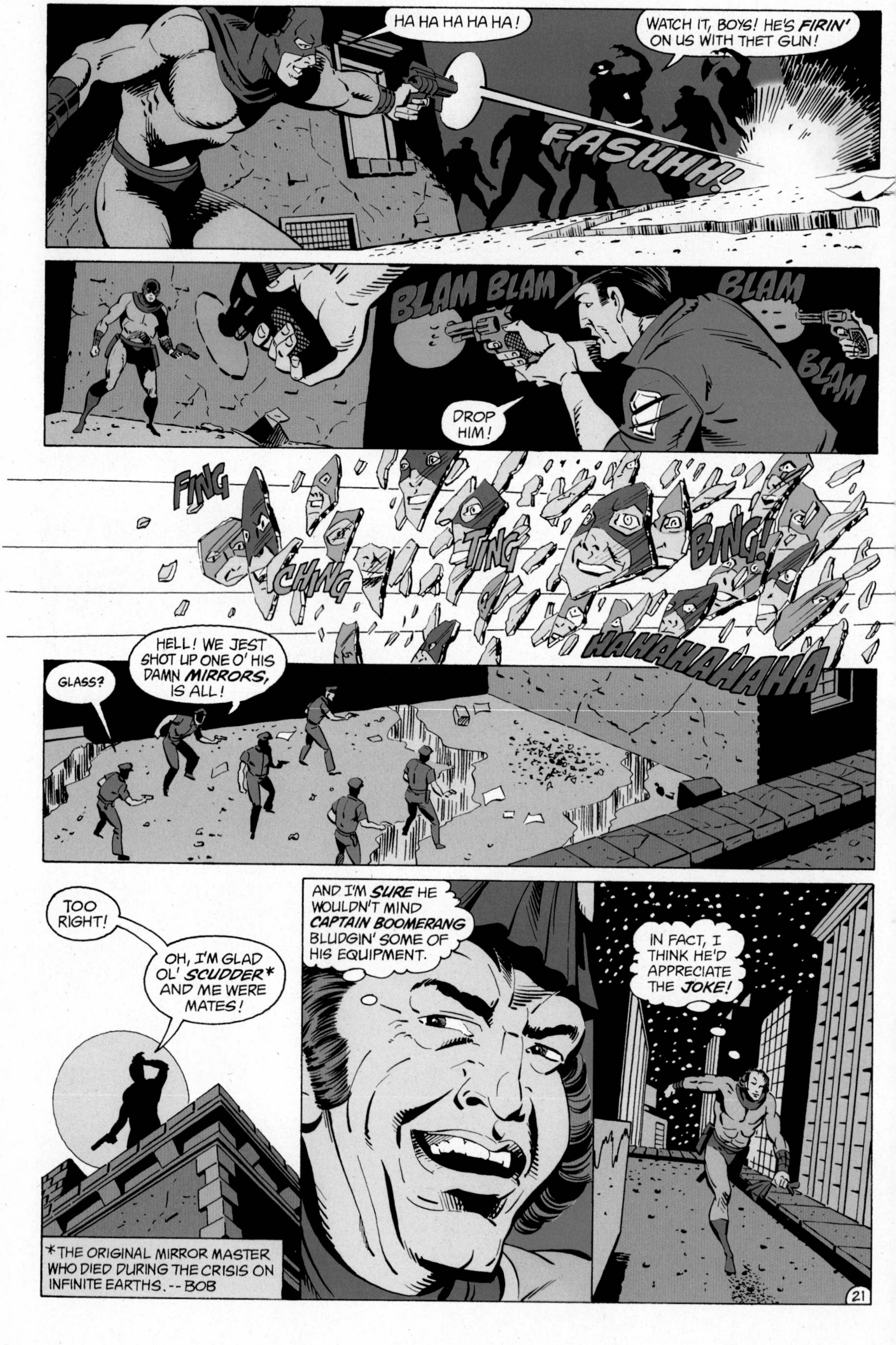
HA HA HA HA HA HA!
WATCH IT, BOYS! HE'S FIRIN' ON US WITH THET GUN!
FASHHH!
BLAM BLAM
BLAM
BLAM
DROP HIM!
FING
CHNG
TING
BING!
HAHAHAHAHAHA
GLASS?
HELL! WE JEST SHOT UP ONE O' HIS DAMN MIRRORS, IS ALL!
TOO RIGHT!
OH, I'M GLAD OL' SCUDDER* AND ME WERE MATES!
*THE ORIGINAL MIRROR MASTER WHO DIED DURING THE CRISIS ON INFINITE EARTHS. -- BOB
AND I'M SURE HE WOULDN'T MIND CAPTAIN BOOMERANG BLUDGIN' SOME OF HIS EQUIPMENT.
IN FACT, I THINK HE'D APPRECIATE THE JOKE!
21

NOW WHEN I GET AN *ITCH* TO DO A *JOB*, I CAN PULL IT AS *MIRROR MASTER*.

MEANWHILE, *CAPTAIN BOOMERANG* STAYS ON THE *GOOD* SIDE OF OL' MAMMY WALLER. ALWAYS ASSUMING SHE *HAS* A GOOD SIDE.

I LET THE FEDS *SUBSIDIZE* ME OFFICIAL LIFE WHILE I *ENTERTAIN* MYSELF AS *MIRROR MASTER*!

WHO *SAYS* YA CAN'T HAVE YER CAKE AND EAT IT, TOO? *HAW!*

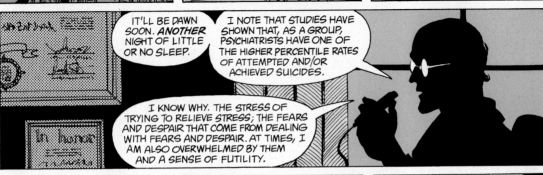

IT'LL BE DAWN SOON. *ANOTHER* NIGHT OF LITTLE OR NO SLEEP.

I NOTE THAT STUDIES HAVE SHOWN THAT, AS A GROUP, PSYCHIATRISTS HAVE ONE OF THE HIGHER PERCENTILE RATES OF ATTEMPTED AND/OR ACHIEVED SUICIDES.

I KNOW WHY. THE STRESS OF TRYING TO RELIEVE STRESS; THE FEARS AND DESPAIR THAT COME FROM DEALING WITH FEARS AND DESPAIR. AT TIMES, I AM ALSO OVERWHELMED BY THEM AND A SENSE OF FUTILITY.

BUT I ALSO HAVE MY *HOME*... MY *FAMILY* AS A REFUGE ... A *BALANCE* TO THAT DESPAIR.

AND I THANK GOD FOR IT.

SIMON?

ANOTHER SLEEPLESS NIGHT?

I'M AFRAID SO, RUTH.

C'MON. I'LL FIX YOU BREAKFAST, OKAY?

WHATEVER ELSE HAPPENS, I KNOW I DON'T FACE IT *ALONE*.

END.

NEXT: MILLENNIUM™

DC COMICS™

"A pretty irresistible hook. What if the good guys assembled a bunch of bad guys to work as a Dirty Dozen-like superteam and do the dirty work traditional heroes would never touch (or want to know about)?"—THE ONION/AV CLUB

START AT THE BEGINNING!

SUICIDE SQUAD
VOLUME 1: KICKED IN THE TEETH

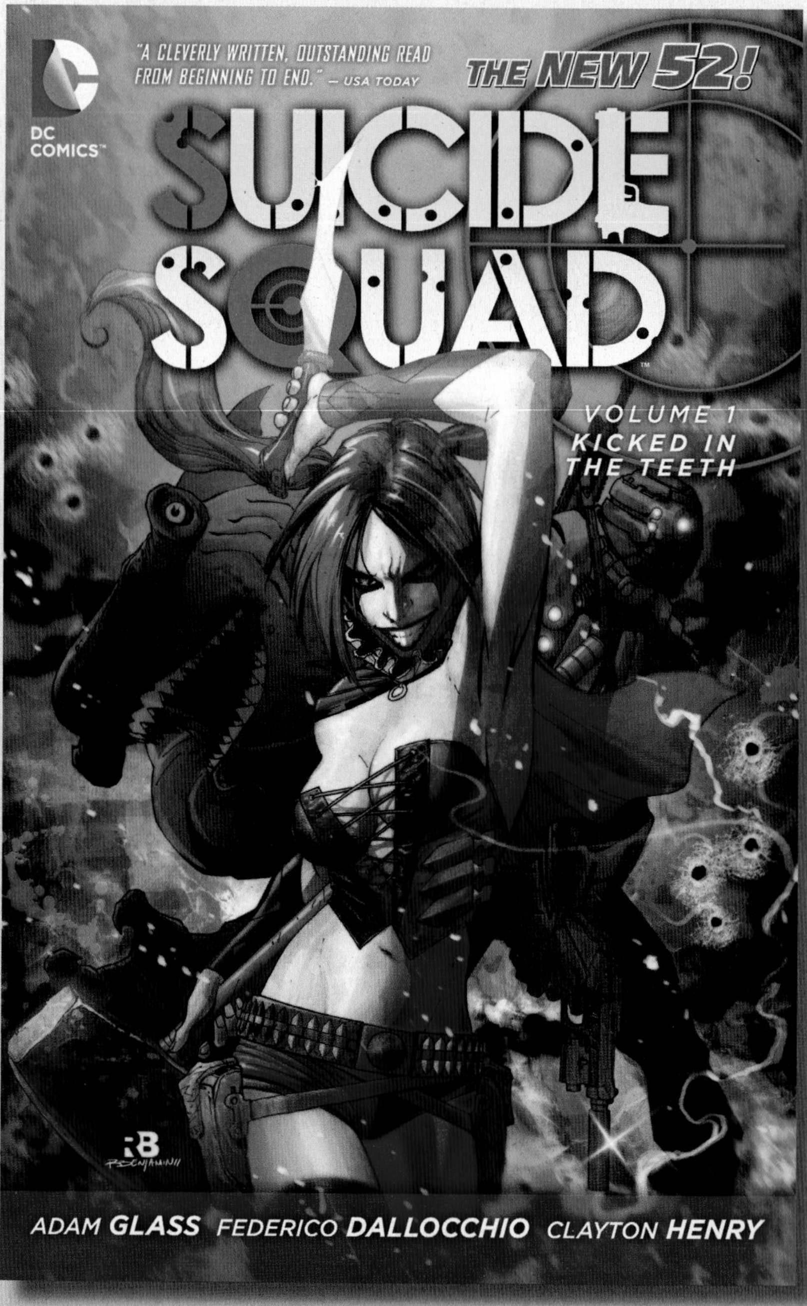

"A CLEVERLY WRITTEN, OUTSTANDING READ FROM BEGINNING TO END." — USA TODAY
THE NEW 52!
DC COMICS
SUICIDE SQUAD
VOLUME 1 KICKED IN THE TEETH
ADAM GLASS FEDERICO DALLOCCHIO CLAYTON HENRY

SUICIDE SQUAD VOL. 2: BASILISK RISING

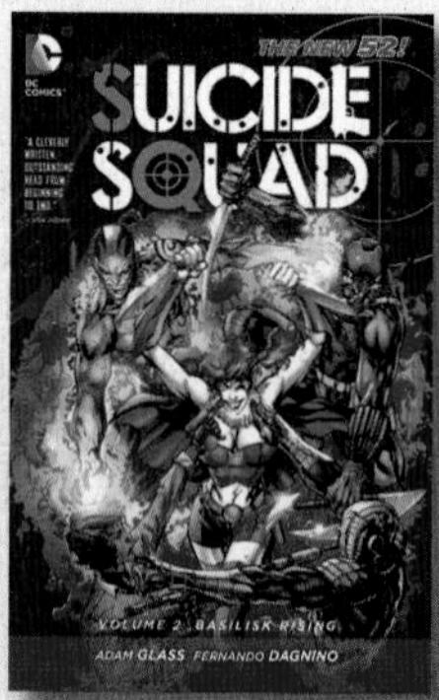

THE NEW 52!
SUICIDE SQUAD
VOLUME 2 BASILISK RISING
ADAM GLASS FERNANDO DAGNINO

SUICIDE SQUAD VOL. 3: DEATH IS FOR SUCKERS

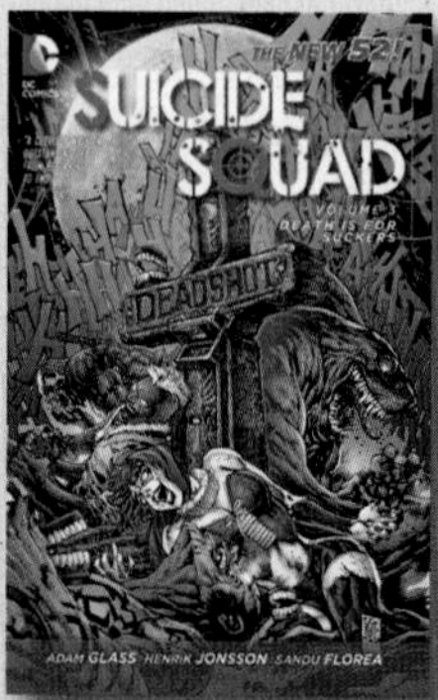

THE NEW 52!
SUICIDE SQUAD
DEADSHOT
ADAM GLASS HENRIK JONSSON SANDU FLOREA

DEATHSTROKE VOL. 1: LEGACY

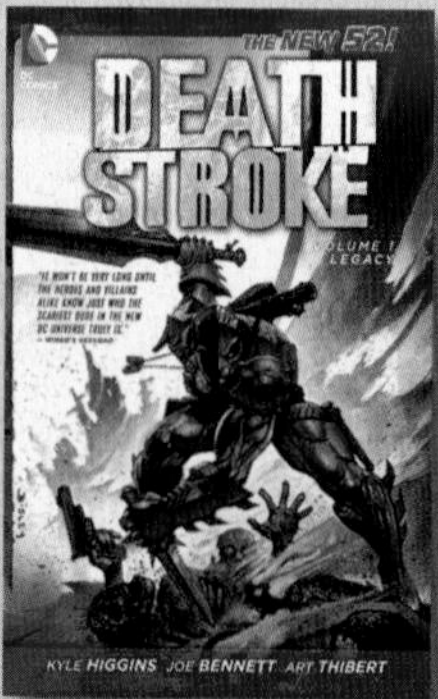

THE NEW 52!
DEATHSTROKE
VOLUME 1 LEGACY
KYLE HIGGINS JOE BENNETT ART THIBERT

DC COMICS™

START AT THE BEGINNING!
JUSTICE LEAGUE
VOLUME 1: ORIGIN
GEOFF JOHNS and JIM LEE

JUSTICE LEAGUE VOL. 2: THE VILLAIN'S JOURNEY

JUSTICE LEAGUE VOL. 3: THRONE OF ATLANTIS

JUSTICE LEAGUE OF AMERICA VOL. 1: WORLD'S MOST DANGEROUS

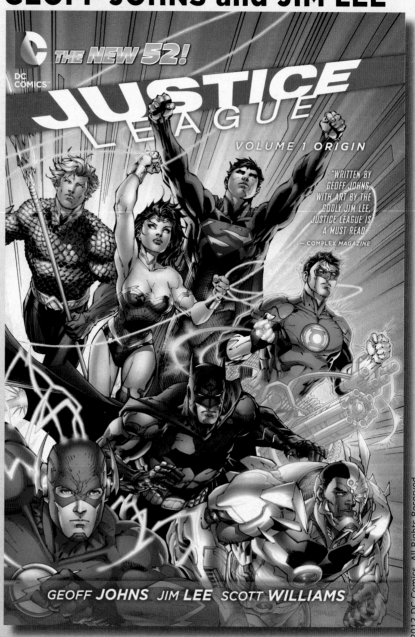